D1327608

THE EARLY VASAS:

A HISTORY OF SWEDEN, 1523–1611

GUSTAV VASA IN OLD AGE

by Cornelius Arendtz

The Early Vasas

A History of Sweden, 1523-1611

MICHAEL ROBERTS

PROFESSOR OF MODERN HISTORY
THE QUEEN'S UNIVERSITY, BELFAST

CAMBRIDGE
AT THE UNIVERSITY PRESS
1968

Published by the Syndics of the Cambridge University Press
Bentley House, P.O. Box 92, 200 Euston Road, London, N.W. 1
American Branch: 32 East 57th Street, New York, N.Y. 10022

Library of Congress Catalogue Card Number: 68-10332

Standard Book Number: 521 06930 0

Printed in Great Britain
at the University Printing House, Cambridge
(Brooke Crutchley, University Printer)

To

Copper *and* Alan

. . . for what is here display'd is no History of the Wars of the *Turks* and the *Roman* Empire . . . whereof the whole World abides the Issue, every man apprehending a general Servitude and universal Thraldom: no, it is no greater matter than a Relation of how things stood in *Sweden* for some few years; which to know is by no means incumbent upon all.

GUSTAV II ADOLF: *Introduction to a History of his own Times*

Contents

Contents

Illustrations

PLATES

The plates are reproduced by kind permission of Svenska Porträttarkivet, Nationalmuseum, Stockholm

MAPS

The maps are adapted from those in the author's 'Gustavus Adolphus', *vol. 1, by kind permission of Messrs Longmans, Green & Co.*

Preface

Though the history of the Swedish Reformation has attracted the attention of a few non-Swedish historians, there seems to be no extended account in English of the general history of Sweden in the sixteenth century. I hope that this book may serve as an elementary introduction to the subject, and may supply some of the information necessary to an understanding of the 'Age of Greatness' which followed. In a work of synthesis such as this there seems little point in distracting the reader by footnote-references to authorities in Swedish, and except at a few points I have made no attempt to do so; but I have tried to provide a bibliography which may be of assistance to any who should wish to pursue their inquiries, and which will also give to those acquainted with the literature some idea of the authors whom I have found most useful. I had originally intended that the book should end with a survey of social and economic developments during the period, in so far as they had not already been touched on in the preceding chapters. But I soon found that I should in effect have been repeating something I had written already; and though it would have been satisfactory to re-write some passages which I could now wish otherwise, it did not seem to me that this was a sufficient reason for extending this volume by an additional sixty or seventy pages. I must therefore ask the indulgence of the reader, and refer him to the chapter on the state of Sweden in 1611 which opens volume II of my *Gustavus Adolphus*; and which forms, indeed, a natural link between this book and that.

I should like to take this opportunity to express my thanks to those who have helped me in various ways in the writing of this volume: to my friends and colleagues who have read all or part of it in manuscript and above all to f. Riksarkivarien Dr Ingvar Andersson, who with unwearied kindness read the whole text, and saved me from many errors; to Professor J. C. Beckett and Principal J. L. Haire; to the Senate of The Queen's University, Belfast, who generously gave me sabbatical leave so that I might finish it; to Svenska Institutet för Kulturellt Utbyte (and especially to Docent Gunnar Ahlström) for innumerable kindnesses on many occasions, culminating in an invitation to spend two months in Sweden as their guest; to Mrs Anthea Orr, for invaluable and long-suffering assistance in preparing the text for the press; to Messrs Longmans, Green and Co. for their permission to reproduce the maps. Some of the first draft was written when I had the honour to hold the Hugh Le May Fellowship at Rhodes University, Grahamstown. It was an extraordinary privilege to be able to spend a year of uninterrupted work in my old University: I can well believe that other holders of the Fellowship have employed their tenure of it more profitably; but I am sure that none has derived from it a more poignant pleasure, or quitted Rhodes at the end of their term with more affectionate regret. For this experience I am deeply grateful. And it is to two Old Rhodians, pupils of long ago, and my friends and colleagues now for close on thirty years, that I venture to dedicate this book.

M.R.

Belfast
December 1967

Glossary

arvförening — Succession Pact.

beställning — an allocation, by way of wages, of specific crown revenues.

frihetsmil — the area within a radius of one Swedish mile of a manor, within which the manor-owner enjoyed absolute freedom from taxes and burdens: lit. 'mile of freedom'.

frälse — lit. 'deliverance'; i.e. exemption from most taxes and burdens, or obligation to render them at only half-rates: the characteristic privilege of nobility. Hence *frälsebonde*, a peasant of the nobility; *frälsejord*, noble land; *frälsestånd*, the Estate of the Nobility, etc.

förläning — allocation of crown revenues and services to an individual, by way of remuneration or reward, the beneficiary having the right to collect them himself (in contrast to *beställning*, where the revenue was collected by the crown's agents, and subsequently paid over).

härad — a county; hence *häradshövding*, a sheriff, with both judicial and administrative functions; and *häradsting*, the county court.

herredag — an afforced meeting of the *råd* (q.v.), often not easily distinguishable from a *riksdag* (q.v.).

hovkansler — court chancellor.

konungaförsäkran — charter given by kings soon after accession, or as a condition of accession.

lagman — a provincial judge.

landshövding — a provincial governor.

landslag — the national code of law drawn up about 1350 by Magnus Eriksson.

landsting — the assembly of the province (cf. *häradsting*, above).

län — a (non-hereditary) fief.

ofrälse — not exempt from taxation; non-noble.

reduktion — resumption by the crown of alienated lands and revenues.

riksdag — a meeting of the Estates.

riksföreståndare — lit. 'representative of the realm'; regent.

rusttjänst — provision of a prescribed number of properly armed horsemen for service with the king's army: cf. knight-service.

Glossary

råd, riksråd — council, council of the realm; a member of this body. Hence *med råds råde*, with the council's counsel.

sammansvärjning — a conjuration, a swearing-in-common, for political purposes.

ståthållare — a governor (of a province or a castle); cf. Statthalter, stadhouder.

sätesgård, säteri — a manor, a private estate of a member of the nobility, to which special fiscal exemptions attached.

utskrivning — a militia-levy.

1. Introduction: the end of the Union of Kalmar

On a broad inlet of Lake Mälar, in the very heart of central Sweden, lies the ancient town of Strängnäs: a cluster of somnolent streets; a few old houses; a famous *gymnasium* dating from the early seventeenth century; a modest cathedral crowning a little rise and looking out over the wooded shores and the wide expanse of water. It is a secure and pleasant place, the very pattern of a small Swedish country town of the better sort. Modern industrialism has passed it by; the tide of tourism stops at nearby Gripsholm. But in former times it was a place of some consequence, with a notable free market; famous men lie buried in the aisles of its cathedral; great events in Swedish history are associated with its name. And none greater, none more pregnant with consequences for the future of the country, than that which was enacted here on 6 June 1523.

Since the beginning of the month the Estates of the realm had been making their way to Strängnäs: a handful of members of the council, a large gathering of the nobility, representatives of the burghers, the miners, the peasants: the little town must have been hard put to it to lodge them all. In Strängnäs too were three foreign observers, all evidently in some way concerned with what was going forward. One of them was Berend von Melen, a German soldier of fortune who had recently deserted from the Danish to the Swedish service; the other two—Bernt Bomhouwer and Hermann Plönnies—were the official representatives of the city of Lübeck. The business which had brought them all together was nothing less than the election of a new king. After more than a century of union with Denmark and Norway, the Swedes felt themselves ripe to resume existence as an independent state. Since 1520 they had been in rebellion against the Danish king, Kristian II, and it was now virtually certain that their movement would be successful. Of that rebellion the leader and inspirer had been a young nobleman of the ancient family of Vasa: by name, Gustav Eriksson. Already in August 1521 the rebels had recognized him as regent; now, with final success almost within their grasp, they accepted the logic of the situation and offered him the crown. No other plausible candidate seemed available; the decision of the Estates was unanimous. The only hesitation, it appears, came from Gustav Vasa himself. But after consultation with von Melen and the Lübeckers he allowed his diffidence to be overborne, and on 6 June 1523 he was elected by acclamation, and took the oath as king. On the following day he celebrated his accession by a solemn mass in the cathedral. It was noted that in the procession the new king walked with Plönnies on the one hand and Bomhouwer on the other, and that it was they who occupied the places of honour in the choir. When the service was over, the king made a speech to the commonalty in the churchyard, in which he took occasion to remind them of the great services which Lübeck had rendered to Sweden; and all the people shouted that they would cleave to Lübeck for ever. 'In this wise', writes Peder Swart in his *Chronicle*, 'in the name of the Holy Trinity, he was chosen, proclaimed and acclaimed as elected king of Sweden, Gothland, and so forth'; and proceeded forthwith to the promulgation of a proclamation to his subjects, wherein he promised to be to them a 'gracious, good and faithful lord, according to the law of Sweden and of St Erik'.

The union of the three Scandinavian kingdoms, established in 1389, solemnly confirmed at Kalmar in 1397, was now broken. It was not the first time, by any means. In the century and a quarter which had passed since Queen Margaret had secured the acceptance of Erik of Pomerania as king of the three realms, Sweden had more than once shown a disposition to take her own road. A native nobleman, Karl Knutsson, had ruled an independent Sweden from 1448 until his deposition in 1457, again from 1464 to 1465, and again from 1467 to his death in 1470: he is reckoned as Karl VIII in the roll of Swedish kings. From 1471 to 1520 three successive members of the noble house of Sture had built up a power in Sweden which enabled them, under the title of regent (*riksföreståndare*), to maintain a virtual independence of the kings in Copenhagen.[1] No doubt it was true that the idea and ideal of union had been growing weaker in the last two or three decades before Gustav Vasa's accession. Yet even so Kristian II of Denmark had in 1520 been able to reassert his authority with a vigour and a success unparalleled for almost a century. Gustav Vasa's seizure of the throne, and the rejection of Danish pretensions which it implied, must to many contemporaries have seemed but one more turn of a wheel that had made notable revolutions in the past: the Union had surmounted similar crises before, and might probably survive another. But such a reading of the situation, however plausible, was in fact erroneous.

[1] Sweden's rulers under the Union were: Erik of Pomerania (Erik XIII), king 1397–1439; Kristoffer of Bavaria, king 1441–8; Karl Knutsson (Karl VIII), king 1448–57; Kristian I, of Oldenburg, king 1457–64; Karl Knutsson, king 1464–5; Kristian I, king 1465–7; Karl Knutsson, king 1467–70; Sten Sture the elder, regent 1471–97; Hans, king 1497–1501; Sten Sture the elder, regent 1501–3; Svante Nilsson (Sture) regent 1503–12; Sten Sture the younger, regent 1512–20; Kristian II, king 1520–3.

This time the Union was really dead. The accession of Gustav Vasa was a turning-point in the fate of the North: here, at Strängnäs in 1523, begins the history of the modern Swedish state.

Nevertheless, it remains a fact that the Union had stood for over five generations, and the accession of Gustav Vasa could not obliterate it without trace. Its strengths and its weaknesses, the factors which had preserved it and those which had contributed to its destruction, remained operative (as to some of them, at least) for many years to come; and even those features of the Union which no longer had relevance to the times, and had become the mere detritus of a former age, gave a bottom on which the new dynasty must build, if it were to build at all.

As far as Sweden was concerned, the initial impulse towards the Union had come from the need of the Swedish nobility to obtain assistance against a king (Albert of Mecklenburg) from whom they had become irretrievably alienated; and it has been suggested that Margaret of Denmark agreed to help them because Denmark and Norway, no less than Sweden, seemed at that time to be in danger of falling under the domination of north German princes. The Union was therefore in one aspect the successful resistance of Scandinavia to German expansion. But it was of course much more than this. For the Union concluded at Kalmar in 1397 was neither the first nor the last of its kind. It had been preceded by a union of Sweden and Norway which lasted from 1319 to 1364, and which from 1332 also included Skåne. The union of Denmark with Norway inaugurated in 1397 was to endure till 1814, and was succeeded in its turn by a ninety-year union of Norway with Sweden. More than one Scandinavian monarch, on either side of the Sound, was to dream of rebuilding the edifice which Queen Margaret had raised. The Union of Kalmar, like those other unions, might seem superficially a mere dynastic arrangement; but it was also the translation into political terms of a cultural and social kinship which made the area distinct, and recognizably distinct, from the rest of Europe: languages so closely akin as to form no barrier and trace no frontier; political institutions and legal systems which, because they were still based on similar social structures, were still on the whole evolving in striking parallelism; economic habits which made light of vague and transient frontiers; above all, perhaps, an aristocracy truly Scandinavian, which intermarried freely, and bought, inherited or acquired in marriage-portions estates on either side of the borders. The Scandinavian peoples felt the North to be a world apart, a unity in itself; and this view of the matter was to some extent shared by observers outside: the friars, for instance, grouped the three kingdoms together into the single province of Dacia. This sense of common heritage and common destiny did something to blunt the edge of intra-Scandinavian conflicts: peasants in the frontier areas regularly made their own local truces, and became non-belligerents in their rulers' quarrels; the great magnates of the councils of state were accustomed, by appeals to community of interest, or by conferences on the frontier, to try to avert the ill effects of royal policies. And for magnate and peasant alike the Union brought a better assurance of quiet times, or at least a cessation of border forays: a consideration important to those who were thriving economically—as the lay magnates generally were, and as the church certainly was. The church, indeed, was for long committed to the Union on the ground simply that it secured peace. With the passage of time the Union acquired the sanction of normality, so that it lived on in men's minds as an ideal, or at least as a political habit, even when the realities seemed to contradict it most peremptorily. It is not until after 1500, perhaps, that it is possible to detect prudent heads of families dividing up their estates so that the one son's share should fall on the Danish side of the frontier, and the other's on the Swedish. But this was a rationalization which was not completed for decades, nor perhaps almost for centuries: a hundred years after the end of the Union the Posse family still had estates in Norway which afforded them a revenue in exile; and their case was not exceptional. There were Totts in Sweden, Thotts in Denmark, Brahes in both; and it was only slowly that men made any distinction between them.

The feeling for the Union was indeed strong: strong enough to survive severe internal crises. It was well expressed by Jakob Ulvsson, archbishop of Uppsala, who at a moment of stress wrote to the Danish council, 'Bethink you that we are all of one speech, and most of us blood-relations, so that we ought to agree peaceably among ourselves, and not go about to do each other an injury, nor seek each other's ruin'. The eviction of a Union king, and even the apparent breaking of the Union, by no means implied hostility to the Union itself: when Erik of Pomerania was deposed in 1439 the Swedish council made this quite clear, though they also indicated to their colleagues in Denmark that they expected that due weight should be given to their views about his successor. They accepted Denmark's choice of Kristoffer of Bavaria in 1441; but it did not therefore follow that they would always automatically follow Denmark's lead. The monarchy was after all elective, though with a preference for the sons or relatives of the last king; and if the line should fail it was perfectly possible that the Swedes might find a Union king of their own choosing. This in fact happened, when Kristoffer died without heirs in 1448: the Swedish council chose Karl Knutsson in a hurry, in order to present the other kingdoms with a *fait accompli* in which it was hoped they might concur. For two years, indeed, Norway did so: it was only 1450, when the Danes chose Kristian I, and so put the House of Oldenburg on the throne which it still occupies, that they found that they had precipitated a schism. But nobody therefore supposed that the Union was at an end: a century which had seen three rival popes and two rival emperors at the same time could accept two Union kings with equanimity, and wait for the death of one of them to resolve the difficulty. Twenty years later the regency of Sten Sture the elder put Sweden effectively outside the Union for thirty years. But nearly everybody refused to acknowledge the fact. On the contrary, at meeting after meeting of the councils of the two kingdoms the Union was reaffirmed; for none of the magnates on either side of the border (except perhaps Sten Sture himself) as yet wished it broken: it was only that they could not agree among themselves upon the terms on which it was to be carried on. As late as 1509 or 1512 its re-establishment in the fulness of its early days was conceivable, and that by way not of Danish conquest but of agreement between the aristocracies on both sides. As late as 1513 a member of the Swedish council could suggest that it was Sweden's turn to choose a monarch for all three. To the last there were men who clung to the Union because they preferred peace to war. And the bitterness, the hatred of the Danes, which was the legacy of Gustav Vasa's war of liberation, and was reinforced by many another war thereafter, never wholly killed the sense of the unity and uniqueness of the North. It flowered anew in the romantic rhetoric and student demonstrations of the 'Scandinavianism' of the mid-nineteenth century; and in the strains and perils of the mid-twentieth has re-emerged on a basis of common ideals, sober calculation and practical utility.

On Sweden's side the Union had been the work of a handful of great landowners, members of that relatively limited circle of families from whom the kings were wont to recruit their council of state (*råd*). These men represented a constitutional tradition which by the end of the fourteenth century was already well established and fully self-conscious: in Albert of Mecklenburg's time the *råd* had overshadowed the crown. They believed it to be their function to curb any tendency towards an extension of the royal prerogative; and an absentee king, far away in Copenhagen, was not the worst sort of monarch from this point of view. It happened, therefore, that the Union was most successful under the rule of such a wholly foreign sovereign as Kristoffer of Bavaria, who did not attempt to make much resistance to the political aspirations of the magnates. But Kristoffer's reign was exceptional. The normal state of affairs was one in which monarch and nobles were at best on uneasy terms, at worst in direct conflict. Rulers who tried to take castles and fiefs into their own hands, rulers who showed signs of emancipating themselves from aristocratic tutelage, could be sure of trouble. And if their foreign policies happened to be expensive, so that the burden of taxation was increased, they would find their noble adversaries able to draw on popular support. This was especially true in Sweden, where royal exactions were sometimes levied by unpopular foreign bailiffs. Thus, one after another, from Erik of Pomerania to Sten Sture the elder, Sweden's rulers came to grief upon the fiscal rocks: it was a lesson which was not to be lost upon Gustav Vasa.

The first great crisis of the Union—that which led to the deposition of Erik of Pomerania in 1439—arose mainly from causes of this kind: behind it lay the financial demands and administrative severities of a king suspected of authoritarian leanings, and determined at any cost to push his struggle against the Hanseatic league to a successful conclusion. In 1434 this anti-Hanseatic foreign policy provoked a rising in the Swedish mining regions (Bergslag), which were dependent upon the Hanse for their markets. The Bergslag had an admixture of German colonists among its inhabitants; and it was a gentleman-miner from Norberg—a place whose ties with Lübeck were demonstrably close—who gave the movement its leader, in the person of Engelbrekt Engelbrektsson. But it was the hatred of the peasants for King Erik's foreign bailiffs that provided the mass support for the rising; and it was the backing of the *råd*-magnates, jealous of the power of the monarchy, that ensured that the affair should yield solid political results. The coalition of these elements, to be sure, did not last even until Erik had been disposed of: a member of the high nobility murdered Engelbrekt in 1436; and thereafter the *råd* directed the movement for its own ends. Those ends were no doubt largely selfish. The Swedish aristocracy did not desire a strong king. They wished to be left alone to run the country, to bargain and squabble among themselves about the allotment of fiefs and the custody of castles. They throve on lack of governance. Yet the magnates, and especially the *råd*, did also stand in some sense for the rule of law against the monarchy's aspirations to put itself above the law, or (to use the phraseology of the age) for a *regimen politicum* rather than a *regimen regale*. When they were confronted with an ambitious ruler in the person of Karl Knutsson—a ruler, moreover, who had risen from their own ranks—it was not surprising that they should seek to make capital out of the schism which followed his election; and hence they played him off against his rival Kristian I. The great families of central Sweden—the Oxenstiernas, the Vasas, and their connexions—dominated Swedish politics in the 1450s and 1460s. Led by Jöns Bengtsson Oxenstierna, the turbulent archbishop of Uppsala, or by Kettil Karlsson Vasa, the martial bishop of Linköping, they made and unmade kings to suit themselves—though indeed they speedily found that Karl and Kristian suited them equally ill. And so it happened that on more than one occasion Sweden was outside the control of either king, a *de facto* aristocratic republic managed by political prelates: both Jöns Bengtsson and Kettil Karlsson for a time assumed the title of regent. Thus in the sixties Karl and Kristian came in or went out, as it might happen, as the result of family coalitions, bargains about fiefs, and perhaps (though this is disputed) alignments of economic vested interests which felt themselves favoured or prejudiced by the policies of one side or the other.

To these factors in the situation was added, at the close of the sixties, another which was destined in the end to be more potent than all the rest: the comparatively new passion of popular nationalism. This was a sentiment which long remained unintelligible to the aristocracy: themselves supra-national, they felt a patriotism (if they felt it at all) for Scandinavia as a whole; and they saw their intermittent controversies with the kings in Copenhagen in terms rather of personal prestige, economic advantage, class privilege, or constitutional law. At lower social levels it was rather different. To large sections of the Swedish population Engelbrekt had been a popular hero; after his death, a martyr; and at last in his own part of the country an unofficial saint. Before the end of the century popular tradition had made him the representative of emergent Swedish national feeling, the first great leader in a fight not so much against misgovernment as against *Danish* government. Whatever cause he had really represented in his lifetime, he came to personify the cause of Swedish independence. Under the inspiration of Engelbrekt's rebellion, Bishop Thomas of Strängnäs had in 1438 written his *Song of Liberty*: probably the only fragment of medieval Swedish literature still known to every Swede, and still powerfully evocative.[1] Karl Knutsson had seen the advantage to be gained from fostering such feelings: by deliberate policy he encouraged a crude xenophobia, and by skilful propaganda and loaded historiography sought to represent himself as in some sort Engelbrekt's successor in the defence of the national cause. The army of peasants which, under the leadership of Kettil Karlsson, chopped up Kristian I's mercenaries at Haraker in 1466, soon seemed in retrospect to have won a national victory. Still more was this the case in regard to the battle of Brunkeberg in 1471, when Kristian was once more defeated, and the way cleared for the regency of Sten Sture. Brunkeberg, soberly considered, was a battle in which Swedes fought on both sides, a spectacular incident in the endless *politique de bascule* of the great, with lucrative fiefs

[1] It has been argued that Bishop Thomas had in mind rather *libertates ecclesiae* which Erik had also been infringing; but on this opinion is divided.

as the prize of victory. But it was not long before those Swedes who had fought for Kristian were represented as traitors to the national cause. It was significant that the victory was followed four days afterwards by the removal of all Germans from the town council of Stockholm. And it was commemorated, a decade and a half later, by the superb equestrian statue of St George and the Dragon which stands today in Stockholm's Great Church—the subject of the monument being deliberately chosen, as a piece of brilliantly effective propaganda, to symbolize Sweden's liberation from the foreign yoke.

The man who commissioned Bernt Notke to carve it was the victor of Brunkeberg, Sten Sture himself. Soon after the battle Sten was chosen by the *råd* as regent; and save for one brief interval (from 1497 to 1501) when King Hans succeeded in persuading a majority of the Swedish magnates to admit him as effective ruler of their country, Sten Sture retained the regency until his death in 1503. He was succeeded by his relative Svante Nilsson; and he in his turn by his son, Sten Sture the younger, regent from 1512 to 1520. The title of regent implicitly acknowledged the continuance of the Union; but it indicated also Sweden's virtual emancipation from the king's control. The Swedish *råd* saw in it an interim measure, a stop-gap arrangement pending a final agreement on the way the Union was to function, an appointment revocable as soon as a solid settlement should be reached. But though such a settlement seemed, on several occasions, to be virtually achieved, it always in the end proved elusive. The regency continued, therefore, in default of any easy and acceptable alternative. And as decade succeeded decade with the position unchanged, the device became a kind of political habit. If the king were not prepared to proceed to extremities and assert his claim by armed force, there seemed no great reason to look for any other expedient—provided the Stures' *régime* was in other respects congenial to the great landowners. It was just here, however, that lay the real uncertainty. Sten had been made regent by a coalition of magnates, most of them linked together by family ties, and like his supporters he sought to increase his revenues and enhance his political importance by adding acre to acre. The ambition was common enough; but Sten and his successors pursued it with an altogether uncommon determination and logic. The Stures, all three of them, were ruthless and long-sighted careerists, indefatigable in the creation and use of opportunities for self-aggrandisement. Through three generations they laboured to build up for themselves a compact block of lands and castles, crown fiefs and private estates, more concentrated in area than the scattered holdings of their rivals, so that they might provide themselves with a firm economic and military basis for control of the country. As the years went by, they showed a disturbing tendency to view their position in dynastic terms: this was one reason why the opposition magnates made a fruitless attempt to break the succession by supporting the candidature of Erik Trolle for the regency on the death of Svante Nilsson in 1512. The Stures' proceedings naturally excited jealousy; but they also provoked constitutional alarm, for the age saw a close correlation between hereditary rule and unlimited power. Hence the Stures' relations with the aristocracy tended to deteriorate; and they began to turn increasingly for support to other elements in society. They adopted and developed Karl Knutsson's propaganda methods; they cultivated with success the art of popularity: Sten the younger, especially, unashamedly played for the support of the masses, and sought to give his election as regent the colour of popular acclamation, rather than of mere selection by the *råd*. All three Stures took care to preserve especially close relations with the Bergslag on the one hand, and with Stockholm on the other. Stockholm was the main port for the export of copper and iron; and the strong economic tie between burghers and miners usually ensured that they should take the same line in politics. That line was the Stures' line: Stockholm, the Bergslag and Dalarna had carried the elder Sten to victory at Brunkeberg; and the coalition long formed the core of the Sture party. No wonder, then, that King Hans should have made it an accusation against the elder Sten that he toadied to the masses. As for Sten the younger, he was frankly a demagogic politician, who used popular emotion at meetings of the Estates, or at more informal gatherings at fairs or markets, to tip the balance against his noble adversaries. There is little doubt that he aimed at a popular, national and hereditary monarchy, with the crown for himself and his heirs; and for a moment it almost seemed that he might achieve it, for he came very near to inducing Leo X to recognize him as king of Sweden.

Under the younger Sten, then, the dispute about the terms of the Union was transformed into a dynastic quarrel between the Stures and the Oldenburgs; and in that struggle the regent did not hesitate to employ the fairly new weapon—partly forged by himself and his predecessors—of national hatred of the Danes. Around the carefully idealized figure of 'young Herr Sten' a strong feeling of Swedish patriotism—by no means all of it factitious—began to gather. To the younger and less opulent of the nobility these developments were not without some appeal; and once Sten was firmly in the saddle he could also count on the support of the *råd* more certainly than his namesake had been able to do—perhaps in virtue of his judicious distribution to them of shares in the newly discovered silver mine at Sala. Yet at bottom Sten's programme was incompatible with the political interests of the nobility as a class—at least, as those interests had been conceived in the previous century. Instead of government by a family ring of magnates under the nominal control of a distant and discreet monarch (which had been the idea of the golden age of Kristoffer) Sten seemed to be aiming at a monarchy free of trammels, authoritarian and strong, and a state which should be more than a mere conglomerate of immunities and privileges held together by a tacit recognition of the advantages of mutual forbearance. Sten, indeed, represented the new idea of the state, as it was manifesting itself in France and England and Castile, and in him the techniques of parliamentary despotism were already implicit. Such a programme subverted the only bases upon which the Union could have continued; for an untrammelled monarchy was repugnant to the aristocracy, and the kind of tumultuary patriotism upon which the Stures throve had no place within the Union as either Queen Margaret or Jöns Bengtsson had conceived it. In the second decade of the sixteenth century it might indeed seem that the attractions of the Union appeared somewhat limp and faded; but if a monarchy in Sten's style was seen to be the only alternative, conservative politicians might be forced in desperation to embrace the Union once more. Their difficulty was that from their own point of view a restoration of the authority of the king in Copenhagen now offered a prospect scarcely more inviting than the other. For since 1513 the throne of Denmark had been occupied by Kristian II; and Kristian, by something more than a coincidence, was pursuing a political programme which in many respects was discouragingly similar to that of young Herr Sten. He too was for an absolute hereditary monarchy: he had indeed, in 1499, been formally recognized as hereditary prince by his reluctant Swedish subjects. Like the Stures, Kristian was on uneasy terms with the nobility, and angled for the support of burghers and peasants. Thus from the point of view of the regent's domestic enemies a renewal of an effective Union under Kristian II looked much less attractive than a renewal of the Union under Kristian I would have appeared to the politicians of the previous generation.

It was no longer true, moreover, that a foreign policy directed from Copenhagen was likely to be in the main accordant with Sweden's interests: one principal reason for the ejection of King Hans in 1501 was the revelation of his alliance with Ivan III, at a time when Sweden was heavily engaged in resisting Muscovite pressure on Finland. Old rivalries for influence in the lands to the south of the Gulf of Finland were reawakening; long-standing disputes about the ownership of Gotland grew more acrimonious with the passing of time. In the years after 1513 Kristian II, as part of his preparations for reconquering Sweden, made great efforts to achieve the diplomatic isolation of Sten Sture by approaches to most of the states of the Baltic littoral, from

Muscovy to Mecklenburg. His success, to be sure, was not great; but his attempt inevitably produced counter-action from Stockholm: Sweden and Denmark thus moved almost inevitably into different camps in international affairs. This was particularly true in regard to Lübeck and the Hanse. By the opening of the sixteenth century the long-standing commercial supremacy of Lübeck in the trade of the Baltic was being challenged by merchants from western Europe, and especially from the Netherlands. The Dutch skippers, by sailing round Jutland and through the Sound, were breaking Lübeck's old monopoly of the exchange of eastern and western European commodities; for that monopoly had been based on the command of the portage-route across the Kiel isthmus. But the sea-route round the Skaw was cheaper and less troublesome for those inexpensive and bulky goods which formed the staple of the Baltic trade; and already in 1429 Erik of Pomerania found the traffic sufficiently heavy to make it worth his while to mulct it: it was in that year that he introduced the celebrated Sound Dues which were for centuries to form the backbone of Danish royal finance—and, incidentally, of the Danish navy. The challenge to Lübeck was the more serious, because it developed at a moment when the Hanse's old outposts in east and west were crumbling: Bruges was declining in the face of Antwerp's competition; Novgorod fell into Muscovite hands in 1478, and Ivan III closed the Hanse's factory there in 1494. Moreover, the Hanseatic League was itself divided in its attitude to the interlopers: the other Wendish towns supported Lübeck, but Danzig grew rich on trade with the Dutch and the English. Such a situation offered obvious opportunities to play off Lübeck against her opponents. Since the mid-fourteenth century Danish kings had carried on an intermittent fight against the economic predominance and political pretensions of the Hanse, and perhaps only Engelbrekt's revolt had deprived Erik of Pomerania of a decisive victory in that struggle. Though in recent years relations had somewhat improved, Kristian II was regarded by the Hanse with justified apprehension. They were well aware of his determination to make Denmark independent of Lübeck's middlemen, and supplant the Hanse as the leading maritime and commercial power in the North. He had inherited from his father an excellent navy. In 1516 he married Isabella, granddaughter of the Emperor Maximilian I, sister of the young man who would soon be the Emperor Charles V. By doing so drew closer politically to the hated Dutchmen; while at the other extremity of the Hanse's commercial empire he was on terms of alliance and friendship with Ivan III. He was thus in a strong position to exert pressure upon Lübeck, and to blackmail her council into support of his policies.

From the moment of his accession Kristian had been determined to reassert his authority over Sweden. His father had attempted it and failed: in 1509, and again in 1512, truces had been arranged which postponed a settlement, and gave the Swedes the option of paying tribute until such time as they chose to admit the Danish king. As early as 1449 Kristian I had constrained Lübeck to bring pressure to bear on Karl Knutsson by forbidding her burghers to trade to Sweden. Hans had several times followed his example, and Kristian II intended to use the same means. But it was by now a question how long the Lübeckers would continue to yield to such demands: in 1510 they had lost patience, changed sides, and waged a brief and unsuccessful war against the Danes. Commercial caution, induced by the strength of the Danish navy and the ability of the Danish king to harry their shipping, might still dictate a policy of appeasement; but the blockade of Sweden cost them a trade which they could not afford to lose. Young Herr Sten and his father were well aware of these economic cross-currents, and of the possibilities which they offered to a ruler in need of allies. Whenever Kristian II enforced Lübeck's reluctant support, Sten Sture courted Danzig and the Dutch; whenever Lübeck was Denmark's enemy, she became inevitably Sweden's friend. Meanwhile, the truce of 1512 was renewed for two years in 1515. Once again the friends of peace had averted a conflict by postponing a settlement. But it was for the last time. Kristian would not be fobbed off again: a decision could hardly be deferred beyond 1518. And already accident had put a new and powerful weapon into Kristian's hands.

In 1514 Gustav Trolle became archbishop of Uppsala, in succession to the aged Jakob Ulvsson, who resigned the see in his favour. The resignation may well have been designed to ensure that Sten Sture should not secure the election of a man of his own, for Jakob Ulvsson had good reason to fear the Stures' attitude to the church. Certainly Trolle, and Archbishop Ulvsson too, belonged to that section of the magnates which resented the regent's high-handed methods and was suspicious of his dynastic ambitions: it was the archbishop's father, Erik Trolle, who had been the unsuccessful rival of young Herr Sten in 1512. The change at Uppsala at once produced a crisis. For more than half a century the see of Uppsala had held in perpetuity the important castle of Almare-Stäket, and also (but only at pleasure) the fief which went with it and was necessary to its support. Almare-Stäket, lying a little to the north-west of Stockholm, commanded the main land-route from Stockholm to Dalarna and the Bergslag at a point where it crossed a narrow arm of Lake Mälar. When Jakob Ulvsson resigned his see, Sten Sture (in 1515) resumed the fief, and was probably within his rights in doing so. Trolle seems from the beginning to have expected a struggle with the regent, and to have taken his measures accordingly. At his consecration in Rome he secured papal briefs authorizing him to use force in defence of the church's interests, and to lay an interdict, if necessary, to enforce his pretensions to the fief—though this was a matter justiciable only in the Swedish lay courts; on his way home he seems to have put himself in touch with Kristian II; and his behaviour on his return was needlessly truculent and provocative: he refused, for instance, to take the usual oaths of fidelity and allegiance. The regent was outraged; the archbishop defiant. In 1516 Sten unearthed a conspiracy designed to bring in Kristian II; and its leader, Sten Kristiernsson Oxenstierna, by his confession implicated Gustav Trolle. This gave the regent a pretext to extend the quarrel. Hitherto he had claimed only a right to sequester the fief: in October 1516 he proceeded to besiege Trolle in the castle. After all, the elder Sten had done as much to Jakob Ulvsson in 1497.

Essentially the Trolle affair was a typical dispute between church and state: the archbishop believed himself to be defending *libertates ecclesiae* against an aggressive ruler who was trying to subject the church, no less than the state, to his arbitrary power; and if the dispute had been kept on that level Sten could hardly have rallied the rest of the episcopate to his side. But Trolle changed the whole aspect of the controversy by trying to play off the king against the regent. In 1517 a Danish expeditionary force was sent to relieve Stäket. It landed near Stockholm, and was ejected. And from that moment the question became involved in the great controversy about the Union. Trolle was looked on as a traitor to the national cause; his episcopal colleagues washed their hands of him in the name of patriotism; and Sten, pressing the moral advantage, in November 1517 summoned a meeting of the Estates to Stockholm, and asked their advice as to how to deal with Trolle. The Estates were solidly in Sten's favour, for the archbishop was already hated by the populace. He was now voted a traitor; and it was unanimously resolved never to accept him as archbishop. It was further resolved that the castle of Almare-Stäket be razed to the ground: the Stockholm burghers had for some time been complaining that it interfered with their trade to the Bergslag. And, finally, they all swore to stand by each other in defence of these resolutions, to accept common responsibility for them, and to resist, if need be at risk of their lives, any attempt which might be made at the papal court to institute punitive measures against them because of their proceedings. It was a formal conjuration, a 'swearing-in-common' (*sammansvärjning*)—a device which had been used by the Stures before. It was a typical example of their tactic of associating the commonalty with their policies; and it was to be revived by another ruler of similar propensities in another great crisis at the end of the century. The step the Estates had thus taken was certainly a grave one, and the consequences might well be serious. Stäket was undeniably church property; its razing involved the destruction of relics and the profanation of holy things; the action seems to have been accompanied by gross brutality to the archbishop, and was followed by his imprisonment. Not surprisingly, Trolle called loudly to Rome for vengeance. Yet the regent could take some comfort from the fact that his stock stood high in Rome. If his actions were arbitrary and violent, Kristian II's treatment of the church was no less so. The chances of resisting Danish intrigues in the curia seemed by no means desperate.

In the spring of 1518 Kristian II returned to the attack, and appeared with a fleet in the Stockholm skerries. The event did not answer his expectations. Beaten by Sten Sture at Brännkyrka, he was glad enough to enter into a negotiation. As an earnest of good faith Sten was persuaded to put into Kristian's hands six hostages, all persons of consequence in his party: among them were Hemming Gadh, an ecclesiastical careerist of ability who in the past had done good services to the Stures in Rome, and Gustav Vasa, then a young man of twenty-two. No sooner had they boarded the Danish fleet than Kristian gave orders to weigh anchor; and with his six hostages safe under hatches he sailed away to Copenhagen, to prepare a better opportunity. Meanwhile he and Trolle were getting the upper hand in the struggle for the support of the papacy. Despite the backing of a papal legate, Arcimboldus, who had come to Scandinavia to sell indulgences, and whom Sten Sture is said to have tempted with the prospect of the reversion to Trolle's see; despite the undeniable fact that Sten Sture the elder had done violent things to Jakob Ulvsson, and Kristian I no less violent things to Jöns Bengtsson, without permanently alienating the papacy; Kristian's influence at Rome was strong enough to prevail. For since 1517 the balance of forces in the curia had changed to Sweden's disadvantage. In 1519 Charles V was elected Emperor, in the face of the opposition of the papacy; and Leo X, hastily adjusting his policies to the new situation, now deemed it imperative to support Charles's brother-in-law of Denmark. Sten Sture was accordingly excommunicated; Sweden was put under an interdict; and Kristian could invest his next campaign with something of the character of a crusade.

Early in 1520 his forces struck northwards across the border; and on 20 January they met and defeated Sten Sture at Lake Åsunden. Sten was mortally wounded, and a fortnight later died in his sledge on the way home to Stockholm. He left behind him a seven-year-old son, Nils, an enterprising and intriguing widow, Kristina Gyllenstierna, and a band of partisans and servants whose future, it seemed, was dark indeed. But he left, above all, a strong loyalty and devotion in the hearts of many of the common people, who had focused upon him their rudimentary patriotism, and had believed that he might perhaps be the strong king who would safeguard them against the illegalities of the great. Not the least of the obstacles in Gustav Vasa's path would be the shade of young Herr Sten.

The death of Sten Sture, and the tender age of his eldest son, offered a last opportunity to those of the Swedish aristocracy who had disliked the implications of the Sture *régime*. Kristina Gyllenstierna, to be sure, still held out in Stockholm; but the very fact of her resistance helped the *råd* to strike a bargain with the invader. At Uppsala, on 6 March 1520, they succeeded in concluding a treaty with Kristian's commander which appeared to leave most of the effective power in Sweden in their own hands. It was indeed an agreement of a type common enough in the last two generations; and if it fell short of all their desires, it seemed at least to make possible a revival of the Union as the old *råd*-party had conceived it. But these calculations were speedily dealt a shattering blow. Stockholm surrendered in September, in return for a comprehensive amnesty to Kristina and her supporters, which covered, among other things, any violence they might have offered to the church, and soon afterwards Kristian forced a helpless *råd* to acknowledge him as hereditary monarch. With the sweeping away of the elective nature of the kingship there was swept away also all hope of confining Kristian within those constitutional bounds which the *råd* was concerned to preserve: at one stroke the treaty of Uppsala was annulled. Kristian had served notice upon his Swedish subjects that they need hope no longer for any *regimen politicum*: the little finger of the Oldenburgs was to be thicker than the Stures' loins.

The victory was also to be exploited in other ways. It put Kristian at last in a position to realize his long-cherished commercial ambitions. On his entry into Stockholm he is said to have remarked, 'We have won one of the gates of Lübeck, and it will not be long before we win the other'. The means he envisaged to this end was the creation of a Northern Trading Company, which should beat the Hanse at their own game. It was to be a joint-stock company, with permanent shares and a dividend payable every third year; it was to establish factories or staples at Copenhagen, Stockholm, Antwerp and Viborg; and it was to use these commercially-strategic vantage-points to draw into its hands all the trade between Eastland and the west of Europe. An important element in this trade was the export of Swedish copper and iron; and here too the recovery of Sweden gave Kristian the opportunity to make far-reaching plans. There was to be a rationalization and reorganization of the Bergslag to bring the mines under effective royal control; mining techniques were to be modernized with the aid of technicians imported from Saxony; the Fuggers were to be approached and tempted to invest their capital. The whole project was typical of that capacity for bold and imaginative planning which gave Kristian in his better moments an undeniable quality of greatness—a quality which is also displayed in his enlightened plans for social and judicial reform in Denmark.

Unhappily this was not the only side to his character, as the Swedes were now to discover. When Kristian entered Stockholm, he brought Gustav Trolle with him; and Trolle, it seems reasonable to infer, came with the fixed determination to see his wrongs righted. He had already a suit depending at Rome against Sten Sture and his associates; but that was no bar to his seeking redress also at the hands of his secular sovereign. He wanted those responsible for the injuries inflicted upon himself and his servants to be brought to book; he desired restitution and indemnity for the church. Kristian was crowned in Stockholm on 4 November; and three days later Trolle notified him that Sten Sture, seventeen of his leading supporters, and the burgomasters, council and citizens of Stockholm, were guilty of 'notorious heresy'. But the property of heretics who suffered death was forfeit to the crown; and Trolle accordingly coupled his notification with a statement of the amount of indemnity which he was claiming, presumably in the hope that Kristian would make it over to him, at least in part: he estimated it at the enormous figure of one million marks. There followed an investigation before the *råd*, at which at least some of the accused seem to have been given an opportunity to make a defence. Among them was Kristina Gyllenstierna, who in an attempt to prove that the proceedings of 1517 had been the work of the Estates as a whole, rather than the particular responsibility of individuals, produced the act of conjuration of 23 November 1517. The effect of this move was disastrous. For the case was now referred to a species of spiritual court (convened for the purpose by the king) composed of Trolle, three bishops and ten prelates; and on 8 November this court pronounced all the accused guilty—not on the grounds which Trolle had adduced in his notification, but as being contumacious excommunicates, and, above all, as having been proved by the act of 1517 to have banded themselves together to resist papal authority. And since by canon law the adherents, aiders and abettors of heretics were to be esteemed equally culpable, the judgment extended the circle of the guilty to any who had concurred in the act of 1517, even though they had not personally participated in its promulgation. All those who had been a party to Sten Sture's conjuration—which meant the entire body of the Estates—were thus liable to be accounted heretics. The whole Sture party, and very many others, were now at the mercy of the secular arm.

And the secular arm was already flexed for service. The *sententia* of the court had no sooner been made public than the king's servants took action. On the afternoon of 8 November 1520, between the hours of one and four o'clock, no less than eighty-two persons were beheaded; and others fell victim in the days that followed. Their bodies, together with the exhumed corpses of Sten Sture and his infant son, were later burnt in three huge pyres on Södermalm. Most of those who suffered, no doubt, were persons specifically named, or generally described, in the indictment, or could be considered as followers and abettors of heretics. But some were quite obscure individuals; some had demonstrably been among the Stures' political enemies in the past; two were inoffensive bishops, of whom one—Matts of Strängnäs—had been prominent in attempting the reconciliation of the *råd*-party with Kristian II; while another ecclesiastical victim was Hemming Gadh, who had turned his coat while in captivity in Denmark, become Kristian's man, and was now rewarded by being executed in Finland on Kristian's express orders.

Such was the 'bloodbath of Stockholm'. Probably no event in Swedish history—unless it be the death of Karl XII—has been the subject of more prolonged controversy. There is scarcely an incident in the events of 7 and 8 November upon which there is an agreed opinion: the weight to be attached to the evidence, the sequence of events, and above all the interpretation to be placed upon them, are all in irreconcilable dispute. In particular historians differ upon the motives for the massacre and the allocation of responsibility for it. At the one extreme are those who see it as the act of a bloodthirsty Renaissance tyrant, or the manifestation of a psychopathic personality; at the other those who regard Kristian as the innocent agent of Trolle's malignity and party spirit, or the loyal executor of the judgment of a spiritual court, bound by duty to implement its decision. One thing, at least, seems clear: that in any legal point of view all the proceedings were hopelessly irregular. If this was a heresy-trial, it was a trial which violated the rules of canon law at almost every point.[1] And on the whole it seems probable that Trolle was concerned, not to compass

[1] Neither the facts in Trolle's original notification, nor the grounds alleged by the court, in fact justified condemnation for heresy; the condemnation of heretics must by canon law be by name, and not by vague categories such as 'the burghers of Stockholm'; it was Trolle's duty to encourage the reconciliation of heretics, if there were a possibility of it, but he expressly rejected reconciliation in advance; the king had no right to convene or constitute a spiritual court; such a court had no right to pronounce a *sententia*, since that duty rested only on the bishop; the king (or his servants) had no right to decide which heretics should be spared, and which not; the execution was not by burning at the stake, as prescribed for heretics, but by decapitation. Trolle had no need to give any grounds for a notification of notorious heresy, and could perfectly well have proceeded in his own episcopal court.

the death of his enemies, but rather to rifle their pockets: it is significant that his list of heretics omitted some of those—and some of the most culpable—of whom he had complained to Rome, but included the utterly unpolitical (but conveniently wealthy) mother of Kristina Gyllenstierna. He brought the matter to the king in order to make sure that the church's claims to compensation should not be lost sight of; and in the end he does seem to have been given a share of the confiscated property. For Kristian, on the other hand, the proceedings offered a chance—especially after the production of the act of 1517—to crush his political enemies, actual and potential, at one blow. The executions did not shatter only the Sture party; they dealt a heavy blow at the *råd*—at the very group, that is, to which Trolle by origin and conviction belonged. The execution of the bishops cannot have been acceptable to Trolle. It has indeed been defended on the ground that some contemporary sovereigns considered that the Roman law entitled them to deal with ecclesiastics guilty of grave crimes as though they were laymen. But this was a theory wholly unacceptable to the papacy; and it is a defence which cannot be put forward simultaneously with the plea that Kristian, as a pious monarch, felt that he had no option but to carry out the sentence of the court. And indeed he did not carry it out: he executed a highly arbitrary selection of victims, chosen either at random or upon some principle which is a matter for conjecture. The papacy certainly blamed Kristian for the bishops' death, and exculpated Trolle; and Kristian felt obliged to explain to an incredulous pope that there had been a 'plot', a tumult, that the bishops had perished by accident, and that it was really all the fault of the legate Arcimboldus for encouraging Sten Sture. The episcopal victims, moreover, were curiously chosen. One of them had probably not been a party to the resolution of the Estates which formed the basis for the charge of notorious heresy. On the other hand two bishops—Hans Brask of Linköping, Otto of Västerås, who certainly had appended their seals to that resolution—appeared in 1520 not among the accused but among the accusers, and also among the judges. And even if the story be accepted that Brask in 1517 safeguarded himself by inserting into his seal a strip of parchment bearing a protest to the effect that he acted only under duress, and was now able to save himself by producing it, this still leaves the sparing of Otto unexplained. Again, the swift haling to execution (without trial or hearing of any sort) of so many burghers of Stockholm implies the existence of a proscription-list prepared before the heresy-charge was brought forward; and the execution of the more important burghers, it has been suggested, may have been a deliberate move in Kristian's grand plan for remodelling Scandinavian trade: their places were to be filled by foreigners whom

Kristian would import. The continued atrocities which accompanied the king's peregrination of his kingdom are certainly in part Kristian's own responsibility; and may be taken to suggest that the Stockholm bloodbath was either part of a deliberate system of terror designed to pulverize all opposition, or the manifestation of an acutely psychotic personality. And not the least significant pointer to Trolle's comparative innocence is the fact that two years later Gustav Vasa (for whatever reason) made an approach to him with proposals for political collaboration. For Gustav Vasa, on that bloody 8 November, lost his father, his brother-in-law, and two uncles among the slain; while his mother, his grandmother, two of his sisters—to say nothing of Kristina Gyllenstierna herself, who was half-sister to his aunt—were now held prisoner in Stockholm castle, and would presently be transferred to Denmark. The civil broils of fifteenth-century Sweden, in contrast to contemporary disturbances in France and England, had on the whole been remarkably bloodless: few battles; virtually none of the assassinations, the political executions of the vanquished, the cold-blooded murder of dangerous innocence, that stained the Armagnacs or the Yorkists. The bloodbath of Stockholm was something new and shocking, which revolted public opinion outside Sweden no less than in it; and Gusta Vasa's propaganda, for many years to come, would shout itself hoarse with easy but telling invective against 'that horrid bloodhound and tyrant', 'that cruel and un-Christian old King Kristian'. To the very end of the reign, the unforgettable lesson of the massacre would remain one of his most well-worn and potent political arguments, deployed over and over again to rally his subjects to his policies, or persuade them to swallow disagreeables; and the prospect of Kristian's restoration would be depicted, with unwearied iteration, as the dire consequence of disobedience, the dreadful alternative to the rigours and caprices of Gustav's own rule.

Gustav Vasa himself might well have shared the fate of his father; for since May 1520 he had been once more on Swedish soil. After his removal to Denmark in 1518, he had remained for some months in easy and honourable confinement; but in 1519 he had made his escape, and at the end of September of that year had taken refuge in Lübeck. Here he had found succour and protection from certain citizens whose economic interests were concerned in the maintenance of Sweden's virtual independence—such men, for instance, as Karl Konig, Hermann Iserhel, and the Stures' old factor in Lübeck, Markus Helmstede. Official Lübeck, though it evaded a Danish demand for his extradition, was understandably reluctant to do anything positive to assist him. The city's relations with Denmark were, no doubt, strained; but it was proving difficult to formulate a policy acceptable to the other Wendish towns, and Danzig, though quite as hostile to Kristian as Lübeck, proved captious and uncooperative. In May 1520, therefore, Lübeck suffered Duke Fredrik of Holstein (who was Kristian II's uncle) to patch up yet another treaty, whereby the city once more agreed to suspend trade to Sweden for the next ten months. Since this was Lübeck's policy, Gustav Vasa had little to gain by protracting his stay; and it was with no very lively hopes of Hanseatic aid that he landed near Kalmar on 31 May 1520.

His coming at first made no impression; nor was there any reason why it should. He had been a Sture-man, like many another, and his family was related by marriage to both the elder and younger Stures; but his father had been politically and personally of little account, and he himself had not hitherto been especially prominent among the younger nobles at Sten Sture's court, though he is said to have fought well at Brännkyrka. His escape from his Danish prison had given him a certain notoriety, and exposed him to Kristian's vengeance: hence Kristina Gyllenstierna took care to have him included by name in the Stockholm amnesty. Failing any other leader—and after 8 November the range of choice was not wide—he might serve as well as another to lead the Sture party until young Nils should be able to lead it. Even so it required the bloodbath of Stockholm, and Kristian's sanguinary progress through the kingdom, to persuade anyone to follow him; and for some months he was a hunted man, with as many hairbreadth escapes and desperate adventures to his credit as Bonny Prince Charlie.

It was in Dalarna that he found his first support. The traditional resistance of the Dalesmen to successive Union kings, their long-established political alliance with the house of Sture, the alarm of the small miners at rumours of Kristian's plans for the control of Sweden's mineral exports, the tales of atrocities committed upon peasants and priests—all these at last stirred up a movement which turned to Gustav Vasa because he seemed to be the only possibility. He proved a skilful leader; and since the men to whom Kristian had entrusted the government in Stockholm were squabbling among themselves, and ineffective in their counter-measures, the rebellion gathered momentum fast. In April 1521 the rebels were able to defeat Kristian's forces at Västerås; in May they captured Uppsala. A push eastward to the sea gave them a port through which supplies could reach them from abroad. By the beginning of the summer Gustav's army stood outside Stockholm; and in July he reached agreement with two typical representatives of the aristocratic party which had made the treaty of Uppsala a year earlier, and had subsequently paid for it so dearly. These were Hans

Brask, bishop of Linköping, and Ture Jönsson (Tre Rosor),[1] governor of the province of Västergötland. Ture Jönsson, no doubt, had been constrained to abandon Kristian II by the threats of the local peasantry; but both he and Brask had already been alienated from the king's cause by his obvious disposition to arbitrary rule. Their junction with Gustav Vasa and his peasants was thus a coalition of members of the old *råd*-party with the new popular patriotism which had hitherto been so alien to them. They counted, it seems, on their ability to control a young and politically inexperienced leader; and perhaps they counted too on being able to drop him when he had served their turn, as their ancestors had dropped Engelbrekt nearly ninety years ago. It may well have been their insistence that led Gustav Vasa to make an overture to Trolle soon afterwards. It was fortunate, perhaps, that Trolle repulsed these approaches: the report of them had provoked a menacing letter of protest from the Dalesmen. Nevertheless, though these aristocratic reinforcements brought their own problems, and though Gustav Vasa must have been galled by the paternal and patronizing tone which Brask adopted towards him, it was their support which carried his election as regent in August 1521; and without it he would hardly have gained the crown two years later.

The successes of 1521 had been facilitated by Kristian's miscalculations: in the summer of that year he had turned his back on Sweden, and departed on a three-months' visit to the Netherlands, there to concert high politics with his Habsburg relations. By the end of the year most of the country was in the hands of the insurgents; and early in 1522 Gustav acquired an important auxiliary when Kristian's commander in Stegeborg, Berend von Melen, came over to his side. But the three main fortresses of the kingdom—Stockholm, Kalmar, Älvsborg—still held out under resolute commanders. Until they were taken, the road remained open for Kristian's return. And it was becoming evident that Gustav had not the resources to capture them without outside aid: his army of volunteer peasants, at first unpaid, and always concerned for their crops and their families, was anxious to return home.

In this situation it was natural that the regent should turn to the Hanse: indeed, he seems to have made his first approach to Lübeck as early as the summer of 1521. The prospects in this quarter had latterly been improving fast. Kristian, by raising the level of the Sound

[1] The use of surnames did not become general among the native Swedish nobility until the first quarter of the seventeenth century, and many were still named only from their father: thus Ture Jönsson's son was Jöran Turesson. In order to distinguish between men of similar names in different families, it is usual to add the surname which they later took, and which was in many cases the simple description of their coat of arms—in Ture Jönsson's case, Three Roses (Tre Rosor).

Tolls, had violated the agreement he had made with Lübeck in 1520. He had for a time so far succeeded in misleading Charles V as to induce him to threaten the Hanse with the imperial ban if they resumed dealings with Sweden. He was the friend and supporter of Albert of Prussia in his quarrel with Danzig. Gustav Vasa was prepared to bid high for Hanseatic aid; and was already promising large commercial privileges in Sweden. In April 1522, therefore, Lübeck and Danzig agreed in principle to give support to the Swedish insurrection. But the government of Lübeck took care not to commit itself, in the first instance, by overt official action. Assistance was indeed organized; but organized on the footing of a private speculation, a *consortium* in which the main investors were Gustav Vasa's personal friends and well-wishers from 1519. In June 1522 they sent 750 trained soldiers, with arms and supplies, in a fleet of ten warships; which on arrival Gustav purchased—on credit. Encouraged by the success of this venture, the Lübeck town council now took a hand; and in October despatched a second fleet, which arrived opportunely to capture a large convoy designed for the relief of the Stockholm garrison. The command of the sea thus passed into the hands of the insurgents; and even on land the Swedes were now so much the masters as to be able early in 1523 to invade the Danish provinces of Bleking, Skåne and Viken.

Meanwhile, a revolution was preparing in Denmark. The Danish nobility had been alienated by Kristian's legislation on behalf of the peasants and burghers; the Danish church was shocked at his flirtation with the Lutherans. They turned for help to Fredrik of Holstein. In March 1523 they elected him king. In April Kristian II, with a characteristically sudden collapse of morale, fled with his wife and family to the Netherlands; and though his partisans continued for some time to resist (especially in Copenhagen and Malmö), from the spring of 1523 it was Fredrik I rather than Kristian II who was effectively king of Denmark. His victory had in great measure been made possible by his alliance, in February 1523, with his old friends the burghers of Lübeck.

The accession of Fredrik meant that Kristian's claims to Sweden passed into his hands. He lost no time in asserting them; and it was disquieting that Lübeck, in exchange for a promise of better privileges in the Scandinavian countries, had bound herself to give at least a partial and conditional recognition to his pretensions to be Union king. But this was perhaps no more than a tactical move; for Lübeck's investment in Gustav Vasa had now reached such dimensions that the city could scarcely afford to abandon him, while he on his side probably held out a better prospect of trade concessions in Sweden than Fredrik was likely to offer. A divided Scandinavia suited their book better than a Union, after all; a king was the best bar to a king; a monarch created at their instigation and enthroned under their aegis might probably provide the best political security for the recovery of their outlay. They had made Fredrik of Holstein king of Denmark; they would make Gustav Vasa king of Sweden—at a price.

The Swedish magnates, led by Ture Jönsson and Hans Brask, may well have reasoned along similar lines. The Union as Kristian II would interpret it was a flouting of all their political traditions; Gustav Vasa was their *protégé*, and might if properly handled be kept reasonably docile: he seemed at least a less objectionable ruler than young Herr Sten had been. And if, when they arrived at Strängnäs on 2 June, they still had doubts and reservations, their hesitation may perhaps have been removed by the news of the Lübeck-Holstein alliance, and by the knowledge that Fredrik I was asserting his pretensions to the Swedish throne. Gustav Vasa himself might have his misgivings—doubts about his 'modest birth', doubts whether he could risk thus flouting the Sture claim—but on the whole he seemed the only possible solution. This conclusion was probably enforced or reinforced by hints from the Lübeck representatives that if he were not elected they might turn for security to Fredrik. On 6 June, therefore, Gustav accepted the crown; on 17 June Stockholm surrendered to him. The surrender was a sufficient sign of Lübeck's authority, for it had been negotiated beforehand by her representatives, and they had come to Strängnäs with the offer of submission in their pockets. Meanwhile, the sparse ranks of the *råd* had been filled by new creations, including Berend von Melen: as a foreigner he was by law debarred from that high office; but his intimate connexions with Lübeck made his choice politic, and perhaps necessary. With a king, with a full council, there was a semblance of regular government again. The Lübeckers had had their way, and now bestowed a qualified and conditional benediction. The country was virtually cleared of the Danish enemy. The reign could begin.

The Union of Kalmar had been an arrangement of convenience, and it had survived only for as long as it suited the interests of the contracting parties. But it had also embodied great ideals: the ideal of Scandinavian fraternity; the ideal of *regimen politicum*. And the Union came to an end because one of the ideals, at least, had been ousted by another: Unionism had been defeated by Swedish nationalism. The fate of the constitutional ideal was in 1523 still undecided, and to men such as Hans Brask or Ture Jönsson there seemed no compelling reason to assume that Gustav Vasa would necessarily try to tread the path of young Herr Sten. No doubt he had climbed to power on popular support; but it was to the *råd* that he owed his election as regent and as king—to the *råd*, and to Lübeck. It was still possible that an independent Sweden might remain effectively an aristocratic republic with an elective monarchy tightly bound by constitutional limitations. But the history of the last half century was in the event too strong for Hans Brask and those who thought like him. In the perilous world of the 1520s Sweden could no longer afford anything less than a strong monarchy; which meant a monarchy rich in revenues, and in the armed forces which revenues could hire. The lesson of the fifteenth century, for all save a narrow circle of ageing aristocrats, seemed to be that Sweden needed more government, a firmer hand, a stronger central authority, an administration less casual and rudimentary. At the end of a century and a quarter of Union, Sweden had emerged as a nation, and must have at least some of the apparatus of a modern nation-state. The Stures had seen this, and they had sought to strengthen their position by appeals to the commonalty and exploitation of the Estates. It was a line of action which must obviously present itself to the new monarch as one possibility for the future. But Gustav Vasa's experiences during the war of liberation and after it might well make him chary of committing himself irrevocably to this alternative, at any rate as a permanent solution: '*Herr Omnes*' could be a useful ally, but was an ill master. Yet the bar to any increase in kingly power and wealth lay in the fact that both church and nobility seemed to have a common interest in resisting a change which could only be at their expense. Perhaps it was only the blunders of Trolle, and Sten's skill in using them, that had prevented a confrontation on these lines in the years before 1520. In the person of Gustav Vasa, as in that of Karl Knutsson, one noble family (and not the most powerful or the most ancient) had ascended the throne over the heads of their social equals; and half a century after 1523 there were still members of the aristocracy who were ready to remind them of it. Thus personal grudges no less than constitutional principles and economic interests might seem to designate the nobility as the predestined opponents of the Vasas; and if this were so, *Herr Omnes* might after all prove inevitable. King Kristian had indeed done his successor one useful service by cutting off some of the tallest heads in 1520; but though the aristocracy had been temporarily weakened, it would recover. Sooner or later Gustav Vasa would have to make up his mind whether he could risk affronting it, or whether he could afford not to do so. Upon his ability to resolve this dilemma, upon the method by which he ultimately did resolve it, hung the fate of his dynasty, and (more important) the fate of Sweden.

2. Gustav Vasa

I. SWEDEN IN 1523

What sort of country was it over which Gustav Vasa was to rule for the next thirty-seven years? Of what nature was the material from which he was to build a new national state?

In 1523 Sweden, more decidedly than today, was a country that geographically and politically faced east rather than west. Access to western Europe was limited and precarious, for only at one place—the estuary of the Göta river, where lay the fortress of Älvsborg and the town of Nya Lödöse—had Gustav Vasa an open window to the North Sea. To the north of Älvsborg, Norwegian territory included all of what is now Bohuslän, and was then called Viken; to the south, the Danish province of Halland thrust up to within a stone's throw of the river. The rich grain-growing province of Skåne was Danish too; and so, to the north-east of it, was Blekinge; and the peasants and townsmen of Swedish Småland, to the north of the border, were linked by strong economic ties to the ports and markets of this region. Up in north-central Sweden, the frontier with Norway, which otherwise ran roughly along the watershed, took a great swerve to the eastward, which brought it within sixty miles of the Gulf of Bothnia, and deprived Sweden of political control of the provinces of Jämtland and Härjedalen, whose inhabitants found their economic focus not in Gävle but in Trondheim. In the Baltic itself, Denmark owned the island of Bornholm, and in 1523 was still in possession of Gotland. Thus the distribution of Danish and Norwegian territory not only came near to cutting off Sweden from the Atlantic—not only enabled Denmark to treat the Sound as a stream running through Danish lands, to be opened or shut at the discretion of the Danish king—but also interposed at least a potential barrier to Sweden's contacts with Germany: a barrier which, forty years later, would become a formidable political reality. Only to the east was Sweden's view relatively unimpeded; and to the east a long historic tradition had directed Swedish interests. The memory of the Varangians had hardly faded before a semi-crusading, semi-colonizing venture had led to the incorporation of most of Finland into the Swedish realm. But a limit was set to advance on this side by the resistance of the Russians; and the treaty of Nöteborg (1323) had fixed a frontier which now, in its northern reaches especially,

English miles
0
50
100
150
200
250
Vardøhus
Vadsø
Varanger Fj.
Fiskar Peninsula
Petchenga
Kola
Loppen I.
Alten Fj.
Malanger
FINNMARK
Tana
Alten
Maals
Enare träsk
Pasvik
Lofoten
Ofoten Fj.
Titisfjord
LAPPLAND
Kandalaks
Jokkmokk
VÄSTERBOTTEN
ÖSTERBOTTEN
Uleåborg
Kajaneborg
Trondheim
JÄMTLAND
ÅNGERMANLAND
Umeå
GULF OF BOTHNIA
Vasa
FINLAND
KEXHOLMS LÄN
SAVOLAKS
KARELIA
HÄRJEDALEN
Härnösand
MEDELPAD
HÄLSINGLAND
Hudiksvall
SATAKUNDA
Björneborg
TAVASTLAND
SWEDEN
Mora
DALARNA
Leksand
Kopparberget
Tuna
GÄSTRIKLAND
Gävle
Dalälven
Raumo
Nystad
FINLAND PROPER
Åbo
Kymmene
Viborg
Kexholm
Ladoga
Oslo
NYLAND
Borgå
Nyen
Nöteborg
Neva
Åland
Kastelholm
Helsingfors
Ekenäs
Kimito
GULF OF FINLAND
Kopore
INGRIA
VÄRMLAND
Filipstad
VÄSTMANLAND
Örbyhus
Sala
Enköping
UPPLAND
Uppsala
Sigtuna
Karlstad
Västerås
Arboga
Mälaren
Vaxholm
Stockholm
Strängnäs
Gripsholm
Södertälje
Örebro
NÄRKE
SÖDERMANLAND
BOHUSLÄN
DALSLAND
Vänern
Mariestad
Lidköping
Skara
Vadstena
Vättern
Nyköping
Norrköping
Söderköping
Stegeborg
Stångebro
Gamla-Lödöse
VÄSTERGÖTLAND
Linköping
ÖSTERGÖTLAND
Lödöse
Göteborg
Älvsborg
Jönköping
Eksjö
Västervik
Vimmerby
Visby
Gotland
Varberg
HALLAND
SMÅLAND
Växjö
Halmstad
Markaryd
Kalmar
Borgholm
Öland
Hälsingör
Hälsingborg
BLEKINGE
Kristianstad
Kristianopel
SKÅNE
Lund
Malmö
Bornholm
BALTIC SEA
Teusina
Jama
Narva
Ivangorod
Tolsburg
Reval
ESTONIA
Padis
Weissenstein
DAGÖ
Hapsal
Peipus
Gdov
Lais
Novgorod
Volchov
Ilmen
Sönnenburg
Pernau
Dorpat
ÖSEL
Karkus
Staraja Russa
GULF OF RIGA
LIVONIA
Pskov
Domesnäs
Salis
Wolmar
Windau
Wenden
Dünamünde
Goldingen
Tuckum
Riga
Kirkholm
KURLAND
Mitau
Libau
SEMGALLEN
Düna
Bauske
Birže
Memel
LITHUANIA

Sweden, 1611

lay well to the west of the actual limits of Swedish and Finnish settlement. By the time of Gustav Vasa's accession, Finland, more or less to its present extent, was *de facto* a constituent part of Sweden, with similar institutions and a similar social structure. Lastly, in the far north lay a vast indeterminate area, where frontier-lines either did not exist or had no significance, with a thinly spread nomadic population of Lapps—the latter still mostly pagan—over which neither Denmark-Norway, nor Sweden, nor Muscovy exercised for the present any continuously effective control.

But if Sweden was thus smaller than in later years, it was still a very large country; and its size was made the more obvious by the difficulty of communications and the paucity of population. By far the greater part of the country was either forest or lake; and the forest still as of old acted as a barrier to free intercourse. Roads were few and bad: scarce one was practicable for wheeled traffic. The isolation of one province from another was mitigated only by the relative facility of water-communication—either within the skerries that fringed much of the coast, or over the huge lake-system that filled much of the centre of the country—and by a winter climate whose severity made sledge-travel easy and comfortable for three or four months of the year. Except in Östergotland, Västergötland and Uppland, where the villages lay close enough together for one parish church to be visible from the next, the areas of cultivation appeared (and still appear) as sparse and precarious islands in a dark sea of conifers which only waited its opportunity to return and engulf them. The impression was illusory, at least in part, for the forest was friend as well as foe. It furnished timber for building and fencing, birchbark for roofing, fuel without stint for domestic consumption or for smelting, lush pasturage in summer, game and berries to diversify a spare diet, and in those too-frequent years when the harvest failed, bread-substitutes in the shape of bark or moss. Within the high walls of timber the village communities practised an agriculture whose yield, under the influence of primitive methods and an unkind climate, was never abundant and usually disappointing. The open-field was distributed among the village householders in strips or patches, and the precious meadowland likewise; an ancient form of plough rather scratched than turned the soil; and a simple alternation of crop and fallow was the usual rotation. The predominant grain was barley: rye came a bad second, though by the end of the sixteenth century it would be gaining ground; and the cultivation of oats was still in the future. Apart from such changes as these agriculture remained static, alike on noble and peasant land; though it is conceivable that the continuous care of monastic establishments may have produced better results than elsewhere. But less than half of the country, after all, was suitable for arable farming. The mining areas of Dalarna, Närke and Värmland, as well as much of Norrland, were regions which had always to rely on imports of grain from other provinces, and were even more dependent than the rest upon eking out their food resources (and paying their taxes) by fishing and hunting. The southern provinces of Västergötland and Småland were predominantly pastoral: they paid their taxes in butter or oxen; drove their stock on the hoof to the markets of central Sweden; and contributed, in the shape of hides and butter, a substantial share of the country's export trade. In all ordinary years Sweden could feed herself; in a few there might be a small surplus. Unlike Norway, the country was not regularly dependent upon importation of foodstuffs. The food was coarse enough (hard bread and salt fish were the staples for the common man); it was rarely eaten fresh; but such as it was it usually sufficed.

In 1500 the population may perhaps have amounted to something like three-quarters of a million. The greatest part of it was concentrated in the centre and south of the country, and especially in the areas of old cultivation round lake Mälar, in the open grain-growing plain of Östergötland, in pastoral Västergötland, and in parts of Småland. It was, overwhelmingly, a peasant population. But it differed much from the peasantry of most of the rest of Europe, in that it was free, and believed itself always to have been so. There had indeed been slaves in old Scandinavia, descendants of defeated tribes and captives taken in raids, and the last handful of them had been freed by statute as late as the mid-fourteenth century; but a majority of the peasantry had from time immemorial enjoyed a freedom which contrasted with the villeinage of feudal Europe. More than half were independent yeoman farmers, owning their own land, and rendering to the crown the standing taxes and burthens that lay upon it; the remainder were tenants of the crown, paying rent instead of taxes; or tenants of the nobility or the church, who paid rent to, and did work for, their lords, and were taxed only extraordinarily, and on a reduced scale. The fifteenth century had seen no real deterioration in the status of the Swedish peasantry. Their freedom remained unimpaired; and despite individual cases of landlords' tyranny the country emerged from the Middle Ages without experiencing anything like a *jacquerie*. In these respects conditions were markedly different from those in Denmark, where the process was already beginning which was to degrade the peasantry to a condition approaching serfdom, and where King Hans could speak of them as a people born to servitude.

It has been estimated that at the beginning of the sixteenth century perhaps five per cent of the population of Sweden may have lived in towns. But the distinction between town and country was anything but sharp. All Swedish towns were strongly rural in character and interests: even in Stockholm goats grazed on the turf roofs of the houses, and the city authorities fought an uphill battle against the pigs. Wood and water pressed close around their walls, wild nature peered in at their gates: as late as 1840 wolves were not uncommon in Stockholm, and a century after that a stray elk turned up in the centre of the city. Since communications were easiest by water in summer, or over the ice in winter, it was natural that most Swedish towns should be situated on the sea-coast, or on lakes and navigable rivers. In the high Middle Ages Sweden had been very much in a commercial backwater: the main streams of trade had passed her by. But there had been a period before that when Viking enterprise had put her at one end of a great trade-route which led by the Russian portages to Miklagård (Byzantium); and it was in this period that the earliest Swedish urban communities arose. A high proportion of them still obviously faced east. A string of ports dotted the long east coast—Tälje, Söderköping, Västervik, Kalmar; at the northern extremity of the Gulf of Bothnia Luleå was already in existence as an outpost in the wastes of Västerbotten; Gävle was a foundation of the fifteenth century. But pre-eminent among them all was Stockholm, successor to the vanished Birka, supplanter of the now-decayed Sigtuna. In 1523 Stockholm presented a somewhat melancholy appearance, with its towers shattered and its population diminished by the long siege, but it was still the only town in Sweden of any consequence when measured by the standards of north Germany. Its normal population was perhaps six to seven thousand, which put it in the same order of magnitude as Wismar or Reval, but was less than half that of Norwich or Bristol. Though a few hundred persons already lived on Norrmalm, and a handful on Södermalm, the town proper was still the town 'between the bridges', and the island on which it stood had limits a good deal narrower than today: the gradual rising of the level of the land, and the reclamations of successive centuries, have by our time added considerably to its area. Massive walls erected in the early fifteenth century made it a place of strength; and its castle was never in its whole history taken by storm. It was a tight-packed, congested place, with houses over-arching the vaulted entrances to villainous side-alleys; but the narrowness of the streets was less apparent than it became a century later, since the habit of building high had not yet established itself: two, or at the most three, storeys seem to have been the rule. With the exception of the castle, the Great Church and the establishments of the Franciscans and Dominicans, the buildings were mostly mean enough: many houses were still only wooden shacks, though a majority, perhaps, were already of brick. Certainly it was extremely dirty, even to a German nose—though not, perhaps, as dirty as early eighteenth-century Edinburgh; for the strong current of the Mälar ensured that some at least of the sewage should be water-borne. Stockholm had thriven as the *entrepôt* between the Bergslag and the Hanse; and from its beginnings in the thirteenth century German influence had been strong. By 1350 it was a half-German town: Magnus Eriksson's Town Law found it necessary to stipulate that half (and thus by implication not more than half) of the town council should be native Swedes. Its connexions with the Hanse had been so close that its representatives had attended a meeting of the League in 1366. But relations between the two nationalities within its walls had not always been easy, despite the tendency for Germans to become Swedes after residence for a generation or two; and as Swedish national feelings grew stronger they turned on occasion against Germans no less than Danes. It was symptomatic that in 1466 a Swedish writer should have complained that 'A German is mint-master, a German has the great customs, a German has the little customs, a German has the ground-rents, so that there is nothing left for a Swede but to be hangman and grave-digger'.[1] Five years later, as we have seen, the victory at Brunkeberg was seized as the occasion to exclude all Germans from the town council.

For the rest, the Swedish towns were either ecclesiastical centres such as Uppsala, Skara, Vadstena or Strängnäs; or local markets such as Jönköping; or places which lived—as Västerås and Köping mainly did—by organizing the food supplies of the Bergslag at markets where the oxen of south Sweden were bartered for iron or copper. Most of them were little more than overgrown villages. But there was one other town which deserves special mention: Nya Lödöse. Nya Lödöse was founded in 1474. It lay on the Göta river, not far from the site of modern Göteborg, nearer the open sea than Old Lödöse, which it supplanted. It gave Sweden her only port on the North Sea, her only route to the markets of the Netherlands and England, if Denmark should ever close the Sound. While the Union of Kalmar subsisted this was not perhaps a matter of prime importance. After 1523 the case was altered. Nya Lödöse's communications with central Sweden were difficult and slow; the town itself hopelessly insignificant; but to a state liable to be imprisoned within the Baltic its retention might well become a vital interest.

Urban communities such as these could not aspire (except of course for Stockholm) to play a part of any political importance in the nation's life. The possession of Stockholm, certainly, was indispensable to any ruler, and never more so than in the latter days of the Sture *régime*: no

[1] Nils Ahnlund, *Stockholms historia före Gustav Vasa*, p. 325.

one who was not master of Stockholm and its castle could be sure of his grip upon Sweden. But the rest did not count for much; though Kalmar had strategic importance. The truth was, that the Swedish towns had missed some of the toughening educative experiences of towns in western Europe. They had never had to fight seriously for their liberties or their privileges; they had never been menaced with subordination to an over-mighty baronial neighbour; they were too tiny to have been ripened by the party struggles and faction fights of Italy or Flanders. The gild merchant had never established itself; and the craft gilds (like so much else) came to Sweden rather late: the oldest seems to date from 1356. It was, of course, an importation from Germany; and German influence and German models are very evident in the Town Law of Magnus Eriksson. For that very reason a large part of it was unsuited for application to any other town than Stockholm: the careful regulations about burgomasters and councils, the attempt to enforce membership of craft gilds, were unrealistic when applied to Växjö or Enköping, whose burghers could never produce the prescribed number of burgomasters, and whose population baked and brewed at home, and could hardly be expected to organize craft gilds on the basis of one smith and a couple of cobblers. And because the towns were small and weak they had from the beginning accepted royal interference as an earnest of royal interest and protection. In every town was the king's bailiff, who kept the municipal officials up to their duties, and regularly sat on the bench in the municipal courts.

In many respects, it is clear, Sweden was a somewhat primitive and backward country. But it was a country by no means ill-endowed with potential sources of wealth, and already awake to the possibility of exploiting them. The days when the herring fishery had made Falsterbo and Skanör the hub of Hanseatic activity might now be over, for the herring had moved further afield; but the soil of Sweden contained mineral resources which were already of great importance, and which were one day to provide the material basis for her emergence as a great power. The least significant of these was silver, mined at Sala from 1510. For the first half of the sixteenth century the Sala mine produced silver in payable quantities, and to Gustav Vasa its output was to be of considerable importance; but thereafter production dropped, and it never came near to repaying the capital which successive Swedish monarchs lavished upon it. They long clung to the hope that they had found a Potosí; but geology was against them. The wealth of Sweden was to come not from silver but from copper and iron. Both industries were of ancient date: the first mining of copper is thought to date from the eleventh century; the first mining of iron from the twelfth. Iron is found dispersedly over much of central Sweden, but at this period was mined and smelted mainly in Närke, Västmanland and southern Dalarna: this was the area known as the Bergslag. Copper, on the other hand, came from a single immensely rich source, the Kopparberg; and here in later years the town of Falun was to arise. The techniques of mining and extraction were somewhat rough and ready by German standards, and output was apt to vary greatly according to the ease or difficulty of winning the ore; but production of each was already considerable, and it was increasing. There was as yet no manufacturing industry in Sweden capable of interesting a foreign buyer: the arms and armour of the nobility seem still to have been mostly imported. What was sold to the Germans who came to Sweden was either plate-copper, or *osmund*—the small, uniform-sized pieces of iron which for centuries provided the excellent raw material for the manufactures of other lands. And it was the increased sales of this latter commodity which in the 1490s caused the Cornmarket in Stockholm to be renamed the Ironmarket.

Mining was in the hands of the local peasantry or lesser gentry: a small-scale affair of individuals with very limited capital, who regulated their own affairs, made rules and allotted shares, in much the same way as village communities decided upon the time of sowing or harvest, or settled the distribution of strips in the common field. The crown had early enforced regalian rights, and in exchange had accorded to the Bergslag considerable privileges and immunities, which included a large measure of self-government, concessions about taxation, and a right of asylum for fugitives from justice who were prepared to work in the mines. The miners, indeed, formed a distinct and highly self-conscious element in Swedish society, which was neither peasant nor burgher; and at meetings of the Estates they were represented by special delegates of their own. Their obvious economic importance to the country gave them self-confidence, and their contacts with German traders afforded them a wider outlook upon matters of state than that of the ordinary peasant. And since the Bergslag included part of Dalarna, and recruited labour from that province, the miners could usually count on being supported by the Dalesmen. Like the miners, the peasants of Dalarna were a little different from peasants elsewhere: for one thing, there were no nobles in Dalarna—and no monastic establishments either. They were sturdy yeomen, recalcitrant to royal bailiffs and kingly authority; formidable bowmen who used a special short and heavy arrow peculiar to them (it figures in the arms of the province), and by no means deficient in a good conceit of themselves—an attitude of mind in which they were confirmed by the prominent part they had lately taken in domestic politics, and especially in the war of liberation that had placed Gustav Vasa on the throne. From the time of Engelbrekt onwards it had been apparent that the views of the Bergslag and Dalarna could powerfully affect the course of Swedish history; and this was a lesson which they were quick to learn and slow to forget. Under the Stures, in particular, when they had cemented their economic and political alliance with Stockholm, they were a force in the background which no ruler of Sweden could afford to ignore.

The Swedish mining industry was of indigenous growth, and in its early stages had been developed by native enterprise; but it soon attracted the attention of foreign *entrepreneurs*, and in particular of Lübeck. German immigrants came to the Bergslag, and German capital came with them. At the Kopparberg this was a relatively short-lived stage: by the end of the fourteenth century the shares in the mine seem all to have reverted into Swedish hands; but in the iron industry the German influence was more enduring. It was the mines and their produce which mainly attracted the Hanse to Sweden, and which led, therefore, to the heavy germanization of Stockholm and some other of the east coast ports. Successive kings welcomed the influx. The earliest grant of privileges to Lübeck dates from 1251; it was confirmed in 1336; and in 1361 was extended to apply to the Hanseatic League as a whole. These grants resulted in the putting into Hanseatic hands of a control of Swedish commerce which at times came near to a monopoly, and which the Hanse would willingly have converted into one. For the policy of the rulers of Sweden was usually to prefer a 'passive' to an 'active' trade: that is, they encouraged the foreigner to bring the goods of which the country stood in need, and to take in exchange the products which Sweden had to offer; while the native merchant was to be content to trade with the Germans on Swedish soil, rather than to venture out on his own. By the end of the fifteenth century this general principle was subject to numerous exceptions; but it remained true that the greater part, and above all the more valuable part, of imports and exports was in foreign hands.

Of exports, the most important in the years around 1500 was probably copper, and this all went by way of Stockholm to Lübeck. Iron, nearly equal in importance to copper, and in some years exceeding it, went both to Lübeck and to Danzig; and so did the only other two exports of any consequence, which were butter, and hides and skins. As to imports, they consisted mainly of one luxury commodity, cloth; one universal necessity, salt; and one amenity, beer. The cloth came from the Netherlands or from England, by way of Lübeck or Danzig; the salt, either from Lüneburg or, increasingly, from Bourgneuf in the Bay of Biscay (the so-called 'Bay salt'); the beer, from Rostock or Danzig. On the whole, the predominance of Lübeck in Swedish commerce was very marked, and Sweden's share of Lübeck's trade not inconsiderable: it has been estimated at about 15 per cent; while perhaps 80 per cent of Lübeck's iron imports were of Swedish origin. From Lübeck Swedish commodities passed to the markets of Germany, the Netherlands and England: it was, indeed, the great middleman upon whom the country depended to keep its trade going. That is not to say that Lübeck had not competitors, actual and potential. There was a considerable trade with Reval, for instance (particularly from Finland), and a much larger one with Danzig. This last was especially important, for Danzig, as we have seen, encouraged the Dutch interlopers, and could within limits be played off against Lübeck and the Wendish towns, politically and economically. It was to Danzig that Karl Knutsson fled on his deposition in 1457, and it was to Danzig that young Herr Sten sent an embassy of desperate entreaty in the final crisis of 1519–20. It is true that Danzig had the disadvantage that it offered no vent for Swedish copper, for it was committed to handling the Fuggers' exports of copper from Hungary. Nevertheless, that section of Sweden's trade which was in Swedish hands—an 'active' rather than a 'passive' trade—tended to be directed to Danzig or Reval: ships from relatively ungermanized towns such as Västervik, ships of great landowners or churchmen who preferred to market their butter themselves, ships of the elder and younger Sten—good businessmen both, and the largest native shipowners of their day. Above all, it was by way of Danzig that Bay salt reached Sweden—a circumstance which substantially moderated the rigour of the trade-bans which Denmark periodically pressed the Lübeckers to impose. And already the Stures had begun to think of a direct trade to the Netherlands, though as yet nothing came of such projects.

It was because the Lübeckers were beginning to fear a potential Dutch threat to their commercial supremacy in Scandinavia that they determined to extract the last ounce of advantage from the extraordinary chain of circumstances which had enabled them to place their clients (and, they hoped, their puppets) simultaneously on the thrones of Denmark and Sweden. In each case the stipulated reward for their assistance was to be a grant of privileges more comprehensive than any that had preceded it. The terms which they secured at Strängnäs in 1523 were certainly extraordinarily favourable: the trade of Sweden was to be reserved to Lübeck, Danzig, and such other of the Hanse towns as Lübeck might agree to include. All other foreigners were to be barred. The Swedes themselves were to trade only with the Hanse: navigation westwards through the Sound or the Belts was specifically forbidden them. Lübeck and the towns approved by her were to have the right to trade free of all Swedish tolls and customs in Stockholm,

Kalmar, Söderköping and Åbo; and in those towns were to be at liberty to trade in luxury goods directly with the Swedish nobility and clergy without the intervention of a middleman. And finally these privileges were without limitation of time: they did not apply only (as perhaps might have been expected) for the duration of Gustav Vasa's indebtedness. They put Sweden's economic development at Lübeck's mercy; and it is obvious that only hard necessity and strong pressure could have extorted them from Gustav Vasa: Hans Brask, for one, had been opposed to the acceptance of Lübeck's terms. In the long run, they would be intolerable; and the event was to show that Gustav Vasa was not disposed to submit to them for longer than he must.

In comparison with the modest circumstances of the native Swedish burghers the nobility and the church appear decidedly affluent, though by western European standards their resources were narrow enough, and their ideas of luxury—and even of comfort—unexacting. A sharp line of demarcation ran horizontally through the whole of Swedish society, dividing those classes who were free of tax (*frälse*) from those who were liable to it (*ofrälse*). The nobility and the church were *frälse*; the peasants and the townsmen *ofrälse*. Exemption from tax had originally been a privilege conferred in requital for service, and any man who provided a fully armed horseman for service with the king's host had been entitled to claim it. But by the end of the fifteenth century knight-service (*rusttjänst*) of this kind was restricted in fact to those who were already in the enjoyment of *frälse*, and *frälse* became the privilege of a class, the mark of noble or clerkly status. This did not mean, however, that the nobility became a closed caste, as was happening about this time in Denmark. On the contrary, though the acquisition of *frälse* by way of *rusttjänst* was now no longer automatic, or even usual, the nobility continued to receive accessions from below. Movement into the ranks of privilege by way of royal favour did occur, and it grew steadily commoner throughout the sixteenth century. In the seventeenth came the great flood of peer-creations, which made a title the normal reward for a successful career in the service of the state. But at the beginning of the sixteenth century the nobility was still comparatively small in number: in 1611 there may have been between 400 and 500 noble families; a century earlier there were probably less. But of these certainly a half, probably more than a half, differed little in social circumstances and economic resources from the richer peasants of their locality. War, harvest failures, or the personal degeneration of the stock could easily depress a family until it retained only the name and privileges of nobility. The absence of any custom of primogeniture led to the constant subdivision of estates among heirs, so that the race which bred vigorously might be hard put to it to maintain its standard of living, while the race which did not was always in danger of extinction. There was never in Sweden, as in England, the characteristic problem of what to do with younger sons, for nobility inhered in all descendants of a noble in the male line; and there was in any case small choice of a career for such persons, apart from the management of their estates: the church, as we shall see, was no longer attracting them as in earlier days; not many, it seems, sought their fortunes in continental armies; and the king's service was as yet so exiguous that it offered few opportunities—though Gustav Vasa, when he came to expand it, would recruit his bailiffs from those *knapar* (petty nobles) whose narrow circumstances drove them to look for alternative sources of income. Higher up the social scale the nobility did indeed act very generally as provincial or county judges at *landsting* or *häradsting*, for in the absence of any class of professional lawyers they were the traditional and indispensable custodians of the law; but this was no more a career in itself than it was for an Elizabethan J.P. or lord-lieutenant. The frequent inability of the poorer nobles to render the military service which was the sign, and had originally been the condition, of noble status was always forcing some of them to drop quietly back into the mass of the peasantry, if only for a generation or so, or leading them to accept solid yeomen, not exigent in the matter of dowries, as husbands for their daughters: in the second half of the century the aristocracy would be increasingly concerned about this kind of *mésalliance*.

As yet there was no real distinction between the nobility of the court and the nobility of the provinces, for all the aristocracy, however great or small their estates, were emphatically provincial in residence and outlook. They might attend upon the king intermittently when his progresses took him in their direction; if they were members of the *råd* they were liable to be summoned to him for counsel; but as yet there was little in the way of a court or court-life: Gustav Vasa had to educate his nobles to it. The habit of buying town property was a good deal more common than the habit of living on it: they bought town houses as an investment, or for convenience of trading with foreigners, and set their servants to live in them. Very few members of the aristocracy maintained a permanent residence in Stockholm. The great magnates formed a quite small circle of families—perhaps twenty-five or thirty of them in all—held together by a complicated web of intermarriages, their social prestige and political power firmly founded on the ownership of great estates. They were not compact estates: on the contrary, they tended to be dispersed widely over the country—often enough, indeed, beyond the Danish border—and they were dispersed deliberately, as an insurance against harvest failure, or for convenience of trading. Between these estates they moved around, as their sovereign also did, in order to consume on the spot some of the perishable commodities which came to them as rents from the peasantry. But even their utmost efforts could not consume them all; and the great landed magnate had usually considerable surpluses, which he bartered at home for other commodities, or exchanged with Lübeck merchants for the cloth, spices, and arms which were the main luxury imports, or from the salt which was the common need of all. A few drove an export trade in their own ships, and resorted to Danzig or Reval with the produce of their lands, or (if their estates lay near the Bergslag) with the *osmund* which they acquired by exacting it as a rent from their tenants, who had themselves obtained it by barter from the miners. And since standards of luxury were modest, and prestige spending (thanks to the absence of any real metropolitan life) was on a comparatively limited scale, such persons had often free capital at their command. They sought to invest it, as a rule, in land. But this was often attended with some difficulty; for the demand for land exceeded the supply. It is true that the imposing territorial empires of the great magnates were less stable than they appeared to be: a good part of them was in the form of revocable fiefs, and there was much buying and selling of the remainder. But the total amount of land available to the nobility was now limited; and in any case the magnates were in competition for it with the church, which was a bigger property owner than any of them. By the time of Gustav Vasa's accession *frälse* had become a privilege which inhered in the land owned by a noble, or by the church, and peasants on such land were exempted from ordinary taxation, since their lords required from them dues and services roughly equal to those which they would have rendered to the crown had they been tax-paying peasants, and it was clear that the land could not support exactions from the king in addition to those of the lord. But since the crown could not well afford to see an indefinite extension of land exempt from taxation, it therefore (in 1396) adopted the expedient of defining what land was *frälse*, and prohibiting any further extension of *frälse* through noble acquisition of *ofrälse* land. And since it was also a standing constitutional principle that the king must not permanently diminish the lands (and hence the revenues) of the crown, the practical effect was that in the fifteenth century the amount of *frälse* land available for purchase was restricted, and could be expanded only with the king's leave. Hence there was brisk competition for such land between those who were entitled to possess it. Nobles anxious to add acre to acre to support political ambitions jostled with churchmen looking for a sound investment for surplus revenues; and perhaps on the whole the churchmen came off best, since land which had once passed into their hands rarely came again upon the market. Even so, the church was also driven to seek investment in *ofrälse* land (which now retained its *ofrälse* character after purchase), and in urban property (to the irritation of burghers), and seems in addition to have developed a considerable business as a money-lender. Already, long before the Reformation, there was thus a latent clash of economic interest between church and nobility: it contradicted that general community of constitutional outlook which had made them both, on the whole, opponents of the Stures and champions of a Union in which they should be the predominant elements. In this latent antipathy Gustav Vasa was ultimately to find the solution to his political dilemma.

For indeed the interests of the monarchy and the aristocracy were to some degree coincident in this matter. The monarchy was poor in comparison not only with the nobility, but also with the church: the church's revenue from tithe exceeded by a large margin the sum of the royal rents. It has been estimated that in 1523 the land of Sweden was divided in the following proportions: 52·4 per cent was in the possession of tax-paying peasants; 21·3 per cent in the possession of the church; 20·7 per cent in that of the nobility; only 5·6 per cent in that of the crown.[1] Since about the middle of the fourteenth century the crown had found that the revenues and services which it drew from the land were inadequate to the business of administration and defence in an age when the cost of both was rising. In these circumstances kings had been ready enough to hand over the custody of a castle, with the administrative areas dependent on it (and on which it in turn depended for supplies), to a member of the nobility, in exchange for his taking upon himself the governmental responsibilities which went with it. Sometimes the crown demanded, in addition, a fixed sum from the local revenues; sometimes it delegated its authority on condition that its agent accounted for and handed over any surplus on the year's working.

There grew up, therefore, the practice of allotting service fiefs (*län på tjänst*) to great magnates who would do the king's work for him. The system fell short of feudalism as the continent knew it, for fiefs were not hereditary, and lapsed on the demise of the crown; status was never determined by tenure; and justice never passed into private hands—in contrast with the position in Denmark, where the fifteenth century saw the development of manorial courts. In the Middle Ages Sweden was not a feudal country. Nevertheless, the *län*-system arose from administrative difficulties analogous to those which feudalism had been devised to solve. The kings were careful to try to keep in their own hands a nucleus of fiefs—the so-called 'larder-fiefs' (*fata-*

[1] In Finland, tax-paying peasants at this time owned 96·4 per cent of the land.

burslän)—to provide the indispensable basis of economic support for their authority; and they did not allow Stockholm castle to pass out of their hands if they could help it. The expense of maintaining castles in a defensible condition against artillery led in the course of the fifteenth century to the decay and destruction of many of them, and fief-holding consequently tended to become more attractive (because less onerous), though for the same reason the crown became less eager to entrust castles to its subjects. It is obvious that the holding of fiefs was closely related to political power, and the struggles between the crown and the aristocracy about the terms of the Union, as well as the quarrels of rival noble groups, turned largely upon their bestowal, and upon the pretensions of this family or that to improve its holdings. Even such ambitious and ruthless rulers as the Stures did not venture to trample too heavily upon noble susceptibilities in this matter. But they did endeavour to amass a compact and stable block of larder-fiefs in central Sweden; and young Herr Sten's fateful attack upon Trolle's fief of Almare-Stäket (though the immediate economic gain was small) may be seen as an aspect of this policy.

The problem was really an aspect of the inelasticity of the fiscal system, and this in its turn of the constitutional situation; for the imposition of any new tax was possible only with the consent of the assemblies of the various provinces (*landsting*). It was a well-established principle that the king must live of his own; and if his regal activities required any extraordinary aid, or if a new tax were in question, it was to the provinces that he must turn. Sweden had emerged as a state through the growing-together of separate provinces; and even at the end of the fifteenth century was still not far removed from a loosely articulated federation of lands and towns. Dalarna had a character, a tradition, and a dialect which were different from those of Småland; Västergötland was a world in itself, whose aristocracy intermarried tightly and long acted as a separate political group; in times of crisis one province would send emissaries to another to concert common policies. Local organs of government, local vehicles of opinion, still counted for much: the *landsting*, and the smaller assemblies of the counties (*häradsting*)—which were the subdivisions of the province—were still politically and judicially active. The governor of a province (*lagman*) and the sheriff of a county (*häradshövding*) were, no doubt, members of the nobility; but the *ting* itself, whether at the provincial or the county level, was a robustly democratic body, in which every tax-paying peasant was entitled to take part. Meetings still often took place in the open air, procedures were rude though formalistic, and the voice of the commonalty could make itself heard with effect. And this primitive democracy was an essential characteristic of Swedish society. It appeared again in the village councils, which regulated petty local affairs, in the elected vestrymen, who managed parochial business, and—perhaps most important of all—in the standing jury of the county, which, drawn as it was from peasants of local weight and reputation, provided a real safeguard for the poor man entangled in the antique complexities of the law.

The provinces had kept their own codes of law until the middle of the fourteenth century, when a general code for the whole country—known as Magnus Eriksson's Land Law—had superseded them in most respects, if not quite in all. And Magnus Eriksson's Land Law had enounced, in memorable words, a principle which by 1500 was already deeply rooted in Swedish society: 'The land' (it said) 'shall be built upon law, and not upon force'. Sweden was still in many ways a country of savage manners, and violence was common in every class of society; but the idea of the rule of law was already firmly grasped, and even in the most adverse times it would henceforth always contrive to maintain itself. It is as fundamental to Swedish as to English history.

The Land Law was not only a codification of civil and criminal law, it was also a formulation of the law of the constitution which crystallized current practice, or resolved points that had in the past been doubtful. The monarchy was declared elective, and the procedure of election was defined. The king was pronounced to be subject to the law and not above it; and a coronation oath was prescribed for him. He was bound to 'govern the land with inborn men after the old law and custom of the realm'. He must live of his own, and see to it that the land be not diminished for his successor. He must maintain the privileges of church and nobility. He was not to give fiefs to men who were not of Swedish birth. 'He shall also hold, confirm and defend all old Swedish law, which the commonalty of their free will and consent has accepted, and which is established by previous kings and by their kingly power, so that no ill custom prevail over their rightful law, especially that no foreign law be set over it and be brought into the kingdom to be law and right to the commonalty, nor shall any new law be given to the commonalty without their yea and consent. He shall also protect and safeguard all his commonalty, especially the peaceable who desire to abide in law and quietness, as well from violent and evil inborn men as from foreigners.' And, finally, in terms which seem familiar to an English ear, 'he shall not imprison nor cause to be imprisoned nor in any way destroy any man, poor or rich, in life or limb, without he be lawfully condemned . . . nor shall he by any means take any property away from him, save by law and lawful doom'.

In thus establishing the principle that the monarchy was limited,

Magnus Eriksson's Land Law provided the basis upon which the whole future constitutional history of Sweden was to repose. By its unique authority and prestige it stood as a bulwark against any reception into Sweden of foreign law, and especially Roman law. It defined the fundamentals for that *regimen politicum* which was to be the constitutional ideal of the aristocracy in the period of the Union. For generations after that it stood as a constitutional norm to which appeal could be made, and against which existing conditions could be measured. It was in itself a constitution; and its influence on the subsequent course of Swedish history is comparable with that of Magna Carta upon the history of England. And, as with Magna Carta, it was capable of being made the jumping-off ground for constitutional developments—and particularly for further restraints upon royal authority—not all of which were necessarily implicit in its text or consonant with its spirit. In 1371, for instance, the *råd* extracted from Albert of Mecklenburg not only a coronation oath, but also a charter (*konungaförsäkran*). It was a precedent which was not forgotten—Svante Nilsson and the younger Sten Sture were both forced to give charters on their election—and it was later to be of great constitutional importance. It was not easy for the Union monarchs to resist developments of this sort. If they tried the high hand, they stood in danger of deposition: between 1397 and 1523 only Svante Nilsson and the younger Sten Sture maintained an uninterrupted tenure of the throne. The *råd* and the nobility (in Denmark, as well as in Sweden) made the most of their opportunities, and tilted the constitutional balance more and more in their favour. In 1441 the Swedish *råd* forced Kristoffer to promise that no new member should be appointed to their body without their consent. In 1442 they secured the promulgation of a revision of the Land Law which was modified in the aristocracy's interest. In 1457 Kristian I was constrained to agree that henceforward the crown should not be permitted to acquire *frälse* land. And in the Recess of Kalmar, the terms of which the *råd* drew up in 1483 as a condition precedent for the recognition of Hans of Denmark's authority over Sweden, they pushed their pretensions to extreme lengths. All castles were to owe fidelity to 'four good men' during *interregna*, and the same good men were also to take charge of the government during the king's absence from the country; if any subject exhibited a grievance against the king, the *råd* was to adjudicate the cause; the *råd* had a duty to admonish the king if he denied justice to a subject, and afterwards if need be the right to resist him; no fief was to be conferred or revoked without their consent; the king was not to hinder 'good men' from fortifying their manors, and such manors were given extensive rights of asylum; it was laid down that 'every good man shall be king over his tenants'—

by which was meant that he was entitled to such fines for misdemeanours as would otherwise have fallen to the king's share; and, finally, the king was to govern through 'good inborn men', and was in no circumstances to 'place any base-born men above them'. The Recess of Kalmar, if it had been accepted and applied (which it fortunately was not), would have been the charter of an all-powerful aristocracy, which under the guise of defending the rights and liberties of the nation would have been in a position to tyrannize over the rest of society, while they safeguarded themselves against royal retribution by producing a licence for anarchy. In the name of *regimen politicum* they aspired to much the same sort of constitution as the Polish nobility were later to achieve in the name of *aurea libertas*. Nevertheless, it was a programme which was not forgotten; and in more or less diluted form it tinctures the whole course of Swedish history for three centuries to come.

Against that programme the rule of the Stures, and especially that of the younger Sten, was a deliberate reaction. Seeking to recover for the regency some of the authority that had been lost to the crown, they ruled with the aid of men of non-noble birth whose fortunes depended on their masters' survival—men such as Peder Jakobsson Sunnanväder, Erik Svensson, Hemming Gadh: it was the first foreshadowing of a type of government which was to acquire notoriety later in the century under the name of 'the rule of secretaries'. Above all, they appealed from the *råd* to the people; and they could plausibly claim that in doing so they were recurring to the real spirit of the Land Law. By the last quarter of the fifteenth century a new constitutional organ was beginning to emerge. As yet it had no defined status, no recognized constituents, the scope of its activity was uncertain, and it can scarcely be said even to have a name; but a later age would call it the *riksdag*. Its origins and early development are obscured by the dust of controversy, as well as by the darkness of the subject itself; but it seems at least certain that it represented the fusion of two constitutional traditions. On the one hand, it descends from those solemn national gatherings at which the representatives of each province exercised their immemorial right of 'taking and breaking kings'; on the other, it can be considered as an extension of the common practice of afforcing ordinary meetings of the *råd* with representatives of other classes of society, to form a so-called *herredag*: the *råd* was long regarded as an essential element in any *riksdag*. So much is common ground; but when it is attempted to establish a date by which this body can be clearly discerned as something new—a date by which it was identifiable as a real national parliament—then agreement is not to be had. Nevertheless, it is probably safe to say that this stage had been reached by the

1460s, at the very latest. The basis of recruitment by Estates seems much older. Its members were still designated by authority, rather than popularly elected; its rights, duties and privileges had hardly begun to be matters of consideration; but it was now clearly an embryo parliament. It comprised nobles and burghers, miners and tax-peasants; though the clergy (unless, as bishops, they were members of the *råd*) were not present. The old-style meetings of the afforced *råd* continued to be summoned on many occasions, and the fact that the term *herredag* was used indifferently for such meetings and for the new-style body which was to become the *riksdag* makes for confusion, at all events in the minds of historians; but the habit was establishing itself of summoning the new body to endorse critical decisions, or to lend the government support at moments of danger. King Hans took care to have Kristian recognized as hereditary prince by a gathering of this sort; and Kristian II himself summoned two meetings of the Estates to reinforce his authority during his brief reign in Sweden. Sten Sture the younger found in such meetings an instrument well suited to his needs: it was the embryo *riksdag* that in 1517 gave popular endorsement to his actions against Gustav Trolle—a very remarkable instance of interference by the *riksdag* in the affairs of the church: there was to be another, still more remarkable, ten years later. And it was in 1518 that Sten told Arcimboldus, in memorable words, that 'what touches all must be approved by all': even if the phrase was less significant than some later historians have imagined, it at least aptly illustrates something which was implicit in his policies.

As yet, no doubt, these meetings of the Estates were for use only upon exceptional occasions, and they by no means superseded the old constitutional principle that required the assent of the *landsting* to new taxes and new laws. The *riksdag* as yet concerned itself neither with the one nor with the other; though it was already beginning to present schedules of grievances. But its proceedings were still relatively formless (the first Proposition dates from 1517), and not seldom its meetings were held in the open air, as at Strängnäs in 1523: indeed, the last occasion when this happened fell as late as 1587. And if a king found he could do his business better by haranguing the crowd gathered at one of the great winter markets, he might well prefer not to put himself and his subjects to the trouble and expense of a meeting of the Estates. For the *riksdag* was still what it had been in its origin—a device of government, to be used or discarded as best might answer; and a device which in the meantime was looked at with some distrust by the constitutional watchdogs of the *råd*.

The administrative machinery of the country was in 1523 hardly more developed than the legislative. Gustav Vasa, like Sten Sture before him, would begin ruling Sweden on much the same lines, and with much the same sort of agents, as he employed in the running of his family lands; for indeed the royal administration was, in ideas and methods, scarcely more than estate-management raised to a higher power. Nobles and soldiers guarded the castles and supervised the administration of fiefs; *lagmän* and *häradshövdingar* combined judicial with executive functions in the province or the county; but the day-to-day business of government out in the countryside was mostly in the hands of the king's bailiffs. The royal revenues were rendered partly in cash, partly in kind, and much of them was spent or bartered locally for local needs. Any surplus would be sent up to Stockholm for safekeeping in the castle there, whence it would be issued to defray demands—such as the payment of Lübeck's mercenaries—which must unavoidably be acquitted in cash. There was as yet no central treasury or exchequer in any real sense. And just as finance was mainly dispersed and local, with scarcely any central organization save in the king and a handful of trusted servants about his person, so justice had a very similar character. The local courts—municipal, county, provincial—dealt with most of it; and though the fifteenth century had produced a novelty in the way of an occasional circuit by the king, or the regent, or by members of the *råd*, who now and then held a sort of General Eyre (*räfsteting*), there was no central court sitting in the capital. Indeed, there can hardly be said to have been a capital at all; for the government centred on the king, and the king was not settled in any one spot. The only appeal from local courts was to the king in person. His dooms might on occasion not only decide cases, but create new law, under the guise of declaring the old. One central administrative office was indeed inescapable, for even a country as simple and loosely articulated as mediaeval Sweden required a chancery. But it was altogether significant that in the time of the Stures there was not one chancery, but two. The Stures had their own private chancery, and their last chancellor, Peder Jakobsson Sunnanväder, was destined to be a thorn in Gustav Vasa's side; but the official chancery was an office attached to the *råd*, and presided over as a rule by the bishop of Strängnäs for the time being. The accession of Gustav Vasa put an end to this dualism; but it did not otherwise alter the administrative arrangements very much.[1] The new king ruled with much the same kind of instruments as the old regent: a handful of clerks and minor ecclesiastics; a rather larger force of bailiffs. Government remained paternal and to a great extent decentralized. The fact that the native aristocracy had neither the taste

[1] There were, in addition, two great officers of state, the high steward and the marshal; but their offices were filled only intermittently, and they had no real administrative significance.

nor the aptitude for participation in the central administration at first drove him, as it had driven the Stures, to rely heavily on members of the clergy. And when the quarrel with the church made such agents suspect or unacceptable he would be faced with a problem of recruitment for his embryo civil service; and the solutions to which he was forced to resort would themselves provide him with fresh difficulties.

It was certainly no easy task that confronted him. At home and abroad the dangers and difficulties were great. But in the person of Gustav Vasa Sweden had acquired a king of no ordinary calibre. He had accepted the government of the country, and he was determined to govern it. He was, no doubt, still young and inexperienced; but he matured with marvellous swiftness. He proved to be a man at once ruthless and crafty, with a dangerous ability to sway the crowd at a fair or the Estates at their gatherings by a natural oratory which was pungent, popular and racy. Despite his public utterances to the contrary, he seems never for a moment to have doubted his capacity to rule, nor swerved from his determination of ruling. From the very beginning he understood that the essential problem of the moment was the assertion and maintenance of a real royal authority. To that end he needed soldiers at his disposal, expensive though they might be, and unpopular as the taxes to maintain them might prove. But most of all he required, from all those concerned with the government, incessant personal application to every sort of business, from the great issues of high policy to the pettiest details of estate-management. He soon discovered that there were few who were qualified or willing to give that application, and that much would depend upon himself. But he took to the profession of kingship as easily as if he had served a protracted apprenticeship. He turned his hand to every kind of business; in great measure, no doubt, for lack of skilled assistance, but not a little because he did in fact delight in the *métier*. For he had, undoubtedly, a real sense of the obligations of his office; and he had a love of ruling, a passion for business, a relish for detail, a satisfaction in the exercise of power, which not all his peevish complaints of the lack of trustworthy collaborators can really disguise.

II. THE OPENING OF THE REIGN: SÖREN NORBY AND THE STURE PARTY

Gustav Vasa was king of Sweden; but it was long before he sat easily on his throne. At home, the old adherents of young Herr Sten were disposed to look upon him as a renegade to the cause of their master's son. Abroad, legitimate monarchs mostly saw in him a usurper. Lübeck, no doubt, was his ally as well as his patron. But the terms of that alliance, though they bound Sweden to come to Lübeck's aid against Kristian II, included no reciprocal obligation on Lübeck's part. If there were a real risk of a restoration, Gustav's best hope probably lay not so much in Lübeck as in Kristian's supplanter in Copenhagen. It was true that Fredrik I, soon after his accession, had given notice of his claim to be king of Sweden as well as of Denmark, and it was also true that Lübeck had made a tepid promise to support that pretension; but once Gustav was chosen Fredrik showed no disposition to dispute the verdict. His heart was in Holstein; and as long as he lived the idea of Union played no part in Danish policy. Common dangers, similar embarrassments, forced him to look to Gustav, as they forced Gustav to look to him: by a strange paradox, the very circumstances which had shattered the Union forced the two countries together anew, and gave to both—now, and for the next quarter of a century—a common outlook on Europe.

For Kristian II threatened the throne of each; and though he might now seem an impotent exile, he was not without resources. The peasants and burghers of Denmark kept his memory in affectionate remembrance: Skåne, Jutland, the towns of Malmö and Copenhagen, looked for the day of his return as the day of deliverance. His brother-in-law the Emperor had but a poor opinion of him; and Margaret, the regent of the Netherlands, seems actively to have disliked him. But both were deeply attached to Kristian's unhappy wife; and Habsburg family pride forbade them to allow Kristian's cause to founder without an effort to retrieve it. His restoration did not rank very high in their list of priorities, and luckily for the Scandinavian monarchs Charles had for the time being more pressing calls upon his attention; but Habsburg memories were long, and to the young Emperor time was still an ally. Yet it might be possible to blunt the edge of this danger by appealing to material interests: the Netherlands merchants would be glad enough to be given a foothold in Scandinavia, and the regent might well be ready to throw over Kristian in return for a satisfactory trade treaty. But here the special circumstances of their accessions hamstrung Gustav and Fredrik alike; for Lübeck would scarcely tolerate any significant infringement of those privileges which had been the price of her assistance. It was certainly true that neither Sweden nor Denmark could as yet afford to dispense with Lübeck's commercial services: at this stage the Dutch provided at best only a complement to the Lübeck trade, rather than a real alternative. It was fortunate, therefore, that Lübeck's hostility to the Dutch was not shared by all the Hanse towns. The Wendish towns might have followed Lübeck's lead; but Danzig, Riga and Reval all had reservations about her policy, or were actually opposed to it.

It was considerations such as these that prescribed the maintenance of good relations, if not the conclusion of a formal alliance, between the Scandinavian kingdoms. But there remained a number of controversies between them which must first be settled. Some were survivals from the period of the Union; some arose from the circumstances of Sweden's war of liberation. For instance, Swedish troops were actually in occupation of Blekinge and Viken; and Gustav Vasa was advancing claims to both these provinces. Even more important was the question of the ownership of Gotland, which throughout the fifteenth century had been in dispute between the two countries. The days when Visby had been the hub of Baltic trade were now long since past; but the strategic importance of the island remained. It commanded the main Baltic trade-routes; it dominated the approaches to Stockholm. At the close of the fourteenth century the freebooting association of the Vitalian Brothers had made it their headquarters, whence they had terrorized legitimate commerce; and when Erik of Pomerania was deposed in 1439 he too had established himself there, and for years had lived very comfortably on the plunder of the seas. In 1523 it seemed very likely that he might have a successor. Kristian II's admiral and commander, Sören Norby, who had been the animating spirit in the defence of Stockholm against Gustav Vasa, had escaped with a small fleet to Visby, and there he had settled down, holding Gotland nominally on Kristian's behalf, but behaving in all respects as an independent sovereign prince.[1] He was a bold and skilful seaman, and in Kristian's name he made war upon the commerce of Lübeck and her allies, proclaiming himself 'the friend of God and the enemy of all mankind'; to such good effect that the warehouses of Visby were crammed to bursting with captured merchandise.

It was equally to the interests of Denmark, Sweden and Lübeck to evict Norby from his pirate stronghold; but it was not so easy to decide how it should be done, and still less by whom. Neither Fredrik nor Gustav Vasa would willingly acquiesce in a conquest of the island by the other; while Lübeck was not anxious to undertake the task herself. There was a real danger that Sweden and Denmark might drift into a war over Gotland; and this the Lübeckers earnestly wished to avoid. Norby, for his part, well understood that the situation afforded possibilities for playing off one party against the other. He sent off appeals for reinforcements to Kristian II; and in the meantime began a secret negotiation with Denmark, in the hope that if he pretended to transfer his allegiance to Fredrik I he would be allowed to hold Gotland unmolested. Early in 1524, however, Lübeck lost patience, decided that

[1] He even struck his own coin ('and very bad coin it was', as Peder Swart sourly comments, 'being mostly copper').

Norby must be disposed of without delay, and urged the Swedes to turn him out. Gustav Vasa needed no urging: it was not the will but the cash resources which were lacking. But the opportunity of acquiring Gotland with Lübeck's blessing seemed too good to miss. By hook or by crook the money was scraped together; an expeditionary force was assembled; and Berend von Melen was appointed to command it. In May 1524 it landed in Gotland and proceeded to besiege Norby and his men in Visby and Visborg. But from the start everything went wrong; desire outran performance. The Swedish army lacked siege-guns and ammunition; Norby intercepted their supply-ships; attempts at storm failed; and at last the German mercenaries struck for arrears of pay. Meanwhile Norby had successfully concluded his negotiation with Fredrik, and had reached an agreement whereby Gotland was to be handed over to Denmark, but Norby was to be allowed to hold it as a life-fief. The immediate consequence of this bargain was, naturally enough, a demand from Fredrik that Gustav Vasa should forthwith evacuate his troops from what had now become a Danish island. This Gustav refused to do. Norby had thus successfully engineered the very situation which Lübeck had been afraid of: an open breach between Sweden and Denmark seemed inevitable.

The result was a prompt reversal of Lübeck's policy. It was clear that either Sweden or Denmark must make concessions if the peace were to be saved; and the Lübeckers quickly made up their minds that the concessions must come from Sweden. Having incited Gustav Vasa to attack Gotland, they now decided that he must not be allowed to take it. This change of front was dictated by concern for their commercial privileges in Denmark, which as yet were unratified, and which could not legally be ratified until Fredrik had been crowned king. On this fact Fredrik played with some skill. He declined, he said, to be crowned king of a mutilated country; Viken, Blekinge and Gotland must be in his hands before there could be any question of coronation; Lübeck must bring pressure to bear on Gustav Vasa.

It was in these circumstances that Lübeck's envoys at last persuaded Gustav Vasa to agree to a personal meeting with Fredrik at Malmö, in the last days of August 1524. Sweden's lack of qualified diplomats was such that she was compelled to avail herself of the services of a member of the Lübeck delegation, and it was Paul van der Velde who acted as counsel for Gustav Vasa in the negotiations. It must be supposed that he did his best for his client; but undeniably his success was small. For the document which finally emerged on 1 September, and which is known as the Recess of Malmö, was a settlement imposed by the mediator, Lübeck; and it was not a settlement in Sweden's favour. It was agreed that the claims of both sides to Blekinge, Viken and Gotland should be submitted to the arbitration of the Wendish towns at a conference to be held in Lübeck next Whitsuntide; that in the meantime Sweden should keep Viken, and Denmark should keep Blekinge; that Gotland should remain for the time being in the hands of whichever side had been in possession of Visborg at the time the Recess of Malmö was signed; and that both Gustav Vasa's and Norby's troops should meanwhile evacuate the island. Norby was at once to lose his fief of Gotland, and was to be moved to some part of Denmark where he could not be dangerous to Sweden or to Lübeck. It was significant, perhaps, of the survival of the old Union feelings, that one clause in the Recess provided for the right of the nobility in each country to continue in possession of estates on the other side of the border. It was still more significant that a month or two later Gustav Vasa and the *råd* should have agreed to discourage this practice, and should have united in condemning intermarriage with the Danish aristocracy.

The Recess of Malmö was a sharp disappointment to Gustav Vasa.[1] On 1 September Norby (as everybody had foreseen) was still in possession of Visborg: the island therefore remained Danish; and, worst of all, Norby remained in Visborg. There is no doubt that Gustav Vasa had been encouraged to believe that Lübeck's mediation would be to his advantage; and no doubt either that the upshot of the affair exacerbated still further his resentment against the Hanse. All he had to show for his compliance with Lübeck's suggestions was an empty pocket. The arbitration-conference at Whitsuntide proved a fiasco; for the Swedish plenipotentiaries arrived late (they blamed it on the weather), and the Danes would not stay for them. Fredrik, on the other hand, had good reason to be satisfied. Already on 7 August—presumably feeling that the game was already in his hands—he had allowed himself to be crowned: the archbishop who performed the coronation was none other than Gustav Trolle, who had temporarily deserted Kristian II, and now professed to be working for a restoration of the Union. Fredrik, for his part, was content with more modest ambitions. He had secured Gotland; he was in occupation of Blekinge. Viken, no doubt, was still in Swedish possession; but he was wise enough to prefer the friendship of Sweden to an immediate settlement of that issue. And thus it happened that the conference at Malmö—against all reasonable expectation—marked a real turning-point in Swedish-Danish relations. On the basis of common fear of Kristian, and common resentment of Lübeck's arrogance, they drew closer together. There was as yet no alliance; but there was understanding. And that understanding proved its usefulness in dealing with the subsequent activities of Sören Norby.

[1] He was still remembering it with resentment as late as 1559.

At the beginning of October 1524 Gustav Vasa's troops were duly evacuated from Gotland. Not so Norby's. Norby rightly suspected that Fredrik had let him down at Malmö. He now demanded money to pay off his troops; he renewed his contacts with Kristian II; and he refused to budge from Gotland. A few months later he passed to the offensive. On the one hand he began to intrigue with discontented elements in Sweden;[1] on the other he invaded Blekinge in the name of Kristian II. His success was immediate: all Skåne rose to support him; he was soon able to form the siege of Hälsingborg; and he appealed to Kristian, more urgently than ever, for naval reinforcements which Kristian was in no condition to send him. The parties to the Recess of Malmö reacted swiftly to the challenge. In April 1525 Norby's fleet was crushed by Lübeck; in the same month his peasant army was cut to pieces by Rantzau in Skåne. But Norby still had one trump in his hand: the castle of Visborg. He played it with great effect. The Lübeckers had at last by this time made up their mind to do what they would have been well advised to do earlier, and take the island of Gotland into their own custody. This naturally did not suit Fredrik; and to avert the danger he was ready to patch up a quick settlement with Norby. In October 1525, therefore, Norby handed over Visborg to Fredrik, and received in exchange Blekinge as a life-fief. Lübeck accepted the *fait accompli*, abandoned her designs on Gotland, and was content to accept Bornholm instead. But by installing Norby in Blekinge, in immediate proximity to the Swedish border, and within striking-distance of Kalmar, Fredrik was certainly violating the spirit and the letter of the Recess of Malmö. And the event proved that he was violating it to no purpose. For Norby, loyal as ever to Kristian II, had no intention of becoming Fredrik's peaceful subject. Once more he collected a fleet, and from the convenient ports of Blekinge once more began his attacks upon shipping. Gustav Vasa and Lübeck were equally infuriated; Fredrik was cured at last of his belief that Norby was a man with whom it might be possible to make a bargain. It was agreed on all hands that he had become a nuisance to be abated. In August 1526 a combined Swedish-Danish fleet sent most of Norby's squadron to the bottom: Norby himself escaped with difficulty to Russia. There his refusal to take service with the tsar led to his being thrown into prison, whence he emerged (at the solicitation of Charles V) only after long and tedious negotiations. In 1529 he went off to join the Emperor's armies in Italy: a year later he perished at the siege of Florence. No doubt he was no more than an audacious and successful soldier of fortune. But his cheerful impudence and his indomitable resilience make him an engaging character, at a distance; and his

[1] See below, p. 56.

fidelity to Kristian II seems really to have been based on principle. He was not the first nor the last to feel passionately in that cause.

In the first few months of Kristian's exile it had seemed very likely that his Habsburg relations would sooner or later help him to recover his throne, if only to the extent of paying him the arrears due on his wife's dowry. He himself expected it; and Charles V did indeed summon a still-born congress in 1524 to concert measures for his restoration. If he was unpopular with the regent of the Netherlands, it might at least have been expected that his cause would be popular with her subjects: Lübeck was their enemy no less than his, and their shipping had been suffering from the attacks of Gustav Vasa's privateers. But unluckily for Kristian the situation in these respects was changing, and changing to his disadvantage. Already by 1524 the eastern Hanse towns, especially Danzig and Riga, were putting pressure on Lübeck to induce her to mitigate her attitude of uncompromising hostility to the Dutch; and they were also demanding that Gustav Vasa should stop his privateering. As a result of their representations (and perhaps because there was a real fear of imperial support for Kristian, or imperial action against the Hanse) Lübeck did in fact modify her policy. Immediately after the Recess of Malmö (that is, in September 1524) she mediated a one-year truce between Sweden and the Netherlands, which provided that negotiations were to be resumed under Lübeck's auspices at Whitsuntide 1525, and that Netherlands merchants were to be free to visit Sweden in the meantime.

In thus yielding to pressure from Danzig, Lübeck may well have intended only that Sweden should be permitted to grant to the Dutch trading rights of strictly limited scope. She probably believed that no great harm would come of small concessions—provided Swedish-Dutch relations were kept firmly under her own supervision and control. But in this, as the event proved, Lübeck had miscalculated. By her own action she opened a crack in the Strängnäs privileges; and she was never afterwards able to repair it. Even worse, the attempt to superintend Swedish diplomacy proved a total failure. It is true that Gustav Vasa sent envoys to Lübeck in the summer of 1525, and that it was in Lübeck that they concluded, in August of that year, a commercial treaty with the regent's emissaries. But that treaty—which provided for freedom of trade for three years on the basis of existing duties—had been negotiated directly, and not (as Lübeck had intended) through Lübeck's intermediaries. The Lübeckers were displeased and disturbed, as well they might be. It soon became clear, moreover, that for Gustav Vasa this was only the beginning: he hoped to transform a temporary settlement into an 'eternal peace'. If he could do this, he would interpose a really solid barrier against any attempt at Kristian's restoration based on the Dutch ports; and he would also make a serious breach in Lübeck's control of Swedish trade. He determined, therefore, not to let the negotiations flag. At Nienburg in 1526, at Ghent in 1527, they went forward with considerable impetus and much good will on both sides. The commercial demands on the Dutch side were more extensive than had been expected, and perhaps more than could safely be conceded; but by the end of 1527 it had been agreed to admit Bay salt to Sweden free of duty, and to permit the Dutch to trade freely, subject to the usual dues, in Stockholm, Kalmar, Söderköping, Åbo and Nya Lödöse. The prospects for an 'eternal peace' seemed not unpromising; another year's diplomacy might well secure it. But at this point negotiations came to a dead stop. Lübeck was angry at Gustav Vasa's proceedings, and irritated by his tardiness in the repayment of the debt due for aid during the war of liberation. By 1528 it was obvious that a permanent treaty with the Netherlands could be had only at the price of a rupture with Lübeck. Gustav Vasa, it seems, was prepared to face that consequence; his *råd* was not. In their view, some decent appearance of respect for the Strängnäs privileges must be kept up, at least till the debt to Lübeck was cleared off. They had their way. The approach to the Netherlands was not renewed; and Gustav Vasa, returning sullenly to his treaty obligations, chalked up a domestic grievance in his unforgiving memory. The chance to neutralize Kristian's most powerful and probable auxiliary went by default: soon, perhaps, it would be too late for another attempt. As long as the Emperor had France on his hands it was possible to count on his having no time over for Denmark; but the news of Pavia had already sent an anticipatory shiver down Swedish spines, and subsequent international developments were not reassuring. Kristian II, to be sure, had temporarily spoiled his chances with Charles by becoming a Lutheran; but to recover his patrimony he would probably be ready to turn Catholic again—or indeed Mohammedan, if that would serve him. The Emperor was surmounting his difficulties one after the other: in 1529 the Turks were beaten back from Vienna; in the same year the triumphant peace of Cambrai freed him for the moment from the French entanglement. Once Germany was settled, it might well be the turn of Scandinavia.

It was no wonder if in these circumstances Gustav Vasa and Fredrik deemed it wise to forget their reciprocal grudges, and convert their *entente* into a regular alliance. This was effected at a typical old-style frontier-meeting between the Swedish and Danish councils, held at Lödöse in August 1528. They could find no basis of agreement about Viken and Gotland; but they cemented a defensive alliance against Kristian II. Two years later, in 1530, the treaty of Varberg assigned

Viken to Sweden for the ensuing six years only. Gotland remained in Danish hands; though the Swedes did not renounce their claims to it. Thus by the end of the twenties a pattern of Swedish-Danish collaboration had been traced out: it was to endure, in tighter or looser form, for most of the reign. It was not a cordial relationship. It did not remove an ingrained hatred of 'the Jute', which was a legacy from the closing days of the Union, and which found an all too easy response in the jealous and devious mind of Gustav Vasa. But it was a political necessity, at least for the present; and Gustav was nothing if not a realist.

In the first three or four years of the reign Gustav Vasa's essential problem in foreign policy had been to safeguard the independence which Sweden had won in 1523. His task at home—and it was even more difficult—was to keep himself on the throne, and by firm government to put Sweden on her legs again; which was indeed another aspect of the same thing. He was called to rule over a country shattered and disorganized by a generation of political uncertainty, and exhausted by the war of liberation. The work of government, such as it was, had been much interfered with; a significant proportion of the high aristocracy—to whom the crown must look to fill the offices of provincial governor and sheriff—had perished in Stockholm's bloodbath; in some provinces there had been no regular payment of taxes for some years; the course of justice had been seriously interrupted; and inevitably, after years of civil war, men had lapsed into habits of insubordination and violence. In the later stages of the war Gustav Vasa had been obliged to take the unprecedented step of paying his local militia-levies; and he was deeply in debt to Lübeck for the wages of foreign mercenaries, as well as for the ships and arms with which he had been supplied. The total sum was alleged by his creditors to amount to over 120,000 marks. In May 1524 he was forced to promise that half of this amount should be repaid by Michaelmas, and the remainder by the following Whitsuntide. But the prospect of his being able to keep this promise was not good. To meet pressing needs, he had been forced to issue a crude and debased coinage. It had quickly depreciated, and it was understandably unpopular; but it was no easy matter to recall it or replace it with a better. Prices were rising, and the commonalty complained bitterly on this head: salt, in particular—the vital commodity—was uncommonly dear. Now that the great effort of the years from 1520 to 1523 had succeeded, and the Danes (as it seemed) had been finally evicted, the peasants expected easier times, and were ominously surly when they found that the times were as bad as ever. Indeed, they seemed to be worse. The king was at his wits' end for money, and he could not afford to be over-nice as to the means by which he raised it. Taxes grew heavier year by year; and the common man was not appeased when he saw the king attempting to tap the hoarded wealth of the church. Bad weather brought suffering and starvation; and the peasant, reduced to eating bark-bread, relieved his feelings by calling his sovereign 'King Bark': it was not a good augury. The Dalesmen, the Lübeckers, the survivors of the old *råd*-party, all considered him as in some sense their creature; and all were beginning to be disillusioned with their *protégé*.

One particularly sore point was the king's choice of servants. At the beginning of the reign, Gustav Vasa was forced to take his ministers and coadjutors where he could find them. If they were prepared to be loyal and proved themselves efficient he could not afford to scrutinize their political pasts too closely. It happened, therefore, that men who had been prominent adherents of Kristian II were now given conspicuous positions: the first chancellor of the new reign was Erik Svensson, who had changed sides twice; the second was Master Lars Andreae, who had been one of the judges who pronounced the verdict that led to Stockholm's bloodbath. Johannes Magnus, designated archbishop of Uppsala in 1524, was of the same party. Berend von Melen, to whom Gustav gave his cousin in marriage, had served in Kristian's army, and was also obnoxious as a foreigner illegally admitted a member of the *råd*. A German count, John of Hoya, who had married the king's sister, was given (again in defiance of constitutional propriety) the important fief and castle of Stegeborg. Gustav Trolle's father had the family estates restored to him, and there were persistent rumours that Trolle himself was to be invited to return. Lars Siggesson (Sparre), the marshal, and Ture Jönsson, the high steward, had likewise been no friends to young Herr Sten. The peasant armies that had borne the brunt of the war of liberation, and the Dalesmen in particular, could not understand these things. They had no notion of the king's embarrassments, and they saw with indignation the advancement of their old enemies. As early as 1522 they had delivered a sharp warning on this head; and their anger was not lessened by the news that reached them thereafter.

It is not surprising that in these circumstances there should have been a revival of the Sture party. It could not fairly be said that that party had been passed over at the opening of the reign: of eight episcopal appointments in 1522 and 1523, at least seven had been given to former partisans of young Herr Sten. Several prominent members of this group were among the new men called to the *råd* at Strängnäs in June 1523; in particular, Sten Sture's chancellor and factotum Peder Jakobsson Sunnanväder, who in March had been rewarded with the bishopric of Västerås, and who was chosen to celebrate High Mass on the king's entry into Stockholm. But Sunnanväder was not contented by these marks of favour. He had been Sten's right-hand man, and he may well have felt his relegation to a less conspicuous position. Perhaps, too, he resented the fiscal demands which were made of him. Certainly it must have been a mortification to him to see men such as Erik Svensson, who had long been his personal enemy, preferred to himself in the new king's service. Sunnanväder was probably the author of Dalarna's warning letter in 1522; in 1523 he was certainly caught conducting correspondence strongly critical of the king. In September of that year he was deprived of his see before he had even received papal confirmation of his election; and the chapter, on Gustav Vasa's instructions, chose Peder Månsson in his place.

Early in 1524 Fredrik I, who had no desire to be associated with his predecessor's misdeeds, released from prison the women captives whom Kristian had taken to Denmark in 1520. First among them was Kristina Gyllenstierna, Sten Sture's widow; and her return to Sweden provided a natural rallying-point for any former adherents of the Stures who might find the prevailing political climate ungenial. It was a fair assumption that Sunnanväder was likely to be among them. Gustav Vasa felt that he could take no chances. Sunnanväder was summoned to Stockholm and forced to give bail for his good behaviour. Eight months later, when Gustav was far away in Malmö conferring with Fredrik I, Sunnanväder notified his sureties that he proposed to violate his engagements, and thereupon betook himself to Dalarna. Here he was joined by another cleric of the Sture party, Knut Mickilsson, the dean of Västerås. Master Knut had taken a prominent part in securing Gustav's election at Strängnäs, and felt himself ill-requited when he was passed over for the vacant archiepiscopal see. He had also committed the indiscretion of protesting against Sunnanväder's deprivation. Like Sunnanväder, he was ripe for mischief; and together they set themselves to stir up rebellion in Dalarna. They found plenty of discontent to work upon, and no lack of grievances to nurse: the dearness of the times, the bad coin, the lack of salt; the story that Trolle was to be reinstated; the presence of foreigners in the *råd*; the plundering of the church. Kristina Gyllenstierna, it was rumoured, was being ill-treated; and it was even said that the king had murdered her son, Nils Sture. A letter from Dalarna to Hälsingland in May 1525 sums up in a sentence the rancours and disappointments of the Sture party, and of the peasants whom they indoctrinated with their resentments: 'All those who faithfully served the lords and realm of Sweden has Gustav hated and persecuted, while all traitors to the realm . . . and all who abetted the country's cruel foe King Kristian, and who betrayed Herr Sten and all Swedish men, these has he favoured.'

At the same time other troubles were developing. It is possible that Kristina Gyllenstierna had no hand in the activities of Sunnanväder and Master Knut; but she was undoubtedly plotting against the *régime*. Her plans involved no less a person than Sören Norby. Norby had made Kristina's acquaintance during her stay in Denmark. He had won her confidence by treating her kindly, and already before her release they seem to have exchanged tokens of affection. She now planned what would in fact have been a restoration of the Union as it had existed in her husband's time, with Kristian II as king and Norby as regent in Sweden until her son should grow up; and she proposed to clinch the arrangement by marrying Norby, who conveniently enough happened to be a widower. The intrigue also involved Berend von Melen. Von Melen had returned from his expedition to Gotland with an uncomfortable (and entirely justified) feeling that Gustav Vasa would hold him responsible for the fiasco. He had therefore prudently kept away from Stockholm, and gone to earth in his castle of Kalmar. It was certainly the case that Nils Sture, the heir to the family's pretensions, was staying with von Melen in Kalmar; and by what looked like more than a coincidence Norby's daughter was there too. Whether von Melen was in touch with Sunnanväder and the movement in Dalarna was uncertain. But what was certain was that at the very moment when it was a main item in the indictment against the king that he gave his favour to men who had been henchmen of the tyrant Kristian, Sten Sture's widow was herself deep in an intrigue with the tyrant's most faithful follower. So strong was the vindictiveness of the Sture party that some of them, at least, would have swallowed Kristian II to be rid of the usurping and renegade Vasa.

In the spring of 1525 Gustav at last succeeded in getting von Melen up to Stockholm, and extorted from him an undertaking that he would hand over Kalmar to the royal forces. But von Melen's brother, who had been left in command in Kalmar, refused to honour this promise, so that the king was forced to despatch a small army to enforce compliance. Berend von Melen was sent down with it, to exert his authority upon his brother; but once he had arrived in Kalmar he escaped by guile to the castle, and thence made the best of his way to Germany. The castle continued to defy the king's commander; and Gustav had to go down in person at the end of July and take it by storm, with considerable loss of life: he did not fail to butcher the defenders after they had surrendered. Von Melen, once safe on the continent, at first entered into relations with his old master Kristian II; but soon settled down into the service of the Elector of Saxony. He devoted the remainder of his life to a protracted political and literary feud with Gustav Vasa, blackguarding him throughout Europe, comforting his enemies, thwarting his policies, fomenting conspiracies against him; and for the next twenty years proved himself certainly one of the most inveterate and dangerous of all his adversaries.

After the fall of Kalmar the king turned to Dalarna. In the autumn of 1525 he went with a show of force to Tuna. The Dalesmen made a timely submission; and by October the disturbances there were over—for a time. In December, Kristina Gyllenstierna acquiesced in the inevitable, confessed her errors, and was reconciled to the king. Sunnanväder and Master Knut remained to be dealt with. When the movement in Dalarna collapsed, they had withdrawn across the Norwegian frontier and found shelter with the archbishop of Trondheim, who was pursuing political objectives of his own and hoped that the fugitives might be useful to him. He proved an unreliable protector. In the summer of 1526 he imprudently delivered up Master Knut, on the rash supposition that he would be tried by an ecclesiastical court. But Master Knut was speedily condemned to death by the *råd*, the king himself acting as prosecuting counsel. In September, the archbishop, untaught by the outcome of his previous action, likewise handed over Sunnanväder. In November the two prisoners were publicly humiliated by a mock-triumphal entry into Stockholm, Sunnanväder being furnished with a straw crown and a battered wooden sword, Master Knut (in reference to his disappointed ecclesiastical ambitions) with an archiepiscopal mitre made of birch-bark. Sunnanväder was tried in Uppsala, the court including members of the chapter, drafted in for that purpose: and in Uppsala he was executed, on 18 February 1527, at a time carefully chosen to coincide with the great winter market. Master Knut followed him to the scaffold in Stockholm three days later.

This, it might seem, was the end of the Sture party. But as Perkin Warbeck rose from the grave of the House of York, so the Young Gentleman from the Dales (*Daljunker*) sprouted from the mutilated stock of the Stures. His identity is uncertain: he claimed to be Nils Sture, and may even have believed himself to be so, for he had been well coached by someone in the part he was to play. Nils Sture he certainly was not, for Gustav Vasa had that unhappy young man at court at a time when the rising was already in progress;[1] but he may possibly have been Sten Sture's bastard. When Kristina Gyllenstierna disavowed him (on the king's pressing invitation), the *Daljunker* explained that she did so because she was reluctant to confess to an indiscretion: it was an explanation which did him no service with his supporters. Whoever he was, he persuaded the men of upper Dalarna to believe in him: the Bergslag, more cautious or less credulous, held

[1] He died—it is said of the plague—soon afterwards.

aloof. He was certainly a personable youth, and not without histrionic ability. 'He was also', Peder Swart tells us, 'of a fair countenance, and had a knavish tongue to speak withal, and the words came easily to his mouth. And when he spoke to any gathering and chanced to mention young Herr Sten (whom he called his father) he straightway wept bitterly. The Dalesmen wept with him. And often in the middle of his parley with them he would bid them for God's sake fall on their knees and say a *paternoster* and an *Ave Maria* for his father's soul'. Even these amiable traits might have availed him little, if he had not been able to half-persuade the Dalesmen that the king was dead. If that were true, support of the *Daljunker* was by no means a political absurdity: better a dubiously legitimate Sture than old King Kristian. So the Dalesmen rallied to the *Daljunker* as the best hope of that national cause which King Gustav seemed to have betrayed; and by the spring of 1527 his movement had become really alarming to the government. The rebels' declarations included a comprehensive collection of grievances, ranging from bad harvests to slashed doublets; and all the old accusations against the king were repeated. But this time they added a new one: Gustav was not only a renegade, the betrayer of the cause, the secret friend of Trolle; he was also (which was worse than all) a Lutheran, a despoiler of churches, and the protector of men who ate meat on Fridays.

For more than three years Gustav Vasa had been faced with a succession of perilous internal crises. His method of dealing with them was a foreshadowing of the techniques which in the years to come he was to develop with conspicuous success. He had argued and explained and exhorted; he had used force only when he must; he had taken care to secure the backing of some form or other of representative meeting —*råd*, *herredag* or *riksdag*; and he had induced these gatherings to solidarize themselves with him in a formal 'union'. And once, in 1525, he had not hesitated to show (though not yet to play) his trump card: abdication. But in the spring of 1527 the rebellion of the *Daljunker* coincided with the culmination of another problem which could no longer be burked. The great question of the relations of church and state was being driven by the king to a crisis. To resolve both questions he turned now to the Estates: they should pronounce judgment in the great controversy between himself and the hierarchy; they should doom between himself and his rebellious subjects. A meeting of the Estates was summoned to Västerås for Trinity Sunday 1527. It was a fair presumption that it would decide the fate of the *Daljunker*. But very few of those that came to it can have foreseen that it would also decide the fate of the church in Sweden.

III. THE CONFLICT OF CHURCH AND STATE

The history of the church in Sweden during the Middle Ages had been singularly placid. Christianity came late to this distant corner of Europe, and while the great contest between *regnum* and *sacerdotium* was being fought out in the West, the Swedish church was still mainly concerned with the struggle against paganism. From time to time kings had quarrelled with popes about the choice of a bishop; but there had been nothing that can be compared with the Investiture contest, or the long-drawn struggles over lay and spiritual jurisdiction. The monarchy made no great fuss about *Unam sanctam*, for Rome was too far off for its principles to be rigorously applied. Just as mediaeval Sweden was never really a feudal country, so it was never as fully integrated into the body of the church as France, or Germany, or England. By the beginning of the fourteenth century the church had indeed secured most of the usual liberties; but in many respects the hierarchy had to reconcile itself to arrangements which would have been considered exceptionable in western Europe. Magnus Eriksson's Land Law, it is true, omitted any definition of church-state relations because the rules which it would have laid down would have been in conflict with canon law; but the practical consequence had been that these matters came thenceforward to be ordered by the provincial law of Uppland, which from the church's point of view was no improvement. In the matter of criminous clerks, for instance, the Uppland law prescribed a compromise which left the clergy justiciable in the royal courts on appeal (even by their own peasants), and which reserved to the crown the trial of all civil cases in which the plaintiff was a clerk and the defendant a layman, as well as of all cases concerning land. The old germanic tradition that property ought not to pass from the family without the family's consent restricted the individual's freedom of bequest, to the church's prejudice. The circumstances of Sweden's conversion to Christianity gave parishioners a greater control of parochial affairs than was usual elsewhere; for since churches had very often been built by the congregations that were to use them, parishioners were able to claim the rights of patrons, so that incumbents were generally chosen by their flocks. Churchwardens were the rule; and by the end of the fifteenth century parish affairs were mostly in the charge of a select vestry of six persons, the so-called *sexmän*.

When compared with western Europe, or even with Denmark, the Swedish church appeared rustic and primitive; its most ambitious cathedrals—Uppsala, for instance, or Linköping—could ill stand comparison with Salisbury or Lincoln; its parish churches were small and rude. This was true also of monastic foundations. The most important of them were Cistercian: the Augustinians and Premonstratensians had never come to Sweden; the Carthusians and Carmelites were each represented by a single establishment. Sweden had, of course, produced her own order, the Brigittines, and Vadstena was the most splendid and best-endowed of all Swedish foundations. But Vadstena had no daughter-house in Sweden, apart from Nådendal on the other side of the water in Finland, and by the close of the Middle Ages it had ceased to give any effective leadership to the order as a whole. The truth was, that Sweden was still on the far edge of western Christendom. Paganism was still an adversary lurking in the background, and the spiritual frontiersman must always keep a sharp eye open for stealthy attacks from that quarter. Heresy was much less important: clergy and laity alike were too ignorant to be in much danger of taking the wrong turning in the theological labyrinth, and Hussitism was no more than a confused story of ill-doings far away. At the end of the thirteenth century a certain Boëthius de Dacia contrived to incur suspicion of Averroistic divagations; but that was in Paris: for a Swede to be a heretic, it seemed, he had first to get out of Sweden. Heresy-trials were exceeding rare: before 1520 the flames of Smithfield or Constance struck no answering glow from the indifferent northern sky.

Despite the local peculiarities of the Swedish church, its relations with the papacy were usually good. There was no great grievance about papal provisions: they were common enough, in Sweden as elsewhere, but it was only very rarely that they thrust in a foreigner. The financial exactions of the curia increased during the fourteenth century: bishops paid the *servitium commune* on their appointment, holders of benefices paid annates, and all paid Peter's Pence; but these impositions were never felt to be so burdensome as to constitute a major ground of complaint. The Swedish church had consistently supported the Roman popes against Avignon during the Schism, and had later as consistently backed the council of Basel against Eugenius IV; but in neither case had it been able to profit from its attitude. After a long struggle of varied fortunes Uppsala had by the close of the fifteenth century emancipated itself from Lund's claim to primacy; but in other respects both church and state seemed to have missed an opportunity. The weakness of the monarchy after 1440, and the attempts of both Oldenburgs and Stures to enlist papal support for their pretensions, prevented Sweden from bargaining with the papacy on advantageous terms. When the conciliar period ended Sweden had not even attempted to secure a concordat. Denmark, indeed, was included within the terms of the concordat with the Emperor Frederick III; but this was not a settlement which Swedes would wish to see extended to themselves.

The church in Sweden was too young to be decadent, too remote from the centre to be the sport of church politics, too lacking in rich plums to invite the attention of the greedy or the speculative, too simple for the more exotic vices. It was a church where scandals were rare enough to be remembered. Celibacy had scarcely been universally accepted before the end of the fourteenth century, and the parish priest was not begrudged the comfort of a housekeeper; but monastic establishments were respectably conducted. The parochial clergy were not remarkable for evangelical zeal, and their intellectual level was low: they preached, indeed; but not often, and not well. Monks and nuns maintained a regular if conventional piety, did works of mercy and charity, transcribed or composed books of devotion. Franciscans and Dominicans were perhaps more active than the rest, though it is to be noted that Swedish Franciscans were not of the reformed Observantist persuasion, and their moral reputation was not high. On the whole, the church's pulse beat only sluggishly: of the *devotio moderna* there was scarcely any. A century and a half before, Birgitta had led a great revivalist movement, and had administered swingeing castigation to delinquents in high places, not excluding the monarchy and the papacy itself; but not much of that spirit now remained. She had never sought to alter the fabric of the church, nor do more than knock away unseemly excrescences. Though her successors followed her rules, the low religious temperature at Vadstena contrasted sharply with the spirit that prevailed in the daughter-house at Syon. There was nothing in the church as they saw it which seemed to tempt the wrath of God, no part so sick as to cry for cautery. But if it was thus a matter for congratulation that the corruptions of Italy had left Sweden relatively untainted, it was less fortunate that Italy's glories should have lain so far below the Swedish horizon. The great surge of the Renaissance had diminished to a ripple by the time it reached these latitudes, and the Swedish church was as little affected by the epicureanism of the humanists as by the enlarged learning and critical approach of the new scholarship. The first Swede to possess a knowledge of Greek is said to have been Gustav Trolle. An occasional Swedish ecclesiastic, long resident in Rome, might speak Italian and write a semi-literary Latin, and Hans Brask seems to have had a taste for contemporary Italian literature of the lighter sort, but for the enormous majority these refined pleasures were still undreamt-of. A small percentage of the clergy had always gone abroad to receive a university education; but only a few of them became doctors of canon law; and scarce any took a doctorate in theology. Yet it was a growing sense that Sweden was lagging behind other lands, a dawning national pride, a determination too to get in ahead of Denmark, that led to the foundation of the university of Uppsala in 1477, one year before the foundation of the university of Copenhagen.

Uppsala seems to have got off to a fair start, and Gustav Vasa is reckoned among its undergraduates; but it foundered in the storms of the last years of the Union: after 1516 we hear no more of its activities. It had lived long enough, all the same, to acquire a printing-press. Printing had begun in Sweden in 1483; but the available reading public was not such as to encourage large-scale enterprise. A press in Uppsala, a press under the control of Bishop Brask in Linköping, others in Vadstena and Mariefred, sufficed to cater for the demand: it would be no very difficult matter for government to establish a monopoly of printing, if that should be necessary.

To a visitor from Germany or even Denmark the Swedish church no doubt appeared mean and meagre; but it was anything but poor in relation to other elements in Swedish society. Despite the restrictions of the law the piety of aristocratic donors had endowed it well, by modest local standards. Its territorial holdings were not much below those of the lay nobility, with whom (as we have seen) it was in growing competition for the limited amount of *frälse* land now available. Its revenues might well excite the envy of a penurious monarchy; its town property provoked the ill-will of the burghers. There is some sign, however, that in the fifteenth century the stream of donations was beginning to dwindle; and this may be related to the decline in the number of members of the aristocracy entering the church. The episcopate, no doubt, was still a desirable object to the scion of a noble family; but even here the proportion of *ofrälse* was considerable (in sharp contrast to the state of affairs in Denmark), while in the chapters as well as in the monastic establishments the tendency towards a predominantly *ofrälse* recruitment was unmistakable. The slow loosening of the social ties between the lay nobility and the church, and the dawning sense of economic rivalry between them, would in the end undermine the political collaboration which had been so marked in the period of the Union. It was a portent of things to come when a meeting of the *råd* in 1491 demanded more effective action to prevent the bequeathing of land to ecclesiastical foundations. A natural result of this movement of opinion was an increased anxiety by church authorities, and especially by bishops, to make the most of the incomes that were still available to them. The church became more preoccupied with profitable investments; it embarked upon the business of money-lending, not least to the nobility; as a landlord it grew more rigorous in exacting what was due to it. The bishops strove pertinaciously to subject monasteries to their control; they appropriated the share of tithe which had hitherto gone to the poor; they waged a petty war against hospitals. Bishop Brask made himself unpleasantly conspicuous in these activities. Already in the time of young Herr Sten it is possible to perceive a strain of anti-clericalism in Sweden: it was an important element in rallying support for his violent measures against Gustav Trolle. But as yet there was no hostility to the church in general, or to the papacy; no hint of popular indignation at the abuses of either; nothing remotely reminiscent of Lollardy. Piety of the cruder type flourished; the cult of relics was popular; Sweden had her own fashionable saints; religious art was imported from Flanders in good quantity. When Arcimboldus came selling indulgences in 1517 he found the market buoyant, and nobody thought of questioning the efficacy of his wares.

The attitude of the Stures towards the church, like that of Karl Knutsson before them, had necessarily been ambivalent. On the one hand they all took pains to cultivate the good will of the curia: the success of their diplomatic agents in Rome, the defeat of the intrigues of Denmark, could do much to strengthen their hold on Sweden. In this struggle they had as a rule been not unsuccessful, at least until 1519. On the other hand they could not fail to look upon the higher clergy in Sweden as probably disaffected to their rule: political bishops jostling for fiefs or fighting pitched battles, bishops with long rent-rolls and private armies, were over-mighty subjects, equally suspect to Stures and to Oldenburgs. Since about 1440 the Swedish church seemed to have committed itself to a policy of keeping the monarchy weak, as the best hope of preserving ecclesiastical liberties. As members of the *råd* the bishops were involved in the constitutional programmes embodied in such documents as the Recess of Kalmar. They had made more than one attempt to play off Oldenburgs against Stures; and in Gustav Trolle their political and ecclesiastical programmes had combined to produce what seemed to be a betrayal of the national cause. Thus in the time of young Herr Sten, when the name of Luther was as yet unknown outside Wittenberg, the clash between church and state had already come into the open. Gustav Vasa inherited the quarrel whether he would or no: it was an issue he could not evade, unless he were prepared to remain a king impotent and bankrupt. A collision might perhaps have been avoided if Herr Sten, or his successor, had been able to induce the papacy to concede something like the Concordat of Bologna; but only a Marignano could extort a settlement of that sort. Any chance of a more limited arrangement was for ever dissipated by the bloodbath of Stockholm, and by the papacy's attitude to Swedish affairs in the years that followed. Any hope of composing the resulting quarrel was wrecked by the injection into it of the new element of Lutheranism, and also by the characters of the leading personages involved. And from the very beginning Gustav Vasa committed himself, more explicitly than ever the Stures had done, to the subordination of the church to the state: he would not suffer two lords in one land. The new monarchy was from its nature the enemy of the church's liberties.

The inevitable confrontation was hurried on, the clash when it came was made more bitter, by the very circumstances of the king's accession. He had mounted the throne by defeating an enterprise sanctioned and approved by the pope; and his victory had confirmed the extrusion of Trolle from his archiepiscopal see. Gustav Vasa insisted that that see was now vacent. Soon after his accession he issued a proclamation pronouncing Trolle for ever excluded from Sweden; and the *råd* followed this up by writing to Rome to demand a new archbishop. It so happened that the sees of Strängnäs, Skara and Åbo had fallen vacant too, either by the eviction of Danish bishops intruded by Kristian II, or by death; and in each case the chapter had chosen a Swedish successor (*electus*) in accordance with the king's wishes. A fourth instance occurred at Västerås; where, after Sunnanväder had been deprived, Peder Månsson—an elderly Swedish ecclesiastic living in Rome—was at the king's instance elected to succeed him. In the autumn of 1523 Gustav Vasa wrote three letters to the pope demanding the confirmation of these *electi*; but asking at the same time that the payment of the *servitium commune* be on this occasion remitted in view of the exhausted state of the country. In exchange he offered to eradicate heresy, convert the Lapps, reclaim the Russians for Rome, and make war on the Turks. Adrian VI was not impressed. He indicated that he proposed to present his own candidate to Skara. He insisted that Trolle must be permitted to return to Uppsala. Nobody in Rome really believed Kristian's cock-and-bull story about the bloodbath of Stockholm, and the papacy had other serious grounds for complaint against him for his treatment of the Danish episcopate and his invitation of Karlstadt to Copenhagen; but however badly they might think of Kristian, Trolle was undoubtedly the only canonical archbishop of Uppsala until an ecclesiastical sentence should deprive him of that preferment. Adrian VI, as might have been expected, took his stand on principle. He sent a papal legate to Sweden to report on the situation, for it was said that heresy was beginning to spread there. He chose a Swede, Johannes Magnus, for the mission. But he had no intention of compromising.

It was unfortunate that neither Adrian nor his successor Clement VII had any inkling of the strength of Swedish popular feeling on this issue. In Swedish eyes the papacy had shown a scandalous cynicism in its attitude to Kristian II's atrocities. Rightly or wrongly, Trolle's name was indissolubly linked with those atrocities in the popular mind. He had defied and betrayed Herr Sten; he had called in the tyrant Kristian;

he had initiated the proceedings which led to the massacre of 1520. Trolle had become the symbol of foreign lordship and national abasement; it was morally impossible for a patriotic Swede to tolerate his return. Bishop Brask soon sensed this: already in 1523 he was writing to Trolle telling him so, and urging him to resign his see. As for Gustav Vasa, on this matter he could not weaken without risking his throne. Thus both king and pope arrived very quickly at extreme positions from which they could scarcely budge with honour or safety. By the close of 1523 Gustav Vasa was threatening that if the pope continued to support Trolle he would govern the church himself 'as might in his judgment be most pleasing to God and Christendom': as to the *electi*, they might be left to be confirmed '*a solo et summo pontifice Christo*'. But Clement VII proved no more persuadable than Adrian VI. He did, indeed, refer the accusations against Trolle to a cardinal for investigation, and he appointed Johannes Magnus as administrator of Uppsala *ad interim*. But when the king induced the chapter of Uppsala to elect Johannes in the hope that this choice of a papal legate might provide the curia with a way out of the difficulty, Clement showed no readiness to take it. He rejected the request for remission of the *servitium commune*; he refused to confirm the new *archielectus*; and of the other *electi* he confirmed only one—Peder Månsson of Vasterås: on 27 April 1523 the pope himself consecrated Peder in Rome, and so (as it turned out) safeguarded the Apostolic Succession to the Swedish episcopate.

As early as 1521 Gustav Vasa had given Bishop Brask a pledge to maintain and defend the rights and privileges of the church. He had renewed that pledge in the oath which he swore at his election as king. In October 1523 Brask had asked and received yet another guarantee that the church's liberties and immunities should be respected. Yet it may well be doubted whether the king ever intended to observe these undertakings further than the necessities of state might require. Already in May 1523 he showed that he intended to keep the presentation to canonries in his hand; and he took care that the elections to vacant sees should be to his liking. He looked upon bishops as rivals and potential enemies, subjects imperfectly amenable to royal authority, who had contrived to amass territorial resources and military potential which had been a danger to the crown in the past, and might well be so again. Such fears were not wholly unreasonable, as the stormy history of the previous century had shown; and it cannot have escaped Gustav Vasa's observation that the bishop of Skara could produce thirty armed horsemen for knight-service, while the great lay magnate Ture Jönsson was liable only for thirteen.[1] If in the end his fear and

[1] I take this illustration from Bertil Broomé, *Ätten Posse*, II, 51.

dislike of bishops was to become an obsession,[1] it was of long standing: it led him in the first three or four years of his reign to the resumption of almost all the fiefs which had been in ecclesiastical hands. But apart altogether from such feelings he was bound to come into collision with the episcopate on other grounds. For the bishops were the natural defenders of the church's privileges; and those privileges he was almost forced to infringe, whether he would or no.

Until Gustav Vasa's time no systematic effort had been made by any Swedish ruler to break through the church's immunity from taxation and tap its large resources for the benefit of the state. Gustav Vasa was driven to attempt it. The war of liberation had left him heavily indebted to Lübeck, and his creditors pressed ceaselessly for repayment. The crown had certainly not the resources to meet these demands, and the country was too exhausted to raise the money by taxation. There remained the church, with its broad acres, rich revenues, vacant preferments, and abundant stores of plate; and very early the king made up his mind that the church must pay its share. From 1522 he sequestered the revenues of Uppsala. Between 1521 and 1523, on five different occasions, he took what were in effect forced loans of superfluous and dispensable pieces of church plate: after all, Svante Nilsson had done as much, in a far less grave emergency, in 1504.

Unfortunately the end of the war in 1523 did not see the end of the piling up of debt. The expedition to Gotland in 1524 proved extremely expensive, and it had in fact been financed only by commandeering silver destined for the shrine of St Catherine at Vadstena, and by putting pressure on bishops to act as agents for the raising of money from churches in their dioceses: Gustav Vasa did not forget that Gotland lay in Brask's diocese of Linköping, and that Brask had been among those who most strongly urged the expedition. Apart from this, the dangers of the times forced the king to keep a small standing army in being, and it was hard to find the money to pay it—indeed, it was impossible, if the debt-payments to Lübeck were to be kept up. As early as October 1524 the king suggested that some of the expense of the army might be saved by quartering troops in wealthy monasteries: after all, Fredrik I, for similar reasons, was doing just this in Denmark. But the *råd* turned down the idea: it was probably illegal; it was certainly contrary to the Recess of Kalmar. Yet Gustav Vasa could not help remembering that for the last half-century or more the Swedish bishops had successfully asserted a right to billet their own retinues in monasteries and parsonages. It seemed intolerable that in a national emergency the same right should be denied to the king. He took no

[1] Of the fate of bishops in the next world he remarked on one occasion that 'they shall have wailing and gnashing of teeth, and their feet well toasted too'.

notice, therefore, of his council's opinion; and early in 1525 the pressure of necessity forced them to think better of it. At the same time they agreed that that portion of tithe which went to the parish churches should this year be diverted to pay the soldiers. Three bishops who were present at this meeting consented to these measures: Bishop Brask, who was absent, sent in a vigorous protest, for he saw, more clearly than any of his colleagues, that the king's policies meant the end of the church's fiscal immunities. He was sharply answered. In a famous phrase Gustav Vasa told him that 'Necessity overrides the law; and not the law of man only, but sometimes also the law of God'.

As one emergency succeeded another—Sunnanväder's revolt, von Melen's defection, Norby's restless activity—the financial situation grew worse. Lübeck's agents were clamouring for their money: the king complained that he scarcely dared show his face outside the castle gates for fear of duns. In January 1526, on the ground that his father was heir-general of Sten Sture the elder, he suddenly claimed the manor of Gripsholm as his private property, alleging that Sten's donation of it to the monastery of Mariefred was invalid, since his heir had never consented to it. He also added, with that ingenuous effrontery of which he was a master, that the monks had asked him to ease their consciences by taking it away from them. A *herredag* at Vadstena admitted the claim; and the king characteristically ordered his bailiff to steal the monastery's plate before the monks quitted the premises. The Carthusian monks accepted, then declined, alternative accommodation; their community disintegrated; their *oeconomus* prudently stayed on as a royal steward. It was all surprisingly easy. The same *herredag* agreed that two-thirds of the tithe for 1526 should be diverted to meet Lübeck's demands; and further consented to the levying of an aid, allegedly to cover the cost of the coronation. Six months later, though Gustav was still uncrowned, the situation was as bad as ever; and in August 1526 he demanded two-thirds of the entire income of the clergy for one year. Bishop Brask, who had excellent reasons for wishing to conceal what that income was, persuaded him to be content with a lump sum of 15,000 marks and yet another aid. By the beginning of 1527 it was clear that Dalarna and Hälsingland would refuse to pay it. The movement in favour of the *Daljunker* was already beginning; the king was desperately laying hands on ecclesiastical funds wherever he could find them—selling benefices, extorting contributions, misappropriating moneys, even tinkering with the will of the late dean of Åbo, who had inexplicably omitted to leave all of his estate to the crown. The quartering of troops in monasteries was extended to nunneries, and became permanent. No progress had been made in securing the confirmation of the *electi*: indeed, the king no longer desired it; he wished bishops to be his own appointees, and to owe their authority to none but himself. A national church under royal control—the fruits of a concordat without the obligations and concessions—was beginning to appear to him as a possible issue from his difficulties; and not an undesirable one either.

The attack on the economic immunities of the church was pushed with the more vigour because the king had by this time found other grounds for his actions than mere necessity, and was able to represent himself as moved by principle. The principle had been enunciated by his chancellor, Lars Andreae, in February 1524. In a famous letter to the monastery at Vadstena he had maintained that the church was the whole community of the faithful; that its resources, having been originally given to it for public ends, might properly be applied to such purposes now; that, in short, the church's wealth was the people's wealth. These were characteristically Lutheran positions; and Lars Andreae was indeed already a Lutheran, though he did not publicly acknowledge it until 1526.[1] Certainly they were arguments which the king found very apt to his needs. Gustav Vasa had no particular desire to break with the papacy. He had little or no interest in doctrinal questions, and none of that theological learning which was to be so characteristic of his sons. His piety was conventional at best. But he saw in the preaching of the reformers a store of argument upon which he could draw to support his attack on the church's revenues and the political position of the bishops; and he did not scruple to make use of it. And since he could not hope to succeed without a measure of popular support, and since he was a firm believer in the power of the spoken word, he countenanced and even encouraged preachers whose doctrinal outlook was likely to assist his political aims. The pulpit should buttress the throne; the preachers, by undermining the authority and the prestige of the church establishment, should make the king's way plain.

Lutheran doctrines came first to Sweden with Hanseatic traders, and seem to have found adherents in Stockholm as early as 1521. There were Lutherans too among the mercenaries sent over by Lübeck to Gustav Vasa's aid: by 1522 Brask was threatening them with excommunication; and it was at his solicitation that Adrian VI despatched Johannes Magnus to investigate Swedish heresy in 1523. The first native Swede to stand out as a Lutheran was Olaus Petri. Son of a blacksmith of Örebro, he had begun his university career at Uppsala, moving thence to Luther's Wittenberg, where he was a student during

[1] In his letter to Vadstena he had written: 'For although little has come to my knowledge of the new doctrines that they call Martin's, I have nevertheless found . . . that Martin is too big a man to be confuted by simple men like ourselves, for his shield is the shield of Scripture.'

the critical years from 1516 to 1518. He returned home a reformer of the stamp of Erasmus: it was only after he had settled down in Strängnäs that his views became clearly heretical. There seems little doubt that it was he who drew Lars Andreae over to Lutheranism: Olaus was secretary to Bishop Matts of Strängnäs (the same that perished in Stockholm's bloodbath), Lars was archdeacon, and the ordinary diocesan business threw them much into each other's company. Olaus was a man of ardent faith, sanguine disposition and brilliant gifts, for whom the church's reformation came to be an all-absorbing question of conscience; Lars was a cool-headed and able canon lawyer, devoted to the royal interest—'a hard-fisted *praktikus*', as a contemporary called him—mainly concerned to increase the king's authority. As chancellor, he was Gustav's right-hand man in the struggle with the church; and no man, certainly, did more to ensure that matters should come to a crisis.

In 1524 the king appointed Olaus Petri town-clerk of Stockholm. It was a shrewd stroke, for Petri, who had been ordained deacon in 1520, had now at his disposal the most influential pulpit in Sweden, and he could be relied upon to preach in favour of the king's church policy—or at least against its opponents. At first he had no easy task: if his sermons veered too obviously towards the new religion he found himself pelted by his congregation. Perhaps it was because he sought reinforcement that he persuaded the king to appoint a certain Nicholas Stecker of Eisleben, an undoubted Lutheran, as pastor of the Great Church. But Olaus did not lack the courage of his convictions: in February 1525 he scandalized the town by taking a wife—an example which Luther himself did not follow until some months later. He would hardly have ventured upon so provocative a step if he had not felt confident of the king's approval. And in fact, from 1524 onwards, Gustav Vasa allowed himself to appear more and more as the protector of the reformers. In 1524 he refused Brask's request that he should condemn Lutheran books out of hand: they must first, he said, be examined and judged by impartial experts. On Lars Andreae's suggestion he resurrected the old printing-press at Uppsala, ordered the bishops to prepare a translation of the Bible, and checkmated Brask's objections by inducing Johannes Magnus to act as general editor. This cooperative venture did not get very far (though Brask and his chapter loyally completed the portions assigned to them); but the revived Uppsala press did not stand idle. Peder Galle, a member of the Uppsala chapter, and a skilful controversialist, seized the opportunity to publish three books denouncing Luther's errors. It was not for such purposes that Gustav had made the press available. His reply was to move the press to Stockholm, where it would be conveniently under his eye, and to order Brask to stop production from his diocesan press at Linköping.[1] Printing was to be a royal monopoly; the Stockholm press alone was to operate; and henceforward it was to be used only in the reformers' interest. The fruits of this policy were not long in appearing. In 1526 came the first Protestant book in Swedish, Olaus Petri's *Useful Instruction*, and later in the year there followed his translation of the New Testament, with a lectionary appended for use in church services. It was a great success: the bishops at once ordered incumbents to procure copies for their churches. By this time mass was probably already being celebrated in the vernacular, at least in Stockholm: it is said that Olaus Petri's wedding was the first occasion. The first Swedish hymns were soon to follow. The king did his best at the end of 1526 to inveigle the champions of the old faith into a public disputation with the reformers: he seems to have shared the common idea that if points of controversy were publicly debated the truth would emerge triumphant, and all difficulties would disappear. Brask and his friends were too wary to accept this proposal, and the king had to be content with the written answers to a set of Ten Questions (later increased to twelve), which he propounded to both sides for their consideration. The questions concerned the value of custom and tradition; the authority of the papacy; the power of excommunication; justification by faith or works; the invocation of saints; purgatory; and the authority of scripture. For Olaus Petri it was a great opportunity, and he did not fail to take advantage of it. In May 1527, on the eve of the critical meeting of the Estates at Västerås, he published his answer. It was a full-blooded enunciation of the Lutheran teaching on all these points (except purgatory, which he still left an open question), written in a salty, sinewy prose which revealed him as the first considerable writer of the modern Swedish tongue;[2] and it probably played no small part in moulding opinion in the debate that followed.

Meanwhile Gustav Vasa had been made aware that his patronage of the reformers might have its inconveniences and dangers, as well as its advantages. In 1526 there arrived in Stockholm a certain Melkior Hoffmann. He came from Livonia, well armed with recommendations from Luther himself, and at first he was well received. He began to preach in Stockholm, and soon attracted a following, especially among the German elements in the town. His sermons were stronger meat

[1] Brask was forced to sell his press. It was bought by Olof Ulriksson, who set it up at Malmö, where it played a notable part in the dissemination of Protestant literature among the Danes.

[2] Something of his manner may be collected from the following excerpts: 'It does not help to tell us how old the pope's authority is: the devil is old, but he is none the better for that'; 'preaching the Word of God is a priest's job, as smithing is a smith's job; and as you cannot call a man a smith who does not do any smithing, so you cannot call him a priest if he does not do any preaching.'

than had hitherto been put before the Swedish public; for Hoffmann was an unbalanced enthusiast of chiliastic leanings, and possibly an iconoclast too. His apocalyptic transports soon repelled the moderate, and the religious hysteria which he induced in his congregation seemed unedifying to many who might otherwise have had some sympathy with parts of his doctrine. Olaus Petri and Lars Andreae, who had at first been attracted, took alarm and withdrew their countenance: they saw clearly that such excesses could do nothing but harm to the Lutheran cause. Those who might be disinclined to believe Hoffmann when he announced the imminent end of the world began to fear that his gospel might involve the imminent end of the social order. This was probably the king's main concern with the affair. To Hoffmann's religious views he was antipathetic; but in any case he could not tolerate a continuous fermentation in Stockholm. The movement reached its peak about the end of 1526: soon afterwards the king shipped off Hoffmann back to Germany (adding, for good measure, Dr Nicolaus Stecker), and the religious temperature in Stockholm dropped to less torrid levels. But the king did not forget that Master Olof and Master Lars had once dabbled in Hoffmann's movement.

The extravagances of Hoffmann's followers make it easy to forget how small the progress of the reformers really was, even in 1527. Lutheranism was still the creed of a very tiny minority, of whom a good proportion was probably German in speech. It was confined mainly to a handful of east-coast towns. With the nation at large it was thoroughly unpopular. Its greatest asset was that it was now almost openly patronized by the king, who sustained the reformers for his own purposes; though he could equally well have extinguished them if he had chosen to do so. But Lutheranism gave a religious sanction to political necessity, and Gustav Vasa soon learned the jargon of reform: his attacks on monks and bishops had all the crudity and virulence which was to be characteristic of Protestant polemic. The main brunt of these attacks was borne by Hans Brask; for Brask was the real leader of the resistance, both to the spread of Lutheranism, and to the king's assaults upon the economic position of the church. Already in 1523 Brask had uttered a warning against clerics who tell the laity that the church exists for the sake of its members, and deduce that congregations have therefore the right to dispose of the church's property. He had pronounced Lars Andreae's letter to Vadstena to be heretical. He had implored Johannes Magnus to establish the Inquisition in Sweden. He had done his best to secure the confirmation of the *electi* at Rome, partly in order to strengthen their authority, partly because he foresaw the consequences of papal intransigence, partly because the king would have been glad to have the *electi* consecrated by the archbishop without confirmation, and so evade the payment of annates. Step by step he had fought the king on the question of quartering in monasteries. If he acquiesced in some of the exactions which were made upon the church, it was because he perceived the impossibility of withholding the church's aid altogether in the prevailing emergency. He saw clearly that each concession was likely to be followed by a more exigent demand; and he knew well that the overwhelming majority of Swedes were hostile to the new religion. He was defeated by the cynical and ruthless tactics of the king, who shrank from no falsehood or meanness in his determination to blacken Brask's character and exhibit him to the country as a proud prelate, a bloodsucker battening on the laity, a defender of the 'pack of hypocrites' who lived lives that were idle (or worse) in over-endowed monastic establishments. Brask was not, perhaps, a very spiritual churchman: duty to the church, as he saw it, consisted in defending her liberties and her revenues. But he was a genuine patriot, and he long remained loyal under much provocation: for Sunnanväder and Master Knut he had only contempt. It was his misfortune that he was but feebly supported by his episcopal colleagues. The *electi* lacked weight and authority; the *archielectus* Johannes Magnus was a man of peace, unfitted to the times, who dealt with heresy by stopping his ears and avowing that he heard nothing amiss. In Peder Galle, indeed, the old church produced one vigorous controversialist who was prepared to enter the lists against Master Olof; but the suppression of the liberty of printing deprived him of the means of reaching the public. There remained only two resources to which the church could now turn: one, the religious conservatism of the peasantry; the other, the church's old political allies among the lay magnates, whom it might be possible to stir to resistance by the argument that the attack on the church's privileges foreboded a general attack upon the concept of *frälse*: it was not unreasonable to hope that the nobility might rally to the support of the church against a kingship which showed signs of becoming dangerously strong. Both expedients were tried. The clergy of Uppsala seem to have incited the visitors to the winter market to clamour for measures against Lutheranism: when the king visited Uppsala in 1526 and delivered a violent harangue against the bishops, the monks and the church in general, he met a hostile audience: 'the people shouted that they wanted to keep their monks, and that they would not have them driven away: rather than that, they would feed and foster them themselves.' The rising in favour of the *Daljunker* showed that this form of resistance might be serious. There is no evidence that Brask or his colleagues had any hand in it; but the king certainly believed that they had, and there were stories of monks from Vadstena slipping away north to encourage the rebels. But whatever Brask's personal connexion with peasant movements, he certainly took steps to form a common front with the lay nobility. Quite early in the reign he appealed to Ture Jönsson to stand firm with him in defence of *frälse*. In the January and February of 1527 he was having secret meetings with him in Västergötland, and Ture Jönsson in turn was meeting the local bishop, Magnus Haraldsson of Skara. The king believed himself to be confronted with a politically monstrous coalition of the church, the old *råd*-party, the Dalesmen, and the remains of the party of the Stures; with 'that old bloodhound King Kristian' in the background.

Gustav Vasa understood well enough that his church policy, if it were to succeed, must have at least the passive acquiescence of the nobility and peasantry. Its unpalatable elements must be sweetened by material advantages, or justified by the necessity for reform. Again and again, in public utterances, letters, proclamations, he disavowed any adherence to the new doctrines—though he usually coupled this with the statement that he was not prepared to condemn them without trial. The preachers, he argued, did no more than preach the Word of God; which was, after all, their plain duty. But there were abuses in the church that required correction: the over-mighty power of bishops was one, as successive rulers of Sweden had found to their cost. Other abuses touched the daily life of the common man: the unfairly favoured position of clerical litigants, for instance; the abuse of ecclesiastical penalties, and especially of excommunication, to secure private and secular ends; the exaction of arbitrary or exorbitant fees. It was to destroy the exceptional position of the clergy which made such abuses possible that his church policy was directed; and since Rome was the defender of that position, and the obstinate assertor of those exceptional rights, the attempt at reform must (for a time at least) entail defiance of Rome. The church of independent Sweden could and should manage its own affairs: it had no need of papal provisions, and still less of Gustav Trolle.

By arguments of this sort, stated often in the most brutal and tendentious form, Gustav Vasa sought to quiet the suspicions of the peasantry. With the nobility he used other tactics, and more solid inducements. To them he held out the prospect of plundering the church. His own proceedings in regard to Gripsholm manor had been an unmistakable hint; and there is some reason to think that more explicit suggestions were made. The arguments were of course based upon state policy: the nobility, it was explained, had grown so impoverished by their forefathers' reckless donations to the church that they were now incapable of rendering to the crown those services which the proper management of the country demanded, and without which it could hardly be effectively run. There was some truth in this; for, as we have seen, the church had for some decades been having the better of it in the increasingly sharp competition for *frälse* lands. And, true or not, to most of the nobility it was an irresistible argument. A few stalwarts such as Ture Jönsson and his friends from Västergötland, who foresaw that the enrichment of the aristocracy would be accompanied by a much greater enrichment of the monarchy, and a consequent disproportionate increase in royal power, were proof against the bribe. But most of them, as the coming *riksdag* would show, were only waiting for the opportunity to recoup themselves. And it was clear, too, that the appeal to self-interest could also be made to the other Estates; for to them the position could be stated as a plain alternative: either the church is fleeced, or taxes must be raised.

The problems which the Estates were now to be called upon to solve were not peculiar to Sweden. They had their analogues elsewhere in the North; and to some of them answers had already been given or implied in neighbouring lands. The dramatic scenes at Vasterås in 1527 were played out against a European, as well as a Swedish, background, and none of the participants (least of all the king) can have failed to be influenced in some degree by the course of events abroad. By the spring of 1527 the Reformation had made great progress in the Baltic lands. Riga, Reval and Dorpat were now Protestant cities; Mecklenburg and Holstein were ruled by dukes whose Protestant sympathies were already evident. Most influential of all was the example of Prussia, where in 1525 Albert of Hohenzollern, with the active collaboration of the episcopate and the church, had turned the lands of the Teutonic Knights into a secular principality, with himself as *summus episcopus*. Soon afterwards the political relations between Prussia and Sweden began to be drawn closer: in 1526 a treaty of friendship and freedom of commerce was concluded, and early in 1527 a Prussian envoy arrived in Stockholm to ratify it. He can scarcely have failed to mention that his master had just taken the bishops' lands into his ducal hands. Albert of Prussia was also on terms of friendship with Fredrik I of Denmark, and in 1526 married his daughter Dorothea; and Fredrik, though he was not prepared to go as far as his son-in-law, had already moved some distance towards an anti-papal position: before the end of the year he appointed Hans Tausen, the leader of the Danish reformers, as his chaplain. His difficulties with the church much resembled Gustav Vasa's. Some of them had already exercised Kristian II. In 1521, for instance, Kristian had limited the size of the armed retinues of his bishops; he had insisted on the clergy's being resident; he had prohibited appeals to Rome, and the use of excommunication in purely civil cases. A meeting of the Estates at Kiel in February 1526 had demanded that the bishops be compelled to take care that the Word of God, and not man-made fables, be preached to the people. Another meeting at Odense in November had resolved that henceforward bishops might be confirmed by the archbishop of Lund, without troubling to seek confirmation in Rome; it had also ordered the confiscation and melting-down of some of the church bells, in order to provide for defence against the expected attacks of Kristian II. Fredrik's attitude to the religious question was largely influenced, as Gustav Vasa's was, by financial stringency, by a desire to divert the drain of funds to Rome into his own pocket and tap the wealth of the bishops and monasteries to meet the necessities of the state; and like Gustav Vasa he excused his patronage of the reformers by insisting that his only concern was that the Word of God be purely preached to the people.

Thus when the Swedish Estates gathered at Västerås in 1527 the tide of religious change was already running strongly in those neighbouring lands with which they had most in common, and of which they were best informed. The burgher of Kalmar or Söderköping who did his business with traders from north Germany, the Småland peasant who sold his cattle or his butter in the Danish ports, would be aware of the strength of the new ideas and alive to the fact that the church was now under attack from other sovereigns than his own. The progress of reform elsewhere prepared the way for the crisis in Sweden; and those who had now to confront it could hardly fail to be affected by the swift current of events swirling past their doorstep.

IV. THE BEGINNINGS OF THE REFORMATION, 1527–31

The Estates had originally been summoned to meet at Söderköping at Whitsuntide 1527; but the date of the meeting was deferred to Trinity Sunday (16 June). The place was changed to Västerås, in order to be nearer to the area of unrest in Dalarna, and to give facilities for representatives of the Dalesmen to attend and state their case if they should wish to do so: with a characteristic touch of irony the king suggested that the *Daljunker* might care to come in person to put forward his claims. The writs of summons alleged the disturbances in Dalarna as a main cause of the meeting, and members of the *råd* were significantly urged to bring armed men with them. But an exhortation to send three or four of the most learned men from every chapter also foreshadowed the discussion of theological issues: in a letter to the commonalty of January of this year the king had sharply attacked Indulgences. And already in the summonses the king gave the moral thumbscrews a preliminary twist by hinting at the possibility of his abdication.

When the *riksdag* was assembled, Gustav laid before it a Proposition.

It took the form of a long exposition of the state of the country, with an invitation to the Estates to give him their counsel upon it: this was the first time that a Swedish ruler had exhibited to his subjects so detailed and comprehensive a survey of the problems and difficulties of his government. It was a document of great political adroitness, masterly in its plainness, its forcefulness, its irony, its seductive logic, and in a certain rough-hewn, popular quality which fitted it well to the tastes and understandings of most of the audience to which it was addressed. It began by describing the perennial disturbances and conspiracies to which the country appeared to be subject, and which caused the king to repent that he had ever allowed himself to be elected. It proceeded to castigate the ingratitude of the Swedes to their deliverer: the Dalesmen, for instance, not content with grotesquely exaggerating their part in the liberation of the country, now presumed to behave as though they had the crown of Sweden in their gift. Next came an exposition of the economic situation, with an explanation of the need for the recent extraordinary burdens and a justification of the quartering of troops in monasteries. It was not Gustav's fault if the times were hard and the price of salt high: was he God, that he should be supposed capable of regulating these things? The plain fact was, that the crown's income was too small for discharging the obligations and shouldering the responsibilities of a modern state. The revenue stood at 20,000 marks against an expenditure of 60,000:[1] was it any wonder that the royal castles fell into ruin? The nobility, too, if they were to play their part properly, must have fiefs; but how could the crown afford to provide them? Only the proud prelates appeared to be well off: king and nobles together, he calculated, had scarce one-third the revenues of the church. As to the accusations against him of favouring heretical opinions, he had done no more than to encourage the spread of the Gospel; but for the quieting of all controversy he demanded that the preachers be confronted with their critics, and that the Estates convince themselves, by a public disputation to be conducted before them, of where the truth really lay. And finally, the Estates were told that the king would bear the burden of government no longer: he would renounce the throne, not being minded to be made a fool and a puppet of, as Karl Knutsson had been in his time; and he asked only that 'a bit of a fief' might be provided to support him in his retirement into private life. His debts, no doubt, he would leave behind him with his crown.

The threat of abdication was decisive. With rebellion in full flame in Dalarna, with Lübeck's agent lurking around the *riksdag* in mute

1 Even allowing for the fact that this was a year of severe distress, these figures seem unacceptably low.

testimony to the king's difficulties, the Estates could not afford to take him at his word, and hope that good luck would throw up another native leader able to relieve them of the need to choose between Fredrik I and Kristian II. (Brask and Ture Jönsson had been in touch already with Kristian and Trolle, but they had soon found the negotiation more than their patriotism could swallow.) Apart from the suggestion for a disputation, and the demand that the Estates pledge themselves to stand by him against the *Daljunker*, the king had made no specific proposals; but his Proposition had been so drawn that most of those who heard it must jump to the conclusion that the easiest way out of all their difficulties (perhaps the only one) was to endorse the king's practice and strip the church alike of its authority and of its 'superfluous' revenues. It took some days for them to come to the resolution for which Gustav was waiting. Brask and Ture Jönsson, backed by a section of the nobility, fought obstinately against odds. It required a temperamental outburst (and a timely flood of tears) from the king, and an abdication which this time really seemed to be definitive, to break their resistance. In spite of protests the disputation was duly held, Olaus Petri *versus* Peder Galle:[1] it resulted, for all practical purposes, in Olaus' being cleared of the charge of heresy—though certainly this was a matter upon which the views of the Estates were void of authority, save upon the strained argument that they were in fact a sort of church council, a *concilium mixtum*. And at last the three Estates, led by the nobility (as the most directly concerned), severally answered the queries implicit in the Proposition. Their resolutions were digested by the *råd* (and significantly touched up) to form a common resolution of the *riksdag*, celebrated in Swedish history under the name of the Recess of Västerås.

The Recess proceeded upon the assumption (which proved to be justified) that the king's abdication would be withdrawn if satisfactory remedies were provided for the 'deficiencies' of which he complained. Those deficiencies fell under four heads: the failure of his subjects to remain faithful to him against rebels and pretenders; the poverty of the crown; the weakness of the nobility; and the country's readiness to credit charges against the king's orthodoxy. As to the first, they offered a pledge of union against all traitors. As to the second, they provided for a drastic curtailment of the political power and economic resources of the church. Henceforth bishops were to surrender their castles to the king,[2] and to maintain only so many armed men as the

[1] The disputation dealt with Indulgences; the worldly power of bishops and their neglect of their proper duties; and the incompetence of human law to regulate matters of conscience.

[2] The reply of the nobility had suggested that this be a temporary measure, until the king should have been able to rebuild the royal castles: the Recess significantly omitted the limitation of time.

king should permit. In consequence of this limitation they would be able to subsist on incomes much smaller than before, and a large overplus of revenue would become available for other purposes. The Recess enacted that this surplus (which it offhandedly referred to as 'a bit of money'[1]) should be given to the crown, after its amount had in each case been agreed upon between the bishop and the king. Similarly, all 'superfluous' revenues of cathedrals and canonries were to go to the king also. Monasteries and nunneries that lived only on their rents, and which were considered by the king to be in general ill-managed, were to be put in charge of 'good knights', who would administer their affairs against a reasonable recompense, decide how much of their income they really needed, and forward the balance to the treasury—a plan of starvation which represented itself as being prompted by a concern for administrative efficiency. It was added that henceforth bishops were not to meddle with these institutions, except only that they might continue to profess nuns—though even that only with the permission of the king.

The crown's necessities being thus relieved, the aristocracy took its reward. By the third point in the Recess it was enacted that all properties donated by the nobility to the church since the year 1454 were to revert to the families of the donor, without compensation. (When those families had died out, as not seldom happened, the king obligingly stepped into their place.) Property sold or mortgaged to the church since 1454 could also be reclaimed, though in these cases compensation was to be paid at a rate varying inversely with the time the property had been in the church's possession. Land which was by nature *ofrälse* was to revert to lay hands without limitation of time. Finally, the Recess recorded the judgment of the meeting (for what it was worth) that the disputation had shown that the reformers were in the right, since they did no more than preach the Word of God; and put it on record that the Estates had entreated the king 'that God's Word may be purely preached everywhere in the realm'.

Gustav Vasa had appealed to the *riksdag*; its doom had been given in his favour. He had accused the old church of ruining the country, he had denied Lutheran heresy in himself or the preachers; and the Estates, with the knife of abdication at their throats, and the prospect of anarchy or foreign lordship before their eyes, had testified emphatically to his veracity. It was an enormous political and constitutional victory; and Gustav took care to exploit it to the full. Within a few days of the conclusion of the Diet, he had caused the *råd* to draw up an Ordinance, designed to give practical effect to the decisions of the Recess. The Ordinance of Västerås certainly did that; but it went far

1 'Ett stycke pengar.'

beyond the letter or the spirit of the earlier document. It provided, for instance, that when the bishop supplied a parish with a priest who was 'unsuitable: as, brawlers, tipplers, or those backward to preach God's Word', the king had the right to deprive the incumbent, and instal a better man of his own choice. It enacted that bishoprics, canonries and prebends were not to be filled henceforward without the king's approval. By a provision which destroyed the last tenuous remnant of the fiscal privilege of the episcopate, the 'bit of money' due to the king by Västerås Recess was no longer to be a matter of agreement between king and bishop: the sum would be fixed by the king. There followed a long list of provisions which revealed the king as exercising what, if he had been a Lutheran, would have been termed his *jus reformandi*: prohibition of excessive fees; relaxation of discipline in certain cases of Sabbath-breaking; the removal of the church's privileged status in cases concerning lay matters, so that priest and layman should henceforth be equal before the law; injunctions against the abuse of excommunication, and against the perversion of spiritual authority for secular ends. A series of clauses appropriated to the crown the fines levied in church courts—for instance, for moral offences, or in matrimonial causes. A notable clause struck a mortal blow at the mendicant orders by restricting the period within which they might beg to ten weeks in the year; and a final paragraph enjoined the reading of the Gospel as part of the ordinary school curriculum. Six further clauses, included in the original draft, it was thought prudent to omit. Three of them, in particular, would have constituted that direct assault upon Rome's authority which, in spite of everything, Gustav had so far contrived to avoid; for one forbade payment of Peter's Pence; another, any payment to Rome by a monastic establishment; and the third, the seeking by bishops of confirmation from Rome. But even without them the Ordinance announced a formidable and ominous programme; and in the event, though there were indeed matters upon which the law had thus preferred to remain discreetly silent, things arranged themselves as comfortably as if it had spoken. No bishop henceforward sought confirmation at Rome, no Peter's Pence trickled into the papal treasury. The king quietly garnered the benefits of an anti-papal policy, while at the same time avoiding the *éclat* of a breach.

The proceedings at Västerås in 1527, and the Ordinance which was their sequel, were a turning-point in the history of Sweden. The struggle between church and state, latent and only occasionally articulate in the Sweden of the Stures, had been forced by Gustav Vasa to a crisis, and that crisis had ended in a decisive and irreversible victory for the crown. The political power of the episcopate was destroyed by the confiscation of their castles, and by the limitation at the king's discretion of the size of the military force they might maintain; the arrangements about their revenues ensured that for the future they would be too poor to be dangerous: it was logical that henceforth the bishops should disappear from the *råd*. A benevolent commentator might remark that in future they would be *episcopi secundum verbum Dei, non secundum verbum Papae*, but the experience of the next few years was to show that they felt themselves rather to be bishops *secundum verbum Regis*, and Gustav would hardly have quarrelled with that description: it would not be long before he was deposing bishops with as little fuss or embarrassment as if they had been defalcating bailiffs. Meanwhile, their fiscal privileges had gone for ever; the king's appropriation of their 'superfluous' revenues meant that they would be subject henceforward to a standing tax; and the Ordinance, by depriving them of the right to negotiate with the king about it, left its size to his good pleasure, and in fact put them economically wholly at his mercy.[1] They were not, indeed, as yet robbed of their property. Their lands remained their own, even though they were now heavily burdened. But they had lost most of their fiefs already, would soon lose more, and stood helpless before the despoiler whenever it should please him to exercise his power to snatch what was theirs. One after another the ancient *libertates ecclesiae* were going by the board: freedom from taxation, free canonical election of bishops, inviolability of the clergy, had all now been taken away; *privilegium fori* was gravely compromised. The attack, it is true, had been concentrated upon the episcopate, the cathedral chapters, and the monastic establishments: the parochial clergy had as yet suffered no economic loss. But their turn would come; and already their juridical privileges were impugned.

The church's losses were the crown's gains; and very considerable they were. They soon required special administrative officers to take care of them; and they had the special advantage from the king's point of view that the superfluous revenues were rendered in specie. But as yet they were substantial rather than spectacular: the developments which were to make Gustav Vasa the richest king that Sweden had so far seen were only just beginning at Västerås. Another twenty years of ruthless litigation *in terrorem*, naked plunder of parochial lands and revenues, and confiscation of church property would be necessary before that state of affairs was attained. Västerås opened the gates and pointed the road; it did not advance very far along it. But in thus providing the monarchy with a new financial basis which grew broader and broader with the passing of the years, the meeting at Västerås took a decision which was to have far-reaching effects upon Sweden's

[1] In fact, negotiation of a sort seems to have taken place, with results which varied with the king's opinion of the bishop's political reliability.

constitutional history. As the Stures had seen, a central authority which lacked an adequate backing of lands and revenues could never be effective: their difficulty had been that such a backing seemed possible only at the cost of alienating the nobility and the church, and that resistance by these classes could plausibly be based on constitutional principles. Already by the time of young Herr Sten it was beginning to become clear that the only escape from this predicament lay in sowing divisions between the privileged Estates. And it was just this that Gustav Vasa successfully accomplished at Västerås. A lucky combination of circumstances presented him with a chance to violate the liberties of the church in the name of the interests of the nation, and he was able to push home his advantage because he could split the potential opposition: the connivance of the lay *frälse*, it appeared, could be bought with ecclesiastical booty. It was a tactic not without its risks, nor was it certain of success; for the church as such was certainly not in ill odour with the mass of the population. Brask may well have been unpopular in his diocese; but he was not, as Trolle had been, an object of general detestation. Moreover, at least some of the nobility penetrated the king's design, descried the snare that he set for them, and strove to avoid it: Ture Jönsson and his friends from Västergötland stood staunchly by the church in defence of *frälse*. But the majority of the lay aristocracy were too greedy, too easily swayed by the king's bluff about abdication, to stick for long to this line; and with their defection his victory was as good as won.

Yet victory brought its own problems. If the monarchy had emerged from the crisis much better endowed than ever before, so too had the great lay magnates. The king's political gains would be hollow if it should turn out that he had committed himself to an alliance with the nobility which was to entail his paying them blackmail at unspecified intervals. But the very way in which the decision at Västerås had been reached gave Gustav Vasa some measure of security against this danger. For the decision had been the work of the *riksdag*: the support of the *ofrälse* Estates had been an important element in his triumph. In 1527, as in 1517, the monarchy had staked its position on the willingness of the representatives of the mass of the nation to follow its lead, and in each case the gamble had been successful. The *riksdag* had given the aggrandizement of the crown a sanction which was already beginning to be recognized as a *constitutional* sanction, not less valid than that older type of constitutional sanction—the assent of the *råd*—which had enjoyed such authority in the previous century. In 1527 the Recess of Västerås was a sound bar to any objections based on the Recess of Kalmar. But the king had no mind to be the prisoner of the lower Estates, any more than he intended to be the tool of the nobility. His object rather was to place himself in a position where he need not fear the tutelage of either, and to maintain himself in that position by using each to check the other. The nobility should safeguard him against the perennial discontents of *Herr Omnes*; the Estates should ensure that in any argument with the magnates he had a constitutional authority and resource behind him. When Brask protested that the great changes that followed the Västerås meeting were 'the negation of law', the king could retort unanswerably that they were the will of the people, legally expressed through its assembled representatives. That the *riksdag* should itself ever become a constitutional check upon the crown such as the *råd* had been in the past was a development which neither Gustav Vasa nor anyone else foresaw.

So it was that Gustav Vasa in 1527 seemed in fact to have resolved the Stures' political dilemma. It might indeed be expedient for the moment to stop the mouths of an aristocracy clamouring for fiefs by granting to them many of those same castles which had been reft from the bishops on the plea that they were necessary to the crown; but the king did not thereby relinquish his designs upon them. Meanwhile the experience of Västerås had clearly established the *riksdag* as an effective organ of the constitution: as yet, perhaps, to be used only in an extremity, but undeniably available to a sovereign in difficulties. It had legislated upon fiscal and ecclesiastical matters of a kind that no *riksdag* before it had been allowed to meddle with. The forms of parliamentary procedure were taking shape: for instance, in the drawing up of a Resolution, in answer to the royal Proposition. The constitutional implications of Västerås were not lost on Gustav Vasa; and scarcely any member of the House of Vasa thereafter ever forgot them.

The *riksdag* of Västerås did not register the triumph of the Reformation in Sweden: far from it. The Recess had by implication *exculpated* Gustav Vasa from the charge of Lutheranism. The commonalty, on the one hand, and the *råd* on the other, were agreed in urging him to preserve and safeguard 'good old Christian customs'. Popular opinion, as shown at the great fairs and markets, was unambiguously on the same side: specific demands were made that no monk or nun should be constrained to quit the cloister. In order to enlist support against episcopal power the king had found it necessary to make great play with the oppressiveness to the people of having 'two lords in one land'; but there is not much sign that the Estates had found it a very telling argument. The burghers, indeed, had some vague grievances against mendicant monks; but of reformed ideas there is scarcely a trace in the *riksdag* proceedings. Apart from such of the clergy as were present very few of those that assembled at Västerås can have had any notion that they were deciding the religious destiny of Sweden.

Nevertheless, it is still true that it was the Recess of Västerås which made the future victory of the Reformation possible. That clause which asked that henceforth the Word of God should be *purely* preached, though it may have been intended by its framers only to absolve the reformers, without condemning their adversaries, in the sequel provided all the opening that they needed. Hostility to episcopal power drew the king into hostility to the rulings of ecclesiastical authority, even where they concerned spiritual things; his practical, utilitarian and philistine spirit was easily induced to measure a priest's usefulness by his assiduity in preaching; and a preacher who based his sermons on the authority of the Bible, rather than on that of pope or council or Fathers, had a good chance of his sympathy—provided he respected the royal authority. He looked at the church with the insensitive and unsentimental eye of an efficiency-expert, saw superfluous fat here, illogicalities or abuses there, and had no qualms about reforming them. Like Laurentius Petri, his future archbishop, he suspected that cathedral chapters were 'crawling with useless priests', and that monasteries fostered 'a pack of hypocrites'. The power over church appointments which the Ordinance gave him he fully intended to use; and in the next decade or so he advanced steadily to a position in which he believed the church to be subject to the state, believed himself to be its supreme head, and believed that this kind of *landesherrliche Kirchenregiment* (to borrow the term that became current in Lutheran Germany) entitled him—and indeed bound him—to intervene to correct abuses wherever he might discern them. He had been led to attack the bishops by wholly political considerations: ultimately, perhaps, by the grave crisis of the *Daljunker's* revolt, in which he really seems to have believed Brask to be involved. His doctrinal indifference did not prevent his sympathizing with some aspects of the Lutheran creed, if only for their practical political consequences, and if only because so many of his political enemies took the other side. His respect for the principle of order ensured him against antinomian divagations, and he was the last man to be beguiled by 'enthusiasts'. By his side stood Lars Andreae, cold of heart, but intellectually a convinced Lutheran; and Andreae at times advanced faster than the king was willing to go: the cancelled clauses of the Ordinance were probably Master Lars' work. Gustav did his best to keep him on a tight rein; but Lars was a hard-mouthed animal: the clauses were indeed suppressed, but they seem in fact to have been acted upon. Formally, there was still no overt defiance of papal authority—no prohibition of payments to Rome, no ban upon bishops' seeking confirmation there. The Ordinance makes no attack on Rome, nor even refers to relations with the Holy See. But what chance was there that the bishops, or the monasteries, would be allowed to retain sufficient revenues to make payments to Rome possible? And what *electus* could now afford the financial demands which confirmation by Rome would entail?

Västerås *riksdag*, among its other effects, ensured the failure of the movements in favour of the *Daljunker*. In the summer of 1527 that young man—in this as in so much else following in the footsteps of Sunnanväder and Master Knut—betook himself to Norway, there to seek support. The Norwegian authorities at first received him with respect; Fru Inger of Østråt, a strong-minded noblewoman of great influence, promised him the hand of her daughter; and the *Daljunker* undertook to cede Viken to Denmark once he had recovered his throne. By the spring of 1528, however, it was clear that the Dalesmen had given him up, and the Norwegians deemed it prudent to ship him off to Copenhagen. On the way there he escaped and fled to Rostock, whither he was shortly pursued by an affidavit from Kristina Gyllenstierna, denouncing him as an imposter. Gustav's brother-in-law, John of Hoya, on his way to negotiate with Lübeck about outstanding arrears, succeeded in persuading the hesitant Rostock authorities to bring him to book; and in the autumn of 1528 they executed him. A desperate attempt to rescue him at the last moment, by a force led (ominously enough) by Berend von Melen, came only just too late. The Pretender's Swedish adherents had already been dealt with. In March 1528 the king moved into Dalarna with a strong force of nobles; and at Tuna summoned his rebellious commons to meet him. He packed them tight together in a dense mass, surrounded them with armed men and artillery, and relieved his feelings in a scarifying indictment of their delinquencies. A few of the leaders were executed on the spot, as a warning to others; for the rest, it was to be hoped that the king's home-truths would suffice.

A month or two earlier, Gustav Vasa had at last allowed himself to be crowned. He used the occasion to extract both religious and political advantages. A coronation required bishops, if it were to be conducted with decent ceremony; and in November 1527 Gustav cut the knot of the long controversy over the *electi* by curtly notifying them that they must get themselves consecrated forthwith if they wished to retain their sees. The *electi* complied, and were duly consecrated by old Peder Månsson of Västerås; but a secret protestation, signed by all three, put it on record that they acted under duress. A new and unprecedented oath was exacted from them: they must bind themselves to preach the gospel and be content with their wages. The coronation, which followed in January 1528, was also notable for an innovation: for the first time the coronation oath omitted the pledge to safeguard the rights and property of the church. Was it for this reason, perhaps, that the king had postponed his crowning until he had the Västerås decisions in his pocket? And it was highly significant that the oath taken by the *råd* omitted the traditional obligation to see to it that the king and people observed the pledges which they had made to one another. The *råd* was no longer, it seemed, to retain its constitutional position of umpire between subjects and sovereign: its prime duty was now fidelity to the king. The constitutional trends of the last two centuries were about to be challenged.

For the church, the months that followed the Västerås *riksdag* were inevitably months of discouragement and confusion. Brask had been defeated at Västerås, had been forced to find sureties for good behaviour, and was now constrained to an onerous 'agreement' with the king. He had lost heart; there seemed no more that he could do. He took the opportunity of an episcopal visitation to Gotland to slip away—to Denmark first, and then to Prussia. Inevitably he was drawn into correspondence with other members of the ever-growing band of Gustav's enemies in exile—with von Melen, with Trolle; but his part in Sweden was played out, and he died in a Polish monastery eleven years later. The king, making the best of the situation, took advantage of his departure to confiscate the episcopal tithes for his own use—an action which coincided neatly with his attempts to explain to the commonalty that the obligation to pay tithe had not (as they seemed to assume) been cancelled by the Västerås proceedings. The Recess appeared to have been misunderstood in other particulars also. The king was forced to issue letters of protection for hospitals in danger of being plundered; to provide maintenance for schoolmasters; to intervene to prevent over-zealous bailiffs from purloining the communion-plate of parish churches; and to draw up a new schedule of fines for those cases where fines had formerly been payable to the church, but had now been appropriated by the crown. There was a good deal of semi-official violence and disorder; ugly things were done by royal agents and private speculators in the name of reform: in particular, Lars Andreae's ruthless proceedings against the monastery at Skänninge were widely and bitterly resented. There was general confusion, moreover, as to the extent to which innovation would be tolerated in the form and order of services. It was in an attempt to clear up this question that a sort of church council was summoned to Örebro for February 1529. It comprised some forty leading clerics under the presidency of Lars Andreae, and its decisions (equally unpopular with conservatives and reformers) were an obvious attempt at compromise. They prescribed the reading of Scripture in churches and schools; they enjoined diligence in preaching; and they entered into a careful exposition of the significance of various church ceremonies—most of them being explained as either commemorative or edifying. But apart from one reference to 'the pope's law' in the matter of prohibited degrees, and a cautious curtailment of saints' days, their report was not provocative of the old church; and as they themselves avoided speaking of 'superstition', so also they deprecated railing from the pulpit. Moderate as this may seem, only the royal authority, visible in Master Lars' person, could have constrained the meeting to go so far.

By the spring of 1529 some of the opponents of the king's religious policies had reached a pitch of exasperation at which they were prepared to run the hazard of rebellion. Ture Jönsson, no less than Bishop Brask, had been defeated at Västerås. His political and religious principles were now both obviously in jeopardy, his property scarcely less so: for Gustav Vasa, who had a strongly litigious streak in his character, and seems to have shared with William Rufus an ambition to be 'every man's heir', had recently secured a verdict which gave him a substantial block of lands (part of the Sture inheritance) which Ture Jönsson had grown accustomed to regard as his own. The nobility of Västergötland—isolated, closely intermarried, exceptionally clannish—felt for Ture Jönsson in his misfortune, and shared his disapproval of the way the church was being treated. Their local bishop, Magnus Haraldsson of Skara, was a churchman of Brask's school, and no friend to the reformers. It happened, moreover, that the economic interests of the Västergötland nobility led them to sympathize with Lübeck at a time when the king's relations with the city were moving to a crisis; and it is not unlikely that Lübeck's agents had some share in stirring up the revolt. But the antecedents of the movement are not wholly clear: what seems almost certain is that Ture Jönsson and Bishop Magnus were already engaged in conspiracy in the autumn of 1528, and that it was they who were the principal instigators of the affair. Some of their grievances, no doubt, had little to do with religion; but it is nevertheless probable that it was religion that provided the main element in the insurrection. Certainly the leaders played on the religious string to enlist the support of the peasantry of Västergötland, Småland and Östergötland. These areas admittedly knew little or nothing of Lutheranism at first hand; but the lack was more than supplied by the lurid accounts of heretical goings-on in Stockholm with which they were furnished by Ture Jönsson and his friends. The peasants of Småland led off by massacring one of the king's bailiffs—a well-tried method of hinting dissatisfaction to the government; in Jönköping the Franciscans incited the burghers to rise; the dean of Uppsala (who happened to be Ture Jönsson's son) began to collect a force in Uppland to support the insurrection; and the clergy of Västergötland imported themselves into the movement with a zeal which they were made to rue when it was all over. At an early stage the rebels acquired a valuable pawn in the person of the king's sister Margareta (John of Hoya's wife), who was intercepted and detained, together with the king's secretary Wulf Gyler, as they were making their way home from Germany. The nobility of Västergötland ranged themselves behind Ture Jönsson, and one of them, Måns Bryntesson, allowed himself to be put forward as a candidate for the throne which they hoped might soon be vacant. By the first week of April, when it began to look as though the revolt might become general, the king was confessing that he hardly knew whether he could count on the loyalty of any of his subjects.

But though the crisis was sharp, it was also short: within two or three weeks it was over. Stockholm remained loyal, perhaps from the strength of Lutheranism there; Dalarna, still smarting from recent castigation, sent letters to Småland virtuously reprehending the sin of rebellion. The king scattered promises, protestations, denials, with a shrewd eye to their immediate effect and a fine carelessness for the future: militarily he was at a temporary disadvantage; diplomatically he ran rings round his enemies. Two trusted agents were sent down to Östergötland to parley with the insurgents. At Linköping the chapter offered them its good offices, and the offer was accepted. The negotiations thus begun led to an agreement with the Västergötland lords and their following, concluded at Broddetorp on 25 April. Its terms reveal how hard-pressed the king had been. He was made to promise a full amnesty for all, and to pledge himself that 'all good old Christian customs may be confirmed and maintained, and the Lutheran heresy and the evil communications that go with it be clean done away'. A fortnight later Gustav ratified these terms. But he slipped into his ratification a couple of lines which made the religious promise of no avail: he would prohibit heresy and maintain the good old Christian customs 'in all respects as in the Recess made at Västerås, and there accepted and agreed to by the *råd* and the commonalty of the realm'. This in fact knocked the bottom out of the Broddetorp agreement. It was sharp practice, very characteristic of Gustav Vasa; and if the simple men of Jönköping and Småland possibly failed to notice how they had been cheated, Ture Jönsson was under no such misapprehension. He prudently put no trust in the king's offer that all should be forgotten and forgiven; and with Bishop Magnus of Skara crossed the Danish border into exile.[1] Måns

[1] When Gustav Vasa tried to persuade Fredrik I to hand them over, Fredrik suggested that they be summoned to answer before a joint meeting of the councils of the three Scandinavian realms—an interesting example of the survival of the political traditions of the Union period.

Bryntesson and two others, unwisely braving it out at home in the hope that no evidence against them would be forthcoming, were soon made aware that they had miscalculated; and Måns with one of his companions in due course paid the penalty for his optimism on the scaffold.

Such was the revolt of the Västergötland lords. Despite the secular grievances it had been in the main a religious movement. The commissioners whom the king had sent down to Östergötland, in a report on the state of public opinion there, had told him bluntly that popular hatred of Lars Andreae and Olaus Petri was the driving force behind it. It may be that this explanation is to be attributed to the suggestions of the Linköping chapter, whose members had no love for Master Lars, and were still resentful of his proceedings at Skänninge. But the commissioners needed no extraneous influence to persuade them to add: 'We tell Your Grace the truth: that the common people will never submit to that doctrine . . . without they be constrained to it by force.' To a dispassionate observer in 1529 this must have seemed no more than a plain statement of fact. But Gustav Vasa knew better. He knew that gradual advances and partial retreats; double-talk confusing to the common man; singleness of purpose against uncertain resistance; vehement protestations as a cover to unpalatable acts; appeals to patriotism, to greed, to fear—all these things can circumvent the use of force. At a *riksdag* in Strängnäs in May 1529 he deliberately put himself in the dock, and conducted a defence of his policies with an unscrupulous virtuosity which it is impossible not to admire. To the accusations of the Västgöta lords, to the grumblings of the peasantry, he answered simply that he acted according to the decisions of Västerås; and that those decisions were approved by the *råd*. Any further changes were unauthorized by him, and he disclaimed responsibility for them—though he was prepared to avow a personal opinion that meat-eating on fast days, and the marriage of monks, need not necessarily be worthy of condemnation. Nor should they forget (he added) that if bishops were to be considered as appointed of God, He had not less certainly set kings in their high seats for His own purposes.

The decisions of Västerås; the legality of actions taken *med råds råde*: these were to be the twin bases upon which the Swedish Reformation was to build for the next few years. Yet neither the one nor the other was broad enough for Gustav: at the coronation, the *råd* protested at the forcing of monks from the cloister and the closing of monasteries. The town of Stockholm was permitted to behave as though it were a member of the nobility, and to reclaim property alienated to the church since 1454, though the Västerås Recess had certainly not authorized any such procedure.[1] The king extended his control of the clergy far beyond anything provided for even in Västerås Ordinance: a royal bailiff was informed that the dean of Skara was 'as much our official as you are', and the dean himself was summarily ordered to sink his objections and accept the office of bishop. Bishops were restrained from issuing pastoral letters. The king not only claimed to nominate to prebends and stalls (the Ordinance had given him the right only to approve), but began to formulate a theory (which he eventually succeeded in establishing as a custom) that the presentation to the major livings was reserved to the crown—the first serious interference by the state in parochial affairs. It is difficult to see what decision at Västerås, or what counsel from the *råd*, empowered him to inform a country congregation that the marriage of their parson was a matter of indifference; still less to pronounce that a vicar's loss of one finger was no impediment to the proper discharge of his pastoral function, 'whatever the pope's law may say'. Recess and Ordinance, in fact, were being operated to achieve results never contemplated by *råd* or *riksdag*. The destruction of the monasteries was one such result: destroyed, not by specific legislation or any single action, but by a gradual process in which the ingredients were lay administration, the granting of monasteries as lay fiefs, their conversion to hospitals, the encouragement of desertion, the deprivation of the means of subsistence, and, on occasion, forcible eviction. The attenuation of cathedral chapters was another: again, by a gradual process of transferring canons, prebendaries, precentors, to parochial cures, and neglecting to provide for their replacement—an operation which made the old sung mass increasingly difficult. Meanwhile, Lutheranism was spreading inwards from the ports; slowly, perhaps, but perceptibly. Gustav Vasa by 1530 was less afraid of the label of Lutheran. Already he had despatched, at the crown's expense, four young scholars to Wittenberg: one of them, Laurentius Petri (the brother of Master Olof), was destined to be his new archbishop. To most of his audience at Strängnäs, his justification of the plundering of the church on the ground that it provided funds for education must have sounded more than ordinarily cynical.

Meanwhile, the genius and industry of Olaus Petri was providing Swedish Lutheranism with its fundamental texts. In 1528 he produced *A Little Book on the Sacraments*,[2] in which he limited the sacraments to two (baptism and the eucharist), demanded the cup for the laity, and

[1] An even more curious case occurred in 1532, when Gustav Vasa gave permission to Tyge Krabbe, a *Danish* nobleman, to reclaim a donation by his family to the Blackfriars in Stockholm.

[2] This is a fairly faithful translation from the *Ansbacher Ratschlag*: the translator may possibly have been Lars Andreae.

condemned the notion of purgatory. Later in the same year his book *On Marriage* condemned celibacy also. In 1529 there followed the *Swedish Handbook*, a service book in the vernacular whose influence—literary, religious and sentimental—may justly be compared with Cranmer's Liturgy. This was followed in 1530 by the *Postilla*; and this in its turn by *The Swedish Mass* (1531). Since the crown controlled the only printing-press, it could control the type of religious literature available to the public. Gustav Vasa used that control to give Master Olof a monopoly of the religious book-market. The *Swedish Mass* appeared, with an appropriateness characteristic of its author, precisely at the moment when the language of the mass had become a main focus of controversy. Already in 1529 the Swedish mass had become so usual in Stockholm that a formal resolution of the town council was required to secure toleration for the Latin. A year later, this concession to the conservatives was revoked; and henceforward only Swedish was permitted. The decision caused scandal elsewhere, and there were many protests against it. The king had no strong feelings one way or the other, for this was not as yet a question which touched his authority; and for some years the official attitude was that congregations might have the mass in Swedish if they preferred it, but that no congregation was to be constrained to it against their will. Olaus Petri himself took the same line. But he added a memorable plea for the vernacular: 'We Swedes also belong to God, as well as doth any other nation; and the tongue that we speak, that hath God given us. He contemneth not us above the nations of the earth, neither despiseth He our speech beyond the speech of others.' Against the emotional pull of custom and tradition he invoked the pride of a young nation, recently liberated from a foreign yoke, and sensitive to the visible manifestations of subjection to external authority. It was not the least powerful element, perhaps, in swinging an increasing number of Swedes to Lutheranism.

As the coronation had precipitated a solution of the problem of the consecration of the *electi*, so the problem of the archbishopric was brought to a head by the king's approaching marriage to Katarina of Saxe-Lauenburg. He wished, naturally enough, that the wedding ceremony should be performed by the archbishop of Uppsala. But in 1531 the see, from his point of view, was vacant. Gustav Trolle was still busily plotting in exile; and Johannes Magnus, the *archielectus* of 1523, was no longer available. Unable to halt the progress of the Reformation, lacking papal confirmation or consecration, looked on with increasing suspicion by the king, weary at once of his impotence and his equivocal position, he had abandoned the struggle. While on a mission to Poland, he seized the opportunity to escape from his embarrassments. His later life was spent in Rome; and in Rome was published in 1554 his *Historia de omnibus gothorum sveonumque regibus*, which was to do so much to give definitive form to the national myth of the glories of the ancient Goths. It was not very easy to find a bishop to take his place. With scarcely an exception they were either opposed to the king's religious policies or lukewarm about them. Some were not averse to measures of reform; scarcely any wished to modify doctrine or renounce allegiance to Rome. In August 1531 two of them (the bishops of Strängnäs and Västerås) drew up a secret protest against Lutheran heresy, and against the consecration of any new archbishop without papal confirmation; and before the end of the month two others (Skara and Växjö) secretly swore fidelity to the pope, and pledged themselves to seek confirmation as soon as might be possible: only one, the newly appointed *electus* of Linköping, could be considered from the king's standpoint as really reliable. Upon the choice of the new archbishop, therefore, very much depended. If he should turn out to be, as most of the others were, at heart a friend to Rome, it was unlikely that the king would suffer bishops in Sweden much longer: it seems that only Lars Andreae's influence had deterred him from abolishing them already.

In this critical situation the king summoned a general meeting of the clergy, over a hundred strong, to make the election. Their choice fell on Laurentius Petri, who had by now returned from Wittenberg. It was an election acceptable to the king, and perhaps in the circumstances it could hardly have been otherwise; but it was also a choice most fortunate for the church. For though the new archbishop was an avowed Lutheran, and made no difficulty about acknowledging the king's *jus reformandi*, he did not therefore believe that the church faced the state stripped of all rights. He had courage, and temper, and patience; and in the years to come he would do more than any man to establish the Swedish Lutheran church on a basis strong enough to survive the caprices of Gustav Vasa and the hectic oscillations under his successors. On 22 September 1531 he was consecrated, without papal sanction and without the pallium; on 24 September he performed the king's marriage and the coronation of the queen. The consecration was a decisive act. Henceforward Sweden would be some sort of Protestant state. Of what particular sort depended in part on the relationship between the king and his new archbishop.

V. THE BREACH WITH LÜBECK, 1529–37

The war of liberation had produced two distinct, but related, controversies with Lübeck. One of them was implicit in the Strängnäs privileges. Those privileges, because they placed Sweden in economic tutelage to the Hanse, created a state of affairs which Gustav Vasa could never look upon as anything but a temporary settlement: sooner or later it must come to a breach on this issue. The other controversy concerned the king's indebtedness; and this, it might have been supposed, was capable of resolution. The total sum, though large, was probably not beyond the king's means; and if he had applied to its discharge all the funds which were raised allegedly for that purpose he might have been quit of it before 1530. But the moneys destined for Lübeck were used for other things (to pay his armies, for instance) and between 1523 and 1528 little or nothing seems to have gone to his creditors. By 1527, moreover, he had begun to query certain items in Lübeck's account; and he insisted that the expenses of the Gotland campaign should be offset against his owings, since that campaign had been undertaken only at Lübeck's instigation. He probably hoped at a fairly early stage to use disputes as to the size of the debt as a bargaining point in negotiations for a curtailment of the privileges; and all along he used the clamour of his creditors as an instrument of domestic policy.

By 1528, however, the remonstrances of the *råd* forced Gustav reluctantly to face the fact that Lübeck had reached the limit of her patience. Within the city a movement of opposition to the burgher oligarchy had made its appearance, demanding a more democratic form of municipal government and a clearly Lutheran religious policy. The leaders of this movement—though they included at least one of Gustav Vasa's old friends—blamed the city authorities for not dealing more firmly with Sweden. They were ready to enter into negotiations with Kristian II (still in his ultra-Lutheran phase), and they gave a warm welcome to Berend von Melen. It was to check these dangerous developments that Gustav Vasa in 1528 despatched to Lübeck his brother-in-law, John of Hoya, and his German secretary Wulf Gyler.[1] The real business of their mission was to try to abate Lübeck's demands to a more reasonable figure; but once the negotiations began they were soon forced to acknowledge to themselves that the king's exceptions to Lübeck's bill of costs had little substance in them and could not be sustained. Gyler therefore returned home to report progress. He succeeded in convincing his master that any further haggling would be futile as well as dangerous; and when he returned to Lübeck he took back with him full powers to sign an agreement. In 1529 it was duly concluded: the sum outstanding was fixed at 69,000 marks; and Sweden was to discharge it between 1529 and 1532 in four equal instalments.

[1] Gyler had been a muster-clerk in Berend von Melen's service, and when von Melen fled from Sweden the king—chronically short of competent civil servants—had been glad to take him into his own.

John of Hoya stood as personal security for the observance of these conditions, and bound himself in the event of default to return to Lübeck with thirty followers and place himself under arrest. The king, whatever his private feelings, accepted the fact and ratified the treaty; and the first instalment was punctually paid. In the course of the discussions Lübeck had held out vague hopes of a relaxation of the Strängnäs terms; and in 1530 there were further negotiations. They led to no result; but relations with Sweden became for a moment more cordial than at any time since 1523. And indeed it was by the benevolent intervention of Hermann Plönnies and Hermann Iserhel that Gustav's negotiations for a marriage alliance, which had latterly appeared unpromising, were eventually successful.

From a very early stage in the reign the king had been on the look-out for alliances or friendly understandings with neighbour states. Apart from the oppressive patronage of Lübeck and the still-dubious friendship of Fredrik I he was wholly isolated; for the princes of Europe were disposed to see in him a usurper whose throne was hardly worth five years' purchase. Yet the play of political and economic forces gave some prospects even to so forlorn a monarch. Charles V from a sense of family duty might now and then give Kristian II his countenance; but Margaret, his regent in the Netherlands, had her subjects' trade to think of, and was not really anxious to quarrel with Sweden. Danzig could probably be played off against Lübeck. Albert of Prussia, though he had been a friend of Kristian in 1520, was drawn to Gustav's side by a common dislike of the Livonian towns of the Hanse, and a common friendship for Poland. Between Sweden and Poland good relations were already a tradition by the time of Gustav Vasa's accession. They were based essentially on common hostility to Muscovy; for Muscovy threatened Polish interests in Livonia, and had for half a century been impending menacingly over Finland's eastern frontier. It was natural, therefore, that Gustav Vasa should turn to Poland in search of a bride. For a moment he had hoped to strengthen his ties with Fredrik I by marriage with a Danish princess; but when this speculation failed, and a less hopeful enquiry in Mecklenburg was equally unsuccessful, he made a determined effort to obtain the hand of Hedwig, the daughter of Sigismund I. It was this business that took the *archielectus* Johannes Magnus to Poland in 1526. But Sigismund had heard ill reports of Gustav Vasa's dealings with the church; and he found in the religious issue a real or a pretended reason for not committing himself. At all events, he let it be known that he would expect convincing proofs of Catholic orthodoxy before he would be willing to entrust his daughter in Gustav's hands. The negotiations hereupon came to an end, and Gustav was forced to look elsewhere.

In 1528, therefore, he sent an emissary to Magnus of Saxe-Lauenburg with offers for the hand of his daughter Katarina. It was an unexpected choice; for Magnus had been the friend of Kristian II, and was connected through his wife with Henry of Brunswick, the Emperor's most loyal supporter in north Germany, and a pillar of the Catholic party. Magnus had serious misgivings about the match (which the Västergötland revolt did nothing to allay), and for a time the negotiations made no progress. But now the king's old friends and protectors in Lübeck put in a good word for him; Magnus's hesitations were overcome; and in March 1531 the marriage-contract was concluded. It proved a very successful political investment. Kristian was deprived of supporters upon whom he might otherwise have been able to rely; Gustav Vasa acquired useful intercessors with the Habsburgs. The marriage was indeed short-lived, for Katarina died in 1535;[1] but her relatives remained for years Gustav's steady friends and champions in Germany, and provided a much-needed antidote to the wide-spreading venom of Berend von Melen.

If the king's improved relations with Lübeck thus had agreeable consequences in the international field, at home their implications were less pleasant. For a final effort had now to be made if the four instalments were to be paid punctually; and that effort involved the country in yet another rebellion. At a meeting of the *råd* in 1530 it had been agreed to require that all urban churches hand over to the king their largest bell, or, if they preferred it, an equivalent sum in copper or silver. Fredrik I had made similar demands in Denmark between 1526 and 1528, in order to obtain metal for casting cannon, and he had got what he wanted without resistance. At first there was no resistance in Sweden either; and in 1531 Gustav Vasa was able to deliver 30,000 marks' worth of bell-metal to Lübeck. Encouraged by this success, he decided in 1531 to extend the levy to country churches upon the same conditions. But in lower Dalarna this new exaction met with strong opposition. The harvest of 1530 had been bad; the copper mine at Falun was in temporary difficulties; the clergy encouraged their congregations to resist, and played upon their dislike of the king's religious policy. Worst of all, the rich miners of the Bergslag, on whose loyalty the king had always been able to count hitherto, now deserted him. Their leaders—Anders Persson of Rankhyttan, Måns Nilsson of Aspeboda, Ingel Hansson of Gylle—had been among the very first to rally to Gustav in 1521; they had fought at his side through the war of liberation; they had stood by him against Sunnanväder and the *Daljunker*. But latterly they had fallen into disfavour; probably because

[1] Gustav Vasa married (i) Katarina of Saxe-Lauenburg (1531); (ii) Margareta Leijonhufvud (1536); (iii) Katarina Stenbock (1552).

the king—it is impossible to say with what justice—suspected them of complicity in the Västergötland revolt of 1529. They now led the resistance, rabbled the king's bailiffs, and sought to enlist neighbouring provinces in the revolt. It was in vain that they were reminded that if they withheld their contribution Lübeck would cut off the supply of salt: perhaps they realized how much salt already came by way of Danzig. At all events, they summoned a *riksdag* to meet at Arboga, and obviously hoped to use it to put pressure on the king. But their success was small. Gustav Vasa overtrumped their *riksdag* by calling another to Uppsala on his own account at the same time; he protested his reluctance to engage in controversy with his subjects and his readiness to pardon the contrite; he explained to the country at large that the root of the trouble was not bells, but the intrigues of Kristian II; and he invited Stockholm to remonstrate with the rebels. Stockholm, dependent on the king's tolerance for its Protestant practices, and newly conciliated by generous privileges, was quite ready to oblige: the traditional alliance with the Bergslag on which the Stures had risen to power was split by the king's religious wedge. By the autumn of 1531 the Dalesmen had come to terms; the king (after a silence ominously prolonged) had consented to accept 2,000 marks in place of their bells; and the more sanguine or the more credulous might believe that their midsummer madness was forgotten.

It was in fact neither forgotten nor forgiven; but the close of 1531 was no propitious time for vengeance. For Kristian II was stirring at last: his long-deferred, long-expected attempt to win back his dominions had actually taken shape; and the upstart kings of Sweden and Denmark were trembling for their thrones. In June 1530 Charles V, for the moment clear of his war with France, allowed himself to be persuaded to give his brother-in-law just sufficient assistance to enable him to mount an expedition for the recovery of his patrimony. He insisted, as a condition precedent, upon Kristian's reconversion to Roman Catholicism, and he exacted a pledge that the old faith be restored in Denmark; but Kristian swallowed these terms without much difficulty. Old and new enemies of Gustav Vasa—Gustav Trolle, Ture Jönsson, Magnus Haraldsson of Skara—made all haste to join him. He made his landfall in Norway. The country was discontented and strongly Catholic, and in a few weeks a great part of it had gone over to him: only Akershus, the citadel of Oslo, with its tiny garrison—a score of men at most—held out hopelessly for Fredrik I. But after this promising start Kristian ruined his chances by irresolution. He made no real attempt to storm Akershus, and feebly granted its defenders a four-months' armistice on condition that they were not reinforced. His invasion of Viken faltered as soon as it came up against

Swedish opposition, and withdrew, leaving Ture Jönsson's decapitated body in the streets of Kungsälv as a memento of the occasion;[1] and while Kristian was busy in the field Fredrik rushed an extra forty men through the pack-ice into Akershus. One by one Kristian lost the ships that had borne him to Norway: by May 1532 the last of them had been burnt by his adversaries. Vacillating, uncertain of himself, lacking the stimulus of a strong personality at his side to inspire him, he deluded himself into believing that he could induce his uncle to step down from the throne by argument and persuasion. The exaggerated optimism with which he had begun the campaign was succeeded by an equally exaggerated apathy, and he parleyed when he should have acted. Fredrik I saw his opportunity and took it. He agreed that the problem was best settled by discussion; he invited Kristian to come to Copenhagen to talk it over. All sorts of guarantees were held out; the most binding safe-conducts were offered. Kristian, his Machiavellian intellect bruised and numbed by disaster, ambled piteously into the snare. On 24 July 1532 he reached Copenhagen: a few days later he entered Sønderborg castle as a prisoner; and a prisoner he remained until his death in 1559.

Though Kristian was thus disposed of with unexpected ease, his incursion into the North had provoked something not far from panic: the report of his arrival in Copenhagen threw Fredrik into such agitation of spirit that he took to his bed. And, as it turned out, it was Kristian's advent that started the train of circumstances which led directly to the complex imbroglio of the Count's War. At first it seemed probable that his coming would cement the reconciliation between Lübeck and her former *protégés*: in May 1532, for instance, Fredrik I concluded an alliance with Lübeck against the Dutch. Without Dutch aid and countenance Kristian II could never have started, and it seemed to the magistrates of Lübeck that they had now a rare opportunity to exploit the indignation of the Scandinavian kings, and so to shut the Dutch out of the Baltic altogether. But this proved in fact a miscalculation. Neither Fredrik nor Gustav was anxious for an interruption of trade relations with the Netherlands, and each valued the presence of the Dutch in northern waters as an offset to the economic predominance of the Hanse. Mary of Hungary[2] for her part felt that quite enough had been done to satisfy family honour, and was very ready to drop Kristian II and patch up a peace. Even before Kristian's capture a conference of interested parties, meeting in Copenhagen at the beginning of July 1532, had arranged a treaty between the

[1] Ture Jönsson is conjectured to have advised Kristian that there would be no resistance, and to have paid the penalty for guessing wrong.

[2] Regent of the Netherlands since 1530.

Netherlands and the Scandinavian kingdoms, whereby the Dutch were once more admitted to the Baltic. Mary's envoys did not hesitate to abandon Kristian to his fate, explaining that the assistance which he had received was purely of a private nature; and Fredrik and Gustav discreetly pretended to believe them. The news of Kristian's imprisonment, which followed soon afterwards, confirmed the wisdom of the reconciliation, and deprived Lübeck of the last hope of inducing her former clients to rally to her side. Lübeck, indeed, was now isolated; and prudence suggested acquiescence in what could no longer be helped.

The Lübeck town council, however, was anything but prudent. The democratic-Protestant movement within the city, which had been gathering force for the previous two or three years, had by now reached a climax. A revolution overthrew the old ruling clique, a new council of a more popular character took control of affairs, and an able demagogue, Jürgen Wullenweber, assumed the leadership and was elected mayor in the spring of 1533. The new men were for a tougher foreign policy; they were prepared to take risks to maintain the city's position of dominance in the Baltic trade; they believed that this was the moment to fight it out with the Dutch. Wullenweber's election as mayor was followed by a declaration of war; and this in turn by a demand that Sweden and Denmark follow Lübeck's lead.

To this summons Gustav Vasa answered neither yea nor nay. He had already made up his mind that he was not going to break with the Netherlands, but it seemed to him that the occasion offered opportunities for blackmail. He accordingly informed Lübeck's envoy that before he could think of entering the war Lübeck must make some concessions in the matter of the privileges; and he hinted that if they were obstinate they might find their privileges cancelled altogether. Worse than this, he began to back out of the agreement of 1529 concerning repayment of the debt. Worst of all, he made a clumsy attempt to put on the screw by levying a toll upon every Lübeck merchant in Sweden, in clear violation of the Strängnäs privileges, and in defiance of most of his advisers. At the same time he renewed his diplomatic contacts with the regent of the Netherlands, in the hope of being able to turn the recent treaty of friendship into a defensive alliance. But the new rulers of Lübeck, hot-headed and pugnacious, were not to be intimidated. They retorted upon Gustav by confiscating a consignment of copper and butter lying in their customs-house: this Gustav had recently shipped to Lübeck with an injunction to his agents that the proceeds were on no account to be applied to the discharge of the last instalment of his debt. Gustav Vasa in turn replied by sequestering all Lübeck property in Sweden, and followed this by arresting all

Lübeckers he could lay his hands on. By August 1533 the breach was complete.

Meanwhile, Lübeck had been equally unsuccessful in Denmark. On 10 April 1533 Fredrik I died; and his death gave the opportunity for a reaction which put power into the hands of an aristocracy preoccupied with its class interests and conservative in its religious outlook. The obvious successor to the throne was Fredrik's eldest son, Kristian of Holstein; but the Danish council was in no hurry to choose him: Kristian was a strong Protestant, and this was in any case a good chance to remind the Oldenburgs that Denmark was an elective and not a hereditary monarchy. They decided, therefore, to postpone the election, and in the meantime to supply the place of the sovereign themselves. The results were disastrous for Denmark: in a few months the country slipped into a state of semi-anarchy. They also constituted a defeat for Wullenweber; for the aristocratic-Catholic elements who had assumed the government in Denmark had no wish to quarrel with the Habsburgs for the sake of a pack of heretical demagogues. They refused to ratify the treaty of 1532 with Lübeck; and in September 1533 they concluded a defensive league with the Netherlands.

The anger of Lübeck was great. Stung by the ingratitude of the Scandinavian kingdoms, seeing perhaps in the confused state of Denmark a last chance to possess themselves of the Sound, Wullenweber and his associates went hard about upon a new tack. They dropped their war with the Dutch, patched up a truce with the regent in March 1534, and concentrated all their efforts upon reasserting their authority in Scandinavia. Remembering the still-continuing popularity of Kristian II with the lower orders in Denmark, they announced their intention of liberating him from prison and restoring him to the throne; they loudly beat the Protestant drum; and they incited the Danish peasants and burghers to rally to the cause of the gospel, legitimism, and social justice. Their appeals met with a lively response. The masses and the middle classes rose; Copenhagen and Malmö declared for Kristian II; much of the countryside was ravaged by a social war. Wullenweber now looked around for possible allies—or at least for possible commanders; for though Lübeck had some confidence in her fleet, she needed professional assistance with her operations on land. A suitable candidate presented himself in the person of Count Christopher of Oldenburg, a distant relative of the Danish royal house; and it is from this insignificant adventurer that the whole confused affair derives its name of 'The Count's War'. Gustav Vasa's unappeasable enemies—Berend von Melen, Gustav Trolle—hastened to avail themselves of the chance to strike a blow at the usurper; and a new enemy appeared in the person of Gustav's own brother-in-law, the trusted

John of Hoya, who slipped away from his Finnish fief and put himself at Lübeck's disposal. His motives seem to have been both intelligible and honourable. He had pledged his faith for Gustav's observance of the debt-settlement with Lübeck; he had done his best to restrain him in 1533; and he felt his personal honour compromised by the king's violation of his undertakings. To crown all, Wullenweber succeeded in getting possession of the person of Svante Sture, Sten's surviving younger son, who happened to be in north Germany at the time. Great efforts were made to induce him to appear as a candidate for the Swedish throne; but Svante, more loyal or more discreet than his mother, was proof against temptation. Could he have foreseen the fate that lay in store for him he might well have lent a more willing ear to Wullenweber's solicitations.[1]

In the face of this coalition of forces, Denmark and Sweden had no option but to sink all minor differences and draw together for defence. In February 1534 the Danish council made a treaty of mutual assistance with Gustav Vasa. The terms were sufficiently remarkable: Gustav Vasa was, indeed, given a guarantee against any revival of the claims of the Danish monarchy upon Sweden, but in return he acquiesced in conditions which seemed to look back to the palmiest days of aristocratic Unionism. All matters of dispute between the kingdoms were to be referred to arbitration by an inter-Scandinavian jury of six or twelve magnates; fugitives from either country were to go free until their cases had been adjudged by a court composed of four members of the councils of each, and the king from whose realm they had fled was to be bound to accept that verdict. There was even a passing allusion to the possibility, at some future period, of the election of a king common to both realms. It is true that, as things turned out, these provisions were never put into force; but they showed that the Danish nobility, at any rate, had not forgotten the political traditions of the fifteenth century. And though in Sweden the times might no longer seem suited to aristocratic-constitutional ideas of this sort—and were certainly not to become so in the years immediately ahead—it seems unlikely that the terms of the treaty can have gone entirely unremarked. They must at least have served to keep alive memories which, a generation later, would quicken into action. Meanwhile the Danish magnates had been brought to face the fact that they could not any longer afford to postpone the choice of a successor to Fredrik I: in July they at last regularized the domestic position by electing Kristian of Holstein as Kristian III. The new king had married a sister of Katarina of Saxe-Lauenburg, so that he was Gustav Vasa's brother-in-law; but there was never much fraternal feeling between them:

[1] See below, p. 236.

Kristian considered Gustav 'a man with whom it is impossible to negotiate, and who understands little or nothing of what he is talking about, or at all events less than he seems to think'. But in this emergency personal feelings took second place to political necessity, and while the war lasted their collaboration was in fact reasonably harmonious. In October 1534 Swedish forces captured Halmstad from Kristian II's partisans; in November Lübeck freed herself from Kristian III's blockade by making a truce with him as duke of Holstein, and by so doing virtually deserted the popular insurrection in Jutland; in December Rantzau effectively crushed the resistance of the Danish peasants. A considerable Swedish victory at Hälsingborg early in the following year paved the way for Kristian III's recovery of Halland. Even more important than these military successes was a significant change in the balance of power at sea. In the ten years since his accession Gustav Vasa had gradually gathered together a small but efficient navy, based on the nucleus of warships which he had bought from Lübeck; and it now intervened with decisive effect. On 9 June 1535 it scattered a Lübeck squadron near Bornholm; a week later a combined fleet of Swedish, Danish and Prussian[1] warships won a great battle in the Little Belt, which annihilated Lübeck's naval power for the rest of the war, and enabled the allies to proceed to the blockade of Copenhagen, Malmö and Landskrona. Finally, on 11 June, Kristian III and the Danish nobility routed Count Christopher's army at Øxnebjerg: John of Hoya was killed in the battle, Gustav Trolle was captured and died of wounds soon afterwards. In September Kristian III made a surprise visit to Stockholm, ratified the Danish-Swedish alliance of 1534, persuaded Gustav to leave his fleet on the Skåne coast over the winter, and in return for a promise to pawn Bohus, Viken and Akershus obtained a loan of very substantial dimensions.

The solid front presented by the Scandinavian monarchs, and the military and naval disasters of 1535, drove Lübeck's leaders to look further afield for aid. They approached Henry VIII, who offered ships; they tried John Frederick of Saxony; they put pressure on their reluctant colleagues in the Hanse. But their only real hope lay in the relatives of Kristian II. His niece's husband, Albert of Mecklenburg, was ready to risk a political gamble; and in due course he appeared in Denmark, much to the irritation of Count Christopher. More formidable in every respect was the threatened intervention of Frederick, Count Palatine.[2] Frederick was being encouraged by Charles V to marry Dorothea, Kristian II's eldest daughter (and in fact he did marry

[1] Albert of Prussia (also a brother-in-law of Kristian III) had joined the coalition against Lübeck. In the previous autumn the Swedish navy had captured five warships lent to Lübeck by Henry VIII.

[2] Afterwards (1544) Elector Palatine.

her, in September 1535), and it seemed probable that he would be able to count on steadier support from the Habsburgs than they had ever been willing to give to her father. It was the news of this development, retailed by Kristian III on his arrival in Stockholm, that had made Gustav Vasa so accommodating about the loan. For the first time, perhaps, both monarchs began to realize that the elimination of Kristian II was not to be the end of the story. The event would prove that in the persons of his daughters and their husbands the cause of legitimacy had a lively future.

All this came too late to save Wullenweber. The democratic revolution had failed to produce the expected results; the Emperor had served on the city what was virtually an ultimatum demanding a change of government. In August 1535 there was a counter-revolution. Wullenweber was thrown from power, and the old men came back again to make the best peace they could: the princes of the Schmalkaldic League had for some time been urging a speedy settlement. In February 1536, therefore, peace was concluded between Lübeck and Kristian III at Hamburg. It was a breach of Kristian's promise to Gustav to make no separate peace; it was negotiated behind Gustav's back; and it was not even notified to him until four months later. He was, indeed, at liberty to adhere to it if he chose; but since the issues that affected him were left unsolved he was not likely to do so. And from his point of view the treaty was in another respect intolerable: not only did it provide for Kristian III's acting as arbitrator upon his controversies with Berend von Melen, and upon the claims of John of Hoya's heir to his father's fief, but it bound Kristian to withdraw his support from Sweden if the judgment should go in favour of Gustav's adversaries.[1] And even for Kristian III the treaty did not finish the business: Albert of Mecklenburg and Christopher of Oldenburg refused to accept it; Malmö did not capitulate till April 1536, Copenhagen not till June; and, worst of all, the Palatine continued his preparations for a naval expedition based on the Netherlands. But Kristian III was now courted by the Protestant princes of north Germany; and having in October 1536 concluded a six-year agreement with some of the members of the League of Schmalkalde, he might feel that his throne was reasonably secure. He so far recognized his obligations to Gustav Vasa as to exert himself to contrive a preliminary truce between Sweden and Lübeck in November 1536; he parried the threat from the Palatine by a three-year truce with Mary of Hungary in May 1537, to which Gustav Vasa was allowed to accede; and at mid-

[1] There was an unpleasant diplomatic incident in 1537, when the Swedish representatives at Kristian III's coronation refused to sit at the same table with von Melen, who was also a guest.

summer 1537 he presided over a conference in Copenhagen to settle the controversies between Sweden and Lübeck. After arduous negotiations it was agreed to present the parties with alternative arrangements. They were offered either a treaty, whereby Sweden was to grant new (and much restricted) privileges to Lübeck;[1] or failing that a truce for five years, the question of the privileges being left in suspense, and the Lübeckers in the interim paying the usual duties imposed on other foreigners. Gustav Vasa, not unnaturally, preferred the treaty, and duly ratified it; Lübeck, still hoping despite this setback to impose her will upon Sweden on some later occasion, rejected the treaty and accepted the truce.

Six years after Kristian II put out on his expedition to Norway, the convulsions produced by that enterprise had at last subsided, and it was possible to take stock of the position. Despite some disappointments, it showed a balance heavily in Gustav's favour. Lübeck had made her great effort; and it had failed. She would never make another. In 1533 the Lübeckers had boasted 'that with 100 marks they had made Gustav king of Sweden; with 500 they could certainly unking him'. By 1537 the day for such vaunts was for ever gone. The decay of the Hanse as a political organization had been made manifest. And though Lübeck still refused to face the facts and reconcile herself to reality, the king had in fact triumphed. It is true that Lübeck's position in the Swedish economy was too strong to be much affected by competition in the immediate future, and in the forties and fifties the town would make a great and successful effort to reorientate its commerce along new lines: some weakening there was, in the years just after the war; but by the end of the reign Lübeck was once more in control of a predominant share of Sweden's overseas trade. But this recovery could only be temporary; for the loss of the Strängnäs privileges gave a stimulus not only to Dutch rivals but to the native Swedish shipping; it threw open the trade westward; it made possible the dream of Gustav's later years, and the policy of his successor—the attempt, that is, to exploit Sweden's geographical position in order to make her the great *entrepôt* between east and west. For twenty-three years yet Gustav Vasa would be haunted by the fear of a counterstroke from Lübeck; crises in Swedish-Lübeck relations would never be far off, and the hope of peace would continue to be illusory; but in fact the critical point had been passed, and the battle won. And though

[1] But to no other of the Hanse towns. They might now import their own goods free of toll; the duration of their visits was limited to six weeks, and their goods must be sold within that period or left behind; Swedish merchants were to be free to sail through the Sound, and to trade with any foreigner. These were in fact better terms than Kristian III had obtained for himself.

Lübeck would still show, under the later Vasas, that she lacked neither the will nor the power to do Sweden a mischief, she could no longer suppose that she had Scandinavia in her pocket.

In regard to Denmark, Gustav could feel much less satisfaction. During the war Kristian III had appeared on the whole as the weaker ally; at the peace he was able to assume almost the air of a benevolent patron. Denmark emerged from the conflict surrounded (it appeared) by solicitous friends and potential allies; Sweden seemed isolated and friendless, admitted to the peace as an act of grace, informed of what was done for her only as an afterthought. Gustav Vasa strongly resented—and never forgot—this treatment. Yet the bond of union which had drawn Sweden and Denmark together—the fear of a legitimist restoration—still remained. Kristian II's only son, Hans, had died in 1531; but the pretensions of his daughters would still be potent for many years to come to perform the miracle of submerging Scandinavian jealousies. And Gustav Vasa could take comfort from the undeniable fact that the war had revealed a quite unexpected and impressive increase in Sweden's real power and resources. It had been the Swedish navy that had played the main part in the destruction of Lübeck's fleet; it had been Swedish money that had financed Kristian III's fight for his throne: in 1535–6 Gustav Vasa lent him—apparently without inconvenience—more than the whole amount of the debt to Lübeck. Lübeck was defeated by ships she had sold to Sweden, by money which was rightly hers, by the swiftly accumulating plunder of the church, and by a new source of income which was to be of great importance in the next decade—the revenues from the silver mine at Sala, which just now began its brief period of prosperity.

The breach with Lübeck had been Gustav Vasa's personal policy, embarked on and persisted in despite the disapproval of the *råd*, despite the warnings of Lars Andreae and Olaus Petri, and despite the obvious reluctance of the mercantile community. The king's repudiation of the outstanding 10,000 marks due to Lübeck, which had driven John of Hoya to high treason, prepared also the fall of the secretary Wulf Gyler, who in a desperate effort to save the country's good name had even offered to raise the money on his own security. In the months of crisis that preceded the war Gustav Vasa gave the first large-scale exhibition of that morbid irritability, that intolerable violence of language, that inability to control his terrifying outbursts of rage, which made him so ill a master to serve, and which passed in such full measure to all his sons. Much of the evidence on this matter comes from prejudiced sources: from men who had quarrelled with the king and quitted his service, and above all from Wulf Gyler himself. We hear of Gustav's administering beatings with a poker, of pummellings and kickings, of tearing out of hair; we hear of a goldsmith who, having taken a day off from the king's work without leave, was called up to the castle and so mishandled by his sovereign that he died, medical aid being refused him; we hear of how the king, dagger in hand, chased an unfortunate secretary round and round the courtyard of Stockholm castle. On the death of Katarina of Saxe-Lauenburg in 1535 the story was current in Germany that Gustav Vasa had killed her with a blow of his hammer, and had himself been murdered in revenge: the belief that he was dead was probably one reason why Kristian III made peace in 1536 without him. It may be no accident that the Lübeckers in 1534 referred to him (in words which are ironically reminiscent of Gustav Vasa's own allusions to Kristian II) as 'that tyrant and bloodhound'. The details of Gyler's accusations tally too well with ascertainable facts for it to be likely that they can be dismissed simply as malicious fabrications. Too many of the king's servants deserted, professing themselves to be in bodily fear, for the similarity of their stories to be mere coincidence. His own family knew him as a violent-tempered and heavy-handed parent: when his daughter Cecilia complained that he had pulled out handfuls of her hair, his reply was not (as it might well have been) that she richly deserved it, but the rather lame explanation that the hair 'had come away of itself, as is well known to all'. As for Gyler, he had incurred the king's displeasure by courageously insisting on the need to honour the agreement of 1529; and when Hoya defected, when the breach with Lübeck became inevitable, his position was obviously delicate and dangerous: he may well have feared ill-usage or captivity. At all events, in August 1534 he fled the country, leaving wife, child and property behind him. The ill-luck of the winds drove him to a part of Denmark which happened to be under the control of Christopher of Oldenburg, and Gustav Vasa branded him as a traitor. But Gyler was no traitor. He was only one of a long succession of faithful servants who broke away from a master whose temperament could at times make him impossible.[1]

Yet, in spite of all, the king's gamble had turned out well. His advisers had been wrong, and he had been proved right. One by one his enemies were disposed of: Kristian II was put away; Ture Jönsson,

[1] Gyler eventually found high employment with Albert of Prussia—to Gustav Vasa's undisguised fury. It is significant that both Albert and Kristian III seem to have taken Gyler's part in the quarrel. Through their intervention he reached an agreement with the king, whereby Gustav promised to restore his wife and family and property in return for a solemn undertaking that Gyler would not publish any account of his experiences in Sweden. Gyler gave the undertaking and Gustav sent over his wife and family; but with characteristic bad faith hung on to the property. Albert and Kristian III, though indignant, would not permit Gyler to go back on his undertaking. The affair led to a coolness between Gustav and Albert which lasted some years.

Gustav Trolle, John of Hoya were dead; Lübeck was beaten. Nor had the Dalesmen gone unremembered. Waiting till they thought themselves secure and their misdeeds forgotten, the king turned savagely on them in 1533, marched his army into Dalarna, and at the Kopparberg held a *landsting* that closed an epoch. The leaders in the 'churchbell rebellion' were haled away to Stockholm; and in Stockholm they were in due course condemned to death. These men had been Gustav's comrades, his oldest political supporters; and, ruthless as he was, he probably felt the prick of compunction. The execution of the sentence was delayed for months; but it was carried out at last.[1] Official historiography, as represented by Peder Swart, charged them with having been in league with Sunnanväder, with the Västergötland rebellion, and even with Kristian II. There is no need to believe all this: the record had to be made as black as possible, so that the removal of these veteran patriots might not appear too shocking. But that they were guilty of rebellion is clear; and the king might well feel that he had no choice: Dalarna had had ample warning, and at least as much lenity as a rebel was entitled to look for in that cruel age. It might be possible in the days of the Union kings for the Dalesmen to maintain themselves as a separate Estate with whom kings and noble factions must parley; but it was an intolerable pretension in the conditions of the 1530s. Their claim that a king must obtain their safe-conduct before entering their province, their hostility to the nobility as a class (for there were no nobles in Dalarna), could not be suffered either by the one or the other; and it was not surprising that Gustav Vasa should have chastised the Dalesmen, on two successive occasions, with forces recruited from the nobility's knight-service. And now the great days of Dalarna were over; the province was split in two; the old forms of self-government which had been peculiar to the Bergslag were emasculated; and royal control became a good deal firmer. For in Gustav Vasa the Dalesmen had found a king who was not prepared to rule over the loose and insubordinate federation of provinces which was their political ideal, nor to permit his policy to be dictated to him by a small section of his subjects: 'better a province laid waste than a province rebellious.'

And what was true for Dalarna was true also for Stockholm. Stockholm, like lower Dalarna, had stood by Gustav at more than one critical moment of the reign, and he was not insensible of what the city had done for him. But the war with Lübeck imposed a real strain on the loyalty of that section of the burghers—very many of them Germans—who depended upon the Lübeck trade for their livelihood.

[1] The widows of those executed, it is pleasant to find, were treated by the king with generosity.

There was also in Stockholm a radical religious element, already somewhat suspect to the king: men who had been formerly drawn to Melkior Hoffmann's enthusiastic sermons, and were impatient of the slow pace of the king's Reformation. Others appear to have sympathized with the popular revolution in Lübeck, and to have been inspired by the examples of Copenhagen and Malmö to work for a Stockholm independent of royal control. It seems extremely probable that some of these men were in treasonable relations with agents from Lübeck. Below the surface there was certainly a conspiracy brewing, and most of the leading actors in it were Germans; but its ultimate aims remain obscure: at least one of those involved (Gorius Holst, arrested as early as the close of 1533) was an old partisan of Kristian II, while others are thought to have been working for the forcible restoration of the old religion. In the spring of 1534 Gustav Vasa received an urgent warning from Kristian III that mischief was afoot; and on 20 April the prevailing tension was heightened by the appearance over Stockholm of that meteorological phenomenon which is known as *parhelion*—a manifestation then generally considered to portend revolutions and civil convulsions. But it was not until a year later, when the plot (whatever it was) had almost certainly been abandoned—Lübeck having by this time made peace with Denmark—that the details came to light and the ringleaders were detected and arrested. It then appeared that their plans had included the assassination of the king by blowing him up when in church, the seizure and partial razing of Stockholm castle, a general attack upon the aristocracy, and the handing over of Stockholm to the Hanse.[1] In consequence of these revelations eight persons were executed, of whom seven were Germans; Gorius Holst ended his days in prison. The names of some others, more or less entangled in the fringes of the conspiracy, the king stored up in his memory against a suitable occasion.

The consequences for Stockholm were serious. The burghers had their guns and weapons taken away from them; the defence of the town was henceforth to be entrusted exclusively to the care of the king's commander and the castle garrison. No longer would Stockholm be able, as in the days of the Stures, to follow a political line of its own, and play an independent part in national politics. A quarter of a century earlier it had seemed likely that Stockholm might make good its footing as a separate Estate of the realm. After 1536 that possibility had gone for ever.

Thus, one by one, those who challenged the king's authority had been struck down: the Sture party, the bishops, the conservative

[1] *Rasmus Ludvigssons krönika*, p. 31.

nobility, Dalarna, Stockholm: the one rebel, often enough, with the aid of the next; until at last the king stood clear above them all. It remained now to provide the theoretical basis for his practice.

VI. ROYAL SUPREMACY IN CHURCH AND STATE, 1531–41

The three or four years which followed upon the consecration of Laurentius Petri brought a slackening in the advance of Protestantism which the reformers had probably not expected. For the first time since the mid-1520s the king applied the brake. His immediate objectives, after all, had been secured: the power of the episcopate had been curbed, the troublesome question of the *electi* was solved, he had an archbishop of his own choosing, and the revenues of the church at his mercy. The Recess of Västerås had made over to him the responsibility for seeing that the clergy were diligent in preaching the gospel, and no man could say that he had been remiss in that matter: the ancient right of parishioners to choose their own incumbent was now more in jeopardy from the king's interference than ever it had been from the pope's. From Gustav Vasa's point of view, then, there was no urgent reason for pushing on with Reformation, and not a few reasons in favour of a temporary pause. The mass of the population, the mass of the clergy, were still Catholic: the archbishop might now be a Lutheran, but there was not one of his colleagues on the episcopal bench who shared his opinions. Of the seven Swedish sees four were held by men who were certainly not Protestants, though some of them—notably Sven Jacobi of Skara—were willing enough to contemplate a reform which should leave the fundamentals untouched. The chapter of Linköping, which had rendered Gustav Vasa such good service in the revolt of 1529, was of the same opinion. They had convinced themselves that the king's measures were anti-episcopal rather than anti-Catholic, and they acquiesced without much trouble in a reduction of their numbers. Gustav Vasa was willing for the present to carry them along with him by lenient treatment. The chapter of Uppsala, on the other hand, led by old Peder Galle, was uncompromisingly Catholic, and Laurentius Petri could make nothing of it. But even here the king for the present made no attempt to remodel it to his liking. In the dangerous years of the Count's War prudence suggested that there was little to gain and much to lose by affronting public opinion unnecessarily: the Västergötland revolt had been a warning which the anti-Protestant cries of the church-bell rebellion had reinforced. Consequently, though the friaries were indeed stripped bare, the pressures upon the establishments of other monastic orders were for a time somewhat relaxed. And if the king seized the chance afforded by the insurrection in

Dalarna to plunder the churches there, as yet there was no general attack upon parochial property. The burdens which had latterly been laid upon the church in the way of aids and quartering were consolidated in 1530 into a single impost; the bishops soon afterwards were successively deprived of the remains of their income and put in the position of salaried civil servants;[1] but otherwise the early 1530s saw no major change. In the autumn of 1532 Lars Andreae left the king's service and retired to private life; and for the next few years Gustav Vasa listened most often to the advice of Sven Jacobi, who in 1535 even ventured to criticize Laurentius Petri for granting a dispensation, on the ground that dispensations could be granted only by the pope. Developments outside Sweden seemed to confirm the wisdom of moderation: 1533 brought, on the one hand, the Roman Catholic reaction in Denmark, and on the other the alarmingly radical Protestantism of Wullenweber's Lübeck, and of rebellious Malmö and Copenhagen. And in 1534 the Anabaptist movement in Münster seemed to reveal, with horrid clarity, the abyss which lay at the end of the reformers' road. There had been a time when even Olaus Petri had felt the attraction of such ideas; but by now he had come to think that little good was to be expected from religious anarchism. And when he condemned the expounding of Scripture in ale-houses by enthusiasts who called in liquor to fortify the light of nature, he could be sure that in this matter, at all events, he and his sovereign were entirely of one mind.

Considerations such as these led Gustav Vasa in 1533 to instruct his archbishop that any further reformation of the church must proceed with caution, and must not be undertaken without royal permission. The order was obeyed. Laurentius Petri's position was difficult, placed as he was between the resistance of his episcopal colleagues and the pressure of the reformers, with a master who kept him in a state of financial dependence, and who in any case looked with suspicion at bishops as a class. It was fortunate for the church that the king had a liking for him personally, for they certainly did not see eye to eye on church government. Laurentius Petri did not hesitate to claim that bishops, no less than kings, were invested with divine authority—an idea which must have been almost as strange to Gustav Vasa as if he had claimed divine authority for bailiffs. But on matters of ritual the archbishop was to prove himself a moderate, and in his respect for tradition a conservative; and for the moment, at least, this made compliance with the king's standstill policy the more easy for him.

By 1536, however, that policy was ripe for a change. The victory of Kristian III had entailed the triumph of the Reformation in Denmark:

[1] Gustav Vasa usually allowed the Västerås agreements to stand until a see became vacant, and imposed a new arrangement upon the successor.

by the deprivation of all the bishops and their replacement by 'superattendents' the Apostolic Succession was deliberately broken; and the church's property was confiscated to the state. It was an example which did not go unremarked in Sweden. If Kristian III's experience went for anything, moreover, it seemed to show that a clear-cut Lutheran policy brought advantages abroad no less than at home. Kristian's friendship was now courted by German Lutheran princes; his entry into the League of Schmalkalde was already being canvassed. Gustav Vasa was not slow to take the hint. When in 1536 Paul III invited him to send representatives to the forthcoming general council, he pointedly replied that he would do as other evangelical princes did. And that the implications of this answer might not be lost upon possible well-wishers in Germany, he underlined his adherence to the Protestant party in a letter to the Elector of Saxony in 1537. The course of affairs at home, as was to be expected, conformed to this new line in foreign policy. Magnus Sommar of Strängnäs had been deprived of his see in 1536 for suspected complicity in the Stockholm conspiracy, and spent the rest of his days as a pensioner in a deserted monastery; old Peder Månsson of Västerås had died in the previous year. The king took care that their places should be filled by men of undoubtedly evangelical principles. The balance on the episcopal bench moved sharply to the left: it was now three to four—or three to two in favour of Protestantism, if distant Åbo and unimportant Växjö were left out of the reckoning. The same trend was observable at the parochial level: clergy of Protestant opinions began to obtain livings in appreciable numbers. The church's doctrinal position no doubt remained officially as undefined as ever; but the publication in 1535 of Olaus Petri's *A little book* could perhaps be considered as a presage of a clearer theological climate. It was the first Swedish discussion of the question of Justification, and it came out clearly for faith and against works. In October 1536, moreover, a church council which met at Uppsala reached decisions which certainly went beyond the cautious formularies of its predecessor at Örebro in 1529. It resolved that every effort should be made to introduce the Swedish mass in all cathedrals (though elsewhere it was to remain optional for the present); it accepted Olaus Petri's *Handbook* as the prescribed order for the service of baptism, marriage and some others; it declared the clergy released from the obligation of celibacy, and ordered those who kept concubines to marry them forthwith.[1] A flood of Protestant literature now poured from the press; and in 1537 Olaus Petri produced, in his *Lesser Cate-*

[1] Johannes Magni, the Reformist bishop of Linkoping, attempted to impose a compromise on his diocese, in the form of a mass which, while omitting prayers for the dead and the idea of the mass as a sacrifice, was otherwise based on the mediaeval mass, and was in Latin; but it seems to have had no influence.

chism (a translation from Luther) what was destined to be one of the most powerful agents for the dissemination of evangelical doctrines among the people.

By 1537, then, the course seemed set and the prospects again fair; and the archbishop and his brother might feel that the king's hesitations had been overcome. If so, they were much mistaken. Considerations of policy, and a degree of indifference to the doctrinal issues involved, might induce Gustav Vasa to tolerate or even to encourage a further instalment of Reformation; but he was none the less uneasy. If Protestantism implied changes in the form and order of service, he had no great objection; but changes of this sort must not be made matters of such importance as to attach an appearance of authority to the churchmen who decided on them. Preaching, after all, was the clergy's real business: it was perhaps the one spiritual lesson which Olaus Petri had instilled into him. Certainly it was a lesson which appealed strongly to a ruler who worked hard at his *métier*, expected to see his subjects work equally hard at theirs, and was inclined to doubt whether prayer and fasting constituted an honest day's labour. But preaching too could be dangerous, if it were provocative of excessive zeal, or if (on the other hand) it aroused embarrassingly antipathetic reactions: the security of the ecclesiastical revolution must not be imperilled by zealots. His doubts, in fact, concerned not so much the reforms as the reformers. He had not engineered the Reformation in order to produce a popular self-governing church, as independent of himself as of the pope. His suspicions were all too easily alarmed by any sign of what he regarded as a hierarchical tendency in his episcopate. It would be a pretty end to his labours if he were to find that he had given free rein to men who were minded to challenge his control of his own church!

These jealous feelings, never very far below the surface, were in 1538 suddenly exasperated by a quite unforeseen humiliation. In April of that year the League of Schmalkalde met at Brunswick. One of the items on its agenda was a proposal that Gustav Vasa be invited to join them. The proposal was sponsored by Kristian III; it had the support of Philip of Hesse; and Gustav Vasa hoped that in view of the recent course of ecclesiastical policy in Sweden there would be no difficulty about it. From his point of view, membership of the League would have at least one immediate advantage, for it would provide him with a guarantee against the ceaseless intrigues of Berend von Melen. But the event proved that he had underrated von Melen's standing with the Protestant princes, and underestimated the damaging effect of his anti-Swedish propaganda. To Gustav Vasa, von Melen might be a 'damned scoundrel'; but to Luther he appeared 'a unique ornament of the knightly Estate, a man warmly zealous against evil, a hero with the spirit of a lion in his bosom, yet withal a man modest and discreet in word and deed'. A man, certainly, with whom it was unwise to quarrel, as the event was now to prove. A deprecatory word here, a doubt insinuated there, a pamphlet displayed or referred to, suffered to dispose of Gustav's chances. Denmark was accepted; Sweden was blackballed. It was a bitter blow. Not that Gustav Vasa was animated by any strong feelings of religious solidarity with the Protestant princes of Germany, or that he saw himself a paladin in the ranks of those who were prepared to fight with secular arms for the spiritual gains of the Reformation. But he needed friends on the continent to balance his watchful enemies, to countercheck those continental powers without whose aid neither Lübeck nor von Melen nor the Palatine could ever hope to achieve very much. But now, against all reasonable expectation, the Protestant gambit had proved a fiasco. For this he blamed Kristian III, whom he suspected (quite wrongly) of playing him false. And it is not altogether surprising that his resentment should also have fallen upon the Swedish reformers, whose activities (he might feel) had been so closely bound up with the policy which had exposed him to this public affront. By the summer of 1538 he was ripe for a quarrel with them. Already he felt that their views of a national church differed from his own. Consciously or unconsciously he was waiting for the man and the opportunity to formulate the doctrine which would express his practice: the doctrine of royal supremacy.

These trends in regard to the church corresponded with similar trends in secular affairs. Throughout the 1530s the monarchy was slowly but perceptibly gaining in strength. It was a sign of this that the king no longer felt the need to associate the Estates with his policies: whereas in the 1520s large representative gatherings had met every one or two years, there was not a single full meeting of this sort between 1529 and 1544. Circumstances were increasingly enabling the king to live of his own: the revenues of the church, the flow of silver from Sala, allowed him to begin that hoarding which for the rest of his life came to be almost one of his basic principles of politics. He could now afford a small standing army of mercenaries: not all the soldiers hired during the Count's War were disbanded at the end of it. The growth of the king's landed estates, the administration of church revenues, necessitated an expanded body of officials, recruited from the lower ranks of the nobility or from the exiguous middle class; and these men, wholly dependent upon the king for livelihood and prospects, were a useful reinforcement of his power. The beginnings of some system of proper accounting told the same tale of a stronger hand upon the government. It was indeed still necessary to conciliate the nobility: their help had proved indispensable for the suppression of Dalarna, and was to prove not less so for the suppression of Småland in 1543. The Reformation, however, had given the king the means of satisfying them, and the 1530s was a period of lavish granting of fiefs. But they were rarely granted, now, for life; and many of them went into the hands of the king's relations by marriage. His second marriage to Margareta Leijonhufvud linked him more closely than before to the great families; soon the royal relatives would form an aristocracy within the aristocracy, upon whom Gustav liked to feel that he could rely. And, lastly, as the king felt himself more and more the master of the domestic situation, he was beginning to reveal that insatiable desire to guide and control every activity of his subjects, every part of the economy, which was to be the most characteristic trait of the personal rule of the forties and fifties. In short, by about 1538 Gustav Vasa was ready, in church and state, for a more formal and explicit assertion of authority than he had permitted himself hitherto.

For such a development he needed no very elaborate administrative devices, nor any very large staff of civil servants at the centre of power: the last decade of the reign would demonstrate how uncomplicated and makeshift his personal rule could be. But even so industrious a monarch needed secretaries, to write his letters in Latin, German or Swedish, as the case might demand. Secretaries, however, appeared to be neither easy to come by nor easy to retain. In 1530 Gustav had tried the experiment of appointing Olaus Petri as his chancellor; but Master Olof (as his master unkindly put it) was as suited to this work 'as a Frisian cow to spin silk, or a donkey to be a lute-player', and the appointment was terminated (to the relief of both sides) in 1533. Very few Swedes had the necessary qualifications for a secretary's post, and there was no means of training them at home. The university of Uppsala, for reasons which are not altogether clear, had died of inanition in the time of young Herr Sten, and since then no effort had been made to revive it. Gustav Vasa devoted some of the crumbs which fell from the church's table to financing the education of promising young men abroad: it was not unusual to assign them the incomes of vacant prebends for this purpose; but the results were hardly proportionate even to the inconsiderable outlay. Luther himself was moved to remonstrate with Gustav Vasa on the derelict condition of the university; and the princes of Schmalkalde found it another convenient pretext for deferring Sweden's admission to the League: no country, they felt, could be deemed truly evangelical which lacked a university to train its clergy in the right theology.[1] The king was therefore forced, in the absence of suitable

[1] In 1530 the university of Copenhagen had expired also; but Kristian III took care to put himself right with evangelical opinion by refounding it in 1537.

native candidates, to try to recruit foreigners for secretaries, as he had already done in the case of Wulf Gyler. But it was unfortunately the case that Gyler had fled; and the stories which he disseminated of the treatment which secretaries might expect in Sweden were not encouraging to potential applicants. In the years after 1534, therefore, Gustav Vasa was almost continuously inquiring of his friends in Germany for a man to help him with his correspondence. He did succeed in persuading Albert of Prussia to lend him Dr Johann Rheyneck, whom he appointed chancellor in 1535; but Rheyneck died within a couple of months while on a diplomatic mission, and the king found himself once more without assistance. He was reduced to writing letters in German himself, and 'racked his brains' painfully over their composition: 'God knows' (he complained) 'what difficulty and embarrassment we suffer from time to time . . . when we send letters in the German tongue (which we often by no means can avoid) . . . sometimes they are written to our satisfaction, sometimes not.' When in 1536 the chancellor of Saxe-Lauenburg paid a visit to Sweden to deal with Katarina's estate, he was shanghaied into the chancery and set to clear off the arrears of German correspondence. In 1537 the scandal of Gyler's flight was repeated, when Olof Bröms, one of the king's leading financial experts, likewise deserted his service and fled the country. In 1538 a Swedish scholar at Wittenberg, Nicolaus Magni by name, was commissioned to look out for possible recruits: indeed he was pressed to take the post of secretary himself. Magni was quite willing to put in a word with Melanchthon; but he was not to be tempted home: he had heard too many reports of what life was like in the king's service. As he wrote to a friend, 'suspicion is risen to that ominous height in Sweden, that a man can hardly fetch a sigh without its being reported'. And he added, 'No, I do not trust my King Gustav, not though he were to write to me with his own heart's blood'.

In 1538, however, the king's luck changed at last. A very eligible candidate offered his services. His name was Conrad von Pyhy. Pyhy came of the famous Augsburg family of Peutinger; he was a knight, a doctor of laws, he had been *Hofrath* and *Kriegsrath* in the service of Charles V and Ferdinand. He had campaigned in Italy and Hungary, and had been employed on diplomatic missions to Spain and the Netherlands. In religion he was indifferent: of late he had been a Catholic; and it was subsequently alleged (by Luther, who on this point showed an unwonted sensitivity) that he was a bigamist.[1] But these blemishes might seem of minor importance in comparison with his solid qualifications for the post. He was undoubtedly familiar with

[1] Gustav Vasa repudiated the allegation, perhaps with justice: it seems possible that von Pyhy was divorced from his first wife.

the latest administrative devices as used in the Habsburg realms, he knew the German pattern of *landesherrliche Kirchenregiment* from the inside, he had a wide acquaintance with continental politics, and above all he was an expert in that Roman law which provided such a convenient repertory of principles for monarchs who aspired to full sovereignty within their dominions. Pyhy's proffer was at once accepted: he was appointed chancellor in August 1538. A year later he was followed to Sweden by George Norman, a don from the university of Greifswald, recruited through Nicolaus Magni. Norman came with Luther's recommendation, as tutor to Prince Erik, and with a general commission to rehabilitate Swedish higher education. Once Pyhy and Norman had taken the plunge others of their compatriots were emboldened to follow, and found employment of one sort or another in the king's service, particularly at court. But Pyhy and Norman were the men that counted, and each in his way set his mark upon Sweden. For they brought with them an approach to the problems of church and state which was clear-cut, logical, free from the moderating influence of Swedish law and tradition, unhampered by any respect for local prejudices or feeling for national peculiarities, and inimical, therefore, to the half-measures which had so far characterized the Swedish Reformation.

It was, indeed, upon the church that the impact of the new ideas fell first. As part of Pyhy's salary he had been allotted the house and revenues attached to a prebend at Uppsala. Laurentius Petri refused to surrender them, on the ground that it was not for these purposes that the confiscation of church revenues had been sanctioned at Västerås. His recalcitrance touched off a formidable explosion of royal anger. In a letter of 24 April 1539 the king attacked his archbishop with brutal violence: 'We mark well what your game is: you would shear the sheep and use the wool for yourselves. But as to guarding the flock—of that we hear nothing. . . . Preachers shall ye be, and not lords! . . . And that we should ever permit things to come to a pass where bishops shall once more get the power of the sword into their hands, that you need not imagine to yourselves.'[1] The accusation that Laurentius Petri and his colleagues were greedily plotting to fleece their flocks was ridiculous, as Gustav well knew; and it came with singular ill-grace just at this time. For the advent of the Germans coincided with a plundering of the church for the benefit of the crown, more reckless and systematic than ever before. Already in the mid-1530s Gustav Vasa had been extending the system of 'agreements' about stipends from the bishops to the parochial clergy; and his presentation to benefices was often accompanied by what in the bad old days of popish superstition would

[1] *Gustav Vasas registratur*, XII, 186.

have been called simony—a practice which had (and perhaps was intended to have) a prejudicial effect upon the bishops' control of their clergy. The king indeed complained (no doubt with justice) that the towns and the nobility were seizing church property and revenues in ways for which the proceedings at Västerås provided no authority; but it is difficult to suppose that his complaint was prompted by any other motive than resentment that his subjects should have forestalled him. From 1539 the appropriation of the movable property and ready cash of the parish churches was systematized and extended, and the crown, which had already taken the bishop's share of tithe, now annexed the church's share also: only the parson's share was still suffered to go to him without interference. The reformers were disgusted by these proceedings. They had hoped that the superfluous revenues of the church might be applied to educational and charitable uses. But of this there was no sign: the derelict state of Uppsala contrasts badly with the foundation of Christ Church and Trinity College Cambridge. In no country in Europe, perhaps, was the Reformation more immediately disastrous for education than in Sweden: Gustav Vasa and Olaus Petri were at one in lamenting the decay of schools and the diminution in the number of scholars. But if the schools were impoverished, the king grew rich. Lars Andreae is said to have asked the king on one occasion what he wanted with so much money; and Olaus Petri made covert but all-too intelligible allusions to his rapacity in the MS *Chronicle* with which he had been busying himself since his retirement from office. These criticisms came to the king's notice. Soon still plainer provocation was added. For in a sermon *On horrid oaths*, delivered in 1538 and published in 1539, Olaus Petri directly blamed the king's example for the bad language of his subjects. Gustav Vasa was certainly not mealy-mouthed, but it was scarcely fair to lay at his door a habit of swearing which has always been a notorious national weakness; and a less choleric man might have been stung by such an attack as this. Coming on top of all the rest it suggested that the reformers were trying to subvert the authority which had raised them up. The preachers were abusing their privileged position to meddle in matters above their concernment: the king complained that nothing was heard from the pulpits but 'tyrants, tyrants, and cruel lordship'. They were for ever preaching about Herod and Pharaoh; though (as he pointed out) he was properly to be likened neither to Herod nor Pharaoh, but to Moses. His reply to all this was to notify the archbishop that he expected that the clergy should preach the duty of obedience to the secular power; to debar Olaus Petri from the use of the royal press; and to order that nothing henceforward be printed without his permission.

8-2

At a church council held in Uppsala in August 1539 matters came to a crisis. Pyhy presided, much in the manner of Thomas Cromwell. The king was seriously ill, as he had been all summer (it was rumoured at home and abroad that he was dying), and there was no memory of past kindness to soften the collision between Pyhy and the reformers. The council had been called by the archbishop in an effort to unite all churchmen in an agreed programme; but the event proved that agreement was not to be had. The bishops of Skara and Växjö still hankered after the link with Rome; the extreme reformers, still led by Lars Andreae and Olaus Petri, were for a more explicitly Lutheran position. Laurentius Petri was above all concerned to safeguard the church against the aggressiveness of the crown; Pyhy was determined to assert the royal supremacy. The archbishop laboured hard to obtain the acceptance of a compromise which would have given Sweden a Church Ordinance regulating dogma and discipline, in exchange for concessions to Pyhy about church government. The bishops at last gave a reluctant consent; but the reformers were not satisfied. The compromise broke down. More than a generation was to pass before Laurentius Petri's Church Ordinance of 1571 provided Sweden with the basic ecclesiastical statute which he envisaged in 1539.

For Gustav Vasa, the reformers' recalcitrance at Uppsala was the last straw; and at the close of 1539 he proceeded to decisive measures. On 8 December he promulgated, 'out of the plenitude of our royal power', a regulation for the government of the church. It was to be organized as a department of state. At its head was to be an '*ordinarius* and *superattendent*', and to this post George Norman was appointed. The *superattendent* bore a strong generic resemblance to Henry VIII's Vicar-General. He was to exercise on the king's behalf jurisdiction over bishops and clergy in all spiritual matters, and was to appoint and deprive clergy at his discretion. Subordinate to him were to be local officials: each diocese would be provided with two Seniors, members of the clergy, who would conduct visitations, maintain church discipline, act as triers and ejectors, and supervise schools and hospitals; and these Seniors would be assisted by a lay *conservator* who would back their actions with the authority of the state. The *conservators* from all the dioceses would constitute a church council, which with the *superattendent* would determine all points of usage and ceremony. Every aspect of church life, from the morals of the clergy to the form and order of services, was now to be regulated by the lay sovereign. The bishops, the chapters, and the existing diocesan organization of archdeacons and rural deans were not abolished; but they were to be left to decay, impotent spectators of a new order of things. It was an arrangement modelled on that of the Lutheran church in the duchy of Glogau, with which Pyhy was familiar; and it implied, without any question, the royal supremacy in ecclesiastical affairs. Nor was the supremacy left as a mere implication; for in a thundering letter to the commonalty of Uppland the king, after comparing himself with Moses and his subjects with the ungrateful Israelites, continued: 'Do you for your parts look after your houses, fields, meadows, wives, children, sheep and cattle, and prescribe not to us what we shall do or say in our government or in religion, since it behoves us, as a Christian king here on earth, in the name of God and of righteousness (and by all natural reason) to set laws and rules for you and all other our subjects, while you, as you hope to avoid our dire punishment and displeasure, shall be attentive and obedient to our royal command, both in worldly things, as also in religious; and you shall do only that which we prescribe to you by our royal mandate, both in matters spiritual, and in matters lay.'[1] The church, in short, was not to be the church of the people; it was to be the church of the king.

Gustav Vasa well knew that this was a position in which the reformers would never willingly acquiesce. He determined to beat them into submission. A *herredag* met at Örebro in December 1539, and the king used the occasion to bring a charge of high treason against Lars Andreae and Olaus Petri. A court of ten laymen and three bishops, presided over by Pyhy, was appointed to try them; and by a cruel stroke Laurentius Petri was constrained to be one of the judges. The articles of accusation, drawn by Pyhy, were a chaotic mixture of serious charges and trivialities, inadequately linked together by deplorable invective and biblical quotations. Lars Andreae was accused of luring the king further along the path of Reformation than he had wished to go, and was compared with Ahitophel, who incited Absalom to rebellion. The indictment recalled that there had been a time when he had maintained that bishops should have no more power than the king allowed them; but (and this can hardly have come from any other pen than Gustav Vasa's own) 'he had stuck to this opinion for about as long as Adam stayed in Paradise, or the ice lasts at Whitsuntide'. He had connived at false coining, neglected the king's finances, enticed him to the fiasco of the Gotland expedition, exposed him to the danger of insurrection by untimely iconoclasm. Olaus Petri was accused of libelling the king by calling him a tyrant, of seeking to provoke a rebellion by his unpublished *Chronicle* (wherein he had written, among other unpalatable things, of the *reciprocal* obligations of king and people); nor was the matter of the horrid oaths forgotten. He had sent his brother the archbishop to hear the king's confession after the death of Katarina of Saxe-Lauenberg—'no doubt with intent

[1] *Gustav Vasas registratur*, XII, 256.

to make ill use of it': Gustav Vasa, we must suppose, felt sensitive about the rumour that her death had been caused by a blow from his hammer. He was accused of inciting the king to break with Lübeck, and then turning against him when he did so; though the truth was rather that he had been set to work in the archives to ferret out a case against Lübeck, had become convinced in the process that Gustav Vasa's position could not be defended, and had tried to dissuade him from hostilities. He was accused of being led by religious enthusiasm to urge the Stockholm municipal court to decide cases by 'the inner light': his religious wild oats here produced their unlucky harvest; yet it is unlikely that there was much substance in the charge, for in fact Stockholm's privileges of 1529 permitted magistrates to decide cases 'according to their conscience' if the matter happened not to be covered by the law. But the main count in the indictment against him was that he had been cognizant of the Stockholm conspiracy of 1534–6 and had concealed his knowledge from the king. He had, however, imparted it to Lars Andreae, who was thus also involved. It was now recalled, as a sinister circumstance, that Olaus had caused a picture to be painted of the *parhelion* of 1535,[1] and had preached a sermon about the possible revolutions which it might portend. No wonder that he had advised Gustav Vasa to deal leniently with the conspirators! Here at last the king's case had some substance; for Olaus had indeed known of the plot. His defence was that his knowledge had come to him by way of the confessional, and was thus confidential—a defence which was certainly somewhat weakened by the fact that he had passed on the information to Lars Andreae. But it seems probable that by the time Olaus learnt of the conspiracy it had already been shelved by the participants; and it is almost certain that the fact of his cognizance of it had been known to the king for some years. It had been kept as a rod in pickle for Master Olof; and it may be that it was Pyhy who called the king's attention to the fact that such misprision of treason was by Roman law (though not by Swedish) a capital offence. At all events it proved useful now. Olaus at first protested his innocence; but later (possibly after ill-usage)[2] confessed his guilt and begged for pardon. The court condemned both the reformers to death, but recommended them to mercy; and the king, having obtained his object, was quite ready to commute their sentence to a swingeing fine.[3] Lars Andreae retired to Strängnäs, to live there half-forgotten until his death in 1552; but Olaus Petri had still a part to play. For the king, having disposed

[1] It hangs still in the Great Church in Stockholm, and provides a uniquely informative guide to the appearance of the town in the early sixteenth century.

[2] Messenius, a well-informed historian of the next century, wrote that the king personally 'hit them often with his hammer'.

[3] Olaus Petri's fine is said to have been paid by voluntary subscriptions from Stockholm.

of him as a possible competitor, was not averse to making use of him. He was soon sitting on the bench in ecclesiastical cases; in 1543 he was made pastor of the Great Church in Stockholm; and he was even encouraged to resume his labours as a historian—though the king did not again trust him with access to the archives, and no doubt expected that this time there should be no nonsense about being impartial.

The fall of the reformers made an immense sensation. The adherents of the old religion saw in it a notable instance of divine judgment. Its effects reached beyond Sweden's frontiers, and Luther himself was moved to write to Gustav Vasa about it.[1] But the king had no difficulty in sending him a reassuring answer. Protestantism was in no danger: on the contrary, it was just about to win its definitive victory. If the reformers had seemed to challenge the royal supremacy, the Reformation was by no means incompatible with it. And on the morrow of the sentence upon Master Olof the king made this perfectly plain. In January 1540 a royal mandate, issued in virtue of 'Our high royal might, power and majesty', enjoined on all Swedish churches a reformation of doctrine and ceremonies, ordered the *superattendent* to remove peccant priests and try the qualifications of all incumbents, and provided for a grand visitation of the whole country, to be carried out by George Norman upon the basis of a Church Ordinance which he was commissioned to draw up. Supremacy, it seemed, was to imply at least some degree of uniformity. The king did not, indeed, style himself 'supreme head' of the Swedish church; but he did call himself 'supreme defender'. The difference was not perhaps very material.

Sweden was now unmistakably a Protestant country. George Norman's Church Ordinance, though it remained a fragment, echoed the theology of Melanchthon. And in 1541 the long-awaited appearance of a complete translation of the Bible—the noblest volume so far to issue from a Swedish press—provided the new generation of evangelical clergy with the broad and firm foundation on which alone a Protestant nation could be built. In ecclesiastical affairs the German ministers, committed as they were to the support of princely authority, had achieved a decision for which the Swedish reformers had laboured in vain. It was symptomatic that in 1540 Gustav Vasa reduced the stipend of the Erasmian bishop of Skara to one-tenth of its former figure. Yet at the very moment when Norman's authority stood highest, the native tradition began to reassert itself. The archbishop's patience and tact enabled him to recover, quite early, much of the ground he had lost in 1540. When in 1541 the Swedish mass and the church *Handbook* were

[1] His indifference to the almost contemporary fall of Thomas Cromwell (executed 28 July 1540) is in significant contrast: his recorded comment on this last event was that 'Master Henry intends to be God and do as he likes'.

published with official sanction, and their use enjoined upon the church, it was essentially Olaus Petri's work that was adopted, and not Norman's proposals. In spite of all probabilities, the future would belong not to Norman but to Laurentius Petri, and the Swedish church, like the English, would speak the international language of Protestantism with an accent of its own.

Two days after the sentence on Master Lars and Master Olof the assembly at Örebro witnessed another scene not less remarkable. On 4 January 1540, in the presence of the king and the young princes Erik and Johan, twelve members of the *råd* and three bishops took a new, circumstantial and unprecedented oath, swearing upon the king's naked sword to be true and faithful, not only to him, but to the heirs of his body. And as they laid their hands upon the outstretched blade the king pronounced these words: 'In the name of God the Father, the Son, and the Holy Ghost, Amen. And by the divine might and power of Almighty God, which to us and all our royal progeny from generation to generation is vouchsafed and entrusted, to rule and reign over you and all our subjects, we stretch forth this sword of righteousness over you for a witness, whereon ye are to swear.'[1] These were new accents in a Swedish monarch, falling discordantly upon the political polyphony familiar to an older generation, vibrating with the overtones of German princely absolutism and with mystical suggestions of Divine Right. They owed much, no doubt, to the new ideas which Pyhy had brought from Germany. Much, but not all. For there had been signs enough since 1526 that Gustav designed to establish a hereditary monarchy; and signs too of the growth in him of a concept of sovereignty which his German servants had only to develop. For instance, in regard to the ownership of land. As early as 1535, by alluding to commonages as the property of the crown, he implied a claim to the ownership of all unappropriated land; though it was only in 1542 that the pretension became explicit in the famous pronouncement which proclaimed, in the new emphatic style, that 'land which lies uncultivated and unsettled pertains to God, to us, and to the realm of Sweden; and to none other'. Yet already by 1539, under the stimulus of the new German ideas, he was writing as though the crown was the ultimate owner of *all* land, present possessors being merely in temporary enjoyment of the usufruct; and two years later the practical implications were made clear in a warning that peasant owners who paid taxes were entitled to their land only for so long as they did not abuse it, since if they did so they would be unable to meet their fiscal obligations and the crown would lose its revenue. In one aspect this contention was a typical example of the king's minute care for the

[1] *Svenska riksdagsakter*, I, i, 253.

economic good behaviour of his subjects, reflecting his land-agent's view of the state and his extreme sensitiveness to the possibility of fiscal loss. But in another it declared a new aspiration to effective royal control of every aspect of the economy. And indeed it implied a new dimension in Swedish theories of monarchy. And these high pretensions were promulgated *ex cathedra*, of the king's mere motion, 'in the plenitude of our royal power'. It was so with the reorganization of the church; it was so with the reorganization of the civil government, of which the arrangements for the church really formed only a part.

In 1538, when Pyhy came to Sweden, the central government was rudimentary. Apart from the king and his entourage of courtiers, secretaries, clerks and cashiers, there was no permanent central government at all. The old great offices of state (steward, marshal) had ceased to be efficient, and were in fact unfilled; the chancellor, when he existed, was of varying importance, and at times of inferior rank to the secretary. The *råd* met as a whole only when summoned to advise the king on matters submitted to it, and such meetings might occur only once or twice a year. It was in no sense a council doing the ordinary business of state. Its members normally lived on their estates, though there would usually be some of them at court to whom the king could turn for assistance in a wide variety of tasks, or to whom he could delegate business at need. The 'chancery' was no more than the place where the secretary and clerks wrote the king's letters; and the letters, it seems, were frequently dictated by the king himself: sometimes they were written by him too. Similarly the 'chamber' or 'exchequer' was simply the room where bailiffs rendered their accounts and received their acquittances, and not at all (as in England) an office of government with entrenched traditions, antique safeguards and thriving interdepartmental jealousies. To a considerable extent government was by word of mouth, by verbal order from the king in person: at times, it is to be feared, it must have seemed like government by shouting. When good secretaries were so hard to come by this was a reasonably expeditious method; though the great series of Gustav Vasa's Registers is an impressive reminder of how much writing even so uncomplicated an administration had to do. But it was all unsophisticated to a degree which makes any comparison with the position in early Tudor England almost impossible. There exists no administrative history of mediaeval Sweden comparable to Tout's great studies; in part because administration by Gustav Vasa's time had not developed so far as to present the historian with comparable problems. As to where the main weight of business lay, or which was the efficient centre of government, or which organ was growing stronger and which decaying—these are questions which it is hardly pertinent to ask. No 'battle of the seals' makes the pulse of the Swedish mediaeval historian beat faster (not even, apparently, when the *råd*, through the bishop of Strängnäs, controlled the Great Seal, while the regent had a privy seal of his own);[1] no dazzling revelation of the transcendent importance of the Wardrobe or the Chamber is ever likely to illumine the undifferentiated obscurity of the institutional history of mediaeval Sweden. Offices do not beget offices; the council (*råd*) engenders no courts; and even its claim to father the *riksdag* is putative at best. In 1538 the Swedish Middle Ages, administratively speaking, had still nearly a century of makeshift life before them: not until 1634 is it possible to see administration clearly going 'out of court'. If Gustav Vasa had been left to himself, he would probably have felt that all he was really needing in 1538 was a few more secretaries who were efficient, a corps of bailiffs whose honesty and zeal were less obviously questionable, some chamberlains and accountants who would do as he told them, and perhaps some provincial governors to look sharply after his interests when his own attention was otherwise engaged. But Pyhy had other ideas. He soon came to the conclusion that what Sweden required was a bureaucracy which would function independently of the person of the monarch. In a state which was singularly ill-adapted to the experiment he aimed at objectives similar to those which have recently been credited to Thomas Cromwell. The king, harassed and ill, painfully mindful of his enforced secretarial labours, was prepared to let him try.

Pyhy, then, began by setting up what he styled a Council of Government. It was designed to be not merely a central executive body, but also a *Hofrath*, a court at Court. The king was still (and long continued to be) the apex of the judicial system; he still heard cases on appeal in person, either alone or with the help of any member of the *råd* who might happen to be present, though he might on occasion delegate his functions.[2] Pyhy now proposed to institutionalize royal justice, and to set up a sort of Aulic Council as supreme court of appeal. In its executive capacity the Council of Government would act for the king in his absence; it would be permanently at work; and its decisions would be collective: it would be, in fact, what the next century would call a *collegium*, a board. Pyhy probably intended that it should ultimately absorb and supplant the old *råd*, eleven of whose members, indeed, appeared in the list of the new Council. In the precise definition of its composition, its duties, its forms of procedure, it contrasted with the informal, hand-to-mouth, *ad hoc* methods that had hitherto pre-

[1] The Great Seal passed to the king in 1523.

[2] Since the first half of the fifteenth century provision had also been made for the king to go on circuit in a kind of General Eyre, holding court in each *härad*; and here too he had often delegated the duty to members of the *råd*.

vailed. Pyhy and Norman, indeed, were themselves the first full-time professional senior civil servants in Swedish history. But the Council of Government was to be only one part of a general system of councils which were to share the work of government between them. There was to be now a properly organized chancery, appropriately divided into a German and a Swedish section. The exchequer (*kammaren*), which had been slowly developing since the mid-1520s, was given new senior officials, the chamberlains or exchequer-counsellors (*kammarråd*), professional administrators with high authority which they were to exercise collectively, as a *collegium*; and they were to be recruited from the aristocracy. Another overdue reform divided the exchequer into an exchequer of receipt and an exchequer of audit. Pyhy intended that there should be a council of war also; but it is doubtful whether it ever came into existence. Finally, the ring of *collegia* was to be closed with the church council, with the *superattendent* at its head. And just as the central authority of the *superattendent* was matched at a lower level in the institution of the Seniors and *conservators*, so Pyhy planned that the pattern of the Council of Government should be reproduced in provincial administration. In April 1540 the king promulgated a provincial ordinance for Västergötland,[1] which set up for that province a collegial executive headed by a lord-lieutenant, or *ståthållare*—a word which here appears for the first time. The *ståthållare* would provide a much-needed intermediate term between the king and his bailiffs; he would have a clearly defined area to control and administer; and he would be essentially a senior civil servant paid by the state for his service, rather than an old-style fief-holder rewarded by concessions for taking the job of government off the king's hands. Implicit in the arrangement was a change in the meaning of the word *län*, which would gradually make good its ground in the succeeding decades: in 1520 *län* had unambiguously meant 'fief'; by 1600 it would be coming to mean 'administrative area'.

Such were Pyhy's reforms. Modelled as they were on German and Burgundian procedures, transplanted abruptly to unprepared Swedish soil, they did not take root easily. The Council of Government (which appears to have transacted its business in German) did not succeed in ousting the old institution of the *råd*, with which its relations were always undefined; the reform of the exchequer made some impression, but seems never to have been sanctioned by the king; the church council seems to have met but once; the provincial organization for Västergötland was never extended to other provinces as Pyhy had

[1] Västergötland seems to have been selected for the experiment as being a frontier province, in danger from Denmark, where strong and efficient government was particularly necessary.

intended. The transition from the primitive to the sophisticated was too sharp, the spirit and method of the new bodies too foreign; and they were not popular. They depended for such success as they had upon Pyhy himself, upon Norman, upon the queen's young brother Sten Eriksson Leijonhufvud (who had from the beginning attached himself to Pyhy), and upon the handful of German fortune-seekers who made the most of the brief sunshine of Pyhy's Swedish summer. But the reforms in chancery and treasury, the idea of provincial *ståthållare*, the concept of the *län* as a unit of local government rather than a fief—these were legacies which a later generation would know how to appreciate and improve.

In the meantime Pyhy seemed to have provided his master with the nucleus of an administration appropriate to the monarchy's new theoretical pretensions. Royal supremacy was to be built upon the firm ground of bureaucratic efficiency and administrative *expertise*. And it is just possible that Pyhy might have succeeded in this programme, if he had had ten years of power in which to carry out his plans. In the event, he had less than half that time. His projects were barely launched before royal supremacy had to meet the most serious challenge it was ever to encounter. The monarchy survived that challenge; but not upon Pyhy's basis. For the great crisis of 1543—in part, at least—was a popular reaction to the activities of the German reformers; and it would number Conrad von Pyhy among its victims.

VII. THE CRISIS OF THE REIGN, 1540–4

The ending of the Count's War in 1537 brought no sure peace to Sweden. A ring of enemies threatened Gustav Vasa's throne: if for the moment their assaults had been beaten off, he could not doubt that they would be renewed. Lübeck, having declined a definitive settlement, did not feel debarred from pursuing hostile intrigues: in the years before 1540 her agents were in touch with unruly elements in Småland. The indefatigable von Melen, not content with securing Gustav Vasa's rejection by the League of Schmalkalde, was doing his best to concert forces for an invasion: in 1538 he made a not unhopeful attempt to interest Henry VIII in the project.[1] Another threat came from Albert V of Mecklenburg. Albert had married a niece of Kristian II; he was directly descended from a brother of that Albert of Mecklenburg who had ruled Sweden from 1364 to 1389; and on both counts he considered himself a better candidate for the Swedish throne than Gustav Vasa. But the main responsibility for championing the legiti-

[1] He did succeed in collecting a body of troops, but in May 1539 the Schmalkaldic League persuaded him to disband them.

mist claim, now that Kristian II was safe behind the walls of Sønderborg, passed naturally to his two daughters; and their chances of making it good would necessarily depend to a considerable extent upon their husbands. The elder daughter, Dorothea, had in 1535 married Frederick, Count Palatine, who was to succeed his brother as elector in 1544. The marriage was still childless, and was destined to remain so; but the Palatine was nevertheless warmly interested in the prospect of recovering his wife's inheritance. It was unfortunate for Gustav Vasa that Frederick happened to be a strong imperialist, for this made Charles V willing to give to Dorothea's pretensions a more active sympathy than he had been wont to bestow upon her father's. Her younger sister, Christina, had been left a widow in 1535 after a brief and childless marriage to Francesco Sforza, and she was by now looking out for a second husband—or rather, her uncle the Emperor and her aunt the regent of the Netherlands were considering how to marry her off to the Habsburgs' best advantage. The question was of importance, since the legitimist claims to Denmark might well pass to Christina's heirs, if she had any. From Gustav Vasa's point of view, therefore, the less powerful and the more distant Christina's next husband, the better. Francesco of Milan had been ideal. The duke of Angoulême (who was for a moment considered) would have been safe enough; James V of Scotland would have done very well; William of Cleves would have required watching. Worst of all, perhaps, would have been Henry VIII; for Henry was already the friend of Gustav's enemies, and probably had the naval and financial resources required for an expedition to Scandinavia. For two years—from 1537 to 1539—Henry was a pressing suitor for Christina's hand; and there were times when all the signs seemed to show that he would be successful. Gustav Vasa might count himself fortunate that in the end the negotiation broke down on the pope's refusal to grant Christina the dispensation made necessary by her consanguinity to Katherine of Aragon. But though this particular threat did not materialize, the international situation at the end of the 1530s was not reassuring. The security of the usurping dynasties in Stockholm and Copenhagen had for some years appeared to rest upon the preoccupation of the Habsburgs with other problems of greater importance, and in particular upon the continuance of the war with France: it was an ominous fact that the peace of Cambrai had been followed very soon by Kristian II's attempt upon Norway. And now the truce of Nice (1538) had freed the Emperor's hands once more. The reconciliation with France seemed complete; the fate of Ghent would make it clear that Charles felt himself able to give time to dealing with some of the minor political problems which hitherto had been allowed to stand over. The truce which Kristian III had concluded with the regent of the Netherlands in 1537, and to which Gustav Vasa had adhered, was to run out in 1540. It had in any case explicitly reserved the rights of Kristian II's heirs. How would it be if Scandinavia should prove to be the item next below Ghent upon the imperial agenda?

The danger threatened Kristian III equally with Gustav Vasa; but each reacted to it (to begin with, at all events) in different ways. Kristian ran for shelter to the enemies of Habsburg: above all, to the League of Schmalkalde. Gustav Vasa, for obvious reasons, could not take a similar course: wounded pride forbade it. Nor was he willing to collaborate with Denmark in common measures of defence. He believed that Kristian had not dealt fairly with him in the negotiations which ended the Count's War; he strongly resented Kristian's willingness to arbitrate upon von Melen's charges on a footing which implied equality of status between the king of Sweden and a mere soldier of fortune. He had other grievances too, all carefully kept warm: the matter of the large loan to Denmark during the Count's War, for which the stipulated security had never been made over; the moral support given by Kristian III to Wulf Gyler, and the more recent harbouring of Olof Bröms; the circumstances of his rejection by the Schmalkaldic League, in which he mistakenly supposed that Kristian was concerned. It was to no purpose that Kristian tried to disperse these clouds; in vain that he used his influence to deter von Melen from his enterprises, in vain that he gave Gustav Vasa warning of them, in vain that he despatched a couple of conciliatory embassies to Stockholm in 1538 and 1539. Gustav Vasa was not to be propitiated. Kristian's envoys were received with suspicion, if not with discourtesy; they were dismissed with speeches which seemed to them 'full of absurdity', and which were certainly intemperate. Kristian III, perhaps, might himself be a man of honour; but who could trust the Danish nation? And was there not always the risk that Kristian III might come to a private arrangement with the heirs of Kristian II? Might he not purchase security for himself at the price of conniving at a Palatine conquest of Sweden?

By about 1540 Gustav Vasa seems to have persuaded himself that he stood in danger of attack, not only from the Emperor and the legitimists, but also—and more immediately—from Denmark, from Prussia (was not Wulf Gyler now on Albert's permanent establishment?) and from von Melen's patrons and backers in the Schmalkaldic League. Certainly he made visible efforts to put the country on a war footing. His commercial agents were instructed to exchange Swedish exports against cloth or specie—two of the indispensable commodities for keeping a mercenary army in fighting trim. Exports across the land-frontiers were prohibited in order to conserve stocks. The fiscal machinery was tightened up; stiffer gressums were exacted from crown tenants; better book-keeping and a more rigorous insistence on punctuality made the best of existing revenues. A large-scale recoinage yielded the crown a satisfactory profit; increased production by the mints reinforced the king's stores of ready money. Finally, in December 1539, a general tax, payable in cash and not in kind, was imposed with the consent of the *råd*. At the end of February 1540 a formal resolution of the *råd* defined the purpose of these extraordinary measures as being the defence of the country 'against Denmark and against the Schmalkaldic League, which Denmark has incited against us'.

It is difficult to resist the conclusion that these alarms were exaggerated. Kristian III was not, in reality, planning an attack on Sweden; nor was he in a good position in 1540 to make private terms with the Palatine at Sweden's expense. Nevertheless, Swedish policy was deflected to meet this imaginary danger. Gustav Vasa embarked upon the very course of action of which he suspected Kristian III: he attempted to reconcile himself quickly with the Habsburgs and their clients. If he could purchase safety for Sweden, he might well find himself able to support with fortitude the prospect of the Palatine's establishment in Copenhagen. This new line of policy is possibly to be associated with the influence of Conrad von Pyhy: as Luther was later to remark, von Pyhy had 'ein burgundischer Kopf'. But however that may be, it appeared to be a serious attempt to come to terms with one group of adversaries. Negotiations were opened with Albert of Mecklenburg; George Norman was sent to Riga to try to win the goodwill of that staunch Habsburg partisan the Grand Master of the Livonian Knights. Above all, Claus von Hattstadt—one of the Germans who had come to Sweden with Pyhy—was sent on an exploratory mission to the Palatinate. Little is known of his proceedings; but it seems a fair guess that he was ordered to investigate the chances of buying off the Palatine's hostility by promises of an alliance against Denmark. That the negotiations were not wholly fruitless was seen when in the summer an emissary of the Palatine appeared in Stockholm; and the implications of the mission were underlined by the fact that the envoy to whom it was entrusted was Hans Bogbinder, in former days the secretary and faithful servant of Kristian II.

These proceedings caused much concern in Protestant Germany; and even more in Denmark. And it is at least possible that this was precisely what Gustav Vasa intended. He had no notion of conducting his foreign relations on a confessional basis: his aim was security, his policy essentially defensive. His prime interest, after all, was now peace: peace which would give him time and opportunity to fatten his lean country and fortify his personal power. If the Protestant world declined to admit him to political fellowship, religious scruple would not deter him from seeking assistance elsewhere: the Habsburgs, the Schmalkaldic League, Kristian III, the king of France—he would turn indifferently to any of them, provided that his friend (whoever it was) gave him what he needed without making over-heavy demands in return. If his flirtation with the Palatine should shock Kristian III into a sense of the impropriety of his recent behaviour, if it should prick him into making really solid offers, Gustav Vasa was still uncommitted, equally ready to conclude with Habsburg's friends or Habsburg's foes, as the balance of advantage might suggest. At all events, whether intended or not, the effect of his diplomatic manœuvres of 1540 was to force Kristian to seek a reconciliation with Sweden in real earnest. He had indeed succeeded in extending his truce with the Netherlands for one further year (to the summer of 1541); but he could not afford to see Gustav Vasa ranged with the Habsburgs when it finally expired—least of all at a moment when the scandal of Philip of Hesse's bigamy had shaken the coherence of the League of Schmalkalde. With trouble brewing in Germany, Kristian could not risk leaving an enemy in his rear.

In the autumn of 1540, therefore, negotiations between Danish and Swedish delegations began at Kalmar. But the Swedish representatives refused to discuss political questions at all until they had received satisfactory assurances about the repayment of Gustav Vasa's loan; and the Danes were at last forced to agree that the whole capital sum, with accrued interest, should be repaid in one instalment in March 1541. Once this matter was disposed of it proved possible to agree upon the draft of a treaty of alliance which might serve as a basis for discussions at a later meeting. The talks were then adjourned, to be resumed in June 1541 at Brömsebro. In the interval, both sides were given sharp reminders of the perils which threatened them. In January 1541 Christina was at last married—to Francis of Lorraine. In May, the Diet of Regensburg endorsed an imperial demand for the liberation of Kristian II; and Philip of Hesse, seeking by vicarious prudence to rehabilitate himself in Germany and appease the Emperor, urged Kristian III to compromise the issue by ceding a portion of his dominions—Skåne, perhaps; or Norway; or even Jutland—to Frederick of the Palatinate. No wonder that the Danes at Brömsebro grew anxious for a settlement; no wonder that the Swedes agreed to drop their claims for the restitution of Gotland. On 14 September 1541 the treaty of Brömsebro was signed; on 30 September the two kings met in all amity.

The treaty of Brömsebro[1] was in the first place a defensive alliance covering all the dominions of either sovereign: in itself a sufficiently remarkable provision, since if literally interpreted it committed Kristian to the defence of Finland, and Gustav Vasa to the defence of Holstein. If one of the parties attacked a third power 'for reasonable cause', moreover, the alliance was to be offensive also. It was to last for fifty years. It pledged either party to abstain from any unilateral settlement with the heirs of Kristian II. In an annexe to the treaty Kristian III bound himself to aid Gustav Vasa if he were attacked by Lübeck before a regular peace between them was concluded; to defend him from any onslaught by von Melen's German sympathizers; and to use his good offices to settle Gustav Vasa's disputes with Albert of Prussia, and with Danzig. Other provisions (in part looking back to the Swedish-Danish treaty of 1534) provided for the arbitration of differences between the two states, and also between individual citizens of each; for mutual aid against rebellious subjects; for a guarantee of the privileges of the nobility in each country; for intervention, by the councils of either state, to prevent their respective monarchs from going to war in violation of the treaty; and for the payment of a fine of 100,000 *riksdaler* for any breach of it. By a very remarkable clause (§ 20), which was obviously prompted by the *affaires* Gyler and Bröms, subjects of one state who incurred their king's displeasure and were exiled in consequence were to be entitled to have their cases investigated by an impartial tribunal made up of judges from both kingdoms. The two realms were now to be considered as '*in ein Corpus verfasst*'. The Union, it seemed clear, had not vanished without leaving its mark upon intra-Scandinavian relations.

The alliance was undoubtedly a diplomatic success for Gustav Vasa. It gave him a measure of insurance against his enemies; and one immediate effect of its signature was to enable him to take an intransigent line in the negotiations with Lübeck which had simultaneously been proceeding, and which he had deferred bringing to a conclusion until he had the Danish treaty in his pocket. The demands of Lübeck were now peremptorily rejected; the truce was continued on the old basis. The treaty of Brömsebro was also something of a turning-point in Swedish foreign policy. It is true that Gustav Vasa did not immediately abandon his attempts to make contact with the Emperor; but within a short time he followed Denmark into the anti-imperialist camp, and perhaps was drawn to a more full-blooded participation in its policies than would have been the case if the Brömsebro alliance had not been made. And though Gustav Vasa himself, by his exaggerated and morbid suspiciousness of all Danish actions, soon for-

[1] *Sverges traktater med främmande magter*, IV, 206–24.

feited the peace of mind which the alliance might have been expected to give him, he gained, in Kristian III, a loyal and long-suffering ally, whose steadfast adherence to the spirit of the treaty (despite one solitary lapse) was of value to Sweden in the difficult years that lay ahead: when the news of Kristian's death arrived in 1559, even Gustav, ailing and cantankerous as he then was, was constrained to admit that he had lost a good neighbour.

It is none the less true that Kristian III's offers of his good offices at Brömsebro, and his subsequent energetic efforts to reconcile Gustav Vasa to potential friends or old enemies, were motivated by his desire to free Sweden from embarrassments in the hope of securing her active participation in the perennial Valois-Habsburg conflict, whose renewal was already obviously impending. Two months after the treaty of Brömsebro Denmark signed an alliance with France; and both partners were anxious that Sweden should follow this example. The idea was no novelty to Gustav Vasa: as early as the summer of 1540 he had sent an agent secretly to France to reconnoitre. A French alliance looked a sound investment against any mischief from Lorraine; and French commercial interests might be presumed to be unsympathetic to Hanseatic or Dutch pretensions. After some hesitation, therefore, he took the plunge. In January 1542 the approval of the *råd* was obtained for the despatch of a great embassy to France: the importance attached to the mission is revealed by the nomination of Pyhy, Norman and Sten Eriksson Leijonhufvud to be Sweden's representatives. The king was eager for closer economic ties with western Europe, and was especially interested in Brouage salt; Norman was friendly to Denmark, and perhaps saw a French alliance as the logical corollary to Brömsebro; while Pyhy may have been induced to abandon the imperialist line by the hope of subsidies for Sweden, and perhaps of a pension for himself. The embassy was received with flattering distinction; the negotiations met with no obstacles; within a short time success was complete. The offensive and defensive alliance of Montiers-sur-Saulx pledged each party to aid the other with 6,000 men, or in extreme need with 25,000 men and 50 ships: for Sweden, it might seem, a rather heavy commitment. The treaty of Rigni-la-Salle gave Sweden the right to import salt in unlimited quantity, with a special concession (for this occasion only) allowing purchase of 6,000 crowns' worth tax-free. Both treaties were signed in July 1542. In that same month the long-expected European war broke out, with attacks upon the Netherlands by France, Denmark and Cleves. And Sweden was now openly ranged with the anti-Habsburg party. Indeed, Gustav Vasa seemed to stand (somewhat diffidently, perhaps) at the centre of a great European coalition; for the treaty of Montiers-sur-Saulx had provided for the adherence not only of the kings of Denmark and Scotland, but also of the dukes of Prussia and Cleves. It was even hoped to attract Henry VIII. For the first and only time during the reign, it seemed likely that Gustav Vasa would be involved by his own choosing in the great clash of arms upon the continent. From this perilous situation he was delivered by the outbreak of a crisis still more serious at home. In June 1542 Gustav Vasa had to meet the gravest domestic situation that ever confronted him, and all thoughts of action upon the continent had at once to be postponed to the overriding need to cope with the insurrection of Nils Dacke.

In 1540 George Norman had begun the discharge of his duties of *superattendent* by starting upon a visitation of southern Sweden. He went first to Östergötland and Västergötland, where the influence of the Reformation had still scarcely begun to be felt; and he found much that called for his attention. The nuns of Vadstena, for instance, had tried to compromise with the times by simply translating the old Latin mass into Swedish: they were forbidden this evasion for the future. Some of the clergy were disreputable; many were ignorant—as for instance that incumbent who answered the question 'Quod est Evangelium?' with 'Est baptismus'.[1] The unworthy were now removed, and the simple were ordered to be instructed. Norman saw to it that the vernacular was used in services, that a measure of uniformity in practice was secured, and that the clergy understood the implications of the changes. He had another concern also, in which perhaps the king took a more immediate interest. For Norman used the visitation to compile a register of church revenues and clerical incomes comparable with Cromwell's *Valor ecclesiasticus*; and he made an enormous haul of those vestments and that 'superfluous' plate which (as he observed) 'had hitherto been so unchristianly misused'. When he had finished, few churches in the two provinces were left with much more than a chalice and a paten. On his return to Stockholm he presented an account of his doings, together with the draft of his Church Ordinance, to a meeting of the new church council, as evidence of his zeal in the king's service. Thereafter his participation in the embassy to France prevented him from continuing his visitation in person; but the work was carried on by his coadjutor, Bishop Henrik of Västerås, who in 1541 extended it to Småland. Småland was a province strongly Catholic, and already dangerously discontented on a variety of grounds. Bishop Henrik found both priests and people notably recalcitrant. They were con-

[1] Compare Bishop Hooper's Visitation of 1551, when of the 311 clergy he examined more than half could not repeat the Ten Commandments, and more than a tenth could not say who was the author of the Lord's Prayer: A. G. Dickens, *The English Reformation* (1964), p. 243.

temptuous of the new services in Swedish: at this rate, they thought, 'every lad on a dungcart will soon be whistling a mass'. They were outraged by the plunder of the churches: 'from the churches and monasteries are taken the monstrances and other ornaments, and all that our fathers appointed and gave to the glory of God, so that it will soon be as sweet to walk in the dreary woods as to go into a church.' It cannot be said that this was an exaggerated complaint: a total of 3,700 kilograms of church plate—or about 85 per cent of the province's total holdings—is estimated to have been carried off from Småland. The splendidly bound volumes of ecclesiastical libraries were gutted, and their leaves used as folders for the royal accounts; and a similar spirit of prudent management was no doubt responsible for the queen's cutting up of copes and altar-frontals to make garments for herself and her children. The visitation was perhaps the last straw to a province already too well provided with grievances. At all events, it was followed in 1542 by what was in many respects Sweden's Pilgrimage of Grace: the revolt of Nils Dacke.

Dacke's revolt was Småland's protest against the new monarchy; the last great gesture of defiance hurled by the old provincialism against a standardizing king. It had both economic and religious aspects; and each was a direct criticism of the king's policies. Economically, it was in the first place a reaction to the recent increases in fiscal burdens which were the result of the king's defensive preparations: the external crisis helped to produce the internal. It was also a protest against the new notions of regalian rights which claimed oak- and beechwoods as royal forests, and led to restrictions upon utilization of the waste. Among the measures that provoked it was a typical attempt by the king to alter the natural course of trade in what he conceived to be the interests of the realm. The recent ban on exports had hit the province hard, for the cattle of the Småland highlands had from time immemorial taken the route to the ports of Halland, Blekinge and Skåne. But apart from such temporary restrictions, it was a longstanding policy of Gustav Vasa (as of Sten Sure the elder before him) to force the trade of south-eastern Småland to go, not to its natural market and port at Ronneby, but to Kalmar: why (he argued) should a Danish port have the benefit of it? The inhabitants of Småland cared little for such considerations; and there had been disturbances in 1539, followed by a new and more stringent order in 1541. But the matter of the cattle-trade was only one aspect of a general feeling of resentment at royal interference in their private concerns. They complained that the king's agents tried to dictate to them the time of their harvesting, and that he even told them which clothes they were to take care of, and which to wear out. There was some truth in this; for certainly the king had but a poor opinion of the intelligence of his subjects, nor did he believe that enlightened self-interest could be relied upon to guide them to the type of economic behaviour which the welfare of the country required. But it was the religious grievance which weighed heaviest and cut deepest: it was an intolerable presumption that the king should interpose his meddling not only between a man and his market, but between a man and his God. Thus the movement was compounded of divers elements, but was upon the whole a rebellion against times out of joint, against a new world which was coming upon them unbidden, and which they felt to be bad; and the rebels summed up their rejection of that world in the famous demand for the 'good old customs'. The population of this frontier region, remote and lawless as Liddesdale or Redesdale, had still not adjusted themselves to the implications of the dissolution of the Union. They had tried to remain neutral in 1520, as Gustav Vasa very well remembered. Many of them were colonizers of the waste and the forest, who found it easy and natural to slip over the border when hard pressed; they could live if need be as semi-outlaws in the forest for months together; they had a history of virtual independence which stretched far back into the Middle Ages. More than once in the late thirties they had given ominous rumbles of unrest. They now found a leader of the true Borderer quality. Dacke was no gentleman-lawyer like Robert Aske; nor did his movement ever command the wide spread of support from the nobility and gentry which Aske had at his disposal. He was a substantial peasant farmer, coming from a family which typically (and conveniently) straddled the frontier. In 1542 he was already in the king's bad books: six years earlier he had for a time been outlawed for the murder of one of the king's bailiffs. His followers were mostly peasants like himself; aided, doubtless, by the local clergy, but rather hostile than otherwise to gentlemen. Courage, resource, audacity and knowledge of the terrain made Dacke a formidable guerilla commander, and militarily he was for a time extraordinarily successful. The king's German mercenaries, with their cumbrous pikes and stereotyped tactics, were utterly at a loss in the ambushed wilderness of Småland. Their lack of woodcraft put them at a hopeless disadvantage in the deep forests; their habit of advertising their approach by marching to tap of drum exposed them to murderous surprises; their professional contempt for peasant armies led them to neglect elementary precautions. And such military assets as remained to them were further diminished by their refusal, as a matter of professional etiquette, to fight on a Monday. By the end of 1542 they had been driven clean out of the province, the rebel forces had overrun much of Östergötland, Gustav Vasa had been reduced to the humiliating necessity of negotiating a truce with his own subject on far from favourable terms, and Nils Dacke kept his Christmas triumphantly in the royal castle of Kronoberg.

It was the kind of situation which always called forth the king's best efforts. His counter-measures, no doubt, ran upon familiar lines: promises of concession, exhortations to loyal provinces to remain loyal, swift and efficient military preparations. But to these was now added a very effective economic blockade of Småland, which revealed how real was the control which the king had acquired over the country. And never, perhaps, was his skill in propaganda displayed to more effect. The fidelity of one province was enlisted to offset the recalcitrance of another: the loyal denunciations of Dalarna, he hoped, would sound louder than the grievances of Småland. The country at large could not know that the Dalesmen's manifesto was in reality of the king's concocting, nor did they suspect that the seal which was appended to it had been affixed without the Dalesmen's knowledge. The rebels' clamour for the good old customs was taken up with dialectical brilliance and telling irony. In a letter[1] to the commonalty of Östergötland and Västergötland the king painted a lurid picture of the Sweden of the good old customs, where light taxation ensured the weakness of the state, where public order and private rights were insecure, where unprotected traders were plundered on the high seas, where turbulent bishops disturbed the public peace, and the good Herr Sten was slain in battle, and cruel King Kristian went his bloody progress through the land. It was effective as propaganda because for all its tendentiousness it was largely true, and because Gustav Vasa himself believed it to be true. It never occurred to him to doubt that his rule was truly for the advantage of his country. If he was greedy and grasping, it was because he saw himself beset by foes; and only money, and the soldiers that were to be hired for money, could make him secure. If he crushed the independence of the church, and advanced unheard-of pretensions to sovereignty in the state, it was because contemporary history seemed to him to show that the safety of the state demanded a strong monarchy. He knew the Swedish peasantry through and through; their obstinacy, their shrewdness, their tough resilient independence of spirit. He used severity against them on occasion, as other kings were wont to use it against their subjects; but only when nothing less than severity availed. By Tudor standards, he was decidedly a merciful monarch. Plain arguments, appeals to common sense, hard words, rough humour, calculated pathos—these were the weapons to which he was inclined first to turn; and he never showed his command of them to more advantage than in the time of Nils Dacke.

The insurrection was serious enough, considered as a purely domes-

[1] *Gustav Vasas registratur*, XIV, 392 ff.

tic disturbance; but it was made far more alarming by the very real danger of foreign intervention. To all Gustav Vasa's enemies, personal and political, Dacke's revolt offered an opportunity too tempting to be missed. For the last decade and more exiles had been gathering in little colonies here and there in north Germany. Wulf Gyler, and later Olof Bröms, had passed into the service of Albert of Prussia. Hans Witte, expelled from Stockholm during the Count's War, was at Danzig, and subsequently in the service of von Melen; and at Danzig too was Hans Månsson, the son of that Måns Nilsson of Aspeboda who had been executed for his share in the church-bell rebellion. Von Melen himself was at this time at the height of his influence: in 1542 the Schmalkaldic League had taken the field against Gustav Vasa's brother-in-law, the Catholic Duke Henry of Brunswick; they had expelled him from his dominions; and they had installed von Melen as governor of the Brunswick lands. There he remained for the next five years, to Gustav Vasa's great indignation and perennial alarm. To the north-east of Brunswick, in the territory of von Melen's former backer Albert of Mecklenburg, was another little group of adversaries and exiles, centring on that Bishop Magnus Haraldsson of Skara who had been a fugitive since the Västergötland rising of 1529. It was from Mecklenburg that the first attempt was made to exploit the disturbances in Småland: in September 1542 Bishop Magnus sent an emissary to Dacke, bearing a letter written by Olof Bröms. The emissary was stopped and executed by Kristian III on his return journey; but the idea of making contact with the rebels was not abandoned. Albert of Mecklenburg eagerly took it up, and in November 1542 sought to enlist the support of Frederick of the Palatinate. But Frederick had ambitions of his own upon Sweden; he had better prospects and more powerful friends than Albert; and Bishop Magnus and Olof Bröms soon came to the conclusion that Frederick was the man for them. Early in 1543 he was canvassing support in Germany for a descent upon Sweden. Christopher of Oldenburg was ready to assist him; and Albert of Mecklenburg, with commendable realism, renounced his own pretensions and professed himself willing to support the expedition provided he were allowed to rule Sweden as Frederick's lord-lieutenant. Mary of Hungary was persuaded to write a letter to Nils Dacke exhorting him to support the legitimist claims; the Emperor's minister Granvelle also wrote to him in a similar strain; and Frederick hurried to Brussels to assemble the men and materials for an invasion. He even conferred a patent of nobility upon Dacke—or at least sent him a message that he intended to do so.

Dacke, for his part, had wit enough to see the possibilities of these foreign connexions; but he did not initiate them. He seems indeed to have made approaches to Lübeck; which was natural enough, since he had earlier been one of Lübeck's agents.[1] But his movement had not originally aimed at Gustav Vasa's deposition; and if events should force him to that extremity his candidate for the throne would be Svante Sture, or even Kristian III, rather than any German prince. He used his newly won authority over south-east Sweden to restore the old trade-routes to Ronneby, to cultivate good relations with the Danish peasantry across the border, and above all to restore the old forms and ceremonies of the church. If Gustav Vasa could have been trusted to observe the terms of the truce which he had made with the rebels, if he had been able to bring himself to give Småland to Dacke as a fief, Dacke would not perhaps have taken much notice of the Palatine or Olof Bröms. But this was a risk which Gustav Vasa could not take. The news of foreign emissaries in Dacke's camp forced him to act quickly: at all costs Småland must not be allowed to become a bridgehead for dynastic enemies; at all costs the rebels must be denied the use of the port of Kalmar, and the easy communications with Germany which its capture would afford.

Early in the new year the king was ready to resume the attack. The truce was denounced; Dacke's attempt upon Kalmar was beaten off; on 20 March 1543 the main army of the rebels was decisively defeated near Högsby, Dacke himself being wounded in the engagement. He withdrew for a while across the border into Denmark, and on his recovery made some attempt to revive the insurrection. But by now the king was too strong for him. At the end of July 1543 his hiding-place was betrayed, and himself slain. With his death the movement came to an end. Royal vengeance proved less bloody than might have been expected: Dacke's family was hunted down and virtually exterminated; and some hundreds of the peasants who had followed him were deported to Finland. The affair was over. Gustav Vasa had fought it down none too soon: had Dacke been able to keep the rebellion alive throughout the summer, there might well have been a Palatine invasion to contend with. Even so, it had been bad enough. Neither the monarchy nor the peasantry would soon forget the name of Nils Dacke.

And perhaps, after all, Dacke had not lived and died altogether in vain. His rebellion had been essentially a protest against that new view of the state with which the king's German advisers had been particularly identified; and within a month of his death he had been in some sort avenged by the political extinction of their chief. The fall of Conrad von Pyhy, in September 1543, was (at least in part) a direct consequence of the insurrection. When the movement was at its height,

[1] And it has been suggested that Gustav Vasa's anti-Lübeck policy was itself one of the motives for the revolt.

Pyhy was on the way home from his mission to France. It was natural that the king should take advantage of his absence abroad to employ him to raise troops for service against Dacke; and he did, indeed, specifically authorize him to recruit 4,000 men, and sent him letters of credit to the Fuggers to cover his expenses in this connexion. Pyhy was perhaps too zealous in executing his commission; but he could justly claim a share of the credit for preventing any expeditionary force from Germany being despatched to Dacke's assistance, for with the troops he had enlisted he attacked and dispersed the mercenary army which Albert of Mecklenburg had been assembling with this end in view. It was almost certainly Pyhy, moreover, who was responsible for the composition and dissemination of a proclamation purporting to emanate from Dacke, which announced an intention not only of restoring Roman Catholicism in Sweden, but also of ensuring that Sweden should join the Emperor to fight the League of Schmalkalde. This adroit forgery caused consternation among the German Protestant princes, and may well have cooled their enthusiasm for the rebels' cause. But these services were offset by serious indiscretions. Pyhy committed his master's credit in the matter of hiring mercenaries to an extent which Gustav Vasa had probably not authorized. He bought jewels on credit on the king's account in France, and pawned them without orders in Germany. He dallied on the continent at a time when he had been urgently ordered home to Sweden. Above all, he embarked upon a private foreign policy designed to commit Gustav Vasa to full participation in the war against Charles V; and he seems in particular to have given undertakings to Otto of Brunswick which he found himself quite unable to make good upon his return home. Gustav Vasa had certainly attached himself to the French party; but he had no intention of involving himself in large-scale military adventures in Germany or the Netherlands, least of all on the morrow of a domestic crisis which had strained his resources to the limit, and which might not even yet be finally disposed of. As the bills for Pyhy's lavish activities in Germany came in, one after the other, the king was appalled at the sums which he was called upon to pay—the more so since all these troops (in his view, at all events) had been intended for use only against Nils Dacke, and now that Dacke was dead seemed a purposeless expenditure which the state could not afford. In the summer of 1543, moreover, Otto of Brunswick made a secret visit to Stockholm at Pyhy's invitation, to discuss the execution of the promises which Pyhy had made to him. He was recognized; the whole intrigue came to light; and the king's anger boiled over. The chancellor was arrested and imprisoned; and in prison he remained until his death in 1553.

Conrad von Pyhy was, no doubt, an adventurer. His haughty and overbearing temper did not endear him to those with whom he had to deal. In foreign policy he proved too reckless, as in domestic affairs he was too doctrinaire, for the circumstances in which Sweden found herself. Yet he was faithful to his master after his fashion, and his fate was harsher than he deserved: it was convenient and politic to make him a scapegoat for Dacke's revolt, and to charge upon him the unpopularity of some of the recent innovations. With his removal, most of his work collapsed. The old *råd* had already, in his absence, ousted his Council of Government; the local government for Västergötland did not long survive; the bishops quietly resumed their authority (though the king persisted in calling new ones 'superintendents'); and of the church council, as of the council of war, no more was heard. Yet this so-called 'German period' of the reign did not disappear wholly without trace. George Norman, more solid, more discreet, less flashy than von Pyhy, was not involved in his fall; and for the rest of his lifetime (until 1552) Norman was indubitably Gustav Vasa's first minister in fact if not in name. And though the machinery which Pyhy had foisted upon the country was dismantled, or allowed to rust with disuse, one essential element from the Pyhy period remained after he had gone. The king took good care not to sacrifice the advances in authority which the crown had made since 1538; nor did he ever relax his grip on that supremacy in church and state which the Germans had helped him to assert. On the contrary, they were given more solemn and formal confirmation by the *riksdag* which met at Västerås in January 1544.

The Västerås *riksdag* coincided with a moment when the king either professed to be, or actually was, seriously apprehensive of invasion; and its essential purpose was to strengthen the state against assaults from without. The legislation for which it was responsible was thus in one important aspect a measure of defence, and this was true even of changes in the church and the constitution. Nor was defence in a purely military sense neglected. One main object in summoning the Diet was to secure consent to new taxation for military purposes. The king was much preoccupied with plans to modernize the fortifications of Stockholm: there must be no doubt about the capital's ability to hold out against another Nils Dacke; its castle must be strong enough to defy any casual tumult or urban sedition. But he also took the opportunity to obtain the sanction of the Estates for changes in the country's military organization which were to have far-reaching consequences. Dacke's revolt had revealed how inadequate German mercenaries were when confronted by the traditional tactics of the Swedish peasantry. They were also extremely expensive; which was a serious matter at a moment when the cost of crushing the insurrection had made heavy inroads upon the treasury. The king decided, therefore, to try the experiment of a permanent native army. It was not intended that it should all be permanently embodied: most of the men would remain on their farms in peace-time, receiving a remission of taxation by way of a kind of retaining fee; others would be employed as garrisons; a permanent regiment (afterwards to become *Svea Livgarde*) would act as a training *cadre* for the rest. Recruitment was at first voluntary, but conscription soon became necessary; and the system developed which by the end of the reign would become standardized as *utskrivning*, whereby every ten or (in the case of peasants of the nobility) every twenty peasants would furnish one man for the forces. The old militia-levies were not immediately supplanted, and for years the new system and the old existed side by side. But the militia had never been bound to serve beyond the frontiers, and it was untrained except for guerilla warfare; so that once the new system had got into its stride its superiority became evident. Thus in 1544 Sweden became the first European country to have a native standing army. A main consideration in its establishment was probably economy; but its beginnings coincided significantly with the enunciation of royal supremacy in the church, and with the acceptance by the *riksdag* of hereditary monarchy.[1] It was Sweden's good fortune, however, that the instrument of military power with which the king thus provided himself, and which in other circumstances might well have been used to transform absolutism into despotism, was of a nature to render such a transformation difficult and unlikely. For this was no ordinary army of mercenaries, bound to the sovereign by strong ties of self-interest, alien to the country in which it served, and indifferent to the constitutional and social implications of royal policies. The men lived too close to the soil, they were too intimately associated with their families and friends, for the spirit of the barracks to develop, or the professional soldier's contempt for civilian attitudes and sensibilities to take root. Between this sort of army and the civilian population the distance was small, at times scarcely perceptible, and their interests and outlooks tended to be the same. It is hardly too much to say that the nature of Sweden's standing army, as Gustav Vasa founded it in 1544, was one of the most powerful negative factors in securing the survival of popular liberties, and in shoring up the concept of the rule of law.

Military problems, important as they were, were by no means the main business of the meeting at Västerås. This was the first full *riksdag* to be summoned for more than a decade; and it is clear that the king

[1] See below, p. 142.

looked to it to give retrospective approval to the important developments in the church which had taken place in that long interval. Without some such approval, indeed, they stood on a doubtful legal footing, for though it could be argued that they had the requisite preliminary consent of the *råd*, most of them had not been submitted either to provincial gatherings or to the Estates. Some care was taken to ensure that the meeting at Västerås in 1544 should be unusually representative of the nation: for the first time since 1527 the bishops and prelates were summoned—not now as members of the *råd*, but as leaders of the clergy; and with them came numerous representatives of the parish priests. The king had been especially anxious to secure a good attendance of the lower clergy, 'and the more papists, the better'; for he intended that they should endorse his religious policy. There was no attempt to pack the Diet with hand-picked supporters of the Reformation: as in so many cases, Gustav Vasa had a lively faith in his powers of persuasion. Constitutionally, the presence of the lower clergy and their grouping with the bishops and prelates was of great importance for the future. The Estate of Clergy here had its beginnings,[1] and it was speedily to establish itself as one of the normal constituents of a Diet. The association of bishops and lower clergy in the same house did much to bridge the gulf between them; it saved Sweden from anything like those head-on clashes between the upper and lower houses of Convocation which were later to bedevil English church politics; and it provided the ordinary parson with parliamentary leaders who could easily be put in mind of their duty to their constituents. The old provincial councils of the church, which in the past had framed and promulgated ecclesiastical legislation, were not abolished. They retained their importance and their functions; but they tended henceforward to be simply the Estate of Clergy meeting under another name for a specific purpose. The church was now represented—numerically, very strongly represented—in the *riksdag*. In so far as the consent of the *riksdag* was deemed necessary to new legislation, the church could be sure of a chance to put her point of view.[2] If the crown should invite the Diet's approval of ecclesiastical measures upon which the provincial council had not been consulted, the clergy had still a forum in which they could air their opinions. The steady growth in the importance of the *riksdag*, the increasing habit of seeking its approval for new laws, the slow crystallizing of its structure into a pattern of four Estates of (theoretically) equal authority—all this ensured that the

[1] Indeed, it is at this *riksdag* that the term Estate (*stånd*) appears for the first time in this parliamentary sense.

[2] Contrast the situation in England, where the clergy in 1547 declined an invitation to sit in the House of Commons, and so weakened the church's ability to influence ecclesiastical legislation.

Swedish church should have a strong influence on the religious policy of the monarchy, even when the royal supremacy was most vigorously exerted.

The proceedings at Västerås opened with a speech from the throne, written by George Norman with pitiless German verbosity, translated into Swedish hardly less crabbed than the original, and dubiously seasoned with numerous scriptural allusions: a speech so turgid and so long[1] that the bemused audience had to be provided with a summary of what was in it. Beneath the intolerable flood of verbiage could be detected the king's familiar propaganda-lines: the bad old days of cruel King Kristian, God's deliverance of Sweden by the hand of King Gustav (the new Moses), the obligation of subjects to be grateful to him, the religious duty of obedience, the terrible expensiveness of government, the political iniquities of bishops, the justification of the plunder of the church by hard necessity, and the king's intention to use the profits for reviving the university—if only Dacke's revolt had not marred all. The specific proposals (apart from the demand for supplies) were two: the confirmation of the Reformation; and the acceptance of hereditary monarchy.

The Estates made no difficulty about either. They endorsed the religious changes of the last few years; they appear to have raised no objection to Gustav Vasa's violent attack upon holy water, monstrances, the worship of saints, pilgrimages, indulgences, the use of wax and salt and incense, and so forth; and they pledged themselves 'never to depart from the doctrines that now prevail'. 'Popish practices' were henceforth to be forbidden; those opposing the new dispensation were to be accounted 'heretics and heathen'. The doctrinal position still awaited precise definition; there was still a virtually complete tolerance of dissenting *opinion*; but the official religion was now no longer Roman Catholic, it was probably Lutheran, and whatever it was, conformity would be expected.[2]

The hereditary monarchy had long been preparing. Young Herr Sten had designed it, Kristina Gyllenstierna had claimed it for her son, old King Kristian had extorted its recognition by the *råd*. For nearly twenty years Gustav Vasa had obviously had the idea in mind: as early as 1526, at a time when he had begun to look around for a wife, he had induced the *råd* to promise that any sons of his marriage should have priority in the succession. In 1537 the *råd* had agreed that in the event of the king's death commanders of castles should owe fidelity to Prince Erik 'and to none other'. It did not need the arrival of Pyhy to set the

[1] Forty large pages, in the printed version: *Svenska riksdagsakter*, I, i, 337–77.

[2] The Estates also forbade 'great oaths and drunkenness', so that Master Olof's sermon had not been in vain.

king thinking on these lines, though Pyhy's counsel may well have reinforced an existing trend. The new oath which was imposed upon members of the Council of Government at Örebro in 1540[1] certainly committed them to the principle of hereditary succession, and from this time onward Gustav Vasa in fact styled himself 'hereditary king'. The Örebro oath presupposed the existence of a valid hereditary right, and in 1544 some stress was laid on Gustav Vasa's descent from a sister of Karl Knutsson, and thus from St Erik. At the end of 1543 the king had consulted the *råd* as to whether a formal sanctioning of the hereditary principle might not be a necessary measure for the quieting of the country and the strengthening of the throne; and at Västerås the proposition came to the Estates in the form of a *råd*-resolution to which their assent was invited. Their acquiescence was expressed in a document, subscribed by the *råd* and the Estate of Nobles, which is known in Swedish history as the Succession Pact (*arvförening*).[2] It pledged the country to be faithful to Gustav Vasa and his heirs male by primogeniture; and it agreed that the king might by his testament assign duchies for the support of his younger sons.

The Succession Pact was undoubtedly a sharp break with the constitutional traditions of the fifteenth century, as they had been expressed, for instance, in the Recess of Kalmar; and perhaps it was a consciousness of this fact which led the king to take care that the procedures laid down in Magnus Eriksson's Land Law for the making of new law were more or less complied with: not only was the consent of *råd* and Estates obtained, but the proposal was subsequently sent to the provinces for approval by their *landsting*. It has been contended that the Pact was drawn up under the influence of foreign models, and opinion has differed as to whether these models were French or German. And it may very well be that the phrasing of the Succession Pact, and perhaps some of its ideas, were borrowed from some non-Swedish source. But the hereditary monarchy was a response to stimuli of a less literary and theoretical sort than these. One potent influence must surely have been the memory of recent events in Denmark, where the maintenance of the elective principle on the death of Fredrik I had opened the way to chaos and catastrophe. And indeed, the external threat to Gustav Vasa's throne was so clearly dynastic in character that a firm dynastic settlement for his own family must have appeared a natural precaution and counter-move. It is to be observed, however, that though the Swedish monarchy now became hereditary, it did not therefore cease to be elective. In the Middle Ages it had been a recognized constitu-

1 See above, p. 120.

2 The Estates as a whole accepted the *arvförening* at a great open-air meeting. The appearance of a rainbow, simultaneously with a sharp snow-shower, was accounted a good augury.

tional principle that election should as far as possible be confined to the sons of former kings; at Västerås in 1544 the range of choice was narrowed until (in fact, but not in theory) it became no choice at all.[1] Or, to look at it in another way, the Estates at Västerås elected, once for all, the male line of the Vasas to be their kings; and this might be considered a natural extension of existing law, rather than a radical change in it. The preservation of the elective principle was not simply a legal fiction of no importance, or a politic tribute to constitutional conservatism. It enabled a later generation to contend that just because the crown was still elective its wearers were still bound by obligations to those who had elected them—indeed, that the very special benefit conferred on the Vasas in 1544 must necessarily entail (and perhaps must have necessarily entailed *then*) a correspondingly greater obligation on the king's part. The proceedings at Västerås, it is true, give little support to such an interpretation, and the word 'election' is nowhere used; but it was perhaps feasible to argue that the oaths of fidelity to the hereditary monarch implied, though they did not explicitly elicit, a reciprocal pledge on his side. The next generation of the Vasas would contend that far from the Succession Pact's entailing upon the dynasty a special obligation to the people, the historic truth was that it had been an expression of the nation's gratitude to the monarch who had delivered it out of the house of bondage. Upon this claim to gratitude Gustav Vasa's sons would base extensive pretensions, while their adversaries would use the argument of obligation to support constitutional theories of equally dubious validity. The truth was that neither king nor *riksdag* cared very much in 1544 for such niceties, or for the theoretical implications of what they were doing. The king was thinking about his young family's future, and was ready as always to remind the Swedes how much they owed him; while the Estates, with danger threatening from outside, and the embers of civil war barely cold, were very ready to concur in an arrangement which seemed to offer stability at home and increased prestige abroad.

Thus at Västerås in 1544 ecclesiastical supremacy was matched by a secular authority which, though it was avowedly bounded by the laws, and though it was well content to work through parliamentary forms, had in the eyes of contemporaries become essentially greater just because it was now based on hereditary succession, and consequently emancipated from the constitutional checks and limitations which the age associated with elective kingship. To this monarchy obedience was now enjoined as a religious duty. From the crisis of Dacke's revolt the crown had emerged stronger than ever. Gustav Vasa, hereditary monarch by free consent of his people, stood in a position which none of his predeces-

[1] This was the view of Karl IX when he drafted his revision of the Land Law.

sors had ever enjoyed. The constitutional revolution had been brought within the framework of the traditional legislative process; and if here and there the Succession Pact spoke in alien accents, the enactment as a whole was now unimpeachable Swedish law. And as long as Gustav Vasa lived neither king nor country would be disposed to employ much exegetical ingenuity upon it.

VIII. FOREIGN POLICY, 1543–60

From 1540 to 1544 the domestic crisis in Sweden had been concerned with a struggle between two views of society. The one was personified in Conrad von Pyhy; the other in Nils Dacke. At the Diet of Västerås that struggle reached its end; not with the triumph of either, but rather the defeat of both. Gustav Vasa, uniting in his own person the conservatism of the one and the ruthless spirit of the other, emerged as the sole victor.

In foreign affairs it was another story. Here, the crisis which had prevailed since 1540 was in 1544 still far from being resolved: indeed, it showed signs of becoming permanent. In this matter the fall of Pyhy made no difference. Gustav Vasa had committed himself to membership of the anti-imperialist coalition; and he must make at least a show of contributing a contingent to the common effort, once the revolt in Småland was suppressed. Kristian III had especial claims on him, for since the treaty of Brömsebro he had been exerting himself energetically on his ally's behalf. At the end of 1541 he had reopened the question of Sweden's accession to the League of Schmalkalde, and in 1542 had persuaded the League to offer membership on the same terms as for Denmark. When in 1541 he began negotiations with the regent of the Netherlands for an extension of the truce between them, he was careful to stipulate that Sweden should be included. At Brömsebro he had offered Gustav Vasa his good offices with a view to coming to some understanding with von Melen; and in March 1542 he actually succeeded in negotiating a composition whereby von Melen was to promise to forbear any further unfriendly actions against Sweden in return for a lump sum of 12,000 *daler*. Indeed, Kristian's zeal for a settlement so far prevailed over his prudence as to lead him to pay over a first instalment out of his own pocket. During Dacke's revolt his behaviour had been all that the most exigent and suspicious neighbour could desire. He had sent threatening messages to the Wendish towns, warning them to give Dacke no assistance. He had forbidden his own town of Ronneby to handle the trade which the rebels were seeking to re-establish. The bearer of Olof Bröms' letter had been intercepted and executed by his order. The Danish nobility had been permitted to raise contingents for service against the Småland peasantry. And, finally, he had refused the crown of Sweden when Dacke offered it to him.

It is clear that in all this Kristian was influenced by his desire that Sweden should be available as an effective ally in his struggle with the Emperor. Already in 1542 he had closed the Sound to Dutch shipping; and in July 1543, just when Dacke's revolt was ending, he made his formal declaration of war upon Mary of Hungary. Whatever his motives, it was difficult to deny that he had comported himself as a loyal ally in terms of the treaty of Brömsebro. But Gustav Vasa would not see it. His suspicion of Danish intentions remained ineradicable; his fear that he might be tricked into action and left alone to bear the consequences warped his judgment and blinded his vision; and he looked mistrustfully on Kristian's diplomatic initiatives. He did indeed avail himself of Danish help to obtain a prolongation of his truce with Lübeck in August 1542, at a moment when Dacke was winning his first successes; but when Kristian transmitted the Schmalkaldic League's invitation, he replied coldly that he would in due course open negotiations with them for himself. As to the settlement with von Melen, he rejected it out of hand on the ground that it did not bind von Melen to discontinue his pamphleteering; nor would he even consent to reimburse Kristian III for his outlay.

It was a policy that was certainly ungracious, and probably unwise; for Gustav Vasa was not in a position to dispense with friendly aid at a moment when the international prospects were growing darker every month. The tide was already turning against France and her allies. In August 1543 Charles V crushed William of Cleves in a lightning campaign; the French invasion of the Netherlands petered out; the Schmalkaldic League refused to come to Denmark's assistance on the ground that Kristian had been the aggressor. It seemed that Sweden and Denmark had backed the wrong horse. Kristian III, for his part, frankly faced the situation and prepared to negotiate with the victor. Gustav Vasa (less wisely) hesitated, fumbled, and missed his chance. Perhaps he trusted that his share in the war had been too inconspicuous to draw the Emperor's vengeance upon him; perhaps he hoped that Denmark, if left to negotiate alone, would have to bear the main burden of defeat. At all events he ignored Kristian's suggestion that he should send representatives to take part in the peace negotiations. No Swedish diplomat was present when the peace of Speyer was concluded in May 1544. It was left to Kristian III to safeguard Sweden's interests; and, to do him justice, he seems to have made a real attempt to do so. If in the face of the Emperor's intransigence he at last desisted from the vain effort, he can hardly be blamed for not sacrificing to his ungrateful neighbour a settlement so satisfactory to himself. The peace of Speyer, which reopened the Sound to Dutch skippers, and fixed—as the Dutch believed, for ever—the dues that might be levied on ships passing through it, on the face of it contained no concession by Charles in the matter of Kristian II's heirs; but by a secret declaration the Emperor made it plain that while reserving their rights in Scandinavia he would not support their claims by force *against Denmark*. Nothing was said of Sweden in this connexion. All that was offered to Gustav Vasa was the opportunity of being included in the peace if he made application within six months. Thus Kristian III was protected against the Palatine by the secret declaration, while Gustav Vasa was not. There can be no doubt that by negotiating a peace of this sort Kristian III had violated his obligations under the treaty of Brömsebro; and Gustav Vasa felt that his interests had once again been sacrificed, as in 1536. But this was in great measure his own fault. Neither his past conduct nor his present attitude gave him much claim to Kristian's consideration.

Nevertheless, it is hardly to be wondered at that he should have refused to adhere to the treaty of Speyer, nor that he should have resolved to try what a separate negotiation with the Emperor might do for him. The prospects were less discouraging than might appear. In Duke Henry of Brunswick, his own brother-in-law, he had a friend who might be willing to do him a service, and who was a prince in good standing with Charles V. Duke Henry had taken the initiative in opening the negotiations which reached fruition at Speyer. Berend von Melen was his enemy, no less than Gustav Vasa's. In the summer of 1544 Henry visited Stockholm in the hope of borrowing money for the recovery of his duchy. In the ordinary way his prospects would have been poor, for Gustav Vasa was not the man to squander his savings on political gambles; but on this occasion he opened his purse, gave Henry a loan, and counted the money well bestowed. That was in September 1544; and in the same month he drew up the instructions for an embassy to the Emperor for which, it was hoped, Henry would prepare a favourable reception. But it was characteristic of his tentative and dilatory foreign policy that he delayed its departure for nine months.

Meanwhile Kristian III had so far improved his relations with the Emperor that at the close of 1544 Charles V was suggesting the possibility of arranging a final settlement of the claims of Kristian II's heirs on the basis of the payment of a lump sum in return for the renunciation of their pretensions to both the Scandinavian kingdoms. Kristian III was very ready to consider terms, and he urged Gustav Vasa to send an envoy to Worms to take part in the discussions. But once again Gustav Vasa declined a joint negotiation. He preferred to bargain for himself, and he had no intention of paying anything if he could help it. He was, however, prepared to make a propitiatory gesture in the Emperor's direction: in 1545, evincing a hitherto unsuspected concern for the Turkish danger, he urged his subjects to remember their duty as Christians and contribute liberally to the *Türkenhilfe*. And at last, in May 1545, the embassy to Charles V got under way. But in the months which had elapsed since its despatch had been decided on, the situation in Germany had undergone important alterations. Charles's willingness to discuss terms for a settlement of the legitimist claims had so angered the Elector Palatine that he had for the moment gone over to the enemies of Habsburg. Henry of Brunswick's attempt to recover his duchy had ended disastrously: the Schmalkaldic League had beaten him and taken him prisoner. Not only had Gustav's money been thrown away to no purpose, but he now stood in danger of public exposure as the subsidizer of one of Protestantism's most inveterate adversaries. The rumour that he had supplied Henry with money so incensed the League that even those members of it who had not previously been disposed to support an enterprise against Sweden were now sympathetic to the Palatine's cause. And the embassy to the Emperor met with disaster before it had well begun; for as it was passing through Worms its members were kidnapped by Claus von Hattstadt, who had quitted the Swedish service after a quarrel with the king. Von Hattstadt was probably acting for the Elector Palatine; and it seems likely that he hoped to find upon the ambassadors compromising documents which would establish the extent of Gustav Vasa's complaisance to Henry of Brunswick. Thus by the end of 1545 the king's refusal to collaborate with Kristian III in the spirit of Brömsebro had landed him in a position in which he had failed to reconcile himself with the Emperor, and had so alienated the Emperor's enemies that he was actually preparing to meet an invasion sponsored by the Schmalkaldic League. No doubt it is true that recent experience had persuaded him of the danger of committing himself wholeheartedly to either the imperialist or the anti-imperialist party. No doubt it was desirable to hold Sweden aloof from the great European struggle, if possible. But to foreign observers the objectives of Swedish policy must have seemed ill-defined, its methods misconceived, its sincerity suspect. Gustav Vasa's caution, his reluctance to spend money, and perhaps a justified feeling that he was dangerously short of early and reliable information about the shifting patterns of continental politics, led him to shrink from close connexions with other powers. Yet it was undeniable that as long as the pretensions of Kristian II's heirs remained alive there would always be one party in Europe ready to back them; and since that was so the safest policy, after all, was perhaps to join the other—

unless, indeed, he was prepared to settle the whole issue for good by diving into his pocket.

For this he was not ready; and it was one of his grievances against Denmark that Kristian III thought differently on this matter. He had, indeed, all too many grudges against his neighbour; some substantial, others the 'bugbears and brain-squirts' of his brooding antipathy for all things Danish. One very typical cause of friction was provided by the case of Kristoffer Andersson. Andersson had started life in humble circumstances, had risen in the king's service, and about 1535 had been made a member of the *råd*—an extremely rare honour at this period for anyone not of noble birth. Like Wulf Gyler before him he had the misfortune to disagree with his master's policy;[1] like Gyler he found the king's temper impossible; and like Gyler he fled. In 1543 he went on an embassy to Denmark, obtained leave for six months, overstayed it, and in 1545 openly broke with Gustav Vasa, having first taken care to get his wife and family out of Sweden. He then appealed to Kristian III to arrange for the trial of the issue between himself and his sovereign according to the procedure which had been laid down in clause 20 of the treaty of Brömsebro for dealing with such cases. The affair thus became a sort of touchstone of the real state of Swedish–Danish relations; a test whether the 'Scandinavian' clauses of the treaty really had sufficient strength of opinion behind them to constrain Gustav Vasa to observe them. The outcome, disillusioning perhaps for some, proved that on an issue of this kind the traditions of the Union would not prevail against a monarch who was determined to ignore them: the spirit of Kalmar Recess was ill-attuned to the political thinking of the mid-1540s. Kristoffer Andersson was accordingly tried and condemned (*in absentia*) by Swedish law. And relations with Denmark were not improved by the fact that Kristian III had in the meanwhile invited the fugitive to his court.[2]

But this, after all, was no more than an irritant between allies. Much more serious was the major divergence of policy over the question of a settlement with the heirs of Kristian II. Kristian III was convinced that to buy off their claims would be a sound investment. He was bound by the peace of Speyer to relax the conditions of Kristian II's imprisonment, and he skilfully entangled this question with the larger issue of a cash bargain. After nearly three years of negotiation he was able to conclude with Kristian II the treaty of Sønderborg (14 July

[1] He seems to have favoured cordial collaboration with Denmark and a compromise with von Melen.

[2] The Swedish *råd* thereupon wrote to Kristian explaining the Swedish point of view. It was presumably with no ironical intention that they observed 'that it would be most unfortunate if the idea were to get about that the king of Sweden showed himself ungracious to anyone without good cause'.

1546), whereby he promised his prisoner a comfortable and honourable confinement at Kalundborg, and obtained in return Kristian II's renunciation, for himself and his heirs, of all claims on Denmark, Norway and Sweden, provided that each of his daughters was furnished with a substantial dowry. Gustav Vasa was now invited to become a party to this agreement. But Gustav Vasa saw no reason why he should pay to extinguish claims whose validity he denied; and in any case it was not he who was the old king's gaoler. Nevertheless, he shrank from rejecting the proposal on his own responsibility. A sense of the gravity of the decision, and perhaps a wish to safeguard himself if the decision should turn out ill, led him to refer the matter to the Diet which met at Strängnäs in January 1547. It is possible that the clergy for a moment suggested that the settlement might be a good bargain; but if so they soon changed their minds. In the end, the Estates rejected the proposal unanimously. So too did the various *landsting* to whom the king took care afterwards to refer it; for the royal bailiffs had been instructed to put it about that if Kristian III's plan were accepted every peasant in Sweden would be asked to pay 200 ounces of silver, and the common man did not warm to that prospect.

Thus the best chance of a settlement of this dangerous question was deliberately rejected, and rejected by what on the face of it looked like an impressive demonstration of national solidarity. And for the moment, at all events, it seemed likely that Gustav Vasa might have made an expensive blunder. For in 1546 and 1547 there was another dramatic change in the balance of forces in Germany. By 1546 the Schmalkaldic League was already wilting before the growing power of Charles V: in that year their leaders found it expedient to address to Gustav Vasa a pressing invitation to join them, and so afforded him the satisfaction of being able to return a contemptuous (and prudent) refusal.[1] In 1547 the Emperor's victory at Mühlberg laid the League prostrate at his feet. Frederick of the Palatinate, by eleventh-hour repentance, succeeded in reconciling himself with the victor. Once again, then, the cause of Kristian II's heirs passed to Charles V's keeping; and never before had the Scandinavian monarchies been confronted with a power more capable of maintaining it.

The triumph of Charles V reinforced the political moral of the peace of Speyer. It was no longer possible to suppose that Gustav Vasa could continue indefinitely to evade normalizing his relations with the Emperor. It was increasingly improbable that he could afford to dissociate himself from the policies of Kristian III: the isolation in

[1] He remarked that 'the evangelical princes would now be glad to have us in the dance with them, although before we had little reputation with them, nor enjoyed much security from them, but one section of our foes was always maintained and strengthened by them'.

which he had enwrapped himself since 1544 could no longer do duty for a policy. In 1548, accordingly, relations with Denmark took a marked turn for the better—as they might have done at any time during the past four years, if only Gustav Vasa had been willing. It was agreed to adopt identical attitudes of cautious approval of the Council of Trent, should Charles V press for an answer on this point; and there were even signs that Gustav Vasa might bring himself to swallow Kristian's policy of killing legitimism by bribery. Fortunately for Sweden, the Emperor was no longer greatly interested in this matter: it was the *Interim* and the problems associated with it that now engaged his attention. With Denmark imperial relations were becoming increasingly cordial: it was significant that in 1548 Charles should have agreed to enfeoff Kristian III with the duchy of Holstein. The marriage of Kristian's daughter Anna to August of Saxony, brother of the new Elector Maurice, drew Denmark closer to the Habsburg party; and when Kristian's younger brother Adolf of Holstein became a suitor for the hand of the widowed duchess of Lorraine there really seemed a prospect that the dynastic feud within the House of Oldenburg might be healed at last. To Gustav Vasa it was not a prospect that afforded much satisfaction; and he was glad enough when Adolf's aspirations came to nothing.

Already in the autumn of 1547 the *råd* had once more debated the expediency of sending an embassy to the Emperor; in February 1548 they decided upon it; in 1550 it actually set out, the cost being defrayed by voluntary contributions from the nobility. Its official purpose was to arrange for the inclusion of Sweden in the peace of Speyer upon a basis modified to suit Gustav Vasa's views; but one important object was undoubtedly to ensure that Charles should not give his support to Lübeck, with whom relations had again reached a critical stage. In 1546 renewed negotiations with Lübeck had left matters as they were: the city refusing the curtailed privileges which were offered, Sweden declining peace on any other terms; so that the best that could be done was to extend the truce for a further ten years, and leave all issues unresolved. By 1549 tension had become acute: in that year the king prohibited any of his subjects from trading to Lübeck; in 1550 he unilaterally modified the truce arrangements by cutting short the length of time a foreign merchant might remain in Sweden. That he was not without anxiety about the reactions to these measures may be seen from his reminder to Kristian III that the treaty of Brömsebro bound him in case of an attack by Lübeck to come to Sweden's assistance. It was against this background that George Norman began his negotiations with the Emperor in Brussels. At one time he had some hopes not only of a separate peace treaty, but also of a commercial agreement;

but Charles would go no further than to agree that Sweden, at long last, should be admitted as a party to the peace of Speyer. On this basis a settlement was reached in 1551—as it might equally well have been six years earlier. Against the heirs of Kristian II it offered no protection; but it did at least seem to give some security against the designs of Lübeck.

The reconciliation with the Emperor heralded the close of an epoch in Sweden's foreign relations. The last decade of Gustav Vasa's reign brought with it new problems, unwonted cares, longer perspectives. The politics of the 1550s look forward to the reign of Erik XIV, and would, indeed, fulfil themselves only under him; while the anxieties and preoccupations of the forties grow dim, and appear increasingly irrelevant to the temper of the times. The old figures pass from the stage: Albert of Mecklenburg had died already in 1547; Bishop Magnus Haraldsson in 1550; Olaus Petri, Lars Andreae, George Norman, all died in 1552; the Elector Palatine followed them, his claims still unsatisfied, in 1556; in January 1559 'cruel old King Kristian' ended his life quietly at Kalundborg, full of years and benignity; and the pretensions of his heirs were henceforth concentrated in the house of Lorraine. A new generation of claimants had arrived; and the marriage of Renata, the eligible daughter of Christina of Lorraine, would soon be a matter of high international concern. The decline of Charles V's power after the peace of Passau, the French occupation of Lorraine in 1552, the marriage of the young duke into the house of Valois in 1559, seemed to portend that backing for these pretensions might now come from a new quarter; the accession of Francis II, and the ascendancy of the Guises at his court, might be expected to strengthen that possibility. As late as 1556 there was indeed a project, quite in the old style, for an attack on Sweden by John William of Weimar and von Melen; but it came to nothing because they could not induce Lübeck to give it support. Von Melen himself contrived to outlive his adversary: he did not die till 1561. But the disaster which had overtaken the Ernestine line in Saxony had crippled von Melen's most formidable patron; and though Gustav Vasa never forgot him (when did he ever forget an enemy?) by 1560 he had ceased to be a serious nuisance, and Gustav was more exercised by rumours of plots in Lorraine than by anything von Melen might be able to compass. Of other old enemies, Lübeck was unfortunately immortal: in 1553 the king was urging accelerated naval construction to meet expected threats from that quarter. In 1556 the truce finally ran out, and was not renewed. The days were gone when the hostility of Lübeck alone could mean real danger for Sweden, the more so since it was now by no means certain that other Hanse towns would follow her lead. But she might still be formidable in alliance with a stronger power: for instance, Denmark.

In the 1540s the Danish alliance had afforded the most solid guarantee against external dangers; in the 1550s it slowly became plain that the alliance was running to its end. It is true that in 1554 there took place at Älvsborg a meeting between members of the councils of state of the two kingdoms, with a view to compromising the differences between them. It was a procedure which had been prescribed by the treaty of Brömsebro, and it looked back to the frontier-conferences of the heyday of the Union. But in 1554 it came too late. The old Unionism was almost obscured beneath an increasingly clamant nationalism: in Denmark the hope was once more awakening of renewing the Union by Danish conquest; in Sweden the feeling was slowly growing that war with Denmark might be inevitable. The old dissensions—as over Gotland—could find no remedy; and new ones were added, casting long shadows before: disputes over the right to tax the wandering Lapps of the far north, where no boundaries as yet had apportioned the wilderness; disputes of yet more explosive tendency on points of heraldry and national prestige. In 1557 Gustav Vasa became aware that Kristian III was quartering the Three Crowns of Sweden in his coat of arms. The Danish view was that this was an emblem symbolical of the Union, and that either country, as a legatee of the Union, was entitled to display it; while Gustav Vasa insisted that it was a Swedish emblem antedating the Union, and that its appearance in the Danish arms implied a claim of right which had been rebutted for ever in 1523. The dispute rankled and festered, and it was to be many years before it was settled. It soon became involved in a violent literary feud between the officially-sponsored historians of both countries. In 1555 there was published in Denmark the third edition of the *Rhyme-Chronicle*, containing highly offensive attacks upon the Swedes. Gustav Vasa was predictably indignant. He put the blame, not on Kristian III, but on his influential chancellor Johan Friis; and there is no doubt that he was right in thinking Friis no friend to Sweden. He thereupon sent to Laurentius Petri to borrow a copy of Saxo, in order to be able to convict the Danes of iniquity by the mouth of one of their own historians; and he set Peder Swart to compose a Swedish chronicle which should demolish the Danish allegations. Swart's chronicle was ready in 1558. It fully answered Gustav Vasa's requirements, and treated Johan Friis, in particular, with such severity that he was moved to reply in scurrilous verse. The publication at this juncture of the second edition of Johannes Magnus' *Historia de gentibus septentrionalibus*—it appeared at Basel in 1558—did something to redeem the controversy from the vulgar level to which it had now descended. The old *archielec-*

tus—in the eyes of Catholics he was the legal archbishop of Uppsala, having been consecrated to that see after the death of Gustav Trolle—had died in Rome in 1544, and his book had been published posthumously by his brother Olaus. Unlike Peder Swart's *Chronicle*, it was a work of curious scholarship and perverse learning, which soon acquired the status of a standard authority. It embodied the first full statement of that mythical history upon which Swedes were for generations to come to base their assertion of their country's pre-eminence; it traced their descent from the ancient Goths; it recited the long roll of Swedish kings (a hundred and more) who had ruled over the country since the Flood. Johannes Magnus was not the first man to propound these ideas—they had been forcibly put to the Council of Basel in 1434 by Bishop Nicholas Ragvaldi—but it is to him that they owe their authoritative formulation, and he was the first man to give them literary form. The influence of his book was immediate, powerful and long-lived: from it stems that 'megalogothicism' which was to be one of the seminal intellectual influences of the Age of Greatness. And in the immediate context of the dispute with Denmark the weight and learning of his volume, the fact that it was obviously not a piece of *ad hoc* pamphleteering, and above all the fact that it came from one of Gustav Vasa's adversaries, made it a most effective weapon. The old *archielectus* might have been a papist, a fugitive and an exile: he had not ceased to be a patriot.

As long as Kristian III was alive there was no need to take these controversies too tragically, for even Gustav Vasa did not seriously suspect him of a desire to emulate Kristian II; but on the accession of Fredrik II in 1559 they mattered much more. Fredrik was a brutal extravert, who succeeded in impressing an English delegation with his 'insolence and monstrous manners'. There is little doubt that from the moment of his accession he rather welcomed the prospect of a war with Sweden. Once more Denmark had a king who corresponded with Gustav Vasa's ideas of what Danish kings were like. It had been stipulated in 1541 that the treaty of Brömsebro was to be renewed upon the accession of a new sovereign in either country. Fredrik made no effort to renew it. This change of temper in Copenhagen constituted a most fateful alteration in Sweden's position. Since the meeting at Malmö in 1524 Sweden had never been in any real danger from Denmark: Gustav Vasa may have frightened himself into thinking so on occasion, but he was mistaken. For nearly twenty years the alliance of Brömsebro had done much to shield Scandinavia from trouble; though Gustav Vasa, unhappily, had probably never looked upon it as much more than a disagreeable necessity. It was certainly a misfortune that the Hotspurs on either side of the border should have so far prevailed over cooler heads as to make possible the erosion of the alliance by suspicion, jealousy and negligence. Among such persons was Prince Erik: it was an error which was one day to cost him dear. But it was not an error into which he fell unaided: hatred and suspicion of the Dane was one of the principles of statecraft with which Gustav Vasa indoctrinated all his sons. On this matter, at all events, there was no clash of generations.

If as regards Denmark the 1550s seem to show a failure of insight on the part of Swedish statesmen, in other directions they disclose an unwonted spirit of enterprise. This was conspicuously so in those fields where foreign policy was determined or influenced by economic considerations. It had long been a part of Gustav Vasa's policy to facilitate Sweden's emancipation from Lübeck by developing trading connexions with western Europe—with the Netherlands, for instance, or with France. In the 1550s this trend becomes more pronounced. The attempt at a trade treaty with Charles V, the marriage of the Princess Katarina to Count Edzard of East Friesland (the owner of the valuable port of Emden), a renewed commercial agreement with France in 1560—were all signs of it. And to them was added a new interest in England: there were commercial negotiations (which came to nothing) in 1548 and 1549, and a Swedish embassy went to England in 1557. This increased activity in the west was matched by a more vigorous policy in the east, particularly with regard to Russia and Livonia. For more than half a century the situation in the lands between the Neva and the Niemen had been slowly moving towards the crisis which matured in the middle of the sixteenth century. The decline in vigour of the Hanse, the decay of the crusading orders, the consolidation of the Muscovite realm, had by the 1550s produced a situation in which a formidable expansive force was banked up in immediate proximity to a vacuum of power. The outward thrust of the Muscovites to the sea had begun: indeed, it had been exerting pressure ever since the last quarter of the previous century. Ivan III had conquered Novgorod in 1478, and had closed the Hanseatic factory there in 1494. In 1510 he took Pskov. These actions had as one of their objects the breaking down of the ring of middlemen which the Hanse had succeeded in interposing between Muscovy and Europe: the Russians wished to be able to trade directly with western merchants, without the Hanse thrusting in their unwanted services and taking their inflated profits. But this first wave of expansion failed to do what was needed. All that happened was that the *entrepôts* for the Russian trade were pushed a little further back, from Novgorod and Pskov to Reval, Narva, Riga and Dorpat. The burghers of these Livonian towns exploited their advantageous situation to the full; they prohibited the trading of guest with guest; they milked the trade to Muscovy of heavy transit-dues. It was a situation which all who had business to do with Russia were concerned to alter: on this matter Lübeck and the Wendish towns saw eye to eye with Gustav Vasa and the Dutch. The weakening of Lübeck's power as a result of the Count's War, and the long minority of Ivan IV, presented the Livonian towns with an opportunity which they were not slow to seize; and in the 1540s they imposed an almost complete ban on direct trading with the Russians. Half a century earlier, Ivan III had tried to get round the economic barrier by the foundation of Ivangorod in 1492; but the harbour there was too shallow to be useful, and it did not answer. Gustav Vasa now hoped to divert the trade by way of Finland; and it was with that end in view that in 1550 he founded the new town of Sandhamn, later to be known as Helsingfors: like Ivangorod, Sandhamn was intended to offer to the foreign merchant an alternative (and perhaps cheaper) access to Russian raw materials. But Sandhamn was slow to thrive; and before much could be done to establish it firmly commercial interests had been thrust aside by more urgent political considerations.

In the last quarter of the fifteenth century there had been sharp clashes between Sweden and Muscovy on the eastern borders of Finland. Swedish–Finnish settlement had penetrated into Karelia, far beyond the most liberal interpretation of the frontier as it had been drawn by the treaty of Nöteborg in 1323; and Ivan III had reacted vigorously against these encroachments. But since 1510, when a peace of sixty years had been concluded, relations had been nominally friendly. The Great Duke felt it beneath his dignity to negotiate with a mere king of Sweden: treaties were signed, on the Russian side, only by his servant the governor of Novgorod. The Swedes, though with an ill grace, swallowed this point of punctilio; and the treaty of 1510 was renewed by Gustav Vasa after his accession. Vasilij III made no difficulty about allowing the Swedes to reopen their factory at Novgorod in 1527, for like his predecessor he was glad enough to extend favours to non-German merchants. His death in 1533, however, necessitated a new negotiation, and in 1537 Sweden was constrained, very reluctantly, to accept another treaty with the governor of Novgorod upon the old terms. But despite official amity the situation on the borders was tense, and raids and counter-raids increased in seriousness during the 1540s: in 1544 and 1545 Gustav Vasa was debating whether it would not be better, as the Finnish nobility suggested, to clear the air during the minority of Ivan IV by launching a preventive war. The Swedes were uncomfortably aware that their position in eastern Finland was untenable in terms of the treaty of Nöteborg; and it was perhaps at this time that they made some effort to rectify it by producing a forged treaty which purported to show a frontier-line much further to the east than that contained in the true one. Gustav Vasa did not allow any scruples to inhibit his forward policy in Finland; and in 1550 he began to give direct encouragement to colonists who pushed into Eastern Karelia and established themselves there. A settlement at Riitimaa, on the Karelian isthmus, was especially provocative. The result was what might have been expected: in 1554 a more than ordinarily severe outbreak of border lawlessness degenerated into open war. Gustav Vasa may not have wished for it, but it may be fairly said that he had caused it; and Ivan IV, who had postponed dealing with the Swedish problem until he had captured Kazan, was at last ready to engage. The ensuing conflict lasted three years (1554–7), and both sides put forth considerable efforts.[1] The Swedes won a victory of some importance at Joutselkä in 1555; the Russians failed in an imposing attempt to capture Viborg in the following year. But the military operations were quite inconclusive. In 1557 the combatants were ready for peace. The treaty which was signed in March of that year left matters much as before. Once again it was in form a treaty between the king of Sweden and the governor of Novgorod; once again it was expressly declared to be based on the treaty of Nöteborg; once again it was agreed that the frontier should be demarcated and beaconed afresh; and once again (as in 1537) the peace was to last until 1597. Nothing was settled; the controversies remained unresolved; the ashes of conflict could at any moment be blown into a flame, as it might suit either side. If the struggle was for the moment laid aside in Finland, it was only because each party had problems of more immediate concern elsewhere. Yet it was not without significance that despite this perennial hostility the peace treaty should have been accompanied by the draft of a commercial agreement which would have provided (if it had ever come into force) for Sweden's right to trade, not only to Russia, but through Russia to central Asia. This proposal (which came from the Russian side) is one of the early signs that Ivan IV had realized that he was the master of the road to Persia and Turkestan, India and China, by way of Astrakhan and the Caspian, and that the traders of north-western Europe might be ready to give him good terms for the use of it.

South of the Gulf of Finland, in that triangle of land which lies between the Neva and the Düna, lay the ill-compacted state of the Livonian Knights. The Livonian Knights were the successors of the mediaeval Knights of the Sword, who at the beginning of the thirteenth century had christianized these remote areas at the sword's point. In

[1] It was significant of the worsening state of Swedish-Danish relations that Gustav Vasa did not trouble to ask Kristian III for the aid which he was due to give under the treaty of Brömsebro.

1237 they had been merged with the more powerful Teutonic Order of Prussia; but they had always retained a measure of autonomy, and in 1513 an enterprising Grand Master had managed to purchase their complete independence for cash. It therefore happened that when the Teutonic Order was secularized by Albert of Hohenzollern in 1525 the Livonian Knights were unaffected by that transaction: they continued in being, retained their mediaeval organization, and remained in an alien world much what they had been in the days of the crusades, with a Grand Master in Livonia, a German Master to look after their property in Germany, a military-religious constitution, and a system of recruitment which drew new blood only from Germany. It would have been better, perhaps, if they had been secularized; for the spirit had gone out of them, recruits came but sparingly, and militarily they were no longer efficient. But the chance was missed; and the Recess of Wolmar (1546) expressly forbade secularization in the future. The Order was weakened by a general decline in morals and morale among its members, by internal dissensions, by its frequent struggles with the archbishop of Riga, by the conflict between a pro-Polish and an anti-Polish faction within it. In 1556 and 1557 these disharmonies led to a civil war, which ended in the victory of the friends of Poland and was terminated by a peace-settlement—the treaty of Poswol—which came near to making the Order Poland's client.

The treaty of Poswol came at a moment when the Order was on the point of being attacked by Ivan IV; and may possibly have done something to make that attack certain. But Ivan had for some time been meditating war, as soon as his Finnish campaign should be off his hands. He had his legitimate commercial grievances against the Livonian towns, and he could also justifiably complain that they had been enforcing against him a virtual blockade not only of arms and materials of war but also of experts and technicians. He had old pretensions to Livonia (which he was in the habit of referring to as his 'patrimony'); and he had specific claims to tribute from the see of Dorpat, for which the Order in an evil hour had agreed to make itself responsible, but which it now refused to pay, alleging that Ivan's demands were exorbitant. On grounds such as these he declared war; and in 1558 he won great successes: in May he took Narva; in July, Dorpat. The capture of Narva was an event of European importance. For the first time the Russians had command of a practicable port; and the Wendish towns, the Dutch, the English—all those traders who had been galled by the economic barrier interposed by the Livonian towns—hastened to Narva to trade directly with the Muscovites, unhampered by vexatious middlemen. It was a major commercial revolution. In Russia, the price of imports from the west fell sensationally; in Reval, the burghers believed themselves to be facing ruin. In an effort to avert it they set privateers to prey upon the merchants who resorted to Narva. The new route to Muscovy was scarcely opened before it was threatened with blockade.

This situation gave Gustav Vasa a chance to renew his attempt to obtain a foothold in the trade to Muscovy. His plan now was to establish Viborg as the staple: unlike the infant Helsingfors Viborg was a well-established fortified city, and in the 1490s it had for a time held an important place in Russian commerce. But the experiment proved no more successful than its predecessor, though for different reasons. Russian and Hanseatic merchants were, indeed, very willing to come to Viborg at a time when access to Narva was subject to interference; but they did not allow much of the trade to pass into Swedish hands. The king found to his chagrin that the Swedish mercantile community in Viborg was too short of capital to be able to function successfully as middlemen: commerce continued to be controlled by the Germans, guest traded with guest, and Viborg was a staple only in name. As he characteristically remarked, 'The Germans leave us nothing but their garbage, to manure our gardens with'.[1] Nevertheless, it might seem that if trade were encouraged to pass through Viborg it might still be possible for the Swedish crown to draw a useful revenue from customs and transit-dues—provided they were not made so heavy as to frighten merchants away. The king's servants on the spot saw clearly that the rates must be kept low; but their views made no impression on their royal master. Gustav Vasa insisted that the rates should be high. It was an expensive business, he explained, to keep the fortifications of Viborg in good order and provide the facilities which the traders expected. Unless he could show a profit on the venture he was not interested in maintaining the staple: the Germans were welcome to move to Narva, for all he cared. Those who tried to persuade him to change his mind were told that they must have got Russian soap in their eyes.[2] This typically pennywise attitude ensured the failure of the enterprise: both Ivan and his customers speedily lost interest in Viborg. In any case, it was no longer the only alternative to the Livonian ports. Richard Chancellor's opening of the White Sea route to Russia in 1553—a route which avoided both the Sound Dues and the Livonian middlemen—was already threatening a radical change in the commercial politics of the Baltic. Gustav Vasa was well aware of this: in 1557 the embassy he sent to England was charged to appeal to Queen Mary to forbid her subjects to sail to St Nicholas.

It is against this background that must be set the attempt of Prince Erik to obtain the hand of Elizabeth of England. It was in the mid-

[1] *Gustav Vasas registratur*, XXIX, 261. [2] *Ibid.* 263.

1550s that the question of Erik's marriage first began to be seriously considered. As acknowledged hereditary prince Erik could reasonably expect to make a better match than his father, and from time to time projects were started for marriage negotiations with Poland, or Hesse, or electoral Saxony. After the return of the mission to England in 1557, however, the idea gained ground that Erik should propose himself for Elizabeth. The speculation was no doubt very much of a gamble: if all went well—if Elizabeth succeeded Mary on the throne without too long a delay—it might prove a brilliant *coup*; if things should turn out ill—if Mary should live, and Elizabeth fall into disfavour—Erik might find himself wedded to an ill-dowered bastard. Nevertheless, the plan captured Erik's imagination. His tutor, Dionysius Beurreus, was sent to England in November 1557 to ask for Elizabeth's hand; and though his tactlessness in presenting himself first to her rather than to the queen angered Mary and caused her to reject the proposal, Beurreus remained in England for the next three years as *legatus perpetuus*. Gustav Vasa was on the whole sceptical about the English match; but the peaceful accession of Elizabeth for a moment encouraged him to think that there might be something in it: it must now surely be a point in Erik's favour that he had sought the new queen's hand at a time when her political future was highly uncertain. Two Swedish embassies accordingly left for England in 1559: the second of them was particularly illustrious, for it was led by Erik's younger brother, Prince Johan, and Johan's maternal uncle Sten Eriksson Leijonhufvud. Johan made an excellent impression in London; and though in April 1560 Elizabeth declined Erik's offer on the ground that she had no intention of marrying, nobody took this very seriously. Erik remained in popular estimation very much in the front rank of possible candidates, being especially favoured by those who wished to avoid a Habsburg or a Habsburg partisan. Gustav Vasa, nevertheless, stuck to his conviction that nothing was to be hoped for from Elizabeth. He was sure that Erik and Johan were reading more into her ambiguous answers than they would bear. He had also justifiable anxieties about the consequences for Sweden of a future union of the crowns. But the enthusiasm of Johan, when he returned from his mission in the spring of 1560, was difficult to resist: he was the old king's favourite son, and to him he yielded as he would never have yielded to Erik. Johan had his own motives for pressing on the match,[1] and perhaps he allowed himself to believe what he wished to believe. At all events, his importunity was successful: Gustav Vasa, much against his better judgment, and with many grumbles at the heavy outlay involved, at last gave his consent to Erik's going to England.

[1] See below, p. 166.

The *riksdag* which met in June 1560 gave its approval to his departure; and the king informed the Estates that the marriage was as good as made.

Among the arguments which Beurreus had urged in support of Erik's suit were some of a commercial nature. At the close of the long Latin oration in which he laid the proposal before the English council (3 April 1560) came a short passage in which he alluded to the ease and convenience of the trade to Muscovy by way of Sweden and Finland, and observed that as long as war was raging in Livonia Baltic merchants could have no trade with the Muscovites without the permission of the king of Sweden.[1] It has been suggested that behind these arguments lay a bold and imaginative design for an Anglo-Swedish monopoly of the trade between Russia and the West: the old sea-route to the Livonian ports, burdened as it was with the Danish Sound dues, was to be superseded by direct access to the Russian vendors by way of Älvsborg and Viborg. The author of the project, it is contended, was Prince Erik himself, who was concerned to exploit the economic advantages of Sweden's geographical position more vigorously and more intelligently than Gustav Vasa seemed willing to do. It is certainly true that Erik had a quickness of apprehension and a breadth of view which were in sharp contrast to the cautious and pedestrian temper of his father. But it is difficult to treat Beurreus' remarks as being the expression of a considered and practical programme. Beurreus' business was to make a Swedish marriage palatable to the English Council. He made the most of the fact that Erik had been Elizabeth's suitor at a time when a marriage with her would have brought no financial or political advantage. He expounded Gustav Vasa's descent from the mediaeval kings of Sweden with anxious particularity: the details no doubt meant nothing to his audience, but it was important to scotch the gibe that Gustav Vasa was 'a clown who had stolen his throne from the crown of Denmark'.[2] He expatiated hardily upon the size, populousness and vast wealth of the Swedish realm. There was an obligatory passage on the peculiar excellences, moral and physical, of

[1] The relevant sentences run: 'Est trajectus ex Svecia in Finlandiam valde brevis ac inde ad interiora Muscoviae non difficilis. Deinde habet etiam Sveciae rex illustrissimus urbes et portus Muscoviae conterminos, in quibus omnis generis merces, quae apud Muscovitas venales habentur, facile reperiuntur. Huc accedit, quod quamdiu bello cum Muscovitis Livonienses impliciti sunt, nullum cum illis commercium habere possint, qui ad mare Balticum habitant, nisi serenissimi regis Sveciae consensu interveniente. Postremo ex Svecia in Angliam tam brevis et compendiosa est navigatio, ut trium dierum spacio, ubi ventus spirat secundus, idque quocumque anni tempore absolvi queat eaque etiam ita libera, a nemine ut impediri possit. Ac proinde et naves et militem instructum tanta copia florentissima duo haec regna sibi mutuo suppeditare possunt, cum opus sit, suis inimicis et hostibus ut terrori maximo futuri sint': *Gustav Vasas registratur*, XXIX, 850.

[2] Quoted in Ingvar Andersson, *Erik XIV:s engelska underhandlingar* (Lund, 1935), p. 29, n. 70.

Erik and Elizabeth, and their eminent suitability for each other. The advantages which the marriage might bring to the common cause of Protestantism were not forgotten. There was even an allusion to the linguistic affinities of the English and Swedish tongues. It was only after these topics had been disposed of that he turned to commercial matters. He could hardly have omitted them altogether: as Gustav Vasa frequently observed, the English were mainly interested in Erik for what they could get out of him. At a time when Reval's privateers were making the Baltic dangerous for English seamen, any suggestion for a safe route to Russia might be expected to make a more immediate appeal than arguments grounded upon Erik's disinterested devotion, or even upon comparative philology. The few sentences on trade, in fact, give the impression of being a tub for a whale; or a final spadeful of argument thrown in to give some body to an otherwise rather tenuous performance. They do not at all read like a precisely formulated proposal. It is certainly true that in October 1559 the Danish agent in London—suspecting the worst, as Danish agents were prone to do—reported a rumour that Sweden designed to secure a monopoly of the trade to Russia by the Gulf of Finland. But it seems scarcely warrantable to read into Beurreus' oration any idea which went much further than the encouragement of English traders to come to Älvsborg. This idea was not new, nor was it peculiar to Erik: in the summer of 1558, under the impression produced by the news of the attempt to blockade Narva, Gustav Vasa himself had declared his intention of making Älvsborg a staple for the Muscovy trade. Erik's parting speech to the *riksdag* in June 1560 would appear to have gone no further than this.[1] And indeed, the practical difficulties in the way of any plan of monopoly were formidable; though that, it may be admitted, would not necessarily have weighed very heavily with a prince whose strength never lay in the judicious correlation of means and ends. The bulky goods—timber, pelts, flax, hemp, wax, grain—which formed the staple of Muscovy's exports were as unsuited as possible for the lengthy overland route through Finland and Sweden: it was precisely because of this kind of difficulty that the Dutch *ommegangers* had been able to steal so much of Lübeck's trade across the Kiel isthmus. Älvsborg itself had such bad land-communications with Stockholm that Gustav Vasa recognized that a programme of road-building would be necessary, if it were to have any chance as an *entrepôt*. After Gustav Vasa was dead, in October 1561, Erik announced his intention to construct a canal across Sweden, to link Älvsborg with the east coast—an idea put forward long ago by Bishop Brask—and so open up a direct water-

[1] We know his speech only by much later report: Sven Elofsson, *Paralipomena* (*Handlingar rörande Skandinaviens historia*, XII), p. 116.

route between Viborg and western Europe. It is difficult to decide how far this was a serious proposal; but it has at least been suggested that Erik's main purpose in making it was to reassure the burghers of Reval, who had in the meantime put themselves under Swedish protection,[1] and who were afraid that Denmark might stop their commerce at the Sound. As to Beurreus' claim that the trade to Livonia was at Sweden's mercy, this was no doubt meant to impress the English; a brag put on for the occasion. Later experience was to show that though Sweden could indeed cause much inconvenience and annoyance by interfering with merchantmen, she could never cut them off from Russia entirely. There were too many alternative channels through which trade could run, some of them obviously superior to the Älvsborg-Viborg route (even assuming a canal), for the idea of monopoly to be anything more than a delusion, at least for the present; and it is hard to believe that Erik did not perceive this. And, after all, any such scheme ignored a fundamental fact of contemporary Baltic politics: the determination of Ivan IV to burst out of the ring of middlemen and sell his country's wares direct to the western buyer. There was no real reason to suppose that he would submit to exploitation by the Anglo-Swedes, any more than to exploitation by the Balts.

Meanwhile, the crisis in Livonia had been deepening, and was now becoming a matter of concern to all the Baltic and north German powers. The Livonian Knights, demoralized by ease and hamstrung by petty quarrels, made but a feeble resistance to the Russian onslaught. In August 1559 the Grand Master, acting for once in concert with the archbishop of Riga, concluded with Poland the treaty of Vilna, whereby the Order ceded to Poland about one-seventh of its territory, admitted Polish garrisons into a number of important castles, and agreed to share with Poland any conquests that might be made from the Russians. A few months later a new Grand Master, Gotthard Kettler, persuaded the Knights to take the final step and agree that the Order might be secularized, if that should prove necessary. Meanwhile the defence of Livonia was paralysed by the selfish scheming of its leaders, by a general tendency in the population to welcome the Russians, and by a feckless optimism and culpable carelessness which led the Order to neglect military preparations in the expectation that some form of assistance from the outside would in the end turn up, if only they appealed loudly enough to the right quarters. In the search for deliverers much energy was expended which would have been better employed in self-help, and the results of these exertions were anything but encouraging. All the neighbouring sovereigns agreed in wanting to prevent a Russian conquest in Livonia, but none was

[1] See below, p. 202.

anxious to undertake the task of stopping it, for none was willing to quarrel with the tsar. Sigismund II Augustus of Poland had a truce with Ivan which was not due to expire until 1562, and no wish to anticipate its ending. His concern was mostly limited to the Düna valley, which was a vital artery for the growing export of Lithuanian corn. He was certainly not displeased to see the old trading monopoly of the Livonian ports breached by the opening of the route to Narva; but at this stage his only interest in Estonia was to take care that it did not fall into the hands of any foreign power. The disintegration of the Order offered an opportunity, too good for any king of Poland to neglect, to extend the limits of his realm: hence the treaties of Poswol and Vilna. But for the present he wanted to take over the rights and territories of the Order without assuming their responsibilities or committing himself to their quarrels. His troops sat tight in the Order's fortresses, and took care to avoid a collision with Ivan's invading armies: as far as assistance in battle or protection of the open country went, they might just as well have stayed in Poland.

Thus there was not much to be hoped from Poland, at least in the immediate future. From Germany, still less; though urgent appeals were made to German patriotism. Ferdinand I was fully alive to his duty to give aid and comfort to this distant bastion of German civilization, but his sense of responsibility was not shared by the imperial Diet. As with the defence of Europe against the Turk, they were content to leave the task to the Emperor, deny him the means to carry it out, and gird at him when he failed. The Diet voted money in 1559, but jibbed at raising it: it sent to Ivan a mediatory mission which he treated with contempt. A year later, in 1560, another Diet voted both arms and subsidies; but before their good faith could be put to the test Livonian resistance had collapsed beyond hope of recovery.

Another possible source of assistance was Denmark. In the thirteenth and early fourteenth centuries the kings of Denmark had played a great part in the history of Estonia, and though thereafter their possessions had mostly been abandoned, they still held the fief of Gute Kolck, and in the closing decades of the fifteenth century had shown a strong revival of interest in this region. Historic tradition therefore made it not unnatural for the Livonians to look to Copenhagen in their hour of need: as early as 1555 the Knights sent an appeal to Kristian III for aid. There was an active pro-Danish faction in Reval, for the privateering of the burghers had not succeeded in stopping the Narva trade, and it seemed to many of them that the best hope now was to give themselves to the power which could cut off that trade by stopping it at the Sound. In July 1558, by a sudden *coup*, Danish partisans got possession of Reval castle, and hung on to it until they were dislodged by troops of the Order in the following December. It happened, moreover, that the feoffee of Gute Kolck, Christopher von Mönnichhausen, had a brother who was bishop of Ösel and Kurland; and the bishop, seeing little prospect of his property's being secure from the Russians, was anxious to sell it while it was still saleable. In 1558, accordingly, Mönnichhausen offered on the bishop's behalf to put the two sees into Danish hands for a reasonable consideration. But Kristian III was cautious: he had no ambitions in Livonia, and no desire to fall out with Ivan IV. He temporized with Mönnichhausen; and when the Grand Master approached him for assistance, demanded terms so steep that they could not be accepted. The furthest he was prepared to go in the way of practical help was to send an embassy to Moscow; and to it Ivan, with his armies already within sight of Riga, naturally paid no attention. The accession of Fredrik II, however, brought a change; for though Fredrik was almost as uninterested in the prospect of Livonian adventures as his predecessor, he had a troublesome younger brother, Magnus, whom he was very willing to shift from his inheritance in Holstein if an acceptable alternative could be found for him. Mönnichhausen's offer of Ösel and Kurland seemed just what was required. In 1559, therefore, Fredrik accepted it on Magnus's behalf; and in the spring of 1560 Magnus landed on Ösel, to begin his long and unhappy involvement in Livonian affairs. At first his prospects seemed good: within a few weeks the bishop of Reval likewise resigned his see into Magnus' hands; the Order's commander on Ösel handed over to him the important fortress of Sonnenburg; and Magnus was able to embark on a rash campaign to extend his dominions to the mainland of Harrien and Wierland. There was even another attempt to surprise the castle at Reval, which only the last-minute intervention of Gotthard Kettler succeeded in defeating. Meanwhile from the military point of view the affairs of Livonia went from bad to worse. The annihilating defeat of Ermes (2 August 1560) really extinguished the military power of the Order; the Russians roamed unhindered over the countryside; by September they were in the Wieck; and Magnus soon found himself a fugitive on his island of Ösel.

Sweden was inevitably concerned in these happenings. Reval had certainly been Viborg's competitor for the Russia trade; but Narva was a challenge to both. It would be dangerous to allow the Danes to get a firm footing in Livonia: from Reval they would be in a position to strike at Viborg and Finland. With southern Finland Reval had close ties: perhaps between a fifth and a quarter of her population were Swedish subjects. For several years now Gustav Vasa had been putting forward claims to interfere on their behalf in the town's internal affairs. In 1556 he actually did intervene to protect the Swedish-speaking peasants of the island of Rågö, off the Livonian coast, advancing the dubious claim that the king of Sweden was its immediate overlord. He had also shadowy pretensions upon Ösel, though as he ingenuously confessed he would have been puzzled to define them, since the documentary evidence was now lost. Hitherto he had held aloof from the civil strife that convulsed Livonia; though his agents kept him well informed of the course of events, warned him of the feebleness and fecklessness of the Order, and from time to time urged him to stake a claim in Estonia while he could. But Gustav Vasa was not to be tempted. He observed the agony of the Order with grim indifference; for he remembered that in 1554 the Grand Master had incited him to make war on Russia, had promised him assistance, and then had left him in the lurch. The boot was now on the other leg, and the Order might shift for itself. His policy was to keep out of the trouble if he could, for he believed Sweden to be in danger of attack—from Denmark, from Lübeck, from the Emperor, perhaps—and he knew her to be politically isolated. He did not much like the expansion of the Muscovite power in Estonia; but he was quite determined that there should be no renewal of his quarrel with the tsar if he could help it. Refugees from Estonia were made welcome in Finland; but for the rest he exerted himself to show that he was a good neighbour. He shared Russian indignation at the depredations of Reval's privateers, took care to punish them when he caught them, and did not fail to inform Ivan that he had done so. To suggestions of intervention in Livonia he steadily replied that however desirable it would be terribly expensive; that it was too risky; and that he would in any case do nothing without being sure of the attitude of the tsar. In February 1559, at the request of Ferdinand I, he wrote to Ivan offering his mediation; and though nothing came of this, it is evidence that the Emperor believed that the king of Sweden was not ill-regarded in Moscow.

Meanwhile the leaders of Teutonic resistance in Livonia were in urgent need of funds, and quite ready to pawn a few castles in exchange for financial assistance. Both the Grand Master and the archbishop of Riga approached Gustav Vasa with propositions of this kind. He did not find their terms attractive. But on Erik's suggestion he replied to the Grand Master's overture (in November 1559) by offering to advance money provided that Sonnenburg and Arensburg (two strongholds on the island of Ösel which did not fall within the episcopal lands of Duke Magnus) were put into his hands immediately, were hypothecated for at least twenty years, and were not to be redeemed before the expiry of that period: if he was to spend money maintaining castles, he must be assured of a reasonably lengthy tenancy. This was more than the Grand Master had bargained for, and the deal accordingly fell through.

If Gustav Vasa viewed the troubles of Livonia as an imbroglio to be avoided, his second son, Prince Johan, saw them rather as an opportunity to be exploited. Since 1556 Johan had been duke of Finland, and as he looked, from comparatively short range, at the growing chaos on the other side of the water, he came to think that there might be a chance for him to carve out a principality for himself from the wreckage. He had his eye on Sonnenburg; his agents were reconnoitring the ground in Reval; he was willing to consider a loan to the Grand Master on easier terms than his father. Gustav Vasa, informed of his proceedings, was angered by his presumption in venturing to engage in a private foreign policy, and impatient at his deplorable political and financial levity: his notions were 'childish'; he would burn his fingers; his money would be as good as thrown into the sea. Johan's projects were firmly vetoed; he was sharply reminded to write to his father at least once a week, and to spend less time imbibing impracticable ideas from the reading of works of historical scholarship. This, however, was not the end of the affair. For by the close of 1559 Johan had secured a secret ally in the person of his brother Erik, who was much in need of his assistance in the matter of his courtship of Queen Elizabeth. The brothers accordingly reached an agreement whereby Johan engaged to do his best for Erik in England, and use his influence with his father; while Erik undertook to forward Johan's ambitions in Livonia. And early in 1560 Erik, after laborious efforts, at last persuaded Gustav Vasa to permit a negotiation to be opened for the pawning of Sonnenburg and Padis to Johan, in return for a loan of 200,000 *daler*: Johan was in no position to raise the money, but it was hoped that once the castles were in his possession the king could be induced to find the balance of the sum. Fortunately for Gustav Vasa's peace of mind the Grand Master was no longer interested. The Order was throwing in its lot with Poland; Johan had missed his opportunity. It would not recur in Gustav Vasa's lifetime. For the old king was suspicious and resentful of his sons' attempts to stampede him into action; he was out of sympathy with their youthful impetuosity; he was wounded by what he considered to be their unfilial treatment. And he had probably a juster appreciation than they of how grave the consequences of intervention might be. In the last months of his life he did indeed move gradually towards a conviction that intervention might after all be unavoidable. But he did so not with any view of territorial expansion, nor with the idea of barring Russia's access to the sea; and least of all because he saw intervention as an element in some grand commercial plan. It was the increasingly tense relations with Denmark, especially after the accession of Fredrik II, that led him to take fright at the prospect of Livonia's passing under Danish control, and forced him to contemplate action to forestall that danger. When he laid the question before his last *riksdag*, in June 1560, his main concern was to bar the back-door to Finland. For him, as for the Estates, intervention, if it must come, would be essentially defensive.

In August 1560 came a development which brought matters to a head. For in that month Reval, in desperation at the loss of trade to Narva, disillusioned alike with Poles and Danes, and alarmed for her independence, sent an embassy to Gustav Vasa charged to enquire the terms upon which he would be prepared to give his assistance. When it arrived in Sweden the king was on his death-bed, and a decision was necessarily postponed until the next reign. But there could be little doubt what it would be. Gustav Vasa, if he had lived, would probably have responded to Reval's appeal. Erik was not the man to reject it. And Johan was rash enough to give the ambassadors, in Erik's absence, a private assurance of his personal protection. As the old king lay dying, Sweden reached one of the great turning-points of her history; for from the intervention in Livonia would spring all that train of events which was to lead, with a persuasive appearance of inevitability, to the foundation, expansion and ultimate collapse of the Swedish empire of the Baltic.

IX. THE ACHIEVEMENT OF GUSTAV VASA

In the church, as in the state, the fall of Pyhy in 1543 was followed by the shelving of some of the innovations which the Germans had introduced. George Norman's commission as *superattendent* expired in 1544: it was not renewed. The new organization of Seniors and *conservators*, which had in any case never established itself in north and central Sweden, was suffered to expire even in the south. Yet in ecclesiastical matters, as in lay, the period did not vanish altogether without trace. The royal supremacy in things spiritual had since 1540 acquired a strength and consistency which matched the establishment of the hereditary succession. Norman remained as influential without the title of *superattendent* as he had been with it; and for the remainder of his life he acted in effect as minister for church affairs, with an influence that was everywhere perceptible, and an authority which threw that of the archbishop into the shade. Had Laurentius Petri been a man of less equable temper they could hardly have avoided a quarrel: as it was, the archbishop suffered his eclipse meekly, and kept on friendly terms with the great man—much as Cranmer had contrived to keep the peace with Cromwell. The other bishops were little disposed to make difficulties. In 1544 the deprivation of the bishops of Skara and Linköping removed the last members of the bench about whose reliability there could be any doubt: henceforward the whole episcopate was avowedly Protestant. In the place of the deposed the king appointed, not bishops, but 'ordinaries and superintendents'; and though the old bishops retained their titles (except for Laurentius Petri, who was degraded from archbishop to bishop), all new appointments for the remainder of the reign were superintendents. This policy was carried a step further in 1557, when (without consulting the bishops) the king ordered the subdivision of dioceses, on the not unreasonable ground that the dioceses were too big for adequate supervision; so that Laurentius Petri, for instance, found himself provided with two superintendents (one for Stockholm, one for Gävle) who took over the administration of substantial portions of the diocese of Uppsala. The distinction between bishop and superintendent was important, for superintendents were at first no more than vicars entrusted by the king with administrative and disciplinary authority. Whereas bishops, as the king remarked, had a tendency 'to assume great authority, dignity and power, and by so doing have brought low mighty nations, realms and principalities', the superintendents would be no more than the instruments of royal control, conducting visitations in obedience to the king's commands. Though they were expressly endowed with all the spiritual authority of a bishop, and not least with authority to ordain, they were not consecrated; and their proliferation consequently represented a real threat to the Apostolic Succession. There are signs that the parochial clergy were at first not too amenable to their control. Nevertheless, the change was certainly designed by the king to weaken the only authority in the church which might conceivably challenge his own; and if he had lived for another decade it might well have been successful. As it was, for the last fifteen years of the reign there seemed to be no very obvious limit to the royal supremacy apart from the king's own conscience, and possibly the discreet counsel of George Norman. Already in 1537 Gustav Vasa had taken it upon himself to grant a divorce, and given leave to contract a second marriage, on the ground of the persistent unfaithfulness of one of the parties; already in 1540 he had dissolved a marriage on the ground of insanity. Seven years later he did not hesitate to pronounce upon a question of legitimacy. In 1556 he arbitrarily reinstated a parson who had been convicted of rape and properly deprived by the ecclesiastical courts. At his order parishes were united for reasons of alleged convenience; churches were pulled down and the bricks sold by his bailiffs, or were by the royal command converted to secular uses: that at Vadstena was devoted to the storing of grain, while the aisles of the Great Church in Stockholm were utilized for the stock-piling of salt. And if we hear nothing of the conversion of ecclesiastical buildings to industrial purposes, we may perhaps attribute it rather to the inability of contemporary Sweden to produce a William Stumpe, than to any superior piety or sensibility on the part of the monarch.

No doubt it is true that Lutheran political theory placed great power and responsibility in the hand of the sovereign: as *praecipuum membrum ecclesiae*, as *custos utriusque tabulae*, his prerogative might be made to stretch very far. But hardly as far, perhaps, as Gustav Vasa stretched it. For the position he designed for himself, it seemed, was that of *summus episcopus*: the church was to be subject to, rather than coördinate with, the state. He would scarcely have acquiesced in Melanchthon's contention that it was the king's business to be *minister et executor ecclesiae*. His practice, in fact, was not in accordance with the best Lutheran thought; nor was it, as the event was to prove, to set the pattern of church–state relationships in Sweden. On the contrary, that pattern would eventually be recognizably Melanchthonian. It was one of the most important of the characteristics of the Swedish Reformation that the traditional organs of the church emerged from the break with Rome almost unimpaired; and this was true of no other Protestant country save England. The moral offences which had previously been justiciable under canon law became by the Ordinance of Västerås offences against the law of the land, since (as Laurentius Petri put it in 1533) 'the Sword —that is, all external punishment—pertains to the king, and not to the bishop'; and the fines which the church courts had previously imposed now went into the king's pocket. But it was still the bishop and his chapter that dealt with them, if only because Swedish law had not as yet framed a code to cover them, and it was convenient (and cheap) to use the old experts in these matters. In 1554 Gustav Vasa made a first attempt to legislate in this field by the issue of a statute on breaches of the peace in churches and churchyards; but a real effort to provide a secular code for moral offences would not be made until the reign of Karl IX, and even then would be unsuccessful.[1] And just as the church-courts survived, so too did diocesan synods and church-councils. The Swedish Reformation lacks any enactment destroying the legislative independence of the church: there was nothing to correspond to the *Supplication against Ordinaries* and the *Submission of the Clergy*. It was the church itself, from 1536 onwards, which undertook the definition of doctrine, in so far as it was defined at all. The episcopate successfully weathered the storm of Gustav Vasa's animosity; the church was occasionally allowed to participate in the choice of a bishop; secular interference, even in this reign, never crystallized into the cynical pretence of the *congé d'élire*. The chapters somehow escaped extinction; archdeacons and rural deans did not, after all, disappear; parochial

[1] See below, p. 438.

self-government maintained a sturdy life. It was no rootless organization with which future kings of Sweden would have to deal; and in the church's conservatism, in the strength it drew from tradition, lay at least one reason for its success in averting a total subjection to the lay power. The danger of such a subjection was certainly never greater than towards the close of Gustav Vasa's reign; and the church had good reason to be grateful to Laurentius Petri for the skill with which he conducted a delicate rearguard action. A decade after the king's death it would fall to him to place state–church relations upon a better footing.

In the meantime it was one of the disadvantages of Gustav Vasa's jealousy of the hierarchy that it inhibited any clear definition of ecclesiastical law, any revised scheme of church discipline, and any satisfactory provision for education. After 1544 one of the church's most urgent needs was a comprehensive Church Ordinance which would deal with these matters: Denmark, for instance, had had a Church Ordinance since 1539. George Norman had pointed the way with his draft of 1542; but no action had been taken upon it. In 1547 the *råd* had scrutinized and approved a revised draft, and strongly urged its promulgation. In the following year a resolution of the *råd* deplored the slackness of the bishops, the inadequacy of the clergy, the lack of uniformity in liturgical use, the indiscipline of the church as a whole, and the decay of schools. As concerned the schools, at all events, the king was well aware of the gravity of the problem. He was not sparing of orders designed to protect their incomes from the rapacity of his subjects: schoolmasters, as he sapiently observed, being no more able to live on air than the rest of mankind. He was lavish of exhortation to send children to school; and in 1559 went so far as to issue letters of protection to the young gentlemen of Åbo, who found themselves exposed to the rude affronts of the rabble while on the way to their lessons. The state of education was indeed of direct concern to him, for he looked to the schools to provide him with recruits to help him to govern the country. The results were perennially disappointing; and he complained on one occasion that the headmasters seemed to select the most unpromising boys for the civil service: '. . . we find that the persons who are sent to help us in the aforesaid high offices are almost less serviceable for such high concerns than if we should have taken such a one as might serve for pearl-embroidery, or become a goodly weaver of gold cloth; for . . . the schoolmasters, who ought to assist us in this matter, choose out the foulest of the whole crowd, namely such as are naught but drunkards and ale-hounds, debauched and beastly tosspots, who would better serve behind the plough or a tree stump than in the high and weighty affairs of the realm. But how possible and tolerable it is for us to rule and manage the realm's urgent affairs with such useless and contemptible persons, who have neither honour nor honesty nor intelligence, that we remit to your and every upright and reasonable man's consideration.'[1] The domestic supply being so poor, the king was forced to continue the practice of sending boys to be educated abroad at the expense of their dioceses, on the understanding that they should keep the home government supplied with news from the continent, and return to lend the king a hand when their education was complete. But these efforts, like the king's lamentations, were beside the point. Schools were decaying, the scholastic profession was coming into contempt (as Gustav Vasa himself remarked in 1540) because the schools were not receiving revenues for their support, and the schoolmasters were not being paid their tithe. It does not seem to have occurred to the king that his own example might have been instrumental in producing this deplorable state of affairs; nor that an effective Church Ordinance might do much to improve it.

But Gustav Vasa was not prepared to sanction any Church Ordinance. Like Henry VIII, in circumstances not dissimilar, he was reluctant to tie his hands. An ordinance would abridge the limits of his discretion; and if Laurentius Petri had a principal hand in it might probably contain unpalatable matter too. The bishops were therefore forced to do the best they could with partial and local regulations: a synod at Stockholm in 1551, for instance, laid down rules about preaching, baptism, public confession, and church discipline; and in the following year the so-called Articles of Vadstena added provisions about liturgical uses. But this was only to tinker with the problem, as the archbishop well knew; and a really satisfactory solution had to wait until the appearance of his Church Ordinance of 1571.

If the royal supremacy as practised by Gustav Vasa had serious disadvantages for the church, at least it claimed no victims. No head fell on the block for denying or impugning the king's authority over the church; no heretic went to the stake for adherence to unauthorized doctrines; no attempt was made to invoke the law of treason to enforce ecclesiastical policy; not a single abbot was hanged. The Swedish Reformation—gradual, pragmatic, easy-going—was notably gentle and humane; perhaps because it was unusually lacking in religious rancours or sectarian passion. There is surprisingly little invective against the papacy in Gustav Vasa's letters: he writes, indeed, of 'papists' errors', or of 'papistical practices'; but the Beast of the Apocalypse and the Whore of Babylon are not among his rhetorical stereotypes. Swedish bishops were never compelled formally to renounce the Holy See; the

[1] Letter to the ordinary of Örebro, 16 August 1559: *Gustav Vasas registratur*, XXIX, 255–6.

king contrived to avoid excommunication; the breach with Rome was never, in this reign, made definitive. The Reformation had come upon the country as a thing imposed from above; there was not any of that background of popular indignation at ecclesiastical abuses that existed in England: Swedish history could show no parallel to the case of Richard Hunne. No one seems to have felt deeply about mortuary fees, or sanctuary, or pluralism. At no time could the king stand back, as Henry VIII was for a moment able to do, and let the tide of popular feeling do his work for him. Nor was there any analogue to *praemunire*, to catch the clergy and bludgeon them into submission. But indeed, the resistance of the church to the king's proceedings had been a good deal feebler than in England: it lacked the traditions, the organization and the theological talents of the Convocation of Canterbury. The stalwarts of resistance, clerical and lay, had too often withdrawn beyond the frontiers (though Peder Galle, for one, remained); and they had never been numerous or effective. On the other hand the reformers in Sweden never seem to have been organized, as was the case in Denmark, as a compact and effective pressure-group. Sweden was never troubled by zealous and impatient souls who desired 'a Reformation without tarrying for any'; and nobody—at least after the expulsion of Melkior Hoffmann—seems to have dreamed of a priesthood of all believers: it was not under banners such as these that the opposition to royal supremacy would develop. No one in Sweden, now or later, seems to have boggled at paying tithe, whether to king or incumbent; the only real enemy of the episcopate was the sovereign himself; the attack on monastic property failed to stimulate anybody to question property-rights in general. Sweden was a country in which there was very little clerical absenteeism;[1] and this circumstance, together with Gustav Vasa's vigorous efforts to secure a godly preaching ministry, helped to prevent the emergence of any form of sectarian voluntaryism: it was perhaps among the most important of the king's services to the church. Gustav Vasa's Reformation was all his own, in the sense that he controlled its beginning, determined its pace, decided its nature. It progressed, on the one hand, by way of his acceptance and endorsement of successive theological positions adopted by a very small number of active reformers—Olaus Petri, Lars Andreae,

[1] It is true that in 1546 the bishops complained of the difficulties of parsons who had to serve several churches, now that they were bound to preach in each as well as to say mass. It may have been this situation which led to the increase in *komministrar* (perpetual curates); but it is in any case surprising to find a complaint which implies a shortage of pastors, for the bishops were at the same time troubled about how former holders of prebends could find a livelihood, and there must have been many ex-monks who turned to parochial work. In the last two decades before 1611 there were forceful complaints of an *excess* of priests, and a wish to limit the number of ordinations. And certainly absenteeism and pluralism never seem to have become a scandal or a grievance.

George Norman, Laurentius Petri; and on the other by way of steps taken by the king in response to his political fears or financial necessities. The part played by other agencies was small: only once—at Uppsala in 1536—did a church council give a strong positive lead. If at Västerås in 1527 the *riksdag* and *råd* seem to us now to have thrown the reins on the king's back, they certainly had not meant anything of the sort. It is one of the striking differences between the Swedish and the English Reformations that in Sweden the movement towards reform proceeds, for long stretches of time, without the participation or consent of the nation as expressed by its representatives. Between 1529 and 1544—in the years, that is, that decided the religious future of the country—there was no full meeting of the Estates. And when, after fifteen years, they gathered once again at Västerås, the terms in which they gave endorsement to the changes that had taken place seem to fall far short of the great issues involved: they record their approval of the prohibition of a number of liturgical practices (for instance, masses for the souls of the dead) which the reformers held to be superstitious; they abolish religious gilds; they enjoin church-going; and they proclaim that 'God's Word and the Holy Gospel shall be generally used'. And this, and no more than this, is the 'doctrine' from which they bind themselves never to deviate. There is no need to emphasize the contrast with the precise, copious and weighty legislation of the Reformation Parliament. No Act of Supremacy ever buttressed the position which Gustav Vasa seized for himself: the royal supremacy rested on proclamation only; a simple act of the royal will. No Act in restraint of Appeals set historians by the ears by proclaiming that Sweden was an empire. The whole structure of rights and claims which the king built upon the inadequate foundation of 1527 was never laid before the Estates for approval: the validity of those claims rested upon the king's mere assertion that they were accordant with the decisions of the Västerås *riksdag* of 1527, though it must have been sufficiently obvious that they were not so.[1] The despoiling of the parishes and the parochial clergy had no statutory basis at all. It is true that the *riksdag* cannot at this period be properly compared with parliament. Its constitutional rights were doubtful, its constitutional importance small and new, the ambit of its resolutions was straitly confined by its total lack of the initiative, and it meddled with religion only when it was invited to do so. Yet in so far as legal sanction of some sort was felt to be necessary, it was from the *riksdag*, and not from the *landsting*, that it was sought. As it had been thought expedient to secure

[1] As late as 1636 Bishop Rudbeckius confessed himself unable to decide whether the Recess of Västerås had abrogated the ecclesiastical sections of the Uppland Law or not: *Svenska riksrådets protokoll*, VI, 309.

its support at Västerås in 1527, so it was thought expedient to secure its endorsement at Västerås in 1544. What was not thought expedient was to give it any opportunity in the interim to form an opinion or express a view on the great principles of politics and theology to which the king was committing the nation.

The vagueness, the reluctance to define, the apparent indifference to implications, which are characteristic of the Swedish Reformation, are no doubt in part attributable to the king's own feelings. For Gustav Vasa the Reformation was primarily a question of the royal authority within the state. Secondly, of ensuring that the clergy properly discharged their duty of preaching: a valid point, since if congregations could not be brought to assume the homespun of elementary Christian conduct, there was little point in weaving the fine tissues of theological controversy. Thirdly, the king became convinced that much in the old religion was superstitious, and much of the administrative and liturgical top-hamper wasteful and inefficient; a conviction which accorded happily with the gaping holes in his pocket. Lastly, and much the least important, he had from time to time the notion that from the point of view of foreign policy it might be an advantage to be explicitly and recognizably Lutheran. But as to doctrine—that was a different matter. Gustav Vasa could never have emulated Henry VIII, and 'confounded them all with God's learning'. It is doubtful if he had any clear ideas upon Justification, still less on the nature of the Eucharist. This side of the affair was played down from the beginning: after the initial clashes between Olaus Petri and the conservatives there is a marked absence of real theological controversy, an absence which is only partly to be explained by the difficulty of printing and publishing. Communion in both kinds had been enjoined in Olaus Petri's *Swedish Mass* as early as 1531, and was well established by the end of the reign; but the sacramental question, at a time when the great debate between Luther and Zwingli was echoing through Germany, seems scarcely to have been a live issue. Sweden moved towards a Protestant position by way of directives on ritual and ceremonies, rather than through theological polemic. Presumably the Swedish church (as distinct from this or that individual reformer, whose views can be ascertained) was by the mid-forties committed to the Lutheran position. Presumably: but the Swedish church had not yet accepted the *Augustana*, and was not to do so for more than a quarter of a century after Gustav Vasa's death. It did, indeed, formally reject the *Interim*, and among the grounds of its condemnation was disquiet at the implications of the *Interim's* attitude to the Eucharist; but still it is true to say that the church, as a church, had no clear doctrinal position of its own—in sharp contrast to the church in Denmark, which since 1530 had taken its stand on the

Confessio Hafnica. But the very purpose of the Reformation, as Gustav Vasa saw it, was to secure the unity of the nation around the throne—that unity which over-mighty bishops and over-privileged clerks had been suffered too long to imperil. And since that was so, to what purpose encourage the return of disunion by plunging into the discussions of the theologues?

In these matters, then, it was the king's habit to proceed with moderation; an attitude which (though he probably did not know it) was certainly proper for a good Lutheran.[1] The priest who persisted in the usages of the old church probably had to fear nothing worse than deprivation, unless his contumacy should prove to have political implications; and in at least one instance a timely contrition secured a reinstatement. The Roman Catholic laity seem to have been under no other inconvenience than was involved in the denunciations of evangelical pastors, and the tart allocutions of their royal master. There was no attempt to constrain opinion. It is a long stretch from this lax and untidy policy to the state of affairs sanctioned by the first Act of Uniformity (1549), whereby a man might lose all his goods for speaking against the official liturgy, and be sentenced to life imprisonment for reiterated refusal to use the Prayer Book; or to that established by the second Act (1552), which rendered him liable to punishment for attending a service which did not conform to the prescribed pattern. In spite of George Norman's visitation, there was no really sustained effort to enforce uniformity. The Catholic clergy often survived, at least in the rural areas; and for some years to come there would be no lack of Catholic-minded congregations, and services not much differing from the old. The Latin mass was still not officially prohibited, except in cathedrals; in many places the old church music was still sung; and much of the old liturgy remained. Though prebends might now be assigned to the maintenance of civil servants or schoolmasters, the cathedral chapters obstinately refused to die; precentors and vicars-choral were still to be met with; in 1549 the exchequer was still ordering the customary payments to the choirboys of Uppsala; and Laurentius Petri himself was inclined alike by his respect for tradition and his taste for music to look more kindly on these old ways than George Norman was able to do. It was still worth somebody's trouble, in the Strängnäs of 1550, to transcribe the text and music of the old *horae canonicae*. The cathedrals and churches retained, to a considerable extent, their old liturgical books, and many of them would not be

[1] Art. 7 of the Confession of Augsburg runs: 'And it is not necessary that the same human ordinances, or those external acts of piety and religious customs which are ordained by man, shall everywhere prevail'; and art. 15 enjoins that those pious usages of past ages which can be retained without sin—as for instance certain Saint's days and festivals—shall be suffered to remain.

destroyed until perhaps as late as the 1590s. The great liturgical revival of the reign of Johan III would be possible because the old traditions had never really become extinct. Despite a few isolated instances, Sweden escaped any serious iconoclastic movement; and Gustav Vasa himself was less Puritan in this respect than might have been supposed: he was quite prepared to allow the peasants of Västergötland to buy from his bailiff a picture which had adorned the altar of St Olof's monastery in Skara; and when in 1552 he gave permission to the superintendent of Linköping to set up 'a splendid ornament' on the high altar of his cathedral, he ordered him to procure a skilled sculptor from Germany, who could be trusted to make a good job of it. Such centres of popular piety as holy wells and wayside shrines had lost little of their hold upon the pious: they survived, in many cases, till the next century. There was still a little life in the monastic establishments, despite the discouraging circumstances; and this was especially true of the nunneries, many of which were foundations for women of noble birth. At Vadstena and Skänninge, Vreta and Skokloster, life for a time continued much as usual, though these places were open adherents of the old ways, and their inmates stuffed their ears with wax when constrained for a moment to follow the new. When in 1545 the elderly wife of Axel Axelsson asked leave to enter Skokloster because (as she said) she was tired of the worry of running her own household, the king not only encouraged her but intimated to her husband that he would be expected to be generous in the division of his property between them. As late as 1558 the abbess of Skokloster was still at her post. And they were not always treated badly: the king did sometimes interfere to protect them against exploitation, and to see to it that their revenues in fish and butter, eggs and ale, were duly paid; and if he also licensed the marriage of nuns who might take the taste for it, there was no constraint.[1] One reason for this state of affairs, at least as regards Vadstena, was the patronage and protection of the king's second wife, Margareta Leijonhufvud, who until the day of her death in 1551 remained an undoubted Roman Catholic. Monks were more strictly dealt with; but their survival is testified to by the sharp measures taken against them in 1549, and the fate of some is indicated by a letter of 1551 in which the king gives leave for one of them to be employed as a tutor in a gentleman's household. As to what happened to the great majority, we are much less well informed than in the case of England. Some may have turned to farming or trading, some may

[1] On 9 Jan. 1550 the exchequer ordered the bailiff at Stegeborg castle to provide the nuns with 'half a *last* of herring, 1 *tunna* of fresh eel, 4 *tunnor* of cod, and if he cannot spare the cod he must bargain with the fishermen till he gets some, and one sack of malt': *Kammarrådet Nils Pedersson Bielkes konceptböcker*, pp. 169–70.

have continued to serve the church as parochial clergy; but no systematic study of the problem seems to have been made. What is certain is that neither the ordinary monks nor the heads of houses were solaced with the relatively generous pensions paid over to their English brothers in misfortune. But by the end of the reign there can have been very few of them left in Sweden, nor any conventual establishment for monks alone: only at Vadstena a handful hung on, as they would continue to do for another generation. But Vadstena, with another thirty years of life still before it, was in every way exceptional, and was soon destined to be the sole survivor of the old regulars in a new religious world.

By the end of the reign, then, despite the relative tolerance of the *régime*, Sweden was beginning to be effectively Protestant, and even self-consciously Lutheran. Thirty years of pressure, even though it were gentle, was not without its effect. Virtually the whole body of the beneficed clergy was by 1560 soundly evangelical. The publication in 1541 of the complete Bible in Swedish translation must have hastened the process; as also the revised edition of Olaus Petri's *Little Catechism*, which came out in 1544. The transition to Protestantism might seem gradual and slow, but at least it was not subject to the hazards and pitfalls created by a royal conscience; and this, no doubt, was one reason why Sweden reached a Protestant *terra firma* before England did. By the late fifties, moreover, the reformers were faced for the first time with the need to justify and defend (and hence, incidentally, to define) the faith which they professed. For Calvinism had made its appearance in Sweden. It came from France, with Dionysius Beurreus, tutor to Prince Erik; it came from the Netherlands, with Jan van Herboville, tutor to Prince Karl; it was reinforced from Emden, with which contacts were now lively. In 1558 these immigrants were permitted their own pastor; in 1559 Calvin himself thought it worth while to dedicate to Gustav Vasa his treatise on the Minor Prophets. The real battle here would not be joined until the next reign. But it was already impending; and it was a sign of the times that Laurentius Petri should in 1558 have published *A Little Instruction ... concerning the Eucharist*, for that book was the first Swedish anti-Calvinist polemic.

On the whole, then, Gustav Vasa left behind him a country which was in process of becoming Protestant, and a church which was decidedly so. But for this evolution Sweden paid a high price. The church and the clergy alike had been stripped terribly bare. Six and a half tons of church silver found their way to the royal vaults. Before 1539 the plate came mainly from the cathedrals, the monastic establishments, the religious gilds, and from 'superfluous' urban churches. Thereafter, as Dacke's countrymen complained, it was the turn of the parishes. Dacke's revolt was scarcely over before Gustav Vasa was touring the central provinces in search of ecclesiastical treasures; as late as 1558 the exchequer was issuing receipts for hauls of silver sent in by zealous bailiffs. And after the plate came the parochial lands and the incomes of the parochial clergy. Between 1545 and 1548 the king annexed the lands with which pious congregations had endowed their parishes in the course of preceding centuries. The gains were enormous: almost half of Gustav Vasa's acquisitions of church lands came from the parishes. At the same time he began to attack the incomes of the parish priests, some of whom were certainly men of considerable wealth. In the early 1530s the obligation to billet the king's troops had been commuted to a standing tax; later, the king began to confiscate the parsons' estates, alleging that he did so in order to relieve them of the burden of secular cares. In return, he cancelled the tax, promised that they should continue to enjoy the labour-services due from their former peasants, and undertook to provide them with an adequate stipend from what had now become the royal share of tithe. But his notion of an adequate stipend fell far short of what some of them had previously been accustomed to, and he did not hesitate to break his promise about labour-services: the concession was withdrawn in 1548–9. Not only that: in 1554 he reimposed the tax, on the pretext of the expenses of the Russian war, and this time at double its former amount. No doubt the whole process can be represented as a levelling and rationalizing of clerical incomes; no doubt the very poorest of the clergy got off more lightly than their richer brethren; but the changes brought hardship to many who had never had any large margin of insecurity against poverty, and were now increasingly to be used as auxiliary unpaid public servants.[1] In Sweden, as in England, liberation from Rome meant heavier financial burdens for the church. If the king wanted a parsonage and glebe for himself, he now simply took it, and told the congregation to find their priest another. Wealthy ecclesiastics (such of them as remained) were encouraged to remember the king in their wills; and if they proved unmindful their executors might find (as in the case of the estate of the last abbot of Varnhem in 1555) that the king forcibly laid hands on any gold and silver. From all these sources, the king's total gains from the church were indeed impressive. It has been calculated that at the beginning of the reign the crown owned (in Sweden proper, excluding Finland) some 3754 farms; the church, 14,340; the nobility 13,922; and the tax-peasants, 35,239. In 1560 the distribution had been dramatically altered. The crown now had 18,936 farms, the church, none; the nobility, 14,175; and the

[1] For instance, the duty of collecting what had by this time become the king's share of the tithe was now laid upon the rural deans; and by the last decade of the reign rural deans were appointed with no option of refusal by simple intimation from the exchequer.

peasantry, 33,130. And of this vast aggregate of lands that thus passed into the crown's hands, no less than 6300 farms are reckoned to have been taken from the parishes. Add to all this, two-thirds of the total yield of tithes; the plunder of precious metals; and the king's personal gains by reclamations (as head of the Vasa family) under that clause in the Recess of Västerås which permitted the nobility to recover property alienated since 1454.

The Reformation impoverished the church for three-quarters of a century; and that impoverishment extended to more than material things. It meant, very often, a barbarizing of the clergy: intellectually and socially the church sank perceptibly lower. Since the fifteenth century, as we have seen, the nobility had been less willing to enter the church, unless they could enter it at the top: now that process was suddenly accelerated. We do occasionally hear (by way of extenuation) that a man of noble birth has been forced to enter the church from lack of means;[1] but soon even these unwilling recruits cease to come forward. The clerical estate comes to be dependent for new blood almost entirely upon the peasantry, for whom it offers for a long time to come almost the only prospect of social advancement. Otherwise, it is now a closed society, self-recruiting in that a high proportion of its members are sons of the manse. And this applies at all levels, from bishops to curates. The immediate consequence of the Reformation for the clergy was thus social degradation and cultural attenuation; for even if a man of superior intellectual calibre should now happen to be attracted to the ministry he would often lack the resources for proper training. With no university in the country any more, inevitably the great majority of the clergy received only the sketchiest of theological educations.

Yet this and other disadvantages were perhaps in the long run counterbalanced by new benefits for which the Reformation was responsible. There was an improvement in pastoral zeal, and perhaps in clerical morality. There was probably an increase in the local influence of the pastor, who was henceforward always resident. This was especially true when (as frequently happened) the now-married parson established a clerical dynasty, which might often rule a parish for three or four successive generations. The closed and homogeneous nature of the clerical Estate, moreover, gave it consistency and strength: when in the second quarter of the seventeenth century the crown began to ennoble the sons of bishops, this was felt, and rightly felt, as something which weakened the church. The strong religious passions of the age, moreover, put the clergy in the forefront of politics; their leaders spoke with a natural authority upon one of the most vital issues

[1] Sten Carlsson, *Mellan Bolmen och Holaveden*, p. 60.

which confronted the country; and this gave the bishops a prestige, and in the end a social status, which cancelled out the obscurity of their parentage. After the Reformation there was not a single churchman employed as a regular minister of state, much less made a member of the *råd*; yet successive sovereigns did in fact consult their bishops on all manner of things, and they did rely to an increasing extent on the voluntary collaboration of the clergy in the work of government, much as the Tudors relied upon the Justices of the Peace. Sixty years after Gustav Vasa's death, the episcopate had so far recovered its self-confidence that to some observers it seemed that after all his darkest suspicions of prelatical ambition might have been justified. And if in the long run the Reformation rather strengthened the church's position as against the upper ranks of lay society, it undoubtedly strengthened its hold upon the lower classes, once the slow process of the conversion of the masses to Protestantism was complete. The pre-Reformation clergy had never been conspicuously unpopular; but their Protestant successors soon stood out as the leaders of what (despite Gustav Vasa) became indeed the church of the people. Popular Protestantism gave the Swedish pastor something of the same prestige and authority in his parish as was enjoyed by his Calvinist counterpart in Scotland. And above all, just because by origin, interests and social standards the clergy were now so close to their congregations, they came to be the champions and defenders of the peasantry against threats to their liberty from a socially and economically aggressive aristocracy. In the mid-seventeenth century this would be a service of great importance.

Meanwhile the spoils of the church enriched not only the crown but the nobility. The process implied both less and more of a property revolution than the corresponding changes in England. Less, because the gains of the nobility were small in comparison with those of the crown: the net increase in their holdings may perhaps have been between 2 and 3 per cent. And less also because the church lands in Sweden did not pass into the hands of new men, nor make gentry of those who had not been gentry before. The terms of the Recess of Västerås ensured that only those noble families which had already donated lands to the church should have a share in the gains: the declared object of the Recess was to make it possible for the old nobility to play its proper part in the life of the state. It was mainly the higher nobility, therefore, who stood to benefit from the opportunity the king had created. There was no rising class of lawyers, financiers and men of business from which alternative aspirants to the church lands might have been drawn; there were no domestic creditors of the crown prepared to take land in settlement of a debt which they had small prospect of recovering in cash. In Gustav Vasa's time the crown was not indebted to its subjects: on the contrary, very many of its subjects were debtors of the crown. And hence as far as the monarchy was concerned the property revolution caused by the Reformation was far greater in Sweden than in England. Unlike Henry VIII, Gustav Vasa kept a tight hold on all his gains; with the result that the Reformation meant a decisive transformation of the position of the monarch in Swedish society. No king of Sweden had ever been so rich; none had ever so clearly overtopped the greatest of his subjects. Even outside Scandinavia the wealth of the Swedish crown seemed to foreign observers impressive: by the mid-century Europe was full of stories of Gustav Vasa's fabulous riches.

But if the king's fortune was large, it perhaps was not superfluously large. The course of events (he might have contended) provided a complete answer to Lars Andreae's pert question as to what he wanted with so much money. The prolonged crisis of the Count's War had impressed upon his mind, so firmly that he never afterwards forgot it, the need for a large cash reserve to meet any emergency. It was no sooner over, than he set about saving: by 1538 he had amassed a treasure amounting to a million marks. But then came Dacke; and the cost of that episode was staggering: when it was all over the king found his treasure chambers almost empty. There was no assurance that Dacke would not have a successor, and every reason to fear attack from outside. The hoarding therefore began again at once, more intensively than ever; the silver from Sala was coined into the new *dalers*, which exchanged at par with the German *Joachimsthaler*, and were thus acceptable not only to foreign traders but also to foreign mercenaries; and the *dalers* were stowed away in the vaults of Stockholm or Gripsholm against a return of bad times. Revenues in coin were now preferred to revenues in commodities: the current expenses of government were increasingly met through assignments on the spot of income in kind; the surpluses of perishable products were disposed of for coin which could be added to the strategic reserve. The process continued until the last decade of the reign, by which time the hoards were so large that the king felt easier in his mind, to say nothing of the fact that the slow oncoming of the price-revolution was beginning to make a fixed revenue more valuable if paid in commodities than in specie.

It is a remarkable and significant fact that this feverish anxiety to accumulate did not lead to the imposition of additional direct taxation. A 5 per cent *ad valorem* duty on imports established in 1536, and a 3 per cent duty on exports, imposed in 1559, no doubt brought in some cash revenue; but it is still broadly true to say that the recovery from the strain of the crisis of the early forties, and the defensive preparations thereafter, were managed on the basis of the ordinary revenue, the yield of the crown estates, and the gains from the church. It is true that some of the crown's ancient rights could be made to stretch without much difficulty: this was certainly true of regalian rights, now extended to rivers, forests and wastes; and it was also the case with labour-services, which Gustav Vasa seems to have exploited ruthlessly, either by commuting the obligation for a cash payment, or by using labour for the building of royal castles. Yet in one province at least (Ångermanland) the forties and fifties are said to have been a period of well-being for the peasantry to which there is no parallel in a hundred and fifty years. The timid and tentative foreign policy of the late forties had at all events the advantage that it imposed no great strain on the exchequer. In 1550 Gustav Vasa's income exceeded his expenditure by as much as 110,000 marks, and of this sum the prudent monarch placed 100,000 to his general reserve, using some of it to balance his accounts three years later. Nor does it seem that 1550 was a unique year in this respect. It is certainly surprising that the heavy expenses of the Russian war in the mid-fifties seem to have been met comfortably out of income and savings. Even if we grant the great disparity between the scale of operations of a Henry VIII and those of a Gustav Vasa, the contrast betwen their financial management is sufficiently striking. It was typical alike of Gustav Vasa's mendacity and of his parsimony that he should have told Prince Erik in 1560 that the crown's expenditure was thrice its annual income. In that year, indeed, he did obtain the approval of a *riksdag* for a special tax to finance Erik's projected embassy to England—the expense of which he never ceased to lament—but otherwise, for the last fifteen years of his reign, Gustav Vasa really seems to have been able to live of his own. Of how many contemporary sovereigns—even including those who had done well out of the Reformation—could the same be said?

Gustav Vasa was too good a business man, however, to be a mere hoarder; and he had no notion of allowing all his treasure to lie dead in his hands. On the contrary, he showed great enterprise and initiative in ploughing back his profits; and no inconsiderable portion of them was devoted to the increase of the nation's wealth through the development of its industry. The leading Swedish export at this period was iron, in the form of *osmund*.[1] Hitherto *osmund* had gone mainly to Germany, where it had been manufactured into bar-iron, and in this form reimported into Sweden for domestic use. It occurred to Gustav Vasa that Sweden might make bar-iron for herself. But the technique

[1] *Osmund*, it will be recalled, was the name given to the small, equal-sized pieces of malleable iron produced, either by direct smelting of the ore, or indirectly by way of pig-iron.

was unknown, the forges required for it were expensive to build, and Sweden was too poor in capital for any native *entrepreneur* to risk the venture. In the king, however, the country possessed at least one great capitalist whose money was seeking an eligible investment. Gustav Vasa seized his opportunity. He imported German workmen to train the Swedes in the new process and construct the new forges; he advanced the capital for their building; he gave interest-free loans to those who were willing to imitate his example; and he initiated the manufacture of bar-iron in Sweden. He himself became the biggest forge-master in the country. The production and exportation of *osmund* still continued to be considerable, now and for long afterwards; but henceforward bar-iron would become of increasing importance. A beginning was also made with the production of steel; and in 1551 the king subsidized the formation of a coöperative manufactory at Arboga for the production of arms and armaments: it was a development obviously related to the new policy of relying on a native conscript army. Gustav Vasa tried to ensure that the quality of Swedish iron should be constant and good; and in 1559 he ordered the iron-producers of Nora and Linde to put distinctive marks upon their products —the first move towards that system of marking and testing which Karl IX was later to establish. Thus, by his intelligent investment, his encouragement of private enterprise and his extension of the crown's activities, he gave to the Swedish iron industry a powerful impetus, which his youngest son was later to reinforce. With copper he was less successful, for in his time the mine was going through a lean period. There were repeated difficulties with water in the workings, and though Gustav Vasa came to the rescue by defraying the cost of a 'great engine' to pump it out, production remained low. It was not until twenty years after his death that copper began to regain its former importance in the list of Swedish exports.

The king was now incomparably the greatest landowner in the country: in 1560 the estates of the Vasa family (as distinct from those of the crown) numbered some 5,000 farms. It was natural, therefore, that he should be not less concerned for agriculture than for industry. He lived close to the soil, was well acquainted with all the details of farming, and had a sound judgment of agricultural techniques. He was not prepared to see the land abused if he could help it, if only because agricultural malpractices must sooner or later make the peasant incapable of paying his taxes. He watched over the Swedish land as though it had been all his own—as, indeed, a sizeable share of it actually was—and imported himself with professional interest into the *minutiae* of estate management. The farmer who was late in getting in his harvest, or slack in his ditching, would find himself admonished, or even mulcted of a fine; the peasant who destroyed the fiscal tolerance of his holding by excessive subdivision among his sons would be exhorted—and bribed by promises of tax-reliefs—to colonize the waste or the forest instead. The country's huge importation of strong beer from Germany vexed the king's economical soul, and he launched a campaign (which proved surprisingly successful) to induce his subjects to grow their own hops. The Swedish breed of sheep was a poor wool-bearer: his agents were ordered to procure 'at any cost' sheep from England and Pomerania; and on his manors on the island of Öland he crossed them with the local race, with results which were sufficiently satisfactory to encourage him to establish in Stockholm the first Swedish cloth manufactory. Towards the end of the reign he grew less ready to let out his farms on lease, and more disposed to keep them in hand; and in the fifties he embarked upon a grandiose programme of state-farming. The intention was to develop farming for a market, in contrast to the prevailing subsistence-farming of the peasantry; but also to make the crown-farms capable of supporting and feeding the standing army. Larger units, better administration, better book-keeping, rationalized methods of production, were the means upon which he relied to produce these results; and in the interests of rationalization he did not scruple to expropriate, against a compensation which was often dubious, the local landholders who stood in his way. The experiment—which was confined mainly to Finland—had but a mediocre success; it was very unpopular; and early in the next reign it was abandoned.

There was, nevertheless, a considerable disposable surplus from the royal manors, and there was an unending stream of revenue in kind which could be realized, in so far as it was not consumed at home, only if it were skilfully marketed. From the beginning of the forties this problem was made more tractable by the establishment of crown warehouses—at Stockholm, Älvsborg, Kalmar, Norrköping, Söderköping, Viborg—where commodities could be stored until the favourable moment arrived for vending them to foreign traders. The king, indeed, was not only the biggest capitalist and the largest landowner in his kingdom, he was also the greatest merchant. He was therefore deeply interested in the techniques of trade, the choice of markets, and the state of the exchanges. He would send his agents to Danzig to market the royal butter or fish, and bring back salt; or he would despatch them to the ports of western Europe to buy cloth and sugar and spices for the use of his court in exchange for Swedish tar and timber; and it was their business to see to it that the commodities they took with them were sold at prices which their master thought appropriate. The experience he gained in this traffic still further depressed his already low opinion of the commercial acumen of his subjects. 'The Swedes are so appallingly stupid', he wrote on one occasion, 'that they have no notion of how to deal with other people'. Gustav Vasa had not spent some months in Lübeck without acquiring insight into these matters. He wished to free Sweden from commercial dependence on the Hanse; he strove to build up trading-contacts with western Europe, and especially with the Netherlands, Britain and France; he did much to encourage the formation of a Swedish mercantile marine. But he was, on the other hand, profoundly sceptical about his subjects' ability to market their goods to advantage; he had a rooted conviction that if left to themselves they would take the wrong commodities to the wrong place at an unseasonable time, would be cheated on their bargains, and would come back either with luxury goods or trash, to the great prejudice of the country's well-being. These gloomy ideas led him as a matter of expediency to prefer a 'passive' to an 'active' trade: it was better that the foreigner should come to Sweden to fetch what he required, for since the duration of his stay was limited by law he must at last buy at the seller's price, or lose his voyage. The king was moreover strongly imbued with the conviction that in the existing state of the country it was imports rather than exports that mattered: he could even contemplate the export of specie without flinching, if it brought back goods of which the country stood in need.[1] The essential economic problem for Sweden, as he saw it, was a problem of provisioning, the building up of stocks against an emergency: in his reign there are numerous examples of the prohibition of exports, none of the prohibition of imports. Salt, in particular, had an importance that was vital; for no salt was produced in Sweden, and if the supply from abroad should fail half the country must go hungry for lack of salt meat in winter-time. But though his prudence thus led him to favour a 'passive' trade, he never ceased to be tempted by the possible rewards which an 'active' trade might bring with it. All through his reign he played with the possibility of direct trading connexions with the west, and he would have dearly loved to see Swedish merchantmen sailing westwards with Swedish goods—if only he had not been so sure that they would bungle their affairs when he was no longer at hand to tell them what to do: as he complained in 1558, the men of Älvsborg and Gävle would not even take care to sail in convoy, so that they fell easy victims to pirates, and then came clamouring to him for relief. There was a moment, in 1549, when he seriously thought of trying to organize his merchants into a Swedish Trading Company. It was a moment when relations with Lübeck appeared to be almost at breaking-point, and no doubt that was why

[1] See, e.g., *Gustav Vasas registratur*, XXI, 44, 56.

he ordered George Norman to draft the scheme which is the Company's only visible memorial. It was to be a voluntary association with an initial capital of not less than 100,000 marks; its main base was to be Stockholm; and it was to maintain factors in Antwerp, Frankfurt, Riga and Moscow: obviously the intention was to obtain a foothold in the trade between Russia and the west. It was, in fact, curiously similar to the plan conceived by old King Kristian thirty years earlier; and it was equally abortive.[1]

The Swedish Trading Company never advanced beyond the state of a prospectus; but it was typical of the king's approach to economic affairs. For indeed, in the last twenty years of the reign he made a sustained effort to bring every aspect of his subjects' economic activity under the control—or at least under the guidance and direction—of the monarchy. For the first time in Swedish history there was a conscious and planned economic policy for the whole country, and a plausible attempt to carry it out. The king tried to ensure an even distribution of the food supplies throughout the kingdom, so that provinces which were suffering from a deficiency should be relieved from those that had a surplus. Industry was to be concentrated in specific towns selected by himself, and other urban communities which might compete with those he had chosen were to be evacuated and abandoned: better a few strong, well-fortified and flourishing towns than a multiplicity of weak ones, which would be too poor to help him in an emergency, and incapable of resistance if another Nils Dacke should arise.[2] Internal trading, too, was to be an urban monopoly; retail trade in the countryside was forbidden under stringent penalties: an ordinance of 1546 (as ineffectual as its numerous predecessors) prescribed death for the third offence. Foreign trade was to be concentrated at staple-towns; foreigners were put under strict surveillance. Exporters were told what to sell and whither to send it, for the king believed that they followed each other like sheep to the same overstocked market, and so were forced to dispose of their goods at less than a fair price. The forties were a period of high prices and scarcity; and the king was much concerned to discover the causes and apply the appropriate remedies. A great *Mandate on the dearness of the times*, published in 1546, embodies his conclusions. The blame was placed on the shoulders of the Swedes themselves. It was their commercial ineptitude that pushed up the

[1] The immediate danger of war with Lübeck blew over; but from 1549 to 1555 Swedish subjects were prohibited from sailing thither. Lübeckers, however, could come freely to Sweden on the usual conditions; so that the effect of the ban was really to reinforce the 'passive' nature of Swedish trade.

[2] In this matter, as in some others, the king's plans proved incapable of fulfilment. No town seems in fact to have been permanently abandoned, and after 1560 royal policy tended in the opposite direction, towards new foundations; for experience showed that fewer towns meant more rural trading.

retail price of commodities: their ships were too small, so that they could not buy cheaply in bulk; they sold Swedish exports too cheap, and were driven to recoup themselves by enhancing the retail price of imports; and they suffered Swedish currency to be valued too low. The remedies he proposed were better marketing, bigger trading units, and price-fixing; and a little later a proclamation was indeed issued, ordering the abatement of retail prices by one-third. Its effect is uncertain; but it seems clear that the price-rise was mainly caused by the king's excessive minting to pay for the expenses of the Dacke rebellion, and by a simultaneous debasement of the coinage which was perhaps made necessary by the contemporary debasements on the continent. In time Gustav Vasa seems to have seen that there might be a connexion between price levels and the amount of money in circulation: at all events towards the end of the forties minting tapered off; more and more coin was withdrawn from circulation for storage in the treasure-vaults; and by the mid-fifties the complaints of the dearness of the times had mostly died away.

In these matters it was not to be expected of Gustav Vasa that he should be wiser than his generation. But within the limits of his knowledge and ideas he did great things for Sweden, watching over his subjects' welfare with tireless attention, discerning with a natural shrewdness their faults and shortcomings, innovating and developing along lines which they would hardly have pursued of their own motion. The trader and the husbandman, no less than the bishop and the bailiff, were made to feel at every instant that Sweden had now a king who was sovereign indeed.

The great increase in the wealth of the crown had obvious political and constitutional consequences. The balance of forces within the state, which had been the political ideal of the fifteenth century, was now upset. The king was able to afford a park of artillery; to indulge in the costly luxury of a navy; to resume the building of castles, since he could now afford to keep them in his own hands: the late thirties and early forties saw the construction of Gripsholm and Vadstena. Even if the Reformation had never occurred Gustav Vasa would probably have had less difficulty than most of his contemporaries in living upon a fixed income, for the price-revolution reached Sweden only slowly; its effects, when at last they were felt, were heavily muted; and it was always open to the king to take the greater part of his revenues in commodities rather than specie. But undoubtedly the Reformation was a great political windfall. Gustav Vasa was able to do what the Stures had tried to do, on a scale of which they had never ventured to dream; he could buttress the throne with a great ring of manors from which he could draw revenues in cash or in kind. As he grew older he became less willing to offer the nobility fiefs of the old type, and increasingly disposed to make grants which were almost in the nature of appointments to administrative posts, revocable at will, and remunerated by drawbacks on the local revenues. The old *län* was beginning to give way to the new *förläning*, which would be nothing more than an assignment of specific local revenues in return for specific services. And since the king now preferred to retain direct control of the family estates and the crown lands, his corps of bailiffs necessarily expanded to meet the new demands upon them: in the course of the reign their numbers rose from about sixty to about one hundred and eighty. The areas under their supervision grew smaller, so that they might be able to do their work more thoroughly. Their accounts were ever more peremptorily required of them, their balances ever more closely scrutinized; blast upon blast of royal commination pursued them as they went about their business; and they lived ever mindful of the possibility that sooner or later their perambulatory and inquisitive master would descend in person upon them, review their delicts on the spot, catch them out in their answers, demolish their arithmetic, shame them by the intimacy of his acquaintance with their proceedings and his knowledge of the state of the markets, and throw them at last into that prison from which only his deathbed pardon would deliver them. The children of men, as the king well knew, are deceitful upon the weights (and well they might be, in the mensurational jungle of sixteenth-century Sweden), but a bailiff must be up uncommonly early to deceive Gustav Vasa for long. That he was cheated he took for granted: in his old age he remarked 'God has given me great riches, but I should be even richer if I had not had so many faithless bailiffs'. Still, he had no intention of being cheated for want of effort to prevent it. He gave to the finances and administration of his kingdom the close, continuous and personal attention of a dealer operating on a precarious margin of profit. No one else, it seemed, was capable of undertaking the immense labour of supervising the whole working of the state. No detail was too petty to escape his attention: he writes to the skipper of *The Bear*, instructing him to ship a cargo of dried peas, cod and flat-fish; he rebukes his subjects for their carelessness in the salting of herring, and adds a daunting description of what happens to improperly salted herring when it is boiled; he orders his bailiff to make sure that all his fish-nets in Bråviken are clearly and securely marked with his name; he gives precise specifications for colour, pattern and quality of the cloth he requires for his servants at court. The lazy, the careless and the inefficient had little hope of escaping the displeasure of such a ruler: their misdeeds might indeed elude the royal eye for a time; but sooner or later there would arrive a letter with the ominous phrase 'We are not a little astonished . . .', and then it was high time for amendment, 'unless' (as the king was wont to add) 'you wish us to hold another language to you'. He was a master sparing of commendation, holding that a man need not expect thanks for doing his duty, and being in any case a correspondent whose epistolary style naturally inclined to asperity; but he probably got more work out of his bailiffs, and lost a smaller share of his income, than anybody could reasonably have expected.

If the bailiff was the typical agent of local government, the central government was largely in the hands of secretaries and clerks. Like the bailiffs, they were usually of modest origins—sons of nobles unable to maintain the social standards of their class, sons of *ofrälse* parents who hoped to rise by their wits and their fidelity to a better social position than their fathers'. Pyhy's plan for the central government had been based essentially on the division of labour, the allocation of specific tasks to specific persons, and the provision of permanent paid senior civil servants. When he fell, the central government relapsed into its old ways, in which the only pattern was imposed by the king's presence, and the only order emanated from the king's will: in 1560 there was still no part of it which functioned independently of the monarch. It is true that the chancery was now better equipped than of old with men who could write a decent letter in German or Latin, and the exchequer began to exhibit a modest degree of specialization as between the man who valued the iron and the man who valued the dried fish; but in all other respects administration was no more developed, no less personal, than in the twenties. Pyhy's system of exchequer-counsellors (*kammarråd*), which in the forties had admitted some of the nobility to a place of responsibility, seems to have come to an end with the death of Nils Pedersson Bielke in 1550. Since it was the king's habit to be frequently on the move, passing with his court from one manor to another in order to consume the edible revenues on the spot, and since (despite this habit) there was also a tendency for government business to centre in Stockholm if only because much revenue was stored in Stockholm castle, such 'central government' as did exist tended to disintegrate, a part remaining in Stockholm, a part following the king: and towards the end of the reign there might even be a third part with Prince Erik. This was especially noticeable with regard to finance; for the king collected and spent revenue wherever he happened to be, and maintained (quite apart from the exchequer) two separate hoards of treasure—very much as a man might have one current account and two deposit accounts at three different banks, and at the same time defray much of his itinerant expenditure by drawing on the Post Office. There were obvious difficulties in operating such a system: for instance, the exchequer officials did not always know whether those to whom the king made loans had, or had not, paid their interest, or indeed whether the loans were interest-free or not. There are agitated and curiously domestic letters in which an exchequer-counsellor at Gripsholm tells his colleague in Stockholm that he has left the key to the exchequer under the folio which stands to the right of the door into the treasure-chamber, or informs him that the king himself is not quite sure whether either of the two keys supposed to give access to the wardrobe will really fit it. But these inconveniences were offset in Gustav Vasa's view by the fact that the system enabled him to keep in close and personal touch with every branch of government and every part of the kingdom.

As long as George Norman lived, Gustav Vasa had at least one coadjutor whom he could treat as a real minister; but when he died, in 1552, no successor took his place. In the closing years of the reign the king turned more and more to his near relations: his most important advisers were now Sten Eriksson Leijonhufvud, his brother-in-law; Per Brahe, his nephew; Gustav Olofsson Stenbock, the father of his third queen; and Svante Sture: to whom may be added the king's two elder sons, Prince Erik and Prince Johan. These aristocratic relatives of the sovereign formed an inner core within the *råd*. But neither they, nor the *råd* as a whole, were permanently available for consultation, nor easily to be assembled in a hurry; and from time to time proposals were put forward with the object of ensuring that there should always be two members of the *råd* attending upon the king, or else—as Erik and Per Brahe suggested in 1557—that a new body, to be styled the *hovråd*, should be specially created to supply this need. Nothing came of these plans; but they serve to make clear how intermittent the share of the *råd* in government really was, and how little it could be considered as providing, at this stage, any sort of central executive, or even an effective council of state.

Nevertheless, Gustav Vasa did, on the whole, conform to the injunction of the *landslag* to rule *med råds råde* (with the council's counsel), in that the *råd* was usually consulted before any step of major importance was taken.[1] A meeting of the *råd* invariably preceded any meeting of the Estates, whether as *herredag* or *riksdag*; and indeed the *råd* was considered to be an indispensable element in these assemblies. But if consultation with the *råd* was obligatory when great issues were to be determined, consultation with the *riksdag* on such occasions was growing to be a habit. The *riksdag*, no less than the *råd*, must throw the cloak of its approval over the king's proceedings with the church,

[1] But not, apparently, before the outbreak of the Russian war.

must endorse the proclamation of hereditary monarchy, and guarantee the king's Testament. Gustav Vasa pushed ahead along the line which young Herr Sten had chalked out, and by the end of the reign the *riksdag* was accepted as a recognized part of the constitution: it was significant that the leaders of the church-bell rebellion tried to call a *riksdag* of their own to legalize their actions against the king. *Riksdag* procedure was beginning to gain shape and consistency: the royal Proposition, prescribing the business of the meeting, and the Resolutions of each Estate, embodying their answers to the Proposition, were gradually establishing themselves as normal. In 1560 comes the first Resolution of the *riksdag* as a whole. The composition of the Estates, and the methods whereby representatives were selected, were still variable and undefined; but on the whole the practice was coming to be that all adult members of the nobility would be expected to attend, and also all the bishops; the bishops would pick representatives from their chapters; the bailiffs would select candidates from the country parsons. Towns which were themselves responsible for collecting the taxes from their inhabitants were allowed to choose their members themselves: in other towns they were chosen by the bailiffs. As to the peasantry, it was assumed that those who were tenants of the nobility would have their interests cared for by their landlords, while those who were tenants of the crown already had access to the king: in any case, neither of these classes of peasants was a fit object of taxation. The peasantry, therefore, was represented only by tax-paying, land-owning yeomen. They were selected in each county (*härad*) by the bailiffs, at a rate which varied between two and six to the county; and it was expected that bailiffs would choose men whom the county would trust to take decisions on their constituents' behalf. But it would be a full half-century and more before men were willing to accept the idea that the resolution of an Estate at the *riksdag* was necessarily binding on its constituents; and Gustav Vasa certainly did not act as though he believed it to be so. In many ways the *landsting* was still thought of as the only body legally competent to commit the country: Gustav Vasa took care to have the *arvförening* submitted to the various *landsting* after it had been accepted by the *riksdag*; and before he took the risk of rejecting the proposal to buy off Kristian II's claims by paying a dowry to his daughters he first submitted the idea to *landsting* and *häradsting*, then laid it before the *riksdag* at its meeting in 1547, and then referred it once again to the *landsting*, despite the fact that the *råd* and the assembled Estates had been unanimous for rejection. So too in regard to taxation: there were already signs that the monarchy might form the habit of asking the *riksdag* for that preliminary approval of new taxation which had hitherto always been given by the *råd* alone; and in 1544 and 1560 the Estates did indeed approve new taxes. But it was still only a preliminary approval, subject to the veto of the real tax-granting bodies in the provinces. Again, the share of the Estates in legislation was still uncertain: ecclesiastical legislation was the concern of the supreme defender of the church, or of church councils which had received his permission to draft it, and would come to the *riksdag* (if at all) only for confirmation; economic ordinances were recognized to be within the scope of the prerogative, and as yet the Estates were content that they should be so. And though the *riksdag* was a representative body for the whole kingdom, it was not necessarily the only one: in Gustav Vasa's time we can see the emergence of the *handelsdag*—a national gathering of towns and traders at which the king could tackle problems of a commercial nature. It is true that in the later years of the reign Gustav Vasa no longer transacted as much business of national importance in the old free-and-easy way at markets and fairs: he was no longer physically equal to the exertion, and in any case the Dacke affair seems to have shaken his nerve for this kind of confrontation, for in 1544 he was talking of suppressing markets altogether, or at least of the need for putting government spies upon them.[1] But though the old king now had lost the taste for stump-oratory, and though Erik would always feel himself too grand for it, the market had still a part to play in Sweden's political history, as the last decade of the century was to prove.

The *riksdag*, then, was still in its infancy in 1560; but already it was an instrument which might be made to serve the monarchy's ends. As early as the time of young Herr Sten there are signs that the *råd* and the nobility realized this, and in consequence looked upon the emergent Estates with no very friendly eye. But in Gustav Vasa's time this suspicion seems to subside; probably because the situation never arose (save for a moment in 1529) in which the king found himself at loggerheads with his nobility. The compact with the *råd*-party which had secured him the throne held good for the whole of the reign; and his second and third marriages, into great noble families, strengthened it. The *riksdag* was never used, and never looked likely to be used, against the interests of the aristocracy; and the aristocracy stood staunchly by the crown against the rustic rabble of Dalarna or Småland. This solidarity of interest between the crown and the nobility helped to save the monarchy from once again becoming the sport of family vendettas; it enabled Gustav Vasa to do things which the Stures could never have attempted without disaster: he was able, for instance, to carry through in 1526 a much-needed revision of knight-service, which

[1] Indeed, he even spoke of buying himself a quiet county in Germany, and retiring from the business of kingship altogether; but it is hard to believe that he was serious.

not only fixed it at a higher rate than before, but also laid down a graduated scale proportioned to the means of the landowner. But in 1560 it was already possible to foresee that this era of harmony was coming to an end. It had depended for its continuance upon the weakness of the old aristocratic-constitutionalists, crushed by the disasters of the years from 1517 to 1520, driven to take shelter behind a strong king; and on the success of Gustav Vasa in providing material come pensations for the obscuring of the old constitutional ideas. Thos- ideas, however, were too deep-rooted to be buried for ever under the plunder of the church, or permanently exorcised by fear of Kristian II and his family. From the point of view of the men who had made the Recess of Kalmar, the spirit of the constitution had been repeatedly violated by Gustav Vasa, and indeed the whole structure of the state had been overturned by the revolution that made the monarchy hereditary. The destruction of the old church had left an imbalance in the body politic, a situation in which the power of the crown outweighed all competitors. Government might indeed continue to be *med råds råde*, but what had become of the historic claim of the *råd* to be the mediator and arbitrator between king and subjects, the regulator of the state machine, the residuary legatee of sovereignty? The king broke the *landslag* with blithe unconcern, depriving subjects of their property without trial; and the *råd* was unable or unwilling to intervene. He told the citizens of Lödöse that 'he cared not one blueberry for them and all their old privileges'. The new oaths demanded had no basis in law. The whole cast of government since about 1540 had been a violent break with tradition. It was a disturbing portent for the future that the king should use the *riksdag* to pronounce on issues between himself and his subjects, and to try cases of treason; and already he had been heard to speculate as to whether such cases could properly be dealt with in any other forum. What prospects of oppression such an arrangement might not hold out, given a king at odds with his nobility, and a *riksdag* which was the docile instrument of the crown! And the very nature of the personal monarchy, its modes of operation and the agents it employed, must be disquieting. The bailiffs and clerks and secretaries were entrenching themselves in the seats of power, to the exclusion of the *råd* and the aristocracy. The country's business now needed more constant attention than the *råd* had been able to give it; and the aristocracy had hitherto been too rude and unlettered to cope with the problems which the secretaries had to handle. But in this regard the position was already changing: a younger generation of nobles was moving up, better educated than their fathers. Gustav Vasa tried to attract the nobility to his court so that they might learn the ways of good society: he wanted them, he said, to be able to treat women politely, and not behave as though they were a lot of drovers; he was anxious that the clothes of his courtiers should conform to current fashion; he wanted to convince foreign visitors 'that we Swedes are no more swine and goats than they are'. He maintained an orchestra of sixteen musicians; he gave employment to a number of painters. The results did not entirely come up to his expectations: in 1559 he refused to receive any foreign envoys because his cellars were empty and he had no gentlemen-in-waiting or pages in attendance upon him. Yet he did make some impression: presentable aristocrats could now be found to send on foreign embassies. Sten Eriksson Leijonhufvud and Svante Sture were distinguished examples of Swedish nobles who had acquired a European polish; and in the generation after them—Prince Erik's generation—such men would grow more common. As the aristocracy became better educated, better able to deal with the increasing complexities of government, its demand to participate would match its capacity to do so. For as the granting of fiefs of the old style grew less and less frequent, they would look for some alternative form of financial recompense; and the natural form that was open to them would be the new *förläningar*—that is, the rewards for the service of the state. All these developments made it virtually certain that sooner rather than later the aristocracy would recall that article in the Kalmar Recess which had laid it down that no low-born man was to be preferred over their heads; for it was just to low-born men—to secretaries, clerks and bailiffs—that the new-style monarchy turned for assistance. By 1560, therefore, the long constitutional truce was drawing to an end. The 'rule of secretaries' was slowly impressing itself on the aristocracy as an abhorrent anomaly to be removed; the possibility of a parliamentary absolutism was already dimly sensed as a menace in the future; and the *råd* would not much longer forget its historic mission. As long as the old king lived, there were no changes; but much would depend upon the character of his successor.

Gustav Vasa was the father of a large family. By his first wife, Katarina of Saxe-Lauenburg, he had but one child, Prince Erik; but by his second, Margareta Leijonhufvud, he had three sons—Johan, Magnus, Karl—and numerous daughters. He was naturally anxious to make suitable provision for his younger children; and in 1544, when the Estates assented to the Succession Pact, they accepted in principle the proposal that the younger princes be provided with duchies for their support, and agreed that the details should be left to be settled in the king's Testament. It was not until 1560 that the Testament in its final form was ready to be communicated to the *riksdag*; but in the meantime Gustav Vasa had already taken steps to provide Johan with a duchy of his own. By letters issued in 1556 and 1557 he was invested with the whole of Finland, which henceforward became a quite separate administrative area: Johan had his own chancery, his own exchequer, he appointed on his own authority to government offices, he granted fiefs without the obligation to consult his father. The Testament of 1560 was in large measure based on these arrangements. It confirmed the provision made for Johan, and created similar duchies for Magnus and Karl: Magnus received a large area in Östergötland and Västergötland, while Karl was allotted Södermanland, Västmanland and Värmland. Within their duchies they were to enjoy all the revenues (including those from fines, purveyances, and tolls) and all regalian rights 'as if we held them ourselves on the crown's behalf'; but they were likewise bound to be faithful to the king and to provide him with men for his army at request, 'as many as they possibly can'. No resolution or action on any great matter of domestic or foreign policy was to be taken, not only by the dukes but also (a remarkable provision) by the king, until all the brothers had been consulted; but on the other hand the dukes were to be entitled to some initiative in these matters if the time for consultation were obviously too short—provided that they used their initiative wisely and for the benefit of the realm as a whole. The duchies were explicitly stated to be still a part of the Swedish realm; they were to revert to the crown on the failure of heirs male; the dukes were to seek confirmation of their duchies on the accession of each new king—though the king was bound not to refuse it. No part of the duchies was to be alienated, for that would violate the Land Law's prohibition of any diminution of the realm; and the dukes were not to employ in their councils persons who might be harmful to the country, nor were they as a result of their marriages to import too many foreigners into their duchies. All were pledged not to depart from 'the pure doctrine' of the Reformation. If any dispute should arise between the dukes and the king, or among the dukes themselves, and if ordinary methods of reconciling it should prove unavailing, the issue was to be submitted to the arbitration of 'the leading Estates'.

Such was Gustav Vasa's Testament. Like the Succession Pact itself, it was probably influenced by foreign models (notably by the Testament of Joachim I of Brandenburg in 1534); but like it too it was also a native growth arising naturally out of the internal political situation. The tendency in recent years to grant large fiefs only to the king's close relations, the tendency to rely on such persons as coadjutors in the business of government, was here pushed a step further.[1] Gustav Vasa expected that the royal dukes could be relied upon to stand together for the defence of the dynastic interests of their house; and he hoped

[1] *Gustav Vasas registratur*, XXVI, 175 (to Erik, 29 March 1556).

that the new arrangements would ease the burden of kingship, which latterly he had felt to be increasingly oppressive. Since his pattern of government was so personal, so little reliant upon administrative institutions, the problem of running the country presented itself to him in simple terms. The question, it seemed to him, was how best the monarchy could control the bailiffs upon whose shoulders so large a proportion of day-to-day administration reposed. One possible answer, no doubt, would have been to delegate the control of them to local governors—and so, incidentally, to associate the nobility with the labours of the crown. And in fact it was in this direction that future constitutional development would lie. But for Gustav Vasa, fast bound in the tradition he had himself created, the solution seemed rather to lie in using the princes to establish what would in effect be three new centres of personal monarchical control: the three duchies, by splitting up the burden of royal supervision, would make the old system viable. At first sight it might seem that the Testament contradicted the Succession Pact, and splintered into fragments the royal authority which had been consolidated in 1544. This was certainly not the king's intention. As Erik Sparre was to put it, more than a quarter of a century later, the duchies were instituted 'so that the realm should thereby have not only honour and dignity, but also a weighty aid and support in all sorts of emergency'. Yet the duchies were certainly enormous; they withdrew from the crown's control most of the richest areas of the country; they cut off the king from access to his southern or eastern frontier. And the wording of the Testament, giving with one hand what it took back with the other, capable of very different interpretations, in essential points probably self-contradictory, could hardly have been more carefully designed to provoke friction. How far did the rights of the dukes extend? Could they claim only those rights which the Testament accorded them, or could they claim all rights which it did not expressly withhold? Were they, or were they not, sovereign within their own duchies? To such questions there was no clear answer. The situation would have been difficult enough if the four brothers had all been well-balanced personalities, warmly attached to each other. It became impossible when it was poisoned by the jealousy of half-brothers, and bedevilled by the congenital instability of the Vasa line. In the sequel, the brothers agreed only in one thing: that the Testament was to be regarded as an inviolable fundamental law. But each would appeal to its letter or its alleged spirit as best might suit the political convenience of the moment; and each would derive from it irreconcilable pretensions and clashing claims of right. The document which the old king had fondly supposed to be the guarantee of fraternal union revealed itself in less than a decade as the exhaustless fount of fratricidal strife. Already in his lifetime it required no very great discernment to predict trouble. The shadows of family strife fell ever thicker around him in his closing years; and the clash of temperaments and generations embittered his relations with his sons: the more so since he was an affectionate and proud father. By 1560 he was an old man, racked with headaches, much given to a querulous self-pity, groaning under the burden of kingship, and feeling himself an incongruous survivor into an alien world. The departure of Erik for England took the heart out of him. On 29 September 1560, after six weeks of weary illness, he died; and was buried, with his first two wives on either side of him, in the cathedral at Uppsala.

Gustav Vasa has left a great name in Swedish history. No doubt it is true that much that is associated with him had been prepared or essayed by the Stures: he was in many respects less of an innovator, more a man ranged in an historical tradition, than used to be thought. But he did what the Stures had had neither the time, nor, in all probability, the character and ability to accomplish. He found Sweden vanquished and prostrate; he left her firmly established as a respectable minor European power. It had been no easy passage. In the course of his long reign he had met and beaten down rebellions and resistances which only a very tough and resourceful ruler could have survived. By his personal authority he had carried through a profound change in the constitution; by a sustained act of will he had transformed Sweden into a Protestant country. However odious may seem his dealings with the church, they were conducted with deadly skill, and they issued in an unqualified political triumph. He had a wonderful faculty for concentrating on the essentials; an extraordinary constancy in his refusal to allow himself to be distracted into peripheral or irrelevant enterprises: few reigns can show so little wasted effort. Yet though he may appear ruthless and purposeful, in one aspect his policy was a kind of compromise, the resultant of two forces which pulled him in different directions. On the one hand was a spirit of enterprise, a thirst for power, a limitless greed for the wealth that gives power; on the other was a long-headed calculation, a dislike of risks, an anguished miserliness which could be pushed even to ignominy. But of the two, it was the latter set of forces that pulled the harder. He was not insensitive to considerations of prestige: indeed, he felt them deeply; but in the end he was usually prepared to sacrifice even reputation for security, or for material advantage. His whole career was one long defensive action against dangers from within and without; and even in the comparative calm of his last decade his main preoccupation was to build up the strength of his country to resist the new dangers which he saw ahead of him. After nearly forty years of incessant effort he could feel that he had given Sweden a unity and consistency to which in the previous century she had been much a stranger; and he might fairly claim that that unity centred upon himself. He was a hard master and a violent man; yet he was perhaps more clement than many of his royal contemporaries. His grasp of facts was wonderful, his memory extraordinary, his appreciation of ideas small; and though he was as shrewd as any man in the kingdom, and in course of time acquired a unique insight into the problems of his country, he was not blessed either with sympathy or imagination. In person he was noble, every inch the king; a man (as Per Brahe remembered) upon whom all clothes seemed to sit well. Though he was so liable to furious outbursts of choler, and though his habitual suspiciousness did not diminish with the years, he had decided social talents: he loved to play the genial host, had the royal gift for the appropriate word, and could when he chose be a gay and charming companion. Despite his attempts to foster the arts at his court he was not a cultured man; though he delighted in pictures, and in music had both taste and skill. He was a born orator, who used his talent unscrupulously for private and political ends. He letters reveal him as a master of Swedish prose; but he would have been astonished to learn that anyone should think so. For he was only too sensible of the deficiencies of his education, and at times felt bitterly his inferiority to his brilliant sons. Paternal affection could not make him either a wise or a dignified parent, and some of his letters to his family are painful reading: it is to be feared that there were moments when Erik was a little ashamed of him. To truth he was perfectly indifferent; his word was decidedly not to be relied on; he thought little of abusing his position to cheat and bully his way to a bargain; and though he was the most litigious of monarchs he had scant respect for the law. He was a materialist rather than an idealist; and magnanimity was not among his virtues. But with all the flaws in his character he was indubitably a great king. For he died with most of his objectives realized, and with things achieved which would have appeared incredible in 1523. Of no Swedish monarch can it be said with greater certainty that his reign was a solid success. 'What he minded he compassed.'

3. Erik XIV

The death of Gustav Vasa placed upon the throne of Sweden one of the most remarkable sovereigns ever to occupy it. Erik XIV was twenty-seven when he succeeded his father: a man in the full tide of vigour, stately and splendid to see; glittering with natural genius and acquired accomplishments; not unequal, as it seemed, to the high destiny of Elizabeth's hand. About his father there had always clung a tang of provincialism; but Erik could bear the scrutiny of fellow-monarchs with credit, if not quite with full assurance. To the *grandezza* of a great sovereign he united the polite arts prescribed by Castiglione. He had Latin at his command, fluent, elegant and pure; on his book-shelves were to be found works in Hebrew and Greek; his modern languages included French, Spanish, Italian and Finnish, as well as German. He was well-versed in treatises of geography, and bought Mercator's maps; well-read in history, not least in that of Commines; interested in technological devices and innovations of all sorts; a collector of strange birds and beasts, an amateur of gardening, a man cunning in the craft of the apiarist. To all the arts he gave his patronage: Vitruvius formed his taste in architecture; he could draw, he could etch; he was a skilled performer on the lute, and as a composer he might certainly stand comparison with Elizabeth's father. With him the culture of the Renaissance at last won a footing in Sweden. Unlike Gustav Vasa, Erik had a mind which turned naturally to the abstract, the theoretical, the logical, the speculative: he had a clear appreciation of theological distinctions, for which his father had cared nothing; he well understood the relevance of the precepts of Roman law to the contemporary political situation; and he seems at least to have had some notion of the quantity theory of money.[1] Machiavelli not only furnished him with a *vademecum* to the profession of kingship, but also directed his attention to the theoretical study of war, in which he was himself to be so notable an innovator. He had the gift of words which was the

[1] Cf. his message to the Estates at Uppsala fair, February 1561: 'Concerning the high prices which now more than aforetime prevail (by no means of the King's desiring), the real cause is that his Majesty in the immediate past (by reason of so many occasions which have been, and still are) has issued so much coin, so that the land is almost full of money, which for that reason is come into contempt'—a statement no less remarkable for its frankness than for its insight: *Svenska riksdagsakter*, II, i, 122.

Estonia, Livonia and Kurland

common heritage of all his house; but his speeches—in contrast to his father's pungent, unstudied outpourings—conformed to the classic rules of rhetoric, just as his personal and political problems fell habitually, in his own mind, into syllogistic form. And it was not the least of his accomplishments that he was full of the precise learning and difficult techniques of astrology: it was a passion which held him throughout life; and it may perhaps have contributed something to his fall.

Though in all this he so little resembled Gustav Vasa, he had, nevertheless, more than a trace of the parental qualities. He took the profession of kingship with proper seriousness, displayed real ability as an organizer and administrator, and had an eye no less sharp to his servants' delinquencies. But he inherited also some less desirable traits:

ERIK XIV

by a Dutch master

JOHAN III
after J. B. van Uther

the wearisome suspiciousness of Gustav Vasa became in Erik pathological and alarming; the lack of self-control was more plainly abnormal; the distrust of subordinates made loyal service burdensome almost to impossibility. He wanted his father's common touch and earthy sense of humour; he lacked his solid common sense, and his ability to weigh the desirable against the possible; and his enemies said that he lacked physical courage too. With all his brilliant endowments, Erik was a tragically unhappy man, tense and nervous, self-questioning, self-torturing; liable to violent changes of humour; at once suspicious and credulous, cruel and timid. The gem was flawed from the beginning; and under a sharp blow was always liable to disintegrate.

One main difference between himself and Gustav Vasa—and indeed it provided something of a key to his character—consisted in the tremendous fact that Erik was born to be king; born after his father's accession, born not of some native noblewoman but of a mother of a princely house: the first king of Sweden to succeed as hereditary monarch. Erik never forgot this; and his pride was unsleeping and insatiable. The 'XIV' after his name revealed how firmly he believed in the mythical history of the early Goths, which Johannes Magnus's book had made popular:[1] a German ambassador found himself cross-questioned upon what memorials of Gothic greatness might still be visible in Italy, and native diplomats did not forget to salt their despatches with suitably Gothic allusions. He was the first king of Sweden to exact the title of 'Majesty'; and his ministers and *råd* found it wise to address him in terms of abject servility which had no precedent in Swedish history. Between himself and the aristocracy he set a great gulf; and it may fairly be said that by his deliberate choice he had no friends. In his own family, too, he stood apart: for his half-brothers and half-sisters, the offspring of Margareta Leijonhufvud, were clearly of inferior timber to the son of Katarina of Saxe-Lauenburg. They were closely connected with the high Swedish nobility, and called Stenbocks, Stures, Bielkes, Brahes their cousins—family ties from which Erik for the most part kept himself free, but family ties which might well become dangerous to him if ever it should come to a struggle between himself and Johan.[2]

Erik had not yet left Sweden for England when the news of Gustav Vasa's death overtook him. By Christmas he was back in Stockholm.

[1] Erik translated Johannes Magnus's book into Swedish while in prison after his deposition.

[2] Margareta Leijonhufvud's sister Brita married Gustav Olsson Stenbock; her younger sister Märta married Svante Sture; Gustav Olsson's daughter Katarina was Gustav Vasa's third wife. Of Svante Sture's daughters, Sigrid married Ture Pedersson Bielke, Anna married Hogenskild Bielke. Per Brahe, who was the son of Gustav Vasa's sister, married Beata Stenbock.

And the first great decision to confront him was upon the urgent problem of Livonia, and the reply to be made to Reval's appeal for aid. As might have been predicted, his answer was favourable. In January 1561 he assured the burghers of his protection and promised to maintain all their privileges; in March Klas Kristersson Horn arrived in Reval to negotiate the terms upon which the city was to put itself into Swedish hands. From Reval's point of view there was one essential object in the whole transaction: to obtain the assistance of the Swedish navy in blocking the trade to Narva. And perhaps if Erik's main motive for intervention had really been the plan to establish a monopoly of the Russian trade-routes he would at once have fallen in with Reval's demands. But it was political rather than economic considerations that had taken him to Estonia, and for the moment Horn was careful to avoid committing his master. This was a bitter disappointment; but Reval had now gone too far to retract. In May the burghers formally accepted Swedish protection; in June they swore fealty to the Swedish crown.[1] In return, they were promised that no extraordinary tolls should be imposed upon foreign merchants; that no Swedish troops should be kept in Reval except in time of danger (a usefully elastic exception); and that such troops should be maintained at the king's charges. On 2 August Erik confirmed their privileges. He also promised to do his best to stop the trade to Narva. But he did not commit himself to doing so by force; and he steadily refused a demand that Reval should be the only staple for the trade to Muscovy. If the burghers had hoped that submission to Sweden would mean the end of attempts to set up a staple in Viborg, they were quickly disabused of the idea. For the acquisition of Reval meant that Sweden was now established on both shores of the Gulf of Finland, and was thus in a position to control it: the situation had materially altered since Beurreus made his famous oration to the English council. Erik could now argue that the Gulf was no longer an international waterway, but a Swedish 'stream'—as the Danes were accustomed to argue that the Sound was a Danish 'stream'. He was determined to extract what advantage he could from the situation, and levy toll—either at Reval or at Viborg: as to that he was indifferent—on all traders to Russia who went that way. It was certainly a nuisance that the route by Narva should still be open; but to block it by force seemed in 1561 too direct a provocation of Ivan IV to be worth risking. Accordingly he tried other means. He proposed to the tsar that he should be allowed to buy Narva from him—a suggestion so innocently optimistic as to border on *naïveté*. As his coronation in July he plied the envoys of

[1] The nobility of Harrien and Wierland accepted Swedish sovereignty at the same time; the nobility of Jerwen soon afterwards.

Lübeck with arguments and good words, and a little later offered them an improvement in their privileges if they would undertake to trade only with Reval or Viborg. When this expedient failed he tried the other tack, and used the threat of interference with the Narva trade as a form of blackmail, in the hope of inducing the Hanse to accept worse terms in Sweden than they were demanding. Not until April 1562, when Ivan was preoccupied by the outbreak of war with Poland, did he pluck up resolution to inform Denmark and the Hanse that he intended to use force; not until the following June did he proceed from words to deeds: in that month his navy captured an entire fleet of thirty-two merchantmen returning home from Narva. Eleven of the vessels taken were from Lübeck; and from the beginning Erik treated the Lübeckers with more severity than the Danes or the Dutchmen, who were usually allowed to go free provided that they agreed to pay toll at Viborg.

The acquisition of Reval had thus involved Sweden in an exacerbation of her already unsatisfactory relations with Lübeck. But it also brought with it a whole crop of new problems. If Erik were now to take over the old Livonian pretension to mulct the Russia trade, this would inevitably draw upon him the ill-will of those who had rejoiced in the breaking down of the Livonian barrier, and who now looked forward to free commercial intercourse with Muscovy. The Danes, the Dutch, the English, were all antagonized by his attempt to blockade Narva; and so too was the Emperor, who in an effort to reconcile his obligation to protect German commerce with his duty to sustain a German Order, proclaimed the Narva trade free for all goods save contraband of war. Moreover, by accepting responsibility for Reval Erik had plunged his country into the polygonal rivalries and anarchic politics of Livonia; he had thwarted the plans alike of the Danish and the Polish partisans. It was scarcely to be expected that he should escape from this tangle without landing himself in hostilities with one or other of the sovereigns who were striving for the reversion to the lands of the Order. For it very soon became clear to Erik and his advisers that they could hardly maintain their hold on Reval indefinitely if their stake in Estonia were limited to the city alone. To be safe, Reval must be provided with some sort of hinterland, if only to deny to possible enemies the bases from which an attack could be mounted against it. But once the capture of neighbouring strongholds was begun, who could define the limits of strategic necessity, or set bounds to the process of expansion? Erik's objectives in going to Reval may have been limited, his aims may well have been essentially defensive, his motive security rather than ambition; but conquests, even for defensive purposes, titillated an appetite for territorial acquisitions, and led him and his successors into political projects or military campaigns which were unambiguously expansionist. The seductive argument of security would henceforth exert its compulsive fascination upon generations of Swedish statesmen; the seed had been planted of a political tradition which only a great national catastrophe would be able to uproot. As early as July 1561 the *råd* was discussing plans for extending the Swedish bridgehead by the capture of Padis and Weissenstein; and in September Padis was in fact taken by Klas Kristersson Horn. It happened to lie within the domains claimed by Magnus of Denmark; and its capture was followed by a Swedish offer to buy off his pretensions in Livonia for a lump sum in cash. The offer was rejected—unwisely, as it now seems—and the Danish stake in Livonia was not abandoned for another twenty years. But the building of the Swedish empire had already begun.

It was apparent from the beginning that Erik could not hope to carry on the struggle in Livonia if he were to fight single-handed against all competitors. He must find a friend and an ally. Very early in the reign he made up his mind that he would choose the tsar. Friendship with Russia carried with it the important advantage that it safeguarded Finland from attack from the east in the event of a war elsewhere. The prospect of good relations with Russia had been one of the arguments which had weighed most with Reval in inducing them to choose Erik as their protector. Yet it was certainly a policy attended by real difficulties. It was scarcely possible to reconcile it with the imposition of a blockade upon Narva: this was one reason why Erik was so slow to take effective action on this point. Moreover, those areas in Estonia which were deemed necessary in order to protect Reval were precisely the areas which were most immediately threatened by Russian invasion and conquest. Erik was not unaware of these contradictions; but to the end of his reign he either pretended that they were not there, or tried to talk his way out of them. What he really wanted from the tsar was a defensive alliance against Denmark and Poland, and an agreement that Russia and Sweden should each give the other a free hand in Livonia. In May 1561 he sent an embassy to Moscow to propose a treaty on these lines. But he had no success whatever. Fredrik II of Denmark was also soliciting Ivan's friendship, and initially seemed much more likely than Erik to obtain it. The tsar, having missed his chance of completing the conquest of Estonia and Livonia before foreign intervention could become effective, was now concerned to play off one foreigner against the other. His truce with Poland was due to expire in 1562, and he could not afford to alienate Denmark by an exclusive compact with Sweden. All that he was prepared to concede to Erik, for the moment, was a renewal of the existing truce upon the old terms. Fredrik, on the other hand, was able in October 1562 to conclude a treaty whereby Ivan recognized Denmark's ownership of Sonnenburg, accepted Magnus as bishop of Ösel and Kurland, and agreed to make no objection if he should capture Padis and Leal—both of which were by that time in Swedish hands; while in return Fredrik promised to give free passage through the Sound to merchants bound for Narva. It was not until the spring of 1564 that Erik was able to persuade Ivan to recognize his rights to Reval, Pernau, Karkus and Weissenstein, and even then only upon very onerous terms.[1]

It may well be that Erik opted for Russia without giving sufficient consideration to the alternatives which were available to him. One such alternative was certainly the alliance of Sigismund II Augustus of Poland; and it was an alternative which could be supported by arguments of some weight. Polish and Swedish commercial interests, for instance, were on the whole coincident rather than antagonistic: each was on bad terms with Lübeck, each stood to gain from stopping the trade to Narva. At first, moreover, the Swedish sphere of influence in Estonia clashed less directly with Polish aspirations than with Danish or with Russian. In the confusion of Livonian affairs, Sweden and Poland had less to divide them, were apparently more natural collaborators, than any other pair of participants. Sigismund Augustus would undoubtedly have been glad to go hand in hand with Erik: in January 1561 a Polish embassy appeared in Stockholm offering friendship and alliance. Erik for his part was not unwilling to be friends; but he could not enter into an alliance without committing himself to antagonism to Russia, and this he was not prepared to consider. He was ready to give Sigismund Augustus an assurance that he would not attack castles in Polish hands; but he made it plain that he intended to attack Padis, Weissenstein, Pernau and Sonnenburg as opportunity might offer, on the ground that Sweden was entitled to indemnity for the privateering activities of the Livonian Knights. Sigismund Augustus, deeming this a mere pretext (as perhaps it was) felt that Erik was being unreasonable; Erik, who had a well-developed talent for arguing himself into a belief in his own rectitude, concluded that the refusal to accept his point of view could only proceed from ill-will. By the summer of 1561 he had made up his mind that Poland was a potential enemy; and he did not afterwards modify that opinion. Within a few months it seemed that he had been right. In November the Livonian Knights dissolved their Order and were incorporated into Poland, Kettler being rewarded for his complaisance with the duchies of Kurland and Samogitia. Sigismund Augustus thus became the sole legatee of all the ill-will which the Order had collected by its privateer-

[1] See below, p. 234.

ing, but also the heir to all the Order's former rights and territories, from the Düna to the Gulf of Finland; while Erik became an encroacher upon a Polish preserve. Sweden and Poland were now confronting one another in Estonia. And one direct consequence of that confrontation was the disastrous quarrel of Erik with his brother Johan.

The death of Gustav Vasa put an end to the working alliance between the brothers: even before that event, the latent tension between them had come to the surface in disputes over the terms upon which Johan was to govern the country if Gustav Vasa should die while Erik was away in England. And when Erik succeeded to the crown, he succeeded also to all his father's cogent objections to any private and personal foreign policy on the part of the royal dukes. After the acceptance of Reval's submission it was obvious that there could no longer be any question of Erik's supporting, or even countenancing, his brother's ambitions in Estonia. Even before his accession he had been jealous of the extensive rights accorded to the royal dukes; and he now saw, more clearly than ever, the danger to the monarchy latent in Gustav Vasa's Testament. Within a few months of his accession he resolutely grasped the nettle. In April 1561 he summoned the *riksdag*[1] to Arboga; and to it he presented that revision of the Testament which goes by the name of the Articles of Arboga.

The Articles of Arboga[2] laid it down that a duke who engaged in any conspiracy against the king should forfeit his right to succeed; they placed the military forces of the duchies under the king's control; they withdrew the right of asylum, forbade the dukes to levy new taxes, regulated their privilege of minting. They prohibited them from appointing bishops, and in general reserved all ecclesiastical policy to the crown; they made it clear that the dukes had no right to confer patents of nobility, nor grant fiefs in perpetuity; they provided for appeals from the ducal courts to the courts of the kingdom, and for a septennial audit of ducal accounts by royal officials. The dukes were forbidden to summon meetings of the local Estates without the king's permission; appointments of *lagmän* were reserved to the crown; no high office might be given to foreigners. All grants of privileges would henceforth require the king's confirmation. More immediately important, the dukes were debarred from conducting an independent foreign policy, except (and it proved a significant exception) in regard to their marriage negotiations; and even in this case with the proviso that their activities were not clandestine, nor prejudicial to the king's interests. These were far-reaching changes. But the king could ask no less, if he were to remain master in his own house; and the *riksdag*, following the

[1] This was the first meeting of the Estates to be officially termed a *riksdag*.

[2] *Svenska riksdagsakter*, I, ii, 9–19.

example of the *råd*, made no difficulty about giving the Articles their approval. The dukes, who had at first shown a disposition to be obstinate, after a short hesitation found it expedient to give way. Yet it was not, as Erik hoped, a final settlement. Duke Magnus, indeed, gave little trouble: he had already shown symptoms of insanity. Duke Karl was still a boy of ten. But Johan was not so easily disposed of. His vanity and his restless ambition would not allow him to be quiet; and in the right to conduct his marriage negotiations he found a loophole in the Articles through which he proceeded to plunge incontinently to destruction.

From as early as January 1561 Johan had been interested in the idea of a Polish marriage: it may even have been suggested to him by Erik himself, by way of distracting his attention from the termination of his hopes in Reval. At all events, Johan sent agents to Poland; and when, in July, the Polish envoy Tenczyński came to Stockholm to seek Erik's alliance, he brought also proposals for a match between the duke and one of the sisters of Sigismund Augustus.[1] Erik made no objection, and so far Johan's conduct had been perfectly unexceptionable. No doubt he had grossly misled Tenczyński about the dimensions of his private fortune and the extent of his ducal rights; but a pedantic adherence to the literal truth has never been considered obligatory in matrimonial politics. But in January 1562 he was indiscreet enough to make a loan of 30,000 *dalers* to his prospective father-in-law, without telling his brother about it. Unluckily for him, the news came to Erik's ears; and it made the worst impression. For only very recently Erik himself had applied to his brother for a loan to finance the military operations in Estonia, and had been refused on the plea that Johan had no money to spare. The irresistible inference was that Johan was willing to give aid and comfort to the potential enemies of his country while denying it to his lawful sovereign. It was no wonder that Erik tried (too late) to stop the transmission of the money, nor that he should now have pressed Johan to drop the Polish match. He even offered to make over to him his own matrimonial prospects with Mary Queen of Scots, to whom he had recently been making tactical advances in the hope of goading Elizabeth to a favourable decision. But Johan was proof even against this inducement. In April 1562 Erik reluctantly gave his consent to Johan's marriage with Katarina of Poland. But he also gave an

[1] Tenczyński was also instructed to ask Erik for a loan. Erik intimated that he was prepared to lend, but only if he were given Wolmar, Wenden and Dünamünde in pawn. These were terms obviously meant to be rejected: the demand for Dünamünde, in particular, was a provocative challenge to Sigismund Augustus in the one area where he was most anxious to make good his footing. Tenczyński also proposed, upon his own account, a marriage between himself and Erik's sister Cecilia, whose reputation had been somewhat tarnished by a court scandal in 1560; but nothing came of the suggestion.

explicit warning that he must be careful to do nothing to compromise the interests of Sweden.

Johan, to do him justice, had probably no such intention. He was certainly most anxious to secure for himself a territory in Livonia which would give him the same kind of independent status as Magnus of Denmark actually enjoyed; but he seems to have thought that he might be able, if successful, to do Sweden good offices as a mediator. He was convinced that the best policy for Sweden was alliance with Poland rather than with Russia; and in this it is at least possible that he was right. But it was folly to suppose that he would be allowed to pursue such a policy once Erik had decided against it. It was certainly unfortunate for him that his matrimonial venture coincided with a sharp change for the worse in Swedish–Polish relations. The responsibility for this development lay mainly with Erik. In 1561 he had begun an unsuccessful intrigue to induce the city of Riga to follow Reval's example and put itself under Swedish protection; and he had followed this by supporting the attempts of the evicted coadjutor of Riga, Christopher of Mecklenburg, to regain control of the archiepiscopal see.[1] Whatever may be thought of Erik's intervention in Estonia, his meddling in Riga can only be regarded as aggression: this was something very different from providing a hinterland for his outpost in Reval by the capture of neighbouring fortresses. And to the Poles it was intolerable: in no circumstances could they suffer a foreign power to establish its influence at the mouth of the Düna. Nevertheless in the spring of 1562 Sigismund Augustus made another attempt to enlist Sweden on his side. This time he began by tactfully admitting that he had not hitherto appreciated the serious nature of Erik's complaints about the privateering of the Order. He therefore offered to summon the Grand Master to explain or defend himself; but he asked that in the meantime Erik should suspend his operations in Livonia. The tone was conciliatory, and the moment well-chosen; for the Swedish advance seemed to have come to a temporary halt. Erik accepted the offer. He agreed to a truce. But he had scarcely done so before the news arrived that his army was actually engaged in besieging Pernau, at that time in Polish hands. The temptation proved more than he could resist. He at once tried to recall his letter to Sigismund Augustus. But he failed to overtake it; and on 2 June 1562 Pernau capitulated to the Swedish forces. Sigismund Augustus, understandably outraged, lost no time in sending an embassy to Fredrik II with proposals for joint action against the Swedes in Livonia. Thus by midsummer, largely by Erik's

[1] By a treaty of October 1562 Christopher agreed to hold the see of Riga as a Swedish fief. But he never in fact recovered it; in 1563 he was taken prisoner by the Poles; and in 1566 the see was secularized and annexed to Poland.

fault, Sweden and Poland were on the brink of war, and only great discretion could save Johan from putting himself into an impossible position.

Discretion, however, was not among Johan's qualities. His reaction to the ominous deterioration of Swedish–Polish relations was to hurry on his marriage before they grew worse. On 26 June he arrived in Danzig; on 4 October he married Katarina Jagiełłonica at Vilna. He had already had the effrontery to assure Sigismund Augustus that he was as independent in Sweden as a prince of the Empire in Germany; he had promised aid against the Russians; he had used his influence to discourage a final Polish attempt to settle the Livonian dispute by amicable compromise. And in return for a further loan to his father-in-law of 120,000 *daler* he had received in pledge seven castles in Livonia. From the point of view of Sigismund Augustus the arrangement had much to be said for it: Johan's castles might serve as a useful buffer-state interposed between Poland and her enemies, whether Russian or Swedish. But as far as Johan's own interests were concerned it was a speculation as unsound as could well be imagined. He had not the resources to play the part of a buffer-state. His chances of acting as a mediator were gone, for Erik no longer trusted him. If his career in Livonia had continued long enough, he would soon have found—as Magnus of Denmark was to find—that small powers are not well-advised to interfere in the quarrels of great ones. Moreover, the possession of the seven castles led him straight to a collision with his brother. One of them, Weissenstein, had been a declared object of Swedish military operations for at least a year: when Johan took it over it was actually on the point of being attacked by a Swedish army. Erik had not the smallest intention of allowing himself to be checked in Livonia for the sake of keeping on good terms with Johan; nor would he tolerate the idea of his brother's being a neutral. In spite of Johan's appeals to desist, Weissenstein was taken by the Swedes in November 1562. Thus the duke's levity and ambition had brought him to within measurable distance of treason. On any evaluation he was guilty of a flagrant breach of the Articles of Arboga.

It was not to be expected that Erik should overlook his offences. Johan had lied to him about his Polish agreements; he had given a shuffling answer to a demand that he assist the king's armies in Livonia. Early in 1563 a former servant of his was caught preaching sedition in Uppland, and his confessions under torture (in Erik's presence) seemed to convict Johan of plotting against his sovereign. His closest friends among the aristocracy hastened to desert him; his attempt to enlist Svante Sture was denounced to the king. It was a significant and ominous circumstance that Erik now turned to the *riksdag* for the trial of his brother: the representatives of the nation were to do justice between the king and the greatest of the aristocracy. Their verdict was speedily reached: on 7 June 1563 they pronounced Johan to have forfeited life, property, and hereditary rights. Erik did not desire his brother's death: all he wanted was to render him powerless to challenge the royal authority or bedevil the royal policy. He offered terms, therefore, which were not unreasonable: Johan might keep his duchy, but he must abstain from politics, stay in Finland, and accept a mentor appointed by the king; he was also to be relegated to a position after his brothers in the order of succession to the throne. The terms were rejected; the royal troops besieged Johan in Åbo castle; on 12 August he surrendered. He was taken with his wife to Sweden; and both were immured in the castle of Gripsholm, where they remained in tolerable comfort for the next four years. Thus Erik had been presented by the weakness and folly of his brother with a political and personal triumph. He used it, on the whole, with moderation:[1] the Articles of Arboga were not made more stringent; the Testament of Gustav Vasa was not further amended. But a royal duke, the centre of the aristocratic cousinhood, was henceforward Erik's bitterest enemy.

Erik had settled accounts with Johan not a moment too soon. On the day after he surrendered Åbo to the king's forces, a Danish herald delivered Fredrik II's declaration of war in Stockholm. Since Gustav Vasa's death, relations between the Scandinavian kingdoms had grown steadily worse. Fredrik II was not the man to make things better; and his appetite for war had not been damped by his hard-won victory over the Ditmarsk peasants in 1559. He had pointedly neglected to confirm the Swedish alliance when he came to the throne, although the treaty of Brömsebro required him to do so; and Erik upon his accession was not sorry to follow his example. The literary feud between the historians of the two countries continued to rage, and Hans Svaning's *History of King Hans* (1561) was considered (in Denmark) to be a telling reply to the libels of Johannes Magnus. Fredrik continued to display the Three Crowns in his coat of arms; Erik retaliated by incorporating the Danish lions in his. And now to these old controversies were added new: the Swedish attacks upon Duke Magnus' possessions in Livonia, the check to Danish designs upon Reval, the blockade of Narva. Of all these disputes, that over the Three Crowns, despite its apparent triviality, really cut deepest. For the assumption of the Three Crowns implied a political programme (as that of the Danish lions did not); and that programme was the restoration of the Scandinavian Union. Fredrik II, like his son Kristian IV half a century later, was out

[1] Except in regard to Johan's unfortunate domestics, some thirty of whom were barbarously executed.

to undo Gustav Vasa's life-work; and what was at stake for Erik was no petty question of prestige, but the continued existence of Sweden as an independent state.

Thus in the years between 1560 and 1563 the two sovereigns moved slowly from peace to war. In September 1561 the Danes accepted an agreement virtually prolonging the treaty of Brömsebro for a further year; but discussion in the Swedish *råd* a month later made it clear that nobody really wished for the alliance to be revived. Erik was playing for time, and he was anxious too that the blame for the rupture, when it came, should fall on Fredrik. The Danish council was in general for peace; but Fredrik was more inclined to listen to the advice of hotheads who told him what he wanted to hear. In January 1563 a Danish embassy left for Stockholm; but its instructions gave it little room for manœuvre. In the following month a scandalous incident put the Danes plainly in the wrong: a Swedish embassy to Hesse, headed by Sten Eriksson Leijonhufvud, was arrested and thrown into prison on its way through Copenhagen. In April the Danish council at last resolved on war, and the first moves were made to organize the blockade of Sweden; in May the guns went off of themselves, when a dispute over salutes led to a sharp naval engagement off Bornholm which ended in the capture of the Danish admiral and three of his ships. In vain did Fredrik's brother-in-law, the elector of Saxony, try to restrain him; in vain did Saxony and Hesse offer themselves as mediators. They succeeded, indeed, in calling a congress to Rostock; but neither Swedes nor Danes appeared at it.

Meanwhile a coalition was forming against Sweden. If in regard to Denmark Erik's attitude was essentially defensive, from the point of view of Lübeck it was clearly provocative. Since 1559 Lübeck's relations with Denmark had been strained: Fredrik II was pursuing an aggressive commercial policy, and in 1560 he wrung from the Hanse a treaty which was a sharp check to their hopes of recovering their former command of Danish trade. There was thus some slight chance of keeping Lübeck and Denmark apart: in October 1561 the *råd* advised negotiation with Lübeck with this end in view. But Lübeck's intransigent attitude made progress difficult. She took her stand on the Strängnäs privileges of 1523, although it was now a quarter of a century since Gustav Vasa had suspended them; while Erik would go no further than to offer small improvements in the privileges which had *de facto* existed in the interim. There followed Erik's blockade of Narva, and the especially harsh treatment meted out to Lübeckers who were caught trying to break it. Of all the trading communities in Europe, it was Lübeck whom the blockade hit hardest: no doubt this was why Erik believed that it could be used to force the burghers to abate their demands for privileges. But in this he proved much mistaken. The Lübeck merchants felt that they must fight or be ruined. Inevitably they turned to Fredrik II for aid. And it was on Lübeck's initiative that an alliance with Denmark was concluded on 13 June 1563. Four months later, it was joined by Poland: as the price of his aid Sigismund Augustus exacted the recognition of Polish claims upon southern Livonia and most of Estonia (the rights of Duke Magnus, however, being guaranteed), and a promise that his allies would insist upon the liberation of Johan. Thus Erik's foreign policy had involved him in simultaneous struggles with three opponents. With Denmark, perhaps, war was unavoidable, and possibly with Lübeck also. But it is difficult not to feel that a more flexible and conciliatory attitude might have saved him the enmity of Poland. Certainly Sigismund Augustus had little in common with his allies but resentment against Erik, and the peace of Stettin in 1570 would show how far he was from approving their war-aims.

The outbreak of war had been preceded by much diplomatic activity, as each side sought to gain friends and tried to isolate the other. Rival embassies competed for the favour of Ivan IV; Swedish and Danish agents struggled for the advantage at the court of Christina of Lorraine. Now that the Brömsebro front against Kristian II's heirs was obviously in process of disintegration, each party to it perceived the desirability of coming to terms privately with Christina. Connected as she was both with the Habsburgs and the Valois, she was a factor in European politics which must be taken seriously: there were plenty of noble adventurers in Germany who would be ready to enlist in her service, if the money were forthcoming. She had every intention of recovering her patrimony if she could; and though her designs were directed equally against Denmark and against Sweden, at the beginning of the sixties it looked as though Denmark might be the more immediately threatened. She was giving harbourage at her court to Peder Oxe, a great Danish nobleman who had quarrelled with his sovereign, and Oxe was inciting her to an anti-Danish policy in the hope of frightening Fredrik II into a reconciliation. It was natural, therefore, that Fredrik should try to safeguard himself. The easiest way to do this was to unite the two branches of the House of Oldenburg: Fredrik would marry Christina's daughter Renata, the legitimist claim would be extinguished, and Denmark and Lorraine could coöperate in the reconquest of Sweden. But this programme proved easier to formulate than to carry out. The blunders and arrogance of Fredrik's negotiators, the counterbids of a Swedish agent, did something to spoil his chances; but really they failed because Christina perceived that she was in a position to play off Fredrik against Erik, and in the end deceive both.

She did not yet think so badly of her prospects as to be ready to compromise: why sacrifice Renata for a half-loaf?

Meanwhile, Erik's endeavours to provide himself with friends against the coming of war had met with no success. It was a long time before he abandoned the hope of an English alliance. Early in 1561 he had sent Nils Gyllenstierna to London to keep the marriage negotiations open; and soon afterwards an English merchant, John Dymoke, had made his appearance in Stockholm. Dymoke had offered to sell jewels which, he suggested, might be sent as presents to Elizabeth; and Erik believed (and was perhaps encouraged by Dymoke to believe) that the offer had a semi-official character. Dymoke was indeed disavowed on his return to England; but Erik was sufficiently hopeful to draw up careful terms for the marriage contract, designed to safeguard the continued independence of Sweden and ensure to him an adequate liberty of action after the wedding. For some months after Gyllenstierna arrived in London he continued to send back to Sweden enthusiastic descriptions of Elizabeth's physical, moral and intellectual charms, and her ardent desire for Erik's arrival; while Erik on his side conducted, in silken Latin, a pastoral-romantic epistolary courtship in the most approved tradition of courtly love. The obvious favour accorded by the queen to Robert Dudley was certainly disquieting; and Erik for a time balanced the alternatives of assassination or single combat as a means of removing him—to the horror of Gyllenstierna, who saw himself cast for the part of Erik's proxy if it came to a duel, and earnestly represented to his sovereign that Dudley was too mean a personage to be honoured by a royal challenge. But on the other hand Dudley's ascendancy had the advantage of predisposing Cecil and the anti-Spanish party at court in Erik's favour. At all events, in the summer of 1561 Erik determined to put his fortune to the test. In September he set sail with a stately fleet for England, where he was expected with considerable popular interest: in London woodcuts were on sale depicting Erik and Elizabeth seated side by side on twin thrones. But fortune was against him; the winds proved contrary; and after some weeks of fruitless battling with the weather in the Skagerrak he gave it up and returned home. The fiasco caused irritation in England, which was not allayed by Erik's announcement in November of his intention to take matrimonial soundings in Edinburgh. Thereafter the marriage project gradually petered out in a *diminuendo* of elegant sighs. Gyllenstierna, who had had much to bear from the king's ungracious letters and changeable humour, quitted England with relief, deep in debt, in April 1562. And Elizabeth gave short and vague answers to requests that English merchants be directed to keep away from Narva.

It was especially important for Sweden, in view of the approaching war with Denmark, to have friends in Germany who could help with supplies if the Sound were shut, balance the influence of Fredrik II's brother-in-law, the Elector Augustus of Saxony, and perhaps even menace Jutland from the south. Erik appreciated this very well. He followed his father's policy of trying to isolate Lübeck from the other Hanse towns; he made friendly approaches to a variety of north German princes, from Oldenburg to Prussia. But when it became apparent that his negotiation with England had little hope of success, he concentrated his attention on Philip of Hesse. His object was double, as it had been in England: he sought at once a political alliance with Hesse, and a marriage with Philip's daughter Christina; and of the two, it was the alliance that interested him most. The marriage negotiations went smoothly enough: despite Fredrik II's imprisonment of Erik's embassy in February 1563 it was expected that Christina would arrive in Sweden in May. But there was difficulty over Erik's insistence that a political alliance should be a condition precedent for the match. The landgrave was perfectly willing to marry his daughter to the king of Sweden; but he resented a stipulation of this sort, which might involve him (as indeed it was designed to do) in the impending quarrel between Sweden and Denmark, and when war actually broke out between them he was less than ever prepared to accept it. On this point the negotiation stuck fast for the rest of the year, until the situation was transformed by a sensational revelation. The news of Erik's approaches to Hesse had caused unfavourable comment at the English court; and Erik, always prone to keep too many political irons in the fire simultaneously, and not yet disposed to abandon hope in England altogether, hastened to write to Elizabeth the letter which the situation seemed to require of the courtly wooer: the Hessian venture, he explained, was only a device to try Elizabeth's constancy; now that her displeasure had demonstrated her love for him, he could assure her once more that his heart was entirely hers. It was the conventional epistolary gesture, the appropriate move in the game of love; and neither he nor she attached any serious meaning to it. By ill-luck, however, the bearer of this missive was captured at sea by the Danes, who promptly forwarded the letter to the elector of Saxony, who in turn sent it on to Philip of Hesse. Philip, not unnaturally, was furious; swore that he would 'wipe the Swedes' noses properly for them'; and proceeded to do so. At the beginning of 1564 the negotiations were broken off; Christina was married to Adolf of Holstein. A generation later, their daughter would become the wife of Karl IX, and in due course the mother of Gustav Adolf. But Erik, with neither bride nor ally, was left to face the hostile coalition alone.

Alone, but by no means unprepared. For some time past he had been engaged in fortifying the three key-fortresses of his realm: Älvsborg to safeguard his outlet to the Atlantic; Viborg to protect his back-door in Finland; Reval to secure his new foothold in Estonia. He had no intention, however, of waging war defensively if he could help it; and with a view to fitting his army to take the initiative he had been carrying through a great programme of military reform. The inspiration came partly from Machiavelli, but even more from Caesar and Vegetius:[1] many contemporary military theorists fell under the influence of these models, but Erik seems to have been the very first commander of modern times to translate their precepts into practice. He organized his infantry into units (*fänikor*) consciously modelled on the cohort; he grouped the *fänikor* into a higher tactical unit which corresponded with the legion. The native army of Gustav Vasa was transformed by being armed (much against its will) with pikes, halberds and body armour, and so was fitted to meet a modern continental mercenary force on equal terms. Erik made the pike the basis of *offensive* infantry tactics, for he considered infantry rather than cavalry to be the battle-winning arm; and he was the first commander since the coming of firearms to employ a true linear formation, instead of the massive blocks which were fashionable on the continent. He trained his troops in the combination of arms—pikes with firearms, halberds with pikes. He reorganized and simplified the wasteful confusion of artillery calibres. It is not too much to say that he had appreciated both the virtues and the limitations of contemporary continental warfare. With no personal experience in the field he had thought out for himself and put into practice solutions to the prevailing tactical *impasse* which were original, which promised to be effective, and which in many respects anticipated by a generation the celebrated reforms of Maurice of Orange: in some ways, indeed, they look forward beyond Maurice to Gustav Adolf.

Erik was even more successful in his work for the navy, though here he was fortunate to be able to build upon the powerful fleet bequeathed to him by his father. He was responsible for some innovations in shipbuilding practice which well illustrate his interest in mechanical and technical problems: it was he who introduced the tumblehome into Swedish naval construction; he armoured his warships at the waterline by providing them with a double hull and filling the intervening cavity with iron-ore; and it is said (with what justice is perhaps doubtful) that in his time Swedish shipwrights were building vessels of a stability unmatched anywhere else in Europe, while for sheer size some of his great-ships may very well have exceeded any other warship afloat in northern waters. It is not necessary to believe the legend which credits

[1] Though not, apparently, from Aelian.

him with the invention of broadside tactics, in order to explain the remarkable successes of the Swedish navy in the war which was now to begin; for it had behind it a king who was receptive to new ideas, convinced of the need for naval strength, and prepared to see to it that the shore administration was kept up to the mark. And there was one other factor too, without which all these reforms would hardly have been possible: the accumulated treasure of Gustav Vasa. The Livonian campaigns cost Erik three and a half million marks in three years; his coronation was of unexampled splendour and costliness; he had to find dowries for a couple of his sisters; he had the expense of his preparations for England, and of an unusually active diplomacy; but he was still able to increase his navy, reform his army, and repair his fortresses. And Sweden stood up to the financial strain of the coming war surprisingly well: better, certainly, than Denmark.

The Seven Years War of the North was on Sweden's side a struggle for survival. Erik had long been afraid of Danish encirclement, and he felt himself confronted with it now. Sjaelland, Skåne, Bornholm, Gotland, Ösel, constituted a chain of Danish strongholds strung out across the Baltic, a barrier shutting him off from his supply-ports in Germany, and now reinforced in depth by Lübeck; while from Jämtland and Härjedalen the Danes were within easy striking-distance of the Gulf of Bothnia, whence it was but an easy transit to Finland. The danger for Sweden was not merely military defeat: it was also strangulation by blockade. Erik's sole means of access to western seas, and western salt, was at Älvsborg; and the war was barely a month old before Älvsborg surrendered tamely to a Danish force. Its loss meant that Sweden was cut off from western Europe; and if Fredrik II could isolate her from Germany too, capitulation might seem to be only a matter of time. Erik's strategy was dictated by this state of affairs. He must break out to the open ocean, if he could; he must somehow keep open his communications with Germany. And in order to make sure that the pursuit of these objectives should not be interfered with by the need to repel a Danish invasion of Småland or Västergötland, he must destroy the concentration-areas and supply-bases of the enemy by devastation of the Danish border provinces. If in the course of these operations he could also annexe (for instance) Blekinge, so much the better. He was not sorry to test the quality of his new army against Fredrik's German mercenaries; and in his navy he was entitled to be confident.

It was a shrewd and sober assessment of the situation and its possibilities, and it was acted on with a considerable measure of success. In 1564 a swift campaign overran Jämtland and Härjedalen, pushed over the watershed, and cut Norway in two by the conquest of Trondheim and the surrounding area. Sweden had broken through to the Atlantic in a broad front; and though the drunken incompetence of Erik's French commander lost Trondheim within a few months, a prospect had been opened which was not forgotten: this exploit looks forward to an article in the peace of Roskilde (1658), to the last plans of Karl XII, to a long-cherished ambition of Gustav III, and to the ultimate union with Norway. Other thrusts in other directions were dictated by the same strategy: in 1565 the loss of Älvsborg was triumphantly offset by the capture of Varberg; and Erik long hoped to take Bohus also. Against Bohus, indeed, two campaigns ended in failure; but in 1567 a great expedition overran much of southern Norway, captured Oslo, and was foiled only by the successful defence of Akershus and the arrival in the nick of time of Norwegian reinforcements from Bergen. By the summer of 1567, it is true, only Varberg ensured Sweden's communications with the west; but if we may judge from the surprising volume of trade which passed through it while it was in Swedish hands, it more than supplied Älvsborg's place. That such a trade was possible was the measure of the achievement of the Swedish navy. From 1565 it dominated the Baltic. In the first two years of the war the country had undoubtedly suffered from the blockade which the Danes succeeded in imposing. The shortage of salt was especially serious. The enmity of Lübeck would not ordinarily have cut off the supply, for most of Sweden's imports came by way of Danzig; but in this war Danzig, although with great reluctance, participated in the blockade, so that Erik had cause to appreciate the forethought of his father, who had stockpiled salt in the aisles of the Great Church in Stockholm. But in 1565 began a series of brilliant naval victories by a great admiral, Klas Kristersson Horn, as a result of which the fleets of Denmark and Lübeck were swept from the seas and the attempt to exclude Sweden from the markets of Germany was definitively broken. The Sound itself was patrolled by Swedish squadrons, the coasts of Denmark were insulted, and Horn took toll of passing ships at his pleasure. And in 1566 the navy brought off a spectacular success by capturing the entire Dutch salt-fleet of fifty-two vessels. It carried enough salt to supply every household in Sweden for a whole year; and its capture broke the back of the blockade for good and all.

By the middle of 1567, then, Erik's prime strategic object had been achieved; and though tactically he met with some reverses—notably a severe defeat at Axtorna in 1565—the balance of fighting on land had been fairly even, and the initiative on the whole had been on the Swedish side. The performance of Erik's new legions had been encouraging: they had overcome an early inclination to throw away their heavy armour, and at Axtorna had covered themselves with glory against hardened German professionals. That Sweden had not done even better was to be attributed mainly to two causes: the prevailing incompetence of the Swedish commanders, and Erik's own lack of practical experience in battle. It was inexperience which led to that disproportion between ends and means which too often vitiated his plans. He relied too much on correct reasoning and paper strategy, and took too little account of human frailty or fallibility. Repeated lessons never cured him of this weakness; nor did his own dubious record in the field give him much charity towards others. It is probably not true that Erik, as his enemies asserted, was a coward; but it is certain that his nerve was not to be relied upon in a crisis, and he was humiliatingly ready to accept his generals' advice to retire to the rear. No doubt he was more intelligent and more efficient than any of his servants in the planning and organization of a campaign, and the supervision of the servicing of his armies. No doubt his death or capture would have crippled Sweden's military power—as appeared clearly enough when he was incapacitated in the last six months of 1567. Nevertheless, these withdrawals made a bad impression. And that impression was not mended by the savage rigour with which he dealt with the shortcomings of his subordinates, and the acerbity with which he reprobated the incompetence of the higher command in public statements to the troops. Nor could it fail to be remarked that among those upon whom he heaped the greatest contumely were members of the high nobility.

Gustav Vasa had become king of Sweden with the consent of the Swedish aristocracy, who had seen in him the only available alternative to Kristian II; and the success of his reign had been in no small measure the result of his ability to retain their support. Apart from the Västergötland rebellion in 1529, all the most serious threats to his authority had come from the lower orders, and all had been mastered because in an emergency the nobility could be relied upon to stand by him: nothing could be further from the truth than the taunt of his enemies that he was a 'peasant king'. Conciliated and gratified by the lands of the church, the magnates had forgotten for a whole generation the political principles which had moved their grandfathers in the age of Kristian I and Sten Sture. After 1529 aristocratic constitutionalism as the fifteenth century had known it seemed as good as dead: the Succession Pact of 1544 appeared to close one epoch in constitutional history and open another. No doubt it was true that by 1560 it might have been predicted that monarchy could hardly continue much longer in the personal and domestic pattern preferred by Gustav Vasa. No doubt the new generation of magnates was more interested in the business of government than the generation which had preceded it. But it must have seemed improbable, at the time of Erik's accession, that the long spell of fair weather was really over, and that Sweden stood at the beginning of a tempestuous period which was to last for more than half a century, in which the central issue would be a violent conflict between monarchy and aristocracy. The origins of this struggle lie in the reign of Erik XIV. It was Erik's relations with his nobility which released once more the old antagonisms which had latterly been dormant; it was his policies and his personality that engendered the sophisticated constitutional movements of the last two decades of the century.

It would be misleading to think of Erik as being in principle hostile to the nobility. He had too high a sense of his royal dignity, too anxious a concern for the splendour of the throne, for any such feeling. For him, as for Gustav III, the nobility must lend lustre to the crown: in this matter Sweden's prestige must not suffer by comparison with the other monarchies of Europe. But though the aristocracy had a duty to be ornamental, it must not be ornamental merely: Sweden lacked administrators, ambassadors, commanders, and it was for the nobility to supply them. The aristocracy, like the monarchy, had obligations to the state; and Erik's attitude to them was much influenced by his view of how they discharged them. On the whole, with certain notable exceptions, they did not stand up well to his scrutiny. He found them slack, inefficient, and indifferently honest. These defects, in his view, necessarily derogated from their status; for the essence of nobility was not birth, nor even breeding, but character. And too often the lack of character with which he reproached them took forms which he was disposed to equate with lack of loyalty towards himself: from the beginning he was prone to mistake mere indifference or ineptitude for sabotage. His exalted notion of the royal office, his care to set a distance between himself and the greatest of his subjects, led him too easily to see a challenge to his authority where none was intended. In essence, no doubt, his rule was no more absolute than that of his father; but his absolutism, unlike Gustav Vasa's, was explicit and theoretical, rather than implicit and pragmatic; and as such it invited the aristocratic opposition which it encountered. His coronation oath was so brief and so vague that it almost proclaimed an intention not to suffer precise limitations upon his freedom of action. As the first hereditary monarch, Erik was sensitive to even the suggestion of a threat to the rights of his dynasty; and if in the end he became a tyrant it was mainly fear that made him so: he had not read his Machiavelli for nothing. The Sture family, after all, still survived; a dynastic revolution was still conceivable, given adequate aristocratic support. From the mass of the people he felt he had nothing to fear: on more than one occasion he intervened to protect them from their masters or his servants, and he continued popular with them even after the final catastrophe. But his was a mind fatally accessible to suspicion; and of the aristocracy he was suspicious almost from the beginning.

All this was not apparent in the early months of the reign. The most pressing domestic problem then seemed to be to safeguard the integrity of the monarchy against the dangers of fragmentation implicit in Gustav Vasa's Testament, and this could be done only if Erik could carry the nobility with him. He went to considerable lengths to conciliate them. Gustav Vasa, in the course of his long and nefarious career, had contrived to amass a great collection of estates in the private possession of his family: some of them were ecclesiastical lands, allegedly donated by earlier Vasas to the church in the years between 1454 and 1527; others were the prize of ruthless litigation or the result of hard bargains and forced exchanges. These lands were kept distinct from the lands of the crown: they were the 'inheritance and property' (*arv och eget*) of the Vasa family, and each of the royal dukes now had his share of them. The title to many of them was questionable; and Erik used this fact with great skill to secure the support of the magnates, and at the same time to weaken his brothers. He simply intimated that he would permit process for recovery of these lands by those who might have a claim to them. The results of the ensuing litigation were startling. Of some 5,000 manors, over 2,600 were now adjudged to have been improperly acquired. The great families regained much that they had regarded as for ever gone; while Erik himself lost much less than might have been expected. For among the plaintiffs in these proceedings was the crown itself, whose representatives were able to establish the fact that many crown manors had in fact been transferred by Gustav Vasa to his private possession. Moreover, the crown was also able to recover a considerable quantity of church lands which had illegally passed into noble hands in the lawless scramble at the end of the twenties. The real losers in the whole affair were the royal dukes, who saw their inheritance diminished to the profit of the crown and the nobility and obtained nothing in return.

Another measure taken in these early months of the reign may also have been designed to attach the magnates to him. On the occasion of his coronation in 1561, he created three counts (among them Svante Sture) and nine barons. This was an innovation, for there had hitherto been no distinction in Sweden between a titled and an untitled nobility; and it is possible that one reason for it was Erik's determination that Svante Sture should be able to talk to English earls upon a footing of social equality. However that may be, it was a step which had important and long-lasting consequences. There had long been a real distinction between the great landed magnates and the poor nobles who owned only a couple of manors, and were hard put to it to do their knight-service when called upon. But hitherto the distinction had been social and economic only: legally, both were in the same position; both enjoyed the same privileges. The coming of a titled nobility, however, was soon followed by a differentiation in legal status and private rights. Erik endowed his counts with only small grants of land, and those mostly scattered, while upon his barons he conferred nothing save the bare title; but his successor would give them substantial estates, and special judicial powers and liberties within them; their privileges and immunities would be greater than those of the ordinary noble; their counties and baronies would descend by the alien custom of male primogeniture. Increasingly they would become a specially favoured nobility within the nobility. And this difference in status and rights would exacerbate the ill-feeling between high nobility and low which already existed as a result of the wide variations of wealth within the noble class. By 1607, the counts would be frankly admitting that they were universally hated; nor did the jealousy of them grow less in the decades that followed. It is not necessary to accept the suggestion that Erik created the counties in order to sow dissension among the nobility; but it is certainly true that the monarchy was able to exploit the bad feeling to its own advantage. The deepening division within the privileged class would in the following century pave the way for an absolutism which after 1680 swept aside, for a whole generation, the constitutional safeguards which it had been the aristocracy's historic mission to contend for. And the creation of the counties had one further effect. The counties were royal donations, gifts of land upon certain defined terms, to which specific rights very soon came to be attached. They were also hereditary; and their holding conferred status. In all these respects they differed from the old administrative fiefs of the fifteenth century. They were, in fact, more like a feudal fief than anything Sweden had ever known—apart, indeed, from the royal duchies, which were closely akin to them, though on a grander scale. It was not long, moreover, before they ceased to be the only examples of this kind of quasi-feudal arrangement. As successive kings rewarded their servants, or appeased their creditors, with donations of land, there came to be an increasing tendency for such land to be granted upon conditions rather than as an allodial holding: among the most significant and the most usual of such conditions were the obligation to seek confirmation at every change of ruler, and the reservation of the crown's right of resumption upon failure of heirs-male. In 1604 Karl IX would find it expedient to formalize and stereotype this development.

The acceptance of the Articles of Arboga by the *riksdag* in 1561, and the consequent ending of immediate danger from the dukes, made it less necessary for Erik to cultivate the nobility's goodwill: thereafter his policy took on a sharper edge. In the days when the monarchy was still elective, the nobility had used a change of ruler as an opportunity to secure a confirmation of old privileges, or extract new ones, as the price of their recognition of the new occupant of the throne. The coming of hereditary succession deprived them—or seemed to deprive them—of their power to bargain; they were reduced to petitioning for better privileges where formerly they had been able to stipulate for them. To Erik they petitioned in vain; and they took his refusal ill. They soon found that he was more inclined to curtail privileges than to extend them. The essential sign of noble status, the essential *quid pro quo* for the favoured position which the nobleman enjoyed, was the performance of knight-service (*rusttjänst*) by the sending of one or more heavy-armed cavalrymen to the king's army, to serve without payment for so long as service was within the limits of the realm. In 1526 Gustav Vasa had introduced the principle of graduated obligation, at the rate of six fully-armed men for every 400 marks' worth of revenue from land. The new scale, however, does not seem to have been effectively or generally applied, and Gustav Vasa was often content with *ad hoc* agreements on a local basis. But in the decade before 1560 Erik began to make the principle of graduation effective in the areas which he administered; the demands for *rusttjänst* grew heavier; and a distinction began to be made between revenues from allodial lands, and revenues which had been assigned to a noble by the king in return for administrative services: such revenue-assignments (*förläningar*) were now to be more heavily assessed than the yield of family estates. The king became noticeably less willing to shut his eyes to evasions, false assessments of revenue, and neglect to perform the service that was properly due. Erik was determined that the nobility should not be permitted to be slack in this matter. At the Uppsala *riksdag* of 1562, after stormy discussions, he imposed a regulation of *rusttjänst* which marked a sharp increase in royal demands. A horseman was now required for every 300 marks' revenue from noble estates, and every 200 marks' revenue from *förläningar*; the force raised was to be liable to serve for three months abroad without pay; service in Livonia was to be considered as service within the realm (and would thus be unpaid, however long the period of service might be); light-armed horsemen would no longer be accepted; and the arrangement was to last for the remainder of the reign. There was, indeed, one apparent concession: ordinary noblemen were to be allowed exemption for one manor (*sätesgård*), barons for two, counts for three; but the purpose of this provision was not so much to confer a benefit as to set a limit to the exemptions that could be tolerated. The whole system was tightened up: proper returns of allodial revenue were insisted on, a register of *förläningar* was to be kept in the treasury, revenue from *förläningar* was to be shown in the bailiff's accounts, which were then to be defalked of an equivalent amount. In 1565 a separate unit of noble cavalry was formed for the first time. These measures were felt as a heavy burden; but despite Erik's efforts they were not really successful. Even in war-time the nobility evaded its obligations: in 1566 they defaulted to the extent of nearly half the service due from them. The odium of the attempt was not offset by the results it produced.

The irritation of the nobility was not lessened by Erik's policy in the matter of the granting of fiefs. In Gustav Vasa's time the process had already begun which was to transform the old administrative fief—granted by the crown in order to disburden itself of the task of government—into an office of local administration under the crown's direct control and supervision. Fiefs were no longer allowed to remain for long periods in the same hands. Large fiefs became rare, and were increasingly restricted to members of the royal family, or its close relations: in one aspect, the royal duchies are to be considered as the last examples of the old-style service-fief as the fifteenth century had known it. Their creation had accelerated the process of fief-resumption and the replacement of fiefs by royal (or ducal) administration—a process which was already visible in the early fifties. After Erik's accession it was carried still further: between 1557 and 1568 the number of counties (*härader*) granted as fiefs to private individuals was halved. For the first time, moreover, the interests of the relatives of the royal family were affected: between 1562 and 1568 they lost more than half of the fiefs which they had previously held. In place of the old fief (*län*) the servants of the state were rewarded with the new *förläningar*; accounting passed out of their hands into that of the royal bailiffs. Hitherto local revenues had been collected and spent by the fief-holder, who had found his reward in the surplus of income over expenditure; now they became a fund chargeable with administrators' wages. In short, the nobility—and especially the high nobility—began in Erik's time to awaken to a realization of the financial implications for themselves of a generation of slow administrative change; and they found those implications decidedly unpleasant. They were losing, or had lost, the opportunities for profit presented by fief-holding; and as yet the monarchy seemed to offer them little in the way of compensation. Not very many of them were fitted by education or training to become regular civil servants: it was Erik's complaint that they were less useful to him than a nobility might be expected to be. And most disquieting of all was the fact that they saw the monarchy turning in its need to other men, drawn from other classes, who usurped the political influence, and annexed some of the material rewards, which they had long been habituated to consider as their own preserve.

It is in Erik's reign that there first appears that long-lived political phenomenon which is known to Swedish historians as the 'rule of secretaries'. Gustav Vasa in his day had relied much upon civil servants of non-noble origin; but though some of these clerks and secretaries had been efficient and honest, and had continued to retain Gustav Vasa's confidence, they had all been men of subordinate status, designed to be the tools of his directing hand, risking no initiative: not one had been of real political importance. Under Erik they acquired a new and sinister significance; for they became—or at least seemed to their enemies to become—for the first time not only the monarchy's administrative *factotum*, but the agents, and perhaps the inspirers, of a policy that was deliberately anti-aristocratic. In these circumstances the secretaries began for the first time to be persons of consequence. And one of them, Jöran Persson, became something like Erik's confidential minister. Jöran Persson was a parson's son from Sala; educated in jurisprudence at Wittenberg, with financial support from Gustav Vasa; commended by Melanchthon. On his return home in 1555 he had made the expected return for the money that had been laid out upon him, and entered the king's service, being in 1558 advanced to the position of secretary. After 1560 he became Erik's right-hand man. He was highly intelligent, highly professional and efficient, greedy of power and arrogant in the use of it; so clearly bound to the king's interest by regard for his own safety and advantage that even Erik could not really doubt his fidelity; ruthless with a dry and passionless cruelty, infinitely dangerous from the use which Erik made of him and the readiness with which he listened to his advice. By the aristocracy he was both feared and hated; for he had usurped the place in the king's counsels which they believed to be rightly theirs, and their interests and his were for the most part antagonistic. He was the very type, and certainly the most formidable example, of a new class of royal servant which throve on the decline of aristocratic influence; an apt instrument of absolutism; a natural enemy to those traditions of aristocratic constitutionalism which the fifteenth century had fought for, and which were now—of necessity—to be exhumed. Among the offices which he discharged—and discharged with relish—was that of procurator-fiscal: it was he who managed the case against Johan, it was he who arraigned those members of the nobility upon whom Erik's suspicions happened to fall, it was he (in a word) who seemed to the nobility the agent of royal tyranny, the personification of a *régime* which they felt to be despotic, and which in retrospect they would condemn as unconstitutional.

The most important of the agencies through which Jöran Persson worked, and the most detested, was a new High Court. In Sweden the king was still the fount of justice, the *summus judex*, entitled to doom his own dooms, bound by his office to be accessible to those of his subjects who might 'go to the king' for legal redress. It was a burdensome and time-consuming obligation, for Sweden had as yet no central court of appeal to which cases might be referred from local tribunals. The High Court was intended to take some of this judicial work off the king's shoulders. Erik had planned it in his father's lifetime, and its creation was among the first acts of his reign. Its business was to hear appeals—even from the courts of the duchies—and to go on circuit once every three years for the convenience of litigants; but it was also a court of first instance. It took cognizance both of civil and criminal cases: among other matters it dealt with claims for recovery of lands from the Vasa family estates. At first the nobility had no complaint against it; and of its sixteen original members almost all were drawn from the high aristocracy. After 1561, however, both its constitution and the character of its business underwent a change. The aristocratic members were replaced by commoners; and the court increasingly occupied itself with charges of treason, sedition, sabotage or negligence, with Jöran Persson appearing as prosecutor for the crown. During the war it functioned as a kind of court-martial, and dealt with cases of indiscipline and accusations of incompetence or lack of enterprise: it was also the agency which the king used to bring to book nobles who defaulted on their *rusttjänst* obligations.[1] Its procedures were perfectly regular, and conformed to accepted Swedish legal standards; but its sentences were unusually severe. Between 1562 and 1567 it pronounced the death penalty in more than 300 cases of the most varied description: men were sentenced to death for speaking taunting words of the king, for adultery, for slandering the king's servants, for leaving the royal service without permission, for painting the royal arms upside down, as well as for the usual offences of negligence, defalcation or embezzlement. It is true that many of these sentences—perhaps a majority—were not carried out: they were commuted to heavy fines, and were indeed often imposed with the idea of their being commuted, as a measure for bringing in revenue. A dishonest or negligent bailiff, condemned to death one month, would often enough resume his duties the next as though nothing had happened. But there was another and more sinister reason for the frequency of death-sentences. There seems no doubt that torture, though

[1] In a number of cases it deprived defaulters of their noble status.

no part of the court's procedures, was employed extrajudicially by Jöran Persson to extract information, and that such information was accepted by the court as evidence, without inquiry into the circumstances in which it was obtained. But torture was applied only to those under sentence of death, and its main purpose was to force the disclosure of guilty knowledge and the betrayal of supposed accomplices. Thus the death-sentence would be pronounced, not with any intention of its being carried out, but because the accused was thought to be in possession of information which might be elicited in the torture-chamber. A member of the nobility upon whom the king's suspicion had fallen might see his menial servant arrested for a trivial offence, condemned to death, and racked until he should implicate his master in some real or imaginary conspiracy. It may indeed be true that the court's most important function was to instil a salutary terror into the lazy or the corrupt, but it is understandable that it should have been feared and hated by the nobility as a tyrant's invention; nor is it surprising that they should have come to the conclusion that aristocratic control of the organs of government was an essential precondition of the continuance of the rule of law.

If the aristocracy thus came to feel that the High Court was a weapon directed against themselves, they had other grounds for anxiety in Erik's use of the *riksdag*. For Erik used the *riksdag*, as his father had used it in 1527, as an ally against political opponents. In the thirty years since 1530 there had been little need for such tactics, and the successors of Ture Jönsson had perhaps forgotten how formidable the alliance might be in a skilful monarch's hand. If so, they were now forcibly reminded of it. Erik went out of his way to take the Estates into his confidence. He explained his policies to them, he discussed the question of the succession with them, he asked their approval of his matrimonial projects, he sent them home happy with presents of salt. And he used them as a court, to give judgment between himself and his adversaries: it was they who pronounced the final condemnation of Johan; it was they to whom he was to appeal for justice upon his aristocratic opponents. In 1566 he even held a meeting of the *riksdag* to which the Nobility was not summoned—an unprecedented step, unique in Swedish history. It was a revival of that union of ruler and Estates which young Herr Sten had once exploited; and it had important constitutional consequences. For the reviving tradition of aristocratic constitutionalism, confronted with that union, saw the *riksdag* as a body always liable to allow itself to become the passive instrument of despotism, or at least as an organ which could not be relied upon to resist it. The memory of the part the Estates played in Erik's time would not soon pass away, and before it grew dim would be reinforced by the still more painful experiences of the 1590s. A division was opened between the representative assembly of the nation, on the one hand, and the aristocratic champions of constitutional principles, on the other. It was a division which would hamper the emergence of a truly constitutional system of government; a division which would not be healed before 1719.

It is not surprising, then, that the high aristocracy should have been forced into opposition to the crown in the years after 1562. They had real grievances and solid grounds for apprehension. It is not so obvious why Erik should have gone out of his way to alienate them. For a generation they had been the faithful allies of the crown; they were no more inefficient after 1560 than they had been in his father's time. The explanation is to be sought in the dark recesses of Erik's mind, in that brooding mistrust which was already casting a creeping shadow over the brilliant promise of his youth. Gustav Vasa had not really doubted his ability to cope with the great magnates, if it should be necessary to do so. Erik was afraid of them. He was nervous of conspiracies against himself; nervous above all of conspiracies against the dynasty. It was dynastic reasons that produced the crisis of 1567; it was the question of Erik's marriage that wrecked the reign.

By 1567, indeed, marriage had become a matter of real urgency; for by now Erik was thirty-four. A succession of casual mistresses, a small brood of royal bastards, gave his conscience twinges which recurred with increasing frequency as the years went by; and dynastically it was evident that the situation called for speedy action. Johan had put himself out of the running; Magnus was intermittently insane; only Karl remained. Erik had certainly been very unlucky in his attempts to find a wife:[1] so unlucky, that the suspicion was beginning to take root that his repeated failures were no accident. Was it not possible, perhaps, that successive negotiations had been wrecked by the agents to whom he had entrusted them? that the aristocracy were deliberately spoiling his matrimonial chances in order to ensure that he had no legitimate heir? It occurred to him that Johan would hardly have turned rebel without encouragement. What more likely than that he had been egged on to treason by his noble relatives, in order to compass his destruction? It had been the crisis over Johan's rebellion, moreover, that had pushed Magnus over the brink of insanity: at one stroke two members of the royal house had been eliminated as potential successors. It was characteristic of Erik that he should forget how large a share of the responsibility for his misfortunes lay at his own door. He had certainly made success more difficult that it need have been. He had been too

[1] Approaches had been made to Poland, Saxony and Mecklenburg, as well as to England, Scotland and Hesse.

clever in trying to combine marriage with political advantage. He had defeated himself by attempting to keep too many projects in the air at once. He was not content to take any suitable healthy princess, irrespective of her personal charms. In this matter his standards were exacting: in 1561 he had told a Prussian diplomat that if it were at all possible he wanted to see his bride before committing himself, having no wish to share the unhappy experiences of Henry VIII. Nor was he prepared to be satisfied with the daughter of a petty German prince: as hereditary king he was looking—in the first instance at all events—for someone better than his mother. All this left him with a range of choice which was not wide; and it was natural to consider whether, if Europe failed to provide a queen, he might not be forced to look for one at home, as his father had done before him. But his father's example seemed rather a warning than an encouragement. The Leijonhufvuds and the Stenbocks, he felt, had had their consideration dangerously enhanced by their marriage into the Vasa family. The last thing that he desired was to strengthen the ring of high nobility on the steps of the throne, and so put the fate of the dynasty into the hands of a close aristocratic clique.

Thus the problem of Erik's marriage became a major political question for the country, and an obsession with Erik himself. Repeatedly he consulted *riksdag* and *råd* about it, seeking their endorsement of his projects, extracting from them undertakings to accept his ultimate choice, wherever it might fall. Already in 1561, when the *riksdag* gave its blessing to the English venture, it also gave a promise to acquiesce in his marriage with any of his subjects, of whatever rank: it was an assurance which was to be repeated in 1565 by the Clergy, and in 1566 by all the lower Estates. If a royal or princely bride was not available, no matter; he would turn elsewhere: his rank sufficed to raise any woman above her fellow-subjects. Did not the *råd* advise him in January 1565 that if he was not to marry beneath him only the Emperor's daughter would serve? It was true that they had also urged him, if he should decide to seek a wife at home, to choose from the nobility; but that was no more than he had expected—and feared. It seemed obvious that they wanted to manœuvre him into a position where he would have no option but to take the daughter of some native magnate; and if they failed in that, to ensure the extinction of the Vasa line. At the great winter market at Uppsala in February 1565 Erik for the first time publicly expressed his belief in the existence of an aristocratic plot against the dynasty: it was a bogy which was to haunt his successors for half a century. Already, perhaps, he had made up his mind that if a foreign marriage should elude him, it would not be to the aristocracy that he would turn for his consort.

At the end of 1565 and the beginning of 1566 there occurred a series of events which brought all these nebulous suspicions to a focus. They centred upon Nils Sture, the eldest son of Svante Sture, who was serving with Erik's armies in the south of Sweden. In December 1565 Nils was sent to Västergötland with orders to compel the local peasantry to do labour-service on the fortifications of Varberg, and punish those who had been remiss in discharging this duty. The work was certainly of the first importance; but it is at least possible that Erik intended the commission to be a trial of reliability, and perhaps he calculated that Nils's punitive measures would have the useful effect of preventing his gaining undesirable popularity with the lower orders. In the event, Nils neglected to carry out his instructions, pleading that he had received later orders of a different tenor which superseded the earlier. He was harshly rebuked and recalled from the army; but his explanations were apparently accepted, and for a little while his relations with the king seemed unimpaired. In June 1566, however, he was arrested, and given the option of a trial by the High Court or a public humiliation. He elected to be tried; his arguments in defence were convincingly demolished; and he was sentenced to the degradation which he had sought to avoid. He was compelled to ride through the streets of Stockholm with every circumstance of ignominy, in the same sort of mock-triumph as once Gustav Vasa had inflicted upon Peder Sunnanväder;[1] he was made to sign an acknowledgment of his guilt; and he was forced to promise to bear no malice. It was ordered also that no one should presume to allude to his humiliation in future on pain of death. There followed a formal reconciliation with the king, and a promise that Nils should marry Erik's bastard daughter Virginia.

There is no doubt that Erik came to fear the pretensions of the Sture family; and it is at least possible that his nervousness was based on astrological grounds. He had read in the stars that he was to lose his crown to a 'light-haired man'; and there is some reason for supposing that he identified this personage with Nils Sture—though to be sure Nils's hair is said to have inclined more to ginger. At all events it may well be that he hoped that the shameful spectacle in Stockholm would make Nils Sture an impossible candidate for the throne. What he did not grasp was that the high aristocracy—or at least that important section of it which was closely linked to the Stures by ties of blood—was bound to feel the treatment meted out to Nils as a gross and inexpiable insult. From this moment Erik was for them a declared enemy: henceforward they would shape their course accordingly. Erik himself did not accept the logic of his actions. It was characteristic of his attitude to the nobility in the next three years that he should

[1] See above, p. 57.

have at first received Nils amicably, then inflicted a savage punishment upon him, and lastly sought to expunge all memory of it in a reconciliation buttressed by written pledges and gilded by flattering promises. He wavered in his purpose, it seems, for two reasons: first because he was not yet fully assured that his nightmare of a noble conspiracy was a reality; but also because, even assuming that it was so, he could not make up his mind about the best way to meet it. Should he strike it down ruthlessly before it could gather to a head, and risk the consequences? Or was it safer to meet it by guile, pretended amity, and—if the worst came to the worst—submission? The problem tortured him for the remainder of his reign. But at least he could put Nils's fidelity to a final proof, and by so doing could establish or explode the theory of an aristocratic plot. The last of Erik's attempts to find himself a foreign bride was already under way: negotiations had already been opened in Lorraine. To Lorraine therefore he would send Nils Sture, to conduct those negotiations as his ambassador; and upon the success or failure of his mission he would base his conclusions and his future conduct. Here at last, it seemed to him, was the acid test.

By 1564 Christina of Lorraine's hopes of recovering her Scandinavian patrimony were beginning to crystallize into something like a precise plan, and that plan contemplated as its first move an attack upon Denmark rather than Sweden. It was obviously much easier to assemble an army to invade Jutland than to transport her forces across the Baltic or the North Sea: her father's solitary enterprise in that line had not been such as to encourage imitation. She believed that she could count on help from Hamburg; and her agents were well received by the restive peasants of Ditmarsk. She was also intriguing with John Frederick of Saxony and his minister Grumbach. John Frederick, deprived of his electorate after the battle of Mühlberg, was always ready to take sides with the enemies of the usurping branch of his house; and since the Elector Augustus was brother-in-law to Fredrik II, and well known as his supporter in Germany, John Frederick was a likely recipient for Christina's overtures. Grumbach, who in 1563 had been put to the ban of the Empire, was a desperate man with little to lose, who was glad enough to cultivate the goodwill of potential employers against the day when Germany might become too hot to hold him. Already in the spring of 1564 Nils Gyllenstierna, who remained on the continent during the war as Erik's ambassador at large, had been empowered to get into touch with him. In these circumstances it seemed to Christina that it ought to be possible to turn the hostilities between Sweden and Denmark to her advantage, and enlist Erik as at any rate a temporary ally. In 1564 her agent von Berg, who was in close touch with Grumbach, arranged a meeting with Gyllenstierna in Rostock, at which the terms for political coöperation were discussed. And at that meeting the suggestion was made for a marriage between Erik and Renata.

At this stage Erik's only concern either with Christina or with Grumbach was a desire to alarm Fredrik II sufficiently to induce him to divert some of his forces from Sweden to the Holstein border. He was quite prepared to strike a bargain with Christina; he was ready to promise to help her to conquer Denmark; but he expected to be liberally rewarded for his trouble. His terms for assistance were that she should renounce all claims upon the throne of Sweden, and that he should be permitted to annex Norway, Halland, Skåne and Blekinge, as well as that old bone of contention, Gotland. It was only after the visit to Sweden of Christina's envoy, in May 1565, that he began seriously to consider the idea of a marriage; and for some months after that he made it quite clear that his interest in Lorraine was much more political than matrimonial. By the close of 1565, however, the prospects for an alliance were looking doubtful, and the Swedish envoys in Lorraine began to put the marriage in the forefront of their negotiation. In March 1566 the Uppsala *riksdag* gave the plan its approval. It would, indeed, have been a brilliant turning of the trick against Denmark. But unfortunately for Erik Christina had never considered him as more than a useful trump in her complex game of political intrigue, and before the end of 1566 she was already beginning to think that it might be wiser to discard him. Her Guise relations had no intention of supporting her schemes; Philip II, by the mouth of Cardinal Granvelle, intimated that he would spare no money for Scandinavian adventures; Maximilian II warned her that Erik was a dangerous man to deal with. The information that reached Stockholm from Lorraine—and communications, as accident would have it, were unusually and infuriatingly slow—was notably lacking in precision: only a very sanguine eye could read much encouragement into it.

It was upon this unpromising mission that Nils Sture was now dispatched. He was to bring back a decision from a court whose interest it was not to give one; he was to clinch a marriage which the other party was already almost determined to avoid; and upon his success or failure might well hang the fate of himself, his family and his relations. The dice were loaded against him from the beginning: not the most devoted and efficient of Erik's servants, not Jöran Persson himself, could have snatched success from such an assignment. Nils Sture, as it happened, was not very efficient, and was far from being a devoted servant. His reconciliation with the king had been forced, and on his side insincere: a letter to his mother makes it plain that what he wanted was rehabilitation and revenge. Already before leaving Sweden he had broken the pledges he had given to Erik. In July 1566 there took place a secret gathering of magnates on an islet in the Stockholm skerries. It was an indignation-meeting, a protest-meeting against Erik's proceedings and particularly against his treatment of Nils Sture. The list of those who attended it included Nils Sture himself, Abraham Stenbock, Ivar Ivarsson Lillieörn, Hogenskild Bielke, Klas Fleming, Sten Baner, and—most ominously of all—Erik's youngest brother Karl. What passed at the meeting is uncertain; but it is clear that strong language was used: Abraham Stenbock was later charged at his trial with having said that Erik hated the nobility and wished to treat them all as he had treated Nils Sture. For the moment no word of these proceedings came to Erik's ears; but they mark the point at which aristocratic resentment passed into organized resistance.

At the turn of the year the slow-gathering domestic crisis suddenly exploded with a violence which made any further pretence of harmony impossible. In December 1566 Nils Hansson, one of the mission which Erik had sent to Lorraine, returned home to report progress. It at once became painfully obvious that there was no progress to report.[1] Erik's suspicions of Nils Sture at once returned in full force, and within a month they received dramatic confirmation. In January 1567 Gustav Ribbing, an unsatisfactory young aristocrat who was one of Erik's pages, was condemned to death for deserting the king's service. Under torture, he accused Svante Sture, Per Brahe and Gustav Olsson Stenbock of conspiring to prevent Erik's marriage by sabotaging his attempts to find a foreign bride; and further accused Sten Eriksson Leijonhufvud of trying to force Erik into a marriage with his daughter. The charge seemed not implausible; and it was deadly. Erik had no doubt that it was true. What more likely than that the Leijonhufvuds should seek to draw him into their family net, as once they had drawn his father? The Vasas were to be dragged back to the level from which they had risen, and to become once again no more than the titular leaders of a ruling oligarchy, as Karl Knutsson had been a century before. Erik well remembered how Sten Eriksson had supported Gustav Vasa's opposition to the English match. His reaction to these revelations was characteristic. On 24 January 1567 he extorted from Svante Sture and Sten Eriksson a written acknowledgment that evil-minded and traitorous men, from a design to root out the house of Vasa, had tried to prevent his marriage, had fomented Johan's rebellion, and had caused the insanity of Duke Magnus; and he further forced them to promise that they would accept a queen of Swedish birth, from whatever class of society.

By subscribing this extraordinary document they put themselves,

[1] He was charged before the High Court with neglect of duty amounting to treason, condemned to death, and sent to work in the silver-mine at Sala.

their relatives, and above all the hapless Nils Sture, at the king's mercy. Nor was this all. Hard on the heels of Ribbing's accusation came another alarming disclosure; for it was now that Erik received—probably from his ruffianly brother-in-law Magnus of Saxe-Lauenburg—information of Nils Sture's fatal meeting on the islet in the skerries. To a man of Erik's mentality it was now hardly possible to doubt that the great families were deep in a conspiracy against him.

Throughout the spring and early summer of 1567 Erik seems to have been in a state of mounting nervous tension: it is easy to see, in the light of what was to follow, that he was already near breaking-point. His irritability and his morbid fears had already passed beyond the bounds of normality. Per Brahe tells us that he could not endure to see his pages smartly dressed, lest they should prove too attractive to the women about the court; and if a courtier put his hand over his mouth, or cleared his throat, or whispered or smiled to his neighbour, Erik was sure that men were laughing at him. A chamberlain was arraigned before the High Court because Erik's sceptre was found broken on the floor of his dressing-room, and because there had been difficulty in securing the services of a pearl-embroiderer to adorn the suit of clothes which he planned to wear at his wedding. He flew into rages if his road took him past haystacks covered with fir-branches; for inverted fir-trees had been used to make a mock-triumphal arch for Nils Sture, and he suspected that his servants were deliberately reminding him of it. One of Svante Sture's retainers, on his way to the gunsmith's with a musket in need of repair, chanced to meet the king in the street: he was arrested, condemned to death, tortured to make him incriminate his master, and sent to work in the mines. Jöran Persson must bear responsibility for the torture; the arrest was Erik's order. Two tent-guards were condemned to death because Erik found a jug, a cloak and a halter on the floor of the royal privy: they had been put there, he said, 'to annoy him'.[1] Examples such as these, all taken from late in 1566 and early in 1567, make it difficult to resist the conclusion that the balance of Erik's mind was already seriously disturbed.

It must be acknowledged, however, that apart from such fancies there were real troubles and real anxieties sufficient to put a strain upon a more equable temper than his: the negotiations with Lorraine, and with Grumbach, hung endlessly in the balance; the expedition to Norway was at a critical point; and Erik's relations with Ivan IV had reached a stage at which he was faced with the need to make a harassing decision. The outbreak of the Seven Years War of the North had been greeted by Ivan with natural satisfaction: at a time when internal

[1] Jöran Persson found it expedient to add crossed sticks to the inventory, in order to give the case a more or less rational appearance of being a matter of witchcraft.

difficulties in Russia were making it impossible for him to push his pretensions to the Baltic lands he saw his competitors at each other's throats. For Erik, of course, the war made the goodwill of Russia more important than ever. Ivan saw this and exploited his opportunity. By the treaty of Dorpat (May 1564)—negotiated, as of old, not with the tsar but with the governor of Novgorod—Erik did indeed obtain Russian recognition of his right to Reval, Pernau, Karkus and Weissenstein, but only at a high price. He was forced to acknowledge Ivan's claims to all the rest of the lands of the Order, Duke Magnus's possessions only excepted, and to promise not to interfere with the trade to Narva. He thus conceded one of the points which had led to the formation of the coalition against him; the war with Lübeck became an absurdity. Repugnant though this surrender might be, Erik did not dare to repudiate it, but gave a general assent to the treaty, reserving only some points for further discussion. It was not until the summer of 1566 that he learnt that Ivan too was having second thoughts, and was now adding an additional condition of the most disturbing nature. This was nothing less than a demand that Erik hand over to him the person of Johan's wife, Katarina. It seems that his intention was to use her as a hostage or bargaining-counter in peace negotiations with her brother Sigismund Augustus; but in Sweden it was generally supposed that he intended to make her his mistress. The *råd*, consulted upon whether the demand could be complied with, were unanimous that it could not. Erik, it seems, could not make up his mind. The friendly neutrality of Ivan was essential to him: it was the indispensable precondition for his whole Baltic policy. Without it he faced disaster and ruin, for he well knew that his resources would not suffice to meet yet another enemy. So strongly did he feel the force of these arguments that when he sent Nils Gyllenstierna to Ivan, in October 1566, he expressly authorized him, in the last resort, to concede the extradition of Katarina. Gyllenstierna, no doubt, did his best; but the treaty which he signed in February 1567 began with an undertaking that she should be handed over, and went on to promise that Denmark and Lübeck should have free access to Narva. In return, Ivan conceded to Sweden a rather larger share of Estonia than before, and promised to use good offices to end the war with Denmark. In April Gyllenstierna returned with the treaty; in May a Russian embassy arrived in Stockholm with a peremptory demand for its ratification, and an intimation that they expected to take Katarina back with them.

Erik was now fairly driven to the wall. He had staked everything on Ivan's friendship, and the result had been to make a nonsense of his foreign policy. He had no doubt of the odium he would incur if he acquiesced in the tsar's infamous demand; and scarcely less of the danger to Sweden if he should reject it. Whichever course he chose could hardly fail to be disastrous. As if this agonizing dilemma were not sufficient, he was simultaneously confronted with another, and one which touched him very nearly. Early in 1565 he had taken as his new mistress a certain Karin Månsdotter. She was of peasant origin; her father had been a gaoler; and she herself seems to have served as a barmaid at an inn. She was a woman of gentle disposition, good heart, good humour, and sound sense, and she was one of the few persons to have any influence with Erik when the black fit was on him. He was deeply in love with her; and in the first half of 1567, on top of all his other cares and obsessions, he was wrestling with the problem of whether he could risk marrying her.

It is against this background of accumulated anxieties and brooding suspicions that we must set the tragic events of May 1567. Erik was by now almost certain that a great net of conspiracy had been woven against him. He was probably mistaken: no precise plot seems to have existed in reality. At all events, he decided to anticipate the expected blow. The Estates were summoned to meet at Uppsala: to them he would appeal, to judge between himself and his adversaries. The peasantry attended in great numbers; the nobility were ominously few. But before they assembled Svante Sture and Sten Eriksson were arrested, and together with other participants in the skerries-meeting (Duke Karl being discreetly omitted) were charged with treason before the High Court. By the time the *riksdag* met on 19 May, Abraham Stenbock and Ivar Ivarsson had been condemned to death; Erik Sture (Nils's brother) had likewise been condemned to death subject to the production of confirmatory evidence; and the case against Svante Sture and Sten Eriksson was undecided. It was intended that the *riksdag* should confirm these sentences; and Jöran Persson demanded (and seems actually to have obtained) a resolution urging the imposition of the death penalty upon all whom the High Court might subsequently pronounce to have been implicated in the affair.

At this point, on 21 May, Nils Sture arrived in Uppsala from Lorraine, having evaded the agents sent out to arrest him. He brought no definite answer from Christina. On the available evidence, he was at least as deeply implicated as any of his relatives in whatever mischief was afoot. It is not surprising, therefore, that he should forthwith have been sent to join his father in prison. By this time Erik's sanity was visibly tottering: he deluded himself into believing that when he landed at Uppsala all his servants deserted him and left him to make the best of his way into the town alone; he mislaid the text of the speech he was to make to the Estates, tried it *impromptu*, broke down, imagined himself hooted by a section of the audience, and accused his servants of stealing his notes in order to compass his humiliation. His mind swung erratically from one line of conduct to another: at times, perhaps under Karin's beneficent influence, he would think of a reconciliation with his prisoners, and promise Svante Sture's wife that no harm should befall them. If his own account of this period is to be trusted, what he feared was that the magnates had determined to make Nils Sture king. But he could keep to no fixed resolution as to how best to confront that danger. The leaders of the Sture-party were now at his mercy; the executioner, it seemed, could solve his problems. But there came moments when he doubted whether it might not after all be safer to make his peace with them while there was yet time. It was under the influence of this feeling that he visited Svante Sture in his quarters in Uppsala castle, on the morning of the fatal 24 May 1567, taking Sten Eriksson with him. On entering Svante's cell, Erik fell on his knees, implored his pardon, and after an embarrassing scene was formally reconciled with him; so that the prisoners, marvelling, prepared for their speedy release. But as the king came out from Svante's chamber, Jöran Persson called to him and spoke something in his ear; and in the next hour or so either this conversation, or a subsequent talk with the superintendent of Kalmar, seems to have led him to a dreadful change of mind. Erik himself afterwards alleged that he had been convinced by Svante's demeanour that no real reconciliation was possible, and had concluded that his only hope now was to strike swiftly. However that may be, when he returned to the castle a couple of hours later, striding quickly up the hill with his hat pulled low on his brow and his armed guards panting at his heels, it was in a very different temper. He went in at once to Nils Sture; a short but vehement altercation followed; and Erik stabbed his unresisting prisoner to death with his own hand.

It has been suggested that Erik looked upon what he had done as a mere act of justice, and himself simply as executioner-extraordinary; but if so his nerves were not of the steely sort which such a theory of the kingly office demanded. The killing of Nils Sture broke his last tenuous hold on sanity. As he rushed frantically from the castle, pelting blindly down the hill to the town, he shouted a confused order that all the prisoners in the castle were to be massacred 'except Herr Sten'. Within the next few hours Svante and Erik Sture, Abraham Stenbock and Ivar Ivarsson had been butchered; while Sten Eriksson Leijonhufvud and Sten Baner owed their survival to the accident that no one knew for certain which 'Herr Sten' was to be spared. Erik meanwhile had made for the open country. A mile or two outside Uppsala he was overtaken by his former tutor and faithful servant Dionysius Beurreus, who had courageously followed in the hope of calming him. But Erik could no longer distinguish between friend and foe. At a word from the king Beurreus was hewn down, and Erik resumed his flight, by this time in peasant clothes. When night fell he was wandering at large, distracted and quite alone, through the forests that surrounded the town.

For six months after this catastrophe Erik's mind remained seriously disordered. He was obviously incapable of ruling; and the government of the country passed for the time being into the nerveless hands of the *råd*. An attempt was made to patch up a settlement with the aristocracy: Erik invited the widows and families of the slain to 'put the best construction on what had occurred', and by way of encouraging them in this difficult feat paid out substantial sums in blood-money. The High Court's verdict upon the victims was formally annulled, and in June their representatives entered into a written undertaking not to seek revenge.[1] It was found convenient to put the blame for what had happened upon Jöran Persson, who was arrested (with Erik's assent), charged with various administrative errors and offences, and condemned to death; though the *råd* deemed it prudent to defer the execution of the sentence. There was no attempt at deposition: if a noble conspiracy had indeed existed, the massacre at Uppsala had robbed it of its candidate for the throne. Failing a Sture, the most obvious alternative was Johan; but Johan was still immured in Gripsholm. In July Erik was induced to discuss the possibility of his liberation. The talks dragged on for months; but Erik was really in no condition to conduct a consecutive negotiation. He became convinced that he had been deposed, and believed himself to be his brother's prisoner: when in October Johan was at last released and brought into Erik's presence there was a scene of painful confusion, as each insisted on kneeling to the other. Nevertheless it was, in appearance, a reconciliation. But it was a reconciliation which was not very likely to prove permanent. For already Erik had taken the step which was finally to alienate him from his family. At some time in the summer of 1567, in a relatively lucid interval, he had privately married Karin Månsdotter. After his recovery he disavowed and reversed much that had been done in his name during the period of his illness: and he came bitterly to regret the liberation of Johan. But he never subsequently seems to have had any doubt about his marriage; and the event proved him right. As a man, if not a king, he had in the end picked the right woman.

About Christmas-time it began to be clear that he was struggling back to sanity; by the New Year he appeared to be fully restored. It was

[1] The signatories were Per Brahe, Märta Sture (widow of Svante and mother of Nils and Erik), Gustav Olsson Stenbock, Erik Gustavsson Stenbock, Sten Baner, Hogenskild Bielke, and Nils Gyllenstierna.

high time. His mental collapse had at once been followed by military paralysis and disaster. A Danish army advanced into the heart of Östergötland, and might even have made its way to Stockholm if it had been better supported: the aristocracy into whose hands the responsibilities of government had fallen showed themselves as negligent and incompetent as Erik had always said they were. When Erik resumed the command, difficulties of supply were already forcing the Danes to withdraw southward; but the vigour with which he reorganized the Swedish defences, and the energy with which he carried on the pursuit, were reminiscent of his best days.

The excitement and exertions of a winter campaign may have done something to restore Erik's morale; the birth of his son Gustav, on 28 January 1568, must certainly have done more. As spring approached he began to feel himself once more in control of his kingdom. By the end of February Jöran Persson had been liberated and reinstated; in March he was ennobled. One of the first instructions issued to him was to obtain the repayment of the blood-money—even from the widow of Beurreus—on the ground that the prisoners had been justly sentenced to death and justly executed. And it was a sign of the effective restoration of royal authority that his demand was complied with, Märta Sture alone refusing obedience. The birth of Karin's son made a public wedding necessary, if the child were to be accounted legitimate, and Erik did not hesitate. The wedding took place on 4 July (Erik wrote an anthem for the occasion), and was followed next day by Karin's coronation: her two children by Erik were beside her under the canopy; her three uncles, poor peasants from Uppland, decked out for the occasion in clothes proper to a nobleman, were prominent figures at the ceremony, and were sent home afterwards enriched by gifts of salt.

The rehabilitation of Jöran Persson, the outrageous reclamation of the blood-money, the indifference to aristocratic feelings manifested in the marriage and coronation, must have appeared to Erik's adversaries as deliberate provocations. It was perhaps in any case too much to expect that the aristocracy should stand quietly by while he reestablished his authority as though nothing had happened; but these events made a rising certain. The royal dukes, in particular, were outraged by the marriage; and they absented themselves from the wedding (as they later explained) because they feared Erik would use the opportunity to murder them. About midsummer they began to prepare a rising; financing it, by a fine irony, with the blood-money which Märta Sture had refused to return. It began at Vadstena, a week after Karin's coronation; and thence it moved slowly but irresistibly towards Stockholm. Erik at first was confident; offered to pardon his brothers and allow them to emigrate; summoned the Estates to Stockholm, and from them received pledges of support. But his commanders served him as ill as ever; his soldiers, discouraged by continual reverses, and disgusted by lack of pay, began to desert. By personal valour he checked his enemies at Botkyrka, and returned to Stockholm with his armour visibly dented; but he could not stem the dukes' advance. Terms not ungenerous were offered to him, and unwisely declined. The burghers of Stockholm were terrified by rumours that he was planning a massacre of all Germans in the city; the archbishop, most of the *råd*, and his half-sisters, all fled to the enemy when it seemed that his cause was hopeless; the Stockholm garrison handed over Jöran Persson to the dukes, who put him to death with tortures worthy of his own ingenuity. At last treachery opened the gates of the capital, and young Duke Karl (for Johan had remained prudently out of danger) entered with his army. In a final parley, Erik's guards treacherously attacked Sten Eriksson, and inflicted wounds from which he died soon afterwards; but this repairing of the omissions of Uppsala served only to deprive the king of the last vestiges of support or sympathy. On 28 September he surrendered; on the following day Johan entered Stockholm and assumed the government;[1] and Erik, Karin and their children began that life of captivity from which Johan and Katarina had so recently emerged. The reign was over. But for nine more years Erik lived on, in conditions which grew progressively harsher; until at last his flame guttered out in solitude, and madness, and an unnatural death.

Erik's fall unloosed a universal torrent of execration. His victorious adversaries had no difficulty in posing as the deliverers of their country from the bloodstained rule of an insane tyrant. And when in January 1569 the *riksdag* was called to pronounce sentence of deposition upon him, Johan's propaganda swelled into a monstrous luxuriance of accusation. Some of it was true, some dubious, much patently absurd—charges flung in regardless of reason or probability, to make a horrid catalogue of iniquity. Erik had wished to turn the Swedish peasantry into slaves like those of Estonia; he had 'etched upon copper the likeness of an ass, bearing a sack upon its back, whereby was signified that the Swedish commonalty should be always in subjection to him'; he had four hundred and eighty names written in a book, of persons high and low, men and women, and intended to murder them all; he had wanted to burn Stockholm castle, with his stepmother and sisters inside it, or at least had wanted to deport them all to a life of infamy in Muscovy; he had pretended madness as a cloak for his misdeeds; but

[1] Only Karl's vigorous intervention saved the envoys of the tsar from plunder and manhandling by Johan's over-enthusiastic supporters.

he had also been possessed, like King Saul, with an evil spirit, to which he gave the name 'Koppaff'. And much more to the same purpose. Royal oratory, public proclamations, never ceased to hammer away at this theme: Erik was a tyrant, a wild beast, the oppressor of his people. What 'cruel old King Kristian' was to Gustav Vasa, Erik was to Johan III: a useful political bogy, to distract men's minds from prevailing discontents by exhibiting the horrors from which they had escaped. The nobility, to be sure, needed no convincing; but other elements in society would be none the worse for frequent reminders. To Erik, scrawling bitterly ironical comments in his prison, this campaign of denigration seemed not only vindictive, but utterly unfair. His conscience absolved him of the charge of tyranny. He did not for one moment feel compunction or remorse for any of his actions. He had no difficulty in demolishing the slanders of his enemies by a succession of cast-iron syllogisms. To himself it seemed that he had always acted within the law: those who had suffered had suffered because they were guilty. On the authority which God gives to kings, on the natural right of self-preservation, he rested his case.

And he had indeed a case. Years later, Gustav Adolf wrote, in that sketch of his history which got no further than an introduction: 'By reason of his suspiciousness he imprisoned King Johan, struck down the Stures, and did to death many others; and because they were many, the world judged that they were all innocent.'[1] But the world, as Gustav Adolf implied, was mistaken: many were in fact guilty. Erik never felt himself in the position of a tyrant who must rule by terror if he is to keep his people in subjection. On the contrary, he identified himself with them to a notable degree, consulted them at frequent intervals in gatherings of the Estates, took them into his confidence: nothing in his reign is more remarkable than the astounding frankness of the open letter to his people of July 1568, in which he gave them an account of his insanity, as he saw it, and of the circumstances which had led up to the killing of the Stures. But he believed himself menaced by a small ring of noble families; and he had no doubt of his right to protect himself against them. It is true that his fear was partly a self-induced delusion; but it was real enough to him. No doubt it was an aspect of that limitless egocentricity which made him regard even indifferent happenings as somehow relating to himself. From his own viewpoint his thinking was always solidly logical; but too often it rested upon premisses as insubstantial as a nightmare. Since he could rarely be brought to admit his own mistakes, he was incapable of seeing in them the cause of his failures, and this forced him to seek explanations in the sinister actions of others; while his innate conviction that he could do

[1] C. G. Styffe, *Konung Gustaf II Adolfs skrifter*, p. 76.

a job better than those to whom he entrusted it (though it might sometimes be true) was equally depressing to himself and them. For all his intellectual vigour, for all his bold strategic and diplomatic combinations, he lacked the judgment, the firm grip on reality, the sympathetic imagination, which are necessary to a successful statesman. His diplomacy was too tortuous, too concerned to keep open alternative solutions, in the last resort too cynical, to be successful; his projects too often seemed born of a hectic fantasy rather than the result of a sober weighing of the desirable against the possible. If at the end his foreign policy landed him in a hopeless *impasse*, not the least reason for his predicament was that he was too clever by half.

Yet his reign, so grievous and so tragic, is not only a story of obsession and personal disaster, nor were its effects exhausted when Erik vanished behind the walls of his prison. For Erik bequeathed two things to Sweden, and both were evil legacies. One was the commitment to imperial expansion, from which no Swedish government would be able to cut free for a hundred and fifty years. The other was the fear and suspicion with which monarchy and aristocracy were to regard each other for the next half-century. Erik's 'tyranny' would provide a stalking-horse for claims of privilege for the nobility; while the alleged design to extirpate the stock of the Vasas would trouble the peace of mind of not a few of his successors. From Erik's morbid imaginings had been distilled a poison, fatal to himself, which would taint the blood of Swedish politics for many a day.

4. Johan III

I. THE AFTERMATH OF REBELLION

On 24 January 1569 the *riksdag* met in Stockholm to settle the government of the kingdom. After discussions with the *råd* Duke Karl signified his willingness to recognize his brother as king and his nephew Sigismund as heir-apparent. The sentences which had been pronounced upon those slain at Uppsala in 1567 were formally annulled. And on 26 January the assembled Estates confronted King Erik for the last time. He was so uncertain of his fate that he had come prepared with speeches appropriate either to a death-sentence or to a restoration; but he might have spared himself the trouble, for he was not suffered to speak at all. The Estates renounced their allegiance; Erik was declared deposed. On the same day the Succession Pact of 1544 was reaffirmed by *råd* and *riksdag*, Sigismund's right to succeed being specifically included. Six months later Johan's coronation took place upon a modest scale suited to the distraction of the times. The revolution was over; Erik XIV disappeared into captivity; Johan III reigned in his stead.

All these proceedings made it impossible to pretend that this was a normal accession. It was certainly very different from the automatic processes of 1560. The Estates had doomed King Erik from his kingdom in a style which recalled their right under the *landslag* to 'take and break kings'; and Johan held the crown upon a title which had undeniably more of an electoral than a hereditary flavour. Despite the confirmation of the Succession Pact, it was obvious that the hereditary principle had received a severe shock. Johan's actions could be used to support an argument for the right of rebellion: it might be difficult in future to confine the exercise of that right to members of the royal family. Moreover, political theories which the Vasas could have wished forgotten had emerged from limbo for an unexpected airing. After a long interval of silence, the spirit of aristocratic constitutionalism had suddenly materialized, uttering antique slogans and brandishing constitutional documents of the fifteenth century. Johan's coronation oath, though in general resembling Erik's, contained two significant clauses which had not been required of his predecessor: he bound himself not to begin a war without the consent of 'the leading Estates'; and he undertook to 'hold the leading Estates in honour, and put no foreigner or low-born person over their heads, or over the heads of the *råd*'. This last stipulation was taken over, almost *verbatim*, from the Recess of Kalmar in 1483.

Johan was well aware of the implications of all this for the dynasty. From the outset of his reign he was understandably anxious to buttress the Succession Pact with guarantees as strong as he could make them, and to recover the ground which the monarchy had lost in 1568. It was one of his main concerns—indeed, it became an obsession—to bind his subjects by reiterated pledges to accept his son as his successor. During the early days of the revolt against Erik the nobility and clergy of Småland had agreed to do so *if* in other respects he proved fitted for the kingly office. Johan wanted some better security than that. There were, indeed, no reservations in the promises of *råd* and *riksdag* in 1569; nevertheless he could not be easy. In August 1572 he took advantage of a meeting of the clergy to extract renewed undertakings from them; in 1574 the Estates promised fidelity to Sigismund, by acclamation; in 1576 the *råd* proposed to allay the king's anxieties by suggesting Sigismund's coronation *rege vivente*. Six years later, another meeting of the clergy gave another pledge, styling Sigismund—paradoxically but accurately—'elected hereditary king'. As late as February 1587 the Vadstena *riksdag* renewed the nation's commitment to the hereditary succession in Johan's line. And in the following year Johan characteristically took exception to the Poles describing his son as '*designatus et electus*': the proper style, he insisted, was '*haeres Regni Sueciae*'.

Since Johan had seized the throne by violence, it was natural that in the months after his accession he should feel it to be politic to propitiate and to reward. He gave new privileges to Stockholm, restoring to them the right to supply themselves with armaments, which Gustav Vasa had taken away in 1536. There was a sudden (but as it turned out, temporary) rise in *förläningar* to members of the nobility, in contrast to the trend under Erik. Donations were given to the families of those who had perished at Uppsala. New barons were created, and for the first time provided with territorial baronies. But the obvious political weakness of the crown presented the aristocracy with an opportunity which was too good to miss. In 1569 they made far-reaching demands. And in the coronation oath, together with the new privileges for the nobility which were granted at the same time, they obtained at least a part of what they were asking.

The man who took the lead in formulating their programme was Hogenskild Bielke. He was a good example of the younger generation of Swedish aristocrats, contemporaries of Erik XIV, who shared the cultured tastes and European interests of that monarch. Educated at the cathedral school of Odense and the university of Wittenberg, he was a scholar well versed in theology and law, a great collector of books and manuscripts, an enthusiastic antiquary. He was well acquainted with the mediaeval history of his country, and looked back with regret to the golden days of the fifteenth century, when the power of the monarchy was checked by effective limitation, when the *råd* was the arbiter of the constitution, and the aristocracy enjoyed in their full extent those privileges which were the fitting reward for their services to the state. Opponents of his views found him a difficult man to controvert, for he had a disconcerting ability to produce—or at least to cite—the text of a grant, or a charter, or a statute, in support of his contentions. These qualities made him a natural leader of an aristocracy which had been frightened into resistance to monarchical power, and was now anxious to erect constitutional barriers against a recurrence of danger. He was determined to recover the privileges of the nobility to the limit that the crown would suffer. In this he was perhaps influenced by the example of Denmark; but he was in any case convinced that without a highly-privileged aristocracy a healthy polity was scarcely conceivable. The demands which, under his leadership, the nobility put forward in 1569 were thus a blending of naked class-advantage with guarantees against royal abuse of power. They claimed, for instance, that they should enjoy a monopoly of high judicial office. Erik's High Court had vanished with his fall; but its record in the later years of the reign had certainly done something to justify the aristocracy in feeling that they could not be secure unless the administration of the law were once again placed in their hands, as it had always been in the past. With the same end in view they insisted on their right to be tried by their peers. They secured an important concession which exempted from conscription all peasants on noble estates who dwelt within a Swedish mile[1] of a manor. They took the opportunity to exact a reduction in the burden of *rusttjänst*, a limitation of the obligation to serve without wages in the king's armies beyond the frontier, and an assurance that the noble who was too poor to furnish a fully-armed horseman should not therefore be deprived of his *frälse*. Nobility henceforward was to be considered as a matter of birth, rather than as dependent upon the performance of service, an inherent quality which could be forfeited only by an act which derogated from it—as, for instance, marriage outside the noble class. Such marriages were common enough at the time among the poorer members of the aristocracy; and the attempt to prevent them, which began in 1569 and was to continue for many years, was one sign among many of a growing corporate spirit. But side by side with demands of this sort were others of a less selfish kind. It was a concern for good government which led

[1] 10·7 kilometres: the so-called *frihetsmil*, or mile of liberty.

them to insist that the old great offices of state—steward, marshal, chancellor—should once again be filled; it was their experience of the irresponsibility of powerful secretaries which prompted a stipulation that 'inexperienced clerks' be not appointed to important positions. They were defending something more important than their own class interests when they cited the Recess of Kalmar in support of their protest against unsubstantiated delations and imprisonment without trial. Nevertheless, though they have some title to be considered as the champions of the rule of law, their position as defenders of the rights and liberties of the subject was weakened by some of the arguments which men like Hogenskild Bielke put forward in support of their demands. He asserted the nobility's right to better privileges as being no more than the recompense due to them by the monarchy for their assent to the introduction of hereditary succession: it was one of their charges against Erik that in his treatment of the nobility he had shown himself 'ungrateful'. What they were claiming was thus nothing more than the belated fulfilment of a constitutional bargain. But this was in fact to ask for constitutional guarantees on the curious plea that they had bartered them away in 1544. Nor was their other main argument much better. They insisted that they were demanding nothing new: all they wanted was a restoration of privileges which owing to the exceptional political situation in Gustav Vasa's time had latterly been in abeyance. There was indeed some substance in this contention; but it would hardly bear close inspection. For in 1569, as on other occasions down to 1613, the nobility did in fact ask for advantages which they had never had before; and the novelty of their demands was one reason for the reluctance of successive kings to grant them.

If, then, Johan was forced by the circumstances of his accession to make concessions, it is still remarkable that he made so few. The constitutional points were granted, as was the restoration of some privileges which had lapsed of late years; but innovating demands were mostly resisted, and only one really new principle (that of the *frihetsmil*) was accepted. Here, as in some other fields, Johan showed a firmness for which historians have not always given him credit. He showed political skill, too, in playing upon the increasing cleavage between higher nobility and lower, so that he was able to break the aristocratic front by concessions to the exclusiveness and pride of race of the counts, the barons, and the great families. With the greatest aristocrat of them all, his brother Karl, it was scarcely possible to haggle. Karl's main concern, of course, was with the extent of his rights as duke. In January 1568, when the formal reconciliation between Erik and Johan had taken place, Erik had succeeded in extorting an acceptance of the provisions of the Articles of Arboga; and a year later Johan would probably have done the same by Karl if he had dared. But Karl made it plain that he expected to return to the letter of Gustav Vasa's Testament, and to hold his duchy 'as freely as H. M. will hold his kingdom'. Johan was therefore obliged to confirm his father's donation, for himself and his heirs; though he succeeded in reserving 'the general oath, fealty, obedience and service' of all Swedish subjects, whether living in the duchy or not. Thus the Articles of Arboga were in effect swept away, and the dangerous situation of 1560 was restored. The result was a vendetta which for twenty years threatened to tear the kingdom apart, which wrecked Johan's policy for the church, and which played a great part in the dynastic catastrophe of the nineties. It was a high price to pay for usurpation.

Moreover, it was by no means certain that the usurper would be able to hold the throne which cost so much to win. King Erik in prison was the natural focus for all who had disappointed ambitions or unsatisfied grievances. In the nine years which intervened between his deposition and his death there were at least seven conspiracies against Johan III, and most of them aimed at Erik's restoration, although only one seems to have been hatched with his connivance. They differed widely in participants and motive. Some were closely involved with foreign policy: those of 1569 counted on buying Danish aid by territorial concessions; that of 1570 contemplated Erik's release from Åbo with the aid of Russian troops. Others began as spontaneous outbreaks of discontent, or protests against heavy taxes, and afford evidence of Erik's long-lasting popularity among the lower orders of society. Such were the movements in Småland in 1570; such were the disturbances two years later in Hälsingland, Dalarna, Uppland and Värmland, in the course of which Uppsala, Enköping and Nyköping were burnt by persons who called themselves Erik's adherents. Others again (as in 1569 and 1570) were led by men who had once been in Erik's service, or in Karin Månsdotter's, and were actuated by simple loyalty to an old master. One incentive that tempted discontented persons into treason was the persistent rumour that Erik before his fall had managed to conceal a vast treasure, which would be available to reward a successful insurrection. The only man besides Erik who was said to know its whereabouts was his former garden-master, Jean Allard, now safely beyond the seas and out of reach of Johan's inquiries; and it is not surprising that Allard's name should crop up from time to time in connexion with these movements. Johan himself seems to have believed in the treasure's existence: at all events he was so pressed for money that he could not ignore the chance that the story might be true. On one occasion only the protests of Queen Katarina deterred him from torturing Erik to make him reveal where it was hidden; and as late as

1588 he was ordering digging operations in Stockholm castle in the hope of discovering it.

Many of Erik's former servants had attached themselves to Karl,[1] and perhaps it was not difficult for such people to bring themselves to think of Karl as a possible king, if Erik's sanity were doubtful. At all events, there is no doubt that Karl himself was involved in conspiracies of various kinds. There was for instance a plan to marry him to Dorothea, youngest daughter of Christina of Lorraine, and then to seize the throne with Christina's aid. And in 1573 he was implicated in the most formidable conspiracy of them all. It was the work of Karl's friend and adherent, Charles de Mornay; a man much trusted by Johan, and by him made *ståthållare* of Älvsborg. De Mornay's plan was to depose Johan by a *coup d'état*, to be carried through with the aid of Scottish mercenary officers who were at that time in Sweden on their way to the army in Livonia. He was in touch with Allard; and the prospect of a share in Erik's treasure made a strong appeal to soldiers of fortune who were anything but sure of their pay. It seems certain that some of their officers—Archibald Ruthven and Gilbert Balfour, in particular—allowed themselves to be inveigled into the scheme. Before it could come to fruition, however, they were moved on to their destination in Livonia; and the affair might have ended at this point had it not been that in 1574 their participation in the plot was betrayed by one of their colleagues. The whole conspiracy then came to light. De Mornay, ordered up to Stockholm to explain himself, sought refuge with Karl; and Karl, on one pretext or another, protected him as long as he dared. But when de Mornay, who had no illusions about his probable fate, made a desperate bid to flee the country, Karl at once took measures to pursue him: his own position was already too delicate for him to be able to risk conniving at his *protégé's* escape. De Mornay was caught and handed over to Johan, who requited this service by contriving that Karl's name should be kept out of the legal proceedings. There could be no doubt about the verdict: de Mornay was condemned, executed, and buried in the Riddarholm church in Stockholm. It was an odd place to choose, one would have thought, for a convicted traitor.[2]

Lastly, there were two other conspiracies, very different in character and objective, but alike in having decidedly sinister overtones. The first was revealed in 1572 to Charles Dançay, the French ambassador to Denmark, by Gustav Baner and Hogenskild Bielke. Its object, according to Dançay, was to restore aristocratic government as it had

[1] Karl, very much to his credit, had provided for the unfortunate widow and children of Jöran Persson.

[2] The Riddarholm church is Sweden's Westminster Abbey.

existed in the fifteenth century, with a prince of the house of Valois as an innocuous regent. The second, of 1576, was the work of Mauritz Rasmussen, a country parson who incited his receptive congregation not merely to rise and liberate Erik, but to also massacre Johan and all the nobility.

The interconnexion of these plots is still to be unravelled, and the persons involved in them by no means certain; but it has been thought that several members of the *råd*, the Princesses Cecilia and Elizabeth, and the bishop of Västerås, Hans Ofeegh, may have been more or less implicated. Historians have sometimes been contemptuous of the timidity which Johan displayed in the face of threats to his throne and his life; but it is scarcely possible to doubt that he was at times in real danger. Soon after his deposition Erik had begged that he might be liberated on condition that he engaged to live abroad: 'the world is wide enough', he wrote, 'for even fraternal hate to be mitigated by distance'. But there were too many possible enemies abroad who would be willing to restore him, in return for concessions to themselves, for such a solution to be safe. There seemed no alternative but to keep him in prison. He was moved from place to place: from Stockholm to Åbo, to Gripsholm, to Västerås, to Örbyhus; brutally maltreated by one of his aristocratic enemies who had been made his gaoler, but thereafter reasonably housed and cared for—though separated after a time from Karin, lest they breed more children to form the root of a rival dynasty. Wherever he was, his presence seemed to call forth a new conspiracy. Little by little Johan came to face the fact that the only safe way with him was to kill him. As early as September 1569 he had induced the archbishop and two of his colleagues to agree that in certain circumstances it would be justifiable to put his brother to death; in June 1573 Erik's gaoler was given authority to despatch him in a variety of ways (all horrifyingly particularized) so as to leave no trace. In March 1575 the *råd*, with the archbishop, four bishops and three of the clergy, assented to his being killed if there were danger of his liberation; adding, with revolting sanctimoniousness, that 'It is to be feared that we have rather offended than pleased God by not killing him so far'. These tender consciences were not left to ache for long. On 24 February 1577 Erik died after a short illness: a recent exhumation has made it all but certain that he died of arsenical poisoning. Karl, it seems, had his suspicions: in 1605 he accused Hogenskild Bielke of advising that Erik be poisoned, and it is possible that the charge was true. Certainly Karl took strong exception to the mean funeral and hugger-mugger interment: 'We are heartily sorry', he wrote, 'that a person so able and a king so mighty should have come to such case as to end his life thus pitifully in prison.' Erik might have been a tyrant; he might have been deposed; but Karl could not forget that he had been a crowned and anointed king.

Even this did not end the business. In 1579 Jean Allard made a brief raid upon the west coast of Sweden, to the alarm of the government. In 1583 he was deep in grandiose negotiations with Henry III of France, to whom he offered two million *écus* in return for warships and troops. As he is said to have laid out 400,000 *écus* in bribing the French nobility, and was offering to pay a further 400,000 in cash before sailing, he would certainly appear to have had resources at his disposal—whether from Erik's treasure or not it is impossible to say. At all events, he was not without a possible candidate for the throne. Erik's son Gustav had been sent abroad to Poland in 1575 to be educated by Jesuits; and from time to time the Swedish government developed anxiety lest some hostile power—the tsar, for instance—obtain control of his person. Boris Godunov succeeded in tempting him to Russia in 1599; but he proved less pliable than was expected. He never became a danger to his Swedish relatives, and died in Russia in 1607. His mother, Karin Månsdotter, who had been given an estate in Finland, lived to marry her daughter into the high aristocracy, was reconciled to the royal family, and survived till 1612.

Johan's treatment of Erik is as impossible to defend as it is difficult to condemn. He was not by nature a cruel man. His threats were often terrible; but his bark was much worse than his bite. Emotionally unstable, like all his family, he was quite as liable as any of them to be transported by passion; but unlike most of them he recognized and regretted his lack of self-control, excusing it by what he called his 'choleric and martial nature'. In his rages he was a dangerous man to encounter: like his father, he kept an iron hammer handy which he was apt to use on those about him. Yet he shed little blood in his reign: indeed, he was much concerned to project his image as the *rex justus*, in contrast to the tyrant Erik, from whose oppressions he had delivered his people; and his ideal of kingship was St Erik. And he had, indeed, many private virtues and attractive qualities. He was a devoted husband and father. When not out of humour he could be an agreeable companion: the English in 1560 thought him 'a good fellow' (perhaps because he played rackets well); Charles Dançay reported to Catherine de' Medici that he was '*fort bénin et débonnaire*'. His aesthetic interests were very strongly developed, his taste in all the arts highly cultivated. He had a perfect passion for building. In a family which more than atoned for Gustav Vasa's lack of learning he was much the best scholar. Compared with Erik's hectic brilliance or Karl's iron grimness his character seems milder and more congenial. It was a misfortune for Sweden that he had none of the hard-headed business sense which

Gustav Vasa transmitted to his youngest son, nor any of that grasp of administration and love of order which was still an essential of Swedish kingship. Vain of his learning, over-tender of his dignity, petty in his resentments, given to thrasonical brags, he had a habit of talking big and acting small which made him seem a weaker man than he really was. Foreign diplomats were exasperated by his apparent vacillation and contemptuous of his sudden changes of mood. But behind these superficial appearances lay much tenacity of purpose; and whenever his interests or sympathies were deeply engaged this tougher grain in his constitution soon showed through. It was so in the matter of religion. And it was so too in regard to foreign policy.

II. THE STRUGGLE FOR LIVONIA

The accession of Johan III brought with it an abrupt change in the political alignments of the Baltic lands. As brother-in-law of Sigismund Augustus he could count on some sympathy from Poland; as husband of Katarina Jagiełłonica he was unlikely to wish to continue Erik's policy of close association with Muscovy. Already in the spring of 1568 Erik had hoped to use Johan to influence Sigismund Augustus in his favour; and when Erik fell, the coalition against Sweden speedily broke up. Poland's attitude to the Narva question had from the beginning been irreconcilable with Denmark's, and it became increasingly clear that the interests of the two powers clashed in other respects also. One of the king of Poland's most cherished ambitions was to make his country a naval power. As yet, indeed, he had no fleet of his own; but he issued commissions to numerous privateers, who in the closing years of the war preyed on Baltic shipping to such effect that Fredrik II found it necessary to take action: in 1569 they received sharp chastisement at the hands of a Danish squadron. To the indignant Poles it seemed that Denmark was barring their legitimate aspirations on the seas: Sigismund Augustus, coining a phrase which was to become famous, accused Fredrik of aiming at *dominium maris Balthici*. In these circumstances Poland was not disposed to continue fighting in Denmark's quarrel. Hostilities in Livonia came to a halt; Johan sent over to invite his brother-in-law to his coronation; and Sigismund Augustus set about trying to bring peace to Scandinavia: it was even rumoured that he might send military aid to Sweden.

In the last few weeks of Erik's reign both he and Johan had made approaches to Denmark, no doubt with the idea of immobilizing the Danish armies until the domestic struggle had been decided; but it was Fredrik's inability to pay his mercenaries, rather than these diplomatic overtures, which prevented his taking advantage of the brief civil war.

As soon as it was over Johan sent commissioners to begin a negotiation. In November 1568 they allowed themselves to be persuaded into signing a peace treaty at Roskilde, though by accepting the Danish terms they undoubtedly went beyond their instructions. The treaty of Roskilde would have restored the *status quo ante bellum* in Scandinavia, a result which not unfairly reflected the run of the fighting; but it would also have bound Johan to surrender the Swedish stake in Estonia to Frederik's brother Magnus; it would have restored to Lübeck the privileges of 1523 in their full extent; it would have saddled Sweden with the whole amount of Danish war-expenditure from 1563 to the moment of ratification. These were terms which could not be accepted. The treaty remained unratified; and both sides, with infinite difficulty and undisguised reluctance, prepared for a final campaign, in the hope that it might improve their bargaining position without involving them in absolute economic ruin. For the Swedes the speculation proved a bad one. In July 1569 a combined Danish-Lübeck fleet bombarded Reval; in November, the fortress of Varberg (captured from the Danes in 1565) which Johan had counted upon being able to exchange for Älvsborg, tamely capitulated to the enemy. Sweden had still considerable naval resources: a great fleet put to sea in 1569; but it fought no important action, and its capture of merchant prizes, however welcome at home, did not help Sweden's prestige abroad. But the truth was that the exhaustion of the belligerents made all of them desperate for peace. The frontier provinces on both sides of the Danish border were devastated—a more serious matter for rich and populous Skåne than for poor, thinly peopled southern Småland; while not a few of the thriving towns on the Danish side had been burnt. The Swedish peasants were short of seed-corn for their spring sowing. The German mercenaries with whom Fredrik II had fought the war were mutinous, unpaid and unpayable; the civilian population in each country exasperated by the requisitions of the soldiery. In January 1570 Fredrik could obtain supplies only by threatening abdication if they were refused; and his authority had been so shaken by the failure of his war-policy that for the rest of his reign the crown would be under the tutelage of the aristocracy. As to Lübeck, she had seen her Hanseatic sister-towns annex the trade to Sweden which had formerly been hers; while her direct loss in bad debts and captured shipping was estimated at over 300,000 *Thaler*.

There was no lack of willing hands to help the combatants to a peace: the elector of Saxony, who had lent Fredrik II a quarter of a million *gulden*, and was increasingly alarmed about his chance of ever recovering his money; Charles Dançay, the French ambassador to Denmark, whose object was to compose Scandinavian quarrels in order to attach both countries to France; the Emperor Maximilian II, whom Sigismund Augustus induced to intervene by persuading him that mediation offered the best chance of saving some rags of imperial authority in Livonia; Sigismund Augustus himself, who had managed the metamorphosis from belligerent to mediator with very little ado—all these played their part in preparing the congress which met at Stettin in 1570. Duke John Frederick of Pomerania presided, at Maximilian's solicitation; the Emperor, the kings of France and Poland, and the elector of Saxony, shared the mediation between them.

The result of their labours was the peace of Stettin, concluded on 30 November 1570. By the terms of this agreement Johan III renounced his claims to Jämtland, Härjedalen and Gotland; while Fredrik II abandoned his pretension to the Swedish throne. Sweden recovered Älvsborg; but only upon payment of the first instalment of an indemnity of 150,000 *riksdaler*, one half of which was to fall due in 1571, the remaining quarters in 1572 and 1573. The controversy over the Three Crowns was to be submitted to arbitration by foreign experts, if no agreement between the two parties had been reached by 1 January 1572. In the meantime each was to be permitted to display the Three Crowns, without prejudice to the rights of the other; but the king of Sweden was debarred in future from bearing the arms of Norway or Denmark. The trade to Narva was to be free to all nations, subject to such limitations in the matter of contraband as the Emperor might from time to time decide upon. Lübeck's merchants in Sweden were to enjoy the old privileges of 1523, with the exception that they were no longer guaranteed a monopoly of Swedish foreign trade within the Baltic; and they were to be paid 75,000 *daler* in settlement of all their outstanding claims since Gustav Vasa's days. As to Livonia—or at least, as to that portion of it which had not been incorporated into Poland—Maximilian seized the opportunity to reassert the rights of the Empire. Swedish and Danish possessions in Livonia and Estonia (including those of Duke Magnus) were to be surrendered to the Emperor, who after refunding the sums which had been spent in defending them against the Russians would hand them over to Fredrik II, as 'protector'. Denmark would thus obtain all the lands held or claimed, not only by Duke Magnus, but also by Sweden; with the exception only of the towns of Reval and Weissenstein, which were to be 'entrusted' to Johan III. In return for this quasi-enfeoffment, the kings of Denmark and Sweden would be expected to assume the obligation to defend imperial interests against the encroaching Muscovite. Lastly, the treaty provided a carefully devised and automatically operating machinery for avoiding future wars between the Scandinavian powers; first, by frontier-meetings between delegations from the councils of each realm (absolved for the occasion from their oaths of fealty), and in the last resort by the arbitration of foreign princes. It was the development of an idea which had been adumbrated already in 1534 and 1541.[1] The inter-Scandinavian aristocracy was not going to be dragged by bellicose monarchs into another War of the North if it could help it.

On the face of it, the peace of Stettin represented the defeat of Sweden at almost every point. Estonia as good as lost; the Narva trade made free; Lübeck triumphant; Älvsborg to be redeemed at heavy cost; small chance of success with regard to the Three Crowns: what remained of the bold foreign policy of Erik XIV? The Poles, when it came to the point, had done little to help Johan III at Stettin: their jealousy of Swedish aims in Livonia outweighed their opposition to the Narva trade. No one else had been prepared to fight hard for Swedish interests—not even the Swedish delegates, who came without much hope and capitulated without much effort; they did not even push the Danes to the limit of concession which their instructions allowed them. Nevertheless, the peace brought one solid gain. Fredrik II had declared war in the hope of restoring the Scandinavian Union by a conquest of Sweden. That, at least, had been prevented. And perhaps Johan might take comfort from the reflexion that what mattered was not so much the terms of the treaty, but how far those terms could or would be fulfilled.

On one thing, at least, Johan was resolved: that he would not quarrel again with Denmark if he could avoid it. Fredrik II, for very similar reasons, was of the same mind. But within the limits imposed by that determination there was room for considerable friction. Johan intended to evade the provisions of the peace as far as possible; Fredrik was resolved to enforce them. The result was a decade of petty irritations and minor crises, temporarily resolved or shelved by a succession of meetings on the frontier. From time to time the Swedes were disturbed—unnecessarily, it seems—by reports of Danish armaments. Occasionally they dabbled in anti-Danish intrigues—as in 1575, when Duke Karl was involved in a plan for common action against Denmark with the perennial Christina of Lorraine; or in 1578, when there was discussion about an anti-Danish League to be headed by Philip II of Spain—but nothing came of these projects. Fredrik II was able to extort the ransom for Älvsborg, for the Swedes could not afford to risk the permanent loss of their only Atlantic port. The sum demanded was not excessively large; but it taxed Sweden's resources to the uttermost to find it. The vital first instalment was paid on time, and Älvsborg was thereupon retroceded. But the second instalment was

[1] See above, pp. 99, 129.

not collected until a year after it was due, the final quarter not until 1578—over five years late; and in order to raise it Johan was driven to selling warships, to using his debased coinage to buy up good silver coin at its face value, and to other lamentable expedients.[1] Lübeck in this respect was less fortunate than Denmark. She was now in no position to enforce her rights under the peace-treaty unless she were supported by an effective ally, and after 1570 she found no ally to assist her. Her relations with Denmark had taken a turn for the worse: disputes about the Sound Tolls, disputes about Bornholm,[2] disposed of any hope that Fredrik II would concern himself with her grievances against Sweden. The indemnity of 75,000 *daler* was simply not paid. The promised privileges were indeed granted; but they were no sooner given than they were whittled away—notably by the giving of equal advantages to Stralsund, which was thus rewarded for standing staunchly by Sweden during the war. Swedish privateers inflicted heavy losses on Lübeck's merchantmen; repeated embassies to Stockholm met with indifference or rude rebuffs. As far as Lübeck was concerned, the peace of Stettin was a hollow triumph.

Upon the thorny question of the Three Crowns, as might have been foreseen, no progress was possible: 1 January 1572 came and went without agreement between the parties. Some attempt was then made to set in motion the procedure for arbitration which had been laid down in the treaty. But the Swedes proved to be masters of the arts of procrastination; and though the conference which was to proceed to arbitration did at last assemble at Rostock in 1574, the Swedish delegates took care to defer their arrival until the other participants had lost patience and gone home. The truth was that neither side relished the idea of arbitration, and both were ready to bury the question for the time being. Accordingly, at a frontier-meeting in 1575 the Swedish and Danish representatives agreed to postpone discussion of the problem for ten years: in the event, the steady improvement in relations between the two countries led to its being shelved for the remainder of Fredrik's reign.

The great question of the trade to Narva was not so easily disposed of. Narva had enjoyed a boom period during the war. The Dutch, the English, the French, the Wendish towns, had all made for the open door to Russia, so that by the end of the sixties Narva had attained an importance in Baltic commerce second only to Riga. Johan III had no

[1] He even suggested that his brother Karl should borrow the sum required—from Fredrik II!

[2] Bornholm had been pawned to Lübeck for fifty years in 1525, in lieu of Gotland; but Kristian III had in 1536 extended the period to 1586. The Lübeckers pursued a policy of ruthless exploitation and extortion; the islanders complained to Denmark; and Fredrik II in 1575 repudiated the agreement of 1536 and reunited Bornholm to Denmark.

intention of allowing the boom to continue if he could help it. Erik XIV had always been embarrassed in his treatment of the problem by his dependence on the friendship of Ivan IV; Johan was free of any such restraints. Maximilian II, torn as always between his concern for German commercial interests and his reluctance to put arms into the hands of the Russians, in 1571 obtained the electors' approval of a list of contraband, and prohibited the carriage of these commodities to Narva; but Johan made no such nice distinctions. Within six months of the conclusion of the peace of Stettin his ships were harrying the Narva trade indiscriminately; and they continued to harry it, with occasional intermissions, for the next eleven years. In the interests of good relations with Denmark he made a point of exempting Danish ships from molestation; but there were always irresponsible Swedish privateers who ignored official policy. Danish vessels would be taken to Swedish ports, or stopped off the Estonian coast; there would be protests from Copenhagen, and apologies from Stockholm. From time to time Johan appealed to Fredrik II to prohibit the Narva trade on his own account; and in 1575, and again in 1579, Fredrik did so, in retaliation for Russian aggression in Livonia. But, as he complained, Swedish policy was not consistent. It was galling to find that at a moment when Danish subjects had been forbidden to sail to Narva, Johan was supplying his urgent need for cash by allowing ships to go through on payment of toll, or by the selling of passes. The Narva question thus remained a perennial irritant in Swedish–Danish relations all through the seventies. To Lübeck it was worse than an irritant; for Johan's commanders treated their ships with especial severity. Their losses were heavy: notably in 1574, when the Swedes captured an entire fleet of sixteen merchantmen. The revenue from these activities was an item of importance to Johan's insolvent exchequer: troops in Estonia could be paid with the booty, captured ships could be made over to diplomats instead of wages, or to importunate sisters clamorous for their unpaid marriage-portions. The trade to Narva continued, in spite of all; for Sweden lacked the naval resources for a fully effective blockade, and the advantage of direct contact with Russian merchants made skippers ready to run the hazard. But as far as Sweden was concerned, the peace of Stettin was in this matter a dead letter from the beginning.

The controversy over the Narva trade was of course only one aspect of the broader problem of Sweden's relations with Russia, and the future of the Swedish venture in Estonia. At the time of Johan's accession, neither he nor Ivan was anxious to add a Russo-Swedish war to his other commitments, and each was ready to smooth over the awkward business of the demand for the handing-over of Katarina Jagiełłonica. Ivan lost no time in explaining that this proposal had been based on the assumption that Johan was dead, and had really been designed to extricate Katarina from prison; and he suggested that Johan might send an embassy to Moscow to negotiate a treaty of amity between them. Johan deemed it politic to receive this explanation in the spirit in which it was offered. He was not unwilling to open a negotiation: in 1569 an embassy was duly despatched to Moscow. Before it arrived, however, the tsar had received news of the attack upon his own ambassadors in Stockholm.[1] He took his revenge upon the Swedish delegation, who were treated with contumely, barbarously mishandled, and for months denied an audience. They returned to Sweden in 1572, broken in health, bearing insulting messages to their sovereign. Johan replied in kind; and there followed an extraordinary exchange of royal Billingsgate which can have few parallels in correspondence between civilized monarchs. Behind the brisk bandying of invective lay an issue of real importance: nothing less than Sweden's status as an independent state. For Ivan was asserting, not only that Johan was the son of a jumped-up cattle-dealer who had stolen the throne, but that the kings of Sweden were his vassals, inferiors upon whom he might justly 'lay his wrath', and that Sweden itself was a province to be equated with Novgorod, rather than a realm to be equated with Muscovy. Johan's refusal to accept this subordinate position was phrased in language more vigorous and uncompromising than either Erik or Gustav Vasa had ever ventured to employ. It was also more successful; for by 1575 Ivan was ready for the first time to negotiate directly, rather than through the governor of Novgorod. A tradition long maintained by the tsars was thus broken, never to be re-established; and the severest ideological defeat that Ivan ever sustained was inflicted by Johan III. Long before this, however, it had become clear that there could be no peace between Sweden and Russia. In 1570 Ivan concluded a three years' truce with Poland, which left him free to deal with his other rivals in Livonia. For the moment, domestic preoccupations prevented his personal intervention; but he pushed forward a pawn in the person of the feeble but ambitious Magnus of Denmark. Magnus had been seduced into playing the tsar's game by substantial bribes and promises: he was given the tsar's niece in marriage; he was presented with the see of Dorpat; he was hailed—in Moscow—as 'king of Livonia'. In return for these favours he was to expel the Swedes from the country (with the aid of Russian troops), in order thereafter to rule it as a Russian puppet. He lost no time in getting to work: in August 1570 his forces laid siege to Reval.

The defection of Magnus to Russia, which provoked indignation in

[1] See above, p. 239, note 1.

western Europe, influenced the decisions taken at Stettin about Livonia; for it was hoped that by putting the country under the protection of Fredrik II some security would be provided against its falling to the tsar—partly because Denmark's relations with Russia appeared to be good, partly because in the past Fredrik had shown that he was willing to curb Magnus's extravagances. The event did not answer these expectations. Fredrik could no longer control his brother; his credit in Moscow was doubtful; he had neither the ambition nor the resources for further expensive campaigns. One basis for the Stettin settlement thus fell away. The others proved equally ill-founded. The imperial Diet would not, and Maximilian could not, find the money to compensate Sweden for the 'reasonable expenses' incurred in defending Estonia against the Muscovite. Failing such compensation it was clearly impossible to insist on the arrangement whereby the Swedish-held areas (except Reval and Weissenstein) were to be transferred to the protection of Denmark. Johan III may well have counted on this when he accepted the peace-terms. But he made a great show of being willing to transfer his rights if only he could get the money that was due to him; at intervals he clamoured for payment; and only in 1577, when it was obvious that no payment would be forthcoming, did he formally repudiate the terms laid down at Stettin for Livonia. In 1579 he intimated to Rudolf II that he considered himself to hold Livonia as '*directum dominium immediate*'. Thus Maximilian's forlorn attempt to preserve imperial authority broke down on the indifference of the German princes and their morbid jealousy of Habsburg. In 1581 Riga, which had clung tenaciously to its status as a German city, at last accepted Polish sovereignty. In 1582 the Diet resolved that the recovery of Livonia was 'not advisable at present'. And though as late as 1595 the imperial representative at Teusina was reserving the rights of the Empire, the future of the Baltic lands no longer lay in German hands.

In so far as any effort was made to save Livonia from Russian conquest, it was made neither by Fredrik II, nor by Maximilian II, but by Johan III. For seven years he sustained single-handed the attacks, first of Magnus, then—after 1572—of Ivan himself. The only assistance came from the Tatars of the Crimea, who burnt Moscow in 1571 and periodically distracted Ivan's attention thereafter. The war was unpopular in Sweden; Johan's resources were quite inadequate to wage it with success; from time to time the *råd* urged him to make peace. But no peace short of surrender was to be had from Ivan. The struggle dragged on, without victory and often almost without hope, dependent for its issue not upon the feeble efforts of the Swedes but upon the degree of attention Ivan was willing or able to give to it. It was a war of devastations, plundering raids, sieges of petty fortresses, in a grim climate and a starving countryside, with amateur strategies, antiquated tactics, and few battles of any consequence; stained on both sides by massacres of the vanquished and barbarous atrocities: after the capture of Weissenstein in 1572 the Russians roasted alive the Swedish commander and some of his subordinates. A war, too, of treacheries and 'practices' by the hungry adventurers who were ever ready to betray their employers for the hope of pay or the prospect of bettering themselves; a war of which the vicissitudes seem irrational, and are certainly unmemorable. At times the Swedish hold on Livonia was reduced to the perimeter of Reval, which stood two great sieges in 1570–1 and 1577; and if Reval was held, that was due quite as much to the determination of its burghers as to any help Johan was able to send from Sweden. There was fighting too in Finland: in 1572 a Russian raid reached Helsingfors; but on this front a two-years' truce, concluded in 1575, gave at least a temporary respite.

It might seem too much to dignify such scrambling campaigns with any intelligible strategic objectives; yet it is true that throughout these depressing operations Johan kept one purpose clearly before him: to capture Narva. But it was to be a long time before he had armies and commanders adequate to such an undertaking. He was forced at first to rely upon mercenaries, whose discipline was as uncertain as their pay. Most of them were Germans, but in 1572 he commissioned Archibald Ruthven to raise 3,000 foot in Scotland, and by the autumn of 1573, after an anxious transit of Sweden, this contingent had joined the main army in Estonia. Within a few weeks of their arrival they were at feud with the Germans; and early in 1574, when the Swedish army was attacking Wesenburg, national jealousies culminated in a pitched battle in the course of which no less than 1500 of the Scots were slaughtered. Meanwhile the Germans were themselves mutinous for lack of pay: by the end of 1573 the king owed them 200,000 *daler*, towards which all he could offer was 26,000 *daler's* worth of silver plate. The Germans felt this to be inadequate. Johan was therefore driven to the desperate expedient of placing the fortresses of Hapsal, Leal and Lode in their hands, as security that the balance of the debt should be met by midsummer. In case of default the soldiers were to be free to dispose of the fortresses to their best advantage, provided they did not hand them over to Magnus or to Ivan. When midsummer came Johan was still without sufficient ready money. The soldiers thereupon came to an agreement with Fredrik II's commander on the island of Ösel, and delivered over the places to Denmark.

The Swedish fortunes in Livonia had now sunk to their lowest point: in 1575 even Reval turned to Fredrik with an appeal for mediation. Johan himself seems for a moment to have been ready to abandon the struggle: at a frontier-meeting with the Danes this year he offered to transfer to Fredrik his rights to Hapsal, Lode and Leal in return for cancellation of the outstanding debt on Älvsborg; or alternatively to renounce all his claims in Livonia in exchange for the cession of Bohus, or Viken, or Jämtland. It is at least doubtful whether he was in earnest; but in any case Fredrik stood out for a harder bargain. It may well be that by doing so he lost his best chance of fulfilling the role for which he had been cast at the peace of Stettin. But in truth it was a role to which he had never aspired. If he could keep a foothold on Ösel and in the Wiek, that was as much as he desired—and, as it proved, more than he could compass. For Ivan IV was becoming truculent in his attitude to Denmark. In 1574 he snubbed a Danish embassy bent on conciliation; he elected to feel affronted that Fredrik should have accepted the custody of the three fortresses; in 1575 he peremptorily demanded that they should be surrendered to him. The demand was rejected; and in 1576 the Muscovite hordes burst into the Wiek, crossed over into Ösel, and devastated Fredrik's corner of Livonia from end to end. Not even Hapsal, Lode and Leal, whose rash acquisition had precipitated this disaster, were saved; for the mercenaries, finding Fredrik as little able to pay them as Johan, forthwith betrayed the strongholds to the enemy. It was the beginning of the end of Danish influence in Livonia. In 1578 the wretched Magnus, terrified by the displeasure of his appalling patron, fled from the Russian service, renounced his thorny crown, and took refuge in Kurland, where he ended his life in obscurity five years later. In 1580 Fredrik II virtually abandoned his rights under the peace of Stettin in exchange for a tacit Swedish renunciation of claims upon Ösel.[1] And in 1585 he accepted a modest cash payment from Poland, in liquidation of such Livonian interests as Magnus might be supposed to have retained after his abdication.

One competitor in Livonia was thus eliminated. But at the moment when Denmark withdrew from the struggle, Poland re-entered it. And the great question for Sweden at once became, whether Poland could be enlisted as a collaborator, or whether she was inevitably to be a rival. If the experience of the last twenty years proved anything, it was that Sweden must find an ally in the Baltic. Erik XIV had chosen Russia: the logic of the situation suggested that Johan III must choose Poland.

[1] In 1575 Johan III, in an effort to be rid of his scapegrace brother-in-law Magnus of Saxe-Lauenburg, had enfeoffed him with the castle of Sonnenburg on Ösel. Magnus, against whom Fredrik II had already strong grievances on other counts, made an unprovoked attack on the Danish commander in the island which ended in the Danes' capturing Sonnenburg. In 1580 the Swedes abandoned their claims to Sonnenburg *e silentio*; but Johan considered that they had exceeded their instructions, and the Sonnenburg question was to have some importance in the future.

As long as Sigismund Augustus lived this had indeed been a not unlikely development. In 1571 Johan sent Anders Lorichs to Poland as *legatus perpetuus*, and in the same year Sigismund Augustus opened discussions with a view to an alliance. But Sigismund Augustus died in July 1572; and with his death the prospects of an alliance receded. Two main obstacles stood in the way of it, one of a fundamental, the other of an accidental nature. The fundamental difficulty (which had existed, of course, in equal force in Sigismund Augustus's time) was that Poland, claiming the whole of Livonia (including Estonia), could not easily be brought to admit the Swedes to a share of it. The accidental difficulty was financial and dynastic. The mother of Sigismund Augustus—as also of Johan's wife, Katarina—had been Bona Sforza, daughter of Gian Galeazzo of Milan and his wife Isabella of Aragon, whose father had been Alfonso II of Naples. Bona had inherited from her mother the duchy of Bari, the principalities of Rossano and Manfredonia, and some other Italian interests. On her death in 1557 she made her son Sigismund Augustus her heir-general; left sums of money to her four daughters; and to the extreme chagrin of her family bequeathed her Italian fiefs to Philip II of Spain. Sigismund Augustus contested the will, put in another will more to his liking (which proved unfortunately to be a forgery), and so initiated a bitter family lawsuit which dragged on for centuries, and never in the end arrived at any decision. On the death of Sigismund Augustus without heirs, Katarina and her sisters became co-heiresses to the estate. The amount of money involved was very large by any standards. It was obvious that Johan could not afford to neglect any chance of recovering his wife's share of it. It was true that when Katarina married Johan in 1562 it had been agreed that she should receive the 50,000 ducats left to her by Bona's will only when Sigismund Augustus had recovered the Italian fiefs from Philip II; it was true too that she had renounced all other claims on Bona's inheritance in consideration of the dowry which her brother was to provide for her. But Philip II flatly refused to surrender Bari and Rossano; the dowry had never in fact been paid; and Katarina had been left without either portion or inheritance. Moreover, apart from the rights of his wife, Johan had claims of his own upon Poland. The 120,000 *daler* which he had advanced to Sigismund Augustus in 1562 had never been repaid. In the closing months of his life Sigismund Augustus had indeed promised Johan security for the debt, but he had died before he could give effect to his intention. Since with him the Jagiełłons became extinct in the male line, and other dynasties must now be elected to the Polish throne, it was easy to foresee that the Poles would wash their hands of these obligations. For the next fifteen years, in fact, Johan's relations with Poland were bedevilled by his obstinate attempts to recover his wife's money and his own. If the successors of Sigismund Augustus had been able to disavow all connexion with the Jagiełłons the question of the Sforza inheritance, at least, would have sunk to the level of a purely private quarrel; but, as it happened, one of the conditions for Stefan Batory's election in 1575 was that he should marry Katarina's elder sister Anna. He thus became a party to the cause and a legitimate target for Johan's reclamations.

To all these problems—the need for Sweden to find an ally, the controversy over Livonia, even the financial disputes—there was one conceivable solution, if Johan were prepared to risk it. This was the radical solution of a union of the Polish and Swedish crowns. The disadvantages and the hazards were sufficiently obvious. But in the early seventies the weakness and isolation of Sweden were such that Johan was driven to take account of it. Hence his vacillating, half-hearted and tardy intervention in the Polish elections of 1572–3 and 1575. On the first of these occasions he was a candidate sufficiently serious for the Polish Protestants to be able to use him to extort better terms for their religion; on the second the support he attracted was negligible. His sole assets were his Jagiełłon wife and his ability to speak Polish;[1] his fatal defect was his lack of ready money, and his consequent determination not to squander large sums on electioneering. In 1572 he did indeed authorize his agents to promise that if he were elected he would hand over Sweden's possessions in Estonia to Poland; but the whole history of his reign suggests that this was a promise which he never intended to keep. It is worth emphasizing that Johan's interest in the crown of Poland was not, either in the seventies or later, a matter of dynastic ambition. It was an uncertain political calculation, directed not to the aggrandisement of his family but to the advantage of his country. He gave no sign of chagrin at the election of Henry of Anjou in 1573, nor at that of Batory in 1575. His reaction in each case was to explore the possibility of an alliance with his successful rival. Batory did in fact make him an offer soon after his election; but the terms he proposed made acceptance impossible. For the price he demanded—now and afterwards—was Sweden's withdrawal from Livonia and the diversion of Swedish military effort to Finland's eastern frontier.

Thus Johan made no progress in his relations with Poland. And since his need of a friend and ally did not grow less, he was forced to look elsewhere for what he wanted. He did not turn, as Erik XIV would have turned, to the Protestant states of Germany or the West, although the *råd* recommended him to do so: certainly he had no hopes of his

[1] Johan was a good linguist. Sir Andrew Keith, who was in his service, wrote that he could 'speak and understand guid Inglis'. But Sir Andrew, of course, was a Scot: James Dow, *Ruthven's Army in Sweden and Estonia* (Stockholm, 1964), p. 82.

sisters' husbands, most of whom were political liabilities rather than useful allies. Neither he nor Karl had any sympathy with the Dutch rebels. Johan twice rejected appeals from William the Silent; Karl in 1574 actually offered to enter the service of Spain, bringing with him men, supplies, and eight warships. There was a moment when it seemed that there might be a chance of an arrangement with France: in 1575 Charles Dançay had a project for marrying Johan's sister Elisabeth to a Valois prince, with a view to establishing the pair as rulers of Livonia. Dançay spent much ink in carefully explaining to Catherine de' Medici that Erik's insanity was not a hereditary taint; but nothing came of it at last. Friendship with Spain, on the other hand, had much to commend it. It fitted in with Johan's religious policy;[1] it offered some hope of persuading Philip II to be more compliant about the Sforza inheritance; it would probably bring better relations with the Austrian Habsburgs, and Spain after all was the greatest power in Europe. In 1576 Johan despatched Pontus de la Gardie to Italy, to negotiate with the papacy on matters of religion,[2] and if possible to enlist papal assistance in the family lawsuit. While in Naples de la Gardie took the opportunity to begin talks with the Spaniards about an alliance. Philip II was interested: in 1578 he sent Don Francisco de Eraso to Sweden to continue the negotiations. What Johan principally wanted was money to hire mercenaries for Livonia; what he had to offer was guns and warships—commodities of which Philip stood much in need, and for which he was prepared to pay. But Philip was also interested in the possibility of shutting the Sound to Dutch and English ships, in the hope of thereby inflicting a crippling blow upon the economy of his enemies. Eraso accordingly came forward with plans for the capture, with Swedish assistance, of Elsinore and Hälsingborg, and the formation of a great anti-Danish league under Spain's leadership which should include both Sweden and Poland. A draft treaty on these lines was actually drawn up and sent off to Spain for Philip's approval. Thereupon a silence descended. The draft, it is to be presumed, was read by Philip, and no doubt annotated; but no reply of any sort came from Madrid. Eraso suffered the usual fate of Spanish diplomats, and lingered for months without instructions from his sovereign, until his continued presence became an intolerable irritant to Johan's short temper, and he was at last packed off in disgrace with nothing accomplished. Johan was glad to be rid of him. Spanish money and Spanish friendship were certainly desirable things, but he had no real wish to see himself manœuvred into a Danish war in order to obtain them. And of Spanish aid inside the Baltic there had been no word. An anti-Danish coalition might be an intelligible policy for Stefan Batory, for Denmark had been

[1] See below, pp. 277 ff. [2] See below, pp. 283-4.

giving aid to the rebellious city of Danzig; but from the point of view of Johan III it was a political irrelevance.

The failure of the negotiation with Spain was more than offset by a change in the prospects in Livonia. The election of Batory gave to Poland a king of great military gifts and strong character, and for the first time confronted Ivan with a really formidable adversary. Whatever the Polish feeling about Sweden's presence in Reval, it was obvious by 1577 that the challenge to Poland's aspirations came not from Sweden but from Russia: Sweden was a nuisance to be abated later; Russia was a serious and imminent danger. Once this fact was faced, coöperation between the Polish and Swedish forces, for temporary and limited ends, became at least a possibility. In the year after his election Batory had his hands full with his attempt to reduce Danzig to obedience; but he kept an anxious eye on the operations of the Russians, and by December 1577 was sufficiently concerned at their progress to resign himself to a compromise with Danzig. In 1578 he turned his attention to Livonia. And on 21 October 1578, at Wenden, the Polish and Swedish armies, in a collaboration which was almost an improvisation, inflicted upon the Russians the first really serious defeat that they had sustained in this war.

The battle of Wenden was true to its name; for it marked a turning-point in the history of the whole Baltic region. It inaugurated a long succession of Russian disasters, which within five years transformed the political and military situation. The coöperation of Poles and Swedes was not, indeed, repeated, despite Batory's urgings: each pursued their own objectives, drawing advantage from the dispersion of Russian forces enforced by the activities of the other; and each won great successes. Batory's strategy was to strike straight for Pskov and Novgorod: in 1579 he took Polock; in 1580, Velike Luki and Cholm; in 1581 he began the siege of Pskov. This left a clear field to the Swedes: already in 1579 Henrik Klasson Horn made the first serious attempt to take Narva. Its failure led to the appointment of a new commander-in-chief in the person of Pontus de la Gardie; and in him Sweden at last found a general of quality. Suddenly all the efforts that had seemed vain became fruitful, all the enterprises that had seemed so formidable became easy. In two brilliant campaigns de la Gardie swept the Russians out of Estonia. Kexholm, on the Finnish frontier, Padis, in the Wiek, both fell in 1580; Wesenburg and Tolsburg in the summer of 1581. In July Klas Henriksson Horn recovered the three fortresses of Hapsal, Lode and Leal. And on 6 September 1581 de la Gardie crowned the work by the storm of Narva. An appalling massacre followed, for unlike Ivan in 1558 de la Gardie spared neither man, woman nor child: before the troops had finished their bloody work over 7,000 persons are said to have been slaughtered. After Narva it was the turn of Ivangorod, Jama and Kopoŕe; and at the close of the year the recovery of Weissenstein provided a fitting epilogue to the campaign. The whole of Estonia was now Swedish; a land-bridge from Reval to Viborg seemed within sight; the Russians were driven from almost all of Ingria; not a single port remained in Ivan's hands. In the exhilaration of success Johan III could cry that the Russians' back was broken. His triumph was premature, for there was more fight left in them than he imagined; but he was entitled to his exultation. Until almost the end of the seventies it had seemed likely that Erik XIV's venture would sooner or later have to be abandoned. As late as 1580 the *råd* had urged a quick peace upon the best terms that could be got. But Johan had clung to Estonia with a flaccid tenacity, struggling along in the vague hope that somehow something would turn up to stem the Russian tide, and he had lived to reap the reward of his persistence. De la Gardie's victories had decided the fate of Estonia for more than a century; and they had been made possible, at least in part, by the king's determination to give his general the best support that he could afford.

To Stefan Batory, on the other hand, it seemed that the Swedes owed their successes to his exertions: 'I set the snare', he remarked, 'but my brother takes the game.' He did not admit Johan's right to his conquests; in particular he grudged him the possession of Narva. Meanwhile, his siege of Pskov made no progress. It was time, perhaps, for a truce with the Russians, if only so that he could bring pressure to bear on Sweden. The papacy was ready to offer its mediation, for a Russian embassy to Rome in 1580 had deluded Gregory XIII into thinking that Ivan was inclined to a union of the churches, or at least that he was willing to participate in a crusade. Antonio Possevino, as a man well-versed in Baltic affairs,[1] was accordingly commissioned to undertake the work of pacification. Under his auspices the belligerents concluded the truce of Jam Zapolski in 1582. Its terms were humiliating for the tsar: for the first time in his career it was Ivan who sought peace, his adversary who granted it. He surrendered to Poland all the areas in Livonia still in Russian occupation, and the city of Dorpat in addition; in return he received back the town of Velike Luki. A half-hearted attempt by Possevino to obtain some discussion of the interests of Johan III was vetoed by the Russians, no doubt to Batory's satisfaction; and it was agreed that either party should be free to keep any conquests—and Narva was particularly mentioned—that they might make from the Swedes. The truce was to run for ten years.

The treaty of Jam Zapolski virtually served notice on Sweden that

[1] For his earlier activities in Sweden, see below, pp. 284 ff.

Poland would attack her as opportunity offered. It was followed by determined attempts on Batory's part to frighten or cajole Johan III into surrendering his conquests. Johan replied with indignation, defying the Poles to do their worst, and for some months it seemed that a war between Sweden and Poland could hardly be avoided. But the Polish Diet wanted peace, and Queen Anna used her influence on the same side. Batory, conscious of empty pockets, allowed himself to be persuaded. The crisis subsided; but the clash of claims remained. In the circumstances, it was prudent in Johan to make up his mind that the time had come for a truce with Ivan on his own account. In 1583 it was concluded, for three years, on the basis of *uti possidetis*; it was renewed for a further three years in 1586.

In the course of the negotiations with the Russians the Swedish plenipotentiaries put forward astonishing demands. In addition to the cession of the areas recently overrun, they asked for Novgorod, Pskov, Gdov, Ladoga, Porchov and Nöteborg. These were pretensions which no Swedish sovereign had ever advanced before, pretensions which were quite unjustified by the military situation. No doubt they were made with the idea of being abandoned in the course of the bargaining, just as the Russians on their side had begun by demanding the retrocession of all the places which the Swedes had taken. But they were something more than a gambit of diplomacy. They represented a new aspiration for the future, a sudden enlargement of Swedish ambitions, a programme of conquest which would not be forgotten. Johan's objective was now nothing less than the acquisition, not only of the ports along the southern coast of the Gulf of Finland, but of the great distributing-centres of north-west Russia from which those ports were supplied. More clearly and explicitly than had ever been the case with Erik XIV, he was aiming at the control of the trade-routes between Muscovy and the West. Experience was already proving that possession of the ports was not enough to ensure it. The capture of Narva had crippled the Narva trade, for the Dutch and the English saw no point in resorting to such a petty and inconvenient port if they were to be mulcted of tolls when they arrived there. For a few months Johan had hoped that Narva might continue as a staple; but he soon learnt better. The eclipse of Narva, however, did not mean that its former frequenters moved *en masse* to Viborg or Reval. Some no doubt did so; but it was soon apparent that the Russia trade was finding alternative channels out of reach of the Swedish customs officials. It went from Dorpat to Pernau, or from Dorpat to Riga, with Batory's active encouragement. And it also went north, to the shores of the White Sea, where in 1584 the new port of Archangel was founded to replace the old St Nicholas. Johan III saw all this very clearly. He saw that any

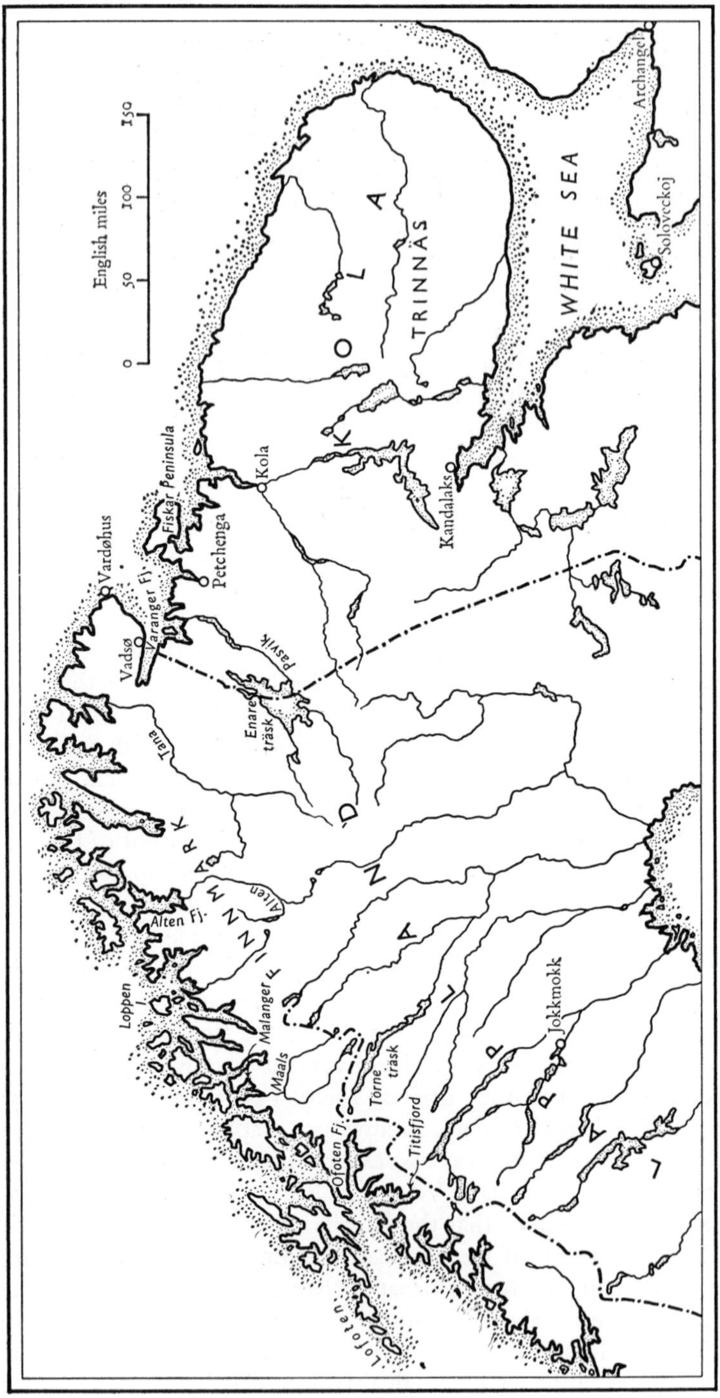

The Scandinavian Arctic

attempt to dominate the Baltic trade-routes to Muscovy must entail, if it were to have any hope of success, not only an attack upon Russia itself, but also the throttling of Archangel. Action in the Arctic, action in Livonia, were but twin facets of one policy.

The opening-up of the route round the North Cape was naturally a matter of concern to Denmark as well as to Sweden, for if it should come to be much frequented it would lower the yield of the Sound Dues. Gustav Vasa had drawn the attention of Kristian III to this aspect of the case as early as 1556; and from 1564 Fredrik II had made repeated attempts to stop the trade by negotiation with the English government. The Danes put forward the argument that the seas lying between Iceland and Norway (both in Danish hands) were to be considered as a Danish territorial waterway, to be opened or shut or tolled at the discretion of the king of Denmark. It was not an argument that impressed Queen Elizabeth. For more than twenty years she succeeded in evading any serious discussion of the question. But as the international situation grew more threatening for England at the beginning of the eighties, she began to feel the need for Denmark's good-will. In 1583 she signified her willingness to negotiate; and the outcome was the treaty of Haderslev, whereby the English were given the right to sail around the North Cape in return for an annual tribute of 100 rose nobles.[1] One effect of the conclusion of this agreement was that the attitudes of Sweden and Denmark to the Archangel trade, which had hitherto been broadly identical, henceforward began to diverge. The Danes had secured their tribute, and were satisfied; the Swedes to their chagrin saw the North Cape navigation in a manner legitimated. And this divergence of view came at a moment when other developments in the Arctic were beginning to threaten the new-found harmony of the Scandinavian kingdoms.

In the Middle Ages, the Scandinavian Arctic had been a no-man's-land, protected against easy access from the south, first by the deep forests of southern Norrland, and then by the inhospitable sub-Arctic wastes that followed when the forest had dwindled to a scattering of dwarf birch; a land rarely visited by pioneers from the south, inhabited only by some tens of thousands of Lapps, and by some few dozens of Swedish traders and trappers, who were organized into the privileged commercial association of the *Birkarlar*. The Swedish crown was by the fifteenth century beginning to colonize the more accessible coastlands, and the crown's bailiffs followed in the settlers' track. To them the Lapps paid tax, not as Swedish subjects, but in return for the use of the land for trapping, or for fishing. As the colonists occupied the coasts the Lapps moved inland to the high fells, abandoned their

[1] The French adhered to the treaty, on the same terms.

former hunting and fishing, and took to nomadism and reindeer-culture. They followed their herds up or down the mountains, according to the season; they moved over the watershed to the Atlantic coast, established settlements there, pushed out fishing colonies to the Norwegian islands. Where the Lapps went the Birkarlar followed, for each Birkarl had his allotted number of Lapp families to whom he was agent, trader and supplier. In the wake of the Birkarl followed the tax-collector. Gustav Vasa, who never lost sight of any possible source of revenue, paid particular attention to these developments. In 1551 he sent up soldiers to defend the Arctic settlements from raids by the Russians; in 1552 he caused to be drawn up a systematic inventory of the yield of all the fisheries in the Arctic, including those on the Atlantic. His bailiffs became regular visitors to the coastal Lapps. By 1560 the Lapps were being regularly taxed all along the Arctic seaboard from Vadsø in the east to Ofoten in the south-west. The economic importance of the area was now considerable, for it produced a large revenue in the form of skins, which had recently become highly fashionable and proportionately valuable: by the third quarter of the century fur-traders were faced with unprecedented demands, and enjoying boom conditions. With the idea of ensuring a firm control of this trade the government in Stockholm began to feel its way towards asserting not merely a right of taxation but a claim to exclusive territorial sovereignty: the first attempt in this direction was made at the Stettin peace conference in 1570. The claim was difficult to substantiate, for in the absence of any other proof the strongest argument was a demonstration that tax had actually been paid over a long period. But in fact Sweden could show no tax-lists before the 1550s. Moreover, the Swedes were not the only tax-gatherers in the field. For the Lapps were also taxed by the Russians and the Danes; and it might happen that the same nomad families paid tax to all three governments. The Swedish successes in the Baltic had direct repercussions on this obscure situation. After the capture of the town of Kexholm in 1580, Johan at once claimed a right to the whole province of Kexholm which was dependent upon it—that is, to a strip of territory extending from Lake Ladoga to the Arctic Ocean. In 1582 he tried to assert his authority over Lapps in this area who had hitherto undoubtedly paid tax to the tsar. In 1588 he claimed the right to two-thirds of any taxation levied in Lappland, on the argument that since Sweden, Denmark and Russia had formerly taken equal shares, he was now entitled to the share which had formerly been Russian, as well as to his own. Two years earlier he had plainly announced his ambition to control the whole Arctic coast from the White Sea to Varangerfjord, and in his negotiations with the Russians at that time it seems clear that he would even have been prepared to sacrifice Ivangorod and Kopoŕe in return for territorial gains in the north and east of Finland. There was more than one motive behind this aggressive policy. Undoubtedly it was his object to secure a larger share of a fur-supply which was already beginning to contract as a result of ruthless hunting. It is possible also that he desired an outlet to the Atlantic. But a third motive, and not the least important, was his wish to annex the Kola Peninsula, to close the White Sea to commerce, and to destroy Archangel: in the last two years of the reign two unsuccessful but carefully-planned expeditions were launched against Kola. The Russians were well aware of what was afoot. The Danes were slower to grasp the implications for themselves, and as long as Fredrik II lived the Arctic question did not seriously cloud his good relations with his neighbour. But within a decade of his death it would have become a major controversy; and ten years after that it would play a part in engendering another war between the Scandinavian kingdoms.

In March 1584 Tsar Ivan's long reign came to an end. He was succeeded by a holy fool under the control of an able upstart: no doubt one of the reasons that led Boris Godunov to renew the truce with Sweden in 1586 was a wish to be free to consolidate his power at home without the distraction of a foreign war. In December 1586 Stefan Batory died also, pursued to the last by dunning letters from Johan III; and with his death the whole question of Swedish–Polish relations was posed once more. Once again the opportunity presented itself of solving outstanding difficulties by a personal union; but this time the prospects were far brighter than in 1575. The widowed Queen Anna had set her heart on securing the election of Johan's son Sigismund, whom she had already made her heir: as the son of a Jagiełłon, as a Roman Catholic and a Polish-speaker, he seemed to many Poles to be the next best thing to a Piast. Johan, however, was troubled and uncertain. It was only after listening to the entreaties of three successive missions from Poland, and after learning that Tsar Feodor would also be a candidate, that he agreed to allow his son's name to go forward. The other candidates were Cardinal Andreas Batory, and no less than four Austrian archdukes, of whom Maximilian soon emerged as the strongest runner; but the election became in fact a contest between Maximilian and Sigismund, supported respectively by the old opponents of Batory and his old supporters led by Chancellor Zamoyski. Zamoyski stood for the continuance of Batory's attempt to incorporate Muscovy into a great Polish-dominated Slavonic state, and his motive in backing Sigismund was frankly avowed. He expected Sigismund to bring to Poland Swedish assistance against Russia, and above all naval assistance: the union of the crowns would enable Poland to emerge as a naval power—indeed, as the predominant naval power in the Baltic. But if

Zamoyski thus intended to use Sweden for Poland's advantage, Johan III intended the exact opposite. From the beginning each side set out to exploit the other; and it was scarcely surprising that in the end both were disappointed.

The contest ended in a double election: on 19 August 1587 a majority voted for Sigismund, three days later a minority chose Maximilian. It was not until January 1588, when Zamoyski defeated and captured Maximilian, that Sigismund's victory could be considered secure. In the meantime he had run into difficulties which soon caused him to envy his defeated rival. At the time of the election Johan had sent over two members of the *råd*, Erik Sparre and Erik Brahe, as Sigismund's agents; and they had immediately found themselves involved in controversy about the future of Estonia. The Poles insisted that the Swedish conquests must be handed over to Poland as the price of Sigismund's election; but the Swedish delegates had been expressly forbidden to agree to this. They succeeded, by fluent but ambiguous eloquence, in carrying the election without committing themselves to an explicit promise, though Erik Sparre came very near to it; but they were at once confronted with the same demand as part of the terms of the *pacta conventa* which was to be required of the new king upon his accession. It is possible, as Johan afterwards asserted, that at this point Sparre again gave verbal assurances in excess of his instructions; but it seems certain that the difficulty was resolved only because Queen Anna pledged the whole of her personal property as security for the demand's being complied with. Johan himself was adamant on the issue. He had accepted Sigismund's election in the first place only after the Polish envoy had exceeded his instructions by giving a written undertaking that Estonia would not be demanded. He refused to allow Sigismund to leave Sweden until he had accepted the terms of the Statute of Kalmar (September 1587), which provided far-reaching securities for Sweden's independence and safeguards against Polish interference,[1] and which explicitly declared Estonia to be 'a Swedish province'. Rather than surrender Estonia Sigismund was ordered to refuse the Polish crown. Accordingly, when he arrived off the Polish coast he declined to land until the *pacta conventa* had been shorn of the Estonian clause; and at his coronation he declared that he would never force his Swedish subjects to cede any Swedish territory. The Swedes argued, shabbily enough, that Anna's pledge of her property was to be considered as an *alternative* to Estonia's cession: since the one was refused, the Poles might now come upon Anna for the other. Before Sigismund had been a month in his kingdom both he and his

[1] Including special provisions for retaining the Swedish calendar and preserving the Swedish language from corruption by foreign idioms.

supporters were regretting that he had ever been elected; within six months, he was engaged in a secret negotiation with the Habsburgs with the object of enabling him to abdicate in favour of the Archduke Ernest. But since nobody in Poland wanted another interregnum, they made the best of a bad business with a compromise that settled nothing: the question of Estonia, it was decided, should stand over until Sigismund should succeed his father as king of Sweden. It was not an encouraging start for the promised new era of Swedish–Polish amity.

The sequel did not belie these auguries. The Union proved a deception to both parties. Johan's truce with the Russians expired in 1590, his hope that Godunov would be frightened into making a peace by the imposing appearance of Swedish–Polish solidarity having proved to be unfounded. The Russians renewed hostilities with disconcerting vigour; the Swedes were caught unprepared.[1] Despite a valiant defence, Karl Henriksson Horn was able to prevent a Russian recapture of Narva only at the cost of surrendering Ivangorod and Kopoŕe. In 1591 an appeal to Poland for aid was rejected on the ground that the Republic had its hands full with Tatar attacks; in the same year the Poles concluded a twelve-years' truce with the tsar. They did indeed exert themselves to arrange a year's truce for the Swedes at the same time; but Johan, who had no intention of allowing himself to be patronized, angrily declined this sop. Yet even he recognized that peace was necessary, if it could be had on decent terms. He did not live to see it; but he was able in August 1592 to make a two-years' truce which provided for the resumption of peace negotiations before its term expired. And at last, on 18 May 1595, thanks in no small degree to the emollient labours of an unbidden imperial mediator, this long war—it had lasted for nearly a quarter of a century—came to an end in the peace of Teusina.

The terms were less favourable to the Swedes than had at one time appeared probable. They abandoned their stake in Ingria; they retroceded Kexholm and its province. But even so their gains were far beyond what would have seemed possible in the sixties or seventies. The whole of Estonia was recognized as Swedish; the Russians accepted Viborg and Reval as staples for their trade with the West. Thus the great struggle for Livonia, which had begun with Ivan IV's irruption in 1558, had ended in the partition of the country between Poland and Sweden. Denmark had voluntarily abandoned the contest; but Russia had been clearly defeated. The objectives of Ivan IV were now more distant than when he had first begun to pursue them. The total exclusion of Russia from the sea, which was to be the fruit of the peace of

[1] Pontus de la Gardie had been accidentally drowned in 1585.

Stolbovo in 1617, had very nearly been achieved, and would henceforth remain an object of Swedish policy. The Gulf of Finland had become a Swedish waterway, through which commerce must henceforth pass on Sweden's terms. And the delusive hope of a total control of the Russia trade had received such encouragement that future generations of Swedish statesmen would always be prone to entertain it. The retrocession of Kexhom might indeed seem to be a check to Swedish ambitions in the Arctic; but other provisions of the peace made that impression misleading. For it had been agreed that Kexholm should not be handed back until the completion of a new delimitation of the Russian–Finnish frontier. When that delimitation was completed, it gave Finland a recognized frontier further to the east than ever before: the treaty of Nöteborg (1323) was abrogated at last. In the far north, the peace of Teusina pushed Sweden's territorial sovereignty for the first time to the shores of the Arctic Ocean. Thereby it implemented the claims to tax which Johan III had advanced in 1588; for the tsar had now surrendered all rights of taxation between Varanger and Malanger, so that in this area henceforward the Swedes could claim that two-thirds of the tax was legally theirs. The Danes, indeed, held that at Teusina the Russians had surrendered what it was not theirs to give; but this was a controversy for the future.

By 1595 the foundations of the Swedish Baltic empire had been laid. Swedish Livonia—to be known henceforth as Estonia—had become a part of the Swedish realm. Since 1583 it had enjoyed an interval of unwonted peace, which the Swedish authorities had used to begin the work of resettlement and reorganization. Swedish law and Swedish administrative practices made their appearance, though they did not wholly supplant local institutions. The wretched peasantry found in the Swedish crown a champion against the tyranny of their German lords; while an impoverished and unlettered clergy could now count on Swedish impulses for the necessary work of church reform. Successful commanders, aristocrats who had deserved well of the crown, began to look for their reward to grants of land in Estonia: expansion overseas was soon seen to carry with it lucrative possibilities for the nobility, and already before Johan was dead there was brisk competition for royal donations. For the first time the possibility appeared that imperialism might be an aristocratic interest. No one as yet foresaw that the acquisition of Baltic estates might implant in their possessors the lower standards of social behaviour, the indifference to law, the contempt for peasant rights and peasant liberties, which prevailed among the Baltic nobility, and might at last begin to taint the aristocracy at home.

It would be unreasonable to place these developments to Johan III's account, whether for debit or for credit; but it is at least clear that the continuation of the struggle until a victorious peace could be made was his personal decision. His country was weary and exhausted, his civil and military advisers had concurred in pressing him to make sacrifices to end the war, he was accused by hostile pamphleteers of being the only obstacle to peace. The accusation was unfair, for it takes two to make an agreement, and the Russians were naturally reluctant to give up the game they had been so near to winning. It is true that Johan's pertinacity was in part attributable to vanity, ambition, and a natural crossness of temper which led him to cling more obstinately to a course of action the more men sought to dissuade him from it; and it may well be that he did not grasp the sacrifices which he was demanding of his people, or was indifferent to them. But it is difficult to deny that he had a clear insight into the political issues at stake, and a sound judgment of the best way to pursue them. He was the first to realize the interconnexion of the Arctic and Livonian theatres. He succeeded in restoring relations with Denmark to a satisfactory footing. His diplomacy, if it could show no striking successes, must be pronounced prudent and judicious. Take it for all in all, his foreign policy was among his most successful achievements. Its results are writ large upon the history of the next century.

III. THE CRISIS IN THE CHURCH

The death of Gustav Vasa closed an epoch in the history of the Swedish Reformation. As long as he lived, the church was helpless, subject, fast bound in the fetters of the royal supremacy. He had enervated its organization; he had inhibited its self-consciousness. His removal brings a sense of liberation: the church breathes more freely; it finds its voice; it begins to feel itself truly a member of the wider Protestant communion: in a word, it becomes adult, and henceforward will expect to be treated accordingly. The decades after 1560 are one of the great formative periods in the history of Swedish Lutheranism, a period when for the first time Protestantism becomes not merely a matter for king and clergy and a few urban congregations, but a faith of the masses, which politicians will ignore at their peril, or exploit to their advantage. The church begins to have a policy *as* a church; it shows a growing resistance to royal dictation: for the first time since the Reformation its relations with the state become a matter of vigorous debate, rather than a question settled by royal *fiat*. And at last the church is driven—reluctantly, and for the most part by outside pressures rather than by inner forces—to attempt some more precise definition of its doctrinal position.

These outside pressures were of two kinds. On the one hand was the threat of a Roman Catholic revival, made explicit by the French religious wars, the struggle in the Netherlands, and the slow swing of the religious tide in Germany: in the face of these things the hatred of Rome took on a sharper edge, and the noses of theologians developed a morbid susceptibility to any whiff of popery in the ritual or formularies of the church. On the other hand, Swedish Lutherans found themselves for the first time involved in the acrid squabbles within the Protestant ranks. However convenient it might be to pretend that there was no difference between Luther and Melanchthon, by the end of the seventies they would not be able to keep up the pretence any longer. Still less could they avoid the challenge of Calvinism, which in the sixties was everywhere on the offensive. It was, indeed, the danger from Calvinism, in the years immediately after 1560, which first galvanized Swedish churchmen into theological activity.

Calvinism, like Lutheranism, came to Sweden with immigrants, who in the fifties and sixties arrived in the country from France, Germany, and above all from Emden, which John a Lasco had made a Calvinist stronghold. Gustav Vasa had provided two of his sons with tutors who were Calvinists—Dionysius Beurreus for Erik, Jan van Herboville for Karl. As part of his policy of encouraging trading connexions with Emden he had done his best to induce immigrants from East Friesland to settle in Sweden. Erik followed his example: in 1562 he issued a general invitation to Calvinists who might be suffering from religious persecution, promising them freedom of worship provided that they did not attack the Swedish church and were otherwise well-conducted. Some Calvinists took advantage of this offer: sufficient, at least, to form the nucleus of a Calvinist movement in Sweden. Beurreus and Herboville were active in writing and spreading Calvinist propaganda: at least one prominent churchman—Hans Ofeegh, the bishop of Västerås, who was Beurreus' brother-in-law—for a time gave them his support. Their zeal, however, outran their theological abilities. The archbishop, Laurentius Petri, in 1562 demolished their arguments in a pamphlet which marks an epoch. After 1562, whatever the precise doctrinal position of the Swedish church might be, at least it was not Calvinist; Calvinism henceforward is heresy; Calvinists are enemies of the faith. And this had consequences analogous to those that flowed from the sharpened hostility to Rome: as the one entailed condemnation of liturgical luxuriance or patristic theology, so the other brought with it suspicion of Melanchthonians, of 'philippists': that is, of those elements in Lutheranism which seemed—especially in their dislike of the strait Lutheran doctrine of the ubiquity of Christ's body and blood—to be tainted with Calvinist 'sacramentarian' opinions. Thus the contact with Emden never meant to Sweden what it meant to England. As the history of the next generation would demonstrate, the main foreign influence was not, as in England, in the direction of radicalism, and the sectarianism which follows from radicalism; but rather towards conservatism within the central Lutheran framework. Sweden's Emden was destined to be Rostock; whence would come a tradition not far removed from the gnesio-Lutheranism of the school of Flacius Illyricus.

As yet this development lay in the future. In the meantime, the archbishop's vigorous intervention perhaps brought home to Erik XIV the impolicy of too easy a hospitality: at all events, his attitude to the immigrants changed in 1563. Two years later he issued a mandate curtailing the liberties of Calvinists and forbidding their propaganda. There was no persecution; but they could no longer count on the king's goodwill. The change would have been even more apparent, had it not been for a sharp controversy in which Erik took the opposite side to his archbishop. Communion-wine, like all other wine, had to be imported into Sweden, and was a special item in the budget of each parish church, defrayed by a special tithe. After the Reformation, the practice of giving the cup to the laity, and also the practice of giving the consecrated wine to the dying in place of extreme unction, put a strain on the vestry's resources. Parochial contributions no longer sufficed to buy wine in adequate quantities. There was a national shortage of communion-wine; and after 1563 it was aggravated by the semi-blockade of Sweden during the Danish war. In an effort to alleviate the distress of congregations who were thus deprived of the Eucharist, some of the clergy advocated dilution, or the substitution of mead, cherry-juice, or even water; and to this the Calvinists could see no objection. They were vigorously supported by Ofeegh. They also had the sympathy of the king, who feared popular disturbances if the sacrament were not available, and in typical Vasa style suspected that the clergy were doing well out of selling communion-wine on the black market. Erik met the immediate need by making wine available from the royal cellars, and by 1565 the worst of the crisis was over. But the 'liquoristic controversy', with its Calvinist overtones, had brought the archbishop into the fray, and his denunciations of Ofeegh and his friends were as pungent as his former attacks upon Beurreus. Erik scented a challenge to his authority; in the last years of the reign his relations with the church were not cordial.

Like his father, Erik had a high notion of the royal supremacy; but unlike him he had an intelligent interest in theology and a real appreciation of the church's needs. Despite the tutoring of Beurreus, despite the liquoristic controversy, he had really no leanings towards Geneva;

but he was inclined to a Lutheranism which was austere, suspicious of tradition from pre-Reformation times, and quasi-Puritan. In this he was not in accord with his archbishop; and early in the reign they differed sharply upon which ceremonies might be considered *adiaphora* (indifferent) and which inadmissible. They disagreed especially about the elevation and adoration of the sacrament: the archbishop (like Luther himself) regarded elevation as an *adiaphoron*, adoration as obligatory; while Erik would have forbidden both.[1] But though Erik might dissent from his archbishop on points such as these, and though he had no intention of relinquishing control of the church, he had none of his father's exaggerated dislike of episcopal government. On the contrary, he restored the bishops to their old authority and reasserted their superiority to superintendents, whose numbers henceforth declined. The episcopate, which had seemed in danger of extinction in the latter years of Gustav Vasa, was thus saved and rehabilitated, and could now resume its place in the leadership of the church: it was a decisive change. It meant, among other things, that the problem of state-church relations, which Gustav Vasa seemed to have settled in the state's favour, was reopened: it was not to be resolved for many a long day. For if Erik XIV and Johan III (though in very different ways) were both Melanchthonians, neither they nor any other Swedish sovereign would easily be content to accept Melanchthon's separation of the lay and spiritual spheres, and his relegation of the king to the position of being no more than *minister et executor* and *praecipuum membrum ecclesiae*; and neither was prepared to tolerate too great a show of independence in the bishops. This, no doubt, was one main reason why Erik refused to allow the *riksdag* in 1561 to accept Laurentius Petri's draft of a Church Ordinance; for it had been drawn without consulting him. The Church Ordinance had accordingly to wait until 1571 to receive official sanction, in a rather different climate of royal theological opinion; but it circulated in manuscript in Erik's time, and had already won practical acceptance in much of Sweden before it was imposed as the general rule of the church.

Despite this disappointment, Erik's brief reign marks a real turning of the tide. The regeneration of the church had begun; its bishops were thinking and acting for themselves as they had not done since the time of Olaus Petri; and in Laurentius Petri it had a leader whose ability and determination could now be deployed with a new freedom, and whose prestige and authority, painfully husbanded during long years of subordination, were now at their height. Laurentius Petri was influenced by Melanchthon's reverence for the traditions of the early church;

[1] Despite Luther's opinion, Sweden was the only Lutheran country to tolerate elevation and adoration.

he believed that the new should grow up within the framework of the old: '*omnis mutatio*', he said on one occasion, '*etiam necessaria, est periculosa*'. His love of music and all beautiful things led him to conserve the old services and the old rich furnishings, where they were not plainly superstitious—and even some of the old saints' days, since the people needed holidays; while his sense of order was offended by the squalor and irreverence of the more evangelical type of Lutheran service. When Johan succeeded his brother the old archbishop found at last a sovereign who in all these things was a man of his own opinions, and whose devotion to the welfare of the church matched his own.

Johan III was the most learned theologian ever to sit upon the throne of Sweden: Olof Dalin, indeed, said of him that he had more learning than he could conveniently use. Like James I, he was proud of it, and he loved to intervene personally in theological disputations. But he was also a man of brooding and mystical piety, who aspired to be a Hezekiah or Josiah to his country. His concern for the church was very real: so real that he easily imputed evil motives to those who opposed the measures he proposed for it. 'If all is well with the clergy', he remarked on one occasion, 'the king and his subjects will be well too.' His visit to England seems to have left him with an appreciation of the Anglican compromise; his marriage to a Roman Catholic who kept her own chapel and her own priests made him familiar with the Roman rite; but the strongest intellectual influence upon him came from his reading of the early Fathers, with which he had occupied himself during the long years of imprisonment in Gripsholm. To this was added, from 1573, the influence of the irenically-minded Roman Catholic theologian Georg Cassander. It happened, moreover, that one of the most trusted of his servants, Petrus Mikaelis Fecht, had received his education at Wittenberg under Melanchthon, and was similarly imbued with philippist opinions: in him Johan found a valuable coadjutor. Johan's ideal was always the primitive church; the opinions and practice of the first five centuries weighed very heavily with him. He would have agreed with Cassander that '*Antiquitas, universitas et consensio*' are the marks of truth. His strongly developed aesthetic sense was attracted by the splendour of the Roman ritual; and his emotional type of religion found the ordinary Lutheran service unsatisfying. In principle he was for a reasonable latitude in matters of ceremonial, and probably really meant to be tolerant; but his exalted view of the kingly office disposed him to react to theologically based opposition as though it had been inspired by a spirit of insubordination, and by a strange paradox he became the first Swedish monarch to persecute for religion's sake. His ultimate goal was noble, for he aimed at a reunion of the churches;

and it is not necessary to impute this (as many historians are disposed to do) to his vanity and self-sufficiency. He knew the Roman church of the post-Tridentine age less well, perhaps, than he thought he did; for his wife came from a Poland more influenced by Erasmian humanism than by the Counter-Reformation. Johan himself was no more a Roman Catholic than Laud was; but his rejection of the doctrine of ubiquity, and his attitude to *adiaphora* and tradition, separated him decisively from the gnesio-Lutheranism of Flacius Illyricus, and he looked with distaste upon the rabid spirit of controversy which affected German Protestantism in the seventies and eighties. But the very eclecticism of his own position made it difficult to find many who entirely agreed with him.

Johan showed his concern for religion very early in his reign: at the time of his coronation in 1569 he presented to the Clergy for their comment thirteen articles concerning matters which he deemed in need of attention. Some of these were incorporated by the archbishop into his final draft of the Church Ordinance, which dates from 1571; and the general trend of that document was certainly in line with many of the king's opinions. It was printed and promulgated by Johan's order, with a preface which stated that the king had confirmed and authorized it, and now enjoined its adoption. In 1572 he laid it before a meeting of bishops and clergy at Uppsala, when all present were required to take an oath to apply it. The author might be the archbishop; the authority was the king's.

The Church Ordinance of 1571 was at once a confession of faith and a piece of practical ecclesiastical legislation. The doctrinal position was deliberately kept almost as vague as it had been from the beginning: the 'pure Word of God', as contained in the Scriptures, was to be the basis of faith; the *Augustana* was neither accepted nor rejected; references to the authority of the Fathers were few. The differences between Luther and Melanchthon, of which Protestant Germany was by now painfully conscious, were simply ignored; though the reading of Melanchthon's *Loci communes* was recommended, and in the critical question of the Eucharist it was Melanchthon's formula that was accepted. Despite the royal authority which imposed it, the Ordinance implicitly assumed the church's independence within the state. The episcopate, explicitly justified on grounds of tradition, was declared responsible for its government. Chapters were retained, and the office of dean approved. The king's share in the choice of bishops was declared to be limited to confirmation of election by a diocesan body which would include laymen. On ceremonial the Ordinance was notably conservative: the meeting at Uppsala resolved that ceremonies received and preserved from antiquity, if without scandal, should be retained. Accordingly, the Ordinance accepted exorcism[1] and vestments, the chalice and paten, the use of the sign of the Cross, adoration and elevation, the canonical hours, Latin for the sung parts of the mass; on the general principle that most ceremonies were to be considered *adiaphora*. Finally, the Ordinance included much-needed provisions for church discipline, and incorporated an important School Ordinance, designed to bring some improvement to the deplorable state of education. It was the archbishop's *nunc dimittis*, for he died in 1573: at once the testament of a liberal spirit and a last brave assertion of the church's rights. Yet in spite of all its merits, the Church Ordinance raised almost as many problems at it solved. Doctrinally, it postponed a decision; in the matter of ritual and ceremonies it soon proved too easy-going for the hardening temper of Lutheran orthodoxy. Its purported character of a sort of fundamental ecclesiastical law, and its lack of precision at vital points, degraded it before long into being a text which could be hurled by one party within the church at another in proof of orthodoxy. Its belief in the church's independence was contradicted by the whole history of the next forty years, and was, indeed, subverted by its final paragraph. For that paragraph stated that though the Ordinance contained all provisions that seemed to be required for the moment, additions might well prove to be necessary in the future, and, if so, further provisions would be added to it. In the king's view, the clergy, having bound themselves by their oath to conform to the Ordinance, were likewise bound to conform to any such supplementary articles. This might mean—and experience would soon reveal that it did mean—that he considered them bound to conformity even if the additions were made by the secular power. In his view, the oath had given a blank cheque to the royal supremacy. The clergy at Uppsala from the beginning took a different view. On the motion of Martinus Olai Gestricius, the bishop of Linköping, the assembly had passed a resolution promising to adhere to 'the ceremonies hitherto in use among us, as now set out in our printed Church Ordinance', and by no means to tolerate 'other, or foreign, ceremonies'. For the clergy, it is clear, the Ordinance was to be an absolute rule; for the king, it might easily be made the basis of alterations.

Within a couple of years the latent divergence came into the open. Until the death of the old archbishop in 1573 Johan made no further move; but in 1574 he caused Fecht to draw up, and to submit to the Clergy, ten articles designed to secure greater order and reverence in church services. Johan himself presided over the ensuing discussions, and his presence no doubt helped to induce the Clergy to accept his

[1] The Danish church insisted on exorcism at baptism, and considered its omission to be a philippist error.

proposals. The resolution in which they were embodied gives some idea of those features in clerical life which the king was determined to reform. It was agreed, for instance, that a parson would do well to abstain from immorality or drunkenness in the period *immediately* preceding a mass-day. Light conversation among the clergy was reprehended. Laymen were forbidden to constrain or persuade clerics to engage in drinking-bouts. The Elements were not to be handled with unwashed hands; vestments must be clean and seemly; the officiating clergy must not 'put their old hats and filthy gloves upon the altar, yea even between chalice and paten'. These were regulations which even those who were unsympathetic to Johan's religious ideals could hardly for very shame oppose. But unanimity was less easy to secure in regard to his next step. Taking advantage of that sentence in the Church Ordinance which admitted the possible need for supplementary legislation, he presented the Clergy in 1575 with the *Nova Ordinantia*. The *Nova Ordinantia* was described as an 'explanation' of the Church Ordinance; but it was in fact a substantial piece of new legislation, wrapped up in a great deal of theological argument. In its emphasis on preaching, its condemnation of the worship of the saints and of images, it was in harmony with strict Lutheranism. It was thoroughly evangelical in its provision for lay participation in church-government, and particularly in a proposed *consistorium ecclesiasticum*, which was to act as a supreme court in ecclesiastical cases. It contained admirable provisions for education, for church discipline, and for the settling of chapters as administrative colleges for the dioceses. It showed a concern for the purity of the Swedish language; it encouraged the maintenance or formation of cathedral libraries; it gave to the bishops a censorship over imported books. But in its treatment of doctrine the *Nova Ordinantia* bore unmistakable traces of the influence of Cassander's mediatory theology: in places, indeed, it follows Cassander word for word. Especially notable (and from the strict Lutheran point of view especially disturbing) was its attempt to reconcile the controversy over Faith and Works.[1] Its frequent appeals to the authority of the Fathers, and its advocacy of the retention of at least one monastery or nunnery in each diocese, marked a new departure; its reservation to the king of a veto on episcopal appointments presaged a new assertion of royal supremacy, and undermined the Church Ordinance. In the matter of ritual, its tendencies became clear when Johan forced Laurentius Petri Gothus, the new archbishop, not only to assume crook and mitre, but also to submit to unction, as part of the ceremony of consecration.

[1] 'Our love of God thus flows from Faith in Him, and the greater our Faith, the greater our Love; but Love manifests itself in Works, for it is the nature of Love that it cannot be unfruitful.'

The question had been hotly debated beforehand, and unction had been generally condemned: indeed, the *Nova Ordinantia* did not prescribe it.[1] Yet almost immediately it was being enforced. To some of the clergy it seemed that the *Ordinantia* was designed to be the point of departure for the introduction of semi-papistical practices. In itself, it was certainly still accordant with Lutheran theology, and the clergy were right to declare, in accepting it, that it 'by no means included anything in doctrine or ceremonies which is popish or sectarian'. Nevertheless, the consciences of many were troubled, especially after the incident of the unction. The king secured the acceptance of the *Ordinantia* only by threats of deprivation for the recalcitrant, and by giving the impression that the whole matter was to be further considered at a general council of the church.

It was not long before those who feared that the *Nova Ordinantia* was only the thin end of a Roman wedge could claim that their suspicions had been justified. In the course of the debates upon it Johan had indicated that he intended shortly to present them with a new Liturgy. Early in 1576 it was ready; in February 1577 it was presented to the *riksdag*. The two lower Estates accepted it by acclamation (only a handful of the nobility attended); the Clergy after a long disputation at last followed their example, all the bishops signing the resolution. But the opposition this time had been tougher: the bishop of Strängnäs (which lay in Karl's duchy) signed '*quantum ad coronam*'; even the archbishop accepted the Liturgy only '*salvo tamen aliorum judicio*'; and the king found it necessary to take steps to ensure that some known leaders of opposition were kept away from the meeting. Even so, the resistance was so stiff that Johan exacted from those present a pledge to use the new Liturgy henceforward, on pain of deprivation; and already the first punitive measures were being taken against the handful of Uppsala theologians and Stockholm parsons who ventured to defy the royal authority.

The disquiet with which some members of the church accepted the Red Book (as the Liturgy came to be called) was caused mainly by the new ritual for the mass. Johan might claim that the enemies he was fighting were '*superstitio*' and '*prophanitas*', and assert that of the two it was the latter which for the moment was the more dangerous, but to Lutherans of the austerer sort it appeared that in the effort to counter the one he was falling into the other. The text of the Red Book was in fact a skilful conflation of the *ordo romanus* and the Swedish masses

[1] To the archbishop's plea to be allowed to escape unction Johan characteristically replied: '. . . And you may as well realize that We, thank God, are quite well enough versed in God's Word to be able to judge that neither ceremonies nor gestures avail to salvation or damnation'—and was given the choice of submission or deprivation. He submitted.

of 1531 and 1537; and it prescribed a ritual richer than Sweden had known since the Reformation. It enjoined the use of the surplice for preaching, and of no less than eight vestments for the celebration of the mass. It aroused misgivings by language which suggested (to less expert Latinists) that the mass was a sacrifice.[1] Lutherans of a Puritan cast—at first a small, extremist minority—were naturally alarmed. To the majority of the clergy—ill-educated, theologically vague, inclined to conservatism—the Red Book was not in itself unacceptable; and the much-execrated Liturgists were probably less hypocritical when they conformed to it in 1577 than when they abjured it in 1593. But extraneous circumstances, whose connexion with the Red Book is debatable, made the Liturgy appear to be what its critics accused it of being—the first overt move towards an apostasy to Rome. For at the very moment when the Red Book was forced upon the church in Sweden—at the moment, too, when continental Lutheranism was redefining its theological position in the Formula of Concord—Johan was engaged in a clandestine negotiation with the papacy.

It was the accident that Sweden had a Roman Catholic queen that first directed the attention of the papacy to the possibility of propaganda in the far north. Katarina on her marriage had received assurances that her religion would not be interfered with; but in spite of this Johan had succeeded in persuading her to communicate in both kinds. Her conscience, nevertheless, was troubled; and she wished to regularize her position by obtaining a papal dispensation. She therefore turned for advice to her countryman, the celebrated Cardinal Hosius. Hosius gave her reprimands rather than encouragement. But in 1574 he sent over a Jesuit, Warszewicki, to strengthen her in the faith; and he took the opportunity to commission him to make a general reconnaissance of the religious position in Sweden. Warszewicki in due time reported that the prospects were not unhopeful: Johan, he thought, could be brought to acknowledge the supremacy of Rome; but only upon condition that the cup was granted to the laity, that clerical marriage was permitted, that the worship of saints was not insisted upon, and that the mass might be said in Swedish. These were terms which could hardly be acceptable to the post-Tridentine papacy; but Rome, it seems, was not discouraged: it was always possible that Johan might in time be persuaded to waive them. At all events, in 1576 Gregory XIII took the decision to send to the Swedish court a certain Father Laurentius Nicolai, a Norwegian Jesuit at that time stationed at Louvain, who was selected, no doubt, for his ability to speak Swedish. His ostensible

[1] It used the word 'offerrimus'. As Johan later scornfully pointed out, if the critics of the Red Book had known their Latin better, they would have realized that *offerre* and *sacrificare* did not mean the same thing. The confusion perhaps arose because the Swedish verb *offra* does in fact mean 'to sacrifice'.

duty was to act as chaplain to the queen: his real task was to begin the reconversion of Sweden. In many ways he was an excellent choice: he had energy, courage and good abilities; he was eloquent, learned and a practised controversialist; but he was over-sanguine, and he was not well endowed with the political sense which might have been expected of one of his Order. He went in disguise; and his arrival was kept a secret by the king and queen, for Johan did not want the prospects for his Liturgy to be prejudiced by the accusation that he was coquetting with Rome.

Laurentius soon found unexpected employment. The disintegration of the university of Uppsala in Gustav Vasa's time had left Sweden without any facilities for higher education, and therefore for the training of the clergy in theology. Erik in 1566 had made an effort to put the university on its legs again, and Johan had given further support in 1572. But it was already apparent that the Uppsala professoriate was likely to be hostile to Johan's religious policy. If he were to be sure of a new generation of clergy of his own way of thinking they must be educated at some other place than Uppsala. He had no great confidence in the Protestant universities of Germany to which the Swedish youth resorted, and least of all in the Rostock of Chytraeus; and in 1575 he had begun an attempt (long persisted in under successive Swedish kings) to exercise a control over visits to universities abroad. Laurentius's arrival seemed to offer a solution to his difficulties in this matter. A college was opened in the former Greyfriars in Stockholm; Laurentius Nicolai was appointed a professor, and soon afterwards rector. From his association with the old cloister he gained the nickname by which he is famous in Swedish history: 'Klosterlasse.'

Klosterlasse, in obedience to his instructions, continued to conceal his religion, and his lectures were skilful *pastiches* of tepid Lutheranism. They attracted pupils, however; and his position was strengthened when Abraham Angermannus, the rector of Stockholm Grammar School, was deprived of his position for his opposition to the new Liturgy, and Klosterlasse's Jesuit colleague, Feyt, was put in his place. In the debates on the Red Book Klosterlasse gave powerful assistance to the king, and Johan soon placed great confidence in him. The Jesuit, on his side, came to believe that if the pope would agree to at any rate some concessions Sweden could be regained for Rome. Johan, for his part, hoped that the Red Book might make a favourable impression on the curia. In the autumn of 1576, therefore, he despatched Fecht and Pontus de la Gardie on an official embassy to Gregory XIII. They were to press for a dispensation for Katarina, to explore the possibility of a reunion of the churches, and to try to enlist the pope's good offices in the matter of the Sforza inheritance. And since Warszewicki had succeeded in implanting in Johan's mind uncomfortable doubts about the Apostolic Succession, they were also to try to regularize the position by persuading the pope to consecrate a bishop, possibly Fecht himself. It unluckily happened that Fecht was drowned while crossing the Baltic, a misfortune which deprived the mission of its theological expert, and was by some contemporaries discerned as a divine judgment upon him for his share in the Red Book.[1] Nevertheless, de la Gardie's overtures were taken seriously in Rome. The pope at once appointed a commission of cardinals to consider the matter; and as a result of its deliberations it was decided to send to Sweden no less a person than Antonio Possevino, a former secretary-general of the Jesuit Order, to explore the possibilities for reunion.

Possevino arrived in Sweden at Christmastide 1577 in lay attire, having fortified himself for his mission by diligent study of Olaus Magnus.[2] He brought two other Jesuits with him: William Good, the inevitable Irishman, and a Frenchman, Jean Fournier. He found Klosterlasse still posing as a Lutheran, but gathering a modest and clandestine harvest of souls: already he had sent off a batch of five for training in the German College at Rome. He was high in Johan's confidence: in November 1577, when the bones of St Erik were re-interred in a silver coffin in Uppsala cathedral, the king had permitted the coffin to be carried by Roman Catholic priests, and had invited Klosterlasse to preach the sermon. His subject, highly appropriate to the occasion, was the worship of saints; which he developed in such a manner as to cause considerable scandal among the Uppsala dons. Nevertheless, he was also on good terms with the archbishop, who regarded him as simply a Lutheran of Liturgist complexion. The prospects seemed decidedly encouraging. The Red Book had been warmly supported by some of the more prominent members of the *råd*, notably by Per Brahe and Hogenskild Bielke (who wrote a defence of it), and it had been actively disseminated by some of the royal secretaries—men whose political importance made them worth cultivating. Klosterlasse believed that the conversion of these Liturgists was either imminent or already accomplished. And it is certainly true that Brahe, Bielke, Erik Sparre and Nils Gyllenstierna gave some grounds for this supposition. Between 1577 and 1579 all of them attended mass according to the Roman rite. Pontus de la Gardie, too, had communicated *sub una specie*

[1] Sven Elofsson, *Paralipomena*, p. 210, where he writes that many thought that Fecht's life was cut short 'because he had sweated and racked his brains over the book of the Liturgy, about which there was such commotion as well before his death as after; but that is as it may be'.

[2] Olaus Magnus was the brother of Archbishop Johannes Magnus, and had accompanied him into exile. His *Historia de gentibus septentrionalibus* (Rome, 1555) was a lively survey of the geography, ethnography and natural history of the Scandinavian lands which became a standard work.

while at Rome; but of him there were less hopes: had he not replied, in answer to a Protestant remonstrance, that he would communicate in one, or two, or fourteen kinds to please his master? It was probably only his candour that differentiated Pontus from his colleagues in the *råd*; for it is likely that Brahe and the rest were moved by somewhat similar feelings. Johan himself had no faith in the religious zeal of the high aristocracy: he remarked on one occasion that they would turn Calvinist or atheist to save their estates. It was natural for Klosterlasse to count these great men as converts; but all the indications are that he was deceived. With the king he seemed to be on much surer ground. From Easter 1577 Johan had forborne to communicate according to the Lutheran rite. He had placed two key positions in the Swedish educational system in Jesuit hands. He had offered no objection to Roman Catholic proselytizing. Possevino found him warmly welcoming, sanguine that the papacy could be talked into reunion on his own terms, eager for theological discussions. He found him also (which pleased him less) intent on a plan for a great international congress, at which the leading Catholic states would meet selected Protestants of good will, in order to hammer out a formula of reconciliation.

Within a very few weeks of Possevino's arrival these hopeful auguries were blasted by a public scandal. One of the king's more disreputable secretaries, Johan Henriksson, after living in adultery with the wife of another man, suborned his servant to murder the husband, and then sought and obtained from Klosterlasse a dispensation to marry the widow. Possevino himself authorized Klosterlasse to give an *oral* dispensation, since the answer to an application to Rome had been delayed, and the secretary was an impatient man whom it was prudent not to offend. Unfortunately, he had constrained Klosterlasse to give him a dispensation in writing, which he had then proceeded to brandish under the nose of the archbishop, who had been threatening him with disciplinary proceedings. The upshot of the affair was that Klosterlasse stood revealed as a papist. The archbishop, who had hitherto been his friend, denounced him in a thundering pamphlet; the church awoke with a start to the strength of Roman Catholic activity in the country. The episode probably also alarmed the king, who began to see that if he were not careful popular hostility to Rome might turn against his own ecclesiastical system. The result was Johan's letter to the pope of 8 March 1578, in which he finally formulated his conditions for reunion. He demanded the cup for the laity, the marriage of priests, the mass in Swedish:[1] that was of course. But he also demanded jurisdiction over bishops for political offences; no interference with the

[1] Oddly enough he based this demand on the argument that St Sigfrid had celebrated mass in English.

Reformation land-settlement; the right to attend all Lutheran services; the abolition of Holy Water; and the recognition that the worship of saints and prayers for the dead were not obligatory. He seems really to have persuaded himself that these terms would be accepted, and his excitement and enthusiasm rose at the prospect. In May 1578, after making his general confession to Possevino, he received communion at his hands. It was on this occasion that he exclaimed, in an irrepressible outburst of sensibility, '*amplector te et ecclesiam catholicam in aeternum*'. But even at this supreme moment he was careful not to add '*romanam*'; and the next day he made it clear that his terms were in no way modified. Possevino left Sweden soon afterwards, bearing Johan's letter with him, and accompanied by another handful of candidates for the priesthood. He had by this time obtained the papacy's approval for the establishment, at Braunsberg and Olmütz, of seminaries designed to do for Sweden what Douai was to undertake for England: unlike Cardinal Pole in Queen Mary's time, Possevino had realized that if Roman Catholicism were ever to be re-established, the first priority was not a revival of monasticism, but the provision of facilities for the training of priests. He departed apparently confident that Johan would abate his demands to an acceptable level: certainly he spread throughout Europe the news that his reconciliation to Rome was imminent.

Five months later, in October 1578, the pope's answer to Johan's ultimatum reached Sweden. On the three main points it was a flat refusal, as it was also in regard to the worship of saints, prayers for the dead, and holy water. The matter of church lands, it was conceded, might be a subject for discussion. Though Johan might listen, if he must, to Lutheran sermons, he might in no circumstances attend a Lutheran mass: the Red Book was thus implicitly condemned as heretical. It was a heavy blow to Johan's pride; and it was keenly felt. The king was, indeed, furious: for the first time he began to be doubtful of ultimate success. In July 1579 he took the significant step of once more attending Lutheran mass: it was the first time for two years.

It was therefore with diminished expectations that Possevino shortly afterwards returned to Sweden, this time in clerical dress. At first Johan refused to see him; and when at last he granted him an audience, he so completely lost control of himself that Possevino fainted in terror. By this time it had become plain that no compromise was likely; and in these circumstances Possevino began to transfer his hopes from Johan to Sigismund. Sigismund had received a Roman Catholic education; but Johan had intended that he should be equipped to make a free choice for himself, in the somewhat naïve expectation that he would choose to follow in his father's footsteps. He was proportionably angry and disappointed when in 1579 the boy absolutely refused to attend Lutheran services and declared his intention of remaining a Catholic. Possevino was sure of Sigismund. The future, he felt, was on his side. For the present, therefore, he confined himself to what was in effect a demonstration. He ordered all Roman Catholic priests in Sweden to throw aside their disguises; and he conducted an ostentatious visitation of the nunnery at Vadstena, which Johan and Katarina were beautifying and rebuilding. But these tactics defeated their object: they were a self-indulgence from which he had better have abstained. Inevitably they entailed a break between the king and Klosterlasse, for Johan had extracted a promise from him that he would keep his religion secret. They provoked panic in the Swedish church, as well they might; and they made it essential for Johan to beat a retreat. There were ugly anti-Catholic riots in Stockholm. Already in February 1580 the *råd* had advised the king to scotch alarmist rumours about his intentions by a proclamation explaining that his purpose was only to effect 'a general union in religion, and not to take up any old error, nor introduce any new'; adding that it might be politic to restore some of the deprived clergy, and that it was essential that Sigismund be brought up a Protestant. And at a *riksdag* at Linköping in March the strength and violence of the attacks on Klosterlasse and the Jesuits sounded a clear warning. Johan did indeed assert his authority by forcing the *riksdag* to endorse the deprivation of the stiff-necked bishop of Linköping; and he could still nibble for a moment at a compromise whereby the papacy should concede the cup for ten years. But he was disillusioned, humiliated, angry; probably he was frightened too. Klosterlasse was deprived of his rectorship, and, being dismissed, made the breach with the king irreparable by openly attacking the Red Book, so that Johan was driven to couple his writings with those of Angermannus, and ban them both. There was now no future in Sweden either for Klosterlasse or Possevino. In August 1580 they took their departure with a few proselytes, to embark forthwith upon an unedifying wrangle about the responsibility for the failure of their mission.[1] In 1581 Gregory XIII made a belated offer to reconsider the question of the cup for the laity, if France and Spain could be persuaded to agree; but to this Johan sent no reply. For another three years the Greyfriars remained under Roman Catholic influence; a half-dozen of priests lingered on in Sweden; but by the end of 1580 the danger from Rome was virtually over—for a time. The death of Queen Katarina in 1583—mourned even by religious adversaries[2] for her estimable personal qualities—removed Johan's last temptation to try again.

[1] It is satisfactory to note that the pope took Klosterlasse's part.

[2] Even Karl could find nothing more to say about her than that she was virtuous and devout despite her religion.

The *missio suetica* had been dear to the heart of Gregory XIII. It had been pushed with determination and discretion—at least, until Possevino's bravado completed its ruin. Its importance for the future history of the Swedish church is undeniable. Yet its tangible results were pitifully small. Its latest historian puts the total number of Roman Catholics in Sweden at 237; and of these a high proportion were foreigners. A few conspicuous converts there were, among the younger generation of the high nobility; a few dozen youths went off to Braunsberg or to Olmütz; some time-serving magnates amused themselves by complaisance to the missionaries. But as Possevino observed (comparing one barbarian country with another) what was this to the 5,000 converted each year in Brazil? If they had captured the king they might (or might not) have done better. It has indeed been contended that they did capture him, that Johan was a real convert, that it was his fear of rebellion which forced him to make his terms for reunion so stiff, and at last timidly to abandon the whole enterprise. But this is to ignore the fact that the king had a theological position of his own to which he clung with a tenacity which sprang from a deep conviction of right. It is easy to dismiss his ecumenism as 'fantastic'. Fantastic it may have been; but it was also sincere: when the way was blocked to reunion with Rome, his mind at once turned to the possibility of union with Constantinople. He passionately desired that the Swedish church should be catholic; and to achieve that end he was prepared that it should also be Roman Catholic—if only Rome would meet him halfway. It was after all an undoubted fact—one of the many loose ends left by the haphazard Swedish Reformation—that Sweden had never explicitly renounced the papal authority, or cut the last tie with Rome. But when Johan angrily denied that he had ever been a 'papist', he spoke no more than the truth. He said on one occasion that he did not believe that the Holy Spirit dwelt either in Rome, or Wittenberg, or Geneva: it dwelt in the Fathers of the church. In pursuit of his ideal he took great political risks; but it was not the danger of the course he was pursuing which persuaded him to abandon it: it was the realization that it was leading to a different goal from that which he desired. He pinned his hopes on compromise; and it was natural that he should believe in the compromise of his own devising. He found he had to deal with men who resisted compromise as a dilution of the truth, and were not impressed by his liturgical patchwork. And if all other obstacles had been removed, it is still difficult to believe that he could ever in practice have renounced the exercise of the royal supremacy over the church, though in his enthusiasm he may for a moment have thought so; nor is it likely that Rome would now have agreed to a concordat so liberal as to make its authority imperceptible.

For Johan the whole affair was tragic, as the wreck of ideals must always be. It left behind it an abiding resentment against Rome, and a dislike for the Jesuits which lasted till his life's end. Upon the church it impressed a deep, indelible mark. It implanted in the minds of all churchmen—even those of the most conciliatory and traditionalist complexion—a lively fear of Rome. It brought home to men for the first time the possible consequences of Sigismund's Catholic education. And it lent increased weight to those men, such as Martinus Olai Gestricius of Linköping, or Abraham Angermannus, or the group of Uppsala theologians led by Petrus Jonae and Olof Luth, who had from the beginning opposed Johan's liturgical innovations as opening the way to popery, and had now as it seemed been proved right. The change of sentiment affected even the nobility. They did, indeed, continue to give support to the Liturgy, though they were as a class probably the most indifferent to religious matters of any in the kingdom; but the Possevino affair was a sudden reminder to them of how great a territorial stake they had in the Reformation.

The most formidable resistance to the threat of Catholicism, however, came from Duke Karl. Karl professed his ideal to be religion as it was practised in the last years of Gustav Vasa; but this was only an aspect of that filial piety which was one of the very few endearing traits in his character. In fact, he was nearer to Erik's Puritanism, and nearer still to that crypto-Calvinism which was one of the by-products of philippism. He desired 'a continuing Reformation'; he was a strong biblicist; an Old Testament spirit of hatred (directed, of course, against Rome) gave a zest and an edge to his creed. His travels in Germany in 1578 and 1579 had given him his bellyful of Protestant polemic; and though he was the last man to be queasy about gross or violent abuse, he was impressed by the need for a common Protestant front, and therefore deplored the unedifying brawling of the theologians. He was not prepared to put himself within the strait-jacket of the *Augustana*, whether *variata* or *invariata*[1]—'the pure Word of God' was good enough for him—and his hope was, that it might be possible to reconcile differences within the Protestant camp by agreeing in essentials, and agreeing to differ on all the rest. Thus like Johan he had ecumenical leanings; but whereas Johan looked to union with those to the right of him, Karl looked to union with those to the left. And as Johan compromised himself by seeming to dally with Rome, so Karl was pursued till his dying day by the suspicion of crypto-Calvinism.

Karl took his stand on the Church Ordinance of 1571 without

[1] His marriage-contract with Maria of the Palatinate (1579) in fact bound him to the *Augustana*; but he ignored the obligation when he got home, and carefully avoided pledging himself on religion to the Estates of his duchy.

modifications or additions. He had indeed acquiesced in the *Nova Ordinantia*, though with reluctance; but the Red Book was more than he could swallow. His duchy, which included the diocese of Strängnäs,[1] was—or at any rate was considered by Karl to be—almost as autonomous in ecclesiastical matters as in lay; and the clergy of Strängnäs, incited by their duke, decisively rejected the new Liturgy. Karl himself, especially after his return from Germany in 1579, made no secret of his opposition to his brother's policy: at the Linköping *riksdag* of 1580 he was among its sharpest critics. It was he who on this occasion put forward the demand that a general council be summoned to settle the controversies within the church: it was a demand to which he returned over and over again in the course of the next decade. Meanwhile, the success of Johan's religious work was menaced by the existence within the body of the state of an autonomous area of dissent. This was made very evident in 1581, when Abraham Angermannus, escaping from the prison to which the king had consigned him,[2] took refuge in the duchy, whither he was shortly followed by Petrus Jonae and Gestricius. All these were given Karl's patronage and protection. The duchy became a place of refuge for those of the clergy who were exposed to the king's wrath, an island of resistance in a Liturgist ocean. For Johan, in the years after 1580, was more determined than ever to enforce the Red Book. The failure to realize the ideal of reunion only attached him the more to his work of church reform; and the eighties saw him proceeding to a sharp persecution of recalcitrant clergy—confiscating their tithes, depriving them of their cures, transferring them to remoter and less eligible pastorates, and in the case of a few of the more obstinate or outspoken, consigning them for a time to prison. Abraham Angermannus and Petrus Jonae, feeling themselves no longer safe even in the duchy, fled abroad, where the story of their wrongs lost nothing in the telling. But though the harrying of the anti-Liturgists was bad enough, it was less severe than was depicted in opposition propaganda and ultra-Protestant historiography. Johan might roar out threats of wheel and stake, or threaten to cut off Gestricius's head, he might accuse his insubordinate clergy of *lèse-majesté* because they would not agree with him on ceremonies, he might try to equate dissent with treason; but the number of persons who suffered, and the extent of their sufferings, have both probably been exaggerated.[3] Of taunts and

1 He later created a new diocese of Mariestad, though only under a superintendent, not a bishop.

2 He was released from his prison, without the king's orders, by Pontus de la Gardie, who was too much of a *politique* to approve of persecution.

3 An example of the atrocity-story put about in this and the next generation is the tale of how Johan, having felled to the ground an obnoxious anti-Liturgist, proceeded to trample upon his prostrate body, declaiming (from Psalm 91) 'Thou shalt go upon the

injurious words there was no lack (on either side); of hardship there was some, of imprisonment a little; but the wheel and the stake claimed no victim. No single person suffered in life or limb. Despite his fulminations the king would have been very willing to allow Angermannus to return and live in peace, if only (impossible condition!) he would engage to keep his mouth shut. Johan was fighting for an ideal and a principle: the principle of royal supremacy, the ideal of a humane and catholic religion. For a time he had great success. It is doubtful how far the ordinary country parson tried to master the new elaborate ritual laid down in the Red Book: copies of the Red Book were scarce, and many churches never possessed one. In the south-west and in Finland—areas where pre-Reformation practice and tradition lingered longest—the Liturgy was accepted readily enough; elsewhere the zealous activity of secretaries and *ståthållare* probably secured a reasonable measure of conformity. As far as the episcopate and the *riksdag* were concerned, Johan seemed in the early eighties to have overcome all opposition. The royal supremacy was explicitly reasserted: the archbishop (as Johan took care to point out) must be subordinate to the king. There was, as it happened, no archbishop at that particular moment; for Laurentius Petri Gothus had died in 1579, and since then the archiepiscopal see had been kept vacant—perhaps because Johan was casting about for a successor of his own way of thinking. In 1583 he found one in Anders Lars Björnram; a man of piety and learning, determined to impose conformity, but better-mannered in his polemics than some of his coarse-mouthed opponents. On the occasion of Björnram's consecration[1] the assembled bishops gave the king an assurance which may be taken to mark the high tide of the Liturgist movement. Not only did they reaffirm their adherence to *Nova Ordinantia* and the Red Book, but they agreed to points which previously they had resisted: unction, the wearing of the cope, greater use of music in church services, sermons based on the Fathers. The work of bringing decency and order into the churches went steadily on; though as late as 1588 Johan, with his usual lack of moderation, could say that the clergy kept their churches 'like sheepfolds or pigsties, so that a man would spew at the stink of them'; could accuse the clergy of 'bawling like troopers'; and threaten them with wheel and stake if they did not amend themselves. But much excellent work was done—in the kingdom, though not in the duchy—in building new churches and repairing old, and in organizing the vestries as regularly functioning

lion and adder; the young lion and the dragon shalt thou tread under thy feet'. The story is told of two different victims, and for one of them rests on no better authority than the laudatory funerary verses composed by a co-partisan.

1 Åbo, to which Erik Erici Sorolainen was consecrated at the same time, had been kept vacant for no less than seven years.

bodies for parochial self-government. These successes in the struggle against *prophanitas* were matched by a new vigour in combating *superstitio*. The Liturgist episcopate, naturally concerned to mark the distinction between itself and the church of Rome, was in the mid-eighties pressing the king to take stronger measures against Roman Catholics. Johan had no hesitation in complying. He was growing anxious about the prospects for religion when Sigismund should succeed him, and must have bitterly regretted having allowed his son to take his own way.[1] When in 1587 Sigismund was elected King of Poland, and the Statute of Kalmar set out the safeguards for Sweden which that event made necessary, religious guarantees took a prominent place. The Lutheran religion in Sweden was not to be interfered with, the number of priests that Sigismund might bring with him to his native country was stringently limited, and they were to be debarred from interfering in politics. It was a combination of this new animus against Rome with the old Adam of royal supremacy that led him to warn his son not to promise 'obedience' to the pope at his coronation, least of all '*cum deosculatione pedum*': *obsequium*, he thought, was quite enough.[2]

Meanwhile it was obvious that the ideal of religious uniformity, which Johan had expounded to the bishops in 1582, could never be realized as long as there was a Cave of Adullam in the very heart of the country. Karl regarded Johan's measures against recalcitrant clergy as tyrannical, and their victims as sufferers for the faith. And in a political point of view he was not prepared to concede to the crown a right to control religion in the duchy, for he believed that under his father's Testament he was entitled to exercise that control himself. His patronage and promotion of the fugitives, his issue of letters of protection safeguarding them from arrest by royal officers, were provocative challenges to the king's authority, involving the whole question of the rights of the duke and the limits of the crown's sovereignty. Thus the religious question became one more grinding discord in the controversy between the royal brothers.[3] And it was a question of ducal rights, rather than any difference on doctrine or ceremonies, that brought matters to a head in 1586 and 1587. In 1585 the death of Bishop Nils left the see of Strängnäs vacant. Johan, appealing to Magnus Eriksson's *landslag* and Gustav Vasa's practice, insisted that all episcopal elections must have his approval;[4] Karl took his stand on the procedure laid down in the Church Ordinance of 1571. He manipulated that

[1] By doing so he had in fact violated the terms of Gustav Vasa's Testament, as Karl and Gustav Adolf were both later to point out.

[2] Aegidius Girs, *Konung Johan den III:des Chrönika*, p. 138.

[3] For the constitutional aspects of this controversy, see below, pp. 300ff.

[4] The Articles of Arboga, of course, had given full control of episcopal appointments to the king.

procedure to produce an election which could hardly have been more flagrantly provocative. His choice—for it was in fact his, whatever the Church Ordinance might say—fell on Petrus Jonae: a fugitive from royal justice; an outlaw. Johan's reply was not only to refuse his approval, but also to outlaw all who had participated in the election. No bishop could be found to perform the act of consecration; Petrus Jonae remained unconsecrated until 1593, when Johan was dead.

Nevertheless it seemed for a moment that a real breach on religion might be avoided. At Vadstena, in February 1587, the royal brothers managed to reach a comprehensive settlement of most of the points at issue between them,[1] not least upon that of religion. On this Johan had clearly the better of the argument. He made good his right of choice of bishops, though henceforth he was to make his selection from three names proposed to him by a joint meeting of the chapters of Uppsala and Strängnäs.[2] On the broader issue, he agreed not to try to force the Liturgy upon the duchy until a general council of the church had met and discussed it; while Karl on his side promised to restrain his clergy from attacking the Red Book and its supporters in the meanwhile. If these terms had been observed, they would at least have afforded an interval for tempers to cool. But Johan, as always, showed no sign of calling a council; and Karl either could not or would not keep the promise to muzzle his hotheads. In May 1587 the clergy of the duchy drew up and published the *Confessio Strengnensis*, which damned the errors of the Liturgists in the amplest terms. Karl for his part wrote to the universities of Leipzig, Helmstedt and Wittenberg for their opinion of the Red Book, and in due course received the condemnatory answer which he had been expecting. And the clergy inside and outside the duchy plied corrosive pens in ever fiercer polemic against their respective adversaries, not excluding the archbishop himself. As far as religion was concerned, the truce of Vadstena was still-born; the battle raged more venomously than ever. Not least from the king's side; for Johan regarded the publication of the *Confessio Strengnensis* as a clear breach of faith on Karl's part. His reaction was more than ordinarily violent: the 'Hard Patent' of 1588 denounced his enemies as 'arch-liars, scatterers of the Faith, bunglers, asses'-heads, limbs of Satan'; it branded them as traitors, and compared them with Nils Dacke; it outlawed the entire body of clergy in the duchy, and sequestered such of their property as might be outside its limits. The concealment or *colportage* of the works of Angermannus became a capital offence—though nobody, to be sure, suffered death for it. Pressure was

[1] For this, see below, p. 303.

[2] They were not to propose anyone who was under the king's displeasure; but on the other hand the successful candidate was to be bound to follow 'the plain and pure Word of God'.

put upon the chapters of other dioceses to sever relations with Strängnäs: Linköping, Skara, Växjö, and later Uppsala, did so; Västerås, though not going so far, declared itself on the king's side. The clergy of the duchy, thus treated as pariahs and outcasts, appealed to their duke for letters of protection; the church was rent in twain; the quarrel threatened once more to bring Johan and his brother to the verge of civil war. Nobody wanted this: not the *råd*, who in 1589 urged the king to call a council and release the imprisoned clergy; not even the choleric and martial royal brothers. Strong political reasons were driving them to sink their differences: in order to be able to fight the constitutional battle side by side they were willing for the moment to postpone the matter of religion. In 1590 they reached a final reconciliation; and as one of its terms agreed upon the calling of a national church council at a time acceptable to each: should that council fail to reach agreement, kingdom and duchy would each be free to practise such form of religion as might seem best to it. This was a substantial retreat for Johan from the terms of 1587: indeed, it was virtual surrender, for it was inconceivable that a general council, attended by clergy from the duchy, should decide unanimously in his favour. It was beginning to look doubtful whether he could even rely upon such a council to give him a majority. For by 1590 the firmness of the Strängnäs clergy, their aggressive polemics, and the attitude of foreign Lutherans, had plainly weakened the Liturgist domination. The death of Archbishop Björnram in 1591 deprived his party of its ablest champion, and Johan had found no successor to him when the reign ended. The anti-Liturgists, who in the mid-eighties had been virtually confined to the duchy, in 1590 appeared formidably in the College at Stockholm (by this time a stronghold of orthodox Lutheranism), where three of the professors went to gaol rather than accept the Red Book.[1] Even in the south, where the Red Book had been accepted with least resistance, a change of feeling had become apparent: in 1592 the clergy of the diocese of Växjö begged to be excused from using it. Johan let them have their way, remarking that he did not wish to be king over any man's conscience. He may have meant what he said; but he had certainly wished it once. By 1592, however, he had given up this particular battle in order to fight elsewhere. Karl was now managing his affairs for him, and he could not afford to revive religious dissensions between them. He could comfort himself with the notion that his reign was ending in political victory (though that perhaps was a delusion too); but he could hardly disguise from himself the fact that he was facing religious defeat. His ideals, mocked, traduced and black-

[1] They were Nicolaus Bothniensis, Petrus Kenicius, Erik Skinnerus; and to them was added Erik Skepperus, the vicar of Stockholm.

guarded by his enemies, were plainly threatened; his compromise was undermined; the next generation was not on his side. It would be long before Swedish Lutheranism learnt to appreciate and sympathize with the real nobility of his programme.

The Liturgical struggle is a good example of the power of a fanatically resolute and intellectually honest minority. The strength of their convictions enabled them to survive persecution in the eighties; in the nineties it enabled them to capture the church. It is probably true that apart from a few men such as Björnram they included among their number the ablest and best educated of the clergy. This was one of their strongest assets; for the modest educational attainments of most Swedish pastors disposed them to follow where they saw a strong-minded or intellectually superior leader. Nevertheless, it is scarcely conceivable that they could have won their victory without Karl's help. The duchy was by no means a land where thought was free; but for those of acceptable opinions it provided a City of Refuge, and if they had lacked it they must have been scattered among the bickering universities of Protestant Germany. It was Karl's jealous defence of his ducal rights that made possible the diversion of the stream of Swedish church history away from the channels in which it seemed destined to run, and made anything like the Anglican settlement out of the question. As far as religion went, Karl and his clergy were by no means at one. On ceremonial they might be in broad agreement; on doctrine they obviously differed. He disliked the narrowness of their Lutheranism; he felt himself invidiously pointed at in their attacks upon Calvin. In the struggle against what they considered to be romanizing tendencies, as in the political struggle against the king, the clergy of the duchy were their duke's indispensable allies; but the differences between them were already marked, and they were becoming deeper. Two great things the clergy of the duchy did for the Swedish church in the eighties: they boldly challenged the royal supremacy, and for the first time since the Reformation effectually asserted the church's autonomy in the state; and they at last cast their anchor into a firm bottom of dogma. However hard Johan might try to convey the impression that the controversy concerned only ceremonies, there could be no doubt that it carried doctrinal implications. To his opponents it seemed that he was trying to do what neither Gustav Vasa nor Erik had ever attempted: to use the royal supremacy to define doctrine. Clerical resentment at the presumption of a layman in usurping what they felt to be exclusively their function was not the least element in the resistance which his reforms encountered. In the face of royal interference in this field the clergy of the duchy were in the end driven to a clear doctrinal statement of their own. The *Confessio Strengnensis* for the first time accepted the *Augustana invariata* as a *symbolum*: with the Church Ordinance of 1571 it would henceforth be the acknowledged bedrock of their creed. They thus declared war on all philippist divagations, and enlisted themselves, if not under the banner of the Formula of Concord, at least on that side of the battle. But these achievements made it certain that their alliance with Karl, always precarious, would be unlikely long to survive the special circumstances that had enforced it. Karl was philippist himself, if indeed he was not already (as some feared) crypto-Calvinist. And whatever his doctrinal position, there was no one in his family—not Johan III, not Gustav Vasa himself—who was a more determined believer in the principle that the church must be subject to the prince. In 1592 Karl may have congratulated himself on the probable defeat of the Liturgists in the near future; but there were ecclesiastical storms ahead of him almost as violent as any that Johan had known.

IV. KING, DUKE AND RÅD

When Prince Karl Filip died in 1622, and the last of the royal duchies fell in to the crown, Gustav Adolf is said to have expressed his determination that the system should never be renewed if he could help it. In 1650, when Queen Kristina was engineering the recognition of Karl Gustav as her successor, she stated flatly that she would not in any circumstances provide her cousin with a territorial duchy. And ten years later, in the course of a discussion in the *råd*, Ture Oxenstierna let fall the remark that 'Gustav Vasa's Testament had such consequences for our fathers that their children's teeth still ache from it'. These remarks give some idea of the impression made upon future generations by the inconveniences and dangers which the existence of the duchies entailed upon the country. It was in the reign of Johan III that Sweden was first afforded an extended experience of them. Before 1568 the implications of the Testament had never been fully apparent: the Articles of Arboga had followed too soon after Gustav Vasa's death; the clash between Erik and Johan had been too short and sharp. But in 1569 the Articles of Arboga were cancelled, and thereafter the crown was confronted with a royal duke determined to extract every possible advantage from his position, and not afraid to push his claims to the brink of civil war. The first twenty years of Johan III's reign were darkened by a nightmare succession of fraternal quarrels. If Gustav Vasa, in creating the duchies, did indeed intend to strengthen the dynasty, the result did not answer the design.

The root of the difficulty lay in the fact that Johan and Karl differed radically in the construction they put upon their father's Testament. Johan, conveniently forgetful of his own behaviour in King Erik's time, held that all rights not specifically conferred upon the duke, all powers not expressly reserved to him, remained as of course in the crown: in particular he insisted that it was never intended to deprive the king of control of foreign policy, taxation, the armed forces, appellate jurisdiction, and the church. Karl on the other hand contended that all powers not expressly reserved to the crown were transferred to the duke. He was not concerned to conjecture what the intention behind the Testament might have been: what mattered to him was what the document actually said. And it said, among other things, that the dukes were to hold their duchies as freely as the king held his kingdom. From this strong but narrow ground Karl declined to be shifted. When in 1578 he went to Germany to look for a wife, he took with him, as warranties for his independent status, his father's Testament, his father's letter of enfeoffment, and Johan's letter of confirmation. He assured the Elector Palatine (whose daughter Maria became his first wife) that within the duchy the king had neither lay nor spiritual jurisdiction. It is likely enough that he believed it; it is certain that he was mistaken. Such statements bore an ominous similarity to the assurances which Johan himself had given to Sigismund Augustus fifteen years before. Karl was indeed wise enough to avoid the false step which had led to Johan's downfall: he took care not to put himself in the wrong by any attempt to conduct an independent foreign policy differing from that of his sovereign; though to be sure the geographical position of his duchy, embedded in central Sweden, offered less scope for this than Finland. His views on foreign affairs did not, as it happened, coincide with his brother's—he was anxious for a peace with Russia, more nervous than Johan about Denmark, and wished for alliance with the Protestant states of Germany—but these differences had no practical effect. Moreover, he did at first do something towards fulfilling his father's hope that the royal dukes might be of service to the crown: he took his place as a member of the *råd*; he did not hesitate to give his brother unpalatable advice which he did not take; he was even prepared to lend the crown money in an emergency. But this coöperation was neither cordial nor permanent: it was not until the last two years of the reign, when Johan sacrificed all other considerations in order to secure his brother's support, that the dynastic solidarity which their father had envisaged became an accomplished fact.

Karl's duchy was organized as a kingdom in miniature. He had his court and residence-town at Nyköping, was assisted by his own bailiffs and secretaries, consulted his own *råd*, negotiated with his own Estates.

In the bishop of Strängnäs he may even be said to have had his own primate. Over clergy and laymen alike he ruled with energy and relish, his self-confident absolutism only thinly veiled by the forms of consultation. He had all his father's love of business, his thoroughness, his suspicious determination to see for himself, and his government compared favourably in point of efficiency with that of Johan III. The duchy flourished under his rule. He did much to assist the colonization of the forest by the establishment of new settlements; he founded the towns of Karlstad and Mariestad; he gave to the development of the iron industry encouragement, capital, and no small measure of practical *expertise*. To protect the economy of his duchy he had no scruples about discriminating against the kingdom: there were complaints that merchants from outside were debarred from the fair at Örebro, and that the duke levied tolls unknown to the rest of the country. His interest in developing new export markets led him to send at least one expedition (which proved a failure) to explore the possibilities in Portugal and Spain. He took his cultural responsibilities with a proper seriousness: schools were set up, scholars sent to German universities at his expense. Certainly he succeeded in winning the loyalty of most of his subjects. Of most; but not of all. For there were at least some of the nobility who disliked his policies. The landholding aristocracy of the duchy fell into two categories: those whose lands were wholly within the duchy's limits, and those whose lands lay both in the duchy and in the kingdom. The former were systematically favoured, and became Karl's steady supporters; the latter felt themselves discriminated against, and showed their resentment. They complained that Karl did not observe the privileges which the nobility had been granted in 1569; they objected to his levying aids upon their tenants without their previous agreement. Karl seems from an early stage to have pursued a policy designed to attach the purely local nobility to himself. He granted them *förläningar* on conditions which bound them to him by quasi-feudal ties; he also gave them donations in perpetuity, although he was certainly not entitled to do so. These measures were so effective that when the crisis came in his relations with Johan the nobility of the duchy gave no sign of being embarrassed by divided loyalties, but ranged themselves unhesitatingly behind their duke. No doubt their support was an asset; but it was more than offset by the alienation of some of those whose estates straddled the border. For among these were some important members of the *råd*; and in the great struggle between king and duke the *råd* would usually be found on the king's side.

Karl's obvious efforts to create an autonomous principality within the kingdom were bound to be resisted by his brother. Their conflicting views of what Gustav Vasa's Testament intended multiplied occasions for strife; their violent tempers, and the unmeasured language which each was prone to use on the smallest provocation, gave a malignant turn to every disagreement. Before Johan had been five years on the throne they were quarrelling fiercely; and they continued to quarrel, to the great distraction of their advisers, for nearly another decade and a half. The cause of a good deal of this friction was Karl's reckless selfishness and insatiable greed. Although Johan at the outset of the reign had 'improved' the duchy—that is, had enlarged it beyond the limits which Gustav Vasa had assigned—Karl was not satisfied. When the Vasa family inheritance was redistributed among the brothers in 1572 (a measure made necessary by Erik's fall) he complained that his share was too small, and pressed for a reallocation. Among other grievances he alleged that Johan had transferred to the crown manors which were properly part of the family estate. There may have been some basis for this complaint: Erik, as we have seen,[1] had done it in 1561; Karl himself was to do it on a considerable scale at the turn of the century. But there could be no justification for trying to extract from Johan compensation for the revenues which Erik had drawn from the duchy during Karl's minority. Still worse was his extraordinarily ignoble attempt to deprive Gustav Vasa's widow, Katarina Stenbock, of the manor of Strömsholm, which she held as part of her dower lands. Strömsholm had indeed been left to Karl by his father's will; but Katarina Stenbock had lived there with the consent of all the brothers since 1560, and Karl had already been given handsome compensation in the form of lands elsewhere. When it is recalled that the object of at least some of the plots against Johan was to put Karl on the throne, and that he was notoriously cognizant of de Mornay's conspiracy, it must be conceded that Johan had no great cause to deal liberally with his brother. Whenever it suited Karl to be loyal he made a virtue of it, hinted at a reward, and harboured a grudge if he did not get it. From time to time he aspired to a wider field of action than the narrow limits of the duchy could afford. He thought for a moment of entering the Spanish service; and when nothing came of that he transferred his attention to Livonia. Here he hoped, as Johan himself had hoped in former years, to carve out a principality for himself, well away from royal interference. In 1572, at a moment when Johan was hard put to it to defend his Baltic possessions, Karl entered into an agreement with him whereby he was to hold Livonia as a revocable service-fief, on condition of his undertaking to defend it. But when it came to the point Karl refused to go, alleging that Johan had failed to guarantee him adequate resources for the campaign. The bargain was called off, with hard feelings on either side. Nevertheless, Karl did not lose

[1] See above, p. 220.

sight of the idea. In 1574 he made the astounding suggestion that he be given Livonia as a hereditary fief, to be held, not of Johan III, but of the king of Poland. He came forward with another offer to take over Livonia in 1577, and again in 1581; but by that time de la Gardie's victories had put Johan in a position where he no longer had any need of fraternal assistance.

These, however, were essentially personal squabbles: the really intractable differences arose out of disputes about the extent of ducal rights. In 1572, for instance, Karl undertook a recoinage without prior permission, and sent agents into the kingdom to buy up old coin by tale for melting down. In the following year there was a great explosion when Johan referred to his brother as 'hereditary prince of *our* realm', rather than as 'hereditary prince of the realm of Sweden'. Karl refused to allow representatives from the duchy to attend the *riksdag*:[1] he was himself, he considered, an adequate representative of his people. In 1575 he infuriated the king by issuing free passes for foreign merchantmen trading to Narva: Johan retorted by confiscating the ships, and the owners came upon Karl for compensation. This episode, and perhaps Karl's implication in de Mornay's plot, moved Johan to a positive attempt to set limits to his brother's pretensions. Karl was informed that the king must retain the right to appoint all *lagmän*; that knight-service, within the duchy as well as outside it, must be due to the king only; and that the king had a right to levy taxes on the duchy at his discretion. Karl flatly denied the first two propositions, and conceded the point about taxation only with the impudent reservation that he must be free to decide whether the tax was advantageous, was reasonably levied, and (above all) whether the inhabitants of the duchy could afford to pay it.

Thus Johan's attempt to assert the royal authority had for the moment no success. In 1575 the conciliatory efforts of members of the *råd* succeeded in obtaining the tacit abandonment of extreme positions, and at least a show of reconciliation. The task of mediation was thankless, invidious, and apparently endless; but the *råd* stuck to it for fear of worse things. Increasingly their sympathies came to lie with the king: partly because they were after all his servants rather than Karl's; partly because they really believed that he had the better case; but also because their personal relations with the duke were in not a few cases strained by private quarrels and family grievances. Karl was involved in litigation about land with Per Brahe, and also with Erik Stenbock. He believed that Erik and Axel Stenbock were making mischief between himself and Johan. It is just possible that he was right: Johan had an unpleasant propensity for listening to tale-bearers, and the

[1] Some of the clergy, however, did attend to discuss matters of religion.

Stenbock family—indeed, all the high aristocracy—were outraged at Karl's behaviour over the Strömsholm affair. Hogenskild Bielke and Erik Sparre were in Karl's bad books because of their zeal in campaigning for the acceptance of the Red Book: Karl later made the preposterous accusation that they were responsible for Sigismund's being brought up a Roman Catholic. Before long he was charging Axel Leijonhufvud with plotting 'the ruin and destruction of our whole family'. This was ominous indeed: it came like a belated echo from King Erik's time, heavy with sinister overtones. It would be caught up, amplified and distorted in the next two decades; and it would at last provide an appropriate accompaniment to the judicial murder of Karl's aristocratic enemies. Already by 1580 Karl had few friends in the narrow ring of great families from which the *råd* was drawn. As his dispute with Johan grew more envenomed, the *råd*, whether they would or no, were dragged into it ever more deeply, if only because they were the natural emissaries and agents of the sovereign in his negotiations with a subject. The ill-will between Karl and the *råd*, which was to plunge Sweden into revolution at the end of the century, was by the eighties already a fact; and of the many causes which contributed to it two were already discernible: one was the involvement of the *råd* in the strife over the duchy; the other was the persistent suspicion that the aristocracy were planning the destruction of the dynasty—a suspicion first engendered in the perturbed brain of Erik XIV, subsequently nursed by Karl's rancorous spirit, and at last (with Karl's eager assistance) implanted also in the mind of Johan.

By the end of 1581 the Strömsholm affair had reached such a pitch, and Karl had put himself so clearly in the wrong, that Johan decided to submit the question to the *riksdag*. Karl had rejected a suggestion that he do nothing to the queen-dowager's prejudice pending a legal decision; he had refused a compromise which would have left Strömsholm to her for her lifetime; he had forcibly sequestered the revenues of the estate: royal commissioners were now exhorting the unhappy peasants to refuse to pay them over to him. The *riksdag* met in Stockholm early in 1582; and on 26 January the *råd* and nobility pronounced decisively in the queen's favour. Johan thereupon took the opportunity to obtain the backing of the Estates for a settlement of the whole question of ducal rights. A statute of 27 January—drawn, it seems, by Erik Sparre and Hogenskild Bielke—provided an interpretation of Gustav Vasa's Testament which reveals by implication how very far Karl's claims had extended. It stipulated that there should be uniformity between duchy and kingdom in the matter of religion; it forbade the duke to nominate bishops without the king's consent; it reserved to the king the appointment of *lagmän* and the right to try nobles accused of serious crimes; it forbade the duke to harbour fugitives from justice, to strike coin without leave, or to make perpetual donations of land; it debarred him from imposing other taxes than those agreed to for the kingdom, and from demanding knight-service for himself; and it affirmed that the nobility in the duchy were to have the same privileges as in the kingdom. In its reassertion of royal authority it took a long step back towards the Articles of Arboga. In its care for the difficulties of nobles with lands in the duchy it well reflected the concern of those who drafted it.

Whatever its merits or demerits, its effect was *nil.* Karl had not troubled himself to attend the *riksdag.* He treated the statute as a mere draft, lacking the force of law until he had assented to it, and in this he was probably correct. Johan shrank from the crisis which would have followed an attempt to constrain him. Nothing was settled, nothing altered. The statute remained no more than a threat, or a programme, deferred to a more propitious season. By 1584 Karl was again levying taxes and imposing customs at different rates from those prevailing in the kingdom. But now a purely domestic matter helped to bring the dispute to a head. In February 1585 Johan married, as his second wife, Gunilla Bielke. The marriage was regarded in the Vasa family as a misalliance: worse, as a political blunder, since it diminished the distance between the high aristocracy and the throne. Acid comments were made by Johan's sisters. As for Karl, he refused to attend the wedding. It was a brutal insult to the Bielkes and their relations: they could not but remember that he had similarly boycotted the wedding of Karin Månsdotter. The high aristocracy from which the *råd* was recruited was still a relatively closed circle of not more than twenty-five or thirty great families, all inextricably linked by a bewildering network of intermarriages. Everybody, more or less, was related to everybody else. By his conduct over Strömsholm, Karl had alienated the Stenbocks; by his attitude to Queen Gunilla he mortally offended the Bielkes: between the two, there can have been few members of the *råd*-aristocracy who had not now a grudge—personal or vicarious—against him.

It was now no longer possible to evade a confrontation. In 1585 Karl again began to strike coin, with no more than a perfunctory inquiry as to whether Johan liked the design. He did indeed offer to go abroad permanently, in return for a large cash payment; but this was a derisory offer, for no one knew better than he that Johan had no hope of raising the money. They had come to the end of negotiations and pretences; they had come, indeed, to within sight of civil war. For Johan only one resort remained: to apply that clause in his father's Testament which laid it down that in the event of irreconcilable division between the royal dukes the issue was to be submitted for arbitration to the 'leading Estates'. At the end of 1586 a *riksdag* was summoned to Vadstena, for the express purpose of deciding the controversy between the king and his brother.

But it never came to an arbitration. Karl had by this time no illusions about the attitude of the leading Estates: if the decision lay with them, it would go against him. The king, on his side, was well pleased if he could avoid the humiliation of being dependent on his subjects' verdict for the enjoyment of what he considered to be his undoubted rights. A private negotiation thus became possible. It was lengthy: obstinate on Karl's part, surprisingly firm on Johan's. At last, on 13 February 1587, an agreement was concluded, without the Estates' intervention, which constituted a victory for the crown on almost all the points at issue. It gave the king entire control of the appointment of *lagmän*—an appropriate arrangement, since in the past these posts had almost always been reserved for members of the *råd*. It ensured that appeals from the courts of the duchy should lie to the king's courts; it permitted the king to conduct a General Eyre (*konungaräfst*) within the duchy if he should think proper. Taxation within the duchy was to be as in the kingdom, except that if the duke could persuade his Estates to give him more he was at liberty to take it. He was, however, debarred from negotiating for aids directly with the peasants of the nobility: in future he must seek the prior agreement of their lords. Economic regulations and customs-dues were to conform to those in force in the kingdom. The duchy was to send representatives to the *riksdag* on the same footing as the rest of the country. The duke was not to make any further donations in perpetuity. He was prohibited from striking coin without the king's leave. All troops in the duchy were henceforward to take an oath to the king, and none were to be raised without his authorization. The bitterly contested question of knight-service, on which no agreement could be reached, was referred to the Estate of the Nobility: they settled it, with no long delay, in the king's favour. Only on two points did Karl succeed in staving off an adverse decision. One was in the matter of the Liturgy: this, as we have seen,[1] was to be referred to a general council of the church which Johan had certainly no intention of summoning if he could avoid it; the other was the purely private matter of the Vasa family inheritance, upon which there were to be further negotiations.[2]

Thus the problem of the duchy was solved, at least for this generation; and it was solved on lines which probably did represent what

[1] Above, p. 293, where the ecclesiastical side of the settlement is discussed.

[2] Karl was in the end defeated on the Strömsholm question: Katarina Stenbock retained the manor until her death in 1621.

Gustav Vasa had intended. But the ultimate success of the crown would hardly have been possible, if Johan had not latterly been able to count on strong support from the *råd*. Indeed, it was a member of the *råd* who produced the most effective presentation of the king's case, in a pamphlet which would be remembered long after the question of the duchies had been forgotten. Erik Sparre probably wrote *Pro Lege, Rege et Grege* in 1582, when the abortive statute of that year was under discussion; but it seems first to have been disseminated in 1586, in the course of the negotiations which led to the final settlement at Vadstena in the following February. It was a vigorous argument for the crown's rights, based upon a firm grasp of Swedish and Roman law, and supported by citations from a very wide range of legal authorities. Sparre argued that the dukes had only a *dominium utile* in their duchies: their claim to enjoy their rights 'as freely as the king does in his dominions' applied therefore only to the 'accidents and conveniences' (*tillhörigheter och nyttigheter*), and by no means implied a sovereign authority. Gustav Vasa's Testament must override the terms of the letters-patent granting the duchy; but it must itself be read in conjunction with the Succession Pact of 1544. Both these instruments derived a superior authority from the fact that they had the sanction of national approval; the one having been confirmed by a *riksdag*, the other being a law which the *riksdag* had itself enacted. Here Sparre left the particular issue of the duchies, and passed to a general discussion of the nature of Swedish legislation. He insisted that consent of the Estates, or at least of 'the leading Estates', was essential to the making of new law. Such consent, moreover, bound 'all Swedes, present or absent, those who swear and those who do not swear, those born and those unborn'. This was an unprecedented assertion of the legislative authority of the *riksdag*, which must have sounded strangely on the ears of many of Sparre's contemporaries: it was to be nearly half a century before men came to accept it as orthodox constitutional doctrine. Implicit in all Sparre's arguments was the idea of the supremacy of law: in particular he insisted that hereditary monarchs were no less bounded by the law than those who were elected. The Succession Pact of 1544 in this respect made no difference, for it was itself a statute; and in making it the nation had had no intention of disturbing the structure of reciprocal obligations which bound king and people together.

Pro Lege, Rege et Grege marks an epoch. Its author may fairly be regarded as the first great constitutional lawyer in Swedish history. Basing himself on the fundamental of Magnus Eriksson's Land Law, keeping always in mind the constitutional traditions of the fifteenth century, he built upon those foundations a political theory which is recognizably akin to current contractualist ideas as they were expounded by Duplessis-Mornay, Hotman and Buchanan. It found convenient instances in Roman law or English practice; but essentially it was designed for, and arose out of, Swedish conditions. After half a century of silence, *råd*-constitutionalism found in Erik Sparre a voice, and a voice less obviously distorted by aristocratic class-interests, more truly concerned with the common weal, than those of the magnates who had drawn up the Recess of Kalmar a century before. There were, it is true, some lines of argument in *Pro Lege, Rege et Grege* about which Sparre would have second thoughts in the light of later experience. But the permanent significance of the pamphlet was not thereby impaired. It was no mere *pièce d'occasion*, and its refutation of Karl's pretensions was in the long run the least important aspect of it. What was really significant was its frank challenge to the assumptions upon which Vasa monarchy had hitherto rested, and its implicit warning to Johan III against any attempt to restore a virtual absolutism on the model of his predecessors. The dynasty's contention that in 1544 the nation had acquiesced in the curtailment of its rights out of gratitude for Gustav Vasa's services was expressly rejected. For the first time since 1523 we are face to face with a real constitutional issue: in 1582 begins a constitutional conflict which will in its course comprehend a violent revolution, and is destined to continue for full thirty years. From 1582 until his execution in 1600 Erik Sparre stands at the centre of Swedish history, the leader of a party, the champion of a cause. The internal struggle which continued all through the reign of Johan III was not a simple issue between king and duke: it was a triangular contest, and the third party to it was the *råd*. Johan had no sooner vanquished his brother than he was confronted with a new antagonist. And as he had found the aid of the *råd* indispensable to his success against Karl, so he would at last find himself driven to seek Karl's assistance in order to fight the battle against the *råd*.

Even during the years when he had made the *råd* his ally against his brother Johan's relations with the magnates had not been entirely easy. In 1569 he had succeeded in restricting his grant of new privileges to a bare minimum, and he was aware that the nobility was dissatisfied with its gains. He was always afraid that if Sigismund should succeed to the throne as a young man he might be blackmailed into inordinate concessions. Twice—in 1576, in 1584—he extracted from the Estate of Nobles pledges that they would not do this. He had real cause for complaint about the nobility's neglect of its knight-service obligations. Though they had been reduced in 1569, and though in calculating them *förläningar* were no longer taken into account, it was notorious that noblemen made false returns of their income, and provided far fewer cavalry than they ought: in 1586 that slippery customer Hogenskild

Bielke assessed his income for knight-service at one-third of its real value. There was incessant trouble about the nobility's abuse of *skjutsning*,[1] and not all the king's endeavours to prevent it could effect much amendment. There were complaints from the clergy that nobles did not pay tithe, that they extruded parsons from their parishes and put in their own candidates instead—practices which Johan, as a good churchman, could ill tolerate. But if the king had cause for displeasure, the nobility on its side had grounds for dissatisfaction. It had been one of their grievances against Erik XIV that he cut down the number of *förläningar* to the aristocracy. In the first years of Johan's reign this grievance had been to some extent met. There was an immediate increase: in 1569 the value of *förläningar* rose to 255,000 marks. But thereafter it steadily declined, and the nobility's share of it declined too: by 1588 the total was down to 88,000 marks; by 1593 only about a third of all *förläningar* were in noble hands. Holders of *förläningar*, moreover, became increasingly the object of financial attack by a king who was desperate for money; for in an emergency Johan would take back a part of these alienated revenues for his own needs: in 1584 he appropriated one-third of the revenues granted in *förläning* and threatened in case of recalcitrance to resume them all; and he did in fact on various occasions resume *förläningar*. In the closing years of the reign such *förläningar* as were held by the nobility were mostly concentrated in the hands of the great *råd*-magnates, so that the crown's raiding of these revenues was felt with especial severity by the most powerful section of the aristocracy. This was certainly one reason for their opposition to policies which put a strain upon the exchequer, and particularly to the war.

It is true that as the number of *förläningar* declined their place was taken to some extent by the newer system of *beställningar*, which were something not very different from wages; but though this had administrative advantages for the crown it often proved no compensation to the recipient. First, because *beställningar* offered none of the opportunities for extra benefits which *förläningar* afforded, since the crown simply paid over the appropriate amount instead of leaving the grantee to collect it; secondly because in fact wages were very irregularly paid. There did indeed remain one other advantage which the nobility might hope to enjoy as an offset to lost *förläningar*, namely the new 'donations', which in this reign first become important. Donations, as their name implies, were outright gifts of crown land or revenues. But in reality there was not much to be hoped for in this way, for donations (especially in conquered Estonia) tended to be bestowed mainly as a reward

[1] The obligation to provide relays of horses or other transport for those travelling on the king's service.

for services of a military nature: in Johan's time the *råd*-families did not secure very many of them.

Dissatisfaction with Johan's land-policy was however only one aspect of a general feeling of discontent pervading the upper classes. The nobility really disliked Johan's whole method of government, and they especially disliked some of the instruments he employed. Their attempt in 1569 to obtain a larger share of responsibility for themselves proved abortive. The revival of the offices of steward, marshal and chancellor was soon seen to have no great significance. Government quickly fell back into the style of Erik XIV; and though the High Court had disappeared, there was no lack of successors to Jöran Persson. Johan was a less alarming sovereign than his predecessor; but essentially he employed the same methods. From the nobility's point of view the revolution of 1568 seemed to have been in vain. The 'rule of secretaries' was as obvious and as odious as in Erik's time. In some ways it was worse: Johan's secretaries were more numerous than Erik's (by the end of the reign there were no less than eighteen of them); Johan Henriksson was a baser creature than Jöran Persson. The aristocracy saw with disapproval an increase in the numbers and influence of subordinate officials in the central government. They were mostly men drawn from the exiguous middle class: sons of parsons or burghers who had somehow contrived a university education and were out to make a career for themselves elsewhere than in the church, a 'useless crew' of 'loose fellows', who entrenched themselves (as the nobility in 1569 had hoped to do) in the chancery or the revenue-services. It was in protest against this state of affairs, and in hopes of changing it, that the *råd* in 1585 put forward a still-born scheme for the recruiting and training of the sons of the aristocracy for entry into the king's service. And if the nobility found themselves poorly represented in the central administration, the case was no better in regard to local government. The bailiff, still the crown's factotum in the countryside, was taking a greater share of the financial administration than ever before. The reign did indeed produce one development in local government of which the aristocracy approved: the increase in the activity and powers of the *ståthållare*. They would have liked to push this process still further, to turn the *ståthållare* into a real provincial governor, empowered to take some of the burdens off the back of the overworked central administration: in particular they urged a decentralization of financial routine whereby the *ståthållare*, with the aid of financial experts attached to his office, should oversee the bailiff's accounts. They would have marked this change of function by a change of nomenclature: the title of *ståthållare* should be replaced by the more dignified term *landshövding*. In the late eighties the *ståthållare* of Finland did in fact become the sort of responsible provincial governor at which they were aiming, with the bailiffs subjected to his authority; but the experiment ended with the disgrace of the *råd* in 1590. Reform on these lines had to wait until the reign of Gustav Adolf.

Behind proposals of this kind—as behind criticism of the 'rule of secretaries'—lay a growing realization that the nobility, if it were to retain (or recover) its political influence, must secure for itself a recognized place in the administration of the state. The old *län*-system had done that, for it had devolved much of the work of government in the provinces upon aristocratic *entrepreneurs*. But the *län* as the fifteenth century had known it was now a thing of the past. The *förläningar* and *beställningar* which had replaced it did indeed offer financial rewards, (often, as in this reign, of a somewhat uncertain character), but in other respects they were no substitute for the old fief-holding, since they were by no means reserved to the aristocracy. By Johan III's time the nobility was beginning to see that what it needed was a guarantee of office. Office-holding was the real substitute for *län*-holding; for it would carry with it the revenue-assignments or wages which they needed to replace their former profits from *län*; it would provide security against the state's falling into non-noble hands; and it might furnish some safeguard against the unconstitutional abuse of power by the monarchy. From this time forward, the demand for a monopoly of the higher offices of government becomes a constant feature of the nobility's programme, reiterated again and again in their proposals for an improvement of their privileges. They were able to urge it with especial force, since they could truly claim that it was also a demand, made necessary by the failure of the crown, for administrative order: noble government meant better government.

It seems likely that the *råd* perceived that the radical weakness in the state was that the business of government and administration was growing too complex for a patriarchal monarchy in the style of Gustav Vasa to be able to control it: by creating the duchies, Gustav Vasa himself had as good as confessed that this was so. Johan tried to meet the situation by increasing the number of secretaries, chamberlains and clerks. But the rule of these minor officials, responsible directly and solely to the king, was tolerable only if the king were in fact able and willing to devote time to supervising them. The event proved that Johan could not or would not do it. The heart of government grew flabby; paternalism faltered under a prodigal father. There was real justification for the repeated efforts of the *råd* to devise a stronger central executive by providing the king with permanent assistance from their own ranks; for long delays in discharging government business were attributable to the king's procrastination, as well as to the mass of affairs with which he had to deal. Hence they proposed in 1585 the setting up of a permanent council of state—a *hovråd*—of four members, half of whom would be always in attendance; the object being to make sure that if Johan were not able to deal with a question, it would not fall to be decided by dubious minor officials.[1] They demanded also a better definition of officials' duties, and the fixing of regular working hours. But these well-meant proposals, like many before them, foundered on the irritability, jealousy and indifference of the king, who preferred theology and architecture to the details of financial administration, and felt his vanity wounded by schemes for reform. In 1580 the *råd* told him plainly that it was his duty to give audiences at least once a week; in 1584 three of them sent in a memorandum complaining of his intolerable bad temper. Imagination boggles at the idea of Gustav Vasa's reactions to such a document.

It was especially unfortunate that Johan's interest in administration should have been so tepid, since his reign was a period of severe financial disorder. This was not altogether the king's fault. He had found himself heir to an impoverished inheritance. The great private hoards which Gustav Vasa had heaped up had all been spent on the Seven Years' War. The yield of the customs had dropped almost to nothing while that war lasted. Johan found himself saddled with the unpaid dowries of his sisters Cecilia and Sophia, and had later to find a dowry for Elisabeth. On top of this came the ransom for Älvsborg. Any hope of recovery was blasted by the endless war in Livonia, for the continuation of which, of course, Johan must bear some of the blame. In 1574, and again in 1583, attempts were made to draw up a reliable balance-sheet of the crown's receipts and expenditure. The work was done with unprecedented care and comprehensiveness, and the resulting statements afforded a view of the financial position such as no Swedish king—and few kings elsewhere—had hitherto had at his disposal. The picture disclosed was devastating.[2] For the year 1573 the total income of the crown was about 650,000 *daler*, the total expenditure 1,008,000 *daler*; for 1582 income was 775,000 *daler*, expenditure 1,120,000 *daler*. These figures included extraordinary income and war expenditure; but even if the comparison were confined to ordinary revenue and expenditure there was still a deficit of 157,000 in 1573 and 133,000 in 1582. Johan managed to fill the gap somehow by *ad hoc* measures and once-for-all expedients: he severely debased the currency between 1568 and 1575, and again from 1590 to 1592; he withheld wages; he resumed *förläningar*; he neglected to pay the bills for imported

[1] There had been a somewhat similar proposal as early as 1571, but nothing had come of it.

[2] The following statistics are borrowed from Birgitta Odén, *Rikets uppbörd och utgift* (Lund, 1955).

luxuries; he extended the *régale* to base metals; he requisitioned commodities from his subjects without paying for them; he increased his demands for compulsory labour-services; he sold warships, or gave them away in lieu of wages. But by 1583, when a list of his debts was drawn up, he was found to be owing over a million *daler*, including 300,000 for arrears of wages to foreign troops, 200,000 to Swedish troops, 245,000 in debts to foreign merchants, and even 45,000 in loans from his subjects. The contrast with Gustav Vasa, whose hoarded treasure had been a legend, and who had been money-lender-in-chief to his people, could not have been more complete: such are the fruits of peace, and of war.

This chronic indebtedness did not arise fom any lack of effort to raise revenue, nor from any resistance by Johan's subjects to fresh taxation. Throughout the reign the king was constantly imposing new burdens on the country. Some were granted by the *riksdag*, but more after piecemeal bargaining with provincial assemblies, in a manner more or less conformable with the spirit of the Land Law. This last method was almost always employed for raising aids (*gärder*), which were payments in specific commodities required to equip or feed the armies in the field. They were levied year after year, and were felt to be especially burdensome. The *råd* contended that they were often unconstitutional too, since the king did not always obtain their approval before proceeding to negotiate with his subjects. The ransom of Älvsborg necessitated special efforts: a capital levy in 1571, a contribution of silver in 1573, the melting-down of the royal plate, and even of the silver shrine of St Erik. Forced loans were resorted to; appeals were even made for free gifts. The nobility more than once waived their exemption from taxation, for themselves and their peasants. Peasants of the crown were in 1582 given the opportunity of buying a title to their land in freehold. For a short time the experiment was tried of farming the revenues; but it did not answer. The crown tried to exploit the rising price and increased supply of copper in the eighties by setting up a royal monopoly, and an attempt was also made to profit by the boom in furs; but despite moderate success the gains were inconsiderable in relation to the scale of royal expenditure. The plain fact was that as long as the campaigns in Livonia continued the budget would never be balanced: Gustav Vasa himself could never have financed a war of twenty-five years.

The *råd* was under no illusions on this head, as appears from their repeated advice to Johan to make peace. But irrespective of the question of peace and war they felt strongly that all was not well with the running of the finances. At the beginning of the reign they had induced the king to appoint Bengt Gylta, a member of the high aristocracy, as lord treasurer (*överste skattmästare*): while he lived they could feel that they had some knowledge of what was going on. But Gylta died in 1574, and no successor was appointed to his office. Finance passed once more out of their purview; and perhaps ignorance made criticism easier. They complained that receipts were not retained, nor proper accounts kept; they were critical of the efficiency of the Audit Office (*räknekammare*). In 1580 they expressed their conviction that aids which had been levied for fighting the war were being frittered away on other purposes. They suspected extravagance, waste and corruption in the management of the royal household. In 1585 they brought forward a comprehensive plan for economical reform: there was to be an end of sinecure offices, reductions in the household, stricter scrutiny of the right to feed at the royal tables. A small committee of nobles was to inspect the royal kitchens; proper schedules of wages were to be drawn up; proper accounts were to be produced. Two members of the aristocracy were to supervise the working of the royal mint. The king was now approaching the crisis of his struggle with Karl, and he could not afford to alienate the *råd* by a refusal. The proposals were therefore accepted, and for a space the *råd* recovered some control of the finances. In 1586 Ture Bielke was appointed lord treasurer. For the next three years he and his colleagues in the *råd* were able to reshape policy to their liking. Some decentralization was initiated by giving the *ståthållare* more control of the royal bailiffs; tolls were lowered in the hope of increasing the yield of the customs; a measure of economical reform was carried through at court. Yet it is doubtful if any significant improvement resulted. Economical reform was based on hopes which proved delusive and suspicions which were not borne out by the facts: where the *råd* expected scandals they too often found only mare's nests. Household expenditure was not grossly extravagant, and had latterly been declining; the wages of household servants were comparatively modest; Johan's tendency to entrust large powers to foreign *entrepreneurs* was not a major element in the problem. Above all, their repeated criticisms of his expenditure on building greatly exaggerated its effect upon the financial position.

There is no doubt that the king's passion for architecture consumed much time and money. In this field, as in that of theology, he was a learned and enthusiastic amateur. He had read Serlio; he followed with attention the trends of fashion on the continent. His marriage to Katarina Jagiełłonica reinforced these tastes, for she brought with her a *penchant* for the Italian Renaissance as it had been modified by passage through Poland and Silesia. The court became a centre of artistic patronage. Foreign architects of distinction made their way to Sweden: Willem Boy from the Netherlands, the brothers Pahr from Italy by way of Mecklenburg. The king personally supervised their activities, exhorting them to impose upon the heavy irregularities of Swedish Gothic the classical order of the Italian models he so greatly admired. Messenius wrote of him that he would have wished to make Stockholm like Rome or Venice. It was characteristic of him, however, that the purity of his artistic intentions was frequently compromised by the extravagance of his own temperament: he could never resist the fanciful or the dramatic. His spires, turrets and weather-vanes; the picturesque jumble of styles in the old castle of Stockholm, where Renaissance arcading contradicted Baltic Gothic; the fantastic castle at Borgholm, so truly Gothic in spirit; were as representative of their builder as the painted sham-rustic of his interiors, or the elegance of the 'chequer-room' at Kalmar. But whatever the stylistic affinities of his buildings, there were certainly very many of them. He carried out extensive alterations in Stockholm castle (where running water and a swimming-pool were installed), at Kalmar, at Västerås, at Älvsborg. Castles—which were indeed more palaces than places of defence—were built or rebuilt at Uppsala, Borgholm, Svartsjö, and above all at Vadstena, that pearl of Swedish architecture. The first Drottningholm dates from his reign, built by Johan as a summer retreat for Katarina. In the field of ecclesiastical architecture he was almost equally active. The dilapidations of Gustav Vasa's time were now repaired; the nunnery at Vadstena put in order; the Riddarholm church in Stockholm rebuilt, St Klara finished, St Jakob begun. It was Johan's filial piety that at last erected the costly tomb of Gustav Vasa in Uppsala cathedral;[1] it is to his historical sense that we owe the tombs of Magnus Ladulås and Karl Knutsson in the Riddarholm church. All this was expensive, perhaps extravagant, and there is no denying that Johan's personal tastes were luxurious. He was a man who would not be denied his whim; a spendthrift by nature, who valued money only for the satisfactions it could bring him. Yet if expenditure be compared to income, it may be doubted whether his outlay on building was relatively much more than the sums which Karl laid out upon his works at Örebro, Gripsholm and Nyköping. A recent calculation suggests that it did not exceed 4 to 5 per cent of the total outgoings. If it attracted the somewhat philistine censure of the *råd*, that was probably because it was so conspicuous, and also because it was persisted in even during periods of acute financial difficulty.

In 1587 the efforts of the *råd* to increase their control of the administration were given a new impetus by the prospect of Sigismund's election as king of Poland. If Johan's successor was likely to be absent

[1] It had been ordered by Erik in Antwerp, but had been held up for years owing to difficulty in paying for it.

in Warsaw for lengthy periods, it would be essential to make provision for the conduct of the government at home—preferably before Sigismund accepted the crown rather than afterwards. The *råd* cannot have been blind to the probability that if the king were to be a semi-permanent absentee, their own share in the government was likely to become greater: for men such as Erik Sparre and Hogenskild Bielke, deeply versed in the political history and constitutional mythology of the fifteenth century, the analogy with the situation under the Union of Kalmar must have presented itself very forcibly. The opportunity was so obvious that it is not surprising that Johan and Karl should later have accused them of deliberately urging Sigismund's candidature to serve their own ends. However that may be, both Johan and Sigismund were alive to the need to make arrangements in good time. In April and May 1587 four members of the *råd*—Erik Sparre, Hogenskild Bielke, Erik Gustavsson Stenbock, Sten Baner—were invited to consider the draft of a plan for the government of the country in the event of Sigismund's election. The result of their discussions, which continued throughout the summer, was an instrument which was signed and sealed by Johan and Sigismund on 5 September: it is known as the Statute of Kalmar. Erik Sparre seems to have contributed substantially to it, but Johan himself was responsible for its final form. As was to be expected, the Statute contained necessary provisions to safeguard Sweden from any danger to her independence as a result of the projected Union.[1] But its arrangements for carrying on the government in Sigismund's absence were both unexpected and remarkable. Sweden was to be governed by what was in effect a council of regency consisting of seven persons drawn from the aristocracy (though not necessarily from the *råd*), who were to retire in rotation 'every two or three years': six of them were to be nominated by the king, one by Duke Karl. They were to act as a board; their decisions would be by majority vote. The great offices of state—steward, marshal, chancellor, admiral[2]—were to be kept filled. *Ståthållare*, recruited from the high nobility, were to take charge of local government. The *råd* would continue to function as before. Its relations to the council of regency were not defined; but whenever a vacancy occurred among the regents, or in the high offices of state, the *råd* would submit to the king a list of three names from which to make his selection. The effect of these provisions would obviously be to put the government of the country, as Erik Sparre and his colleagues had desired, into the hands of the great magnates. There were, however, some further stipulations, which perhaps owe their origin to Sparre's belief that the *riksdag* was to be

[1] See above, p. 270.

[2] He here appears for the first time as the equal of the others.

regarded as the proper organ for the expression of the nation's will. The Statute provided, for instance, that no negotiation affecting the interest of Sweden should be undertaken save with the consent of the Estates; that without such assent no Swede should be conscripted to fight in Poland's wars; and that no royal mandate or prohibition made in Poland should be valid in Sweden until it had the Estates' approval.

It had been intended that the Statute itself should be presented to the *riksdag* for confirmation. This was not done. It was not even submitted to the *råd* as a whole. Above all, it was not communicated to Karl, who did not hear of it until April 1588, and does not seem to have seen the text (though he had by then become aware of its nature) until December 1590. It is no matter for surprise that Johan should have tried to evade his brother's inquiries about it, for one of the most startling features of the Statute was its virtual exclusion of the duke from any share in the government. He had, indeed, one representative among the seven regents; but this was small consolation to a man who considered that he had a natural right to be sole regent himself. If Sweden was to be governed by 'the leading Estates', Karl was in his own person the most exalted Estate of the realm, for he was the sole effective representative of the Estate of royal dukes. But his rightful place was destined to a small circle of oligarchs, drawn from families which, having once been the equals of the Vasas, now grudged their pre-eminence, or even (he suspected) sought to destroy it. The fear of an aristocratic plot against the dynasty, which had driven Erik to murder the Stures, now revived in him in full force. He came to believe that Kalmar Statute was the logical sequel to Kalmar Recess; that it was designed to provide the basis for the rule of the *råd*, perhaps for a return to electoral monarchy, or even for an aristocratic republic. This belief he transmitted to his son: in the sketch of his history which Gustav Adolf began many years later he asserted that it had been intended to give the seven regents the status of the electors in the Empire, and to reduce the monarchy to insignificance under their tutelage. Yet it was natural that Erik Sparre and his colleagues should think in terms of precedents from the previous century: similar situations suggested similar devices. It was not surprising if they recalled the Recess of Kalmar, nor was it remarkable that they should grasp the opportunity to strike a blow for their idea of orderly and efficient government—which implied, in their view, aristocratic government. But the Statute of Kalmar in its final redaction was, after all, the work of Johan and Sigismund: Erik Sparre afterwards pointed out that he was not present in Kalmar when it was signed. The most interesting question about it is why the king should have gone so far towards Erik Sparre's political ideas. And the only possible answer to that question seems to be that he was less fearful of the constitutional pretensions of the nobility than of the prospect of Karl as regent: a usurpation looked a bigger risk than an oligarchy. The *råd*-members naturally agreed with him. If fifteenth-century precedents were to guide them, it would have been natural to appoint a *riksföreståndare*, who could hardly have been anyone other than Karl; but this they pointedly avoided. Karl's clamorous assertion of his rights as duke now told against him: if the king must not meddle in the duchy, neither must the duke meddle in the kingdom. To Johan, barely emerged from an exhausting struggle with his brother, dependent for success in that struggle—as also in the Liturgical controversy—upon the backing of the *råd*, it must have appeared that he had chosen the lesser of two evils. As yet he did not share Karl's notion of an aristocratic conspiracy against his house: another crisis, of a yet more poignant kind, would be needed before he could be brought to that conviction. In the meantime, as rumours about the nature of the Statute supplied the place of information, Karl chalked up yet another injury in his long score against the *råd*.

Whatever truth there may be in the charge that Erik Sparre and his friends supported Sigismund's candidature in Poland in the expectation of getting rid of him and having Sweden to themselves, there is no doubt that they really expected that his election would mean Polish aid against the Russians. In the event, as we have seen, it meant no such thing. Sigismund's election brought no advantage to Sweden; it brought nothing but trouble to Sigismund himself; and about Erik Sparre's neck it hung the charge—never to be allowed to sink into oblivion—that he had been willing to sacrifice Estonia. By the spring of 1589 Sigismund had already determined to abdicate, if he could find a suitable political innocent to take his place: in May of that year he began his not unhopeful attempt to inveigle the Archduke Ernest. As for Johan, he had no sooner let Sigismund go than he began to think of how to get him back again. He loved his son dearly; he felt himself growing old; he wanted the boy at home. For political advantage or disadvantage he now cared little, when set against the cravings of parental affection. As far as Johan was concerned, the Statute of Kalmar became irrelevant within six months of its signature; which no doubt was sufficient reason for his neglect to submit it to the *riksdag*. But before Sigismund returned it seemed worth while making some attempt to exploit the union of the crowns in order to frighten the Russians. Early in 1589 Johan began to prepare for a meeting with Sigismund in Reval. He planned to take with him a large military force, and he hoped that Sigismund would do the same; the expectation being that a really massive demonstration would so impress Boris Godunov that he would be willing to convert the truce into a permanent peace.

Sigismund, after announcing his abdication in Ernest's favour, would then return to Sweden with his father. All would be again as it had been before this unhappy interlude; the Statute of Kalmar, with all that it implied, could be forgotten; Karl's ambitions would be checked; and Sigismund would become the support and stay of Johan's declining years.

It was a political fantasy, touching in its *naïveté*, and requiring for its realization a concatenation of fortunate circumstances not very likely to occur. The *råd*, as yet unapprised of these designs, sensibly suggested that Johan had better take Karl with him to Reval; nor could they resist the opportunity to add some tart comments about misgovernment, the squandering of money, and the need for reform. These ill-timed observations Johan brushed aside: his main concern now was to raise as many troops as possible. But the results of his efforts were very disappointing: mainly, he considered, because the nobility were culpably slack in doing their duty. Certainly the forces he took to Reval were not such as to frighten anybody, unless it were the exhausted inhabitants who had to support them. He landed at Reval on 5 August 1589, accompanied by eight members of the *råd*: Erik Sparre, Gustav and Sten Baner, Ture and Klas Bielke, Erik Gustavsson Stenbock, Axel Leijonhufvud, Klas Fleming. Three weeks later Sigismund made his appearance, bringing with him a small entourage of reluctant Polish senators (who complained that they had been 'dragged hither as it were to Babylon'), but no great Polish army. Relations between Swedes and Poles were not good: there was constant brawling in the streets. The rumour that Johan intended to take Sigismund home with him had already leaked out; and Poles and Swedes, agreeing at least in this, heard it with equal consternation.

There followed a month of dreadful tension, which stretched the nerves of all the participants to the limit. From the point of view of the members of the *råd*, the issue was quite simple. They were themselves opposed to Sigismund's abdication; but if it should prove to be inevitable they insisted that it must be done decently: there must be no precipitate or clandestine evasion in the manner of Henry of Anjou. At all costs Sweden must have peace, the sooner the better; and the best hope of peace, they believed, lay in the alliance of Poland. The essential point was therefore to avoid offending the Poles; for they feared that if the Poles were badly treated they might revenge themselves by allying with the Russians. There was sound sense in these arguments. Upon Sigismund, who saw the difficulties (and kept his temper) better than his father, they soon made an impression. On Johan they had no effect whatever. He had come to Reval to recover his son: nothing else mattered. Those who sought to dissuade him he regarded as enemies of a peculiarly personal kind. On 5 September a great petition, signed by the *råd*, by nearly fifty members of the nobility, and by eight army commanders, appealed to him to abandon his scheme, and castigated his failings as a ruler in terms of extraordinary harshness.[1] The king's only reply was to threaten them that if they persuaded Sigismund not to abdicate he would persecute them as long as he lived. Ten days later the members of the *råd* tried again, urging him at least to have a little patience until the matter could be arranged with goodwill on both sides, and a successor found who would be a friend to Sweden. At the foot of this document they added, in large and tactless capitals, the seasonable exhortation 'VINCAT AFFECTUM RATIO'. But of this there was no hope. In a furious answer the king told them that his affairs had always gone well when he had ignored their advice; that he knew better than they did; that none of the consequences they foresaw would occur. He was resolved to pursue his purpose; he would return to Sweden 'and be and remain an absolute king, as well hereafter as heretofore'—'or if not' (he concluded, with the reckless inconsequence of a man in a passion), 'both I and Sigismund will take ourselves off, and they can choose a king where they will'. Erik Sparre might shrug off the last sentence as a typical absurdity; but its predecessor was something more than a burst of choler. The antagonists were getting down to fundamentals: the reply to *råd*-constitutionalism, now made explicit for the first time, was a claim to absolute power.

Nevertheless, for all his strong language, Johan was losing the battle at Reval. Erik Sparre and his friends were concerting measures with the Polish senators, who may have been unenthusiastic about their king, but preferred to keep him rather than have another election. There were ominous stirrings in the Swedish army. The man in the ranks, sick of the war and longing for home, with pay hopelessly in arrear, had got hold of the idea that the short road to peace lay in the Union with Poland. Members of the *råd* were in touch with the officers around Narva, and may have done something to incite them to action. At all events, they now petitioned the king, while the soldiers refused to march until they were assured that Sigismund would not abdicate. The army was on the verge of mutiny. The *råd* was by this time threatening to quit Reval; the Archduke Ernest had intimated that he required time for consideration; Sigismund himself had virtually surrendered. At this moment the news of a Tatar invasion of Podolia gave irresistible force to the arguments of the Polish senators who were pressing Sigismund to return to Warsaw. On 30 September he tore himself away, while Johan shut himself up in his house '*pro dolore*', that he might not

[1] The petition was formally addressed to Sigismund, Johan having said that he would receive no representations in the matter.

witness his son's departure. He was never to see Sigismund again. Two days later, beside himself with rage and grief, he started for home, leaving his advisers behind him to shift for themselves. The humiliation was complete; the fiasco total.

The events at Reval were unprecedented in the experience of the Vasa dynasty. For the first time the king had been constrained by the open opposition of members of his *råd* to abandon a course of action which he had determined to pursue. His policy had been thwarted, his personal conduct rebuked. The conventions of the Swedish constitution certainly obliged the king to rule with his council's counsel; but as yet it was by no means certain that he was bound to follow the advice that they gave to him. Johan was entitled to feel that the *råd* had put a force upon the crown. But the meeting at Reval can also be seen as the return of the *råd* to the independent status which it had enjoyed in the previous century. It was no longer the king's docile instrument; it was once again a representative body holding the balance between king and people. As such it had rights of its own: Erik Sparre insisted that its members must be free to speak their minds without fear of the consequences. On numerous occasions in the past two decades it had not hesitated to do so: the arraignment of Johan's administration at Reval was only the last and most forthright of many expressions of disapproval. What was new at Reval was not the acerbity of the criticisms, or the self-confidence of the opposition, but the capitulation of the king. Erik had been overthrown by a rebellion within the royal family; but Johan was the first Vasa to have his will thwarted by the resistance of his subjects. It was not long before he formulated the appropriate reply. Against their insistence upon the right and duty to oppose he invoked a new constitutional principle: the principle of ministerial responsibility. For the ill-effects which (he was sure) would come of the fiasco at Reval, the *råd* should be held accountable: accountable to himself, but also in some degree to the nation. And it followed that if the responsibility lay on them, it could not also lie upon him: ministerial responsibility, monarchical irresponsibility, were complementary ideas. No doubt it would be a mistake to attach too much importance to this constitutional dialogue: the events that were to follow in 1590 were acts of power rather than the result of constitutional argument; the precedent they created, though it may have been remembered in 1600, lay dormant thereafter till 1680; a real concept of ministerial responsibility would not establish itself until the eighteenth century. But still it is true that Johan's conflict with the *råd* at Reval in a sense closed a period of Swedish history and opened another. The euphoric atmosphere of national solidarity which had marked the later years of Gustav Vasa is gone; the solid permanencies of political life are shaken. The year 1589 ushers in a period of revolutionary violence which will last until 1611. And the issues which lay at the root of the revolution would be neither dynastic nor religious, but constitutional.

Johan returned from Reval with only one idea: to seek vengeance on those who had separated him from his son. To obtain it he was prepared to abandon much that he had striven for, and to forget quarrels that were now of minor importance. To ally with Karl had obviously become his best policy: his brother's animus against the *råd* became a positive recommendation. The men of Reval saw the danger, and did their best to avert it. In November 1589 Erik Sparre, Sten Baner and Ture Bielke, in a desperate effort to ward off the coming storm, signed a statement in which they confessed that they had been wrong, and gave the king a promise that they would not oppose the cession of Estonia if by that means Sigismund could be disencumbered of the Polish crown. But they were too late. Before the month was out Johan and Karl were reconciled.[1] The dynasty had closed its ranks and was preparing for battle. Erik Sparre, Ture and Hogenskild Bielke,[2] Gustav and Sten Baner, Erik Gustavsson Stenbock, were displaced from the *råd*, dismissed their offices, deprived of their donations and *förläningar*. The first steps were already preparing to blast their reputations in the eye of the nation.

For Karl the quarrel between Johan and the *råd* offered an unexpected opportunity to recover from his defeat at Vadstena in 1587. He was not slow to grasp it. He hoped by supporting his brother to recover some of the ducal rights he had lost; and he hoped too to secure his position in the next reign, which he rightly suspected to be jeopardized by the Statute of Kalmar. Johan was visibly ageing; the accession of Sigismund would probably not long be delayed. Karl's policy in this situation must be to identify himself with his brother, to feed his resentment against the *råd*, to prevent if he could any reconciliation between them. It was important that the men of Reval should be politically isolated, that the mass of the nobility should be induced to dissociate themselves from them, that the nation at large should be taught to look upon them as evil counsellors and disloyal subjects. In January 1590 the king addressed an open letter to his people in which he accused the *råd* of wrecking the prospects of peace with Russia by their failure to provide a sufficiently imposing concentration of troops at Reval. At market-meetings and county-courts the commonalty was given so unfavourable

[1] Karl even made the king a loan—from his daughter's dowry!

[2] Hogenskild Bielke had not been at Reval, but Johan was right in thinking that he could not be separated from the others.

an account of their behaviour that Hogenskild and Ture Bielke were forced to beg the king for letters of protection against the peasantry. The nobility were called up to Stockholm in batches, that they might by personal discussion with Karl and Johan be brought to a proper frame of mind. The resources of popular agitation and official propaganda, which Karl in the next decade was to show himself so well able to wield, were now deployed with determination. The campaign of denigration in 1590 furnished a useful training for the campaign of 1596.

By the spring of 1590 the royal brothers were ready to appeal to a *riksdag*. A preliminary assembly of nobles and burghers in February expanded to become a full meeting of the Estates in March: on this occasion Karl saw to it that representatives from the duchy appeared in force. They were addressed by the king and the duke in speeches of indecent violence: Johan's, disjointed, passionate, almost hysterical; Karl's, so gross in its attacks on Erik Sparre as to incur even Johan's disapproval. The main charges against the *råd* were that they had prolonged the war by sabotaging the demonstration at Reval; that Erik Sparre had betrayed his country by offering to cede Estonia to the Poles;[1] that they had fomented quarrels between Karl and Johan for sinister purposes, and tried to exclude Karl from the succession; that they were all involved in a plot to deprive the Vasas of the throne, of which the Statute of Kalmar was sufficient evidence; and that they had at Reval virtually threatened Johan with deposition. The last two charges give a good idea of the methods and mentality of their accusers. Karl had still not seen a copy of the Statute: indeed, he made its concealment a charge against its authors. It was not, as might have been expected, in the chancery: for some unexplained reason it was in private custody. Karl supposed that Hogenskild Bielke had it, and in February ordered him to produce it; Bielke replied that it was in the possession of Sten Baner. Sten Baner, who was abroad, professed to be unable for the moment to put his hand on it. It was not until December 1590 that Karl actually saw the text of the document on which he was expending his denunciations. When he applied to his brother for information, Johan made the staggering reply that he was afraid he could not really remember very much about it.[2] The last charge had an almost equally curious history. The petition which the *råd*, nobility and army officers had handed to Sigismund at Reval on 5 September had been drawn in two parts, of which the first contained censure on Johan's extravagance and inefficiency, while the second dealt with the international

[1] This within a few months of Johan's extracting from him a promise not to oppose the cession, as the price of recovering Sigismund!

[2] In one of his speeches to the Estates he remembered so little about it as to deny being its author.

consequences of Sigismund's projected abdication. The original draft of the latter section had contained a sentence which suggested that if the war with Russia continued, and a breach with Poland resulted from Sigismund's accompanying his father home, Johan's subjects might 'become ill-disposed to both Your Majesties, and even (which would be still more to be dreaded) that they might take upon themselves to *shut us all out of the country*'. This passage they had found it prudent to excise. But a report of it had gone from one of the *råd* to a relation at home; from him it had reached Karl's ears. Karl interpreted it as an accusation that he was ready to dethrone his brother; and Johan, when in due course the story was passed on to him, saw in it a confirmation of Karl's view that the *råd* was trying to create bad blood between them. The objectionable passage was now made an article of accusation against the very men who had been responsible for its deletion. These were absurdities; but they were not out of place in a list of crimes which included the Articles of Arboga (1561), the imprisonment of Johan (1563), the draft statute on ducal rights (1582), the Vadstena accommodation of 1587, and the rifling of the archives in order to destroy documentary evidence of hereditary succession.

The *riksdag*, receiving the recital of these enormities with a decent show of concern, hastened to dissociate itself from them. But it would go no further than to say that if indeed the members of the *råd* were guilty of the crimes which were laid to their charge, they were deserving of the king's displeasure. The explicit condemnation for which the royal brothers had been hoping was pointedly avoided. This was the more striking because an obvious attempt had been made to secure the nobility's good will by an 'improvement' in their privileges. The improvement was, indeed, no great matter: ordinary nobles would henceforward be entitled to the same share of fines as had been enjoyed since 1569 by counts and barons; their peasants would not be liable to *corvées* if domiciled within a Swedish mile of a manor. Karl had wished that the king should promise that aids should not be levied upon peasants of the nobility without their master's consent; but this Johan refused to concede. And not only was he somewhat tight-fisted with his bribe, he also made it quite clear that no further instalment was to be expected. The new privileges contained a warning that they would immediately be cancelled if any attempt were made to screw better terms out of Sigismund on his accession.

Meanwhile, measures had been taken to preserve the dynasty from the perils with which Johan and Karl professed to think it was surrounded. On 7 March 1590 the Estates accepted a new Succession Pact. It provided further security against a relapse into electoral monarchy ('for', as the Nobles recorded, 'we can well understand what dangers have always attended a free election') by extending the right of succession to the female line. It took account of the fact that Johan now had a son (also called Johan) by Gunilla Bielke: his place in the order of succession was fixed; and he was provided with a substantial apanage. The domestic disputes of the last two decades, it appeared, had been so entirely obliterated by the misdeeds of the *råd*, that the king could deliberately resolve on the perpetuation of the anomaly of the duchies.[1] Karl was given some acknowledgment of his senior status by a clause which prescribed that if a regency should become necessary, the regent was to be the 'oldest and most nearly related' male member of the royal family. This provision did not explicitly promise him a share in the government on Sigismund's accession, but it certainly strengthened his claims. And one possible bar to his aspirations was removed next year by the king's abrogation of the Statute of Kalmar, when at last it was extracted from Sten Baner.

Soon after the acceptance of the new Succession Pact Johan took another step designed to strengthen the monarchy. The *råd* had already been purged of its most obnoxious members; those that remained were for the moment frightened and docile; the opportunity for exacting a formal submission was too good to miss. They were accordingly presented with (and meekly took) a new oath of office, which included a clause of so abject a nature that it is difficult to know which was the more censurable, the king who exacted it or the counsellors who accepted it. It ran: 'But if His Majesty, of the superior understanding which God has given him, should follow any other counsel [*sc.* than that of the *råd*]—and since His Majesty's own opinion has always hitherto (thank God) proved the best and most serviceable—I will never say anything against it, either secretly or openly, nor will I disapprove it or object to it, but will conform to the same His Majesty's opinion, and not set mine, nor any other of my colleagues' views, alongside it, and still less above it.'[2] Johan had told the *råd* at Reval that experience had shown that he was always right: they were now to be bound by oath to that doctrine. What remained now of the obligation to rule *med råds råde*? If these were to be the terms of service, to what end did the *råd* exist at all? Johan's threat at Reval to go home and rule as an absolute monarch seemed indeed in a fair way to realization. The last two years of the reign saw sweeping confiscations of *förläningar*, taxation of dubious legality, a stop to the magnates' king-yoking notions of economical and administrative reform: Sweden, as Karl observed, had got along for centuries without *landshövdingar*, and

[1] Karl at this time had still no legitimate issue, and the expectation was that at his death his duchy would lapse to the crown. Magnus, now hopelessly insane, was childless also: he died in 1595.

[2] *Svenska riksdagsakter, 1571–1592*, p. 953.

could well do without them in future. Yet it may perhaps be doubted whether Johan really planned to turn himself into an absolute monarch: in this, as in so much else in his career, the words were worse than the reality. What he wanted was to humiliate and to punish, to soothe his wounded vanity by proving that he was master and could do as he liked with his own: to show, for instance, that no subject should prevent him from building churches, if he chose to do it. His absolutism was an expression less of political theory than of personal vindictiveness.[1]

And in the ordinary course of events his anger would probably have proved short-lived, as in the case of similar tantrums in the past. Unluckily the whole issue was kept alive by the quite irrelevant circumstance of Karl Henriksson Horn's surrender of Ivangorod to the Russians,[2] news of which reached Stockholm in February 1590. Horn had yielded Ivangorod to save Narva; but his personal enemies—notably Klas Fleming, who though a member of the *råd* had contrived to retain the king's favour—asserted that he had been negligent or worse in his conduct of the defence, and Johan was quite ready to believe them. He at once leapt to the conclusion that the surrender had been concerted with members of the *råd* at Reval, and in particular with Sten Baner. This was the purest fantasy, with not a shred of evidence or probability to support it; but it became an *ideé fixe* both with Johan and with Karl. Horn was recalled, tried, and by a narrow majority condemned to death. He was not executed; for indeed it was not he who was the real quarry. Johan and Karl persisted in hoping that by threats of torture, hard imprisonment, or offers of liberty, they might induce him to betray his supposed accomplices, and so involve the former members of the *råd* in a charge of treason. Fortunately for them Horn was a man of courage and honour, unmoved alike by threats or promises. The disgraced members of the *råd*, who had been imprisoned, then confined to their estates, were now imprisoned again. They were repeatedly brought up to be examined in the hope of extracting from one or the other of them a confession of guilt. But as in fact they had nothing to confess, and were not conscious either of disloyalty or dereliction of duty, there was not much to be got out of them. They refused to incriminate either themselves or each other. In the end there was nothing for it but to give them their liberty, under a greater or less degree of surveillance.

It does not seem likely that the life of any of them was very seriously threatened: Johan was not that kind of tyrant; but it is probable that

[1] It is significant that he does not seem to have resented Karl Henriksson Horn's reminder that he was forbidden by the Land Law to imprison without trial.

[2] See above, p. 271.

their misfortunes were mitigated by the exertions of friends whose pleadings could not be ignored. The queen, Gunilla Bielke, naturally did her best for her family. Old Queen Anna of Poland spoke up to clear Erik Sparre from the charge of having offered to abandon Estonia. Most important of all, Sigismund himself repeatedly intervened in their favour. That slow and stolid youth was perfectly well aware that his father had put himself into a passion on quite untenable grounds. He knew, none better, that Erik Sparre and his associates were not guilty of what was laid to their charge. He had no desire to inherit a throne ornamented with the relics of constitutional martyrs. The uproar seemed to him all the more unnecessary because in 1590 and 1591 he still had high hopes of ridding himself of his Polish kingdom. The Archduke Ernest was willing; the Emperor was in favour; and if the Archduke Maximilian protested that he had prior claims, it was reasonable to expect that Habsburg family pressure would compel him to swallow his objections. In 1592, when Sigismund drew closer his ties with the Habsburgs by marrying the Archduchess Anna, the affair seemed to be as good as arranged. Unfortunately for him, Maximilian was not prepared to see Ernest in his place, nor were the Poles willing to be made the object of a bargain behind their back. Maximilian had only to drop a few well-placed intimations of the plan, and within a few weeks Sigismund found himself forced to declare publicly that he had never entertained it. The unwanted crown was once more rammed firmly on his head; and he was left to face the disquieting prospect of ruling Sweden from Warsaw. If justice and humanity had hitherto dictated his intercession with his father on behalf of the former *råd*, their claims were now reinforced by considerations of policy. No provision existed for the government of Sweden after Johan's death, now that the Statute of Kalmar had been abrogated; but it required no great prescience to foresee that Karl might put forward a claim to the office, if not to the title, of *riksföreståndare*. The history of the Union of Kalmar was sufficient warning against that solution, and nobody with any knowledge of Karl's character could imagine that it was likely to be an easy arrangement. From Sigismund's point of view the best hope was perhaps a government in which Karl's ambitions would be balanced by a strong *råd*. In order to secure this, the reinstatement of Erik Sparre and his colleagues was probably indispensable. At the very least, it was now sound tactics to establish a claim to their gratitude. It was certainly ironical that by 1592 few can have more sincerely regretted Sigismund's absence in Poland than the men whose actions at Reval had helped to keep him there.

For from 1590 to 1592 Karl was effectively the ruler of Sweden. It was he who planned the unsuccessful campaigns in Estonia; it was he who carried through the debasement of the currency. The king mortgaged the province of Dalsland to him; he undertook the management of the copper-trade on the crown's behalf. The continued persecution of the fallen *råd* was mainly his work. The aristocracy, increasingly disturbed by the relentless harrying of their leaders, well knew whom they had to thank for it. Despite government propaganda, public opinion began to veer to the side of the *råd*. Pamphlets and pasquinades passed from hand to hand, seditious writings were found in public places. The most violent of them, which appeared anonymously in 1592, was specifically directed against Karl. He was reminded of the fate of Kristian II and Erik XIV, and even of that of Henry III of France; he was blamed for all the illegalities of the *régime*. 'It has come to this, that no one dares speak openly anything but what you choose to hear, and everyone must agree that you are in the right in all your actions and undertakings; and if any venture to do otherwise, he must stand in danger of his life, or be decried for a rogue and a traitor.'[1] The author of this pamphlet was Count Axel Leijonhufvud, one of the men of Reval. He was, to be sure, a scoundrel with a grievance, prepared at one moment to incite Erik Sparre to revolt, and at the next to betray him in the hope of bettering himself, a man whose future career would show him to be without scruple and without principle; but on this occasion at least he seems to have told something like the truth.

Nevertheless, there were limits to Karl's ascendancy. The king, weary and disheartened as he now was, did not place himself unreservedly in his brother's hands. If he relaxed his efforts for the Liturgy, he made no important concession on ducal rights. He was prepared to confirm the donations which Karl had already given, if his brother should predecease him; but he still declined to acknowledge Karl's right to make donations in future. He rejected Karl's advice about the new privileges for the nobility. Circumstances might for the moment draw the brothers into collaboration; but the old suspicions died hard.[2] One very significant indication of this came at the beginning of 1592, when Johan ordered the preparation of the draft of an engagement which would have bound Axel Leijonhufvud to be faithful to Sigismund in the event of Karl's refusing to recognize him as king. As Johan's life drew to an end, it is clear that he was not free from anxiety about the danger of usurpation. Almost his last act was one which Karl cannot have approved: on his deathbed he pardoned the men of Reval, and also

[1] Lars Sjödin, 'En pamflett av år 1592 mot Vasahuset' (*Historisk Tidskrift*, 1930), p. 330. Karl blamed Queen Gunilla and Johan's daughter Anna for fomenting them, and in his *Rim-Chrönika* attacked both (and especially Anna) with extraordinary scurrility.

liberated Karl Henriksson Horn. He died on 17 November 1592; in charity with all men, save perhaps with those bitter-end anti-Liturgists for whom the hour of opportunity was now to strike. To his unfortunate son he bequeathed an inheritance so beset with intractable difficulties and irreconcilable demands, that it may be doubted whether there was a sovereign in Europe who could have coped with it successfully.

5. The Revolution, 1592–1600

I. THE UPPSALA ASSEMBLY

The old king lay on his catafalque in the great courtyard of Stockholm castle; in Warsaw the new king wondered when his disillusioned Polish subjects would permit him to go across to assume his father's crown. No arrangements existed for carrying on the Swedish government in the interim, now that the Statute of Kalmar had been rescinded. Duke Karl, to be sure, lacked neither the will nor the power for it: as his brother lay dying he had made military preparations too formidable to be easily ignored or defied. The men of Reval, but yesterday released from surveillance, had not as yet resumed their places in the *råd*; the *råd* itself, lacking their presence, had latterly been no more than an echo of the royal voice. But for it too Johan's death had brought emancipation; or at least the opportunity of independence. King, duke, *råd*: the triangular constellation dominated the heavens in the new reign, as in the old, the successive oppositions or conjunctions of each luminary determining the political climate. The accession of Sigismund, so far from resolving this conflict of forces, only shifted the lines of tension: the struggle took on new aspects, the participants sought fresh allies. But the fundamental matter at stake remained unchanged: the clash between a dynasty jealous of opposition, and an aristocracy which combined the pursuit of its own advantage with the championship of constitutional principles. This clear-cut issue, however, was blurred as before by the divisions within the dynasty itself; for Karl was to quarrel with Sigismund even more violently than once he had quarrelled with Johan. In that quarrel the *råd* would once again be driven to take sides. But as the crisis deepened into revolution, the traditional guardians of the constitution would prove their essential consistency by opting for the less flagrantly illegal of the antagonists.

The immediate uncertainties were removed within a month of Johan's death as the result of Karl's initiative: before the end of November he made contact with Erik Sparre and his colleagues. However ungracious and recriminatory the tone of his communication, it amounted in fact to an offer of reconciliation which they felt it would be imprudent to decline. But before they could meet him the waters were troubled by the ill-considered activities of Count Axel Leijonhufvud, who went down to Västergötland and there began an agitation which seemed to be designed to persuade the province that the duke was preparing a usurpation. Karl immediately accused Erik Sparre of being behind this feeble and futile demonstration. Sparre was able to persuade him (as was indeed the case) that he had no hand in it; a squad of Karl's troops sufficed to drive Leijonhufvud over the Danish border; and, with this obstacle removed, duke and *råd* could exchange assurances of collaboration. On 8 January 1593 they established a joint interim government, Karl being recognized as 'leading personage' in the realm. A message from Sigismund, which arrived soon afterwards, explained that his return must be delayed for some months, and made it clear that an arrangement of this sort had his approval, at least for the time being.

So began that political partnership of duke and *råd* which was to dominate the history of the next two years, and was not finally dissolved until 1597. It was from the start an uneasy and fragile alliance. The *råd* had entered into it with many misgivings, moved mainly by the obvious need to organize a provisional government and by a justified belief that they would have a better chance of controlling Karl as collaborators than as opponents. They hoped that it might still be possible, with Karl's goodwill, to salve some of the more useful provisions of the Statute of Kalmar:[1] the participation of the high nobility still seemed to them to be a prerequisite for good government. And the alarming experience of dynastic absolutism, from 1590 to 1592, made it more than ever necessary that the *råd*, as the guardians of the nation's rights and liberties, should recover its share in the control of affairs. The opening of a new reign, moreover, was the best moment for extracting from the crown a further instalment of privileges for the nobility; to which end the stronger their political position, the better their chances of exploiting the opportunity. There was substance in all these arguments. But they could not alter the stubborn fact that the only feeling which the *råd* had in common with the duke was a determination that Sweden should not be ruled from Poland. For the rest, he was sundered from them by deep, unbridgeable divisions. He had latterly been their most implacable persecutor; he had clashed with them repeatedly on major issues for the last dozen years; the undying memory of personal grudges made any real confidence impossible. To their view of the state, their constitutional ideas, their plans for administrative reform, he was essentially hostile, as he was also to their more selfish claims for greater privileges; while they on their side could never come to terms with the demagogy by which he sought to give to despotism the appearance of popular consent. For them, a check on the prerogative exercised through 'the leading Estates'; for him, mob

[1] Karl himself began to think that there might be something of value in the Statute: early in 1593 he ordered it to be disinterred and scrutinized.

oratory, the abuse of ignorant prejudice, and the sweaty nightcaps of *Herr Omnes*. It may well be that at the close of 1592 they had no real alternative to a pact with Karl. But in retrospect it appears as a fatal miscalculation which at the outset placed them in a false position: the irretrievable initial mistake which led many of them to political ruin and brought some of them to a traitor's death upon the scaffold. Yet if, even so early, the issue were to be thought of as in some sense a choice between Karl and Sigismund, it was not obvious whom they should choose. Their relations with their new sovereign had remained good even under the strain of events at Reval, and they certainly felt gratitude for his efforts on their behalf in the following years. Their respect for law, their recognition of their duty as counsellors of the crown, would always keep them loyal to the king as long as Sigismund observed the law himself. But if he should follow his father in taking an absolutist line, if he should attempt to rule his hereditary kingdom by irresponsible advisers, if he should prove too susceptible to alien influences, they would have no option but to oppose him. Already they foresaw this possibility; and the event would justify their prescience.

The other partner in the government, Duke Karl, was now in a strong political position. He was the richest man in Sweden; he had good military and naval forces at his command, drawn from his duchy. For the last two years he had been effectively the ruler of the country. As the only member of the royal family resident in Sweden who was capable of conducting the government, he considered that he had the right to conduct it. When in 1560 there had seemed a real chance that Erik might become king of England, it had been agreed that the senior male member of the royal family should be regent in Sweden during his absences; and the precedent now seemed to be very much in point. Karl intended if possible to apply it, and it is probably not too much to say that from the first he designed to be regent in the style of Sten Sture. All the signs pointed to Sigismund's being compelled to spend most of his time in Poland; a regency might well prove semi-permanent. But Karl was also as determined as ever to secure what he believed to be his ducal rights according to his father's Testament; and the political arrangement he desired would in effect have given him control of the whole of Sweden upon much the same terms as those which he had contended for as duke. It was not in nature—not in his nature, certainly—that he should for long be content with merely a single share in a collaborative *régime*. His hatred and suspicion of the Sparre-Bielke-Baner group was no whit diminished, as his reaction to Leijonhufvud's activities made plain. It was therefore conceivable that he should try to achieve his ambitions by way of a policy of dynastic solidarity: an alliance with Sigismund might seem a natural sequel to his alliance with Johan. But to such a policy there was one formidable objection: Sigismund's religion. Karl's fear of Rome, reinforced by memories of Klosterlasse and Possevino, forbade any union with his nephew until the position of Swedish Protestantism had been buttressed by all possible guarantees; and he had no doubt of his right and duty to lead the nation in the effort to secure them. Thereafter, a dynastic pact would be a possibility; for the moment he needed the support of the men of Reval. And one reason why he moved so quickly to secure it was in order to prevent Sigismund's capitalizing on their gratitude, and their detestation of the duke, to win them for himself.

Sigismund was something of a sport upon the family stock: if one had not known he was a Vasa one would have said he was a Habsburg. He was the only member of his family for three generations to be blessed with an equable temper; perhaps also the only one not to be cursed with the sin of ambition. His Polish subjects, who found him heavy going and disliked the German atmosphere at his court, inquired irritably 'who is this dumb devil that they have sent us from Sweden?', and coined the famous phrase, '*Tria T fecerunt nostro Regi vae: Taciturnitas, Tarditas, Tenacitas*'. He had his father's pride and melancholy; he inherited the aesthetic interests of both his parents, and was himself (to the contempt of his Polish subjects) a painter of talent; but he lacked the Vasas' gift of words and their ability to come to terms with the common man. Stiff and withdrawn, he had none of the easy affabilities and trivial insincerities which smooth human relationships. Probably he did not miss them. The dominant interest in his life was his religion: the core of his character was a profound seriousness and a fundamental integrity. In the last resort he could contemplate without any sense of personal sacrifice the loss of two kingdoms, provided that he were assured of gaining the kingdom of Heaven. The calm certainty of his faith distressed and irritated Jesuit advisers who liked also to keep their powder dry: as Malaspina complained, he was too inclined to trust to the righteousness of his cause and leave the rest to God, accepting consequent failure with pious resignation as one more cross which it was his duty to bear. Slow he often was, and vacillating too; diffident of his own judgment, prone to accept bad advice. But he was a good man in a sense in which none other of the early Vasas can be called so; and a good man beset with cruel difficulties. He was, finally, one of those who seem born to be unlucky—not least in having to confront, in his uncle Karl, a master of the baser arts of politics.

It was in the nature of things almost impossible that any confidence should exist between them. Karl could place no faith in a sovereign bullied by his Jesuit confessors; Sigismund's attitude to his uncle was already warped by the fear that he planned to usurp the crown. His

SIGISMUND
by C. de Vos

KARL IX

engraving by H. Nützal

father had shared that fear; foreign observers from the outset of the reign discussed Karl's actions in the light of it; Axel Leijonhufvud, fleeing ignominiously to Poland, poured tales into Sigismund's ear which reinforced it. Nevertheless, though the suspicion was natural, it was probably unjust. Karl was too convinced a legitimist to wish to seize the throne as long as any other road to his objective was conceivable; and even when usurpation had *de facto* taken place, his naked dynastic conscience clung irrationally to such tattered rags of legality as he could drape around it. Not the name but the power of monarchy was what he desired, nor would he be satisfied with less. To Sigismund the distinction naturally appeared specious and irrelevant; to Karl it was essential. Certainly it enabled him to believe himself loyal to his sovereign long after others had abandoned the attempt to believe it.

One of the first acts of the interim government—it was done the very day after Karl and the *råd* reached final agreement—was to summon a church council to meet at Uppsala at the beginning of March 1593. An assembly of this sort was certainly overdue. Karl had been demanding it for more than a decade; it had been promised as part of the Vadstena settlement of 1587; it had been one of the terms of Karl's final reconciliation with Johan in 1590. The need for reunion in the church was now urgent: they could not afford to face a Roman Catholic sovereign with divided ranks. The lamentable polemics of Liturgist and anti-Liturgist could not be suffered to continue; the split between the clergy of the duchy and those of the kingdom must somehow be healed. Karl certainly believed in the necessity for closing the ranks of Protestantism; and he probably expected that a general assembly would result in the defeat of the Liturgists. It has been suggested, however, that his motive in summoning the Uppsala Assembly was essentially political rather than religious. His object, on this theory, was to strengthen his position by enlisting the support of some representative body of the nation. He had at first wished to summon a *riksdag*; but this the *råd* had opposed, on the ground that the calling together of the Estates was a royal prerogative which the interim government was not empowered to wield. Baffled in this (it is argued) he fell back on a church assembly: if he could not have the Estates as a whole, at least he would secure the Clergy. It is certainly reasonable to suppose that he was not unmindful of this kind of consideration; but it does not follow that it provided his main motive. His anxiety for a church council was after all of long standing, and it had proceeded from his fear that Liturgism might open the road to Rome. His purpose in 1593 was probably a good deal less political than the motives which induced the *råd* to concur in the summons. It may well be asked what it was that in

December 1592 led that former champion of the Liturgy, Hogenskild Bielke, to urge the recall of Abraham Angermannus. What persuaded these religiously-indifferent aristocrats to pledge themselves, on 8 January 1593, to maintain religion according to the Confession of Augsburg?[1] They had resisted the calling of a *riksdag*, as illegal; but the summoning of the Uppsala Assembly was equally an infringement of the rights of the crown. Why so scrupulous in the one case, and not in the other? It can only be supposed that they, too, saw the need for a quick ending of the divisions in the church, and that their political sense told them that the day of the anti-Liturgists was at hand. It may well be that they felt the need for a national demonstration in the face of a possible threat to their interests as beneficiaries of the Reformation. And if it should come to hard bargaining with Sigismund, they were at least as conscious as Karl of the advantages to be derived from the backing of the clerical Estate. Protestant zeal is at least a conceivable motive with Karl; it can hardly be so with Nils Gyllenstierna and Hogenskild Bielke, both of whom had been willing enough to play the Roman with Possevino, and bow in the house of Rimmon. More than half a century later there occurred a curious dialogue in the *råd* between Queen Kristina and Jakob de la Gardie.[2] They were debating the English Civil War and the motives that lay behind it; and after de la Gardie had remarked that there was a *spiritus vertiginis* abroad in Europe, the discussion continued as follows:

KRISTINA: *Religio* is a *praetextus* . . . a kind of raincoat.

DE LA GARDIE: Not to be put on save in case of necessity—as the late King Karl did against Sigismund.

KRISTINA: *Hoc non propter amorem religionis, sed propter statum*.[3]

Now in regard to the later phases of the Swedish revolution, there can be little doubt that this was a just judgment. But it was less than fair to Karl's conduct in 1593. When he summoned the assembly to Uppsala, when he accepted the resolution which that assembly drew up, what moved him most was not ambition, but the fear of Rome.

It is another question how far that fear was justified. Sigismund's devotion to his religion was obvious to all who knew him. It was recognized as a precious asset by the papacy, which saw in him the destined instrument for the recovery of Scandinavia for the church. The recatholicization of Sweden was, indeed, one of the most cherished objects of Pope Clement VIII. Soon after his election in 1592 he appointed Germanico Malaspina as nuncio to Poland, with the special

[1] Karl's reciprocal pledge on the same day significantly couples 'the pure and clear Word of God' with the *Augustana*.

[2] He was the son of Pontus de la Gardie.

[3] *Svenska riksrådets protokoll*, XIII, 17 (21 February 1649).

task of forwarding the design; on the news of Johan III's death he set up a special council of six cardinals for Swedish affairs. These are incontrovertible facts. But nobody in Sweden at this time had any inkling of the true nature of Malaspina's mission, nor was there any reason for the world at large to suppose that Sigismund had plans for making Poland the fortress of the Counter-Reformation, or the spring-board for an attempt to reconvert Sweden. Poland was still a country where the rights of Protestants were very effectively safeguarded: at this time, indeed, there were twice as many Protestant senators as Catholic. Apart from some action against Protestant churches in Prussia, Sigismund seemed determined to advance the Catholic cause more by force of example and indirect social pressures than by direct means: certainly there was as yet no persecution. And it is at least possible that his plans for Sweden went no further—in the first instance, at all events—than the securing of a good measure of toleration for those of his faith. It has therefore been contended that the danger to Swedish Protestantism was in fact small, or even non-existent: Sigismund's difficulties in Poland would always have prevented any serious attempt to put Malaspina's designs into operation, and in any case the crypto-Catholic element in Sweden was far too weak to provide a basis on which to build. The bogy of popery, it is suggested, was deliberately conjured up for political purposes.[1] But this is an explanation which ignores too much. Whether the dangers were great or small was not what mattered. What mattered was men's opinions. And as to that there could be no doubt, least of all since the exploits of the *missio suetica*. It was a bare twenty years since St Bartholomew; the freedom of the northern Netherlands was still in the balance; the story of treason and plot in Elizabethan England could not be presumed to have ended with the Armada; the death of William the Silent (and, it was currently believed, of Don Carlos) spoke its lesson to all. Not for nothing did Nils Gyllenstierna, in his opening address to the Uppsala Assembly, invite their attention to contemporary France, as an example of the consequences of two religions in one realm. Even Johan III had thought it necessary to insert strong safeguards against Roman Catholicism into the Statute of Kalmar. It was in vain that Sigismund on 9 January 1593 addressed an open letter to his subjects, guaranteeing his protection of the faith which 'for some years past' had been prevalent in Sweden, and assuring them that he would 'neither hate nor love any for religion's sake'. Fear of Catholicism may have been exaggerated and irrational, but it was not to be conjured away by such promises as these. As the debates at Uppsala were to show, it was a string already vibrant: there was no need at this stage for Karl to harp upon it.

[1] This is the underlying argument of Harry Hermerén, *Uppsala möte*.

The meeting which gathered at Uppsala at the end of February 1593 was attended by over 300 of the clergy, a handful of representatives of the other Estates, and nine members of the *råd*. Karl held himself aloof, so that he might not seem to put a constraint upon their freedom; but it was impossible not to be conscious of his looming figure in the wings. The precise status of the Assembly was not very clear: it was, no doubt, a general council of the church; but it was also more than that, for the presence of members from the other Estates, and above all of nearly half of the *råd*, gave it something of the character of a national assembly, entitled to speak for the country as a whole in the particular matters within its competence. The church had been promised a 'free council'; and from the beginning the more active members took care that it should be so. The *råd* was not suffered to fix the agenda; the *praeses*—Nicolaus Olai Botniensis—was elected by the members; attempts to curb freedom of debate—for instance, out of regard to the particular religious susceptibilities of Duke Karl—were boldly and successfully resisted. The business with which they had to deal fell into two main sections. They had in the first place to heal the wounds of the church by settling the controversy over the Liturgy; and in the second place they had to draw up, if they could, the *confessio* which Protestant Sweden had hitherto lacked. The first task gave them little trouble, for the anti-Liturgists were in an overwhelming majority. The trumpet for the assault had been blown loud and long at one of the preliminary meetings by Erik Skinnerus, who in a great sermon of two hours (without notes) denounced the Liturgy as *metropolis et turris regni Antichristi*; and the victory of his party was sealed at the end of the sessions by the election of Abraham Angermannus (still in exile) as archbishop. The Assembly condemned the Red Book as *monstrum horrendum*; the few Liturgists who had the courage of their convictions were overwhelmed with execration;[1] almost all those who had conformed under Johan hastened to turn their coats, and confessed their errors—led by the bishops of Linköping and Åbo—in a style which their auditors no doubt found edifying, but which makes but an abject impression upon posterity.[2] The diocese of Strängnäs was once more received into communion with the rest of the church; which meant in fact that the duchy had imposed its will upon the kingdom. But it proved easier to define what they would not have than what they would. The question of ceremonies remained sharply controversial: some which the zealots wished away had to be retained for the present, until un-

[1] It was unlucky for them that the boldest of them, Petrus Pauli, had a moral character not above reproach.

[2] Hogenskild Bielke had the effrontery to remark that this should be a warning to the clergy not in future to approve so lightly, and without proper examination, the things that were enjoined upon them by the king.

regenerate congregations could be weaned from them. Exorcism, in particular, proved a stone of offence and an occasion of stumbling; not least to Karl, who declared that if any priest tried exorcism in his house he would chase him out with the poker, and made an unwise attempt (firmly rebuffed) to impose his views on the meeting. Exorcism was in the end retained, though with some verbal modifications.[1] On matters of ritual and ceremonies in general, their final determination represented approximately a return to the Church Ordinance of 1571.

In regard to doctrine there was less division of opinion. The leaders of the church had come determined to provide Sweden with a confession of faith; and the precedent from Strängnäs in 1587 was there to show them the way. The *Augustana invariata* was therefore unanimously adopted—with the less difficulty, perhaps, because for a considerable proportion of the assembly it had all the charm of novelty: some time was spent by the president in translating and explaining it, clause by clause, for the benefit of those of feeble genius. With the Bible, the three creeds, and the Church Ordinance (but not the Formula of Concord) the *Augustana* would henceforth be the basis of belief. And when the final vote on this point was taken, Nicolaus Olai Botniensis pronounced the famous words: 'Now is Sweden become as one man, and we have all one Lord and God.' As a natural corollary they proceeded to condemn all papists and Liturgists; they demanded that the government take steps to 'root out' Roman Catholic priests, and suppress the nunnery at Vadstena; they resolved that public worship by heretics be forbidden, and that railers against the established religion be punished. For the first time the church had officially affirmed the principle of intolerance and pronounced in favour of persecution. The long misty morning of the Swedish Reformation was over: a harsher light revealed the sharp outlines of the fortress of the faith. There remained, however, one delicate question: was the term 'heretic' to include Calvinists and Zwinglians? The meeting had explicitly condemned 'sacramentarians', which might seem to be sufficient to comprehend both; but a section of the clergy, not unwilling, perhaps, to aim an oblique thrust at Karl, carried a resolution that Calvinists and Zwinglians should be specifically mentioned. Their action nearly split the Assembly: Botniensis resigned the chair in anger. But they forced the sending of a delegation to the duke, charged to obtain his agreement to the alteration in order (as they tactfully put it) 'to quiet those who suspected him of Calvinism'. Karl was predictably enraged; but he found it prudent to give way, although with characteristic asperity. 'Then his Grace replied, "By all means", saying, "put in the whole lot of them for all I care, and the devil in Hell too, for he

[1] Instead of 'depart from hence' the formula was henceforth to be 'keep away from here'.

is also my enemy". Whereupon they returned with gladness to the council, and told them of the gracious answer which the prince had given.'[1]

On 20 March the final resolution, embodying all the previous decisions, was signed by the participants. But they were far from being the only signatories. For after the Assembly had ended, copies of the resolution were disseminated all over the country, so that all might testify to their faith by seal or subscription. It was eventually endorsed by Karl, by fourteen members of the *råd*, seven bishops, 218 members of the nobility, 137 officials, 1,556 of the clergy, the burgomasters and councils of 36 towns, the representatives of 197 provinces and counties. The Uppsala Resolution became a great national act of faith, a declaration of religious rights, the cornerstone of Swedish Lutheranism. It holds a place in Swedish history analogous to that of the National Covenant in the history of Scotland. Sweden awaited Sigismund's arrival in a spirit of religious exaltation which was none the less real for being slightly factitious. The Assembly had delivered, the nation had endorsed, an explicit warning to the absent king; a warning which after his assurances he might be forgiven for thinking gratuitous and uncalled-for. And the warning was accompanied by something very like a threat; for at the first session of the Assembly Nils Gyllenstierna had carried a motion which seemed to imply that Sigismund must accept such resolutions as they might adopt, if he wished for recognition as king. It was a resolution pregnant with misfortune. It involved the purely religious settlement in a constitutional issue of the greatest import. By making acceptance of the Uppsala Resolution a precondition for coronation, it reopened the whole question of the status of hereditary monarchy. It implied—or at least it would naturally seem to Sigismund to imply—a denial of that automatic succession which was the essence of the Pact of 1544. Whatever Sigismund's attitude to the purely religious question, he was bound to resist to the uttermost a demand of this sort. Gyllenstierna had used religion as the stalking-horse for those ideas of limited monarchy for which the *råd* was contending; he had pushed Sigismund into a corner where he had no room for manœuvre, and by doing so had made a *constitutional* conflict almost inevitable. The significance of what had happened became plain when the Stockholm government sent Ture Bielke over to Poland at the end of May. The main purpose of his mission was to urge Sigismund to come to Sweden as soon as he could do so without offending the Poles; but his instructions also enjoined him to impress upon the king the fact that even in hereditary monarchies it is lawful and customary to remind sovereigns of the rights and privileges of their subjects. Bielke

[1] *Svenska riksdagsakter*, I, iii, 77.

was therefore to ask for guarantees that Sweden should have religious liberty 'as it had existed in the last years of Gustav Vasa and the first years of Johan, and as it has most recently been agreed at Uppsala'; that Karl should hold his duchy according to Gustav Vasa's Testament; and that all Estates should be assured of their privileges. Karl on his own account added a request for the confirmation of Angermannus (or, failing him, of Botniensis) as archbishop. Thus the cause of Protestantism, ducal rights, class privilege, constitutional principles, were all conjoined in a frontal attack upon Sigismund's most cherished convictions and susceptibilities.

He had, indeed, much reason for dissatisfaction with the authorities in Stockholm. They had called the Uppsala Assembly without his leave; they had carried through a recoinage which, however necessary to end the inflation, was an infringement of a right which was generally recognized as essentially a *régale*; without consulting him Karl had taken steps to meet one of the most earnestly-pressed demands of the clergy by reopening the University of Uppsala. Almost worst of all, they had gravely compromised themselves by their attitude to Klas Fleming. Klas Fleming was at this time governor and commander-in-chief in Finland; he was also marshal, admiral, *lagman* of Uppland, and a member of the *råd*—a cumulation of offices which caused resentment among his colleagues, and moved the town clerk of Stockholm to tart comments in his minute-book. Fleming was not an attractive personage: crude, brutal, uncivilized,[1] crafty and unscrupulous, but undeniably a man of forceful character and much ability, with the saving virtue of absolute loyalty to his sovereign. He had dissociated himself from Erik Sparre and the others at Reval in 1589, and thereafter had sided with the king; perhaps because he genuinely believed in absolutism as a method of government. He had been a main instigator of the proceedings against Karl Henriksson Horn. The other members of the *råd* hated him as a renegade and detested him as a man. Unluckily for himself, he was also on bad terms with Karl, with whom he had quarrelled on military matters in the last years of Johan's reign. A common hostility to Fleming, indeed, was now one of the few ties which bound Karl and the *råd* together. Already in the first months of Sigismund's reign Fleming seems to have suspected Karl's loyalty: at all events, in January 1593 he addressed an open letter to his province of Uppland which urged fidelity to the lawful king, and was construed by Karl as a reflexion upon himself. When in the same month a truce with the Russians was concluded, Fleming took care not to disband his troops. Defying the orders of the Stockholm government, he distributed them at free quarters upon the Finnish peasantry, who were

[1] He boasted of his ability to eat a whole ham at one sitting.

in no condition to maintain them. Karl, anxious to avoid driving the peasants to desperation, gave them letters of protection which Fleming proceeded to ignore. He ordered the troops to be paid from other sources: Fleming took no notice. He even sent over an agent to incite the men to disobey their commander, though without success. Meanwhile, in February 1593, Johan Sparre arrived in Finland from Poland, commissioned to take oaths of allegiance to Sigismund from the commanders of fortresses there—a measure obviously inspired by doubts of Karl's intentions. At this point Karl put himself clearly in the wrong by ordering the troops in Finland to refuse any engagement until authorized by the government in Sweden to take it. By that time Fleming had secured full powers from Sigismund, and could afford to treat Karl's orders with contempt. The situation had now become really dangerous: the Stockholm government appeared to be refusing not only to acknowledge the authority of the king's commander, but also to obey the king's commands. On the original points at issue Karl and the *råd* were certainly right; but they had allowed their animus against Fleming, and their suspicion of his motives, to lead them into a course of action which was really indefensible. As Sigismund prepared for his visit to Sweden, it was clear that he could hardly avoid a crisis upon his arrival. But it was clear also that the crisis was not of his making.

II. SIGISMUND IN SWEDEN, 1593–4

At the beginning of August 1593 Sigismund arrived in Danzig. His departure from Warsaw had been delayed by serious difficulties with his Polish subjects, who still feared that he might use the opportunity of absence to renounce the crown; and it was probably only the direct intervention of Clement VIII which removed these domestic obstacles. Even so, he was forced before his departure to give a written promise to cede Estonia, and an undertaking to return before St Bartholomew's Day (24 August) 1594.

As he waited for the fleet in which Klas Fleming was to carry him over, he had his first experience of the pressures to which he would be subjected in the following months. On 30 August there arrived in the city Powsiński, an envoy extraordinary from the papacy. He brought with him a gift of 20,000 *scudi* as a contribution towards the expenses of recovering Sweden for Rome; but he brought also the pope's commands that Sigismund must at all costs avoid giving any guarantee of freedom of religion—or at the very worst must confine himself to a promise which might seem to assure religious equality, but which could later be interpreted '*in senso buono*'. This instruction was already too late.

Not only had Sigismund made such a promise in his letter of 9 January, but he had recently reinforced it by an undertaking to respect the *Augustana* and the Church Ordinance. It was true that he had avoided pledging acceptance of the Uppsala Resolution, which would have debarred him from efforts to advance the Catholic cause; but from the point of view of Rome he had already shown culpable weakness. It was as well, perhaps, that Malaspina was to accompany him; for Malaspina, as the official representative of the papacy, could be relied upon to administer unpalatable moral tonics as might be required.

Of this Erik Sparre and Klas Bielke—who arrived early in September—were probably well aware: at all events, they tried hard to persuade Sigismund not to take him to Sweden. They had come to Danzig to escort the king home; but they had come also in the hope of inducing him to make concessions without delay. Their business was to try to get him to accept the Uppsala Resolution and confirm the election of Angermannus as archbishop; to which end they did not fail to insinuate that prompt compliance on these points might be the best means of parrying the designs of Karl. Sigismund, however, would make no promises. Erik Sparre's arguments confirmed his suspicion that the reconciliation between duke and *råd* had no solid bottom. Klas Fleming, on his arrival, warned him against Erik Sparre, and suggested that a bargain with his uncle was still a possibility. He determined, therefore, to keep his hands free for the present, and if possible to play off the one against the other. He had, indeed, no extravagant hopes of what could be immediately effected in Sweden. He would be well content this time if he could obtain a reasonable measure of toleration for Roman Catholics: Malaspina's heroic intransigence was not likely to prove appropriate in the existing circumstances.

On 30 September, after a tempestuous voyage,[1] Sigismund arrived in Stockholm. It was at once apparent that the religious issue was to be exploited to the uttermost. Sigismund's assurances had made no impression on his Swedish subjects, for they had omitted the two things which everyone now seemed to regard as a *sine qua non*: the acceptance of the Uppsala Resolution, and the confirmation of Angermannus. Within four days of his arrival Karl and the *råd*, in a joint *démarche*, told him plainly that until these points were conceded there could be no coronation. At the end of October the Nobility put forward a memorial to much the same purpose, stipulating also that all offices be reserved to Lutherans and that no Roman Catholic priests be permitted in the country. On 1 December the Clergy produced a lengthy

[1] If Sigismund's repeated experience be a guide, the winds were as Protestant in the Baltic as in the Channel.

list of *Postulata* which went further still. They required a promise that Sigismund's eldest son be brought up in the Lutheran faith, that no more than ten Roman Catholic priests be permitted at court, that a Lutheran pastor be assigned to the nuns at Vadstena, that the restoration of the university be confirmed, and that the election of bishops be free. They claimed the right to hold church councils without the king's permission; they wanted criminous clerks to be tried, for all offences short of felony, in the bishop's court, without appeal; they even demanded that Sigismund, as a non-Lutheran, abstain from making clerical appointments. Any hope that the fire of Protestant enthusiasm might die away of itself was destroyed by the presence in Stockholm of the king's Jesuit confessors and the papal legate, by the Roman Catholic services in the castle chapel and the Riddarholm church, and by the indecent brawling for the possession of the pulpit between the clergy of the two denominations. If Sigismund was playing for time, he had better have imposed discretion upon his priests; if he meant to assert the right of Roman Catholics to hold public worship, he should have come equipped to enforce it.

Faced with an agitation which showed no signs of diminishing, the king perforce fell back upon diplomacy and procrastination. It might be possible, perhaps, to disrupt the alliance of Karl and the *råd*. Malaspina believed that the best policy would be an approach to Karl; Sigismund preferred first to try the other alternative. On 2 November he issued 'letters of protection' to safeguard the men of Reval from attacks upon their reputation, in which he declared them innocent of all the charges brought against them by 'evil men' in 1590. This measure certainly infuriated Karl—he later said that Sigismund had given the lie to his father's ashes—but it entirely failed to win over Erik Sparre, who had no intention of losing a uniquely favourable opportunity for the sake of a royal testimonial:[1] indeed, after 3 October it was the *råd* who took the lead in putting pressure on the king, while Karl kept himself in the background. Having thus failed with the *råd*, Sigismund tried the other tack. In December he inquired of Karl whether there was any prospect of toleration for Roman Catholics if the Uppsala Resolution were accepted in its entirety—a question which the duke prudently referred to the forthcoming *riksdag*; in January he attempted to secure him by offers of special religious privileges for the duchy, and even hinted at the succession to the Polish crown. But Karl courteously returned this poisoned chalice; nor was he willing (for once) to dissociate the duchy from the kingdom. *Råd* and duke exchanged messages in which each renewed the pledge

[1] This did not prevent its being made an article of accusation against him at his trial in 1600.

to stand by the other: the opposition front remained unbroken. And if diplomacy had failed to dissolve it, procrastination failed to weaken it. It was in vain that Sigismund promised to give guarantees at his coronation; in vain that he remitted the Clergy's memorandum to the *råd*. The *råd* sent it back to him, toned down a little, but substantially the same. And when he informed them that the memorandum should be considered at the forthcoming meeting of the *riksdag*, they flatly refused to transmit his answer. It was an open breach. One last possibility remained: an appeal to public opinion. In November Sigismund had issued an open letter to the nation, denying any intention to change the country's religion: it had no more effect than its predecessors. In January he sent Klas Fleming and Jöran Posse to the winter markets to talk the commonalty into a better humour: they were not listened to. The peasantry already knew what to think of these matters, for their pastors had told them: Sigismund's propaganda-offensive was a full year too late.

The king had good reason to feel that unprecedented things were being asked of him. With what right, for instance, could the *råd* claim to impose Angermannus upon him, when Karl freely chose bishops in the duchy? Nobody had contested Gustav Vasa's right to pay to his clergy stipends fixed by himself, which varied with the merit of the parson; Johan had freely withheld or curtailed stipends as a measure of church discipline; only now was the king's discretion challenged. The religious clamour could not disguise the fact that the real object of attack was the prerogative: 'under the cloak of religion much was demanded of us that touched our royal majesty too nearly'.[1] Sigismund was an absolutist more serious in his convictions than his father, and not less tenacious of purpose. His experience of the humiliating impotence of Polish monarchy made him determined to resist any tendencies towards *aurea libertas* in his hereditary kingdom. He believed that Erik Sparre and his friends wished to import something like a *Wahlkapitulation*, a *pacta conventa*, into the Swedish constitution; and that was one important reason why—apart from all questions of conscience—he strove to keep himself free of pledges until after his coronation. He told the *råd* on 5 December that he would have given them the religious guarantee they demanded, if he had not been so pressed to grant it; but now it was necessary to show that his was a hereditary kingship. We may perhaps be excused from believing this; but there is no doubt that he felt himself to be defending his natural rights as king, as well as advancing the cause of God. The constitutional issue was one to which Karl himself was not indifferent: though he assured the *råd* that his own view of hereditary monarchy did not posit a king

[1] *Svenska riksdagsakter*, I, iii, 265.

untrammelled by the law, he was plainly uneasy at the Clergy's challenge to the royal supremacy, and he had as little sympathy as his nephew with Erik Sparre's ideal constitution. Malaspina, who believed that Sparre aimed at '*un Re debilitato et quasi depinto*', drew the conclusion that Karl could eventually be rallied to the king's cause. And no doubt if Sigismund could have brought himself to pay Karl's price this might have been a solution. But such a payment would have meant abandonment of hope and acquiescence in impotence, the escape from one type of servitude through the acceptance of another. Victory with Karl as ally would be as fatal to the royal authority as defeat at the hands of Erik Sparre. There was no way out of the dilemma.

The Estates were summoned for 1 February 1594, when the body of Johan III was to be interred in Uppsala cathedral; and it was intended that the coronation should take place immediately afterwards. Before the end of January it had become clear that this programme could not be carried out. The Estates might indeed be persuaded, out of respect for Johan's memory, to attend the funeral; but thereafter the prospects were sombre and uncertain. The funeral itself became something of a demonstration by the opposition: Malaspina was not allowed to be present, and his life was threatened; Klas Fleming, though marshal and admiral, was not permitted to bear any of the regalia; the funeral sermon, by a stroke of retrospective malice, was entrusted to Abraham Angermannus. Thereafter the business of the *riksdag* could begin. But it began in an atmosphere of painful tension, and in circumstances which from the start destroyed the king's ability to resist. Despite Malaspina's advice, Sigismund had taken to Uppsala only a small body of troops; Karl, on the other hand, had 2,000 men behind him, though he had given his promise to come with no more than five hundred: militarily, he was in command of the situation. Politically, he used the occasion to make himself the leader and idol of the Estate of Peasants, who might be useful one day if he should fall out with Erik Sparre: here begins that infrangible alliance which was in the coming years to be fatal alike to Sigismund and to the *råd*. Already he was cultivating the arts of the stump orator, already utilizing the threat of mob violence. It was ominous for the future that at one of his open-air rallies a voice in the crowd should have hailed him as king. Against Karl's popularity, against the vehement Protestant enthusiasm of the commonalty, Klas Fleming's attempts to recruit a party of the crown had no chance. The four Estates were at one in their religious demands: the Nobility led the way by pledging themselves to disinherit any son who should defect from the Uppsala Resolution; the Clergy was inflexible in resisting the smallest concession to Rome: not a church, not a house, not a service, not a priest should be allowed them outside the chapel royal. For a fortnight Sigismund struggled for an acceptable compromise; for a fortnight he staved off a decision. The temper of the Peasants grew more menacing from day to day. Malaspina, who seems to have resigned himself to martyrdom, and thereafter still to have had ample vicarious stoicism at his disposal, resisted the slightest concession to expediency, and pressed remorselessly upon the king's conscience. But on 15 February the Peasants threatened that if the king did not yield within twenty-four hours they would go home. It was an ultimatum; and it was backed by Karl. On the following day, after who knows what travail of spirit, Sigismund at last gave way. But two days later Malaspina so far relented as to permit him to make a secret protest, revoking the promises he had made, as having been extorted from him by force. There still remained the question of the confirmation of Angermannus' election; but after the great surrender of the 16th Sigismund had no heart for further resistance. On 18 February he confirmed the election; at 8 o'clock on the following morning the new archbishop was consecrated to his office. The long-delayed coronation followed in the afternoon. Once again Angermannus preached the sermon; once again the regalia were borne by the leaders of the victorious *råd*. It fell to Erik Sparre to administer the coronation oath; in the course of which one final incident completed the king's humiliation. As he recited the oath, his upraised hand chanced (perhaps from exhaustion) to droop: Karl at once stepped forward and roughly ordered him to hold it well up until the oath was finished. And with that public expression of no-confidence the ordeal came to an end. Sigismund was king at last; and he could now begin to assess the measure of his defeat.

It was, indeed, very heavy. The coronation oath, though far more circumstantial than that sworn by his immediate predecessors, was taken directly from the Land Law, and contained no innovations of importance. The really significant document was the Accession Charter (*konungaförsäkran*). It fell into two halves: one religious, one secular. In regard to religion, it was an almost complete capitulation to the demands of the Estates. Sigismund promised to maintain his subjects' freedom of religion according to the *Augustana* and the Uppsala Resolution; he undertook that no office, lay or spiritual, should be given to any person who was not a member of the Lutheran church. There was to be no infringement of the Lutheran monopoly of education. Non-Lutherans might indeed be tolerated, provided they kept quiet; but liberty of worship was denied to them. In regard to secular matters, he promised to rule Sweden 'with the advice of Karl and the *råd*'; to maintain good relations with Poland, but never to sacrifice Sweden's interests; not to employ foreigners or low-born persons, but rather the Swedish nobility; not to make peace, war or alliance 'or undertake any other important matter' without the consent of all the Estates; not to impose new taxes save with the goodwill and assent of 'those who are concerned' (a vague formula which here makes its appearance for the first time); 'and for the rest, as long as we are king of both realms, the government of this kingdom in our absence shall be so arranged as may be agreed and decided between us, Duke Karl, and our well-beloved *riksråd* acting on behalf of the lower Estates, and according to the written ordinance and assurance which is now forthwith to be drawn up'.[1]

How much was there in this document that was really new? All the religious provisions, certainly: they constituted a limitation of the king's freedom of action in spirituals such as Sweden had not seen since the Reformation. The secular clauses, on the other hand, were less obviously innovating. The provision requiring the consent of 'those concerned' to taxation was really no more than an attempt to find a comprehensive formula to replace the outmoded provisions of the Land Law.[2] The clause debarring foreigners and low-born persons from office had appeared in Johan's coronation oath—and indeed, as far back as the Recess of Kalmar in 1483. So too had an undertaking not to make war or peace without the consent of the 'leading Estates'. This time, however, it was the assent of the Estates *tout court* that was specified, and the range of actions which were to be subject to their consent was so widely defined that it might be taken to include virtually every non-routine decision of the government. But it mattered little whether this clause or that had a precedent from some earlier occasion: what mattered was the implication of the document as a whole. It is clear that both in the Charter and the coronation oath a conscious effort was made to recur to the letter and the spirit of the Land Law. One cardinal principle of the Land Law was consent; and in 1594 that principle was not only stated more explicitly than ever before, but was given a wider ambit. Government by consent, the idea of the rule of law—these were the two ideas which for long had lain at the heart of Swedish political thinking, and it was these ideas which were embodied in the pledges which had now been extorted from the crown. Yet even this was not, perhaps, the most important aspect of Sigismund's defeat. What made 1594 a turning-point in Swedish constitutional history was the fact that a Charter had been secured before Sigismund's recognition as king. In some sense, it was a turning

[1] *Svenska riksdagsakter*, I, iii, 332.

[2] The Land Law provided that consent be sought from a jury of the province, consisting of the bishop, *lagman*, and six members each of the nobility and the peasantry; but it was now many years since such a body had met for this purpose.

backward; for the idea of a Charter was a fifteenth-century idea, now once more put into practice after the lapse of nearly a century. But whereas before 1523 the grant of a Charter as a precondition for coronation had been the distinguishing mark of electoral monarchy, it had now been engrafted upon the stock of hereditary succession. For the first time the principle had been established that a hereditary king was not less bound by the laws of the land than any other man. The victory of 1594 was a decisive precedent: from the accession of Gustav Adolf in 1611 to that moment when Karl XI came of age in 1672, every Swedish sovereign would recognize the obligation to give an Accession Charter to his people. Sigismund was quite right to feel that it was an innovation of crucial importance. From his own point of view it was plainly unconstitutional. But Erik Sparre was no less right in his belief that it revived a sound constitutional tradition. What Sigismund saw as innovation, Sparre saw as restoration: in 1594, as on other critical occasions in Swedish history, a revolutionary change was made easy by relating it to an already-existing constitutional norm. And the revival of the Charter as a check upon the crown had been made possible by the rehabilitation of another piece of constitutional machinery which had grown rusty in the half-century after 1523. The *råd*, impelled by its unhappy experiences under Erik and Johan, had once more resumed its traditional function as the guardian of the nation's liberties, the mediator between crown and people—and, it might be, as the ephorate in whom alone inhered the right of resistance to tyranny. It was not surprising that the monarchy should look on this resurrection with foreboding, and foresee the return of an oligarchy which would make the crown its tool—if indeed it permitted kingship to survive at all.

The constitutional theories which lay behind the Charter had been memorably expounded by Erik Sparre in the weeks immediately before the coronation. The Nobility, like the Clergy before them, had seized the favourable opportunity to draw up a list of *Postulata*; and when these were presented to the king they were prefaced by a lengthy and magnificent oration, in which Sparre developed, with eloquence and learning,[1] those views on the nature of the state which he had already adumbrated in *Pro Lege, Rege et Grege*. Reduced to its essentials, the Oration is really a plea for the rule of law. Justice, he says, is the basis of monarchy; a king's reputation rests on the law's authority; his liberty is to deal justly, his freedom of action exists only within the law's bounds. And this limitation (which to the just king is no limitation at all) applies with peculiar force to hereditary monarchs, for they are bound by an obligation additional to those which bind kings who are elected:

[1] Among the authorities to which Sparre appealed were Hesiod, Seneca, the Bible, Claudian, Alfonso of Aragon, the Salic Law, and English history generally.

the obligation of gratitude for the benefit conferred upon them by their subjects in permitting hereditary succession. Absolutism above the law has no place in the well-ordered state; the king *legibus solutus* is unknown to Swedish history; the examples of the kings of France, England, Scotland and Bohemia enforce the argument that hereditary monarchy is below, not above, the law. But it is no puppet king that he desires, nor does he claim for other elements in society more than their just share: the ideal of monarchy, after all, is *rex non pictus, neque fictus, sed legibus addictus*.

The *Postulata*, to which Sparre's Oration provided the introduction, made constitutional demands similar to those embodied in the Charter. But in at least one respect they showed a significant variation. They asked 'that no other statutes or ordinances be enjoined, than those which are agreed and accepted with the *unanimous* unconstrained free will of all the Estates, and are properly negotiated and resolved upon *in each province*'.[1] The final words, suggesting as they do the retention of the older practice of local negotiation and decentralized assent, side by side with the newer practice of taking the assent of the *riksdag* as committing the nation, is probably to be regarded as the first indication that Sparre was no longer so ready to pin his faith on the *riksdag* as he had been ten years before. The experience of 1590, reviving painful memories of 1567, had shown how easily the Estates could become the subservient instruments of the crown; and perhaps the spectacle of Karl's use of the Peasantry at Uppsala may have reinforced such impressions. Certainly these doubts and misgivings were to be confirmed, over and over again, in the years that lay immediately ahead. The lower Estates—and particularly the Peasants—were too ignorant, too dependent, too anxious to get the business finished and go home, to be a reliable check upon an unscrupulous popular ruler who was able to play upon their loyalty and their prejudices. Experience was very soon to convince aristocratic constitutionalists that the cause of liberty was not safe in such hands. When Erik Sparre wrote *Pro Lege, Rege et Grege* it had seemed to him that the best road to limited monarchy lay through parliamentary control. By 1594 he was not so sure of it; by 1600 he would have the best possible reason for believing the exact opposite. The history of the years after 1594 would force him to the conclusion that parliamentary proceedings, so far from safeguarding legality, offered dangerous facilities for its betrayal. The effect of this realization would be to ruin the cause for which Sparre stood by divorcing the *råd* from the nation. Isolated, fatally obnoxious to misrepresentation, they would be made to appear not as the champions of the constitution but as men who were prepared for their own advantage to

[1] *Svenska riksdagsakter*, I, iii, 402; my italics.

desert the cause of the nation and of religion. In this collapse of his constitutional ideals, in this enforced alienation from the *riksdag*, lay the tragedy of Erik Sparre's career.

The other new feature of the *Postulata* was the insistence on unanimity. It was a principle not wholly unfamiliar in Swedish history: it had underlain the confederations (*sammansvärjningar*) of the time of Sten Sture the younger, and would soon be invoked against the *råd* itself by Karl. But as an ordinary precondition for valid consent it was less Swedish than Polish. Sigismund accused Sparre and his colleagues of borrowing Polish political ideas, and this requirement of unanimity suggests that he may have been right. Such ideas were certainly present in a constitutional project, generally ascribed to Axel Leijonhufvud, which seems to date from 1593, and which included, among many other anti-monarchical features, the legalization of the right of rebellion. It had little influence, and no discernible effect; but it was not without significance as an indication of trends of thought in at least some sections of the high aristocracy.

The *Postulata*, apart from its proposals for restraining the arbitrary actions of the crown, contained provisions designed to make government more efficient. The administrative reforms which the *råd* had urged in the eighties were now revived: it was expressly demanded that the relevant arrangements in the Statute of Kalmar be put in force. And this implied, of course, the entrusting of the major offices of government to the hands of the aristocracy. If in its constitutional ideals the *Postulata* looks back to the fifteenth century, the same is true of its claims for the position of the nobility in the state. To men like Hogenskild Bielke, less interested in constitutional questions than in the privileges of his order, the period of the Union was a Golden Age which might not, even yet, be quite beyond recall. The *Postulata* accordingly contained not only demands for a noble monopoly of high office, proper definition of administrative functions, prompt payment of *beställningar* according to fixed scales, and so forth; it contained also extravagant claims of privilege which, if granted, would have relieved the nobility of a great part of the burdens of society, and would have left their peasants wholly to the jurisdiction of their lords. Yet to Bielke, with his eyes always on the fifteenth century, it seemed that they were asking only for the restoration of what they had lost since 1523. In a remarkable letter to his brother in June 1593 he gave his view of what had happened: 'King Gustav degraded the Estate of Nobles, which was the foremost in the kingdom, and all the seniors of the *råd* were executed by that bloodhound King Kristian. Ture Jönsson fled . . . After that there were not many left who dared to say a word against it [*sc.* royal tyranny], . . . and so liberty declined the one year after the other, so that it came to be clean forgot what the old freedom had been, and no one cared to look into it and consult old documents, and such as were found in cathedrals and monasteries were all confiscated and kept hidden from others, so that they might not come to the eyes of those whom they most concerned.'[1] The ordinary nobleman, less familiar with the archival material than Hogenskild Bielke, was being educated by him into thinking that his forefathers had been the victims of royal oppression, or somehow cheated of what was rightly theirs: in their memorial to the *råd* on 30 November 1593 the Nobility had written: 'and since there are very few of us who have any knowledge of our ancient liberties, we ask the *råd* to give us what information they have about them, since we in some sort understand that our ancestors were a very free people, above all others, which now (God amend it) is greatly altered.'[2] Even Erik Sparre, among the more serious matter of his Oration, could not neglect the opportunity for inserting a long lament over the decay of his order: 'Where is the great treasure, which could indeed be reckoned at many millions, which existed when King Gustav died? It is all consumed. Where is now the rich and powerful nobility, the ornament and glory of the kingdom, which aforetime could ride in its hundreds to court, to the service and honour of king and country? They too are seen no more: a great part are fallen upon the edge of the sword during so many years against so many and various enemies; some has the aforesaid tyrant [Erik XIV] persecuted and done to death; and they who survive are much impoverished.'[3] And from his argument about the obligations of hereditary monarchs he drew not only constitutional implications, but also the practical conclusion that 'if elective monarchs, who are transient, give good privileges, hereditary monarchs, who are eternal, should give better'. Thus at a moment when Karl was justly suspected of aspiring to re-enact the career of Sten Sture, the aristocracy revived the spirit of Kalmar Recess: for Sigismund, apparently, there remained nothing but the deplorable role of Union king.

The coronation oath, the Charter, the Oration, the *Postulata*, together form the climax of the great revival of aristocratic constitutionalism which had been gathering head since 1567. But the *Postulata* also marks the beginning of the turning of the tide. Preoccupied with the desperate struggle for the Charter, the Nobility (and the Clergy too) had neglected to wrest from the king, before his coronation, his assent to the demands of their order. After that ceremony it was no longer possible to blackmail him into acceptance of pretensions so extreme. Sigismund did indeed give a general promise, as part of his coronation

[1] *Handlingar rörande Skandinaviens historia*, viii, 56.
[2] *Svenska riksdagsakter*, I, iii, 178. [3] *Ibid.* I, iii, 382.

oath, to confirm all *former* privileges; but by that he did not mean what Hogenskild Bielke meant. Hogenskild Bielke had in mind the good old times of Kristoffer of Bavaria or Kristian I; Sigismund meant no more than the privileges of 1569, or at worst of 1590. And in this matter, at least, Sigismund could count on the support of Karl; for Karl was quite as hostile as his nephew to all such claims, and seems to have gone out of his way to advise Sigismund not to accede to them. Thus encouraged, the king contrived to avoid taking any action at all on the demands of the Clergy; Erik Sparre's *Postulata* were quietly pigeonholed; and the only fruit of the Nobility's efforts was a grant of privileges—left behind in the chancery when Sigismund departed, and subsequently unearthed by the *råd*—which left matters virtually unchanged, and totally ignored all the constructive proposals which the *Postulata* had put forward.

The great question still remaining to be settled was that of the powers and constitution of the government which was to exercise the royal authority after the king's return to Warsaw. In the Charter Sigismund had promised that after consultation with Karl and the *råd* he would issue a written Ordinance of Government; and in the spring and early summer of 1594 discussions did indeed take place between them. Karl's attitude was that there was really no problem, or any real need for an Ordinance: his position in the royal family made it natural that he should be regent with full powers; though he would of course rule, as the king did, with the council's counsel. But he recognized that such an arrangement might be unpalatable to Erik Sparre; and it was probably in an effort to sugar the pill that in his draft for an Ordinance of Government he included concessions to the aristocracy's plans for administrative reform. For the *råd*, on the other hand, the problem was delicate and difficult. They foresaw very clearly that in any government which included Karl they were in danger of being pushed into a subordinate position, and they had no wish to curb the king's power of interference in order to benefit the duke. They still hoped, moreover, to be able to introduce administrative arrangements of the type provided for in the Statute of Kalmar—to which, after all, Sigismund had once agreed. Their proposal was therefore for a joint government with limited powers. It would be debarred, for instance, from taking decisions on foreign policy, and forbidden to legislate, or tax, or grant *förläningar*, without the king's approval; the commanders in the more important castles would be irremovable during good behaviour; letters of protection issued by the king would be respected 'if not contrary to law'. Foreseeing the probability of friction with the duke, they provided that no member of the government should take individual action independently of his colleagues; and proposed that any irreconcilable dispute between them be referred to the arbitration of 'the leading Estates'. To this draft they appended a scheme of administrative reorganization more precise than any that they had hitherto brought forward: it included a plan for recruiting young members of the nobility to junior posts in the chancery (and hence safeguarding the country against the 'rule of secretaries'), the creation of seven *landshövdingar*, the tying of salaries to posts rather than to persons, and the establishment of numerous new offices in the central government, all restricted to members of the aristocracy.

Sigismund might have been wise to accept these proposals. They preserved the essentials of his authority. They went far to neutralize Karl's potentialities for mischief. They could hardly have failed to lead to quarrels between Karl and the *råd* which could only have been to the crown's advantage. But Sigismund was no more anxious to put himself in the hands of the *råd* than he was prepared to abdicate his sovereignty in favour of the duke. His immediate concern was to play off one against the other until he had made sure of his return to Poland. Disquieting rumours that his departure might be prevented by force had led him to send urgently to Poland for troops and a fleet: until their arrival should put him in a stronger bargaining position it was his policy to defer a decision. The *råd* meanwhile was beginning to feel itself increasingly isolated. Its proposals for the government made no impression. There were alarming indications that Sigismund might try to come to an understanding with his uncle. In June, the arrival of the Polish fleet, with 1,500 troops on board, secured Sigismund's line of retreat. At the beginning of July his departure was clearly imminent. And still no settlement had been reached. In their anxiety lest the country might after all be left in Karl's charge the *råd* made a final offer. In return for keeping Karl grouped, they were prepared to make substantial abatements from their earlier proposals: none of Sigismund's appointees should be removed from office without informing him in advance; no one was to be denied the right to communicate directly with the king; the whole plan for aristocratic administrative reform was tacitly abandoned. All they asked was that Karl should be only one element in a joint government, the members of which were to meet and report twice a year; that two members of the *råd* should always be in attendance on him; and that no member of the government should act independently of his colleagues.

But it was now too late. Sigismund was by this time in a position to avoid a choice between Karl and the *råd* altogether. The Ordinance of Government which he promulgated soon afterwards made Karl and the *råd* collectively regents; but it circumscribed their powers in such a way that they were left with little more than routine business under their control. The king's letters of protection were to have absolute validity; no officer appointed by Sigismund was to be removed without his leave; the principal castles in the country were to be held by commanders responsible directly to him, who were forbidden to admit anybody to these strongholds (even members of the government) without his permission. It was now clear what Sigismund was after: while the two elements in the central government effectively prevented each other from doing anything important, he would retain control of Sweden—if necessary, in the government's despite—through command of strategic key-points, and through a select body of officials whom he could trust: the example of Klas Fleming in Finland had shown the way. In July he proceeded to appoint some of them: Arvid Gustavsson Stenbock was made *ståthållare* of Östergötland; his brother, Erik, *ståthållare* of Västergötland; Erik Brahe, *ståthållare* of Stockholm, Uppland and Norrland. Brahe was an avowed Roman Catholic; and the Stenbock brothers both gave undertakings to put no obstacle in the way of Roman Catholic services. Granting that it was impracticable to rule Sweden directly from Warsaw, Sigismund had by these arrangements at least assured himself that he would be able to intervene at any time to thwart the actions of the government in Stockholm. His solution was a central government checked by restrictions on its powers, and so counterbalanced by irremovable officials devoted to the royal interest that it would have little chance of developing a dangerous independence—even without allowing for the probability that Karl and the *råd* would not long pull well together. What he failed to foresee was the possibility that this solution—which to the Swedes must appear as no solution at all—might drive Karl and the *råd*, in their exasperation, into a renewal of their collaboration. What he unwisely ignored was the indignation which would inevitably be provoked by his flagrant violation of the Charter in appointing a Roman Catholic as *ståthållare*. If he had been able to find a team of sound Lutherans to rule his provinces and keep his castles, if he had not ostentatiously given his trust to such a universally unpopular person as Klas Fleming, his plan might have had some chance of succeeding. As it was, it was bound to run into trouble.

Neither Karl nor the *råd* was anxious to assume responsibility on these terms. But there was still the hope that their letters of appointment might be so drawn as to enlarge their authority to tolerable limits, and it was upon this that they now concentrated their efforts. Karl agreed in principle to act, declaring that he would hold himself responsible to 'God, His Majesty, and' (significant addition!) 'the Estates of the realm'; but he pressed the king to give him a commission styling him 'regent and *föreståndare*', with powers which would have destroyed the whole basis of Sigismund's carefully calculated arrangements. And he backed his appeal with an open threat: if Sigismund refused, he would refer the matter to the Estates, so that they might decide how they should be ruled. This was the last thing that Sigismund was prepared to tolerate: throughout all the discussions he had peremptorily refused to admit that the Estates had any say in the matter. In any case, he had already embarked, and only waited for a wind to carry him to Danzig. His reply to Karl made some verbal concessions: he was now styled 'hereditary prince of the realm' and 'leading personage'; but in essentials it gave him powers more restricted than ever: he was authorized to govern the kingdom together with the *råd* by joint *and unanimous* resolution; all legislation was forbidden, unless with Sigismund's previous consent; and he was explicitly prohibited from summoning the Estates in the king's absence. Since Karl's tactics were to appeal to the *riksdag*, Sigismund countered them in advance by declaring that any such appeal was unlawful. Here, in a nutshell, lay the seeds of civil war. To this communication Karl returned a vigorous protest. Sigismund did not tarry to receive it: on 4 August he took the wind of opportunity and sailed away for Poland. By lingering in Sweden he would perhaps have risked his throne in Warsaw; by returning to Poland he certainly jeopardized his future in Stockholm.

III. KARL AND THE RÅD, 1594–7

As the members of the *råd* watched Sigismund's fleet making sail through the southern skerries, they might well feel not only exasperation but anxiety for the future. They were saddled with the burden of government in conjunction with a prince from whom they had little reason to expect an easy collaboration; they were left to run a country with powers inadequate for running it. Peace with the Russians was still uncertain; the finances were in poor shape; but they could not raise taxes in an emergency without reference to Warsaw—a delay which might well prove disastrous. In Sweden were royal *ståthållare* independent of their control, whose orders were unknown to them and whose powers had not been revealed; in Finland their old enemy Klas Fleming was both *ståthållare* and commander-in-chief. Somehow or other they must contrive to provide Sweden with a government; but the question was whether any tolerable arrangement could be devised without disobeying the king's commands. From the beginning this problem was insoluble, as perhaps Karl already saw: it was the tragedy of the *råd* that they did not realize it until too late.

It was at all events quite certain that there could be no government at all if they quarrelled with Karl. The immediate necessity, therefore, was to come to some understanding with him about the future. In the middle of August, at their earnest request, he came to Stockholm to discuss what was to be done; on 2 September 1594, after very difficult negotiations, they were able to formulate an agreement which took the form of an exchange of pledges of reciprocal support. In order to obtain it, the *råd* were forced to make one vital concession: the recognition of Karl as sole *riksföreståndare* and head of the government. This they justified by stating (what was certainly untrue) that Sigismund had asked Karl to act for him, and had appointed them to assist him. On the other hand, they did their best to protect themselves by various safeguards: Karl's status as *riksföreståndare* was to be subject to Sigismund's approval; their 'oath, fealty and obedience' to the king were explicitly reserved; they were described as representing the king 'next to *and with*' the duke; their right to give counsel without incurring his displeasure was explicitly admitted; above all it was clearly laid down that he was to rule, not only 'with the council's counsel', but with their consent.[1] On these terms they bound themselves, now and in the future, to 'stand by and defend' the actions of the regency, 'all for one, and one for all'.

It might seem that the *råd* had not done badly. Sigismund's authority was formally preserved; their loyalty to the crown was emphasized; Karl was grouped in a balanced government of the kind that Sigismund had intended. But there was no getting over the fact that they had directly disobeyed the king's orders in accepting Karl as sole regent; and the offence was not made less by their submitting the arrangement for ratification to the handful of nobles and clergy who happened to be in Stockholm at the time. Both Karl and the *råd* felt the need to write to the king, explaining and excusing what had been done. The *råd*, with many apologies, adduced as their main reason Karl's refusal to serve in the government on any other terms; Karl, with no apologies at all, complained of the 'other governments' in the country, justified his action by the inadequacy of the powers Sigismund had conferred on him, and again demanded an ampler commission. And once more he threatened that if he did not receive it he would refer the matter to the *riksdag*. He may well have hoped that Sigismund would give way: his marvellous capacity for believing that what he wanted was morally and legally correct may well have fostered that hope. But the full powers which he desired would have made him regent in a very different sense

[1] 'And inasmuch as His Grace has promised that in the affairs of the nation, spiritual or lay, he will undertake nothing, nor take any private determination, without our faithful advice and consent, and that it shall be free and lawful for us to speak and advise without incurring displeasure . . .': *Svenska riksdagsakter*, I, iii, 500.

from that in which he now held the office: there was a wide difference between the government by consent to which he had now pledged himself, and the quasi-monarchical government *med råds råde* to which he aspired. What Erik Sparre hoped might be a permanent basis, a viable compromise, was for Karl a means to coerce his nephew, or a *pis-aller* to be discarded as opportunity might offer. He was careful in his letter to Sigismund to make the point that he had accepted the government at the earnest solicitation of the Estates: this is the embryonic stage of a tactic which would serve him well in the future. As justification for illegal actions he would adduce the popular will; individual guilt would be discreetly merged in corporate responsibility; a personal ambition would assume the aspect of a national cause. Erik Sparre and his associates were soon to experience the effectiveness of these devices. Appeal to the *riksdag*, they would find, could be a weapon against themselves as well as against the king; a popular assembly was as liable to endorse unconstitutional procedures as to condemn them: it was a disillusioning discovery.

Meanwhile the common front of January 1593 had to all appearances been renewed. Measures were taken to explain to the country what had happened; the commonalty were informed, with considerable *suppressio veri et suggestio falsi*, that Sigismund had invited Karl, as senior hereditary prince, to undertake the government. In defiance of the king's prohibition, negotiations for a tax were opened on a provincial basis; the inhabitants of the duchy were notified that Karl, rather than Sigismund, would dispense justice on appeal. Two problems, apart from finance, engaged the regency's immediate attention. One was religion; the other was Klas Fleming. As to religion, the bad impression made by the appointment of Erik Brahe (and of some other Swedish Roman Catholics to posts about the king's person) had been reinforced by Sigismund's provision for the holding of Roman Catholic services after his departure at Drottningholm, and at a house in Stockholm. The *råd* remonstrated with the king about this, and Angermannus complained to the regency. At a church synod held in February 1595 there were demands for trenchant action against Vadstena, and a more vigorous application of the Uppsala resolutions against semi-popish ceremonies. The regency, however, behaved with notable moderation. Karl was so little worried about Erik Brahe that in September 1594 he had provisionally recognized his appointment as *ståthållare*.[1] There is no sign that Brahe ever made any attempt to advance the Catholic cause; and in any case he discreetly resigned his office in the spring of 1595. The obnoxious Roman Catholic services stopped at the same

[1] Brahe probably owed his appointment quite as much to his position as premier nobleman as to his religion.

time. The danger from Catholicism, in fact, was for the moment obviously so small that even Karl could recommend patience in dealing with Vadstena; while as to elevation and other controversial ceremonies, they were still too rooted in custom simply to be abolished out of hand. Karl and the *råd* told the zealots that they were not prepared to risk popular disturbances by taking precipitate action. The only one of the clergy's requests to which any attention was paid concerned the university, which in February 1595 was granted privileges and endowments—a step which the regency was probably not competent to take. Not until the crisis of the summer would Karl feel the expediency of courting the clergy's support by beating the Protestant drum.

The difficulty with Klas Fleming was both more intractable and more dangerous. Apart from all personal animosities, it was natural that all the members of the regency should feel particular concern about Finland. Its isolation made it an especially suitable area for Sigismund's policy of remote control, and the character and ability of Fleming made him a more formidable rival to the Stockholm government than Erik Brahe or the Stenbocks. The regency could not possibly acquiesce in a situation which deprived it of any influence in an area which was an actual theatre of war, and which might well continue to be so, if the truce-negotiations broke down. Yet Fleming was now established in Åbo with a commission which made him virtually independent of any but the king's authority. It was an appointment bitterly resented in Sweden. One of the earliest acts of Karl and the *råd*—unanimous in this at least—was to summon him to Stockholm to swear fidelity to the regency: they seem also to have intended to deprive him of his command. But Fleming, who had no intention of taking orders from them, returned a rough answer; and the regent did not venture to press the point while the negotiations with the Russians remained in the balance. With the conclusion of the peace of Teusina on 18 May 1595, however, these prudential considerations ceased to operate. For some months Karl and Fleming had been engaged in acrimonious correspondence about finance. Fleming had latterly been using the local revenue in butter to pay his troops—as he was fully entitled to do, for he had been given specific authority for it by Sigismund himself. Karl, who at first was unaware of this circumstance, accused him of appropriating part of the king's revenue to his private purposes, and insisted that it must be paid over to the bailiffs, be properly accounted for, and be applied to maintain the troops only after official authorization. Fleming's army resented this as an attempt to deprive them of their pay, and in consequence became disaffected to the Stockholm government. Thus the situation which Karl and the *råd* had most feared—an independent commander in Finland, hostile to themselves, and with an army devoted to his service—had been brought nearer by the very measures which had been designed to prevent it.

At midsummer 1595 Karl received Sigismund's reply to his letter of 17 September: the delay is a good example of that habit of procrastination which was the despair of those who had to deal with him. The answer was none the sweeter for keeping. Sigismund refused to amend the powers given to his uncle, and plainly told him that if he persuaded the Estates to do so his action would be null and void. Karl had now no hope of obtaining what he wanted by legal means; no hope, therefore, of being given an authority which would permit him to bring Klas Fleming to heel. He was alarmed and angered by reports that Sigismund projected a marriage between his sister Anna and John George of Brandenburg, with the idea of making John George (a Lutheran) regent of Sweden. The reports were true, though the project had not as yet advanced very far; and they may have helped to determine Karl's course of action: if he were to safeguard what he considered to be his rights, he could no longer afford to be too tender of the king's prerogative.

In July 1595, therefore, he called the *råd* to a meeting in Stockholm. He reported Sigismund's answer, informed them of his intention to defy it by summoning a full *riksdag* at Michaelmas, and threatened that if they did not concur in the summons he would resign the government until the *riksdag* should meet. He bitterly attacked the *råd* for their failure to give him adequate support in his dealings with Klas Fleming —a failure which he regarded as a breach of the agreement between them; he is said even to have threatened to drag them bound before the *riksdag* for trial. The *råd* was at no loss for a reply. Even if it were admitted that his commission from the king left something to be desired, that was no reason for an act of defiance: Karl had carried on the government before Sigismund's arrival without any commission at all. It was intolerable that they should be accused of violating their undertaking to him simply because they happened not to agree with his opinion. What became of his promise to rule with their consent? What of his guarantee that they should be free to give their opinion without fear of the consequences? As to Fleming (whom they certainly disliked as much as he did), it was unfortunately the case that he had Sigismund's authority for appropriating the butter-revenue, and it was vain to suppose that he would pay any attention to thunderbolts from Stockholm. This was the language of reason. But they were dealing with a man who could now gain his ends only by turning his back upon reason. Karl was struggling to give to his conduct some show of legality while enlarging an authority dubiously acquired, and his need for self-justification forced him to believe in the malignity and bad faith of those who were unimpressed by his arguments. On such a character their temperate representations impinged feebly and left no trace. He was a stronger personality and an astuter politician than any of them; he meant to have his way. They soon realized this. And since, if there must be a *riksdag* whether they would or no, it was clearly better that Karl be not left to do what he liked with it, they at last reluctantly surrendered. The Estates should meet at Söderköping in September, as Karl desired: it would be their task to prevent him from rushing them into desperate measures.

There was something to be said for this policy, as subsequent events were to show. It at least preserved the *façade* of a national government. To permit an open breach with Karl would be to play Sigismund's game, if indeed it did not prove the prelude to administrative anarchy and even civil war. It was not difficult to foresee what Karl might do with a *riksdag* if he were able to confront it as the only remaining authority in the country: his threat of resignation, so ominously reminiscent of his father, was a pointer to the kind of pressure he would be able to bring to bear. But the fact remained that by capitulating to Karl they had for a second time broken their oath as subjects and as councillors. In 1593 they had refused to consent to a *riksdag* in the king's absence: in 1595 they found specious reasons for agreeing to it. They had not now the excuse of real necessity which they could plausibly adduce in mitigation of their actions in the previous September. They were deliberately flouting a reiterated prohibition for the sake of keeping their government together: the first illegality entailed the second, the second would soon exact a third; nor was there any limit to the series short of rebellion, as long as Karl could coerce them to follow him by a threat to abdicate and appeal to *Herr Omnes*. They did not like *Herr Omnes*, least of all in politics. Sooner than that, sooner than Sigismund's remote control, they would stick to Karl and the agreement of September 1594. But to Sigismund it could not but seem that though they might save their government, they failed to save their honour.

The *riksdag* assembled at Söderköping on 29 September 1595. The three lower Estates, and especially that of the Peasants, were more numerously represented than usual: it was among them that Karl hoped to find his supporters. The Nobility, on the other hand, made a poor showing: a bare hundred seem to have put in an appearance. Karl had prepared an elaborate agenda of 87 items, covering almost every aspect of government from the problems of foreign policy to the protection of sea-bird's eggs; and this had been sent to Sigismund for his comments. No word, however, came from that taciturn monarch, either for praise or blame. After a week's delay, therefore, proceedings began with an address from Karl to a joint session of all the Estates. He confronted them at once with an ultimatum: he must have, and must be seen to have, supreme authority, or he would resign the government; all Roman Catholics, clerical or lay, with their aiders and abettors, must quit the country within six weeks; Klas Fleming and the Stenbocks must be summoned for trial by the Estates. These shock-tactics were at first successful: the lower Estates assented by acclamation; the misgivings of the others were unheard. But when he came to develop his demands in a formal Proposition, when the Estates had leisure to consider their written replies, it was a very different story. His Proposition asked them to accord him the title of *riksföreståndare*, with the right to appoint to all offices in the kingdom; it proposed that any orders from Sigismund be scrutinized and approved by himself and the *råd* before promulgation, and that judicial appeals to the king be forbidden; it demanded that all those who had absented themselves from the *riksdag*, or who should decline to conform to its Resolution, should be punished; and it requested that the Estates consider what compensation could be made to him for his trouble and out-of-pocket expenses in conducting the government. There was also an indication of the crimes with which Sigismund's *ståthållare* were to be charged: they had separated themselves, it appeared, from previous decisions of the Estates; they had tried to poison Sigismund's mind against Karl; they had set themselves up as more loyal subjects than anybody else, and as a result had obtained from the king on false pretences powers which were hurtful to the country and to their own consciences, 'if they have any'.

The replies which the Estates made to these representations revealed the latent differences of opinion among them. The Nobility, after four attempts, were unable to produce an answer favourable to Karl in any single point; the Clergy's answer was so hedged with reservations that it could hardly be palatable; Stockholm (which sent in a reply of its own) returned what was in fact a blank negative. On the other hand, the Peasants assented without hesitation to everything that was offered, adding on their own account the suggestion that Karl should be compensated by the confiscation of 'useless' *förläningar*—the first foreshadowing of what a later age would call *reduktion*; and the towns other than Stockholm on the whole supported his proposals. At this point Archbishop Angermannus took the initiative. It seemed to him a matter of prime importance that in this crisis the *riksdag* should speak with a single voice. The oath of fidelity he had sworn to Sigismund eighteen months before lay heavy on his conscience; only the need to defend Sweden against the danger from Catholicism could have carried him thus far in disobedience to his sovereign. He was persuaded that the safety of the church could be secure only as long as there was a united government: the alliance of duke, *råd* and clergy, which had wrested the Charter from the king, must not be suffered to disintegrate. Any decision of the *riksdag* must be taken in the context of the agreement between Karl and the *råd* which for the past year had stood between the country and anarchy. From the point of view of the *råd*, too, this was now the best policy available to them. They were neither able nor willing to run the country themselves, with Karl menacing them on the one side and Fleming on the other. They were horrified at the reckless violence of the duke's demands, and perturbed by his courting of the Peasantry: they would not leave him in sole charge of the government if they could help it.

With the assistance of *råd*, Nobility and Clergy, Angermannus was therefore able to produce a joint answer to Karl's proposals, which was delivered to him on 17 October. It accepted some of the most important of them: Karl should be entitled *riksföreståndare*; he should have the right to appoint to vacant offices; there were to be no appeals to Warsaw; the king's commands must be filtered in Stockholm before they could be binding; Roman Catholic priests must quit the country within six weeks. But against these concessions—which they probably considered as indispensable to orderly government—there were rebuffs, reservations and stipulations in such number that from Karl's point of view their complaisances lost all value. Thus, though they agreed to recognize him as *riksföreståndare*, they insisted that their recognition should be saving the sovereign authority of the king, and in accordance with the agreement between himself and the *råd* of 2 September 1594. The former reservation Karl might swallow as only decent; the latter dragged him back to the partnership from which he was trying to escape. Though they agreed that Roman Catholic priests must depart, they rejected Karl's proposal for expelling Roman Catholic laymen and the aiders and abettors of popery [*sc.* Sigismund's *ståthållare*]: such persons were to be tolerated if they made no trouble. They took care to specify that Karl must exercise his authority, not only with his council's counsel, but with its consent. They reminded him that he must govern by the law of the land: Sigismund's officials, for instance, were not to be removed until convicted in a court of law. But although they would have nothing to say to his demand for vengeance upon political dissenters and absent parliamentarians, they offered him instead what appeared to be an acceptable substitute: they suggested that all those who *in future* should dissociate themselves from the decisions of *this* meeting should be regarded as 'unruly and lopped-off members' of the body politic, and that efforts should be made 'by lawful and proper means' to abridge the authority of such of them as held office. To Karl, no doubt, this seemed to promise a free hand against Fleming and the Stenbocks; and Sparre and Angermannus perhaps hoped that it might placate him. But they intended it, not as a blow against the *ståthållare*, but as the basis for a national rally round the pact of 2 September 1594: the nation was to endorse the arrangement whereby the *råd* was hung round Karl's neck. To all appearances, it was a winning hazard. But they failed to take into account the duke's ability (and readiness) to pot his opponent's ball.

For the moment, Sparre and Angermannus carried all before them. The Resolution of 22 October was in substance the affirmation of the joint reply. In one particular it was even more restrictive, for at the last minute Sparre slipped in a clause which limited Karl's authority to the period of Sigismund's absence: it was a shrewd thrust which Karl did not forgive. Moreover, in return for the acknowledgment of his position as head of the government, he gave two important undertakings: he renewed his promise not to victimize the *råd* because of a difference of opinion; he bound himself to take no important step without their consent. The clause about political proscriptions was incorporated into Karl's declaration, with a slight but significant change of wording. Karl engaged to treat those who would not 'make one with us' as 'unruly and lopped-off members', and if they were office-holders promised to abridge their authority 'by such lawful and proper means . . . as we may *collectively* find appropriate and reasonable'; and a separate category was now created for those who might *defect* from the Resolution, or actively work against it: such persons, if they used violence (but apparently only then), were to be held for 'unrighteous, rebellious and unfaithful men, and destroyers of their country', and Karl would help to 'resist and pursue' them.[1]

Such was the famous Resolution of Söderköping. Despite his initial advantage, Karl had gained little or nothing from the *riksdag*. His title had been recognized by a fuller assembly than that of 1594; but for the rest he remained no more than the leading member of a collaborative *régime*. It was a check, rather than a victory. In the next eighteen months the meaning of the Resolution—and particularly the intention of the punitive clauses—would become a matter of sharp dispute; but originally there can be little doubt that it was designed to range the nation behind the arrangements of September 1594. All over the country meetings were held to declare adhesion to it: the religious

[1] Perhaps because the original idea for this vital clause had come from Karl, it appeared in the Resolution in the form of an undertaking given by him alone. In the sequel, it was accepted without question as binding all participants.

covenant of Uppsala, it seemed, was to be completed by the political covenant of Söderköping.

Sparre and Angermannus had scarcely time to congratulate themselves on their success before they were brought face to face with reality by the arrival on 4 November of a letter from the king, prohibiting the holding of a *riksdag* and declaring its proceedings illegal if it should already have been held. The *råd*, it seems, had been rash enough to take Sigismund's prolonged silence for acquiescence. The shock of his letter for a moment braced them to undertake the experiment of action. They now joined Karl in declaring Arvid Stenbock deprived of his office: he took no notice, it is true, but at least they could feel that they had made a beginning in the lopping-off process. They concurred in finally dissolving the nunnery at Vadstena.[1] They made no protest when Karl high-handedly sequestered Karl Stenbock's *förläningar*. But further than that their brief collaboration with the regent did not go. They had undoubtedly been badly shaken by the implications of Sigismund's letter for themselves; and they began to consider how they should answer for their conduct when next he should return to his hereditary kingdom: there were strong rumours that the event would not long be delayed. They shrank from adding to the score of their offences by tackling the one problem which to Karl now seemed all-important: the problem of Klas Fleming. Their attitude in this matter was to him the acid test of their sincerity at Söderköping. If Fleming were allowed to continue to ignore their orders, the 'lopped-off' clause stood revealed as a political fraud.

Fleming had dissuaded all but a handful of Finns from attending at Söderköping; he had protested against the Resolution. He had therefore put himself within reach of its punitive clauses, and Karl was determined that they should be applied. This, however, was not easy. In vain he attempted to induce the Finnish Estates to adhere formally to the Söderköping Resolution; in vain he tried to tempt the Finnish troops to desert their commander. Fleming was too strong to be shaken. He had an army of 5000 men at free quarters upon the country; in February 1596 he received from Sigismund a new commission authorizing him to resist—by force if need be—any attempt to curtail the royal authority. Thus buttressed, materially and morally, he snapped his fingers at his enemies in Sweden, and dealt ruthlessly with his opponents in Finland. Those who had been at Söderköping were victimized when they returned home. Peasants who had ventured to complain to Karl about their sufferings were savagely punished; and Fleming's hungry troops committed atrocities upon them of a less official nature. Sigismund was compromised by his association with this

[1] Karl urged the nuns to turn Protestant.

reign of terror; while Karl appeared (and took care to appear) as the peasant's friend.

As to the *råd*, in their private correspondence they did not conceal their disapproval of Fleming's doings—not least because of their disruptive effects in Sweden. Unless the *råd* coöperated with Karl in Fleming's suppression, they could hardly hope to preserve the joint government which they had established at Söderköping. But however much they might try to persuade themselves that Fleming was exceeding his instructions, and that Sigismund would disavow him when he learnt the truth, they were gradually forced to face the fact that any attack on Fleming would be regarded as levying war against the king. Karl, with his fearless realism, saw this long before they did, and did not flinch from the consequences. He did not believe that such an attack could make Sigismund any angrier than he was already: if the joint government firmly applied the Söderköping Resolution, he thought, the king would in the end give way. At no price would Karl tolerate two governments in one realm. If Fleming were allowed to go unpunished, his example would shortly be followed by Sigismund's *ståthållare* elsewhere: indeed, there was danger that Finland might be made the base for an assault on Sweden. His own conscience (as always) was perfectly clear: if the members of the *råd* professed that theirs were troubled, it could only be because they were disloyal to their obligations to him, and were plotting mischief.

It must be admitted that Karl was perfectly right in feeling that he had been getting less coöperation from his colleagues than he was entitled to expect: in the spring of 1596 the members of the *råd* found it convenient to have pressing business on their estates, and became noticeably shy of his invitations to confer. The only course of action which they seemed to be prepared to recommend was the sending of appeals to Sigismund to bring Fleming to book, and the despatch of emissaries to Finland to remonstrate—futilities of which Karl was entitled to be contemptuous. He had thus real reason for complaint; but as usual he spoilt his case by the extravagant and unbalanced nature of his reactions: his furious accusation that the *råd* were secretly in league with Fleming was both preposterous and unhelpful. And when he charged them with violating the Resolution of Söderköping by refusing to take military action against its opponents, they could make the unanswerable reply that the Resolution provided only for 'lawful and proper' action which had been agreed upon by all. By the summer of 1596 the issue between them had really narrowed down to a single point: the *råd* was not prepared to risk civil war, even for political objectives which it thought justifiable; while Karl had no such scruples.

Throughout July and August a correspondence of ever-increasing acrimony exhausted the patience and increased the resentment of both parties.[1] Karl had by now convinced himself that the Söderköping Resolution bound everyone to coöperate in enforcing it whenever he should call upon them to do so. Since the *råd* denied this, he could go on with them no longer. He threatened to take action against Fleming on his own account, whether the *råd* backed him or not; he even threatened to patch up an agreement with Sigismund and permit the imposition of Roman Catholicism on Sweden, provided that Protestantism were secured in the duchy: he was weary, he said, of twenty-six years of fraternal strife. And at last, on 17 August, he played his final card: he would resign the government, summon another meeting of the Estates, and explain to them the grounds for his decision. It was not difficult to foresee that his explanation would take the form of an indictment of the *råd*.

Thus the Resolution of Söderköping, which had been designed to maintain the joint government, had become the instrument whereby it was irrevocably broken. The *råd* could now make no concessions to save it; for they had at last realized that it could be preserved only on Karl's terms. And Karl's terms meant open rebellion. In the late summer of 1596 Sigismund bestirred himself to send two embassies to Sweden, whose instructions made the position unambiguously clear. Karl must either resign his position as *riksföreståndare*, or he must conform to the Ordinance of Government which Sigismund left behind him.[2] Any attack on Fleming would be regarded as an attack on the king himself. The *råd* in their reply (23 October) made a last attempt to fight on a constitutional line: it was not illegal, they contended, to summon a *riksdag* in the king's absence, if the king himself did not stick to his coronation oath. Karl for his part answered with a syllogism in the style of Erik XIV: 'That is a lawful assembly', he wrote, 'in which nothing is decided but what the law allows. Söderköping was such an assembly. Therefore it was lawful.' But these answers were really beside the point. It was not the legality of what had been done already that mattered now: what mattered was whether they were prepared to push their dissatisfaction with Sigismund's government to the point of revolt. Karl certainly was; the *råd*, no less certainly, was not.

In September a meeting of representatives of the upper Estates assembed in Stockholm in answer to Karl's summons. In the absence

[1] Hogenskild Bielke, who had already realized that it would be prudent to keep copies of all correspondence with Karl, grew weary at the labour involved: 'I hardly think', he wrote, 'that our ancestors in centuries wrote as much as we have done in our times.'

[2] This was the tenor of Sigismund's instructions; but his emissaries, frightened by the reception which Karl gave them, suppressed this point, and toned down the rest of the king's communication for fear of making the situation worse.

of his peasant supporters, however, it went badly for him from the beginning. The *råd* took care to leave the initiative in his hands: if there was to be a breach, the responsibility should not lie on them. They did indeed say (and may even have said truly) that they wished him to stay in the government; but they had no intention of acceding to his conditions. The Estates took the same line. They would not countenance a ruthless application of the Söderköping Resolution; they refused to agree to send a military expedition to Finland; nor would they approve the summoning of a full *riksdag* in the face of *råd*-opposition and royal veto. They showed no sign of being moved by Karl's reckless accusations against the *råd*, nor of capitulating to his menaces. This time the threat of abdication failed to bite. And when at last, on 29 October, Karl in a final message informed them that he would withdraw from the government, summon a *riksdag* to Arboga early next year, and to it submit his demands and his grievances, they received the communication with wounding stoicism. They pointed out that Erik Stenbock had intimated that he would be prepared to adhere to the Söderköping Resolution, and must be presumed to mean what he said; that Arvid Stenbock had already been deprived of office; that they had offered to write to Sigismund requesting him to remove Karl Stenbock from his post as *ståthållare* of Kalmar. If after all this the duke persisted in flouncing out of the government, they must 'leave things to God and time'. It was not what he had expected. It left him isolated from the politically responsible part of the nation, exposed to Sigismund's vengeance when he should return. Before that happened he must somehow secure some sort of legal sanction for his actions, some broader basis of support for his resistance to royal authority. The barely concealed hostility of the Stockholm meeting drove him to desperate measures. From the responsible part of the nation he turned to the irresponsible, from the prudent constitutionalism of the nobility to the ignorant partisanship of the 'grey multitude'. The appeal to a *riksdag* was an appeal to violence. It was an appeal to revolution.

Karl had never had the slightest intention of retiring into private life and leaving the *råd* as masters of the field. He soon let it be known that his withdrawal from the regency was to be considered only as provisional; he continued to interfere in administration: for the last two months of 1596 there were in fact two rival governments in the country. The Christmas season he spent in vigorous political campaigning in central Sweden, in preparation for the forthcoming *riksdag*. He was not over-nice in his methods. His open letter of 4 December deplored the expensiveness of an absentee sovereign, and blamed the *råd* for it: had they not deliberately engineered Sigismund's election 'for the desire and lust that they have to rule'? The old accusations of 1590, sprung from his resentment at the Statute of Kalmar, were refurbished, and so too were the alarmist stories of Roman Catholic designs: Sigismund's promises were part of a popish plot to sow dissension in the country; if the papists got the upper hand they would clap on heavy taxes in order to buy relics and rebuild the monasteries. The *riksdag*-summons accused the *råd* of sabotaging the Söderköping Resolution, and alleged that Sigismund's orders and commissions were disseminated by 'unruly spirits'. At the Uppsala market in January Karl's incendiary oratory against the *ståthållare* moved his audience to shout 'scrap the lot! chop their heads off!'. And all the time he was careful to make the point that the remedy for prevailing evils was the return of the king. It is quite possible that he really thought so. Carried away by his own propaganda, he may well have believed already (as he certainly believed later) that if only he could meet his nephew he would be able to convince him of the threat to the dynasty from the sinister designs of Erik Sparre. There would be a family reconciliation; the dynasty would close its ranks; and Sigismund, in gratitude for the defence of their common interests, would give him the ample powers that he desired. It was one of the few fantasies of an unimaginative man; and it died hard.

This torrent of unscrupulous denigration and inflammatory appeals was remarkably successful. The men of Dalarna declared that it was against the law to have two rulers in one land; provincial gatherings exchanged pledges of solidarity and messages of exhortation to stand fast for Duke Karl and the Protestant religion. Against this factitious excitement, nebulous patriotism, and smouldering class-hatred the *råd* could make little impression. In December some of them arranged a secret meeting in Stockholm with Angermannus to discuss tactics and organize resistance. It had little effect. The archbishop, deeply perturbed at the course of events, was already in touch with Sigismund; but his chapter was not behind him, and he was still uncertain whether even yet the best solution might not be to try to re-form the national front of 1594. Under strong pressure from Karl he eventually agreed to attend the market at Enköping, where the duke was holding a great political rally; and there he put his name to an appeal to other provinces to send representatives to the *riksdag*. It was the last time that duke and archbishop coöperated; but it deprived the *råd* of support on which they had been counting. Their only success was in the far south, where at a meeting of all classes at Växjö the province of Småland promised to support them, and offered them a place of refuge in the event of civil war.

If anything were lacking to complete the success of Karl's propaganda, it was furnished by the disastrous news which arrived from Finland in mid-January. Throughout the whole of 1596 the situation in that country had been building up to an explosion. Harvest failures, billeting of troops, outrages on the civilian population, the severities of Klas Fleming, had brought the peasantry to desperation. At the time of the meeting of the Estates in October 1596 Stockholm had been filled with refugees and petitioners from Österbotten. Karl made useful political capital out of their sufferings. His agents incited them to threaten that they would give themselves to the Russians unless something was done for them. And when they asked for soldiers to protect them, the duke replied (3 November) that he could send none; but added, with a cynical recklessness of the consequences which needs no underlining: 'I know no other way than that you should deliver yourselves by your own exertions; for you are indeed so many that you are able to beat them off—if by no other means, then with stakes and clubs. Do you look after yourselves on land; I will take care of the sea.'[1] The purpose of this cool incitement to civil and social war is quite clear: it was to keep Fleming's troops so occupied that they would be unable in the next few months to intervene in Sweden. The results were immediate. Within three weeks of this speech Österbotten rose in that bloody rebellion which is known in Finnish history as the 'Club War': a rising in southern Finland followed soon after. In Österbotten the peasantry received some assistance from other classes, especially the clergy; elsewhere it was a real social war of poor against rich. The rebels had no properly constituted armies: it was an affair of burnings and atrocities by guerrilla bands, massacres and reprisals by the regular troops, frightful while it lasted but relatively soon over. Fleming's victory at St Michel in January 1597 broke the back of it; the battle at Santavuori on 24 February finished it off. By March Karl was urging the peasants to make what terms they could: from his point of view the rising had now served its purpose. At the winter markets he had made great play with it as evidence of what might happen in Sweden if Sigismund's *ståthållare* were allowed to remain; at the Arboga *riksdag* he used it to rally the Peasants round him. The whole affair afforded a useful opportunity to demonstrate his sympathy with the lower orders. He had need to appear sympathetic, for upon their support now depended his political survival.

On 18 February 1597 the Estates began to assemble at Arboga. As at Söderköping, the Burghers and Peasants were heavily represented. All the bishops save Sorolainen of Åbo attended. But the Nobility,

[1] Erik Anthoni, *Till avvecklingen av konflikten mellan hertig Karl och Finland*, I, 112; Nils Ahnlund, *Från Medeltid och Vasatid*, pp. 166–7.

apart from those of the duchy, were strikingly few, and the *råd* was represented by a single member—the crooked and ambitious Axel Leijonhufvud, who had made his peace with the duke, and once again deserted his brethren at a crisis. The other members of the *råd* boycotted the meeting, and their absence was probably in itself sufficient to make it illegal. They had been insulted by Karl's neglect to send them the usual individual writs of summons, and stirred to anger by rumours that he had declared that if they did not come they should be fetched by force.[1] Early in February letters had arrived from Sigismund forbidding attendance, accepting Karl's resignation from the regency, and entrusting the *råd* with the government of the country. The *råd* saw little prospect of ruling in Karl's despite, and made no haste to act on this commission; but they were resolute in their determination not to go to Arboga. In a letter to the assembled Estates they complained of the threats to their liberty and the slanders on their honour: attendance under constraint, as they pertinently pointed out, was an evil precedent which kings might make use of in future. They were willing to engage to stay quietly on their estates; but they claimed that protection of the law to which every citizen was entitled.

They did not mistake the issue. What was at stake at Arboga was that rule of law which Erik Sparre had championed for so long. Karl might declare indignantly that he was no tyrant, but his methods were the negation of constitutional procedures. His weapons were the terrorization of opponents, the use of mob hysteria, the exploitation of class-divisions, a totalitarian rejection of the right to differ; his object, in the eyes of his enemies, appeared to be a tumultuary dictatorship. His speeches at the *riksdag* were carefully pitched to catch the popular ear; he met the Peasantry separately and in secret, to make their blood run cold with horrific stories of doings in Finland; he used their economic and social grievances to incite them against the nobility; he tempted them with the prospect of a *reduktion*. Addressing a meeting of the Peasants on 28 February, he gave them his own version of his quarrel with the *råd*, and asked them 'if their tales and rumours about him had been true? Herr Omnes answered: they have lied. Then the prince asked them if they would help him to have them punished? Herr Omnes cried with one voice, Yea, yea, yea!'[2] When he failed to carry the upper Estates with him, he told the Peasants that it was the fault of Angermannus, and denounced him as Sigismund's agent. And when at last

[1] This Karl angrily denied: 'For we have as yet laid violent hands on no one, in defiance of the law; nor are we any tyrant, as they lyingly assert . . . but a Christian lord and prince, who cares not so much about their presence or absence that he will act illegally against them. . . . Such a thing is more comprehensible of those who go about with many arts and seek the ruin of this family and wish to put themselves above it as rightful heirs to kingdom and government': *Svenska riksdagsakter*, I, iii, 841.

[2] *Ibid.* 861.

he was able to inform them that a fair copy of the Resolution would soon be available for their signature, he added: '"And then you will see who sides with the king and me, and who with the nobility and the bishops. For if the nobility get the power into their hands, and the bishops have their way, you will see what a blood-bath they will prepare for you". And the commons cried with a loud voice, demanding that His Grace take them into his protection. The prince said: "Will you stand by me?" And the peasants answered, "Yea, yea, yea", each one holding up his hand.'[1] It is difficult to keep in mind, in the face of these Hitleresque transports, that the matter in dispute was the extent of Karl's personal share in a usurped and illegal authority.

Despite all his efforts, despite the absence of the strongest champions of legality, the three upper Estates put up a determined resistance to his proposals. Karl came to Arboga resolved to extort unconditional recognition of his authority as *riksföreståndare*: he did not obtain it. Though they defied Sigismund's order to acknowledge the authority of the *råd*, and declared for Karl as sole ruler in the king's absence, they insisted that he govern with the council's counsel. He had quarrelled with the *råd* because they would not sanction military action against Fleming: the *riksdag* would not sanction it either. All they were prepared to recommend was the sending of a conciliatory embassy to Finland, and to this the *råd* would certainly have had no objection. Karl had also proposed the despatch of an embassy to Sigismund: he had the mortification of finding that when the Estates concurred in this idea, they recommended that its members be drawn from the *råd*. They insisted on eliminating from their Resolution all the accusations which Karl had made against his enemies. But they were not able, in the end, to resist the inclusion of a sanction which offered the duke the opportunity he was seeking to strike at his opponents: after asserting that they were taking no new step, nor in any way going beyond the Resolution of Söderköping, they resolved that all absentees from the *riksdag*, and all who should not within six weeks declare their adherence to its Resolution, should be liable to the punitive clauses of Söderköping. Thus the Arboga Resolution was declared to be legal because it was substantially the same as the Söderköping Resolution: to dissent from the one was to dissent from the other. The *riksdag* was to be given an *ex post facto* varnish of constitutional respectability by compelling, under threat of persecution, the adherence of those members of the *råd* whose absence had really invalidated the proceedings from the beginning. No matter that it was patently false to assert the conformity of the one Resolution with the other; no matter that Karl's interpretation of Söderköping conveniently ignored its text. The issue no longer

[1] *Ibid.* 862.

hung upon truth, or logic, or consistency; it hung upon force. At Arboga the last shreds of legality are discarded: ahead lies only civil war.

IV. CIVIL WAR, 1597–8

Though Karl had in part got his way at Arboga, he was well aware that the absence of the *råd* from that meeting was very damaging to his claim to be acting within the limits of the law. In the weeks after the *riksdag* ended he made great efforts to secure, by threats or persuasion, their public adherence to the Resolution. A long and embittered correspondence ensued, in which Karl raked far into the past for injuries real or imagined. The *råd*-members answered him with moderation; but on the main issue they were firm: they would not subscribe to the Arboga Resolution. But here their unanimity ended. Conferences among themselves, visits to each other's houses, a flurry of gloomy and indignant letters, brought them no nearer to agreement upon a positive policy for the emergency. They saw very clearly what was at stake: 'If the sovereign [wrote Erik Sparre] and those who stand in his place, are to be permitted in this way to have their will and impose their decision in regard to what they desire, we can look to no aid or protection from law or privileges, now or in the future.'[1] The specious argumentation with which Karl allayed the qualms of the upper Estates, his deliberately emotive appeals to the peasantry, could hardly have been more clinchingly answered than in Gustav Baner's letter to Hogenskild Bielke: 'I am not aware that I ever subscribed to the Söderköping Resolution with the idea that the thing should be so interpreted or understood that all those who did not agree with us were to be constrained by force, and thus Swedes set at the throat of Swedes, as is now resolved at Arboga . . . We have one bound that we may not pass, whatever we must (though innocent, thank God) afterwards endure; our circumstances are evil on all sides, but in such a case it is safest to follow St Paul's doctrine: suffer, but not for ill-doing . . . Who has in fact taken upon himself to depart from Uppsala *concilium*, or the king's oath, or acted against the Söderköping Resolution in any way, except by advising against the expedition to Finland? Is the Söderköping Resolution made any more binding in Arboga than it was? *Vix*. God grant that we do not push the religious issue so far that we run up against the law of the land . . . What encroachment upon religion has been made now in the last two years? I know of none of any consequence. That there is a danger of it is always true, but we must not for that reason start anything, much less agree to what can provoke such danger. *Nam de futuris contingentibus non judicat philoso-*

[1] *Svenska riksdagsakter*, I, iii, 971.

phus.'[1] Law and loyalty, the code of behaviour of their class, spoke with one concordant voice: 'Whatever happens', wrote Gustav Baner, 'we must so carry ourselves that we lay fast hold upon our honour.'[2] But upon the practical application of these excellent principles they could reach no determination. Erik Sparre seems for a moment to have thought of armed resistance; but he soon abandoned the idea. They had no resources, military or moral, to sustain a struggle against the duke, backed as he was by the control of the finances, the levies of the duchy, and the blind devotion of *Herr Omnes*. Nils Gyllenstierna was old and ailing, Gustav Baner was ill, Hogenskild Bielke shammed sick as the easiest way of tiding over the crisis without committing himself, Gustav Oxenstierna chose this opportune moment to die. They felt themselves isolated and powerless, their only hope the speedy return of their lawful sovereign. In March 1597 Erik Stenbock and Erik Sparre slipped across the Danish border to seek aid in Poland; in May, Sten Baner and Jöran Posse followed their example. Gustav Baner, Ture and Klas Bielke hung on, strong in a good conscience, striving as best they could to keep resistance alive, exhorting Hogenskild Bielke and Nils Gyllenstierna to be staunch. But Gyllenstierna, who had served the dynasty for more than thirty years, and endured much in that service, was too weary to face another struggle, and in no condition to cope with Karl's incessant badgering: 'In all this confusion', he wrote, 'I hardly know whether I am coming or going, or what I ought to do; and I wish to God I might be spared His Highness's letters and left in peace, for age and weakness can stand it no longer.'[3] The Bielkes soon saw that they could not count on him: 'God forgive the poor gentleman.'[4] There was still plenty of life in brother Hogenskild, despite those convenient circulatory disorders which confined him to his bed at Ulfåsa whenever Karl summoned him for consultation; but frontal opposition had never been Hogenskild's way. He preferred more devious means: simulated agreement, a policy of appeasement, ambiguous phrases, subterranean intrigue. To his brothers he gave advice to answer 'so that it can be in some measure justifiable to the king, and yet not an irritation to him who now cares for no honest answer or excuse'.[5] Such tactics were beyond—or beneath—Ture Bielke; but they were the only tactics Hogenskild knew. It was a question whether even he could make much of them now: in July Karl was demanding that he 'clearly declare his opinion, and no longer *mum, mum*'.[6]

While the *råd* was thus at sixes and sevens, their adversary was at no

[1] *Svenska riksdagsakter*, I, iii, 980–1. [2] *Ibid.* I, iv, 61. [3] *Ibid.* I, iii, 993. [4] *Ibid.* 978.

[5] *Handlingar rörande söndringen mellan Hertig Carl och Rådsherrarne 1594–1600* (*Historiskt bibliotek* ii), p. 328.

[6] *Svenska riksdagsakter*, I, iv, 95.

loss how to proceed. His immediate objective was to secure effective military control of the country: by the middle of June this had been achieved. The flight of Erik Stenbock had put Älvsborg in his hands; but Karl Stenbock still held Kalmar for Sigismund, and as long as he remained there the most convenient port would be open for the king's return. At the end of May, therefore, Karl sailed south with his fleet to Kalmar and summoned its commander to surrender. With no prospect of reinforcement or relief in the near future, he was in no position to make much of a defence. On 1 June the fortress capitulated; Karl Stenbock was led away a prisoner; and the duke began to sound public opinion on the legitimacy of violating the terms which he had accorded to his captive.[1] At this news Arvid Stenbock fled to Poland. The last of Sigismund's *ståthållare* had quitted the field; the door of Sweden had been slammed in the king's face.

Two other measures seemed necessary, however, if Karl were to be safe: he must protect himself by arranging for the formal trial and sentence of the *råd* by the *riksdag* (a bad precedent from Erik XIV's time); and he must reduce Finland to obedience, lest it be made the base for an attack on Sweden. It was with these ends in view that he called members of the Estates to meet him in Stockholm on 24 July. It was not a full *riksdag*, for this time no representatives of the Peasantry attended: it would not do to disgust his steadiest supporters by taking them away from their farms too often, least of all at the height of the summer. In their absence he did the best he could with Clergy and Burghers, against strong opposition from all but a small minority of nobles. The Nobility were not favourably impressed by his bullying tactics; they resented his insults to some of their members who ventured to think the king's commands a better authority than the duke's will.[2] Gustav Baner, Ture and Klas Bielke, refused his summons to come and stand their trial; Hogenskild Bielke and Gyllenstierna failed to put in an appearance: as at Arboga, Axel Leijonhufvud was the only member of the *råd* to be present. In the absence of the accused, the Estates flatly refused Karl's demand that they should be deprived of their membership of the *råd* (an action which, as they pointed out,

[1] Some insight into the nature of Karl's case against the *ståthållare* is afforded by his list of charges against Karl Stenbock. He was accused of writing to the king accusing Karl of improper behaviour and actions prejudicial to royal authority; of advising him to come to Sweden with an armed force; of unlawfully possessing himself of Kalmar castle [for which he had Sigismund's commission!]; of obtaining orders from the king in blank, for appointments and dismissals; of intending [*sic*] to blow up the powder magazine; of having libels against Karl in his possession; of embezzling the king's revenues [*sc.* refusing to pay them to Karl]; of adultery; of being mentioned by common report as having some years ago murdered a jeweller.

[2] When Henrik Soop warned him not to encroach on the king's authority Karl answered 'You don't know what you're drivelling about' ('Du vet icke, vad du bjäbbar').

they were in any case incompetent to take): the furthest they would go was to agree to a virtual suspension until the culprits had answered Karl's charges.[1] But though he was rebuffed on this point, he did elicit a recommendation that he go to Finland to restore order. It was an important gain: henceforward he would be able to take refuge behind their authorization if he should be called to account for levying war against his sovereign. No doubt it was also with this idea in mind that the introduction to the Resolution of the meeting advanced the startling constitutional doctrine that the Estates were competent to act in place of the *råd*, now that its members had been suspended—a pronouncement which conveniently forgot that four of the *råd*, still in Sweden, had not been suspended at all. After this, it comes as no surprise to find them declaring that their Resolution was in accordance with the Resolutions of Söderköping and Arboga, though this was obviously untrue. Any qualms about the legality of a measure, it seemed, could be set at rest by a mere statement that it accorded with what had been done at Söderköping: illegalities thus became legal, innovations acquired the sanction of precedent. A prudent man would inquire no further. It was a device of noble revolutionary simplicity.

The Stockholm meeting had not given Karl all that he hoped for; but at least he could go to Finland. That unhappy country had recently had a change of ruler. On 13 April 1597 Klas Fleming had died, worn out by his exertions; and in July had been succeeded by Arvid Eriksson Stålarm. The change was for the better. Stålarm was a gentleman, while Fleming had been a brute; he was disposed to be conciliatory as far as his loyalty would permit; he was uncompromised by participation in the Club War; he was not on terms of personal enmity with Karl or the *råd*. But he had not come to Finland to betray his master; and when Karl appeared with his expeditionary force at Åbo early in September, Stålarm immediately took steps to resist him. His measures, however, proved ill-judged: by 30 September Åbo was in Karl's hands.[2] In October he induced a meeting of the Estates of Finland to recognize him as *riksföreståndare*. But these successes were anything but solid. If he wished to make sure of keeping a foothold in the country, he must either embark on a regular campaign or leave behind him a garrison able to stand a siege. In fact he could do neither the one nor the other. He dared not linger in Finland for fear of plots at home, nor could he

[1] Twenty-three members of the Nobility interceded for them and offered to stand surety, but without effect.

[2] There was a number of women in Åbo castle, including Klas Fleming's widow. Karl had the happy inspiration of planting his ordnance so as to shoot into the rooms they were occupying, by way of hastening a surrender. The calculation proved erroneous: Fleming's widow refused to be frightened. This paternal trait is recorded with relish by Karl's bastard: *Egenhändiga anteckningar af Carl Carlsson Gyllenhielm rörande tiden 1597–1601*, pp. 264–5.

afford to put an adequate force into Åbo. Finland was neither conquered nor conciliated; the resolution of the Estates at Åbo was not worth the paper it was written upon. By 29 October Karl was back in Stockholm, carrying his prisoners with him: those that were 'incorrigible' were to be tried by the Estates. With his departure, Finnish royalism soon reasserted itself: at Christmas Åbo capitulated to Stålarm's forces without any real attempt at resistance. Sigismund's writ once more ran unchallenged; the effects of Karl's foray were effaced. And the problem of the *råd* was still unsolved.

It is not easy to believe that by this time Karl was unaware of the real implications of what he was doing. Nevertheless, easy or not, the effort to believe it must be made. Karl was perhaps the most baffling, as he was certainly the most odious, of all the Vasas. He had unlimited faith in his own rectitude, and no man was more readily convinced by his own arguments. If he saw himself now as the champion of orderly government, it is obvious that he had some ground for thinking so. He was quite sincere in his belief that his actions had been necessary in order to save the dynasty from the intrigues of those who did not wish it well. To Gustav Baner he wrote that he had no quarrel with Sigismund save that which the *råd* had provoked: the mandates and prohibitions which came with increasing frequency from Poland could be disregarded, because they had been cozened out of a credulous sovereign by unscrupulous persons. All that was required was that the king's eyes should be opened to the true state of affairs, either by a special legation which could be trusted to correct his impressions, or better still by his coming over to see for himself. Karl did not disguise from himself the difficulty over religion; but here the solution was to be found in a concordat within the dynasty: 'If His Majesty really wants to advance his religion, let him negotiate with me . . . Except for religion I will do all His Majesty asks; I am of his blood and wish my own blood no ill.'[1] But this sweet reasonableness easily gave way to menace; religion soon became an instrument of politics. To Sigismund's contention that it was the royal authority which was really at stake Karl replied by remarking that 'the horrid condition of France and the Netherlands shows that when the pope has wished to spread his religion in any land he has never gone baldheaded at it, but first stirred up internal dissension, so that he may remove those from whom he expects most resistance, as has been done here.'[1] It was a good example of his blending of sincerity with hypocrisy: undoubtedly he shared the common Protestant dread of papal machinations; but he can scarcely have believed that this was the main issue in Sweden—though that did not prevent him from trying to persuade Protestant Europe of it.

[1] *Svenska riksdagsakter*, I, iii, 887.   [2] *Ibid.* I, iv, 186.

Karl brought to the commission of illegalities a passion for the letter of the law and a virtuoso facility in arguing from it to his own advantage. Since he was the king's representative, it followed that opposition to him was treason. If he ignored Sigismund's letters of protection, that was because they had been unlawfully obtained. His quarrel with the *råd* was waged almost as a civil action in which he was plaintiff and the *riksdag* cast for the part of jury; his differences with Sigismund he wished to submit to the judgment of a bench of impartial foreign princes. This preference for quasi-legal forms by no means inhibited him from assertions which could hardly have been safely made upon oath or substantiated in a court of law: he did not shrink from telling the Estates that the *råd* was responsible for the deaths of thousands of Finnish peasants, nor from alleging to Gyllenstierna that they were seeking his life. He strove hard to persuade himself and others that what he really had at heart was the safeguarding of constitutional principle: he, rather than Erik Sparre, was in his own view the real defender of the rule of law. The king had violated his oath by infringing religious liberty: it was not reasonable, therefore, to expect his subjects to be faithful to their oaths to him. When this argument wore thin he was ready with another: the argument of *salus populi suprema lex*. Obedience was no longer obligatory if the king's orders were contrary to the welfare of his subjects; against the divine authority of the monarch he invoked the will of the people. But of that will he was to be the sole interpreter—and, indeed, the sole manipulator. These were not the arguments of a champion of the idea of limited monarchy: they were a sham constitutionalism, affected to give a semblance of decency to revolutionary proceedings. He made the commonalty drunk with oratory that he might push it forward as arbiter of the law. His self-justification was a shifting and treacherous compound of irreconcilable attitudes: the will of the people, the safety of religion, the wrongs of the poor, the solidarity of dynastic interests—all were appealed to in turn (and sometimes simultaneously) as might best suit the occasion or the drift of his argument; and up to a point he believed in them all, though with unequal fervour. It was no wonder that men accused him of Machiavellianism.[1] From time to time the web of sophistry was swept aside by a sudden fierce gesture which revealed the realities behind it: in February 1597 he told an envoy of Sigismund that he 'would not tolerate' government by the *råd*; the instructions for a projected embassy to Poland in August insisted that all the major fortresses must be put in his hands; when he went to Finland he left

[1] In the royalist tract *Avsa . . . Caroli* (1598) his arguments were described as 'doctrina Macciavelli, seditionis plena, non orthodoxa, nec vlla sapientibus cognita': Karl Nordlund, *Den svenska reformationstidens allmänna statsrättsliga ideer*, p. 232.

orders that Sigismund was not to be admitted to them until his return. An effective and recognized sovereignty he meant to have: it was his natural right; it was essential to good government; it was to the advantage of the dynasty; he would take no less. And the sign and precondition of such authority must be the crushing of his personal enemies. If he must strain the law in order to do it, so much the worse for the law. Against the law he would appeal to those by whom the laws were made; or if need be to that Natural Law which transcended statute and precedent, and of which he could trust himself to be the casuistical interpreter.

It was in some such state of mind as this that he once more summoned a *riksdag* to Uppsala at the beginning of February 1598. The Nobility came early for the funeral of Queen Gunilla, and Karl took the opportunity to take counsel with them. Should Gustav Baner and the Bielkes be called to stand their trial? Should a legation be sent to Sigismund? The reply was not encouraging: it recommended him to admit the *råd* to pardon; it urged that they be sent as delegates to the king. Karl made a show of agreement; but it was on conditions which made agreement a mockery: he would restore the *råd* to favour, provided that they confessed their fault and begged his pardon; and provided also that they returned from their embassy by Easter with a favourable answer. By way of ensuring that they should have no chance of doing so, he defined their instructions in terms to which it was inconceivable that Sigismund should accede. Compared with this, Erik's treatment of Nils Sture had been straightforward and magnanimous.

At this moment, when the *riksdag* was on the point of opening, Sigismund at last intervened. By the summer of 1597 he had come to the conclusion that his return to Sweden must not be delayed if he wished to save his crown. As one after the other his *ståthållare* made their way in flight to his court, as Erik Sparre and his colleagues of the *råd* poured their tales of Karl's proceedings into his ear, he was confirmed in that conclusion. The history of the past three years had given him no great cause to put his trust in the *råd*-aristocracy, but at least they were preferable to his uncle. And they all concurred in urging him to come home as the only remedy for the evil. But, as always, it was extremely difficult for him to get away. On his return to Poland in 1594 he had promised to remain there permanently thenceforward. The Poles, though they no longer suspected him of a design to abdicate, feared that if he went to Sweden he might be prevented from returning. Karl's propaganda had convinced many of them that the trouble in Sweden was a constitutional conflict, with the duke representing something akin to the *aurea libertas* to which they were themselves committed. And if Sigismund had thus to face opposition at home, he could not now count on assistance from abroad. Spain was sympathetic, but too distant to be helpful; the other Catholic powers were indifferent; even the papacy was too preoccupied with the project for an anti-Turkish league to have energies to spare for Scandinavia. If it came to military action, the prospects were dubious: an essential preliminary would be the command of a large fleet of transports, with ships of war to protect them. A half-hearted attempt to induce Karl to send the Swedish fleet across to Danzig, in July 1597, naturally had no success. It was partly in order to find out what the chances of obtaining the use of the fleet really were that Sigismund in October 1597 commissioned Samuel Laski to go over on an embassy of reconnaissance. He was instructed to disseminate proclamations condemning Karl's usurpation of authority, to prohibit any further meetings of the *riksdag*, to forbid any trial of political prisoners until Sigismund should return, and to avoid any sort of negotiation with the regent.

Laski arrived in Linköping on 25 January 1598, to learn that a *riksdag* had indeed been summoned to Uppsala. He at once issued an open letter forbidding it to meet. Staying only for a brief conference with the contumacious *råd* in Östergötland, he hurried to Stockholm, where he made contact with Hans Bilefelt and others of the city magistracy who had shown themselves hostile to Karl's government.[1] From Stockholm he went to Uppsala, where he arrived to find the *riksdag* just begun. To Karl and to the Estates he delivered Sigismund's messages, not mincing his words. He was met by the tactics which had served so well in the past: the duke took cover behind the Estates. Karl intended that they should send Sigismund an answer justifying his actions and refusing all real concession. But this time he ran into difficulties. Laski was in close touch with Angermannus, whom conscience had at last made a royalist, and through him was able to exert influence upon the *riksdag*. His messages had left no room for doubt of the gravity of the position: perhaps for the first time men were made to face the fact that they stood on the brink of rebellion. A majority of the Nobility was for patching up a reconciliation at all costs; and even the minority quarrelled fiercely with the Clergy in an effort to avoid taking the lead in drafting the kind of answer that Karl expected. In vain Karl tried to entangle the envoy in argument: Laski was not to be drawn; '*ad subtiles atque acutas quaestiones*' he would make no reply. It took ten days before Karl could push the Estates into framing an answer to Sigismund in a form which he found tolerable. The final version promised that the fleet should be at Sigismund's disposal on due notice;

[1] The magistracy being mostly German, Karl set about undermining their authority by stimulating the latent xenophobia of the lower orders in the city.

but for the rest it made no concessions: the king was given to understand that the regent had the nation behind him. Karl for his part promised to liberate his Finnish prisoners (though only, of course, with the assent of the *riksdag*!) provided that Sigismund guaranteed that they would adhere to the Resolutions of the Estates and obey the Stockholm government—conditions which were tantamount to incarceration for an indefinite period. To all intents and purposes it was a defiance: Laski had now no illusions. He hurried back to Poland, picking up on his way Gustav Baner and Ture Bielke. It was plain to them that the crisis was approaching: if they did not wish to find themselves prisoners, the sooner they crossed the border the better. By the end of March they were out of the country. Of their former colleagues, only four now remained within reach of Karl's persuasions.[1]

Laski returned to Poland impressed by the strength of Karl's position, and convinced of the unwisdom of a direct attack upon him. But his report had the unexpected effect of alarming the *sejm*: for the first time they began to fear that the Union was in danger; for the first time they took active steps to preserve it. Troops and money were voted on a generous scale; preparations for an invasion were put in hand immediately. Strong diplomatic pressure was brought to bear on Danzig, Lübeck and Rostock to break off trading relations with Sweden; Swedish ships were seized in Baltic harbours, or rounded up on the high seas by Polish privateers; an economic blockade was gradually organized. Erik Sparre was sent to Pomerania and Mecklenburg to solicit their benevolent neutrality; and from Mecklenburg proceeded to Copenhagen in the hope of persuading Kristian IV to intervene actively on Sigismund's behalf. For a time it appeared that his mission might be successful. Kristian had no sympathy with rebels, nor was he much impressed by Karl's efforts to represent himself as the defender of the Protestant cause. He had already declined to intercept the correspondence of the exiled *råd*; he now curtly rejected an application for Erik Sparre's extradition. Active assistance, however, was a different matter. His council advised against it, and their advice prevailed. Kristian was prepared to allow Polish troops to pass through Denmark, if that should be found necessary; he offered mediation, with a broad hint that he would decide in Sigismund's favour: further than that he would not go. But both he and his council expected Sigismund to have an easy victory.

In Sweden, meanwhile, Karl was preparing for the worst. On the last day of the Uppsala *riksdag* he launched a violent attack upon Angermannus, with the idea of discrediting him with the members and neutralizing his influence in the country. The archbishop's defection had

[1] Nils Gyllenstierna, Hogenskild and Klas Bielke, Axel Leijonhufvud.

made nonsense of the pretence that the church was in danger; it gave dangerous encouragement to all compromisers and Laodiceans; it was resented on personal grounds, as a client's betrayal of his patron.[1] Henceforward Karl would pursue Angermannus with a rancour scarcely less than the hatred he felt for Erik Sparre. In March he finally broke the resistance of another dangerous opponent by forcing upon Stockholm a magistracy of his partisans. The remaining members of the *råd* were plied with pathetic or minatory appeals not to desert him in the hour of need; the commonalty were kept in good heart by a timely remission of taxes. And finally, that nothing might be wanting in the way of political insurance, he called the Estates together once again—those of the southern provinces to Vadstena in June; those of the northern to Stockholm in July.

But now came an unexpected *intermezzo*. At the last moment, with his preparations all but complete, Sigismund suddenly decided to send Laski back to Sweden. He seems to have hoped that the imminence of civil war might have brought his uncle to his senses: he little knew his man. Laski's second mission revealed how hopeless the prospects of a peaceful settlement had become. The old arguments and accusations were exchanged to no purpose; the Estates at Vadstena sent Laski home with an answer of Karl's devising; the members entered into a solemn union, reminiscent of the days of young Herr Sten, to stand by each other in all circumstances; and Karl's fist gave a bloody nose to one nobleman who was less unanimous than his colleagues. Laski did indeed use his visit to broadcast an open letter from Sigismund, masterly in its pungent polemic—the only occasion in the long wrangle, perhaps, when the king's propaganda bettered the duke's; and Angermannus secured the promulgation of an explicit guarantee of the safety of the Protestant religion. But this was a high price to pay for a delay which went far to ruin Sigismund's chance of a quick victory. For already royalist elements were stirring in Västergötland in expectation of his imminent return; already Stålarm was preparing a descent on Uppland from Åbo. Laski's mission gave Karl time to chase the disaffected Västergötland nobility across the border into Denmark; time to summon waverers and neutrals to meet him in Kalmar, or take the consequences. It enabled him to get Angermannus temporarily out of the way by sending him on an unhopeful mission to Finland. If Sigismund's armada had cast anchor in Kalmar roads in June—as it

[1] Karl's bitterness is reflected in the comments of his son, Karl Karlsson Gyllenhielm, who wrote in his memoirs that Angermannus turned against the duke, 'so that if the king had got the upper hand . . . and had afterwards wished to impose the popish religion on Sweden, it was feared that the archbishop would also readily have fallen in with the king's wishes. So far can covetousness prevail with learned men, yea, with the spiritual estate!': *Egenhändiga anteckningar af Carl Carlsson Gyllenhielm*, p. 268.

easily might have done—the subsequent history of Sweden might have been very different.

As it was, the king waited impatiently for Laski's return: he did not arrive in Danzig till mid-July. There Sigismund had scraped together a fleet of eighty transports (many of them Dutch and English ships commandeered for the service) with a handful of warships to protect them. He had with him between 4,000 and 5,000 troops, mostly cavalry; a few Polish senators; most of the exiled *råd*; and a trio of impecunious German cousins. On 23 July his armada put to sea; eight days later, after a voyage unusually benign, it anchored off Kalmar. The castle surrendered without a fight; its commanders were made prisoner; and Sigismund, despite all Karl's precautions, had gained his foothold in Sweden.

It has been said that the bond of union entered into by the Estates at Vadstena signified the formation of a solid national front: 'The entire Swedish nation stood united'; 'against Duke Karl and his followers, fighting as they were for the sanctity of the law, Sigismund was powerless'.[1] A strange verdict. It is true that all four remaining *råd* eventually subscribed the bond; but three of them were certainly acting under constraint. Sigismund had on his side all the *råd* except one, a great majority of the nobility, the archbishop, the city of Stockholm, a considerable portion of the army, especially the Uppland cavalry. In Småland and Västergötland almost all classes were in his favour; Östergötland was evenly divided. The peasants, except in the south, were for Karl: Dalarna fanatically so; while most of the burghers and clergy were of the same party. In Finland the upper classes feared Karl as the inciter of *jacqueries*; Estonia still resisted all his solicitations. This was no case of united national resistance to tyranny: it was a civil war of parties not ill-matched, in which each could feel a consciousness of right; and as to tyranny, that was an accusation which came home more nearly to Karl than to his nephew. Certainly 'the sanctity of the law' was not the monopoly of either side. It was neither ignorance nor miscalculation that led Kristian IV to expect that Sigismund would prevail; for everywhere a feeling of loyalty to the lawful sovereign remained alive, ready to swell the king's party if it should be victorious, a reserve available to mitigate possible defeat: though they should beat the king a hundred times, yet he would be king still. Even yet men clung to the hope that fighting might be avoided: Sigismund had proclaimed that he came in peace, he had apologized in advance for bringing in foreign troops, he had promised to send them home as soon as he could. At the very moment of his landing he encountered an embassy of mediators—the fruit of an initiative of the Hohenzollerns and the Duke

[1] Axel Jonsson, *Hertig Karl och Sigismund 1597–1598*, pp. 178–9.

of Mecklenburg, who had no wish to find themselves involved in a Swedish–Polish war, and foresaw the difficulties of neutrality. Events were to prove that conciliation was more difficult still; but as long as the ambassadors remained they kept alive the hopes of many for a solution by compromise.

Sigismund's plan of campaign had been designed to make the most of his geographical advantages. It had been intended that Karl's attention should be distracted, at the moment when the king landed in southern Sweden, by a simultaneous descent by Stålarm on the coast of Uppland. The delay in waiting for Laski's return threw this plan out of gear: Stålarm came over before the king had left Danzig, found the prospects unpromising, and beat a hasty retreat. The false start had however one good effect, for it drew Karl's respectable fleet into the waters around Åland, where it lay wind-bound for several critical weeks. Sigismund was thus able to cross to Kalmar without interference: if he had used the opportunity to sail on to Stockholm, he might perhaps have settled the issue at a stroke. Instead, he made for Stegeborg, a hundred miles or so northward up the Östergötland coast: mainly, it seems, because he was anxious to meet his sister Anna, who was living in Stegeborg castle. The move was carried out with success: by 23 August all the army and most of the transports were in Stegeborg, within striking distance of the centre of Karl's power. But a few ships, including that in which Laski was sailing, were separated from the others in a storm, and were driven so far to the north that they found themselves in the Stockholm skerries. Laski had good friends in the capital; Karl was away in Östergötland organizing his army; the chance was there for the taking, and they took it. Stockholm was won without a blow; and Laski, with the zealous coöperation of Angermannus and Klas Bielke, began to re-establish the king's authority in the surrounding countryside.

In the weeks after Sigismund's landing both sides made efforts to attract waverers and win over opponents. In this the king at first seemed to have the greater success. The southern nobility, who had come sulkily to Kalmar at Karl's summons and were still there when Sigismund appeared, rallied to him in a body. A general insurrection in Västergötland forced the hated Axel Leijonhufvud to seek refuge in Karl's duchy. Before the end of August the royalists could triumph in the news that Älvsborg was in their hands. Sigismund's troops were kept in good order; his commanders paid punctually for all they requisitioned. There was for a time a fair prospect of inducing Karl's levies to desert: it was one thing to side with the duke when Sigismund was in Poland; it was quite another to oppose the king to his face. To meet this difficulty Karl spread the report that Sigismund was dead, and that his army was led by an impostor: it was a story which gained much credence among the simple. As the weeks passed, however, Sigismund's initial advantage dwindled away. Not only was Karl able to prevent serious defections from his own army; he succeeded in seducing some of those who had at first rallied to the king. His propaganda depicted the royal forces as a horde of foreign bandits, unloosed upon the country as a punishment; the clergy of his party terrified their flocks by tales of the shiploads of the monks and Jesuits whom the king had brought over. In Dalarna and the adjacent provinces such stories found ready acceptance, reinforced as they were by memories of the Club War and fears of a landing by Stålarm's army. Attempts by Laski to bring the Dalesmen back to their duty provoked a popular rising, in which one of the king's agents was murdered, not without Karl's direct encouragement and approval. Once again, as in King Kristian's day, Dalarna turned out in force to defend itself against what it esteemed to be the threat of foreign tyranny.

It was not by such side-shows as this, however, that the outcome would be decided. Karl had concentrated his forces around Linköping; Sigismund lay in Stegeborg, anxiously awaiting the news of Stålarm's arrival, hoping in the meantime for a demonstration from Stockholm to annoy the duke in rear. Meanwhile the mediators were about their thankless task. Karl, who at first received them with insulting discourtesy, soon found it expedient to avail himself of their good offices; Sigismund was prepared to negotiate to gain time. The mediators did their best; but they soon began to despair of success. Sigismund considered Karl to be a rebellious vassal—a term which Karl took extremely ill—and demanded that he should stand his trial. Karl on his side put forward terms which the mediators felt to be preposterous: Älvsborg, Kalmar and Vadstena must be put in his hands; both sides must disarm (which would have meant that Sigismund, once his troops had been sent home, would have been at his uncle's mercy); six of Karl's bitterest enemies among the aristocracy[1] were to be placed in his hands as hostages; and the mediators were to give their personal guarantee for the observance of these terms. It was in vain that they pointed out that it was outrageous to demand as hostages men whom he regarded as defendants in actions in which he was plaintiff, and for whose trial he was clamouring: Karl was indifferent to such legal niceties; and in any case he was now hoping for a victory in the field.

On 8 September he made a bid to win it. But his attack on Sigismund's position was bungled, and his army was beaten back with loss. Only the intervention of the *råd*—who were anxious to avoid bloodshed, and in an untimely access of humanitarianism persuaded Sigis-

[1] Erik Sparre, Ture Bielke, Gustav and Sten Baner, Gustav and Erik Brahe.

mund to break off the pursuit—saved him from serious defeat. It had been the exiled *råd* who had induced Sigismund, against the advice of the Poles, to bring no more than 5,000 men to Sweden; and now, by a tragic irony, it was they who ruined the best chance of victory which his party was ever to be offered. A truce was agreed upon; negotiation began again. Within a week it had run so hard aground that the mediators, losing patience, washed their hands of the business and set off for home. They had scarcely left before the situation was suddenly transformed. Up in the Åland islands the wind, after weeks in the southwest, had at last shifted; and Karl's fleet was able to sail southwards to his assistance. On 20 September it lay off Stegeborg. Sigismund was trapped between a superior army and a fleet which he had no means of attacking. By swift action he extricated himself from his predicament: on 21 September he broke out of Stegeborg and made his way to Linköping before Karl realized what was happening. But he left behind him his baggage and his wounded; and his transports, with a few exceptions, fell into enemy hands. He was still in good heart: despite numerical inferiority he expected that his professional troops and experienced commanders would be able to dispose of an amateur opponent and a peasant army. And if it had come to a formal battle he might well have been proved right. But on 25 September, as the two armies lay encamped on either side of the Stånge stream near Linköping, skirmishing developed between patrols and outposts on such a scale as to draw Karl into a general advance on the two bridges held by the king's troops. Before he came up to them, however, he proposed a truce, and the reopening of negotiations. Sigismund at once accepted. His forces were withdrawn to their camp; but Karl, having thus lulled his enemy into a sense of security, continued his advance under cover of a mist, and so was able to overrun one of the bridges before Sigismund could take any measures to save it. Thus caught at a disadvantage by treachery and surprise, the king's army was thrown behind the river in disorder. Karl did not venture to follow it; but the victory was undoubtedly his. The king's position was now desperate: the morale of his troops was cracking, total defeat stared him in the face. There was nothing for it but to ask for a truce. To this Karl would agree only on one condition: that his personal enemies in the *råd* be surrendered into his hands. No appeals or remonstrances could move him on this point: the only concession he would make was to give an explicit pledge that they should be tried by a court of impartial foreign princes. Impotent, humiliated, ashamed, Sigismund at last brought himself to swallow these terms. Erik Sparre, Ture Bielke, Gustav and Sten Baner, Jöran Nilsson Posse—the heart of the royalist party in Sweden, the men who had done more than anyone to give to the king's cause the sanction of law and justice—were handed over to an adversary who had that morning demonstrated just how much reliance was to be placed on his pledged word.

Upon his vanquished sovereign the victor now imposed the treaty of Linköping. It provided that past disputes should be buried in oblivion; but Sigismund was to rule according to his oath and his Charter in future. He was to summon a *riksdag* within four months, at which any differences between Karl and his opponents were to be tried by a bench of impartial foreign princes; but it was expressly provided that the disputes between Karl and Sigismund were not to be tried at all. Both sides would disband their forces. Persons appointed by Karl to office were to retain their posts until the *riksdag* should meet. The five members of the *råd* were to remain in his custody for the present, with treatment suitable to their rank. Sigismund recorded his intention of proceeding shortly to Stockholm: on his arrival, Karl engaged to restore any royal property at present in his possession. And lastly, by a provision which Karl had long pressed upon the mediators in vain, the Estates were made guarantors of the treaty, empowered (but not, as Karl had wished, obliged) to resist whichever of the parties might break it.

The treaty of Linköping was signed on 28 September. At the beginning of October Stålarm at last appeared in Stockholm harbour: the stroke which might have tipped the balance in the king's favour had come a week too late. There was nothing for it but to order the Finnish army back to Åbo. Karl, with the game in his hands, was able to allow himself the rare luxury of a show of magnanimity: he could now afford to play the loyal subject and the reconciled uncle. Sigismund made the best of a bad business, conscious perhaps that a show of cordiality now offered the best hope of doing something for Karl's unfortunate prisoners. All the evidence suggests that in the period immediately after the conclusion of the treaty he was firmly resolved to keep it. His measures tell their own tale: he directed that taxes be paid to Stockholm; he sent his servants and effects there. The Finns were ordered home, and a real effort made to find shipping to take the foreign troops back to Poland. But soon after 8 October something happened to make him change his mind. His preparations for moving to Stockholm were now complete; but when on 11 October he at last embarked, it was not to Stockholm that he directed his course. He went to Kalmar; and there he was shortly joined by his sister Anna. On 22 October they put to sea again, leaving Johan Sparre and a foreign garrison in Kalmar castle; and this time they steered their course for Danzig. Neither of them was ever to see Sweden again.

We do not know what prompted this dramatic change of plan. Perhaps it was the arrival of an urgent summons from Poland; perhaps some disturbing rumour of Karl's intentions: it must at all events have been no light matter. For it was a decision of fateful import. Sigismund might try to persuade himself that his flight did not involve a breach with Karl; he might argue that it did not imperil Erik Sparre and his colleagues, since all judicial sentences were subject to the king's revision. But in fact he had torn up the treaty of Linköping; he had thrown the *råd* to the wolves. By one fatal action he had made the loss of his throne practically certain, and for the first time in this long struggle deprived himself of all sympathy. Hitherto the moral advantage had been on his side, and many a man outside the *råd* had stuck to his cause for that reason. But now that advantage had been squandered; nor could he ever regain it. Karl himself was thunderstruck and incredulous at the news; Sigismund's supporters felt it as a shattering blow. Under the impact of what seemed a wanton perfidy the royalist party lost hope and courage. In the next few months it rapidly disintegrated. Those who were less compromised hastened to make what terms they could with the duke—as Abraham Brahe did, for instance, who had been Sigismund's standard-bearer at Stångebro; for others the prospects were now gloomy indeed. In Finland Arvid Eriksson Stålarm and Axel Kurck braced themselves to meet an attack which was unlikely to be long delayed; in Sweden the imprisoned *råd* prepared their defence and clung to the delusive hope of impartial judges. The flight of the king was a decisive event. The reign was as good as over; the constitutional issue virtually decided: all that remained was in the nature of a blood-stained epilogue.

V. THE REVOLUTION COMPLETED, 1598–1600

The treaty of Linköping had done nothing to determine how Sweden was to be governed. The powers of the duke had been left undefined; the measure of control to be given to the king was nowhere specified: all was remitted to the *riksdag* which was to be summoned within four months' time. When Sigismund's evasion made the treaty a dead letter the most immediate problem was to find an authority capable of saving the country from anarchy, and to this problem there could now be only one solution. Both king and *råd* were for the moment impossible: only Karl remained. All but the most irreconcilable of his opponents soon recognized this. Älvsborg submitted to him in November; the Uppland cavalry went over to him on the same day; a little later Stockholm accepted the inevitable. In Västergötland, indeed, Axel Leijonhufvud proceeded with rigour against the local royalists; but elsewhere Karl showed a conciliatory spirit: it was obvious policy to try to rally all moderate men behind him. No one, not even Karl himself, had at first any clear idea of what the final outcome was to be, once this interim period was over. A meeting of the Nobility and the episcopate at Jönköping, in January and February 1599, though it expressed strong doubts whether Sigismund's authority could ever again be accepted, nevertheless offered him a last chance: if he would return to Sweden, and promise to stay there permanently, they were ready to return to their allegiance. But they did not expect him to take their offer; and the event proved that they were right. When in July the Estates met in Stockholm, no answer to their terms had come from Warsaw. They therefore hesitated no longer: by unanimous resolution they renounced their allegiance and declared Sigismund deposed. But the disposing of this question at once raised the problem of a successor. Sigismund had a young son, Władysław, born in 1595, and it by no means followed that his deposition must necessarily entail the rejection of the claims of his heir. If, however, that was really the intention, then the next in order of succession according to the Succession Pact was not Karl, but Sigismund's half-brother Johan, the son of Johan III by Gunilla Bielke; and for a time the Nobility seem to have been inclined to favour his claims. But the obvious candidate was Karl himself. There is no doubt that most men would have preferred to take a king of mature age, Protestant principles and tried administrative ability, rather than gamble on the character and capacity of either of two small boys. In July 1599 Karl had only to make a sign, and the crown could have been his. But he was well aware that his detractors believed that he had long been planning just such an usurpation, and he was not anxious to give them the satisfaction of being proved right. As a convinced legitimist, he wished the revolution to be fitted into the dynastic structure with as little disturbance as possible. The dynasty had suffered one shock already, in 1568; the Succession Pact had already been once violated; to weaken its authority still further would be to subvert one of the bases upon which the rights of all the Vasas were founded. Effective power he meant to have; security, also, for his wife and his young son; but he was not as yet convinced that these things could not be obtained without a usurpation repugnant to his principles. It was still possible that Sigismund might agree to send over Władysław to be educated as a Protestant under his tutelage: at all events, he insisted that the offer be made. In the face of his intransigence the Estates had no choice but to give way. It was agreed to inform Sigismund that he would be given six months to signify his acceptance of Karl's proposal, and a further six months to send Władysław to Sweden: if he refused, or made no answer, his line would be excluded from the succession.

A final decision was thus postponed until next year. In the meantime, Sigismund's position underwent a rapid deterioration. One of his first acts on his return to Poland had been to arrange for the reinforcement of the garrison in Kalmar; but thereafter he suffered his cause to go to ruin with scarcely an effort to save it. Pessimistic about his prospects, stinted of money by his Polish subjects, he sank for a time into a mood of apathy or resignation in which he failed to make the best even of such limited opportunities as were available to him. Kalmar was virtually left to its fate: on 1–2 May 1599 the town was taken by storm, Karl personally leading the attack at the head of his troops; on 12 May the castle capitulated. The three senior officers were executed as traitors, and their decapitated heads affixed to spikes upon the walls. Four months later, when the Stockholm *riksdag* had been disposed of, it was the turn of Finland. The two commanders there, Arvid Stålarm and Axel Kurck, could make little effective resistance. In September and October Karl successively captured Åbo, Helsingfors and Viborg; Stålarm and Kurck became his prisoners; before the winter set in the whole country was brought under his control. His victory was accompanied by savage severities. The vanquished paid the penalty of their loyalty on the scaffold; old enemies from the Club War (including at least one parson) were decapitated or impaled; and Karl permitted himself the private luxury of executing the young son of his old adversary Klas Fleming. The proceedings culminated on 10 November in the 'blood-bath of Åbo'. Åbo had surrendered upon promise that the garrison should be tried by the Estates: Karl's interpretation of this undertaking was to constitute a local tribunal of thirty-seven of his own adherents, which sent fourteen of the accused to immediate execution. Arvid Stålarm and Axel Kurck, though condemned to death, were brought over to Sweden to stand a grander inquest; and Bishop Sorolainen of Åbo, a harmless necessary conformist, accompanied them as fellow-prisoner. By way of justifying his actions, Karl informed the Finns that their country's troubles were due to 'the pope and the lesser nobility'.

Meanwhile Sigismund had at last roused himself to take advantage of Karl's absence by striking a blow at Sweden. In October he sent a fleet, scraped together with much difficulty, to attempt the seizure of Älvsborg. But nothing now went right for him. The defenders were alerted in time; and since success was considered to depend upon surprise, the attack was abandoned before it had well begun. On its return journey the expedition took refuge from the threat of Karl's navy by putting in to Copenhagen, with the idea of wintering there; and in Copenhagen it remained, for its commander soon found himself compelled to sell his ships in order to pay his sailors' wages. Finally, the autumn of 1599 saw the beginning of the collapse of Sigismund's authority in Estonia. On 24 October partisans of Karl seized Narva by a *coup de main*; after the New Year his troops began to overrun the country. In a last desperate attempt to save the situation, Sigismund now informed the *sejm* that he consented to the transference of Estonia to Poland. The Poles, however, showed neither gratitude for the acquisition nor readiness to defend it; and in any case the concession came too late. On 24 March Reval declared for Karl, and with its defection Sigismund lost the last remants of his Swedish patrimony.

Three weeks earlier, the Estates had gathered at Linköping for what must clearly be a decisive meeting. The size of the assembly reflected the importance of the occasion: upwards of 800 members attended. They had before them two great matters for decision. In the first place they must settle the crown; in the second, they must pronounce judgment upon those whose support of Sigismund had exposed them to a charge of treason, and in particular upon the captive members of the *råd*. As to the first point they were no longer in any doubt. Seven months had now elapsed since they had made their offer to Sigismund, and still he had given no answer. Without more ado, therefore, they resolved upon the perpetual exclusion of his family from the throne. In regard to Prince Johan, too, there was now no hesitation. Though they professed to depart from the Succession Pact with the greatest hesitation, they felt that they could not risk giving the crown to one so nearly related to Sigismund: it was even suggested that Johan III's religious policy justified the exclusion of all his descendants. They therefore proposed that Johan be compensated by the creation in his favour of a new royal duchy, though they did not permanently bar his right to succeed. Having thus eliminated the only possible competitor, they unanimously called upon Karl—who, they said, had delivered them 'from popish bonds, and foreign yoke and thraldom'—to accept the crown for himself and his heirs: only if his line should fail was the crown to pass to Johan. They further resolved that in future no person should be capable of succeeding unless he were a member of the Swedish Lutheran church. As far as the *riksdag* was concerned, the revolution was over: all that remained was for the new dynasty to ascend the throne. To Karl, however, the matter did not appear so simple or so obvious. His legitimist qualms, though they were weakening, still embarrassed him, and he was certainly concerned about the effect of a usurpation upon foreign Protestant opinion. However ready he might be to enlist the coöperation of the Estates when it suited his purposes, he could hardly help reflecting that their action recalled constitutional practices which his family had for the last half-century been endeavouring to consign to oblivion: in a manner uncomfortably reminiscent of the fourteenth century they had elected a king from among the family of his predecessor. Undoubtedly he hoped that his young son, Gustav Adolf, would be king one day; but for the moment his solution was that he himself should be recognized as *riksföreståndare* for life on behalf of a monarchy for the time being in abeyance. But the *riksdag*, which did not share his reservations, and was impatient to get the matter settled, would have none of this suggestion. Even yet, however, he continued to find pretexts for delay. It was possible, he urged, that though Sigismund had not replied within six months, Władysław might arrive within the stipulated twelve, of which five still remained to run. Until the twelve months were up, he would take no decision. And with that, for the present, the Estates had to be content. It was unsatisfactory, but there was no remedy. They could not make him king against his will. They dared not make anyone king in his place. He stood between them and confusion, as he well knew. All they could do was to resolve that he was 'Sweden's ruling lord and king', and hope that the efflux of time might bring him to accept the title which they accorded him.

Meanwhile the great drama of the trial had begun. For a year past Karl had made up his mind that there was to be no nonsense about trial by impartial foreign princes; and at the Stockholm meeting of July 1599 the Estates had carefully resolved to invite foreign princes only as observers. Invitations had accordingly gone out to a fair selection of Protestant courts; but the response had not been encouraging. Attendance at the trial was felt to be compromising; it would certainly entail bad relations with Poland. In the end only Karl's brother-in-law, John of Holstein, sent observers to represent him, and it is doubtful whether even they were much edified by what they saw. For the court was a monstrous tribunal, hand-picked by Karl from all the Estates except the Clergy (who refused to act in a capital case) and numbering no less than 155 persons. Its members were indeed freed for the occasion from their oath of loyalty, but it may be doubted whether this gesture had much effect upon their behaviour. The court held its sessions in the presence of the whole *riksdag*, and to the *riksdag* its judgments were submitted for confirmation. Two members of the *råd* acted alternately as presidents of the court: the one (as might have been expected) was Axel Leijonhufvud; the other was, of all people, Erik Brahe—Erik Brahe, the Roman Catholic, the former *ståthållare*, whose appointment had been one main ground for the charge that Sigismund had violated his pledged word. He had recently contrived to reconcile himself with Karl; but it might perhaps have been expected that he should abstain from participating in the sending of his former colleagues to the scaffold. The manager of the case was Karl himself, who opened every day's proceedings with an address to the court, and in his interrogation of the accused displayed considerable forensic ability of the Old Bailey order. In his own view he was acting as Public Prosecutor, or leading counsel for the Swedish people; but this attempt to remove the affair from the level of a personal vendetta wore very thin at times.

The accused were the five members of the *råd* handed over at Stångebro, together with Hogenskild Bielke, Klas Bielke, Erik Leijonhufvud, Krister Klasson Horn, and Bengt Falk; while the case of Arvid Stålarm and Axel Kurck was to be subject to the tribunal's review. The charges against them included all the old accusations against the men of Reval (among whom, it will be remembered, was Axel Leijonhufvud himself!); but the gravamen of the indictment lay in their refusal to conform to the Resolutions of Söderköping and Arboga—particularly in that they had declined to recognize Karl as sole *riksföreståndare* by natural right; their libelling of Karl in their private correspondence (among other items, Karl had the effrontery to complain that they had charged him with being mixed up in the de Mornay plot);[1] their inducing and soliciting Sigismund to invade the country with a foreign army; their conniving at attempts to introduce Roman Catholicism; and, more generally, their wish to restore electoral monarchy and their design to root out the whole House of Vasa.[2] In an attempt to substantiate these charges Karl had recourse to methods which did not improve his case: denial of access to relevant documents, selective quotations designed to mislead, deliberate distortion, loud invocation of constitutional idols such as the Land Law, Gustav Vasa's Testament or the Succession Pact (whether relevant or not), hardy mendacity when driven into a corner. His junior counsel, Erik Göransson Tegel, was to be seen during breaks in the hearings priming members of the court with legal authorities in rebuttal of the defence. Axel Leijonhufvud distinguished himself by the nonchalance with which he combined the normally disjunct functions of judge, prosecuting counsel, and perjured witness for the crown.

The accused were in reality condemned before the trial began; but they made so strong a defence that even this tribunal was not wholly unaffected. They pleaded above all their duty to the king: as Erik Sparre observed, when they found themselves in the position of being called upon to serve two masters, they had no option but to choose the sovereign to whom they were bound by their oaths. They reminded Karl that the Resolution of Söderköping expressly guaranteed their right to give their advice freely without fear of the consequences; and

[1] See above, p. 247. He also tried to saddle them with responsibility for Sigismund's propaganda-piece, *Ausa Caroli* (see above, p. 374, n. 1).

[2] Karl repeatedly accused them of seeking to compass his death.

they made a telling point when they insisted that it was Karl himself who had first broken the Resolution by his resignation of the government—an act which automatically released them from their obligations under it.[1] Gustav Baner protested—with truth—that he had always opposed Sigismund on the religious issue. Sigismund's return to Sweden in 1598, they said, was his affair, not theirs; but in any case he had brought so few troops with him that it was ridiculous to suppose that he had intended to make war upon his subjects. They offered these observations as a commentary rather than as a plea, for in fact they denied the competence of the court. It was packed with partisans who ought to have recused themselves; it denied the right of every nobleman to trial by his peers; above all, it was a flagrant breach of faith, a violation of the pledge which Karl had given when they became his prisoners: the pledge that they should be tried by impartial foreign princes.

In this defence there was only one weak point: their disclaimer of responsibility for Sigismund's invasion. The king would no doubt have attempted the recovery of his authority without their encouragement; but Karl was perfectly right to charge them with having incited him, and their answer on this head was an unworthy equivocation. For the rest, the dialectical as well as the moral advantage was overwhelmingly on their side. Not that it mattered. Their refusal to acknowledge the court was interpreted as an impudent challenge to the authority of the representatives of the nation. Their appeal to their duty to the king was brushed aside on the ground that their councillor's oath bound them to keep the king to the observance of the law—though in fact it did no such thing.[2] As to the promise at Stångebro, Karl tried hard to confuse it with the similar promise in the treaty of Linköping (now, of course, to be considered as abrogated); when this subterfuge was exposed he denied the promise altogether; and finally he contended that even if such a promise had been given it would have been invalid as conflicting with Gustav Vasa's Testament (!). For truth and consistency he cared not at all, and the court not much more. It was indeed vital to him to secure a conviction. What was on trial at Linköping was not only the conduct of the *råd* over the last six years: it was his own conduct too.

[1] Karl did not scruple to allege that he had renounced the government in consequence of their urging.

[2] It was quite true that the Land Law prescribed such an oath for members of the *råd*. But since the accession of Gustav Vasa this clause had been consistently omitted, as it was also in 1594: it would have implied a recognition of the claims of the *råd* to be mediators between king and people, custodians of the constitution, ephors—a claim which Karl no less than Sigismund rejected. Karl cannot have been unaware of the true state of the case, and his charge against the *råd* was particularly iniquitous, since in 1594 Erik Sparre had in fact prepared a draft oath incorporating this particular clause, and Sigismund had refused to accept it: *Svenska riksdagsakter*, I, iii, 369.

Their acquittal would be his condemnation; their guilt was necessary to set him right with his countrymen, with European public opinion, perhaps also with himself. If they would confess it, he was always prepared to admit them to pardon: justification was even more important to him than vengeance. It is true that he threatened that if they denied the competence of the court he would not hesitate to apply the laws of war, and execute the defendants as prisoners taken in battle. But this was by no means the outcome he desired: his menace was rather designed to impress waverers with the uselessness of trying to save the prisoner's lives. Plaintiff and defendants alike felt themselves in a sense to be standing at the bar of history: the issue was nothing less than their reputation and good name. It was also, of course, more than that: for Karl, political survival; for the *råd*, constitutional principle, on which they could not compromise without betraying their ideals and denying their past. What to Karl was treason was to them law.

The secondary figures among the accused, those who had never borne the brunt of the battle and were thus less committed, might be forgiven if they accepted Karl's offer, and confessed their error. Most of them in fact did so, and were pardoned. Hogenskild Bielke's skill in covering his tracks defeated all efforts to bring any serious charge home to him, and the case against him, though it was kept open, was for the moment dropped.[1] But for Erik Sparre, Ture Bielke, Gustav and Sten Baner, evasion and capitulation were alike impossible. They fought their case doggedly to the end, intransigent, resourceful, sustained by a conviction of right; but the verdict was never in doubt. The court condemned them all to death, together with the Finnish prisoners Arvid Stålarm, Axel Kurck and Bengt Falk. Stålarm and Kurck were respited after being led out to execution. But on 20 March 1600 the other five went bravely to their deaths in Linköping market-place, Erik Sparre protesting his innocence from the scaffold. The unruly members had been lopped off at last.

The proceedings at Linköping make distasteful reading. No doubt they were no worse, if also no better, than many a Tudor attainder. But for Sweden they were a novelty. The political vicissitudes of the fifteenth century—unlike similar upheavals in England—had never been followed by the quasi-judicial murder of the leaders of the losing side: in 1600 the defence protested that the imputing of criminality to those who were worsted in political conflict was an innovation repugnant to native traditions, and that the proceedings were unprecedented in the history of Swedish law. Yet in this they themselves bore at least a share of the responsibility. It was they who, in an attempt to shore up

[1] It had included charges of imposing Johan's Liturgy upon the country, and conspiring to have Sigismund educated as a Roman Catholic.

the joint regency, had first secured the approval of the *riksdag* for the punitive clauses of Söderköping; it was they—the champions of legality—who had first substituted parliamentary resolutions for the ordinary process of law: in essence, if not in form, something closely akin to attainder. The pit into which they now fell was of their own digging. Yet from another point of view their condemnation can be seen as the first hint of an important constitutional principle, pointing the way forward to later developments. For they suffered because, among other crimes, they had failed to prevent Sigismund from taking action considered to be illegal: upon them was laid the iniquity of the king's misdeeds. It was to be many years yet before the correlative ideas of ministerial responsibility and royal irresponsibility were clearly formulated—how many, may be seen from the fact that their immediate successor in misfortune was probably Görtz in 1719—but it was not quite without significance that in 1600 the *riksdag* should have decided that obedience to the king's commands was not a complete defence.

But if amid the tragic events at Linköping it is possible for us to see, if only with the eye of faith, the seeds of a constitutional doctrine, that was not a consolation available to contemporaries. To them it must have seemed that the cause of law and liberty had suffered a grievous defeat. The constitutional traditions of the fifteenth century, resurrected by Erik Sparre, and by him refashioned and reformulated to meet the needs of the age, seemed to have been extinguished. Aristocratic constitutionalism, as it had developed in the last forty years, had been brutally rejected by the nation. The authority of the *råd* had been broken, its claim to be an indispensable element in policy-making denied. Yet at the same time, by a reckless paradox, the *råd* had been condemned for failure to discharge its historic function as guardian of the law: the ephorate which refused to revolt was stigmatized as the enemy of the people. Nevertheless, the disaster, great though it was, was not definitive. The principles for which Erik Sparre had fought were not invalidated by his death. Within a dozen years they would spring once more into vigorous life; and thereafter they would be a leading influence in the development of the constitution. One achievement, at least, would remain long after the executioner of Linköping had retired from business. The Charter of 1594 was a precedent which was not forgotten, even when absolutism seemed to have won a final victory: it would provide one of the bases upon which the constitutionalism of the Age of Liberty was to be built.

For the moment, however, the constitutional aspects of the revolution were of secondary importance; or at least, every effort was made to make them appear so. To the men who attended as members of the *riksdag* at Linköping, to their constituents up and down the country, the fall of Sigismund and the punishment of his counsellors was represented as the salvation of Protestantism; Karl was the nation's deliverer from the bonds of popery and superstition; the executioner's sword was the avenging sword of Gideon. This, as we have seen, was but a small part of the truth; but when so much hung upon the support of the lower Estates it was necessary to simplify the issues to their understanding. The Protestant cause was a cause with which the masses could identify themselves; it provided both the heat requisite for revolution, and the sanction to justify it. At Linköping Karl extracted from the Estate of Clergy an opinion that if Sigismund had been victorious in 1598 Protestantism would have been in danger. In this they were, as it happened, perfectly right; for Sigismund seems to have told Malaspina before the expedition set out that if he were compelled to reduce Sweden to obedience by force of arms he would impose his religion upon his subjects. But he had added that unless he should be driven to that extremity he desired no more than toleration; and it is clear that the responsibility for civil war cannot be laid at his door. It was certainly not the least important result of the revolution that it should have made the monarchy for ever Protestant; but in 1596, when the revolution really began, this was far from being the main issue. It is probable that a crisis of some sort was inevitable: Sigismund's arrangements for the government of his kingdom could hardly have been tolerated indefinitely. But there might quite well have been formed a national front so strong that the crisis would have been painlessly and quickly resolved. The formation of such a front was indeed attempted; that it failed was the fault of Karl. The *råd*, however reluctantly, had been prepared to collaborate with him; even to accept him as regent. The fact that he in the end refused to work with them was due not to anything so simple as ambition (though that entered into it too), but to other defects in his character: his intolerance of disagreement, his incomprehension of impartiality, his blindness to the possibility that others besides himself might have consciences that constrained them; so that he was fatally prone to regard doubt and dissent as personal affronts, treacheries to himself, and finally, by a supreme egotism, as treason. It is possible that Karl did not perceive where his actions were leading him; and his protestations of loyalty may well have been sincere. But it was always loyalty on his own terms.

The form taken by the crisis of the nineties was not inevitable, nor was its coming spontaneous: it was induced. As far as any great movement can be considered the work of one man, the Swedish revolution was the work of Karl. He emerged as the sole victor. And to him went the spoils.

6. Karl IX

I. EUROPEAN REPERCUSSIONS: THE LIVONIAN WAR

It is difficult to read the story of the Swedish Revolution without at times being struck by its similarity, in many important features, to that more celebrated revolution which occurred in England ninety years later. In each case a dynasty was deposed by the act of a representative assembly; in each, the new sovereign held his throne upon a parliamentary title. In Sweden, as in England, religious and constitutional questions were tightly intertwined, and a policy of attempted toleration was resisted, not only because it seemed to imperil the established church, but because it was deemed to violate the spirit of the constitution and appeared to presage an attempt to rule absolutely in the law's despite. The clash between the duties of a subject and the interests of religion, between fidelity to the church and loyalty to the king as God's vice-gerent, produced as poignant a personal crisis in Angermannus as it was later to do in Sancroft; Tyrconnel seems like a distant, muffled echo of Klas Fleming; Ireland is England's Finland. The results of the two revolutions, it is true, were very different: in Sweden the usurper sealed his victory in the blood of the champions of the constitution; and the first Swedish Whigs, by a paradox which would have staggered Sydney or Russell, suffered death upon the scaffold for their defence of the king's cause. It is true, too, that social tensions and class antagonisms were both more obvious and more important in the Swedish crisis than in the English. But even so, the two occasions have perhaps more points of resemblance than of difference; and not the least of them is that both had a historic significance which far transcended the domestic politics of the countries in which they occurred. Each was an event in the history of Europe. No doubt the fight at Stångebro, a trivial skirmish on a petty stream, lay too far below the mist-shrouded northern horizon for many statesmen to remark it. When Karl led out his army to the attack, 'on Michaelmas Day in the morning, in fine calm weather, as the dew sunk to the ground, and the sun moved to his rising',[1] Europe did not wait with bated breath for the outcome, as on that June morning when King William affronted the dark waters of the Boyne. No foreign contingent in the duke's army testified to his membership of a great coalition; nor did

[1] *Egenhändiga anteckningar af Carl Carlsson Gyllenhielm*, p. 278.

the news of his success elicit congratulation from the courts of the continent. The deposition of Sigismund was certainly a check to Spanish hopes of preying on Dutch commerce from the safe harbourage of Älvsborg or Hälsingborg; but this had been a bogy for a quarter of a century, and it was losing something of its power to terrify. Karl worked hard to persuade Europe that his triumph was a victory for the Protestant Cause everywhere; but whatever his success at home—and it was considerable: the next generation, and not least Axel Oxenstierna, accepted the official propaganda without question—he made little immediate impression abroad. Protestant Europe declined to identify Karl's grievances with the cause of God; nor could his success make respectable German princes forget Luther's denunciation of rebellion.

Yet in the long run, and in its own despite, Karl's propaganda told the truth. The opening of the new century is also the opening of a new era in Swedish foreign policy. The country's narrowly national interests indeed remain unaltered; but more and more they come to run parallel to wider European causes, and finally to coincide with them. Before the next decade was out, the lines of division between Protestant and Catholic states would be drawn with a harsher emphasis than at any time during the preceding half-century, as central Europe braced itself for the disaster which its statesmen foresaw. The uncommitted foreign policy which Sweden had followed under Johan III was becoming more difficult to pursue than in the past: James I, among the greater princes of Europe, Kristian IV among the lesser, would find the world a colder place for temporizers, neutralists and Laodiceans. The ruler who for one reason or another was politically isolated would in the future find it easier to grapple friends to himself with hoops of doctrinal steel. Karl's wholehearted commitment to the ideal of Protestant solidarity became more relevant to actual conditions in the years after his usurpation than it had ever been before; and sooner or later it would range Sweden, despite the fastidious shrinking of German Lutherans, in a politico-religious camp. In 1600, it must be confessed, this was not yet apparent, nor did Karl live to see it. It took a whole generation before Europe was prepared unreservedly to accept the dynastic struggle between the two branches of the house of Vasa as an admitted aspect of the great question which was moving to the climax of the Thirty Years' War. For the rest of his life Karl knocked perseveringly at the doors of the Protestant courts, importuning his co-religionists to admit him to an evangelical *bloc* which was never as solid as he imagined it to be. But he knocked in vain; his too-eager proposals were received with a chill only partially tempered by politeness, and he had as little success in thrusting himself upon the party of the zealots as his father had had in insinuating himself into the League of

Schmalkalde. A more urgent sense of peril, a more impressive demonstration of Swedish power would be required before the princes of Germany came to welcome Karl's son as an ally and solicit him as a deliverer. But the change of dynasty in Sweden, and the conscious Protestant alignment which was its consequence, proved decisive for the fate of central Europe. In itself the victory of Karl might seem insignificant; yet without Stångebro there could hardly have been a Breitenfeld.

As early as 1599 Karl had made overtures for an alliance to England and to the Dutch. Queen Elizabeth, who had her own grievances against Poland, and had recently demolished a Polish ambassador with an impromptu broadside which rang round Europe, expressed her sympathy; but she took care to remain studiously vague. The Dutch were scarcely even sympathetic. They were irritated by Swedish privateering; they were fearful of the effect upon their Danzig corn-trade if they offended Sigismund; if they must have a friend in Scandinavia they looked to Denmark, as the stronger naval power in the Baltic, rather than to Sweden. Henry IV of France, who in his own person represented the triumph of legitimacy, could have little fellow-feeling for a usurper: so little, that as late as 1608 he was putting himself to some trouble to avoid according to Karl the royal style. He was, indeed, not uninterested in the dynastic feud of the Vasas; but his object was to settle it by some sort of compromise which would restore Sigismund to his throne. He saw with alarm the prospect of Poland's gravitating into the Habsburg orbit,[1] and in the hope of arresting this declension was prepared to be busy in Sigismund's favour: in 1605 he sent an ambassador to Sweden in a fruitless attempt to frighten or cajole Karl into compliance. In the first years of the century, then, no hope of French patronage or protection: Henry's diplomacy had more important objectives than the enrolment of Sweden among his clients. To a treaty of amity there could be no objection; but an alliance was another matter.

In Germany the outlook was not much better. The German princes found themselves unable to grasp, or at least to approve, the constitutional arguments with which Karl tried to convince them of the legality of his conduct. They were unmoved by his diplomatic circulars, sceptical of his appeals to confessional solidarity, and by no means impressed by the Estates' repeated renunciations of their allegiance to Sigismund. The Protestant states of the north-east had no desire to jeopardize their good relations with Poland. This was especially true of Brandenburg; for the Hohenzollerns' prospects of retaining the duchy

[1] Sigismund's first wife, Anna, daughter of the Archduke Karl of Styria, had died in 1598, but he was to marry her sister Constantia in 1605.

of Prussia in the family depended upon preserving the goodwill of the king of Poland, who was the duke of Prussia's feudal overlord.[1] There were, indeed, two German princes who were prepared to accept Karl's account of himself at its face value, and from the beginning gave him their moral support. One was the Elector Palatine, who was the brother of Karl's first wife; the other was Maurice of Hesse, who was first cousin to his second. They represented the extreme left wing of German Protestantism. Both were Calvinists, and as such excluded from the protection of the religious peace of Augsburg; both sought to build up a strong Protestant party for the struggle which they believed to be imminent; neither was as committed as their Lutheran colleagues to the ideal of legitimism or a belief in the iniquity of revolution. But even they had more important political objects than the maintenance of the Swedish revolution. They were most anxious to attract the elector of Brandenburg to their party; and this they could hardly hope to do if they advertised themselves as the champions of Sigismund's enemy, for the elector would never risk losing Prussia by offending the king of Poland. If it came to a choice between enlisting Brandenburg and supporting Sweden, a statesman as judicious as Maurice could hardly mistake where his best interest lay.

There remained Sweden's two neighbours, Kristian IV and Boris Godunov. It was perhaps in an attempt to conciliate their good will that at the close of 1600 Karl asked the advice of each of them as to whether he should take the crown which the *riksdag* had offered him. Boris, who had himself usurped the throne, had no hesitation in recommending Karl to follow his example; but he had no intention of committing himself to political support. In 1600 Sigismund, reviving an old project of Stefan Batory, made elaborate proposals for a treaty of eternal alliance with Muscovy, to be followed by an eventual political union of the two states; and though Boris was not to be beguiled by fantasies of this sort he was willing enough to conclude a twenty-year truce in 1601. The divisions in the Vasa family seemed to him an opportunity to play off one branch against the other, and perhaps to recover Narva in the process. Kristian IV had similar ideas. His sympathies lay with Sigismund rather than with Karl; and if his policy was still neutrality, it had hitherto been a neutrality which leaned to Sigismund's side: in 1599, as Karl very well remembered, he had permitted the Polish fleet to sail through the Sound on its way to the abortive *coup* on Älvsborg. He had a long list of scores against his

[1] The duke of Prussia had no children, was hopelessly insane, and was in the custody of a guardian appointed by the king of Poland. It was vital for the elector of Brandenburg to ensure, first, that the successor to the guardianship should be a member of the Hohenzollern family, and secondly that when the mad duke himself died the elector should be enfeoffed with his duchy.

neighbour. The civil broils in Sweden might give him a chance to settle them; while in a longer perspective he looked forward to a war which should restore the old Scandinavian Union, if only he could carry his council with him. The Danish councillors, no doubt, were determinedly pacific; but even they disliked Karl and the cause he represented. Themselves strongly imbued with a Danish variety of aristocratic constitutionalism, and bound by not-too-distant ties of blood to the Swedish nobility, they looked on Karl with the eyes of Erik Sparre, and predicted with satisfaction the speedy termination of his rule. Thus neither Denmark nor Russia could be counted on as an ally, or even relied upon to be quiet. Indeed, it appeared for a moment that Kristian and Boris might be moving towards an alliance with a point against Sweden. In 1602 a Danish prince went to Moscow to marry the tsar's daughter; and only the happy accident of his death from plague soon after his arrival prevented a connexion which Karl was bound to view with alarm. Dr Richard Lee, Elizabeth's busy ambassador, who was concerned to appease the rancours of the North in the interests of free trade for Englishmen, might delude himself that Swedish participation in a Danish-Russian system was feasible; but he was probably alone in his opinion.

Since the international prospects were so unpromising, it might perhaps have been expected that Karl would make every effort to avoid involving himself in a war with Poland. His quarrel with Sigismund by no means necessarily implied a breach with the Polish Republic: on the contrary, most Poles had no desire to be dragged into war for the sake of their king's dynastic concerns. Zamoyski, no doubt, still hoped for some benefit from that union of the crowns of which he had been the chief architect, and he had encouraged Sigismund's return to Sweden in 1598 so that he might himself have his hands free to pursue Polish ambitions in Moldavia. Less obsessed by fear of an increase in the power of the crown than the majority of his countrymen, he was able to grasp the fact that Sigismund's private interests were not necessarily alien to the interests of his subjects: in particular he realized that if Poland really desired to acquire Estonia, this was the moment to do it. But few Poles were as clear-sighted. By mid-June 1600 Karl knew for certain that the *sejm* had refused Sigismund assistance to recover Sweden, and he knew too that they had declared themselves opposed to any attempt to conquer Estonia. Without the support of the *sejm* Sigismund's prospects were almost hopeless. If Karl could contrive that his army and navy should be in good trim, while keeping a wary eye on Livonia, he could feel reasonably secure, at least for the present. In 1600 the revolution settlement was in no danger from without; the frontiers of Estonia were unmenaced; the prospects looked fair for peace.

Yet in August of that year he began the invasion of Livonia, alleging as his reason the refusal of the Polish commander to give an undertaking that peace would be preserved. But this was a mere pretext: Karl had 17,000 men in Estonia to defend the province against 2,000 Poles, and even for the Swedish army as it then was this was a sufficiently comfortable margin. The real reason for what in the sequel came to look like a piece of disastrous and wanton folly is by no means clear. It may be that Karl hoped that an invasion of Livonia would constrain Sigismund to agree to some sort of compromise: at the end of the year he certainly proposed that their dispute be submitted to arbitration, though it may be doubted whether he would have relished being taken at his word.[1] Again, it is possible that he felt a war with Sigismund to be necessary to his position at home: no nation can long remain grateful (and obedient) to the deliverer from a non-existent menace. Karl had thriven too well on crises and emergencies, on Protestant panics and banausic fears, to be willing to deprive himself of such useful assets. Or, finally, he may have had the deliberate purpose of extending Sweden's grip upon the southern Baltic shore, and seized a moment when Poland was weak to effect it. The Düna offered a much more defensible frontier than that which Estonia possessed; Livonia was a Protestant province which might be expected to prefer a Swedish to a Polish ruler; most tempting of all, it included the great trading city of Riga. Erik XIV in his day had coveted Riga, and Karl certainly coveted it now, for its possession would greatly improve Sweden's chances of achieving a dominant position in the trade of the Baltic.

Whatever the true explanation of his action, there is no doubt that it was a naked aggression upon a peaceful neighbour. Karl's propaganda, therefore, was directed to putting the blame on his adversary. He assured his subjects that he had done his best to keep the peace: his efforts had been defeated by the 'fearful malice' of Sigismund and the papacy, who had plotted the war as long ago as 1598. He had need to lie boldly, for the war was from the beginning most unpopular in Sweden. The more intelligent of his subjects found his inventions hard to swallow. In 1604 the *riksdag* did indeed endorse the official version, though it may be doubted whether they really believed it. But by that time Karl had evolved the ingenious argument that the war was really not his but theirs: they could put an end to it at any time by accepting Sigismund as their sovereign; if they were unwilling to do that, it must be presumed that they wished to carry it on. Whence followed the practical conclusion that they had no grounds for refusing supplies.

[1] In August 1601 Karl wrote to Rudolf II, offering to hand over Livonia to the Archduke Maximilian against financial compensation, but the proposal can hardly have been seriously intended.

Karl's attack caught the Poles quite unprepared. It did indeed convince them that Sigismund's quarrel was now their own; but the *sejm* was slow to grant supplies, most of the Polish forces were in the far south, and for six months there was little effective resistance. Karl was able to overrun most of Livonia without difficulty. In October 1600 he captured Pernau and Dorpat; in the following spring he advanced to the Düna. But his conquest of Livonia was not complete: the castle of Kokenhusen held out, though the town was taken; and though in May 1601 his fleet began the blockade of Riga, his army could make no impression upon it. In the summer of 1601 Sigismund, who had pawned the crown jewels to raise an army, took the field in force. Karl, though greatly superior in numbers, did not stay to dispute with him, but hastily decamped to Estonia. A sharp defeat inflicted on the besiegers of Kokenhusen suggested that he was prudent to do so.

For in fact the Swedish army was incapable of meeting the Poles in battle, unless safeguarded by enormous numerical superiority. The military reforms of Erik XIV had been one of the first casualties of the rebellion which deposed him. His regimental organization was allowed to lapse; his tactical innovations were forgotten. The Swedish infantry made all speed to discard the pikes and body armour which he had compelled them to bear, and robustly asserted their right to be slaughtered in their own fashion, unconstrained by royal tyranny. Johan had at first no option but to acquiesce in a reaction which was so popular; but the experiences of the Russian war soon convinced him of its unwisdom. His attempts to reintroduce the pike, however, broke down on the resistance of the soldiery; and in his reign the Swedish forces declined both in quality and in numbers.[1] The army with which Karl began the Livonian war was in every respect inferior to that which Erik XIV had commanded. Its tactics and its arms were alike antiquated: the foot, for instance, was still armed with the arquebus, though in most of western Europe this had already been replaced by the musket. Above all, its lack of pikes made it incapable of offering any effective resistance to a cavalry charge. It is true that by 1600 cavalry charges had dropped out of fashion: the contemporary cavalryman was a degenerate pistoleer whose ineffective discharges need cause no apprehension even to the rawest of infantrymen. But, as it happened, one of the very few countries which still used cavalry in the way in which cavalry was meant to be used was the country which Karl had chosen to attack. The Polish horse was the best in Europe; its weapons were the lance and the sabre; it shattered its enemies by charging home.

[1] Johan did more for the army than has sometimes been appreciated: he improved the system of pay, standardized for the first time the method of selecting men for the militia, and in 1590 organized his forces into regular regiments for the first time since the death of Erik XIV.

If Karl had searched the whole continent he could not have found an adversary whom his soldiers were less fitted to confront.

To do him justice, he was quick to realize this, and soon made up his mind that his army must be drastically reorganized. It was a sound instinct which led him to offer to abandon the system of militia-drafts, in exchange for an arrangement which would provide him with something like a standing force: as one continental ruler after another discovered, a standing army offered far better opportunities for training in the new drill and the new discipline than could be afforded by casual annual levies. The *riksdag*, however, was unwilling, and Karl did not venture to press the proposal. Nor was he any more successful than his brother in persuading his infantry to trail the pike. The defeat at Kokenhusen clearly demonstrated the need for it. Even though the Swedish cavalry, with their pistols and their caracoles, would never be a match for the Polish lancers, the foot might well have had reasonable prospects if properly armed, and especially if they could be trained in the new Dutch tactics. Those tactics, like Erik's before them, restored linear formations to the battlefield; they provided much flexibility, intensified fire-power, and good pike-protection; they posited strict discipline, elaborate training, and—since the tactical unit was much reduced in size—numerous officers and N.C.Os. Karl lacked the experience to carry through such a change himself; but in the summer of 1601 chance offered him the services of a man who had all the details of the new system at his fingers' ends.

It happened about this time that Philip III of Spain conferred upon Sigismund the Order of the Golden Fleece. His action was interpreted as presaging a closer Spanish concern with the affairs of northern Europe: there were rumours that Spain was to send Sigismund naval aid. The Protestant powers noted these things with alarm; and Maurice of Hesse, conceiving Karl to be most immediately imperilled, sent John of Nassau to give him a friendly warning. He arrived in the Swedish camp in July, was warmly welcomed, and was eventually persuaded to enter Karl's service and take command of the army, with the specific purpose of reorganizing it upon Dutch models. John found it a depressing task, and soon came to the conclusion that it was almost a hopeless one. He insisted, as a condition of undertaking it, that the numbers of the army be substantially increased; but this was in fact the least of his problems. Though he recognized that the fighting quality of the Swedish soldiers was potentially high, he had the poorest opinion of their discipline, training and equipment. In the few months he remained in command he was able to correct some of these defects: he taught them drill; he even taught them the rudiments of Dutch tactics. But Dutch tactics were worse than useless—indeed, they were positively dangerous—as long as the men had an inferior firearm and no pike-hedge behind which they could take cover. When in the summer of 1602 he threw up his command and returned to Holland, to spread reports of his experiences which did no good to Karl's prestige abroad, he left behind him a force upon which he had imposed a reorganization which lacked the basic requirements for its proper functioning. The army had been half-reformed; and the last state of it was arguably worse than the first.

Certainly it was in no case to meet the slow-gathering Polish counter-offensive which developed towards the end of 1601. The Swedes had still a great superiority in numbers, and they had at their disposal a terrain not unfavourable to Fabian defensive tactics; but they proved incapable of using these advantages. The Poles bundled them out of Livonia as quickly as they had come, so that by the summer of 1602 only Dorpat and Pernau remained in Swedish possession. Estonia itself was now invaded: in July the Poles took Weissenstein. The country was so devastated by famine that families had to be moved to Sweden to save them from starvation; the army was mutinous. In a desperate attempt to find a competent commander to replace John of Nassau, Karl took the risk of appointing his old enemy Arvid Stålarm, a prisoner since his trial at Linköping; but Stålarm was no match for Chodkiewicz, who in 1603 took Dorpat despite all his efforts to save it. By the middle of that year Sweden's hold upon Estonia had been reduced to the immediate environs of Reval and Narva.

Three years' experience of the performance of conscripted troops had by this time finally disillusioned Karl with the system of *utskrivning*. He was determined in future to fight the war with professionals; and at the Norrköping *riksdag* of 1604 he persuaded the Estates to grant him for three years a special tax—the 'contribution'—sufficient to hire an army of 9,000 men.[1] The new troops could not be raised in a hurry, and in the meantime it was obviously essential to stand on the defensive. Karl realized this, and he forbade Stålarm to risk a battle; but as he simultaneously harassed him with demands for action, and bitterly criticized him when action proved unsuccessful, Stålarm's position soon became impossible. Threatened with recall and disgrace unless he did better and showed results, he was goaded at last into disobeying his instructions, and rashly engaged Chodkiewicz near Weissenstein (15 September 1604). The result was disastrous for his army, and for himself. Only a fortunate 'confederation' among the victorious Polish troops saved the remnants of Swedish dominion in Estonia; and nothing now could save Stålarm from Karl's vengeance.

[1] The change had its disadvantages. A resolution of the *riksdag* in 1609 granted Karl an aid 'since H.M. has to use a large number of foreign troops, who must always have their full pay, if they are to be of any use': A. A. von Stiernman, *Alla Riksdagars och Mötes Besluth*, I, 634.

Stålarm's failure once more forced Karl to take command himself, though his previous record in the field was not inspiring, and the Estates, who foresaw confusion if he were killed, were very reluctant to let him go. But the international situation was threatening, both on the side of Russia and on the side of Denmark, and he was anxious to be quit of his Polish war that he might be free to deal with other emergencies. He wanted a quick victory, and a decisive one; and he believed that he could get it. His plan was to march upon Riga, force the Poles to give battle in order to save the town, and then to crush them by sheer weight of numbers. And it seemed, indeed, that he might be successful. Early in September 1605 he arrived before Riga with an army of over 11,000 men; against him Chodkiewicz had no more than 3,400. At Kirkholm he drew up his army for battle, and Chodkiewicz obligingly attacked him. The result was decisive indeed, but not in the sense that Karl had predicated. Tactical dispositions which made the worst of both worlds, the inability of the Swedish cavalry to meet their opponents on equal terms, the insufficiency of pikemen among the Swedish foot, and sheer bad generalship, combined to achieve the seemingly impossible. The Swedish horse was routed, the Swedish foot cut to pieces, Karl himself escaped with the greatest difficulty from the carnage. When the day was over his army was virtually annihilated: their losses in dead amounted to at least 7,600—more than twice the total Polish forces engaged—against a mere 900 on the other side. It was probably the severest defeat ever to be experienced by a Swedish army; it was certainly one of the most brilliant victories ever to be won by a Polish commander. But just as the issue of the battle was against all probability, so its consequences were other than might have been expected. Kirkholm did not mean the end of the war in Livonia; it brought Sigismund no nearer to recovering his throne, though for a brief moment of jubilation he permitted himself to think so. At the very time when Kirkholm was fought, his domestic opponents were already preparing an insurrection; and before the end of the year their discontent erupted in the complex crisis which is known as the *rokosz* of Zebrzydowski. The fruits of victory were snatched from him just when they seemed to be within his grasp; the Polish army in Livonia was paralysed; the Swedish, beyond all expectation, reprieved.

Thus the Livonian war, which ought to have ended in 1605, continued to drag on for the remainder of Karl's reign, and for nearly two decades thereafter. After Kirkholm it became a desultory affair, punctuated by truces, and increasingly merged in the larger question of the struggle for ascendancy in Russia.[1] But in its heyday it had shed a disturbing light upon the military weakness of Sweden. The methods

[1] See below, p. 454.

which sufficed for Johan III's campaigns against the Russians would not serve against a more sophisticated foe; the empire of the Baltic could hardly be defended by such means. It would be one of Gustav Adolf's main preoccupations to remedy the defects against which his father had struggled in vain. Sixteen years after Kirkholm he would succeed where Karl had failed: in 1621 Riga became, and for nearly a century remained, a Swedish city.

II. THE DYNASTIC SETTLEMENT AND ITS ENEMIES

In 1600, despite the pressure of the Estates, Karl had contrived to avoid committing himself to an assumption of the crown; and a further four years were to elapse before he could be brought to accept what to most men seemed the irresistible logic of the situation. Temperamentally conservative, at times something of a constitutional pedant, he was unwilling either to appropriate the spoils of victory or to forgo them. He had no liking for revolutions, and was a harsh judge of those who rebelled against their lawful sovereign: Engelbrekt to him was an 'unruly spirit', with whom the magnates should never have allowed themselves to come to terms. To take the crown at the hands of the Estates, moreover, might seem to assort oddly with his vigorous denunciation of electoral monarchy. The least that the situation demanded was a decent hesitancy: he must be pressed to ascend the throne, if only to make it plain that he had not sought it. The responsibility for the violation of the legitimist proprieties must rest, and must be seen to rest, on the Estates' shoulders: hence his insistence that they must promulgate a printed renunciation and a formal act of deposition, as a precondition for his acquiescence; hence his demand that before his coronation they should send embassies to the principal European courts to explain their actions. By forcing them to agree to these things he committed them before European public opinion, and so in a measure insured himself against their changing their minds. The Estates were now dependent upon him if they wished to have a king at all; and he could—for a time—postpone a decision in the knowledge that the very uncertainty of the situation would make them more pliant to his will. He exploited his advantage with a realism reminiscent of his father. Opposition to his policies, reluctance to comply with his demands, was met with threats to lay down the government, or ironical suggestions that they should either reconcile themselves with Sigismund or turn to Johan. These tactics did not lose their effectiveness even after his acceptance of the crown in 1604; for the anxiety of the Estates to hurry on his coronation made them equally vulnerable to blackmail thereafter, and he seems to have deferred the coronation precisely because their desire for it gave him a hold over them. It is clear that his conscience was not at ease about the exclusion of Johan. There may even have been occasions when his urging of Johan's claims—as distinct from those of Sigismund or Władysław—was seriously meant. But it is difficult to believe that after 1600 he would willingly have forgone the position he had won. Certainly he expected that his son would be king after his death: in 1601 a codicil to his Testament of the previous year fully accepts the Estates' designation of Gustav Adolf as the successor. On the whole it is probable that he had by then made up his mind to be king, though after a seemly interval; but this did not for a moment stop him from complaining bitterly of the 'ingratitude' of those he had 'delivered' when he wished to establish a moral advantage; or from frightening them with talk of compromise with Sigismund; or from petulant outbursts against the congenital faithlessness of the Swedish people and the especial laziness and incompetence of those upon whose help he had to rely. Every handle that could exert pressure was adroitly grasped; any line of attack, however unfair, was utilized without scruple, with a fine disregard for mere consistency. Gustav Vasa himself never played the injured monarch with more cynicism or more effect.

But indeed the situation was not one in which he could afford to be over-nice in his choice of means. His rule rested on the upport of only a portion of society: the peasantry, the poorer townsmen, a part of the army command, his own personal following among the nobility; and of these the lower orders were always liable to be alienated by the burdens which his foreign policy entailed upon them. The clergy were suspicious; the aristocracy divided, a majority of them at best acquiescent. Beyond the frontiers in Denmark and Norway, across the sea in Poland and the Baltic ports, was a group of *émigrés* who saw in Karl not merely a political adversary but a personal enemy, and would pursue him with their hatred beyond the grave. There had been Swedes in Poland since Sigismund's election in 1587, some of them attached to that Swedish chancery which he persisted in maintaining for many years after 1600; but the real emigration had come in three later waves —after the Söderköping *riksdag* of 1595, after the Arboga *riksdag* of 1597, and after Stångebro. There were perhaps three to four hundred of these exiles. Some were common soldiers, personal servants, court musicians and the like; but there was also a strong contingent of senior civil servants from the chancery and exchequer, many of whom had reached Poland by way of Finland and Estonia; there was a handful of men of learning; and above all there was a disproportionately large element drawn from the nobility: they numbered perhaps a hundred, or more than a quarter of the whole. Most of the great *råd*-families were represented: two Brahes, four Sparres, two Bielkes, three Stenbocks, three Gyllenstiernas. The latest of Axel Leijonhufvud's tergiversations had led to his flight abroad soon after the Linköping trial; the Posses would follow in 1603. The fugitives left behind them relatives who had either reconciled themselves to Karl (as Abraham Brahe did), or who somehow contrived to keep out of politics altogether (like Lage Posse), or who were in secret sympathy with the exiles and maintained a clandestine correspondence with them. The aristocracy was indeed tragically divided: the network of marriages was so intricate that there can scarcely have been a single great house which could not point to a near relative beyond the seas, and not a few shared with Axel Oxenstierna and the Bielkes the grim experience of being called upon to vote the death of a cousin or a brother. No family had more cannily avoided the dangers of the revolution period than the Oxenstiernas; but Elisabeth Oxenstierna was in Poland as lady-in-waiting to Princess Anna; the Posses and Erik Gyllenstierna were Axel's first cousins; and his mother, Barbro Bielke, came within an ace of being involved in the great treason trial of 1605. Inevitably there were comings and goings between the exiles and those they left at home; inevitably Karl's suspicions, kept alive by a succession of conspiracies, came more and more to embrace almost the whole aristocracy. The material circumstances of many of the fugitives were often straitened; many of them lived penuriously at Danzig and had no real contact with Sigismund at all; but at court in Warsaw there was a hard core of determined men who had the king's ear and were constantly busied in schemes to recover his kingdom. He had agents and spies in Sweden who sent him the kind of intelligence he wished to hear; and he had very able pamphleteers at his command who filled Europe with the story of Karl's atrocities.[1] Until Karl recruited Johannes Messenius to his service in 1609, the polemical advantage remained on Sigismund's side; and that perhaps was one reason why the search for foreign friends proved so unrewarding.

Thus Karl found himself faced, for the whole of the last decade of his life, with an irreconcilable band of exiles, whose connexion with discontented elements in Sweden was undoubted, though its extent was largely unknown. To the threat which they presented he reacted in different ways at different times. The revolution was accompanied by

[1] The most venomous of these productions, *Hertig Karls Slaktarebänck* [*Duke Karl's Shambles*] seems to have been written by Gregorius Borastus, from information supplied by Jöran Knutsson Posse. It was not published until 1617, and was soon withdrawn because its untruths were too gross even for a friendly public: among other crimes it charged Karl with being responsible (through war, as well as executions) for the deaths of 66,997 persons—a figure which for precision and imagination far transcends the accusations brought against Erik XIV.

confiscations of lands on such a scale that a special administration had to be created to deal with forfeited estates; the houses and personal effects of those who suffered at Linköping were ransacked and plundered with impunity by some of the more disreputable of Karl's servants; and Karl himself was capable of persecuting their wives and families with an ignoble rancour: throughout his reign he tried at intervals to persuade the *riksdag* to visit the sins of the fathers upon the children by depriving them of their hereditary estates, debarring them for ever from office, or even by driving them into exile. Yet on the other hand in the years immediately after 1600 he made a real attempt to reconcile former opponents. The Finnish nobility, which had been virtually in the dock *en masse* at Linköping, was admitted to grace in 1601; Bishop Sorolainen was restored; many state prisoners were released in 1602, among them Stålarm, Skepperus and the cousins Jöran Knutsson Posse and Jöran Nilsson Posse. Exiles were offered a safe-conduct if they chose to return within six months to have their cases investigated. There were considerable restorations of forfeited estates. It is true that this conciliatory policy was of short duration; but it was abandoned only because events seemed to show that no measures would avail to abate the hostility of the defeated loyalists. In 1603 came the first of a series of plots which put an end to any hope of winning them over by leniency. It was hatched among the nobility of Västergötland (a province which had been hostile to Karl for years), and its leaders were Tord Bonde and the Posse cousins, who thus made an ill requital for their recent enlargement. It was alleged at Bonde's trial that he was aiming at an electoral monarchy, and Jöran Knutsson Posse was reported to have declared that he had as good a right to the throne as Gustav Vasa's offspring. If so, he did not stay to maintain it. The Posses fled headlong to the frontier as soon as the plot was discovered; and another member of the family, Nils, who had no connexion with it at all, followed their example 'in pure panic'. When the Estates met at Norrköping in 1604 Tord Bonde and some of the other conspirators were tried by a special tribunal on the Linköping model; but it proved impossible to bring home the charge of treason to most of them, and in the end Tord Bonde, though condemned to death, was let off with a prison sentence.

The Bonde-Posse plot was something of a turning-point. Henceforward Karl makes no attempt to win over his enemies; repression, growing increasingly harsher in the next two or three years, is now seen as the only remedy. It is likely, moreover, that the plot did something to influence him towards a decision on the question of the kingship. Already in 1603 he had begun to style himself 'elected king'; at the *riksdag* of 1604 he formally signified to the Estates his readiness to take the crown they offered him. It was not done without the usual threat of abdication, the usual suggestions that they make their peace with Sigismund, the usual offers to stand down in favour of Johan; it was preceded by bitter complaints that he received no assistance from his counsellors, and a comprehensive commination of the upper classes—'faithlessness in the nobility, faithlessness in the clergy, faithlessness in the army, faithlessness in the bailiffs, and no punishment for any'[1]—but when the explosion was over, when the last ounce of advantage had been extracted from the situation, and not least when Johan had formally renounced his claims upon the throne, it was done at last.

Karl's assumption of the crown made necessary a revision of the arrangements for the succession. The Succession Pact of Norrköping accordingly laid it down that the throne should pass after Karl's death to Gustav Adolf and his heirs male, then to Karl's younger son Karl Filip and his heirs male, then to Johan. If Johan should die without a son, it was to revert to Gustav Adolf's daughters, if of age and unmarried; and they were recommended to choose husbands from among the Protestant princes of Germany, or at the very worst to refrain from marrying a Pole or a Dane. Adherence to the Lutheran religion was to be a precondition for accession; defection from it was to forfeit the crown. The opportunity was taken, in the preamble to the Pact, to decide the long-standing controversy as to the true nature of the original Succession Pact of 1544, which was now firmly stated to have proceeded from the 'gratitude' of the Estates for the great 'beneficences' of the house of Vasa.

The settlement of the dynastic question was welcome to the *riksdag*, whose patience had latterly been showing signs of wearing thin; but it did nothing to damp the energies of the partisans of Sigismund. The Bonde-Posse conspiracy was scarcely disposed of before it was succeeded by others. In the autumn of 1604 an ensign in the Uppland cavalry—hostile to Karl since 1598—was detected in treasonable correspondence with Sigismund. The discovery was held to compromise Stålarm, whose failures in the field had already led Karl to think that he might be losing battles on purpose; and who was now summoned home to stand his trial. Almost at the same time came the revelation of the intrigues of Hogenskild Bielke. Having narrowly escaped the block in 1600, Bielke had latterly been living in retirement on his estates, busily accumulating evidence to prove the illegality of Karl's proceedings, and hoarding up a great mass of very plain-spoken correspondence: one chest of this inflammatory material was in the safe-keeping of Axel Oxenstierna's mother, who shared her relative's political opinions. Hogenskild had been in touch both with the exiled court

[1] *Register öfver Rådslag i konung Carl IX:s tid*, p. 27.

and with the Posses, and undoubtedly he was a dangerous centre of intrigue. Early in 1605 Karl came upon the track of his activities. His papers were impounded, and himself imprisoned. The same fate overtook his brother Klas Bielke and Krister Horn. The wives of the accused were strictly interrogated; their servants were tortured to make them incriminate their masters; old enemies such as Abraham Angermannus and Bishop Bellinus were retrieved from obscurity for further investigation; and the whole complex of real and supposed conspiracy was referred to a *riksdag* summoned to Stockholm in the spring of 1605. The letter of summons was eloquent of Karl's anger and alarm. Once more he threatened abdication; once more he dilated, in language of unusual vehemence, upon the ingratitude and perfidy of his subjects: sooner than continue to rule over men who 'knew neither oath nor troth, he would go live among wolves and bears'. The *riksdag* proceedings did nothing to soften this ominous exordium: Karl's opening address was a frontal attack on the whole aristocracy. Another extraordinary tribunal—this time of 274 members—was constituted from the assembled members to try the accused; and once again, as at Linköping, it obliged with the appropriate verdict. Stålarm was condemned to death, tortured in the vain hope of extracting further information from him, led out to execution, and once more reprieved: he ended his life in prison, a victim to an unwise attempt to run with the hare and hunt with the hounds.[1] Krister Horn, less guilty than the others, was spared; Klas Bielke was banished into exile, with the angry exhortation to 'pack yourself off to the Pope in Rome or the Devil in Hell'. But Hogenskild, now an old man broken by illness which this time was not feigned, had reached the end of his long and devious career; and for him there was no reprieve. The archbishop was sent to him in prison, to bring him to a proper sense of his guilt in favouring Roman Catholicism, disseminating the Liturgy, and absenting himself from communion; and in the end he wearily confessed to these enormities, not without some characteristic attempts at evasion. But his last speech on the scaffold was a warning to his countrymen to take care what they wrote or spoke; it totally disappointed Karl's hope that it might disclose a conspiracy—indeed, it expressly exculpated Abraham Angermannus and others who were under suspicion; and it stoutly denied the legality of his sentence. Hogenskild confronted death with a firmness which does something to redeem his reputation. But he came to the block at last, and his decapitated head for the rest of the reign ornamented the South Gate of Stockholm, a grim admonition to

[1] Stålarm's servant stated at his trial that he had boasted 'It can all go to Hell for what I care, I'll fix things so as to keep my job!': E. Anthoni, *Konflikten mellan Hertig Karl och Finland*, II, 276.

all advocates of electoral monarchy and champions of aristocratic privilege.

The plots of 1604 and 1605 gave a violent stimulus to that pathological suspiciousness which was hereditary in the Vasa family, and was quite as strongly developed in Karl as in his father. During the sitting of the *riksdag* of 1605 at least a hundred persons are said to have been in prison without trial. Virtually all the old nobility was under suspicion. Prudent men sent their sons to court to enter the king's service as an earnest of sound political principles; and some were plainly told to send them, as hostages for their parents' good behaviour. It was rumoured that Karl designed 'so to root out and oppress the Swedish nobility that there shall be no one found who will venture to avow himself a Swedish nobleman'. The court lived in a murky atmosphere of delations, anonymous accusations and blackmail. Men were condemned without trial upon anonymous reports; their property was taken from them without due process of law; they might find themselves tried twice over the same offence. One of Sigismund's spies drew a famous picture of the terror of the times: 'Here is great inquisition, misery and persecution, with search for letters and writings, racking and other lamentable tortures, with cuttings off of ears and hands, with hot irons and tongs . . . with quarterings on wheel and stake, and sundry other torments . . . The leading families are in great pain, as well women as men; the foremost countesses and other ladies, and especially the wives of the gentlemen lately executed, are separated one from another, and each kept in separate custody, and before that their keys taken from them, their houses, chests and desks ransacked for letters and writings, and they have moreover been forced to make oath that they have no letters or writings anywhere concealed, but would show and produce everything.'[1] We need not take this account too literally: the opportunity for damaging propaganda was too good to miss. Karl's terror was bad enough, and in its disregard of the forms of law full as tyrannical as Erik XIV's; but it claimed far fewer victims. It was the response to a danger which was no mere phantom of Karl's imagination; and he was entitled to regard what he did as legitimate self-defence. But it gave to the reign a sense of stifling oppressiveness which the nobility felt to be intolerable: henceforward they, and ever larger sections of society with them, would look forward to the day of Karl's death as the moment of deliverance. Only in an atmosphere charged with fears and rumours could a government have proceeded to such severity as was used against the unfortunate Petrus Petrosa in 1606. Petrosa was a pupil of the Jesuits, 'theologically syncretist and

[1] Lars Sjödin, 'Hans Bilefeldts rapporter till Knut Persson åren 1602 och 1605', *Historisk Tidskrift* (1939), pp. 433–4.

politically inoffensive', who had obtained employment in the chancery because the shortage of qualified men was so great as to outweigh even these dubious antecedents. His only crime was to have tried to obtain an audience of Sigismund while on a diplomatic mission; but it was sufficient to ensure his condemnation and barbarous execution for a plot which had no existence save in the perturbed imaginations of those who sentenced him. His death coincided with a vindictive investigation into the political opinions and past record of the chapter of Uppsala, who were now called to account for their failure to make adequately determined resistance to the activities of Angermannus in 1598. They came miserably out of the ordeal, each seeking to cast the blame on the other, and in particular upon their former chief; and for once it is possible to feel some sympathy for the misanthropic contempt which Karl clearly felt for the whole crew of them. The upshot was that Angermannus was once more committed to prison, where he died two years later; that Laurentius Paulinus Gothus (a future archbishop) was deprived of his chair at Uppsala; and that the university, which had difficulties enough in any event, found itself branded as politically unreliable.

By the end of 1606, however, the worst of the panic was over. The affair of Petrosa had given Karl yet another opportunity to deploy his now threadbare tactic of threatening to abdicate, coupled this time with a demand that the Estates should pledge their aid in hunting down traitors. They gave him the assurance that he sought; but they extorted in return the promise of an early coronation. In a Testament drawn up in 1605 he had indeed inserted a recommendation that in the event of his death they should choose Johan rather than Gustav Adolf to succeed him; but this seems to have been intended as a safeguard against confusion if he should happen to be killed in the forthcoming campaign in Livonia; and since he contrived to survive the slaughter of Kirkholm the contingency never arose. The Testament was therefore quietly shelved; Johan's claims were once more passed over; and on 18 March 1607 Karl took the final step, and suffered himself to be crowned in Uppsala cathedral.[1] Two years later he made the ceremonial progress round his kingdom (the so-called *eriksgata*) prescribed in the Land Law: since the coming of the Vasas it had fallen into desuetude, and its revival is a good example of Karl's capricious respect for the letter of the law, even when his actions were most repugnant to its spirit. And with that tribute to antiquity the dynastic revolution was at last completed, and the reign could formally begin. But by 1609 Karl had only two more years of life before him.

[1] The points he put to the Estates on this occasion provide a convenient repertory of some of his more deplorable propaganda lines: they are printed in *Handlingar rörande Skandinaviens historia*, xxvi.

III. KARL AND THE CHURCH

The coronation, though it settled the dynastic question, marked the culmination of disputes with the church which had been almost continuous since Karl's assumption of the government. In the generation which followed the Church Ordinance of 1571 and the liturgical reforms of Johan the contours of Swedish Lutheranism had acquired a sharper, harsher definition. On the one hand it had developed an awareness of doctrinal issues and a distinct position in regard to them; on the other it had gained a new self-confidence in its relations with the state, and a clear idea of what those relations ought to be. The Swedish Reformation in its origins had been a controversy about authority, a collision between the prescriptive rights of a largely independent church and the determination of a necessitous monarch to exercise a real sovereign authority; and the victory of the monarchy in that struggle had at first appeared decisive. Not the least attractive feature of Protestantism in Gustav Vasa's eyes was that its political theory could be made to endorse the pattern of state–church relations which he desired to impose. By 1600, however, the church was no longer willing to accept the absolute subjection to lay control which had been its lot in the middle decades of the century. Assertions of the royal supremacy by Johan had provoked defensive reactions which had gathered strength until they became a programme of ecclesiastical autonomy, a denial of the king's right of dictation in matters of spiritual concern whether doctrinal or administrative. The Church Ordinance of 1571, though it had been imposed by royal authority, had provided a basis for this transformation; while other aspects of Johan's church policy had given it encouragement. Among the most important features of the Church Ordinance had been its reassertion of that episcopal authority which Gustav Vasa had wished to destroy, and with it the mediaeval tradition of episcopal control of the church. Moreover, by reducing the king's share in elections to the exercise of a right of veto, the Ordinance (whatever Johan's actual practice) had been designed to ensure that the episcopate should reflect the feelings of the church rather than of the sovereign. Certainly in the course of the next generation the bishops became once more the real lords of their dioceses; and the revival of chapters as effectively functioning bodies (for which Johan was responsible) helped to strengthen ecclesiastical self-government. This was a Melanchthonian arrangement; for Melanchthon had conceived the government of the church not as a royal dictatorship, still less as a democracy, but as an aristocracy. At the end of the sixteenth century the church's leaders all believed in the necessity of this kind of organization: the newer theories of state–church relations which were being evolved within the Lutheran world had as yet made little impact in Sweden, and the typical *landesherrliche Kirchenregiment* of the German states did not appear to Swedish churchmen to be a model to follow. The Church Ordinance had taken it for granted that church and state were distinct and separate spheres, the church being a self-determining area within which the king's duties were more important than his rights. It was his business to protect the church against its enemies, material, moral or doctrinal; he must be ready with assistance if the episcopate should happen to invoke his aid; and he had a residual emergency power which his position as a Christian sovereign bound him to use, whether invoked or not, when the interests of religion plainly demanded intervention. The bishops were indeed beginning to call upon the king for aid with increasing frequency, in order that the secular arm might lend weight to the application of church-discipline, and provide real sanctions against evil-doers: by the turn of the century considerable progress had been made in persuading the state to treat sin as no less liable to punishment than crime. But in the definition of doctrine, in the day-to-day administration of the church, the Ordinance no longer allowed to the king a preponderant voice.

The Uppsala Assembly of 1593, and the *Postulata* which the Clergy put forward in 1594, provided the first large-scale public demonstration of the new spirit. The Uppsala meeting had insisted that it was a free council; it had gone out of its way to show that it took no account of the opinions of Duke Karl. The *Postulata*, with their assertion of the right to summon councils of the church without royal permission, their reservation of all clerical offences short of felony to the bishop's court, their demand for state enforcement of tithe obligations, were essentially a claim that the clergy formed a community with special rights and privileges which it was the state's duty to safeguard. It may well be that in 1594 they pitched their pretensions so high because the situation was exceptional, in that they had to do with a Roman Catholic king; but it is significant that in 1595 Angermannus, to Karl's great annoyance, summoned a church council on his own authority. It is unlikely that either Laurentius Petri or Björnram would have ventured on such a step. We are at the beginning of a period of strong, authoritarian bishops, men neither disposed to moderate their voices to the tender ears of royalty, nor willing to suffer usurpation of their authority by the laity in silence. Prelates such as Angermannus, Olaus Martini, Laurentius Paulinus Gothus, Johannes Rudbeckius, ruled their dioceses with masterful assurance, for they had no doubt about the legitimacy of their authority and no notion of shrinking from a conflict with the state on issues of principle. Increasingly they tended to draw the appointment of parish priests into their own hands, to the prejudice of the ancient rights of the congregations, and in conflict sometimes with the newer patronal rights of the nobility, or the king's claim to a *régale*: Olaus Martini declared flatly that a priest who was no more than a royal nominee had no divine calling to his office. It was a sharp repudiation of the pattern of church–state relations as Gustav Vasa had conceived it.

The Church Ordinance had also marked the beginning of a revival of the church's claim to legislate for itself within its own sphere. In the next hundred years that claim was to develop along two lines. On the one hand, just as it was usual for kings to issue ordinances for the towns after consultation with the Estate of Burghers, so the custom would establish itself of regarding the Estate of Clergy assembled at a *riksdag* as a proper legislative body for the church. On the other hand the struggle to obtain a grant of privileges for the clergy, which begins in 1594 and was to continue for half a century, can be considered as an attempt to secure what was in fact legislation in the church's favour, and of the church's devising, under the guise of a privilege-grant: in this matter, of course, the Nobility and the towns had shown the way. Either method involved the important consequence that it virtually excluded lay participation in ecclesiastical legislation. In this respect the Uppsala Assembly, with its important lay element, proved to be the exception rather than the rule.

The development of the church along lines such as these is to be explained as a response to the strains and dangers to which it had been exposed under successive rulers during the last quarter of the century. The highly personal nature of Swedish kingship made it inherently probable that the religious colour of the country would reflect the views of the monarch. Since 1568 the resulting variations had been exceptionally violent; and the experience was sufficiently unpleasant to discourage the church from any easy acquiescence in the principle of *cujus regio, ejus religio*. And as the effects of monarchical idiosyncrasy strengthened a determination to recover effective self-government, so also they forced the easy-going pragmatical churchmen of an earlier generation to define their faith, or allow it to be defined for them by their colleagues. In the eighties and nineties the church was captured by a brand of strictly orthodox Lutheranism, fostered in the school at Gävle and the university of Rostock, and represented by such men as Angermannus and Gestricius. In a sense they stood for a middle way between the quasi-Calvinism of Karl and the Liturgism of Johan, a middle way which some found too narrow for comfortable walking. Though for the moment they stopped short of the ultra-orthodoxy of Flacius Illyricus, they had much the same rigidity and intolerance, and they brought to the Swedish church the strength as well as the weakness which flows from these qualities. As yet the acceptance of the Formula of Concord was not a part of their programme—it was not even mooted at Uppsala in 1593—but it would soon become so. The rising religious tension of the age was driving men to extreme positions; there was a growing disposition to believe that militancy was not the least of Christian duties; and to these trends Swedish Lutheranism was no exception. In the two decades after the Uppsala Assembly orthodoxy hardens, its intolerance becomes more marked; and at the first *riksdag* after Karl's death, in 1611, the Estate of Clergy would demand that the state accept not only the Formula of Concord, but the whole *Liber Concordiae*.

After 1600 the episcopate was faced with a ruler who was antagonistic to almost all the current movements within the church. In Johan's time, and also in Sigismund's, political as well as religious considerations had made Karl the supporter of Lutheran orthodoxy. He had provided them with an ally inside the royal family, and had thus in a measure mitigated their defiance of the sovereign and made opposition respectable. After 1600 there was no such convenient figure behind whom they could take cover. Once the danger from Catholicism was repelled, the ties which had bound Karl to the clergy loosened at once—indeed, they had loosened already, by his breach with Angermannus—and the real incompatibility between them became apparent. It was Karl's boast that his religion was the religion of his father. As far as doctrine went this was a mere filial delusion; but in regard to relations between church and state it was substantially true. Karl inherited all Gustav Vasa's dislike of hierarchical tendencies, and at least a trace of his monomania against bishops. It seemed to him that one sound argument for the royal supremacy was that it provided a security against the church's falling victim to episcopal tyranny: a notorious visitation by Angermannus in 1596, in the course of which measures of unusual severity had been applied against moral delinquents, provided a convenient example of the sort of thing of which he complained. He had not the slightest intention of accepting the theory of the separateness of the spheres of action of church and state: he had never done so in the duchy, and would not now do so for the kingdom. He did not believe that bishops ought to be permitted to rule their dioceses without control. He saw himself as the representative of the religious interests of all his subjects, responsible to God for his care of the national church; and this responsibility seemed necessarily to carry with it a right of interference in the church's affairs. A king who took his religious duties seriously would not hesitate to judge criminous clerks; he would freely exercise the right of presentation to livings; he would appoint and translate bishops; he would not think twice about depriving ecclesiastics whose conduct merited deprivation. This kind of intervention had become common enough among German Lutheran princes; but in Sweden it had by now come to have an alien ring, evocative of half-forgotten but wholly unfavourable memories of George Norman and his German devices. Yet it was difficult to deny the evangelical merits of some of its corollaries; as for instance Karl's insistence upon lay participation in the government and legislation of the church: without it, as he remarked on one occasion, the ecclesiastical structure remained characteristically popish. And there may well have been some of the clergy who shared his view that chapters were otiose adjuncts to episcopal power, and who wished as he did to reduce their numbers and set them on to useful work in the field of education.

There was matter enough here for friction and conflict; but the resulting wounds were envenomed beyond hope of healing by the differences between sovereign and clergy on points of doctrine. Karl was certainly no Calvinist, for he rejected predestination; but his sacramental views put a Calvinist colour upon him in orthodox Lutheran eyes. The suspicions of the church's leaders were probably exaggerated and sometimes ungenerous; but whether right or wrong they added acerbity to differences of opinion on less fundamental matters, and effectually ensured that in the ecclesiastical field, as in so many others, the reign should be barren of any constructive achievement. The eclecticism of Karl's religious opinions had effects both good and bad. On the one hand it isolated him, and so confirmed him in a belief that everybody was wrong but himself; on the other hand, by a strange paradox, it made him tolerant. In a man so absolute and so impatient of opposition it is an unexpected virtue; but its exercise was strictly confined to theological differences. It was probably an aspect of his profound reverence for the Bible: provided an opinion was not in clear conflict with Holy Writ he was prepared to suffer it, even though he might personally dissent. For Roman Catholics, of course, there could be no charity; but the divagations of fellow-Protestants he preferred to meet by argument rather than by suppression. Everything turned therefore on the exact words of Scripture; and Karl was understandably anxious for a Swedish translation of the Bible which should be strictly literal, even at the expense of intelligibility. His tolerance had also more practical applications: thus he deplored the clergy's hostility to mixed marriages; and though he had no patience with the doctrine which condemned unbaptised infants to damnation, he was angered by the church's refusal to baptise the infants of Calvinists in cases where no priest of their own faith was available to them.

Karl's difficulties with the church were a kind of retribution for his own political past. It was under his auspices that the fugitives to the duchy had formulated the first rigidly Lutheran declaration of faith, in the *Confessio Strengnensis* of 1587; he more than any man was responsible for the meeting of the Uppsala Assembly of 1593; for his own purposes he had induced the religious excitement which carried the defiance of Sigismund to its conclusion at Linköping in 1600; his own ranting against popery had powerfully assisted in establishing the atmosphere of panic in which the growth of Lutheran extremism became possible. But if he now quarrelled with the episcopate he was not conscious of any inconsistency: his opposition to Archbishop Olaus Martini after 1602 was grounded upon the same distrust of prelatical pretensions as had formerly led him to quarrel with Angermannus and with Björnram, even though the doctrinal issues had changed. He believed he was, and professed himself to be, a Lutheran: it was only that so many Lutherans in high places had fallen into the error of erecting the work of human hands—the *Augustana*, the Church Ordinance, the Formula of Concord, the Resolution of the Uppsala Assembly—into *symbola* of equal authority with the Bible and the Creeds. This he was not prepared to swallow. And since he had a sufficiency of theology at his command, he was prepared to argue the point until he had been proved wrong—which meant in fact, given his obstinate self-sufficiency, that he would argue until either his opponents confessed themselves in error, or death silenced his controversial pertinacity for ever.

The first issue to bring him into conflict with the clergy was liturgical. In Karl's opinion there was still a good deal of 'popish leaven' in the service-books of the Swedish church. In 1595 he had demanded a revision of the *Handbook* and the mass; in 1599 the new version of the *Handbook* was ready; at the Linköping *riksdag* of 1600 it was discussed. To Karl it seemed that the proposed changes did not go nearly far enough, and by way of indicating what he thought was required he put in drafts of his own for the service of baptism, and also for communion. They met with strong condemnation. The Clergy detected in these amateur performances unmistakable signs of Calvinistic error, and were in any case quite satisfied with the alterations already proposed. Karl was able to induce the Estates to include in their Resolution a clause ordering a new version to be laid before the next *riksdag*; but the spiritual Estate felt so strongly on the matter that 126 of them signed a protest against the decision. When the Estates met again in 1602 the battle was joined once more. Karl now not only submitted his own version of the *Handbook*, but imposed its use in the chapel royal; the archbishop publicly denounced it as doctrinally unsound;

Karl retorted by condemning the official *Handbook* as superstitious and unscriptural. By this time the text of the mass-book was also in dispute: in 1602 Karl secured a *riksdag* Resolution that it be revised, and revised not by the Clergy only, but by a mixed commission with lay representatives. The Resolution, however, included the proviso that no alteration was to be made in the sacraments or the articles of faith, which meant in fact that Karl's victory was more apparent than real. The Clergy obviously were in no hurry for further changes, and neither the vote of the *riksdag* nor the pungent adjurations of the king availed to produce results. At last, in 1608, Karl required of them an immediate and explicit answer as to whether they were prepared to do anything in the matter. Olaus Martini, prudently avoiding a direct negative, agreed to proceed with the work of revision—but only on condition that it was left in the Clergy's hands. And with that Karl had perforce to be content. The revision they eventually produced was so unsatisfactory to him that it seems not to have been made public; the whole project came to a dead stop; the Clergy were now obviously playing out time. They had not long to wait. Once Karl was dead progress was rapid: the revised version was submitted to the Nyköping *riksdag* at the end of 1611; the Estates accepted it with little ado; in 1614 it became law. Against the united resistance of the church and the procrastinatory tactics of its leaders Karl's Puritan zeal had battered itself in vain.

It was much the same story in regard to the catechism. Luther's Shorter Catechism had been available in a Swedish translation from as early as 1537, and it had soon come to occupy a central position in the pastoral work of the church. The Swedish Bible was both too big and too expensive for the ordinary man; the Shorter Catechism—portable, memorable, bound up as a rule with the hymn-book—very largely took its place. The Church Ordinance, in this following George Norman's lead, had ordered that sermons be planned to coincide with the various heads of the catechism; and the phrase 'preaching the catechism' was a common locution in the latter half of the sixteenth century. The catechism was indeed 'the poor man's Bible', and was regarded not only as a text-book for teaching the Christian his duty, but also as a succinct compendium of the Word of God. Its authority in Sweden never perhaps reached the heights it attained in Germany, where one drama of the Reformation period could include a scene in which God the Father was displayed examining the souls of the dead in its subject-matter;[1] but it was still one of the most potent forces in the process of turning Sweden into a truly Protestant country.

It followed, then, that changes in the catechism might have far-

[1] I borrow this illustration from F. Böök [etc.], *Svenska litteraturens historia*, I, 167.

reaching effects upon the religious education of the country, and hence upon its doctrinal complexion: clearly they were not to be lightly undertaken. But the gravity of the question seemed to Karl the best reason for tackling it: there were elements in the Heidelberg catechism, he considered, which might well be incorporated, and Johan a Lasco, too, had matter worth the borrowing. In 1604 he accordingly drew up, under the cloak of anonymity, a catechism of his own. Its reception was no more favourable than that of his *Handbook*. The archbishop at once accused the anonymous author of Calvinistic heresies, and the *råd* had to intervene tactfully to prevent the publication of his strictures. Nevertheless in 1607 Karl caused his catechism to be printed; in 1608 he challenged the Clergy to prove that it was in any way heretical; and if they jibbed at that he demanded that at least they should undertake a revision themselves. But Martini and his colleagues had no intention of giving their disputatious sovereign so tempting an opportunity. They preferred to fall back on their usual stone-walling tactics; and by prolonging them until the end of the reign they contrived to defeat Karl on the catechism, as they had defeated him on the Liturgy.

These clashes were only two of the more conspicuous episodes in a continuous guerilla warfare between king and church which raged for almost the whole of Karl's reign. There were of course faults of temper on both sides. The clergy's incessant sniping at Karl's dubious orthodoxy would have provoked a more patient man. Their negative and patronizing attitude to his liturgical proposals was not calculated to conciliate. In 1600 the spiritual Estate had the audacity to declare his punishment of Bishop Sorolainen and the Finnish clergy illegal. Two years later, they did not hesitate to attack his court preacher, Micronius. Micronius was a German whom Karl had imported from Livonia; he was undoubtedly a Calvinist; and his appointment naturally gave great scandal. At the Stockholm *riksdag* of 1602 the Clergy demanded that he be brought before them for examination on his tenets; and soon afterwards resolved that he be expelled the country. It was in vain that Karl asked that Micronius be at least given an opportunity of defending himself in a public disputation with his adversaries: the archbishop declined altogether to engage in a disputation with a heretic. In the end, Martini carried his point: in 1603 Micronius was sent on an ostensible errand to Germany from which he did not return. Karl felt that his clergy had been impertinent; but worse was to follow. Though he was not as learned a theologian as his brother Johan, Karl had read widely (and, his critics would have added, dangerously) in current theological literature; he had a buoyant confidence in his ability to justify his opinions and confute those of his critics; and he seems to have enjoyed theological argument for its own sake. At all events, in the years between 1604 and 1607 he published—at first anonymously, later without attempting to disguise his authorship—a succession of polemical writings designed to establish his orthodoxy. Whether anonymous or avowed made no difference to the archbishop, who took it to be his duty to demolish error wherever he found it. Every publication by the king was followed by a counterblast from Martini, who castigated his sovereign's lapses with exemplary thoroughness, no doubt on the biblical principle that chastisement should be proportioned to love. The nation was presented for some years with the unusual but hardly edifying spectacle of a battle of the books between the king and the leader of the church: it was perhaps fortunate that illiteracy was so widespread. From time to time, in the heated exchanges of biblical texts, the king managed to register a telling hit; but he was after all no more than an enthusiastic amateur who had rashly taken on a professional, and perhaps it was inevitable that he should have the worse of an encounter in which he was so clearly out-gunned. It says a good deal for his intellectual honesty that he did not seek to bolster up his arguments by an appeal to force; and it says even more for him that he seems throughout the affair to have retained a genuine esteem for his intrepid opponent.

This did not prevent him from directing at his bishops and clergy from time to time attacks of the most violent and sweeping description, in a style only too reminiscent of his father. In 1602, for instance, exasperated by their attitude in the matter of Micronius, he retorted by accusing the whole spiritual Estate of gross dereliction of duty: the hospitals, he said, were so neglected by them that the poor died pitifully in the streets; the clergy mulcted laymen of excessive mortuary fees; they excluded from communion those who would not contribute to the Easter offertory, 'thereby making a merchandise of the sacrament of Christ'; the bishops allowed the fabric of their cathedrals to fall into ruin because they were too greedy to spend money on restoration; and, not least, they ordained 'for the sake of gifts and bribes' far more clergy than the needs of the country required. That the poor were dying in the streets was true enough, for 1602 was a year of famine; but it took Gustav Vasa's son to insinuate that the real reason for the mortality was that the parsons were robbing the poor-box. The complaint about an excess of clergy may have had some substance: at Uppsala in 1593 Bothniensis had observed that 'a man had only to beat the bushes, and out popped ten priests'. That some cathedrals were ruinous was true; that few had now the resources to undertake major repairs was unfortunately true too. It may well be that Karl had something of a case in his censure of the clergy, if only he had not spoiled it by the intemperance of his language. But like his brother Johan he found difficulty in measuring his words, and he suffered from an unworthy and unresisted urge to impute base motives.[1]

No doubt he had reason to be displeased with them; but they on their side had much to bear from him. He was for ever meddling in what they considered to be their business; as in 1607, when he issued—without consulting them—an ordinance regulating the method of preaching, and enforced it on pain of deprivation. He had no scruple about exercising the royal supremacy in the matter of appointing and depriving bishops. Olaus Martini, no doubt, was in 1600 regularly elected archbishop by the chapter of Uppsala and all the other bishops, Karl's share in his appointment being confined to exercising that right of approval reserved to the sovereign by the Church Ordinance. But in 1609 Laurentius Paulinus Gothus was translated to Strängnäs by simple royal *fiat*, and at the same time the bishops were curtly told that it was the king's wish that Kenicius should succeed Martini in Uppsala. And if it came to deprivations, whether of bishops or clergy, Karl made no pretence of consulting any ecclesiastical authority, but simply did as he thought proper. Bellinus of Kalmar was deprived of his superintendency in 1606; Sorolainen of Åbo had been deprived of his see in 1600, and was to lose it again in 1605; and in each case the action was taken on dubious political grounds. In 1605, that year of plots and panic, not a few priests found themselves imprisoned without trial, despite the archbishop's courageous protests; in 1607 Skepperus was forbidden by the king to exercise his priestly functions, and Olaus Martini threatened with deprivation if he ventured to interfere. In all this Karl was doing no more than Johan had done in his day, to say nothing of Gustav Vasa; but the temper of the church had changed in the last twenty years. And as Karl claimed the right to remove priests, so too he claimed the right to appoint them. In the past half-century the custom had grown up—despite a protest at Uppsala in 1593—of reserving to the king the presentation to urban benefices, and to the larger and more important benefices in the country. Karl obviously wished to extend the application of this *régale* to include all parishes. He argued that the bishops had latterly usurped the traditional right of the congregation to choose its pastor (which was true enough), and represented himself as being concerned to safeguard

[1] When in 1604 Olaus Martini was in arrears with his taxes, Karl wrote him a letter which included the following passage: 'And since we see that with religion you are concerned not at all, but your intent goes only to ensuring that in the name of religion you may have a parlour, Christmas fare and high living, so will we for our person let religion go as it will, and write thereof to the king of Poland, and so the quarrel which is between him and us shall soon be stilled. Or if that does not like you, you may yourselves go off and make your peace the best you can, or (again) go out with your clergy to battle and resist the enemy, while we sit at home and enjoy the same situation that you now have. And whichever of the two seems the more tolerable to you, that may you inform us of': *Handlingar rörande Skandinaviens historia*, viii, 10–11.

the interests of parishioners (which was a good deal more questionable). In 1606 he issued an ordinance—another example of ecclesiastical legislation without consulting the church—to prevent the bishops from appointing to any benefice: henceforward the congregations were to choose, and the king would approve. The ordinance proved in fact unenforceable; but its object was not so much to protect the rights of the parish as to increase the king's control of the church at the bishops' expense. That object was also strikingly exhibited in his demand that no ordination should take place in future without his permission, a pretension which the bishops naturally considered to be intolerable. And in the draft of privileges for the Clergy, which he thoughtfully drew up for them in 1607, he suggested an expedient which was certainly designed as a blow to episcopal authority. He proposed the setting-up of a central church council appointed by himself, composed of laymen as well as of clerics, to which all ecclesiastical causes were to be referred; and at the same time the establishment of a 'national *concilium*' to consider 'all important matters concerning religion'. Thus the juridical authority of the bishop within his diocese, the still-surviving structure of church courts and ecclesiastical law, the old administrative functions of the chapter, would have been merged in a central tribunal of the king's nomination; and the determination of great issues of church policy would have passed into the hands of a body of uncertain composition and unknown competence. There was certainly a real need for a central authority for the church and a supreme appellate court for ecclesiastical causes, and something like Karl's proposal was to be revived by Gustav Adolf, in the project for a *consistorium generale*; but even in those more propitious times it was destined to founder on the opposition of the bishops to lay participation, and their distrust of any scheme which seemed to imply danger to their authority. In Karl's reign the prospects were hopeless from the start; and in fact no attempt was made to proceed with the project.

To most Swedish Lutherans the Confession of Augsburg, the Church Ordinance and the Uppsala Resolution had by this time become fixed stars in their confessional firmament. The Uppsala Resolution, in particular, was regarded as the charter of the country's spiritual liberty, the palladium of their religious constitution, hardly less venerable than the *Augustana* itself. It had been the central document of the revolution; indeed, if Karl's interpretation of that revolution was to be credited, and the struggle against Sigismund had really been a struggle for religion, then the Resolution was its Declaration of Right, duly converted into a Bill of Rights by the terms of Sigismund's Charter. At Söderköping and Arboga the nation—or at least that portion of it which followed Karl's lead—had solemnly pledged itself to maintain it, and to take punitive action against any who might defect from it or seek to subvert it. With these events still fresh in everyone's mind, it must certainly have come as a shock to find that Karl was now advancing very different opinions upon the proceedings at Uppsala, and displaying an increasing unwillingness to consider himself bound by the Assembly's decisions. Having used the religious question to secure his own political ends, he was now coolly kicking away the ladder by which he had climbed to power. In 1602, 1604, 1607, stormy meetings of the *riksdag* tried in vain to pin him down to an acknowledgment of the authority of the *Augustana* and the Uppsala Resolution. In each instance the pattern of events was the same: demands by the Clergy, resistance by Karl, renewed pressure culminating in a violent eruption of the Vasa temperament, and in the end a compromise which in fact left the issue undecided. In 1602 the question arose because the Estates were considering the terms of a possible Accession Charter if Karl should agree to accept the crown, and the Clergy seized the occasion to ask that it should include a promise to adhere to the *Augustana invariata*. Karl refused an unconditional promise: all he would agree to was a pledge to accept the *Augustana* 'in so far as it was in accordance with Scripture', and from this position he was not to be shifted. As yet he did not venture to refuse the Uppsala Resolution; and the Clergy at last accepted this as at any rate going some way to meet their demands. In the event the discussion proved irrelevant, for Karl postponed a decision on the crown, and the matter of the Charter was for the moment left in abeyance. Two years later, at the Norrköping *riksdag* of 1604, the discussions about the Succession Pact produced a very similar situation. The Pact was to contain provision for excluding those who might lapse from the Lutheran faith, and it became a question how such a lapse was to be defined. It seemed natural, in the light of recent history, to specify that defection from the Uppsala Resolution should be a sufficient ground of forfeiture. But Karl now flatly refused to agree to this: he was not prepared, he said, to treat the Resolution as though it were on the same footing as the Creeds. It was in vain that the Nobility (perhaps maliciously?) reminded him of the punitive clauses of Arboga.[1] He was prepared to concede that defection from the Confession of Augsburg 'in so far as it was accordant with Scripture' might be a bar to the succession; but certainly not the other. The best the Clergy could obtain was a provision which stipulated for adherence to 'God's pure and clear Word as manifested in the prophetic and apostolic books, and to the Confession of Augsburg which is grounded upon them'.

The final crisis of 1607 was once more concerned with the terms of the Charter which Karl was to give in connexion with the coronation.

[1] See above, p. 368.

As things turned out, he did not give it until after the coronation was over; and the Charter was consequently not—as had been the case in 1594—a precondition for allowing the coronation to take place at all. The political situation was now such that it was the Estates who solicited the coronation and the new king who consented to it: in 1607 the trumps were all in Karl's hands. Nevertheless, there was to be a Charter, of sorts; its most important provisions concerned religion; and its terms were the subject of fierce and protracted argument between Karl and the Estates. The battle-ground was the same as in 1602 and 1604; but this time the Burghers and the Peasants gave their support to the Clergy, while the Nobility pursued a politic neutrality. In the course of these exchanges Karl scandalized the orthodox by assertions which he would scarcely have tolerated ten years before from a member of the *råd*. The Uppsala Assembly, it now appeared, had not been a real council of the church; its Resolution was no more than a pact concluded for the temporary purpose of defence against the designs of a Roman Catholic king; once that danger was scotched, it lost its validity and binding force, and became irrelevant. The truth was, of course, that Karl had never forgiven or forgotten the clause in the Resolution directed against Calvinists and sacramentarians. In the nineties the exigencies of politics had forced him to swallow it; in 1607 he could afford to vent an accumulated resentment which had not grown less bitter for its long suppression. He justified his attitude by an argument which was characteristic of his proneness to look at political questions as though they were actions at law between himself and those who disagreed with him. The leaders of the church, he contended, by their failure to resist the 'treasonable' activities of Angermannus, had given ample evidence that they no longer adhered to the Uppsala Resolution themselves; their defection had broken the national front and dissolved the compact; it was therefore inequitable to demand that he should bind himself to observe it.

As if this were not enough, he also took the opportunity to deliver a sharp attack upon the Church Ordinance. Laurentius Petri had from the first acknowledged that the Ordinance might one day stand in need of supplementation; it was by this time common ground that some action of the kind had become necessary; and since 1602 Karl had been demanding that the Clergy set about the work of revising it. The difficulty was that any version they were liable to produce was not likely to be acceptable to the king. Karl wanted drastic alterations to strengthen the power of the crown; the bishops desired mainly changes which would enhance their own authority. It was perhaps exasperation at their attitude which now led him to declare that the Ordinance was not in accordance with the Word of God, had never been accepted by the king or indeed by any other Estate than the Clergy, and involved an attack on the rights of the crown. In a historical point of view this was a statement as inaccurate as could well be imagined; in the context of 1607 it inevitably had the effect of exacerbating the king's already deplorable relations with the church. Certainly it did nothing to encourage the bishops to accelerate their revisory labours. In 1607, indeed, it seemed possible that king and Estates were moving to a head-on collision. But though the crisis was acute, Karl could safely calculate that it would not be pressed to a breach. The usual threat of abdication at last frightened Burghers and Peasants into capitulation; the Clergy, thus left isolated, did not venture to prolong resistance. In the end the Charter pledged the king to maintain the unaltered Confession of Augsburg and the Uppsala Resolution 'in so far as they are based upon the pure and clear Word of God and are in accord with it' —a qualification which, however unexceptionable to the Clergy (who had no doubt that they were) and however essential to the king (who believed they were not), served really to underline the irreconcilable differences between them. The last hope of forcing the sovereign into the straitjacket of Lutheran orthodoxy was gone; for the few years that remained the church must school itself to endure a king more than half suspected of heresy. It was not for this that they had defied the persecution of Johan and driven Sigismund into exile; but as long as Karl lived there was no help for it.

After 1607 both sides seem to have reconciled themselves to the impossibility of effecting any real change in the other's attitude. In 1608, indeed, Karl put up an exiled Scottish Presbyterian, John Forbes, to defend the tenets of his faith, and this time constrained the archbishop to meet him in a public disputation before the university of Uppsala. But from the king's point of view the result was disappointing, for Martini kept the argument to the issue of predestination (on which Karl and Forbes disagreed), and having flattened his adversary with biblical quotations emerged victorious from the encounter. It hardly mattered. King and church now observed a sort of armed truce, and neither was anxious to renew old conflicts. Karl had so thoroughly frightened the bishops in 1607 and 1608 that they did not venture to continue their polemics against his publications; while the king on his side no longer busied himself with theological pamphleteering. The great controversies remained in suspense; the long-promised revisions of the *Handbook*, the catechism, the Bible,[1] the Church Ordinance,

[1] Since 1594 Karl had been pressing for a new, literal translation, and in 1600 a committee of four ecclesiastics began the work of revision. But the version of the New Testament which was published in 1605 was essentially based on Luther's Bible of 1545 (it reproduced even Luther's obvious errors), and was by no means what Karl had been looking for.

seemed no nearer achievement than they had ever been. The royal draft for a revision of the Land Law[1] showed that Karl's view of his ecclesiastical authority had not mellowed with the passing of the years; but it too remained a project without hope of acceptance. Olaus Martini died in 1609, his death eliciting an unusually generous tribute from his sovereign, but the removal of the leader of episcopal opposition came too late to make any difference.

And so, in frustration and weariness, the church waited for the king's death, which alone could open the way to progress. The new reign would indeed see the solution of some of the problems which had bedevilled the old. The accession of a sovereign whose orthodoxy was beyond dispute restored, after the lapse of many decades, a spirit of confidence between the clergy and the monarchy. In a more genial climate of reciprocal trust the church blossomed as it had failed to do in the nipping airs of King Karl's time. Yet even under Gustav Adolf enough ground of difference remained to remind us that the sterility of the earlier reign was not merely a question of personalities. Under Gustav Adolf a clash between church and state was avoided only with difficulty; the revision of the Church Ordinance was even yet not accepted by the crown; the problem of a central government for the church defeated even Oxenstierna. The danger of over-mighty bishops was as real to Gustav Adolf as it had ever been to Karl; and Rudbeckius proved more truculent than Martini. But one of the church's anxieties was certainly removed by the change of ruler. If they had been apprehensive in the face of Karl's interventions in their affairs, one reason for their nervousness had been the possibility that the royal supremacy might be exercised, not only by the king in person, but by his irresponsible agents. The clergy might conceivably have reconciled themselves to a king who acted as *summus episcopus*; but they dreaded the devolution of his powers to chancery officials. The death of Karl relieved the church, as it relieved the nation, of the fear of another 'rule of secretaries'.

IV. CONSTITUTIONAL QUESTIONS

When the heads of Erik Sparre and his colleagues fell to the executioner's sword in the market-place of Linköping, when in the years that followed their sympathizers fled into exile in Poland or Denmark, these events meant more than the defeat of a faction, more even than the overthrow of a dynasty. Aristocratic constitutionalism had been struck down in the persons of its champions. The triumph of Karl registered the rejection of a political theory; it implied—at least in appearance—the bankruptcy of a political ideal. So much was clear. What was not

[1] See below, p. 438.

quite so clear was the colour of the doctrine which was now to replace them. It might seem at first sight that the principle of hereditary monarchy, unbounded by election-pledges, had reasserted itself; that the state was henceforward to be a kind of parliamentary despotism. Karl's Testament of 1605 declared that the source of all the evils of the body politic was the high nobility's craving for electoral kingship. The absence from his Charter of any sort of constitutional guarantees or any grant of privileges, the fact that it was given after the coronation and not before it, showed how much the constitutional ideal had been weakened since 1594. And his ability to use the threat of abdication to force through his wishes put him in a political position so strong that serious constitutional opposition became almost impossible in practice.

Yet it remained true that he owed his throne to a revolution which had flouted the Succession Pact and justified itself (at least in part) by contractualist arguments. There was no gainsaying that Karl was an elected rather than a hereditary sovereign; indeed, in the propaganda which he directed to foreign countries he found it convenient to emphasize the point that he held his throne by the will of the nation: it was the only argument open to him in the face of the claims of legitimacy, and perhaps he used it with the less repugnance because it had been his father's argument in 1523. The circumstances of his accession, in fact, landed him in a dilemma from which he never succeeded in escaping. He had to convince his contemporaries that his revolt against Sigismund and subsequent usurpation of the throne were morally justifiable and intellectually defensible; but at the same time he had no intention of submitting to the same sort of contract as he had extracted from Sigismund in 1594. Past and present were in conflict; rebel and monarch necessarily spoke with different voices; and the exigencies of foreign policy ensured that the polemics of revolution should continue to be employed after the revolution was over. It is therefore not really surprising that some of Karl's secretaries should have written in a style curiously reminiscent of Erik Sparre: Petrus Petrejus, for instance, has much to say of tyrants and the rule of law, accepts the concept of an ephorate, and implies the contractual basis of the state. For Petrejus, who had entered Karl's ducal chancery in 1595 as a young man, the events of the nineties must still have been a vivid memory, and it seems reasonable to suppose that they coloured his thinking: the extortion of a Charter from Sigismund in 1594 could best be justified on a contractualist theory; the rebellion of Karl became almost a civic duty if he could be represented as chief ephor. But if it were a question not of historical argument but of present practice neither Karl nor his ministers were liable to be much concerned with notions of this sort. When Karl launched his project for translating foreign classics into Swedish, the first volume he selected for the operation was James I's *Regium Donum*; and if he was accessible at all to contemporary trends of political thought it was not to the monarchomachists that he listened, but rather to the school which proclaimed the unrestricted authority of God's vice-gerents. At bottom his political creed was probably independent of any external influences. It was domestic, traditional and unsophisticated; its twin pillars were the Land Law and Gustav Vasa's Testament. To them he attributed a literal inspiration comparable with that of the Bible; from them, as from the Bible, he drew texts to justify what he wished to do. And if there was one virtue upon which he felt that he was entitled to preen himself, it was filial piety. All of which did not inhibit him from turning Erik Sparre's arguments against him when it suited his purpose.

Karl's attitude to the problem of the *råd* in the years after 1600 provides a good illustration of how these different theoretical approaches could be made to lead to the same conclusion. On the one hand the *råd* must not be allowed to deprive him of his position as chief ephor. On the other hand he was not prepared to admit its right to impose constitutional limitations upon an adult sovereign. And what he wanted, in practical terms, was that its relationship to the crown should be as he imagined it to have been in his father's time.

After 1600 there was for some time no *råd* at all: most of the old members were either dead, or in exile, or politically suspect, and Karl made no attempt to revive it as a consultative body. For the work of government in the provinces he relied on the *ståthållare*, for the central administration upon chancery and treasury officials. During his absences in Livonia he left the running of the country in the hands of Mickel Olofsson, the leading spirit in the chancery, or to a very informal collection of persons which included *ståthållare*, treasury clerks, secretaries, and the archbishop. On one occasion the lead was taken by the Stockholm clergy, who under the archbishop's chairmanship dealt with an urgent matter of foreign policy and even summoned a meeting of the Estates.[1] Some more regular arrangement was obviously desirable; and already in 1601 Karl on occasion entitled some of his close advisers *riksråd*. In 1602, despite his obvious suspicion of the institution, he made up his mind that the *råd* must be revived. After all, it had for centuries been a part of the constitution—was it not entrenched in the Land Law itself?—and as a traditionalist and a conservative he must be reluctant to dispense with it altogether, especially since he was now anxious to normalize political life after the upheavals of the previous decade. It happened, moreover, that the lack of a *råd* was an obstacle to his attempts to put his relations with Denmark upon a more satisfactory

[1] They cancelled it before it met, however.

footing; for the treaty of Stettin (1570) had provided for frontier meetings between the members of the councils of the two countries as a device for settling differences between them, and there was some danger that the Danes might decline to negotiate (and hence by implication to recognize the legality of Karl's rule) on the pretext that the Swedish representatives on these occasions were not members of the Swedish *råd*. For all these reasons Karl now approached the *riksdag* with the proposal that the *råd* be reconstituted, and staggered them by inviting them to nominate the members themselves. This was an unprecedented suggestion, which he motivated on the ground that since he had not yet assumed the crown he was not entitled to make the appointment. It acutely embarrassed the Estates, who had no wish to exercise themselves in such great matters, and lost no time in declining the responsibility and remitting the choice to Karl. Having thus secured a free hand, he put before them proposals which had certainly some novel features. His nominations he limited to twelve (the figure provided for in the Land Law, but of recent years usually exceeded), but proposed that in addition six members be added from the Estonian nobility, by way of integrating that province more firmly into the Swedish realm; he suggested the appointment of six supernumerary councillors, to be entitled *hovråd*; and he insisted that it be a condition of appointment of the new *råd* that they be pledged to 'advise and *not* to govern'. The Estates made strong resistance to his plan for recruiting Estonians, and in the end Karl had to be content with their agreement that he might summon some of the Baltic nobility to attend the council 'at need'. But they accepted his other proposals; and their resolution included a famous clause which laid it down that 'since aforetime much confusion and disorder has arisen from the fact that those who are members of the *råd* have not only given counsel, as their office requires, but have also governed: Therefore we have resolved that their power and authority shall reach no further than is laid down in the Law Book: namely that they shall counsel the king to that which they know to be useful and advantageous to God, himself and the realm'.[1]

Thus the *råd* was resurrected upon terms which showed Karl's determination to correct what he considered to be the abuses of former years: like Erik Sparre, he could maintain that his object was to restore the constitution rather than to change it. But it was significant that the new *råd* took an oath which corresponded closely with that sworn by the *råd* to Sigismund in 1594: that is, that they omitted the historic pledge to see to it that the king observed the law of the land—the very pledge which Karl had falsely accused Sparre of failing to honour.[2]

[1] A. A. von Stiernman, *Alla riksdagarsoch mötes besluth*, I, 536.

[2] See above, p. 390 and n. 2.

Indeed, to all appearances the new *råd* was remarkably like the old. No attempt was made to introduce any precise allocation of work or any specialization of function among its members, nor to give them a more important place in the day-to-day business of government. When Karl was away in Livonia in 1604 they did indeed function as a standing executive body in more or less continuous session; but ordinarily they were, as they had been in Gustav Vasa's time, a collection of counsellors rather than a council. The new *hovråd*—which was perhaps set up to provide a consolation for magnates who had been omitted from the *råd* by the restriction of its numbers—was never given defined functions, never seems to have met as a separate body, and was certainly not the standing committee of councillors permanently at court which had been envisaged in the proposals for a *hovråd* under Erik XIV and Johan III. The title of *hovråd* survived as a useful distinction which could be conferred upon diplomats of foreign origin in the Swedish service; but as an institution it never had any significance. As to the *råd* itself, Karl was too suspicious of it to wish to see its members charged with any new duties or equipped with any new powers which might lead them to magnify their office, even though the new men had been hand-picked from those upon whom he believed he could rely. After 1602 the only new function which they were called upon to perform was to act as a supreme court of appeal, meeting in more or less regular session in Stockholm town-hall—an activity which was administratively useful and politically neutral. For the rest, the *råd* was never allowed to develop so as to present a challenge to the royal authority. Its members for the most part lacked administrative experience and were uncomfortably aware of their deficiencies. Prudence suggested that they should refrain themselves and keep themselves low, and they habitually replied to Karl's propositions in terms of studious submissiveness: the days were gone when they could venture to oppose royal policy and castigate monarchical misgovernment. They showed themselves understandably shy of assuming responsibility, being mindful of the fate of their predecessors in 1590 and afterwards. It is true that Karl on occasion asked them to do things which they felt themselves incompetent to undertake—as when he called for their advice upon strategy, or the choice of commanders; it is true too that they were well aware that he sought counsel freely elsewhere; but there was probably some justification for his complaint that they gave him little assistance, and that tardily. But after all they were what he had made them, and it was unreasonable to expect much backbone in a council which from the outset he had been concerned to keep supple.

It might seem, then, that the constitutional struggle between monarchy and *råd* had been finally decided in the king's favour. But the long discussions on the project for revising the Land Law[1] showed that even the disaster of 1600 had not been able wholly to stifle the principles for which Erik Sparre had lived and died. The draft of a revision which Karl prepared, or caused to be prepared, in 1603, adhered to the traditional view of the place of the *råd* in the constitution, in that it recognized it (despite the precedent from Arboga) as an essential constituent and natural leader of the Estates, and accepted the need for its assent to new taxation and major decisions in foreign policy. But it was at the same time expressive of his continuing fear of the *råd* as a focus of oligarchical ambitions; for it would have prohibited more than two members of one family from sitting in the council at the same time, and it would have expressly entrenched the king's right to dismiss any member found guilty of serious crime. Yet Karl's draft included provisions which undoubtedly seemed to curb the royal authority more sharply than before. In part these were the outcome of his need for a theoretical justification of his attitude to Sigismund, and even to Erik: it was clearly considerations of this sort which lay behind the clause which for the first time defined the grounds upon which a hereditary right to the crown might be forfeit. Those grounds included the breaking of the oath which the king had sworn to his people; the diminishing of the realm without the commonalty's consent (*sc.* Sigismund's cession of Estonia to Poland); *mésalliance* (*sc.* Karin Månsdotter and Gunilla Bielke—the latter instance entailing the consequence of barring Prince Johan's claim); cruelty and tyranny (Erik again); seeking aid abroad against one's subjects, or bringing a foreign army into the realm (Sigismund's crime in 1598). So too with the reiteration of the old clause in the Land Law binding the *råd* to see to it that king and people observed the oath which each had sworn to the other: having chopped off Erik Sparre's head for failing to do this, Karl now (somewhat belatedly) endorsed the obligation. But there were also other clauses in Karl's draft which might certainly suggest an acceptance of the idea of limited monarchy, clauses which seem to lay a broader basis for control of the power of the crown: for instance, that which laid it down that the consent, not only of the *råd*, but also of the people (through their representatives) should be necessary to the making of war, peace or alliance, and indeed to *all* royal actions 'which concern the welfare of land and people': to this end he proposed a modernizing of the now antique forms for provincial consultation which the old Land Law had prescribed. And it is certainly true that Karl was usually careful to lay matters of this kind before the Estates. But though it could be argued that we have here a constitutional step forward, inasmuch as it could be construed to open

[1] See below, p. 438.

up at least the possibility of a parliamentary check upon the crown, it seems most unlikely that Karl had any such idea in mind. If he seemed to expand the ephorate to include the Estates or the *landsting*, he did not thereby strengthen it: rather the reverse. The constitutional functions of the *råd* were being diluted rather than reinforced: if the experience of the nineties went for anything, the people would be much less of a clog upon the monarch than the *råd*. It is true that Karl in fact found the *riksdag* less pliable after 1600 than in the last years of King Sigismund; but he had a deep conviction that there existed a community of interest between monarchy and people based upon common antagonism to an aristocracy which was a danger to each, and it was this feeling, rather than any notion of chalking out a pattern of limited monarchy, or even a design to outbid Erik Sparre's constitutional programme, which lay behind the emphasis which he placed upon the people in his draft. A very different spirit animated the draft prepared by the revising committee. This affirmed the right and duty of the *råd* to give advice even when not called upon to do so; it bound the king to accept that advice in matters which redounded to the public weal; it stipulated that they were not to be victimized if the advice proved unpalatable. The *råd* would have become once more the sole regulator of the machine. More than this, it would have recovered something of its historic position as arbiter between monarch and people; it would have been entitled once more to see itself as the tongue of the constitutional balance. For a very remarkable clause in the committee's draft would have given to the *råd* the right to judge between the king and his subjects in all cases where there was a complaint that he had deprived a man of his land or property. That a provision so redolent of the Recess of Kalmar could be put forward within a decade of Sparre's death reveals how little the blood of Linköping had availed to extinguish the ideals of those who shed it. The historic revenge of 1611 was already plainly foreshadowed at the very moment when Karl's authority seemed most secure. But in the meantime the *råd*, especially during the closing years of the reign, had no easy time of it; and when Karl was dead it would seek guarantees for the free exercise of what it believed to be its essential function within the constitution.

Two things, in particular, weakened its authority and lowered its prestige. The first was Karl's constant recourse to his secretaries and chancery staff for the shaping of policy and the obtaining of advice; the second was the use which he made of the *riksdag*. Despite the terms of his revision of the Land Law, Karl's practice precluded the *råd* from resuming the leadership of the nation which it had lost since 1596. Indeed, all the signs seemed to indicate that in this matter Karl intended that the *riksdag* should retain the position which it had then usurped, and speak for the nation on its own account. Gustav Vasa had used the Estates as the extreme medicine of the constitution; Karl IX made them its daily bread. The experience of the nineties had imbued him with the idea that the *riksdag* was a serviceable tool in the hands of a monarch who knew how to use it, and he saw no reason why a device which had stood him in such good stead in a crisis should not be exploited in quieter times. After 1600 he summoned the Estates almost as frequently as before: between 1600 and 1611 they met no less than six times. Their sessions as a rule were short—they averaged three to four weeks—but they were called upon to take decisions on a great variety of topics, and to give their opinion on matters which had hitherto been considered as essentially the responsibility of the executive. They settled the crown and the succession, recommended fresh taxation, expressed their views on religion, acted as a court of law in state trials, accepting these tasks as reasonable assignments; but when it came to nominating members of the *råd* or advising upon army appointments they were inclined to feel that they were being imposed on, and that the king was shuffling out of what was properly his affair. This was a delusion, for Karl had no intention of allowing real decision-making to pass out of his hands; but he found it convenient—as his son was also to do—to spread the burden of responsibility for actions which might conceivably have unpleasant repercussions, and thus to arm himself in advance against *ex post facto* criticism.[1]

The frequency with which the *riksdag* met, and the wide variety of matters which it was called upon to discuss, had the effect of accelerating developments which had already been adumbrated in previous decades. In Karl's time the *riksdag* was visibly growing up. The process had begun in 1596, when the Estates for the first time met without the leadership and guidance of the *råd*; but it continued even after the *råd* had been restored. In one respect, it is true, the situation became less precise than before; for in the first decade of the century it seemed at least possible that the bailiffs and the army officers might succeed in establishing themselves as separate Estates, in addition to the now-accepted four;[2] but otherwise the constitution and procedures of the *riksdag* acquired a new firmness and definition. Members were now more likely to be the real choice of their localities, rather than persons designated by the king's agents; they were sometimes armed with power to assent on their constituents' behalf; the expense of attendance

[1] An extraordinary instance of this was his reference to the university of Uppsala in 1605 of the French proposals for mediation with Poland.

[2] And Karl tried (as he had tried with the *råd*) to secure the attendance of representatives from Estonia.

was now usually borne by the member's constituency. Parliamentary procedure begins to crystallize into the forms familiar to a later generation: meetings of all four Estates *in pleno*, the rudiments of a system of committees, the regular provision of Speakers for the upper Estates. The individual lists of grievances with which each constituency was in the habit of charging its members are now on occasion conflated into a general petition from each Estate; the Estates' independent resolutions are digested by the chancery (and sometimes altered in the process) into a consolidated resolution of the entire *riksdag*.

These developments went hand in hand with a gradual increase in self-confidence and a slow augmentation of authority. By 1611 there was a tendency—it was no more than that—to regard the *riksdag* as the best place (though still not the only one) for the grant of extraordinary taxes, and there was a disposition to acknowledge its right to determine the duration of any such grant. In the course of Karl's reign it provided several examples of a spirit of independence and a readiness to criticize: it did not hesitate to show its disapproval of the Polish war, or the risky provocation of Denmark;[1] it rejected Karl's plans for reorganizing recruitment to the army; it turned down his draft Poor Law in 1607; it sabotaged his attempt to revise the Land Law. But these advances towards constitutional maturity were subject to important qualifications, one of which is well exemplified in the last of these instances. The *riksdag* from the beginning insisted that a question as important as that of a general reform of the law ought to be submitted to provincial gatherings for their approval. Members were still very chary of committing their constituents; local consultations were still very much an alternative method of eliciting popular consent. This was indeed the method which the Land Law enjoined; and the continuing importance of these provincial gatherings is shown by Karl's anxiety to revise the constitution which the Land Law prescribed for them so as to bring it into conformity with contemporary conditions. Gustav Adolf's Charter of 1611 would still leave open the possibility of local negotiations instead of *riksdag* legislation, and recourse was in fact had to them as late as the reign of Karl X. Meanwhile, the *riksdag* was still in a sense the king's creature: it met only at his summons; it discussed only such matters as he laid before it in his Proposition; it lacked the initiative, and would continue to lack it for at least another forty years. Attendance was a burden rather than a right; and the frequency of Karl's summonses was felt as a nuisance rather than as an opportunity. Use and wont might exert their educative effect, the Estates might be growing more accustomed to parliamentary life and its possibilities; but this was a matter of practice only:

[1] See below, p 457.

in 1611 their powers were legally no more clearly defined than in 1560. Karl certainly had no wish to define them. He had not the smallest ambition to associate his name with constitutional innovations. As long as the Estates did what he required of them, he looked no further.

But the *riksdag* proved in fact far less easy to manage than in the years between 1595 and 1600. The alliance with the *ofrälse* Estates which had been the precondition of Karl's success did not long survive his usurpation. They had rallied round him as the defender of the faith, they had seen in him an ally against the nobility. But now his orthodoxy was suspect, and he seemed a good deal less concerned to champion peasants against their lords than in the days of the Club War. New taxes were imposed upon them to fight a war for which they cared little; men were taken from their homes for army service, so that farms became more difficult to work; they were for ever plagued with the trouble and expense of sending representatives to attend meetings of the *riksdag*. On occasion the peasantry could still respond to the kind of rabble-rousing appeal which he had used so effectively against Sigismund and the *råd*—an instance occurred as late as the *riksdag* of 1610—but the device was undeniably wearing thin. Karl had never been the 'peasant king' of popular historiography: he had used the peasants' grievances, and played upon their emotions, to serve his own ends, and now that he was king indeed he had too great a need of the nobility to follow that line much further. When the *émigré* pamphleteers derided his reliance upon the *ofrälse* Estates, and called them his 'yes-men' (*jabröder*), they had in their mind's eye a political constellation which had already sunk below the horizon. And with its setting the propitious hour for using the *riksdag* as Karl hoped to use it had gone. In 1600, and certainly by 1602, what the nation wanted above all was a return to normality; and in their idea of normality a hectic succession of *riksdag*-meetings was not as yet included. Thus Karl's relations with the Estates were often uneasy (there was not one meeting at which he did not lose his temper), his hopes of them were not seldom disappointed, and his frequent sessions in the end became a popular grievance.

But though in his use of the *riksdag* Karl made the mistake of clinging obstinately to revolutionary techniques after the revolution was over, he was at heart a thoroughly conservative ruler. This appears very clearly in his approach to the problem of administration, both central and local. After 1598 Karl was in a position to remodel the machinery of government to suit himself, for vested interests and bureaucratic conservatism had been weakened by the flight of so many civil servants to Poland. He did indeed replace the fugitives by men of his own way of thinking, some of them recruited from his ducal chancery, but he made no other innovation of importance. The defeat of Erik Sparre, here as in other fields, meant the end of any hope of progress. The civil service remained royal rather than national, the plans for rationalization and systematization which the *råd* had propounded in the eighties were further from realization than ever. No real attempt was made, for instance, to build a central government round the great officers of state. Between 1602 and 1604 the offices of admiral, chancellor and treasurer were revived in favour of members of the high aristocracy, and at the Örebro *riksdag* of 1608 Karl by implication accepted the idea of reviving the offices of steward and marshal; but only the treasurer had any real administrative work to do: the others were for show. The pivot of the administration was not the chancellor, but the *hovkansler* Dr Nils Chesnecopherus, who was essentially Karl's personal servant. The central offices of government still comprised only the chancery and the treasury; and though Karl made them more efficient, he introduced no changes and promulgated no general regulations for the conduct of business. No advance was made towards Sparre's ideal of the permanent allocation of specific duties to specific posts, with a regular predetermined salary attached to each. On the contrary, government proceeded on the old amateur, *ad hoc* basis, whereby any of the king's servants might be entrusted with any job, financial, administrative or judicial, as the exigencies of the moment might require. Sweden had to wait until 1612 for the first royal recognition of the principle of a fixed wage for office-holders, and until 1614 (when *Svea Hovrätt* was set up as a new supreme court) for the first great example of a government office created for a specific purpose and confined to a strictly demarcated sphere of action.

The characteristic instruments of government in Karl IX's time were the same as in Johan III's: senior clerks in chancery and treasury, and above all the king's secretaries. It has been said that under Karl there was no 'rule of secretaries' in the pejorative sense in which that expression is habitually used, that men such as Nils Chesnecopherus, Mickel Olofsson and even Erik Göransson Tegel are not to be equated with such notorious figures as Johan Henriksson or Jöran Persson.[1] Certainly they were hard-working, well-informed and able men, capable of turning their hands to all sorts of business, better men morally and intellectually than their predecessors in Johan's time. But though the personnel might be more respectable, the system was the same. The secretaries were the mere projections of the royal will, accountable to the king alone, the appropriate executants of a method of government which was by choice improvisatory and unorganized. They were an irresponsible element in the constitution, unknown to the law, usurping by their influence with the sovereign the constitutional

[1] Sven Ljung, *Erik Göransson Tegel*, p. 48.

right of the *råd* to give counsel to the king. Upon them, as formerly upon Jöran Persson, fell much of the odium of unpopular measures. The nobility disliked them as upstarts; the *råd* resented them as rivals; only the favour of the king sustained them. If contemporary opinion be a criterion, there is little doubt that there was a 'rule of secretaries' under Karl IX. Nor would he have wished it otherwise. His conception of kingship was the same as his father's: personal and paternal rule, operating through subordinate agents who could be cast aside as easily as they had been raised up. If personal monarchy in his father's style was still possible at all, he was as likely a man as any to make a success of it; for—unlike his brother Johan—he had a real concern for good government, considerable administrative ability, a mastery of detail, and long experience acquired in ruling his duchy. He had also more respect for the letter of the law than Gustav Vasa had ever had. But he was not a whit less determined to control every aspect of the nation's life, and he had no intention of impeding his freedom of action by the organization of an independently-functioning bureaucracy. And just as he turned his back on plans for the remodelling of the central government, so too he was content with a local government which left existing arrangements undisturbed. A suggestion that it might be worth while to consider the revival of Pyhy's provincial ordinance for Västergötland fell unfruitfully on the stony ground of his indifference.[1] The provinces were governed, as before, by *ståthållare*, the revenues managed by the king's bailiffs; and no concession was made to Erik Sparre's notion of empowering the *ståthållare* to audit their accounts on the spot. Karl had all his father's distrust of their honesty—'a pack of thieves', he called them on one occasion—and he made real efforts to protect the peasantry from their exorbitancies, force them to produce their accounts in good time, and stop their evil practice of deducting their wages before forwarding the revenue to the exchequer: a significant resolution of the *riksdag* of 1604 forbade them to levy taxes without specific authorization. The inconvenience of making every bailiff come up to Stockholm to obtain his acquittance did indeed eventually induce Karl to devise a system whereby special commissioners were sent down to pass their accounts; but this interesting innovation, which might conceivably have produced something like the French *commissaires*, had as it turned out no future. The future lay rather with Sparre's scheme for *landshövdingar* and local accounting; but for that Sweden had to wait until the next reign.

The only sphere of government in which Karl made a conscious and persevering attempt at reform was in the administration of justice. Here there was much need of reform. The civil disturbances at the

[1] Stiernman, I, 558. See above, p. 123.

close of the century had interfered with the workings of the courts; there were arrears of cases for trial; the absence of the king in Poland, at a time when he still constituted in his own person the only supreme court, had been a serious hardship to litigants. Karl made several attempts to deal with the question of appeals, and in the end, as we have seen,[1] succeeded in delegating this function to the *råd*; but it was obvious that Sweden could not much longer afford to be without a regularly-constituted supreme court which would in all ordinary cases relieve the king of this part of his duties: it was one sign among many that the day of personal monarchy was drawing to a close. He also tried to meet the need for the revision of judgments in the provinces. Two *riksdagar* resolved that *rättareting*[2] be held twice a year, at Uppsala and Linköping; but for reasons which are obscure[3] their resolutions remained without effect. One major cause of disorder was the widespread uncertainty as to what the law really was. The Land Law had never been printed; it was available only in manuscript copies, not all of them accurate; both Magnus Eriksson's and Kristoffer's versions of it were in use in the courts. The need for a standard text was obvious: as early as 1595 Karl had pressed for the publication of a modern definitive edition. But the law had been made to suit a social and political situation which had long since passed away; its language was already antique and obscure; its provisions no longer covered all cases that might arise. Publication of a definitive text, though desirable, was not enough: what was required was a revised, modernized and expanded version of the law as a whole. Karl fully appreciated this. In 1602 he induced the *riksdag* to agree in principle to a revision, and to recommend the appointment of a small committee to do the work. Not content with this, he began the work of revision on his own account, with the aid of Peder Nilsson and Nils Chesnecopherus; and by 1604 he was able to present the first instalment of his draft to the Estates. The committee, which had shown no perceptible sign of doing what it had been appointed to do, was now stimulated to begin its labours. By 1605 it too had ready a draft (the so-called 'Rosengren Draft') of a portion of the law. By this time the want of an agreed text of the old law had become a real handicap to the work of revision; and in 1608 Karl accordingly caused to be printed a critical edition of Kristoffer's Land Law, to which was added an appendix, designed to provide interim guidance for the courts in cases of serious moral offences of a type which had until the Reformation been dealt with by the church courts, and for which the Land Law had accordingly made

[1] Above, p. 430.

[2] Revising courts.

[3] The *riksdag* of 1602 recommended that the revising courts be not holden until the king's subjects should be in a better condition to bear the expense: Stiernman, I, 538.

no provision. It was now recommended that they be dealt with according to the Mosaic Law, at least until the new code should appear; and with that recommendation the leaders of the church were not disposed to quarrel.

Meanwhile the work of revision made slow progress; and in 1609 Karl, who had by that time rejected the Rosengren Draft as unsatisfactory, laid his own version before the *riksdag*. It was still far from complete: only the sections on constitutional and ecclesiastical law were ready.[1] The Estates promptly seized on this as a pretext for shelving the matter. At first they declined even to read Karl's version; and they steadily refused to debate it. They had never manifested any real enthusiasm for the undertaking, and they now showed that they actively mistrusted it. It was a pointed snub, and Karl was understandably enraged. In an angry message he washed his hands of the whole business; the work of revision came to a dead stop; and the much-needed recodification of the law had to wait until 1734 for its completion, with the unfortunate result that for more than a century the principles of the Mosaic Law were half-engrafted upon the stock of the law of Sweden. Thus the only fruits of what was certainly an effort of enlightened statesmanship remained the printing of Kristoffer's Land Law, and a new code of Municipal Law which was promulgated about the same time.

Some light is thrown upon Karl's approach to the problem of administration by his dealings with the nobility. Despite the slanders of the *émigrés*, it was no part of his purpose to oppress the aristocracy, provided they refrained from plotting against him. He was not so foolish as to imagine that it was possible to establish his *régime* on a purely *ofrälse* bottom. He had no design to rule Sweden in the nobility's despite: on the contrary, he intended if possible to rule with their collaboration, for like his predecessors he felt the need of educated men for his service, and looked to the aristocracy to supply them. In his view, the social status and economic privileges which they enjoyed imposed special obligations to serve the state, and he meant to see to it that those obligations were discharged. Johan Skytte spoke with his master's voice when in his *Oration* defending Karl's treatment of Sigismund (1603) he observed that the nobility ought to remember that they had not been given their grand titles and their 'exalted position in order that they should escape more lightly than other Estates, and live out their days in idle luxury, and (as they say) lie up by the fire and roast apples, but so that they, above all others, should exert every effort to defend and fight for their beloved fatherland'. And if they would not

[1] The section on ecclesiastical law was the work of Gustav Adolf's tutor, Johan Skytte.

or could not fight, they must serve the state in other ways: Karl's draft of the Land Law contained a provision binding the nobility to educate its sons for state service, and specifically obliging them to take care that they should be taught Finnish, German and Latin—the three foreign languages which a civil servant would be likely to require. As to those with neither the taste for war nor the capacity for letters, they might at least seek upon the continent to acquire so much of the conventions of polite society as might equip them to adorn the unexacting court of Sweden. In any event it was their duty to take an intelligent interest in politics: Karl strongly disapproved of nobles who absented themselves from meetings of the *riksdag*, and steadily resisted a request that they be allowed to elect representatives instead of appearing *en masse*.

There were, however, political difficulties in the way of realizing this ideal of state-service. A majority of the nobility had certainly sided with Sigismund at the time of Stångebro; they had acquiesced without enthusiasm in the dynastic revolution; and they felt no great obligation to put themselves out for a usurper. The high aristocracy, in particular, who had been most committed to the constitutional programme which had been vanquished at Linköping, was of dubious loyalty. Karl's problem was how to rally to his support a class which had hitherto had little cause to love either his person or his policies; he had to cajole and reward those who were accessible to persuasion, and ensure that the recalcitrant be denied the chance to make mischief.

The most obvious means of persuasion at his disposal were grants of *förläningar* and gifts of land; and here the confiscated estates of the *émigrés* furnished him with ample resources. He employed them on a liberal scale: 800 farms in Sweden, 2,300 in Finland, were given as donations to his adherents; the number of *förläningar* rose sharply, until by the end of the reign it was larger than at any time since 1570. The effects of this calculated generosity were so marked that in 1612 and 1613 there were complaints that the crown had alienated almost all of its revenues. The complaints were exaggerated; but they reflected the magnitude of the bid for noble support which Karl had felt obliged to make. The process of alienation had been facilitated by a deliberate change in the law. The Land Law had contained a clause forbidding the king to diminish his realm: as a life-tenant, it was his duty to hand over the estate intact to his successor. Even after monarchy became hereditary there had been a flavour of illegality over permanent alienations of crown property: in particular, the gift of land to a noble, which would entail its exemption from ordinary taxation, might seem to infringe the law since it permanently diminished the royal revenues. But on the other hand it could be argued that in such a case the crown was really only exchanging revenues for services, and might even be a gainer rather than a loser by the transaction. The argument was specious; but it was convenient. At all events, it does something to explain why it was that the Norrköping *riksdag* of 1604 allowed itself to be persuaded into passing a resolution which was to have far-reaching consequences. The Norrköping resolution legalized, for the first time, donations of land in hereditary tenure[1]—which might mean in fact alienation on a semi-permanent basis. It did, indeed, attach important safeguards: the recipient was bound to seek confirmation of the donation at every change of ruler; selling or mortgaging of the land was forbidden unless the crown had first been given the option of recovery; failure of heirs male entailed lapse to the crown. It is true, too, that the resolution only legalized and codified Karl's practice in the past few years. Nevertheless, it was an act of great importance, both in its immediate and in its more remote consequences. Immediately, it provided Karl with a useful hold over those to whom he gave land: the beneficiaries were henceforth bound to him by quasi-feudal ties hitherto unknown to Swedish law; they held their land on strict terms, which in Karl's time usually included a stringent obligation to provide knight-service (*rusttjänst*); and they had no guarantee that their donation would survive the accession of a new king. In a longer view, the Norrköping resolution, by removing legal doubts about donations, opened the way to those massive alienations of crown land and revenues which were to reach their climax in the reign of Kristina, and were eventually to make necessary a *reduktion*. And when the *reduktion* at last arrived, the year 1604 would be the natural starting-point for its operations: noble land held before 1604 was 'old *frälse*', and rested on a securer title than the 'new *frälse*' which had been alienated upon the Norrköping terms, and was liable (as many a rueful owner found, in the years after 1680) to resumption by the crown if those terms—whether by royal negligence or private evasion—had not been strictly complied with.

For the moment these measures did have the political effects they were designed to secure. Karl was able to build up a solid body of aristocratic supporters, and at the same time was able to exploit existing differences within the nobility as a whole. There were already clear signs that the lesser nobility were jealous of the great magnates, and especially of the titled aristocracy of counts and barons. In 1607 they demanded equality of privilege for all within the Estate of Nobles; and Karl, in his draft of a revised Land Law, pandered to this feeling by proposing that in future no titles should be granted without popular

[1] This is not quite exact: counties and baronies had from the beginning been granted in hereditary tenure; but they were very few in number.

approval. His grants of *förläningar*, his donations of land, did not usually go to the high aristocracy: they went to the lesser nobility, and also to those foreign nobles—mostly from the Baltic provinces—who entered his service in considerable numbers in order to carve out a career for themselves.[1] On the whole, then, Karl's land-policy brought no advantage to the great families. They were not conciliated; they were temporarily tamed. Some had changed sides; some sent their sons to enter the king's service, either avowedly as hostages for their family's good behaviour, or as a prudent measure of insurance, as in the case of Axel Oxenstierna. They bided their time, nursed their grievances, and by no means forgot the principles for which Erik Sparre had contended. Their hour would come in 1611. The lesser and middling nobility, on the other hand, had to all appearance been won over: their new donations had given them a vested interest in the revolution.

But this appearance was delusive. Despite the benefits they had received, they were by the end of the reign almost as sour as their betters. Karl's attempt to secure their goodwill was contradicted by other features of his rule which squandered the political advantage which his donations brought to him. One such feature was his own hereditary greed for land. He had never ceased to regret and resent those proceedings in Erik's High Court which had led to the recovery by the aristocracy of much land which Gustav Vasa had incorporated into the Vasa estates;[2] just as he had never forgotten or forgiven what he considered to be the inequitable partition of those estates in 1572. As early as 1596 he had used his political ascendancy to initiate process for recovery of allegedly Vasa lands which had reverted to aristocratic hands; and the political upheavals of the following years had given him his chance to appropriate much of this disputed property. His methods were as high-handed as his father's: when noble owners protested, or asked for an investigation, he put the onus of proof of ownership upon them, and demanded that they produce their title-deeds for his confirmation. This they were often unable to do, even in cases where there could be little doubt of their rights. By such arbitrary proceedings he was able to make very large acquisitions: between 1596 and 1611, it has been calculated, he recovered 1373 farms for the family, so that when he died he had regained possession of more than half of the great accumulation which Gustav Vasa had left behind in 1560. But in doing so he had undoubtedly alienated many, and alarmed more. Moreover, though he at first gave *förläningar* with a liberal hand, he was so strict in his limitations upon the revenues which might be

[1] Karl placed great reliance upon them: he even intruded one of them—Lubert Kauer—into the *råd*, although it was strictly illegal to do so. Such men as Kauer were not popular, least of all with the high aristocracy.

[2] See above, p. 220.

included in the income to be derived from them that any feeling of gratitude or sense of obligation must soon have become a little blunted. Holders might well feel, moreover, that their tenure was precarious: around 1608 there were ominous indications that Karl might be contemplating a wholesale resumption of *förläningar* in the style of his brother Johan. Above all, they strongly resented his insistence that their incomes from *förläningar* must be reckoned when assessing their liability to *rusttjänst*. This was an old quarrel; but it was characteristic of Karl's tactlessness (as well as eloquent of his need) that he should have demanded that such income be assessed at twice the standard rate.

The dispute about *rusttjänst* was indeed one of the most potent factors counteracting Karl's wooing of the nobility. He had certainly right on his side: the nobles notoriously made false returns of income; they failed to produce even the forces with which they were assessed. In 1601 Karl reckoned that *rusttjänst* did not yield more than a hundred horse, and this at a time when there was an urgent need for heavy-armed cavalry to stiffen the Swedish armies against the onslaughts of the Polish lancers. Karl took care to make *rusttjänst* a strict condition for his new donations; he refused to exempt even young girls and widows. But the nobility remained incurably remiss. It is possible that some of them were moved by personal hostility to their sovereign; but this cannot have been the principal explanation, for the difficulty continued under Gustav Adolf, who like his father was in the end defeated by a general tacit conspiracy of laxity which it was impossible to punish wholesale. Commutation was suggested from time to time, and on one occasion accepted; but Karl tried to drive too hard a bargain, and no permanent settlement could be reached. The nobility felt that they were being badgered; Karl was sure that he was being cheated.

In 1607 the controversy over *rusttjänst* became a main element in the broader question of the privileges of the nobility, which it was expected would be confirmed or improved upon the occasion of the coronation. The nobility, as had come to be their habit in the past half-century, put forward claims for ever wider exemptions and ever greater economic advantages; but they also added a demand of more sinister import, when they asked that they be given the right to seize and imprison their peasants and domestic servants, judge them on their own manors, and retain any fines they might choose to inflict. This demand they grounded on the long intervals between sessions of the local courts, and the desirability of more expeditious handling of minor offences. They may have had something of a case; but the inconvenience they experienced was far outweighed by the serious social consequences which would have followed if their proposal had been accepted. The whole social and legal position of the *frälsebonde* would have been undermined; a 'Livonian servitude' might well have established itself in Sweden.[1] But it was typical of the nobility that though many of their demands were inspired by the crassest self-interest and class-feeling, others revealed the same genuine concern for liberty and the rule of law which had inspired the constitutional idealists of the last generation. They insisted, for instance, that there should be no imprisonment without fair trial; they demanded that reasonable bail be accepted. True, they were asking these things only for themselves; but that they should have found it necessary to ask them at all is a commentary on Karl's methods of government. And if the nobility were not safe from illegalities, what security had the *ofrälse* Estates? As so often in the past, a demand for privilege incorporated a constitutional principle.

In the event, they secured neither a guarantee of liberty nor the advancement of their selfish interests. For two years king and nobles wrangled about the new privileges, in exchanges which grew ever sharper; but no agreement was to be had. In March 1609 they reached complete deadlock, and abandoned the discussions. The king was angry, the nobility frustrated; neither would give way. The reign ended without either the confirmation of the existing privileges of 1590, or the promulgation of new ones.

Thus the attempt to conciliate the nobility had failed. Karl's lavish bestowal of donations was spoilt by his own territorial acquisitiveness, by his rigour over *förläningar* and *rusttjänst*, by the controversy over privileges. The old aristocracy was further alienated by his favours to the new; all, new and old alike, were alarmed by his arbitrary actions; all disliked and mistrusted his use or abuse of the *riksdag*. These contradictions go some way to explaining why it was that his effort to enlist the nobility as servants of the state was only partially successful, and why for many of them their collaboration with the king was constrained and distrustful. Yet even so, their reluctance is at first sight surprising; for if Karl wished them to serve the state, he was doing no more than endorse a policy which the nobility themselves had propounded. Both had realized that without the active coöperation of the aristocracy the old administrative devices could hardly support much longer the weight of business which was being put upon them. Gustav Vasa's methods of personal supervision were now scarcely possible, and certainly inadequate; the question had become whether the bailiffs and the clerks should be supervised by royal secretaries or by aristocratic officials. Karl's answer to this question was implicitly to deny the necessity for choosing between them: he wanted, not one or the

[1] It is worth noting, in view of Karl's reputation as the peasants' friend, that at one stage in the negotiations with the nobility he was prepared to accept this demand.

other, but both. But however possible this might be in theory, it was not an available solution in practice. Noble participation in administration, as Erik Sparre had envisaged it, was not compatible with a rule of secretaries, *ad hoc* arrangements, and a snubbed and submissive *råd*. It was against the rule of secretaries and the lack of regular forms that Sparre had reacted when he produced his programme for administrative reform; and in this matter his political heirs inherited his aversions and his prejudices. Karl, as usual, was trying to have it both ways; and his refusal to see that this line was not open to him destroyed any prospect of the cordial integration of the aristocracy into his service. The solution to the administrative problem, as the future would show, lay in a serving aristocracy manning a reorganized central government on a collegial basis, and governing the provinces as responsible *landshövdingar*; an aristocracy which would as a matter of normal practice recruit itself from rising officials who looked to a peerage as the natural end to their career. But that solution was too radical for Karl's conservatism, and it involved too much reliance on the old *råd*-families for his suspicious temper; nor did he perceive that (as his son was to demonstrate) such a solution need not necessarily imply the diminution of royal authority, but only the easing of its burdens.

V. WAR ON TWO FRONTS

Throughout the period of the revolution Sweden's relations with Denmark had given no great cause for anxiety. The later years of the reign of Fredrik II had seen the slow growth of a tradition of intra-Scandinavian good-neighbourliness, and that tradition had not been disturbed during the minority of his son. Despite a perceptible sympathy with Sigismund as the representative of the cause of monarchy, Kristian IV had resisted any temptation to exploit the civil strife to his own advantage: outwardly, at least, he remained neutral. In 1600, neither side seemed anxious for a conflict. Yet by 1611 the two countries were at war once more; and, once more, as in 1563, the issue was nothing less than the survival of Sweden as an independent state. This abrupt transformation was the result of the character and policies of Karl and Kristian, acting upon a situation which, though it did not lack the materials for an explosion, ought not to have been beyond the control of prudent statesmanship. Kristian IV undoubtedly willed the war of 1611; but without Karl's miscalculations and intransigence he would scarcely have found an opportunity of waging it. Karl's policy was provocative; but without Kristian's determination to force the issue he might conceivably have escaped its natural consequences. The antagonism of the two countries had valid grounds; but with different rulers a major conflagration could probably have been avoided, at least for a time.

The treaty of Stettin (1570), which had given the Scandinavian kingdoms a whole generation of amity, had virtually entrusted the preservation of peace to the councils of the two realms. Its elaborate arrangements for the settlement of disputes by frontier meetings between council-members, its provision for arbitration by a joint tribunal constituted from the councils of each, were designed precisely to prevent what actually happened in 1611. Peace was a direct interest of an aristocracy which was still in its upper reaches Scandinavian, and which had seen its estates imperilled during the Seven Years War of the North. The failure of Fredrik II's attack upon Sweden, and the economic disruption which attended it, after 1570 put the Danish monarchy more or less under the tutelage of a pacific aristocracy. From that tutelage Kristian IV was now determined to escape; and one method of doing so lay in enhancing the monarchy's authority and prestige by the waging of successful war. Untaught by the example of his father, Kristian dreamed of reviving the Scandinavian Union: his aim was not only the defeat, but the conquest, of his neighbour. For the crown of Sweden, unlike that of Denmark, was now hereditary; and he might fairly hope that its acquisition would strengthen his hand against aristocratic constitutionalism at home. In one important aspect, then, Kristian's aggressive foreign policy was a move in a domestic constitutional struggle. But it remained true that he could hardly venture to begin a war without the consent of his council; and this could be obtained only if he could convince them that there was no alternative. He must be able to persuade them that Karl's behaviour was so intolerable, and his attitude so challenging, that peaceful means would serve no longer. By 1611 this stage had been reached; and the War of Kalmar was the result.

The fundamental issues were simple. In the Baltic what was really at stake was the relative status of the two countries within the area. It was a struggle between them for primacy; it was a question of *dominium maris*. Before the 1560's the question hardly arose, for in European opinion, as in actual fact, Denmark was clearly the stronger power. But the failure of Fredrik II's attempt at conquest, the achievements of Erik XIV's navy, and above all the success of Sweden in Livonia under Johan III—contrasting so sharply with the abandonment of Danish pretensions—had changed the picture; and the union with Poland, fragile as it proved to be, had confronted Danish statesmen with a new situation. As Sweden established her footing on the southern and eastern shores of the Baltic, the possibility began to take shape of a Swedish economic empire which might be a real challenge to Denmark's position. If the kings of Denmark had grown rich by tolling western merchants at the Sound, the king of Sweden appeared now to be aspiring to a position in which he could mulct them at the great Livonian end-ports. Reval and Narva were in Swedish hands; Riga might easily follow them one day. In its most intractable aspect, then, Danish-Swedish antagonism was a struggle for the control of the sea, and of the Russian trade that was carried upon it; an attempt by Denmark to deny to Sweden the customs-dues of foreign merchants, and prevent her from acquiring the naval and military strength which those dues would permit their owner to develop. This basic rivalry found superficial expression in a congeries of controversies, some old, some new, but all related directly to the underlying issue. One long-standing dispute was the great question of the Three Crowns, still unsettled and plainly insoluble on any agreed basis. Sigismund had been glad to put it into cold storage after Stångebro, and had accepted a proposal to defer it for the lifetime of himself and Kristian IV.[1] Karl was less accommodating; and Sigismund's complaisance was made an article of accusation against him in the act of renunciation which the Estates drew up in 1605. Another old controversy concerned Sweden's rights to Sonnenburg on Ösel;[2] and yet another was provided by a renewed Swedish attempt (in response to Reval's demands) to close Narva to foreign shipping. Besides these, new matters of disagreement arose out of Karl's war in Livonia: there was much resentment at the undiscriminating activities of Swedish privateers, and loud complaint at the attempts of the Swedish navy to maintain an effective blockade of Riga. Denmark felt herself doubly concerned: on the one hand because of the direct interference with her own merchantmen, and the violation of her territorial waters;[3] on the other because interference with foreign traders might frighten them off from the Baltic, and so reduce the yield of the Sound Dues. All Danish kings conceived that their levying of the Sound Dues imposed upon them a duty to keep the Baltic free of piracy: Kristian IV now contended that he had likewise a duty to ensure freedom of navigation within the Sound to ships plying on their lawful occasions; and he was prepared to discharge it by providing them with a convoy into Riga.

The other main theatre of conflict was the Arctic. Before the mid-nineties the government in Copenhagen had attached only minor importance to the Lappmark question, and the Swedes had been able to establish themselves upon a long stretch of Atlantic seaboard with very

[1] Erik Sparre's share in this arrangement was made a charge against him at his trial in 1600.

[2] See above, p. 259, n. 1.

[3] The blockade of Riga was made difficult by Danish possession of Ösel, for foreign shipping took refuge from Swedish warships in Danish territorial waters—hence the anxiety of the Swedes to recover Sonnenburg.

little opposition. But the treaty of Teusina, with its formal cession of Russian tax-rights between Varanger and Malanger, had administered a sharp shock to this indifference, and when in 1599 Kristian IV made his celebrated journey to the North Cape, he obtained a first-hand view of a situation which from the Danish angle was increasingly disquieting. Karl had for some years been interested in pushing Swedish pretensions in this area. His immediate objective was to make good his right to tax the Lapps of the Atlantic coast, as well as those of the mountain region. In his view, the treaty of Teusina gave him a strong case; but he was aware that the Danes did not think so. In the years after 1595, therefore, he began an intensive campaign to collect on the spot evidence to prove that Sweden had in fact enjoyed, from time out of mind, the rights which he was asserting. He hoped to show that the Birkarlar had for centuries acted as the crown's tax-gatherers in the Arctic; or alternatively that the area was Swedish in virtue of its conquest by Finns during the early Middle Ages. The truth of these contentions was at least dubious, and the attempt to prove the second of them was soon abandoned; but Karl's agents did not find it difficult to collect sworn testimony in support of the other, nor did they hesitate to manufacture 'evidence' to suit his purpose: on at least one occasion Karl personally indicated exactly what it was that his witnesses were expected to depone. Lapps and Birkarlar, bailiffs and pastors, were all pressed into service, and by the opening of the new century Karl had at his disposal an imposing mass of ambiguous or falsified testimony for use as ammunition against the Danes.

This paper campaign was reinforced by a policy of colonization, and by the gradual extension of civil and ecclesiastical control. Settlements were founded (Lycksele, Arvidsjaur, Jokkmokk and Karesuando were all established in 1605–6), bailiffs were sent up; churches were built to minister to the needs of the population, pastors installed to reinforce the civil power with their spiritual authority; communications northwestward from Torneå were improved, and shelters constructed for travellers, in order to make the country more accessible to government. In part this programme was an attempt to oust the Birkarlar from their privileged position as the sole authorized traders with the Lapps, and to bring the effective control of the suppliers of furs into the hands of royal agents; and it was prosecuted with characteristic unscrupulousness by means of vicious propaganda against the Birkarlar's personal morality and financial integrity. But this aspect of Karl's policy ran into difficulties, partly because he needed the assistance of the Birkarlar to substantiate his political claims, partly because the Lapps had no wish to exchange their mutually beneficial relationship with the Birkarlar for dealings with government officials new to the ways of the trade, and inadequately provided with ready cash. Nevertheless, the process of colonization went on; and by the end of the reign Lappland east of the mountains was well on the way to being integrated into the general administrative structure.

There was a moment, indeed (in 1601), when Karl, like Johan III, seemed prepared to put forward a claim to territorial sovereignty over the whole of Lappmark, including those Atlantic coasts which were visited by his tax-collectors. But to this the Danes made such decided opposition that the claim was speedily dropped. By 1603 Karl had made up his mind that the best tactic for the future was to avoid a direct challenge on the territorial issue, and to agree that Sweden and Denmark–Norway enjoyed a kind of joint sovereignty over certain common areas where both took tax. If he could establish Swedish tax-rights on the Teusina basis, and by infiltrating the region with Swedish settlers and officials make it effectively Swedish without giving the Danes a clear issue on which to stand, they would find themselves one day in the position that their right to tax was regarded as no more than a servitude on acknowledged Swedish land. The Danes, however, were not misled. They were aware of the danger to their rights implicit in the extension of Swedish colonization; and their officials in the Arctic reacted by razing the new Swedish blockhouses and burning the new Swedish churches. Local clashes beyond the Arctic Circle, reciprocal allegations of outrage, began to play their part in envenoming the relations of the two governments.

It may well be asked why Karl should have been so determined to push forward in Lappmark, and what gains he could reasonably expect from a policy which was bound to be regarded in Denmark as provocative. The revenues yielded by the disputed right of taxation were certainly no adequate object, even when to them are added the prospective profits from a royal monopoly of pearl-mussels, rock-crystal, and above all the fur-trade. More important were considerations of a geopolitical order. For a country in Sweden's position, with her direct access to the open ocean restricted to a narrow neck of land at the estuary of the Göta river, the possibility of breaking out to a warm-water port in the far North was obviously attractive, and the chance of evading for ever the barrier of the Sound too important to be ignored. In existing circumstances, however, the idea was a pure delusion: Swedish Lappland offered such formidable geographical obstacles to the movement of men and goods that free communications here had to wait for the coming of speculative finance and English railway engineers in the last quarter of the nineteenth century. The notion that trade might go that way was a fantasy; and the schemes for establishing a naval base and a shipbuilding yard on the Alten or the Pasvik little better. Nevertheless, fantastic or not, such ideas do seem to have counted for something in Karl's calculations. But there can be little doubt that what he was mainly concerned to do was to put himself in a position to dominate the sea-route to Archangel, and ultimately to close it: the reign ends, as Johan III's reign had ended, with abortive expeditions against Kola. This is a policy which had obvious connexions with the struggle in the Baltic proper. As Johan III had divined, Lappmark and *Balticum* were but two aspects of the same question, two wings of the same operation; and the objective to which success on either wing was designed to lead was the control and financial exploitation of the Russian trade-routes. The edification or destruction of rude blockhouses or pitiful little churches, the lonely violences of rival tax-gatherers in the inhospitable wilderness, may seem *trivia* on the outermost periphery of discernible history, as obscure as the Arctic night that involved them; but Kristian IV was right to feel that they formed but a portion of a larger pattern, and correct in believing that they could not be ignored.

For a decade he fought the struggle with Karl by diplomatic means. At times suggestions were made for the submission of these disputes to foreign arbitrators; but in the early years of the century the debate was conducted mainly at those frontier-meetings which the peace of Stettin had prescribed. Karl on the whole accepted this procedure more readily than Kristian. The Swedish representatives were firmly under his control; they could be relied upon to stick to their instructions and avoid prejudicial concessions; and if it came to the last resort of arbitration by the councils of the two realms they could be trusted to give a judgment on robustly partisan lines, without allowing themselves to be influenced by the adversary's arguments. Kristian, on the other hand, could never be quite sure that the members of his council, in their desire for a peaceful settlement, would not permit themselves an ill-timed impartiality; and in any case he had no love for the Stettin procedure and all its constitutional implications. Meetings took place in 1601, 1602 and 1603; and the mere fact that the Danes were prepared to attend them was in one respect a success for Karl. It implied a recognition, however reluctant, of his regal authority; and only the desire to secure the abolition of a Swedish tax on all transactions with Danish merchants induced Kristian to go so far.[1] At the last of these conferences, that of 1603, the procedure was carried to the full length stipulated for in the Stettin treaty: the representatives of both sides, after fruitless negotiation, constituted themselves a court of arbitration, and delivered formal judgments on the points at issue. But as might

[1] His representatives got no satisfaction from the Swedes on this point. The obnoxious tax remained, an irritant in Swedish–Danish relations, long after Karl was dead.

have been foreseen, they found it no easier to agree as arbitrators than as negotiators; and the court in fact pronounced two sets of judgments, each representing the national standpoint of the members: the arbitration procedure had been reduced to a formal farce.

Nevertheless, it was apparent that the Danish members were more ready to give ground than the Swedish. Though they were rightly sceptical of Swedish evidence on the Lappmark question, they were aware that the Danish position was equally difficult to substantiate, and they had no intention of allowing matters to drift to a rupture. At Sjöaryd in 1602 they gave a pledge to observe the peace of Stettin until the next frontier-meeting, and thus (to Kristian's chagrin) guaranteed Karl against attack in the interim; at Flabäck in 1603 they explicitly admitted that the Swedes had a right to tax the coastal Lapps. At the same meeting, while protesting at the blockade of Riga and insisting that Swedish privateers must not violate Danish territorial waters, they undertook that Kristian should not order any of his subjects to sail to Riga, nor give passes to foreigners to do so, nor be entitled to complain if Danish skippers who tried to run the blockade were stopped by the Swedish navy. The obvious divergence between the attitude of Kristian and that of his council did not escape Karl's observation. Until the meeting of 1603 he had been afraid of a Danish attack; when it failed to materialize he made up his mind that it would never happen, that the Danes could always be pushed into concessions or acquiescence, since the Danish council could always be relied upon to hold back their sovereign. In the strength of that belief he pursued a policy of pinpricks which in the end undermined the safeguard upon which he counted. At his coronation in 1607 he assumed the title of 'King of the Lapps of Nordland'. In the same year he appointed a *ståthållare* for Lappmark, with instructions to build a fort at Vadsø big enough to take a hundred men. In 1608 he gave to the Dutch settlers in his new town of Göteborg the right to fish off the Atlantic coast of Lappmark. As early as 1603 Kristian had tried to persuade his council to agree to a declaration of war. He tried again in 1604. He would go on trying; and one day, if Karl were not careful, he would succeed. But before that point was reached, Karl had committed himself deeply in Russia.

As long as Boris Godunov was alive, relations with Russia gave Karl no serious concern. It could indeed have been wished that Boris had ratified the treaty of Teusina; but it had never been the practice of the tsars to ratify treaties with Sweden. It was disturbing that he seemed so anxious for the friendship of Denmark; but at least he could be relied upon to be hostile to Poland. In the last years of his reign, moreover, when he faced a threat to his throne from the first false Dmitri, Boris had shown such obvious willingness to improve his relations with Sweden that Karl had already begun to speculate upon how high a price he might be able to command for his assistance.

But Boris died on 13 April 1605, his son Feodor was deposed a month later, and Dmitri ascended the throne in triumph. As seen from Stockholm, it was a revolution fraught with menace. For Dmitri had been patronized by Sigismund, he was a convert to Roman Catholicism, he had married a Polish wife, his invasion of Russia had been launched from Polish soil and stiffened with Polish volunteers. It seemed reasonable to suppose that his victory would mean the ascendancy of Polish influence in Moscow, the end of the old quarrel between the two realms, and conceivably the enlistment of Russia in support of Sigismund's attempts to regain his Swedish throne. In alarm at the prospect, Karl opened negotiations with the Turks; and at the same time addressed a stream of letters to the towns of north-west Russia, warning them of the danger to their religion and their nationality from a heretic and alien tsar. But though these anxieties were intelligible, they were in fact superfluous. Though Karl could not know it, Dmitri had no intention of being Sigismund's client, or even his ally. His main concern in foreign policy was the formation of an anti-Turkish league (a project peculiarly untimely, at a moment when Rudolf II had made up his mind for peace); such Polish followers as accompanied him to Moscow were drawn from sections of Polish society which were hostile to Sigismund and would shortly rise in rebellion against him in the *rokosz* of Zebrzydowski; and it may even be that in the closing months of his reign Dmitri was planning an attack upon Sigismund in association with these malcontents.

Nevertheless, it was no small relief to Karl when Dmitri's career was cut short by his murder, just twelve months after his usurpation. His successor on the throne, Vasilij Shuiskij, suited Karl much better. Shuiskij was the choice of the Moscow boyars, disliked by the provinces and the service-squires, personally suspect as the probable murderer of the true Dmitri at Uglitch in 1591, and hated as the representative of the selfish interests of the unpopular boyar class. He had not been tsar for six months before he was faced by a rising of the Volga Cossacks and a revolt of the lower orders led by Bolotnikov. The 'Time of Troubles' had begun; in July 1607 a second false Dmitri emerged, as a focus for the hopes and rancours of all who felt the times were out of joint; he was soon joined by Bolotnikov, by Zarutskij and the Cossacks of the Don, by the wreckage of the Zebrzydowski *rokosz* and other Polish outlaws; and in May 1608 he established himself at Tushino, whence he threatened Moscow itself. That the Bandit of Tushino (as his enemies called him) was an impostor was obvious, even to his supporters; but this did not matter. That he was a serious threat to Shuiskij's authority was a fact which the tsar in the end found himself unable to disguise. Shuiskij's relations with Poland were bad; his position at home was growing precarious. For two years he resisted the proffers of assistance which Karl pressed upon him, well knowing that such aid would entail unpopular sacrifices; and for a moment it seemed that he might be able to evade it by means of a settlement with Sigismund. In 1608 he was able to conclude a four-years' truce with Poland: the exiled Poles who supported the Bandit were as much Sigismund's enemies as his own; and Sigismund now pledged himself to recall them from Russia. But he could neither promise their obedience to the call, nor enforce it in practice. Lisowski, Rożyński and the rest ignored their sovereign's summons, and remained with the Bandit, whose cause continued to prosper. The Polish truce, as far as Shuiskij was concerned, was nearly worthless; there was nothing for it but an agreement with Karl. In August 1608 he at last brought himself to entreat it. It was indeed high time. In the autumn of 1608 Ivangorod, Pskov, Nöteborg and Kexholm all accepted the Bandit's authority: unless Shuiskij could obtain reinforcements, he might find himself cut off from the Baltic altogether.

Karl had been waiting for this moment. In the weakness of Shuiskij and the growing chaos in Russia he saw an opportunity to repair the omissions of Teusina and resume the ambitious designs of Johan III.[1] As early as 1606 he formulated the terms on which he would be prepared to give assistance to the tsar: the cession of Nöteborg, Kexholm, Jama, Ivangorod, Kopoŕe and Kolahus. He did not expect Shuiskij to swallow them; and at this stage he would have been prepared in the last resort to be content with Kolahus alone—a choice significant of the importance he attached to barring the route to Archangel. His propaganda was directed to inducing the towns of north-west Russia to seek security from anarchy in the acceptance of a Swedish protectorate. He revolved plans for seizing Kexholm and Nöteborg by a *coup de main.* He used the chance presented by Russian weakness to delimit the long-disputed frontier in the Arctic. It was with satisfaction, therefore, that he learned that Shuiskij's relative Skopin had concluded a provisional agreement with the Swedish commander in Livonia. That agreement was shortly embodied and formalized in the treaty of Viborg (28 February 1609), which was to remain the basis of Swedish policy in Russia until 1617. By the treaty of Viborg, the peace of Teusina was confirmed; the tsar renounced for ever his claims on Estonia and Livonia; an eternal alliance against the Poles was concluded; and in return for the assistance of 5,000 Swedish troops Shuiskij undertook

[1] See above, p. 265.

to hand over Kexholm and its *län* three weeks after the troops crossed the frontier. And on this occasion, against all precedent, the tsar personally ratified the treaty.

Shuiskij seemed this time to have made a good bargain. His writ no longer ran in Kexholm, and its inhabitants refused to be handed over: in the end the Swedes had to capture it. Meanwhile, the advent of the Swedish forces under Jakob de la Gardie rapidly changed the position to the tsar's advantage. After a victorious campaign Skopin and de la Gardie were able to enter Moscow in triumph on 12 March 1610; the insurrectionary coalition at Tushino disintegrated; the Bandit fled ignominiously to Kaluga. As a reward for his assistance Karl had already (16 December 1609) extorted from the tsar a promise of further territorial compensation (as yet, however, undefined) in exchange for increasing his army in Russia by a further 4,000 men; and already he was pressing for the cession of Nöteborg and Kolahus. His speculation in Russian anarchy seemed to be on the point of paying rich dividends.

But Swedish interference in Russia had already produced reactions which Karl had not foreseen. To Sigismund the treaty of Viborg appeared as a violation of his truce with the tsar; and now that Żółkiewski had subdued the last sputterings of the *rokosz* he was in a position to show his resentment. In September 1609 his army crossed the Russian frontier and laid siege to Smoleńsk. Thus the immediate consequence of Karl's Russian policy was precisely what he was most concerned to prevent—an official Polish intervention. Unauthorized Polish support for the Bandit had been sufficiently alarming; but this was much more serious. The danger which had seemed to threaten Sweden in the time of the first pseudo-Dmitri had now become a reality; the struggle between the two branches of the house of Vasa had been transferred to Russian soil. This was immediately apparent: the fighting in Livonia, which had latterly been going in Sigismund's favour (his troops took Pernau in 1609) dwindled and died away, for each side was now concentrating its efforts on the campaign in Muscovy. All this was bad enough; but worse was to follow. The dissident boyars at Tushino, disillusioned with the Bandit and the Polish outlaws, began to cast about for another expedient. In February 1610 they came to the conclusion that the most effective reply to a Polish invasion might well be the election of a Polish tsar; and they accordingly agreed to offer the throne to Sigismund's eldest son, Władysław. The move proved in fact to be a miscalculation, for Sigismund could only hope to secure the support of his subjects for intervention in Russia if he held out to them the expectation of the acquisition of borderlands to which the Poles considered themselves to have claims. He was understandably attracted by the prospect of placing his dynasty on the throne of the tsars; but he dared not allow the election of Władysław to turn him from the siege of Smoleńsk. Indeed, he would willingly have substituted his own for his son's candidature, and so realized in his own person the dream of a Polish–Russian union which Batory had cherished, and which he had himself revived in 1600. The offer to Władysław, in fact, raised more problems for Sigismund than it solved. This, however, was not yet apparent in Stockholm. To Karl, Władysław's election could only mean a Russia subordinate to Polish policy, the encirclement of his realms by his dynastic enemy, an easy way opened to Sigismund's return through Ingria and Finland. As if this were not enough, the victories of 1609 were now followed by military and political disaster. In April 1610 came the death of Shuiskij's ablest and most popular supporter, Skopin—poisoned, perhaps, by those who envied and feared his talents. On 24 June the Swedish–Russian army was annihilated by Żółkiewski at Klushino: de la Gardie was forced to capitulate on terms, and with a bare 400 men struggled back to Estonia, while the remaining survivors of his mercenary force, mutinous for want of pay, transferred their services to the victor. On 17 July a boyar rising deposed Shuiskij; on 17 August Władysław was formally chosen as tsar. A Russian delegation made its way to Sigismund's camp at Smoleńsk to invite his agreement; while Żółkiewski and his forces were installed in the Kremlin. It would be difficult to imagine a more disastrous outcome to Karl's rash policy of fishing in troubled waters.

In the year after Klushino Karl and de la Gardie were driven to improvise expedients in the hope that they might do duty for a policy. There was an idea of allying with the Bandit, on the basis of common hostility to Sigismund; but the Bandit was murdered in December 1610. De la Gardie then on his own responsibility launched the plan of securing the election of Karl's younger son, Karl Filip. For a moment it seemed to have possibilities: the first National Rising, in its need for a candidate to pit against Władysław, was favourably disposed, and formally endorsed Karl Filip's candidature on 23 June 1611. But within a month its leader, Ljapunov, had been murdered by his Cossack allies; the National Rising disintegrated; the prospects for Karl Filip grew dim. All that remained, it seemed, was for the Swedes to grab what could be grabbed while there was yet time: on 2 March 1611 Kexholm was taken at last; on 15 July de la Gardie seized Novgorod. But by pursuing a system of precautionary plunder, while at the same time sticking to Karl Filip's candidature, Karl was falling into the same error as Sigismund himself. His information about the rapidly-changing course of events in Russia was often fatally out of date; and he allowed himself to be dragged along by de la Gardie into a self-defeating policy which he had neither planned nor desired. And at the very moment when his Russian venture was collapsing in costly confusion, his provocation of Denmark was bringing its long-deferred retribution.

The expansion of the Swedish commitment in Muscovy did not seem to Karl to be any reason for relaxing his efforts in the Arctic or on the seas. The years 1609 and 1610 had seen the advantage in both areas swing to the side of the Danes: their navy convoyed foreign merchantmen into Riga unmolested; their tax-gatherers had a good season in Lappmark. Karl's reaction was to stiffen his attitude and redouble his efforts. In vain the *råd*, disturbed by the tone of recent Danish protests and the rumours of Danish armaments, in May 1610 warned him against risking war on two fronts, and urged temporary and tactical concessions: Karl's reply was to threaten abdication; and as always the threat sufficed to carry his point. He did, however, take measures to improve his diplomatic position. The year 1608 had seen the formation of the Protestant Union in Germany; and in 1609 France, England and the Dutch had linked themselves together in alliance. Karl was anxious to be included in either or both of these groups. In August 1609 the Estates agreed to his proposal to despatch embassies to France, England, the United Provinces, the Palatinate and Hesse, to inquire the prospects and seek their mediation in the Polish war. The missions to Germany were never sent, and that to France was prevented by the news of Henry IV's murder; but in April 1610 Johan Skytte and Jakob van Dijk set off for the Hague and London. The Dutch, mindful of Swedish privateering, proved cold; and though James I was cordial, his council was not. James recognized Karl as king in virtue of the choice of the Estates; but he would promise no support against Poland, no assistance in Russia, no alignment with Sweden in the event of Danish aggression; while as to Karl's acceptance into the alliance, he referred him to separate negotiations with the other parties to it. Thus the embassy to England brought no practical benefit. But at least it did no damage, which was more than could be said of a mission by Chesnecopherus to Copenhagen. Chesnecopherus was the leading agent and supporter of Karl's anti-Danish activities, and was thus hardly the most suitable emissary to choose, if anything effective were to be done. He went to Copenhagen with a closed mind; he returned with a temper exacerbated, less disposed than ever to moderate the habitual asperity of his master.

Towards the end of August came the news of Klushino. It did not shake Karl's determination to persist in his Russian venture; but it must certainly have encouraged Kristian IV to bring matters to a head. In July Kristian's council had once more—and for the last time—refused his demand for war; but they had sanctioned his sending of an open letter to the Swedish Estates, which was in effect an appeal to the

Swedish people to repudiate the policy of their sovereign. And in October he advised James I, in strict confidence, of his intention to declare war next year.

The *råd*, by now thoroughly alarmed, appealed to Karl to cut his losses in Russia, to send no more troops there and recall as many as could be spared, to concentrate the fleet, to accelerate his armaments, to try what diplomacy could do to stave off a crisis. They had no quarrel with the objectives at which he aimed; it was the recklessness of his methods that appalled them. In a final desperate memorandum of December 1610 they insisted that another war, on top of the Russian and Polish commitments, would be 'intolerable, indeed impossible to endure', and pleaded for immediate concessions in the Arctic and off Riga. Karl's reply was to appeal to the Estates against them, to hint that they were alarmists of dubious loyalty, and once again to threaten to lay down the crown. The Estates were in fact no happier than the *råd* about the situation, but by crude appeals to unthinking patriotism he stampeded them into a kind of endorsement of his policy and a promise of substantial supplies of men and money. Fortified by this achievement, he now replied to Kristian's open letter in terms which played straight into his adversary's hands. On 30 January 1611 Kristian at last extracted his council's assent to a declaration of war; on 4 April his herald crossed the frontier to deliver it.

Thus Karl had involved himself in a struggle which neither he nor his country was in a fit state to wage. He had attempted to conduct two major enterprises simultaneously; with the result that he faced failure in both, and was strong enough for neither. The promised levies came in slowly; the best part of the army was overseas, while that which was in Sweden was largely untrained, and no match for the Danish mercenaries; even the fleet, upon which he had lavished much care and money, was enervated by administrative inefficiency and corruption. Apart from Kalmar and Älvsborg, the country's fortresses were in no condition to offer a protracted resistance. Not all Karl's hectic but waning energy, not all his bitter sarcasms, could now repair the accumulated negligence of years, the torpor of his admirals, and the inexperience of his native commanders.

Karl's foreign policy was all his own: neither Chesnecopherus nor any other of his ministers was sufficiently influential to be debited with a share of responsibility. But it was also, of course, to some extent dictated by the circumstances of his accession; and in another aspect it is to be seen as the continuation of the now-traditional attempt to put Sweden in command of the Russian trade-routes. The one entailed the hostility of Poland, and the cultivation of confessional ties; the other revived the hostility of Denmark. It was quite natural that in this situation Karl should recur to the policies of Erik XIV, and seek the friendship of the tsar on the one hand and the Protestant states on the other: if all had gone well, the diplomatic alignment in 1611 might have been broadly the same as Erik had hoped for in 1563. But the peculiar viciousness of Karl's foreign policy lay not so much in its underlying principles as in the manner in which those principles were applied. From start to finish it was marred by grave errors of judgment and apparently ineradicable misconceptions. It was foolish to force the Poles to support Sigismund by wantonly invading Livonia; it was foolish to reject any idea of compromise, despite growing dangers elsewhere, and a military inferiority which had been clearly demonstrated. It was reckless to offer to Kristian IV an opportunity of attacking Sweden while the Swedish forces were fully committed against the Poles, whether in Livonia or in Muscovy. And the miscalculation which cleared the way for Kristian's declaration of war had been preceded by the similar error which gave Sigismund a chance to intervene in Russia. No doubt it was extraordinarily difficult to evaluate the international implications of all the twists and turns of the Time of Troubles; and certainly it was of great importance to Sweden to prevent Russia from becoming Poland's satellite. But in fact that danger (in so far as it was ever a real danger at all) was provoked by the very policy which sought to avert it. And as to Denmark, it is plain that Karl was the victim of self-induced delusions. He believed that the Danish council would always shield him from the consequences of his provocations; he believed that Kristian IV was in any case not formidable unless he were aided by a Swedish fifth-column, and that anyone who doubted this was half-way to treason; he believed that concern for the Protestant Cause would force the western powers to intervene to prevent a Danish attack; he believed, finally, that the main danger against which he had to guard was a conjunction of Kristian with Sigismund—though in fact Kristian proclaimed that he was setting out to conquer Sweden in order to safeguard it from falling into Catholic hands, and Sigismund tried hard by diplomatic means to avert Kristian's attack upon his hereditary kingdom.

The truth was that Karl was as little fitted to the conduct of foreign affairs as to the command of an army in the field. His calculations were often faulty; his knowledge defective; and, above all, his obstinacy and wrongheadedness invincible. His failure was at bottom a defect of character. For it was his inability to appreciate any point of view but his own—that quality which had made him so formidable a politician in the domestic sphere—that, in the last analysis, was the ruin of his foreign policy.

VI. THE END OF THE REIGN

It was beyond Karl's capacity to ride the storm which he had conjured up. At no time had he shown any sign of military ability, and now he was physically scarcely equal to the burden of command. He was sixty-one; his health was breaking. In August 1609, after one of his furious outbursts of passion, he had had a stroke which disabled him for several months; and though he resumed the direction of affairs in the spring of 1610 he was never the same man again. At the *riksdag* of 1610 he had great difficulty in addressing the Estates: an enemy reported of him, with evident satisfaction, that he 'could neither speak nor hear, but was worse than a brute beast'. Karl himself felt his time was running out: the appearance of Halley's Comet in 1607, he considered, had been an indication of his approaching end. In broken, halting phrases he told the Estates that God had punished him.[1] They showed no disposition to dispute the diagnosis.

The temporary incapacity of the king marked the beginning of the slow disintegration of his system of government. The *råd* began to discover a mind of its own, and a voice to utter remonstrance; a change which is perhaps to be associated with Axel Oxenstierna's entry to it in 1609. Certainly Oxenstierna quickly emerged as the effective leader of the council, the spokesman of a group of men who only bided their time to recur to the programmes of Erik Sparre; and inevitably, therefore, he became the principal opponent of Karl's confidential *hovkansler* Nils Chesnecopherus. And just as the *råd* was growing restive, so too was Duke Johan. He was irked by Karl's careful surveillance, annoyed by his refusal to allow him to travel, discontented with the duchy which had been assigned to him. Already he was looking forward to the moment when, on the accession of his cousin Gustav Adolf, he would be able to strike a good bargain for himself as the price of making no trouble. Even Karl's shrewd and masterful wife, Kristina of Holstein, scented changes upon the wind, secured a better settlement for herself while yet there was time, and set herself to make friends with Oxenstierna and the aristocracy against the day when she might need their assistance to maintain the rights of her son.

Despite his disabilities Karl clung grimly to power. The last six months of his life saw a government which was perhaps more purely personal than at any time since the revival of the *råd* in 1602. For the *råd* was now neither consulted nor admitted to his confidence; Chesnecopherus and the secretaries executed the king's orders; from January to April Oxenstierna and his colleagues were left to live on their estates in ignorance of the desperate state of relations with

[1] It is interesting, if fruitless, to conjecture which particular delinquency he had in mind.

Denmark. Already in March 1610 Joachim Frederick of Mansfeld had written: 'Der König ist sehr schwach. Die Reichsräthe nehmen sich nichts an. Keine Sache wird expediert. Es steht nicht wohl zu.'[1]

It was not only the *råd* that had become alienated from the sovereign. Discontent with the government, disquiet at the king's policies, affected almost every section of the community. The nobility were smarting at their failure to obtain fresh privileges, resentful of their lack of influence, angry and afraid at the delations and illegal imprisonments which had marked Karl's treatment of them. The clergy were at loggerheads with the king on doctrine and ceremonies, and disturbed by royal interference with church appointments; the university lamented its lost privileges and unpaid salaries. Among the commonalty, too, strong dark tides of unrest were flowing. A seditious pamphlet of 1609 complained of the intolerable illegalities of royal officials, called Karl a tyrant, and threatened him with revolt if there were no amendment.[2] Similar pamphlets which circulated immediately after Karl's death condemned his wars, complained of the weight of his taxes ('priests are become no better than peasants, and peasants mere beasts'), the prevalence of foreigners in the administration, and the burden of his frequent summonings of the Estates: 'One meeting is scarcely ended before another is in contemplation . . . God in Heaven preserve us here in Sweden from so many *herredagar* and from such another bloody and oppressive reign as this last has been.' The king's death was followed by tumults in the northerly provinces, by hateful libels against the queen, by a wave of hostility to the nobility among the peasants. It was a sick society which Karl was soon to leave behind him.

Meanwhile the war opened disastrously. The Danish attack in the end took him by surprise, and he was ill-prepared to meet it. Already in May 1611 the town of Kalmar fell to Kristian's forces; and two months later the castle was lost also. The most important stronghold in Sweden had thus fallen without Karl's being able to strike a blow to save it; and the subsequent campaign did not belie this gloomy beginning. But by the time the armies were ready to go into winter quarters it was already apparent that Karl would not live to see any turning of the tide. He had reached the limit of his physical resources. As he made his way northwards from the battle-front in Småland he fell ill; his condition became rapidly worse; and at Nyköping, on 30 October 1611,

[1] Quoted in W. Tham, *Axel Oxenstierna. Hans ungdom och verksamhet intill år 1612*, p. 216.

[2] *Ett gott råd här i Sverige*, printed in Stiernman, Bihang, pp. 262–8. Karl took the curious step of printing the pamphlet, together with his refutation of some of its charges, and thus gave it a much wider publicity than it would otherwise have secured—perhaps because its attacks on the bailiffs, the clergy and the Uppsala dons coincided with his own views of them. It is remarkable that he acted on the advice of the author in removing Raumannus from Stockholm to Uppsala.

he ended his violent and crooked career. The volcano of his temperament had rumbled fitfully almost to the last. He left a successor not yet seventeen years of age, a country exhausted by half a century of war, a *régime* in discredit and disarray. His eldest son and his bastard might revere his memory with filial piety; but when he died there can have been few of his subjects, save for those personal servants and foreign adventurers upon whom he had relied, who did not feel his death as a release from tension, and as offering the hope of setting right much that was amiss. The control of the government, which he had claimed so vehemently, and for which he had striven so long, had brought him few satisfactions when at last he attained it; but to his subjects, perhaps, still fewer. In eleven years of personal rule he had contrived to alienate his old ally *Herr Omnes*, without appeasing those to whom *Herr Omnes* was abhorrent; and it was his misfortune that even those features of his government which were most enlightened—his attempted reform of the law, his genuine if limited religious tolerance—did not commend themselves to his people. As Gustav Vasa had found in old King Kristian his chief asset in dealing with the fractious, so Karl had tried to make use of King Sigismund as a spectre to daunt the devout: experience had persuaded him that the best estoppal to a charge of unconstitutional behaviour was to raise a Protestant panic. The danger from Sigismund was real enough, as his subjects well knew; but the political tactics which Karl based upon it had before his death become cruelly transparent, and the cynicism with which he used them had long been obvious. Since 1600 the saviour of Protestantism had drawn recklessly upon the gratitude, and played too often upon the fears, of those whom he professed to have delivered. By 1611 his essential contribution to Swedish history, whatever we may think of it, lay clearly in the past. His part was played out; it was full time for him to be gone.

7. Conclusion

Throughout that sombre Christmas season, while the new king was bargaining with the Estates about the terms of the Charter which was to be the price of his recognition, Karl's body lay in state in the great hall of the castle of Nyköping. It was not until April 1612, when the pressure of domestic politics had slackened and the spring thaw put a stop to campaigning, that time could be found for his funeral. With a last remembrance of his former position as duke he had ordered that he should be buried, not in the Riddarholm Church in Stockholm, or near his father in Uppsala, but in his own cathedral of Strängnäs; and his order was obeyed. There was a certain appropriateness in the choice. At Strängnäs Gustav Vasa had been chosen king, eighty-nine years ago; and at Strängnäs, with the interment of his youngest son, the age of Gustav Vasa at last came to its end.

For the year 1611 in many ways marked the close of an era. The death of Karl IX entailed the passing away of much that his father and his brothers had striven for; it brought the solution of some of the great issues in which they had been engaged. It may be taken, for instance, more naturally perhaps than any other date, as the point at which the Swedish Reformation was completed. By 1611, the Swedish church had assumed its final form. There might still in the future be dissension as to the precise degree of rigidity of Lutheran orthodoxy; men might differ on whether or not to accept the *liber concordiae*; it might be necessary to temper the requirement of conformity in the interests of economics, and wink at Calvinist services among unregenerate incoming Dutch; but to all intents and purposes Sweden was now a monolithic Lutheran state, and all office-bearers, from the sovereign downwards, must profess the state religion—as Queen Kristina was one day to find. Henceforward there would be no place for ecumenical divagations, whether of Johan's sort or of Karl's: the syncretist movement of the mid-century was damned in advance. The church emerged from forty years of tribulation with its authority rather strengthened than diminished. It had beaten off the encroachments of the lay power, and that battle would not need to be fought again; for the absolutism of Karl XI and Karl XII—unlike that of Gustav Vasa—would be of so exemplary an orthodoxy that only the most captious ecclesiastic could cavil at it. The church's right to legislate in its own concerns was now acknowledged. Episcopal authority had survived the disfavour of Karl and his father, and it would be long before it was seriously challenged again. Parochial self-government was vigorous and effective; and in matters of church discipline the secular power—especially now that there had been a quasi-reception of Mosaic law—was in a fair way to becoming the church's provost-marshal. Gustav Adolf's Charter gave guarantees against the arbitrary deprivation of bishops; it promised that there should be no improper interference with their appointment; it conceded to them an unrestricted right to ordain: the royal attack on the episcopate had been decisively repelled. But this was not all. For the accession of Gustav Adolf meant also the end of the doctrinal disharmony between church and king. For the first time since the Reformation Sweden had now a sovereign whose religious views agreed with those of his clergy; and the change meant that the sovereign in future would be less tempted to exercise the royal supremacy, and the church less vigilant against the crown.

Just as Gustav Adolf's Charter, in the ecclesiastical sphere, represented the attainment of an equipoise between the claims of church and state, so too it marked the striking of a balance in the constitutional debate which had dominated the past half-century. At first sight this was far from being obvious. On the contrary, Gustav Adolf's accession might seem rather to register the victory of the aristocracy over the crown, the triumph of *råd*-constitutionalism over its enemies, the rehabilitation of the victims of 1600. The Nyköping *riksdag* of 1611–12 did indeed pronounce an ample, explicit and detailed condemnation of the illegalities and violences of the rule of Karl IX. The oath of fidelity which the *råd* swore to the new sovereign on 4 January 1612 bound them, as of old, to see to it that the king observed his pledges and conformed to the law. The Charter of 1611 provided that *no* business concerning the realm was to be undertaken without the advice of the *råd*, that new or increased taxes were not to be levied without the consent of the *råd* and 'those who are concerned', and that any advice which the *råd* might give to the sovereign was not to be judged *ex eventu*. At the same time, the proposals for administrative reform which Erik Sparre had put forward in 1594 were now in a measure adopted; for the Charter assured security of tenure to all civil servants until lawfully convicted of delinquency, while the privileges granted to the Nobility on 10 January 1612 promised that none but nobles should be appointed as exchequer-councillors (*kammarråd*), that nobles should henceforth be employed in the chancery, and that a fixed salary should be attached to every post. And if the constitutional programme of the aristocracy was thus largely implemented, their more selfish class-interests were also taken care of: the long dispute over *rusttjänst* was settled by the promise that the emoluments of state service should not be liable, and that *rusttjänst* was not to be exacted from widows or girls; donations were to be confirmed without question on the accession of a new king; the principle of trial by peers in all serious cases was reaffirmed (no more extraordinary tribunals hand-picked from the Estates!); and the king undertook that in future there should be no arbitrary confiscations of noble property.

Thus the *råd* resumes its historic place in the constitution; the 'rule of secretaries' is repudiated; and the monarchy, once more held to ransom and constrained to grant a Charter as a condition of recognition, seems destined to be the prisoner of the aristocratic reaction. But in fact this did not happen: the appearances are misleading. On the contrary, the settlement of 1611–12 inaugurates an era of harmonious coöperation between monarchy and aristocracy such as Sweden had not known since 1560. The *råd*-party used its victory with moderation; the monarchy disarmed its adversaries' suspicions by frankly taking them into partnership. The close collaboration of Gustav Adolf and Axel Oxenstierna, the reciprocal esteem and intimate confidence which subsisted between them, took the sting out of the Charter, and transformed it from being the *diktat* of a victorious constitutional opposition into a mere precautionary agreement which there was happily no need to invoke. In part because of this, in part in its despite, the constitutional struggle in 1611 reached a provisional ending; and for the next generation it became a memory which no one cared to stir into life. Not until 1719 would a Charter of comparable stringency be exacted from a successor to the throne. Meanwhile, the monarchy had turned its back for ever on the administrative methods of the early Vasas: after 1611 the attempt to maintain a personal and paternal control of the whole business of government is finally abandoned. In 1611 the state at last ceases to be the king's *votchina*. Instead, Gustav Adolf and Axel Oxenstierna evolve new administrative forms to deal with the growing complexity of business: at the centre the ring of *collegia* which takes definitive shape in 1634; at the periphery the *landshövdingar*, very much as Sparre had envisaged them. And the key to the success of these new developments lay in the enlistment of the nobility in the service of the state. The accession of Gustav Adolf ushers in a period of more than a century and a half in which the nobility stands out as the great serving class, perennially revivified by the practice of giving peerages as the reward of a successful career, whether civil or military. Thus the settlement of 1611, despite superficial appearances, turned out to be a compromise which neither infringed the legitimate prerogative nor stimulated constitutional agitation; and it cleared the way for administrative developments without which Sweden could hardly have coped with the strains and responsibilities entailed by her emergence as a great power. And it was an especially fortunate circumstance that the compromise did not imply a check to the emergence of parliamentary institutions. Despite the complaints of over-many *herredagar*, despite the general revulsion from Karl's exploitation of the *riksdag*, the reaction of 1611 was not strong enough to undo the work of the revolutionary years. The *riksdag* was now too well established for any return to an antique provincialism; and though the Charter contained a clause designed to prevent its abuse, it was already true that the best safeguard against royal manipulation of the Estates was to make them stronger rather than weaker.

Yet the posthumous victory of Erik Sparre, and the alliance of crown and nobility which was the unexpected outcome of that victory, were by no means wholly beneficent. The days when the crown was a creditor rather than a debtor were now for ever past: no Swedish king would ever again enjoy the commanding financial position of Gustav Vasa. Half a century of warfare had already taxed the resources of the monarchy; and ahead of it lay commitments on a scale which would have made Gustav Vasa's hair stand on end. The crown would be able to meet those commitments only by paying for services through alienations of revenue on an ever-increasing scale—partly by way of *förläningar*, as in the past, but more and more by donations: the Norrköping resolution of 1604 had opened the way. As a result of this process, crown peasants would be paying their rents, tax-peasants their taxes, to private individuals who would usually be nobles; and this situation would ultimately imperil the social position and constitutional liberties of a considerable section of the fourth Estate. The reign of Gustav Adolf opens with an urgent and explicit cry for a *reduktion*, and that cry was never wholly to be silenced until the absolutist revolution of 1680. The year 1611 inaugurates the great crisis of the Swedish peasantry; it marks a dividing-line between its relatively secure position under the early Vasas, and its struggle to keep its foothold in the Age of Greatness. But it was not only the peasants who were affected by these developments: for the nobility and for the crown they were to have serious long-term implications. The entrenchment of the nobility in the state's service, which had been one part of Sparre's programme, was to make them especially sensitive to the possibility of royal insolvency, but also clamorous for the donations which steadily eroded the royal revenues. In the end they were torn in two between those who had been paid (and often very handsomely paid) by alienations, and those who feared that they might not be paid at all unless the alienations were revoked. And when to these latter were added a peasantry which believed itself threatened with degradation to servile status, a clergy and a *bourgeoisie* resentful of aristocratic pretensions, then the monarchy would have at its command enough support to upset the constitutional balance, and destroy the constitutional safeguards, more completely than at any other period in Swedish history. The realization of Sparre's plan of administrative reform, in fact, created conditions which would ultimately threaten what was even more important to him, namely the rule of law itself.

The crisis of 1680, like the crisis of 1650 which formed the prelude to it, was in the last resort the penalty which the aristocracy paid for collaborating in, or conniving at, a foreign policy too expensive for the ordinary revenues of the crown to bear; and here at least 1611 was no turning-point. Erik's dissipation of his father's hoards, Johan III's deplorable finances, had both given sufficient warning that native resources had limits too narrow for grandiose adventures. It was only the hope that expansion would pay for itself—by tolls on foreign shipping, by monopoly-control of trade-routes—that kept the sons of Gustav Vasa constant to their enterprises. That there was a strong defensive aspect in their policies is certainly true: Erik, like his father, feared Danish encirclement; Johan was legitimately alarmed at the threat from Ivan IV; and though Karl may have misjudged the situation in Russia, he could hardly remain passive before the possibility of a Polish tsar. But each one of them passed easily from a defensive to an aggressive policy; each nursed the hope of something like an empire of the Baltic. In 1611, to be sure, the prospects for it looked bleak enough; and it may be doubted whether any foreign observer would have considered a great imperial future for Sweden as a possibility which demanded much serious consideration. Estonia was in peril, as so often before; the Swedish forces were bogged down in the morass of Muscovite factions; the dynastic quarrel within the House of Vasa seemed to ensure that for the first time Sweden would have to reckon Poland as a permanent enemy. The prospect of milking the Russia trade seemed as far off as ever: indeed, it seemed further off, for the attempt to realize it had given Kristian IV his chance to put the very survival of the Swedish state in question. The least he hoped for from his war was that it might effectually scotch his neighbour's Baltic ambitions. He failed, indeed, in his attempt to subject Sweden altogether; but the peace of Knäred in 1613 was more onerous than the peace of Stettin in 1570. So onerous, that it might well have suggested to Swedish statesmen that a return to the cautious and insular policies of Gustav Vasa now offered the best hope of recovery, and therefore the best security for the future. But the dynastic quarrel with Sigismund stood in the way of any such conclusion: the struggle in Russia must go on, Estonia must be defended, Livonia (if possible) be conquered, lest Gustav Adolf find himself confronted with a legitimist invasion backed by forces too great for him to master. And the quarrel was not dynastic only: it was—or at least was esteemed to be—religious, and thus one aspect of a great international crisis. As Europe drifted to the catastrophe of the Thirty Years War, the struggle in Livonia took on a new dimension, and became less amenable than ever to suggestions of compromise. Thus religious as well as dynastic considerations barred the road back to the hedgehog policies of Gustav Vasa. It is true that in 1611 Sweden stood quite alone: not a Protestant hand was raised to save her. But her defeat and humiliation at the hands of the Danes would at least have the good effect of attracting the support of the Dutch, who had no desire to see the master of the Sound as master of the Baltic too; and from that beginning it would not be difficult to extend the circle of Protestant patrons and backers. Commitment to the Protestant Cause, and hence involvement in a major European conflict—which Gustav Vasa with his tepid confessional interests had almost always managed to avoid—came in part from the purely domestic circumstances of the dynastic revolution; but in part also from the more positive Lutheranism of church and people which had been both a factor in that revolution and a consequence of it, and which was now incarnate in the person of the new king.

Thus the War of Kalmar, disastrous as it was, did not terminate Sweden's Baltic ambitions, and even contributed to her entanglement in the affairs of the continent. It certainly increased the economic difficulties in the way of an active foreign policy; but even in the difficult opening years of the new reign it was possible to perceive that the country's war-potential was greater than Gustav Vasa would have thought possible. The importance of naval power had been grasped, not least by Erik and Karl; the navy was on the eve of a great revival; all that was really needed to make it the instrument (and it was an essential instrument) of an expansionist foreign policy was better administration. The army, it is true, was in the doldrums, wavering dispiritedly between old methods and new; but a military genius who was also a great organizer would find material here with which to build the finest fighting force in Europe. As to the indispensable economic resources without which the achievements of Gustav Adolf would have been impossible, the prospects were not unpromising. The revenues of the crown might already be severely stretched, but new industrial developments promised greater resources in the future. Iron-mining was flourishing and expanding, exports of bar-iron were rising; while the greatly increased international demand for copper was soon to make Falun the richest jewel in the Swedish crown. Already cheap labour, ample water-power readily available, and tempting government concessions, were attracting foreign capitalists and *entrepreneurs*: a native, self-sufficing armaments industry was already conceivable. It is true that Sweden's mineral wealth never became adequate in itself to support great-power status: the systematic exploitation of occupied territory, heavy tolls at Baltic ports, subsidies from foreign powers, would always be necessary; but home resources soon became adequate to support those involvements out of which greatness would arise. And in foreign trade Sweden was clearly leaving the world of Gustav Vasa behind: the cautious 'passive' policy was already looking old-fashioned; and Karl's plantation of Dutchmen in the first Göteborg (though it was destroyed in the War of Kalmar) showed a determination to increase active trade with the West, quite independently of the old idea of making Sweden an *entrepôt* for the trade to Russia.

In other respects, it is true, a predominantly stable agricultural society had changed little in the past century. Stockholm in 1611 was not much bigger than in 1500; the new towns which Johan III had founded with such enthusiasm throve ill. Population grew only slowly; and though the development of the iron industry may have opened up the country in some areas (notably in Värmland), and though an immigration of Finnish settlers which Karl encouraged may have brought burn-beat cultivation to tracts which before had been mere forest, the limits of settlement had not been greatly expanded. The new industries, the new mines, did not affect more than a numerically insignificant proportion of the population. Society was uncommonly static, social mobility was small. The numbers of clergy were rising sufficiently noticeably to be a matter of complaint, but the professions were otherwise conspicuous by their absence. Except in Stockholm, and one or two of the less insignificant towns, there was still hardly a middle class at all. Within the nobility, no doubt, there was movement up or down, and the creation of counts and barons had superimposed upon the old untitled aristocracy a thin upper-crust which was already regarded with jealousy; but this schism, which was later to be so important, was only just beginning to be discernible. At the summit of society manners were a little less rude than of old, and tastes more cultivated; but though with Erik and Johan the Renaissance had at last made good its footing, cultural levels were generally low. A few native painters and goldsmiths there were, but without royal patronage and imported masters the arts could hardly have sustained themselves; and in literature the sixteenth century is a desert. But here too a new age was dawning. Gustav Adolf's great endowment would put the university at last upon a solid footing; and the coming of the *gymnasia* in the 1620s would do much to repair the grievous wounds inflicted upon education by the Reformation. Compared even with Denmark Sweden was still backward and barbarous; but the men who made the age of Kristina possible—Johan Skytte, Messenius, Laurentius Paulinus Gothus, Rudbeckius, Axel Oxenstierna, Gustav Adolf himself—were awaiting their opportunity, and the first great Swedish poet—Georg Stiernhielm—had already been born. The Ancient Goths were not yet forgotten: on the contrary, the cult of gothicism was just about to take on new dimensions and advance claims of unheard-of scope; but whereas this national myth had before been essentially a fabrication designed to conceal present poverty and compensate for present insignificance, it was soon to become a more positive creed. The day was not far distant when Gustavus would appear not only as the heir (and anagram) of Augustus, but as the reincarnation of Totila.

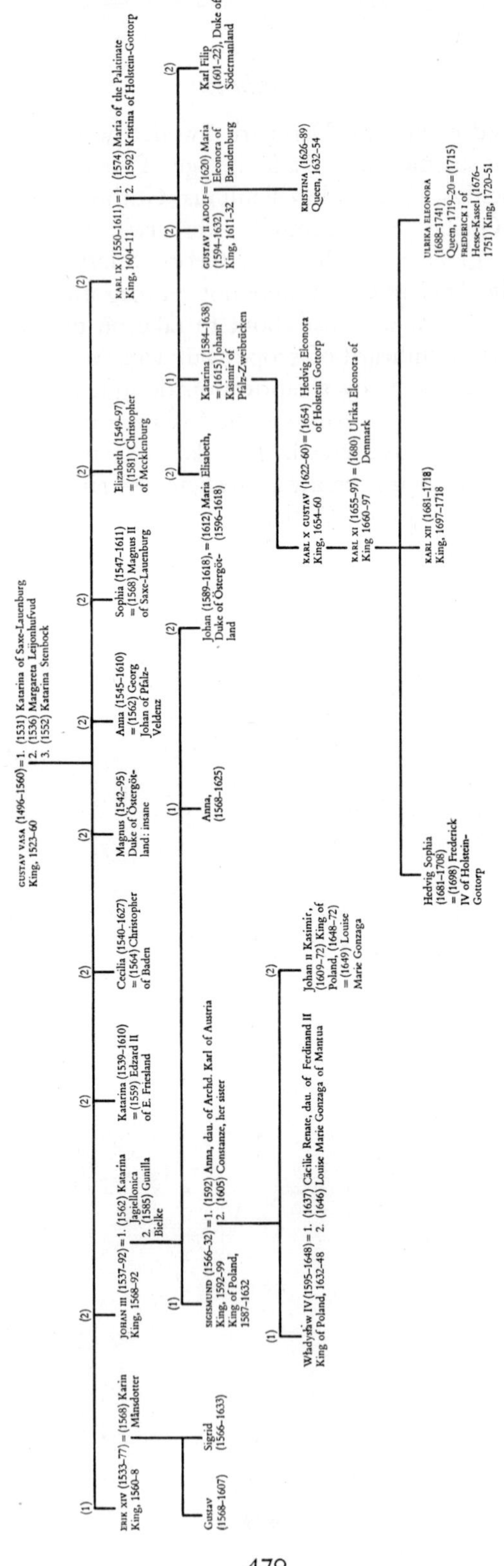
GUSTAV VASA (1496–1560) = 1. (1531) Katarina of Saxe-Lauenburg
King, 1523–60
2. (1536) Margareta Leijonhufvud
3. (1552) Katarina Stenbock
(1)
ERIK XIV (1533–77) = (1568) Karin Månsdotter
King, 1560–8
Gustav (1568–1607)
Sigrid (1566–1633)
(2)
JOHAN III (1537–92) = 1. (1562) Katarina Jagiellonica
King, 1568–92
2. (1585) Gunilla Bielke
(1)
SIGISMUND (1566–32) = 1. (1592) Anna, dau. of Archd. Karl of Austria
King, 1592–99
King of Poland, 1587–1632
2. (1605) Constanze, her sister
(1)
Władysław IV (1595–1648) = 1. (1637) Cäcilie Renate, dau. of Ferdinand II
King of Poland, 1632–48
2. (1646) Louise Marie Gonzaga of Mantua
(2)
Johan II Kasimir, (1609–72) King of Poland, (1648–72) = (1649) Louise Marie Gonzaga
(1)
Anna, (1568–1625)
(2)
Johan (1589–1618), = (1612) Maria Elisabeth, (1596–1618)
Duke of Östergötland
(2)
Katarina (1539–1610) = (1559) Edzard II of E. Friesland
(2)
Cecilia (1540–1627) = (1564) Christopher of Baden
(2)
Magnus (1542–95) Duke of Östergötland: insane
(2)
Anna (1545–1610) = (1562) Georg Johan of Pfalz-Veldenz
(2)
Sophia (1547–1611) = (1568) Magnus II of Saxe-Lauenburg
(2)
Elizabeth (1549–97) = (1581) Christopher of Mecklenburg
(2)
KARL IX (1550–1611) = 1. (1574) Maria of the Palatinate
King, 1604–11
2. (1592) Kristina of Holstein-Gottorp
(1)
Katarina (1584–1638) = (1615) Johann Kasimir of Pfalz-Zweibrücken
KARL X GUSTAV (1622–60) = (1654) Hedvig Eleonora of Holstein Gottorp
King, 1654–60
KARL XI (1655–97) = (1680) Ulrika Eleonora of Denmark
King, 1660–97
Hedvig Sophia (1681–1708) = (1698) Frederick IV of Holstein-Gottorp
KARL XII (1681–1718)
King, 1697–1718
ULRIKA ELEONORA (1688–1741)
Queen, 1719–20 = (1715) FREDERICK I of Hesse-Kassel (1676–1751) King, 1720–51
(2)
GUSTAV II ADOLF = (1620) Maria Eleonora of Brandenburg
(1594–1632)
King, 1611–32
KRISTINA (1626–89)
Queen, 1632–54
(2)
Karl Filip (1601–22), Duke of Södermanland

Bibliography

Och effter nu till thet första, här effter förmält warder om nyttige Böckers Läsning, Så skall man thet weeta, at Werlden är full aff Böcker, om allehanda Ting, som Menniskligit Förnufft hafwer kunnat uptänckia . . . Så måste man uthwälia sig the alldrabäste och förståndigaste *Authores*, som man hafwa kan at läsa uti.

Per Brahe d.ä., *Oeconomia*

I. BIBLIOGRAPHICAL AIDS

The standard guides to printed material and secondary works are S. Ågren and K. Setterwall, *Svensk historisk bibliografi (1771–1874)* (Uppsala, 1937); K. Setterwall, *Svensk historisk bibliografi (1875–1900)* (1907);[1] K. Setterwall, *Svensk historisk bibliografi (1901–1920)* (Uppsala, 1923); Paul Sjögren, *Svensk historisk bibliografi (1921–1935)* (1956); Harald Bohrn and Percy Elfstrand, *Svensk historisk bibliografi (1936–1950)* (1963). This series is continued as an annual supplement to *H[istorisk] T[idskrift]*. A useful single volume, fairly full up to its date of publication, is S. E. Bring, *Bibliografisk handbok till Sveriges historia* (1934).

II. MATERIAL FOR THE WHOLE PERIOD 1523–1611

Of fundamental importance is *Svenska riksdagsakter jämte andra handlingar som höra till statsförfattningens historia*, I Series, I–IV (1887–): though mainly concerned with *riksdag* proceedings, it contains in addition much collateral material, and is particularly rich for the last two decades of the century: publication has unfortunately halted at 1599, and there follows a gap until 1611, when II series begins. For Karl IX's reign, therefore, reference must be made to A. A. von Stiernman, *Alla riksdagars och mötens besluth*, I and Bihang (1728, 1743). Documents concerning the organization and functioning of the administration are collected in *Samling af instructioner för högre och lägre tjänstemän vid landtregeringen i Sverige och Finland*, ed. C. G. Styffe (1853), and in *Samling af instructioner rörande den civila förvaltningen i Sverige och Finland*, ed. C. G. Styffe (1856). Ordinances and proclamations concerning economic matters are gathered together in A. A. von Stiernman, *Samling utaf Kongl. brev, stadgar och förordningar angående Sveriges Rikes Commerce, Politie och Oeconomie uti gemen, ifrån åhr 1523 in til närwarande tid*, I (1747), and concerning

[1] The place of publication is understood to be Stockholm, unless otherwise indicated.

the execution of justice in J. Schmedemann, *Kongl. stadgar, förordningar, brev och resolutioner från åhr 1528 in til 1701 angående justitiae och executionsährende*, I (1706). *Kyrko-ordningar och förslag dertill före 1686*, in *Handlingar rörande Sveriges historia*, I Series, II (1872), prints church ordinances and drafts of ordinances. Treaties with foreign powers, with additional related material, are printed in the series *Sverges traktater med främmande magter*, of which vol. IV (1888) covers 1521–71, and vol. V (1903) covers 1572–1632.

The standard political histories for the period are: Emil Hildebrand, *Gustav Vasa* (1920), and Idem, *Gustav Vasas söner* (1923), forming vols. V and VI of the series *Sveriges historia till våra dagar*; Helge Almquist, *Reformationstiden och stormaktstidens förra skede* (Lund, 1922), which forms vol. III of *Svenska folkets historia*. Shorter and more modern surveys are provided in Jerker Rosén and Sten Carlsson, *Svensk historia*, I (1961), and in Ingvar Andersson, *A History of Sweden* (trans. Carolyn Hannay), (London, 1956). For Finland, see Eirik Hornborg, *Finlands hävder*, II (Helsingfors, 1930); for Denmark, the standard histories are *Det danske Folks Historie*, ed. Aage Friis, Axel Linvald, M. Mackeprang, IV (Copenhagen, 1928); and Erik Arup, *Danmarks Historie*, II (Copenhagen, 1932). Foreign policy is covered in two volumes of the excellent new series *Den svenska utrikespolitikens historia*: vol. I: i, *Tiden före 1560* (1956), by Nils Ahnlund, is a brilliant introductory sketch, but vol. I: ii, *1560–1648*, by Wilhelm Tham, is a full but compact survey. The struggle for the Baltic, from mediaeval to modern times, is treated in Eirik Hornborg, *Kampen om Östersjön* (1945), and the particular question of the mastery of the Sound in Otto Lybeck, *Öresund i nordens historia* (Malmö, 1943). Charles E. Hill, *The Danish Sound Dues and the Command of the Baltic* (Durham, N.C., 1926), is mainly concerned with their effects on international relations. C. Sprinchorn, 'Om Sveriges politiska förbindelser med Frankrike före Gustav II Adolfs tid' (*Historiskt bibliotek*, VII (1880)), is a sketch of early Franco-Swedish relations: a similar sketch is the same author's 'Om Sveriges förbindelser med Nederländerna från äldsta tider till år 1614' (*HT*, 1885). Arnold Munthe, *Sjömaktens inflytande på Sveriges historia*, I (1921), discusses the influence of sea-power on Swedish history. For the Swedish Navy: A. Zettersten, *Svenska flottans historia*, I (1890) is now superseded by *Svenska flottans historia*, ed. Otto Lybeck, I (Malmö, 1942), and by Generalstaben, *Sveriges krig 1611–1632*, Bilagsband I (1938). The development of the Swedish Army in the sixteenth century is discussed in *ibid.* I (1936), and, more fully, in Bertil C:sson Barkman, *Kungl. Svea Livgardes historia*, I–II (1937, 1939), which also gives the best account of campaigns during the period; though Gustaf Petri, *Kungl. första Livgrenadiärregementets historia*, I (1926) is also valuable. For the military service of the nobility, see P. Sörensson, 'Adelns rusttjänst och adelsfanans organisation' (*HT*, 1922).

Swedish historiography is curiously poor in constitutional histories. The fullest, and still the best, is Emil Hildebrand, *Svenska statsförfattningens historiska utveckling* (1896), though inevitably now superseded in some respects. A concise and meaty textbook is Nils Herlitz, *Grunddragen av det svenska statsskickets historia* (1928). Frederik Lagerroth's *Frihetstidens författ-*

ning (1915) has much to say on this period, and is essential reading, though not all his views would command general assent. Important examinations of contemporary constitutional ideas are Karl Nordlund, *Den svenska reformationstidens allmänna statsrättsliga ideer* (1900), and Erland Hjärne, *Från Vasatiden till Frihetstiden* (Uppsala, 1929), though this last is concerned mainly with the seventeenth century: both these represent different viewpoints from that of Lagerroth. The development of the *riksdag* in this period is covered by two volumes in the collective work *Sveriges riksdag*: Tor Berg's *Riksdagens utveckling under den äldre Vasatiden 1521–1592* (1935), and Nils Ahnlund's *Ståndsriksdagens utdaning 1592–1672* (1933). A short but good history is Nils Edén, *Den svenska riksdagen under femhundra år* (1935). An important investigation into the role of the market as an alternative to the *riksdag* is Nils Staf, *Marknad och möte* (1935). The development of the central government has been analysed by an indispensable work of Nils Edén, *Om centralregeringens organisation under den äldre Vasatiden (1523–94)*, continued to 1611 by the same author's 'Den svenska riksstyrelsens organisation 1594–1602' (*HT*, 1901), and his *Den svenska centralregeringens utveckling till kollegial organisation i början af sjuttonde århundradet (1602–1634)* (Uppsala, 1902). A broader but slighter survey is A. B. Carlsson, *Den svenska centralförvaltningen 1521–1809* (1913). Special studies of the history of the chancery and the exchequer respectively are O. Wieselgren [etc.], *Kungl. Maj:ts Kanslis Historia*, I (1935), and Nils Edén [etc.], *Kammarkollegiets historia* (1941), though neither really adds to Edén's own books. Three studies deal with the judiciary: Nils Edling, 'Den högsta rättsskipningen under 1500-talet' (*HT*, 1938); R. Kjellén, *Riksrättsinstitutets utbildning i Sveriges historia* (Uppsala, 1895); Hjalmar Haralds, 'Konungsdom och konungsnämnd' (*HT*, 1927). The structure of local government is dissected in minute but illuminating detail in J. A. Almquist, *Den civila lokalförvaltningen i Sverige 1523–1630*, I–III (1917–22). The introductory chapter in Olof Sörndal, *Den svenska länsstyrelsen. Uppkomst, organisation och allmänna maktställning* (Lund, 1937), is too brief to be of much assistance. A very useful article on the administration of the towns is Folke Lindberg, 'Fogde, råd och menighet. Några drag i den svenska stadsförfattningens utveckling under medeltiden och 1500-talet' (*HT*, 1941). On taxation, see P. E. Bergfalk, *Om utomordentliga penningehjälpen till kronan under sekstonde århundradet och början af det sjuttonde* (Uppsala, 1893), and the opening of A. Thomson, *Grundskatterna i den politiska diskussionen 1809–1866* (1923): the beginning of Fredrik Lagerroth, *Statsreglering och finansförvaltning i Sverige till och med Frihetstidens ingång* (Malmö, 1928), which surveys the administration of the finances until the eighteenth century, deals with this period. A broad survey of a long-lived theme in Swedish constitutional history is M. Roberts, 'On Aristocratic Constitutionalism in Swedish History 1520–1720', in *Essays in Swedish History* (1967). Two suggestive short studies are Fredrik Lagerroth, 'Revolution eller rättskontinuitet?' (*Scandia*, 1936), and Nils Herlitz, 'Ett och annat om självstyrelsens betydelse i svensk förvaltningshistoria' (*Statsvetenskaplig tidskrift*, 1921). A survey of the development of Swedish law is presented in K. G. Westman, 'Från landskapslagar och folkting till rikslag och ämbetsmannamässig rättstillämpning', in *Minneskrift ägnad 1734 års lag* (1934), and in two books by Henrik Munktell, *Det svenska rättsarvet* (1944), and *Brott och straff i svensk rättsutveckling* (1943). Finally, the basic constitutional document, Magnus Eriksson's *landslag*, is conveniently accessible in Emil Olsson, *Utdrag ur Magnus Erikssons landslag* (Uppsala, 1929), which prints all the portions of real interest to the non-lawyer.

For ecclesiastical history, the volumes by L. A. Anjou, *Svenska kyrko-reformationens historia*, I–II (1850–1), and *Svenska kyrkans historia ifrån Upsala möte år 1593 till slutet af sjuttonde århundradet* (1866), are old-fashioned standard works which can still be read with profit, though their place has really been taken by Hjalmar Holmquist's *Reformationstidevarvet 1521–1611*, I–II (Uppsala, 1933), which forms vol. III of the series *Svenska kyrkans historia*. A shorter survey by the same author is *Från Reformationen till romantiken* (1940). John Wordsworth, *The National Church of Sweden* (London, 1911), was a good synthesis of the state of the subject at that date. Otto S. Holmdahl, *Studier över prästeståndets kyrkopolitik under den tidigare frihetstiden*, I (Lund, 1912), though really concerned with the eighteenth century, has a valuable introductory section on the Reformation period. There is a short history of the church in Finland, Wolfgang Schmidt, *Finlands kyrka genom tiderna* (1940). Special aspects are dealt with in Robert Murray, *Stockholms kyrkostyrelse intill 1630-talets mitt* (1949); Ragnar Askmark, *Svensk prästutbildning fram till år 1700* (1943); Hjalmar Holmquist, 'Tillsättningar av gäll i Sverige under reformationsårhundradet' (*HT*, 1933), which deals with presentation to livings. The opening of Hans Cnattingius, *Den centrala kyrkostyrelsen i Sverige 1611–1636* (1939) deals with the central government of the church in this century, and the first chapter of Ragnar Gullstrand, *Bidrag till den svenska sockensjälvstyrelsens historia under 1600-talet* (1923) does the same for parochial self-government. Hilding Pleijel, *Katekesen som svensk folkbok. En historisk översikt* (Lund, 1942) is a short introduction to a subject of some importance. Herman Lundström, *Skisser och kritiker* (1903), is a collection of essays, mainly on this period; other collections of a similar character are two volumes by Hilding Pleijel, *Vår kyrkas bekännelse, Studier i symbolik* (Lund, 1941), and *Svensk Lutherdom. Studier i luthersk fromhet och svensk folkkultur* (1944).

Economic history is still dominated by the great pioneering work of Eli F. Heckscher, though his conclusions are now beginning to be modified in a number of respects. The fullest survey of the period is in his *Sveriges ekonomiska historia från Gustav Vasa*, I: i (1935–6): the author revised some of his conclusions in his shorter work *Svenskt arbete och liv* (1941). Reference should also be made to his collections of essays *Ekonomi och historia* (1922), *Historie-uppfattning, materialistisk och annan* (1944), *Ekonomisk-historiska studier* (1936); to his 'Det äldre Vasakonungadömets ekonomiska politik och ideer', in *Studier tillägnade Ludvig Stavenow* (1924); and to his 'Natural and Money Economy as illustrated from Swedish History in the Sixteenth Century' (*Journal of Economic and Business History*, 1931). For agriculture, see H. Forssell, *Anteckningar om Sveriges jordbruksnäring i sextonde seklet* (1884); and for the forests, the classic studies of Bertil Boëthius, *Skogen och bygden* (1939), and *Ur de stora skogarnas historia* (new edn., 1955). Wool-production and -manufacture are exhaustively dealt with in Sven T. Kjellberg, *Ull och ylle. Bidrag till den svenska yllemanufakturens historia* (Lund, 1943). Mining and its associated industries have naturally attracted much attention from Swedish economic historians, though copper has been more fortunate than iron, which still lacks a good modern study of developments in this century. For copper, the principal works are Tom Söderberg, *Stora Kopparberget under Medeltiden och Gustav Vasa* (1932); K.-E. Forsslund, *Falu gruva och Stora Kopparbergs bergslag* (1936); K.-G. Hildebrand, *Falu stads historia till år 1687*, I (Falun, 1946); Sten Lindroth, *Gruvbrytning och kopparhantering vid Stora Kopparberget intill 1800-talets början*, I (Uppsala, 1955). See too Bertil Boëthius, *Dalarnas bränsleskatter och Stora Kopparbergs bergfrälse under äldre Vasatid* (1957). For iron, see Jalmar Furuskog, *Det svenska järnet genom tiderna* (1939); id., *De värmländska järnbruken* (Filipstad, 1924); M. B. Swederus, *Bidrag till kännedomen om Sveriges bergshantering under Karl IX:s tid*, I–II (1905); Märta Eriksson, *Järnräntor under 1500-talet* (1940). A first-rate study of workers in the mines and forges is Bertil Boëthius, *Gruvornas, hyttornas och hamrarnas folk* (1951), which extends to the later eighteenth century. For the development of the brass industry, see K. Malmsten, 'Den svenska mässingsindustriens uppkomst' (*Med hammare och fackla*, 1939), and S. Erixon, *Skultuna bruks historia*, I (1921); for the armaments industry, Å. Meyersson, *Vapenindustrierna i Arboga under äldre Vasatid* (1939). Folke Lindberg, *Hantverkarna. Medeltid och äldre Vasatid* (1947) is a valuable study of craftsmen. Important aspects of the regulation of trade and commerce are the subject of O. Fyhrvall, 'Om det bottniska handelstvånget' (*HT*, 1882); Richard Matz, 'Hur bestraffades landsköpet på 1500-talet?' (*HT*, 1952); C. Danielsson, '1500- och 1600-talens svenska tullpolitik' (*Statsvetenskaplig tidskrift*, 1924). For the small effect of the price revolution in Sweden, see Ingrid Hammarström, 'The "Price Revolution" of the Sixteenth Century: Some Swedish Evidence' (*Scandinavian Economic History Review*, 1957); for the importance of two key-commodities, K.-G. Hildebrand, 'Salt and Cloth in Swedish Economic History' (*ibid.* 1954). The foreign trade of Finland during the latter part of the century is examined in T. S. Dillner, *Studier rörande Finlands handel under tidsrymden 1570–1622*, I (Helsingfors, 1897). Sweden is fortunate in possessing numerous town-histories of high quality: of towns which were important in the sixteenth century only Stockholm, by an odd accident, lacks one, for Nils Ahnlund's *Stockholms historia före Gustav Vasa* (1952) stops short at the threshold of the period: it would take too much space, however, to list them here. For suggestive remarks upon relations between the crown and the towns, see Lars-Arne Norborg, 'Krona och stad i Sverige under äldre Vasatid. Några synpunkter' (*HT*, 1963); see also C. T. Odhner, *Bidrag till svenska städernas och borgareståndets historia före 1633* (Uppsala, 1860).

Turning now to social history, a modern, lavishly illustrated, and authoritative collaborative series is *Svenska folket genom tiderna*, ed. E. Wrangel (Malmö, 1938), of which vol. III covers the sixteenth century. For the nobility, their privileges, aspirations and obligations, two studies by Sven A. Nilsson are of special value: *Krona och frälse i Sverige 1523–1594. Rusttjänst, länsväsendet, godspolitik* (Lund, 1947), and *Kampen om de adliga privilegierna 1526–1594*

(Lund, 1952); to which may be added Stig Jägerskiöld, 'Förvärv och förlust av frälse' (*Statsvetenskaplig tidskrift*, 1945), and Idem, 'Adelsprivilegier i Sverige och Danmark' (*HT*, 1934). Bertil Broomé, *Ätten Posse. Studier och undersökningar*, II (1960), sheds light on the fortunes of a leading noble family. A splendid guide to the ideals and standards of value of the aristocracy is Per Brahe the elder's *Oeconomia, eller Huuszholdsbook för ungt adels folck* (Visingsborg, 1677). In the absence of any full study of Stockholm in the later sixteenth century, Ahnlund's book, cited above, is indispensable for life in the capital, and so is H. Schück, *Stockholm vid fjortonhundratalets slut* (new edn., ed. T. O. Nordborg, 1951); though for the third quarter of the century there is now a valuable study by Birgitta Lager, *Stockholms befolkning på Johan III:s tid* (1962): for German influences in Stockholm see the short study by Nils Ahnlund, 'Svenskt och tyskt i Stockholms äldre historia', in his *Från Medeltid och Vasatid* (Uppsala, 1933). The slowly-emergent middle-class is the subject of an interesting but all-too concentrated study by Tom Söderberg, *Den namnlösa medelklassen. Socialgrupp två i det gamla svenska samhället* (1956), and the career of one of them is examined by Birgitta Lager in 'Lille Jöns Andersson, en storköpman i 1500-talets Stockholm' (*Personhistorisk tidskrift*, 1964). On a slighter and more popular scale is Sven Ulric Palme, *Stånd och klasser i forna dagars Sverige* (1947). As to the peasantry, E. Ingers, *Bonden i svensk historia*, I (1943) is rather thin on this period. A good insight into the living standards and diet of the people is afforded by Nils Keyland, *Svensk allmogeskost*, I–II (1918–19). Three studies by Lars Levander, *Fattigt folk och tiggare* (1934), *Landsväg, krog och marknad* (1935), and *Brottsling och bödel* (1936), though drawing their illustrations mainly from a later period, are sufficiently applicable to the sixteenth century to be recommended reading. The best guide to poor-law administration is G. Lindstedt, *Översikten af den svenska fattigvårdens historia* (1915). In regard to education, G. Brandell, *Svenska undervisningsväsendets och uppfostrans historia*, I (Lund, 1931) is a standard work; and so, on a rather different level, is Claes Annerstedt's majestic *Uppsala Universitets Historia*, I (Uppsala, 1877). For Swedish literature the sixteenth century was a lean period. What can be said of it is said in *Svenska litteraturens historia*, ed. F. Böök [etc.], I (1929), or in the brilliant survey by E. N. Tigerstedt, *Svensk litteraturhistoria* (1948). For a sidelight on the history of the stage, see Erik Wikland, *Elizabethan Players in Sweden 1591–92. Facts and Problems* (1962). For art and architecture, see Henrik Cornell, *Den svenska konstens historia från hedenhös till omkring 1800* (1944), or Andreas Lindblom, *Sveriges konsthistoria från förtid till nutid*, II (1944). Of studies particularly directed to the sixteenth century may be mentioned A. Hahr, *Studier i Vasatidens konst, och andra nordiska Renässansstudier* (1920), and Idem, *Vasatidens borgar* (1917), which discusses the castle-building of the period; while Martin Olsson, *Kalmar slotts historia*, II A *Tiden från 1300-talets mitt till 1611* (1961) is a magnificent and sumptuous investigation of the building-history of a single castle. Painting is dealt with in K. E. Steneberg, *Den äldsta traditionen inom svenskt porträttmåleri* (1948). The only general history of music appears to be Tobias Norlind, *Svensk musikhistoria* (1918), but the same author has a valuable special study for this period: *Från tyska kyrkans glansdagar. Bilder ur svenska musikens historia från Vasaregenterna till Karolinska tidens slut*, I (1944). On the history of ideas, Henrik Sandblad, *De eskatologiska föreställningarna i Sverige under Reformationen och Motreformationen* (Uppsala, 1942), is important; and so, for the origins of 'Gothicism', is Johannes Nordström, *De yverbornes ö* (1949). See also S. Lindroth, *Paracelsismen i Sverige intill 1600-talets mitt* (Uppsala, 1943).

III. INTRODUCTION: THE END OF THE UNION OF KALMAR

While there can be no question of attempting a full bibliography for the later fifteenth century, it may be appropriate to indicate some of the more prominent of recent secondary works. The volume in the series *Sveriges historia till våra dagar* which deals with the period is Salomon Kraft, *Senare medeltiden II: tidsskedet 1448–1520* (1944). The interpretation of the period of the Union has recently been the subject of lively debate, centring round the relative importance of interests and ideals: the revisionists found a leader in Erik Lönnroth, whose point of view can be collected from his *En annan uppfattning* (1949) and his article 'Är Sveriges historia oföränderlig?' (*HT*, 1950); the more conservative approach is temperately expressed in Bertil Boëthius, 'Behöver vår historievetenskap lägga om sin kurs?' (*HT*, 1950). Among recent contributions to political history may be mentioned Gottfrid Carlsson, *Kalmar Recess 1483* (1955); Sven Ulric Palme, *Sten Sture den Äldre* (1950), a briskly iconoclastic biography; Gunnar Olsson, 'Sverige och Danmark, 1501–1508' (*Scandia*, 1950); Gottfrid Carlsson, 'Sten Sture den yngre' (*Scandia*, 1929); Greta Wieselgren, *Sten Sture d.y. och Gustav Trolle* (Lund, 1949); Gunnar T. Westin, *Riksföreståndaren och makten. Politiska utvecklingslinjer i Sverige, 1512–1517* (Lund, 1957); Gottfrid Carlsson, *Hemming Gadh, 'electus' i Linköping* (Linköping, 1945); Lauritz Weibull, 'Hemming Gadhs "avfall"' (*Scandia*, 1951–2); Rudolf Bergström, 'Sturetidens historia i ny belysning' (*HT*, 1937); besides Ahnlund's history of Stockholm, listed above. For the evolution of the *riksdag*, see Sven Tunberg, *Riksdagens uppkomst* (1931), being vol. I of the series *Sveriges riksdag*; Nils Ahnlund, 'Till diskussionen om 1400-talets svenska riksmöten' (*HT*, 1944); and Kjell Kumlien, 'Problemet om den svenska riksdagens uppkomst' (*HT*, 1947).

The final crisis, from 1520 to 1523, has produced a controversial literature of its own. Two excellent general surveys are Rudolf Bergström, *Studier till den stora krisen i nordens historia, 1517–1523* (Uppsala, 1943), and Lars Sjödin, *Kalmarunionens slutskede. Gustav Vasas befrielsekrig*, I–II (Uppsala, 1943, 1947). The baffling and fascinating personality of Kristian II has been analysed by a professional psychologist in Paul J. Reiter's *Kristian Tyrann. Personlighet, själsliv och livsdrama* (Swedish translation, 1943), a good example of its kind; and by Erik Arup, 'Kong Christiern 2. Et Portraet' (*Scandia*, 1947): for a historiographical essay, see Nils Ahnlund, 'Kristian II i svensk och dansk historieskrivning', in his *Från Medeltid och Vasatid* (1933). The obscurities involving Gustav Vasa's early career are partly cleared up by Lars Sjödin, 'Gustav Vasas barndoms- och ungdomstid', in *Historiska studier tillägnade Sven Tunberg* (1942): see too Nils Ahnlund, 'Vasaäventyren', in his *Svensk sägen och hävd. Kulturbilder* (1938). In his article 'Uppsalafördraget 1520' (*HT*, 1944), Sven Ulric Palme provides a fresh interpretation of the treaty between Kristian II and the Swedish magnates. On the great controversy about the Bloodbath of Stockholm it may perhaps be sufficient to list the more recent contributions. The following selection is representative of most of the tenable points of view: Gottfrid Carlsson, 'Stockholms blodbad. Några synpunkter och reflexioner' (*HT*, 1920); Lauritz Weibull, 'Stockholms blodbad' (*Scandia*, 1928); Josef Sandström, 'Några bidrag till Stockholms blodbads historia' (*HT*, 1929); Rudolf Bergström, 'Stockholms blodbad och det svenska unionspartiet' (*Svensk tidskrift*, 1939); Lars Sjödin, *Kalmarunionens slutskede*, I (Uppsala, 1943); Kauko Pirinen, 'Källorna till Stockholms blodbad i kanonistisk belysning' (*HT*, 1955); Sven Svensson, *Stockholms blodbad i ekonomisk och handelspolitisk belysning* (Lund, 1964); Niels Skyum-Nielsen, *Blodbadet i Stockholm og dets juridiska Maskering* (Copenhagen, 1964); Curt Weibull, 'Gustaf Trolle, Christian II och Stockholms blodbad' (*Scandia*, 1966); to which may be added Nils Ahnlund, 'Brasklappen', in *Från Medeltid och Vasatid*. As is apparent from the text, I have found Pirinen's thesis the most persuasive. The much-debated *Relation of the Canons* is printed in *Handlingar rörande Skandinaviens historia*, II (1816). For Gustav Vasa's election as king the main source is 'Berättelse om den Lybeckska beskickningen i Sverige sommaren 1523', which has been edited by Sven Tunberg in *H*[*istoriska*] *H*[*andlingar*] 26: 2, (1923); the background to the election is discussed in Hugo Yrwing, 'Lybeck, de nordiska rikena och konungavalet i Strängnäs 1523' (*Scandia*, 1958); and Kjell Kumlien, 'Gustav Vasa och kungavalet i Strängnäs 1523' (*HT*, 1960): see also Allan Etzler, 'Gustav Vasa och Sturehuset' (*HT*, 1935); Folke Lindberg, 'Varför misslyckades det svensk-lybeckska krigsföretåget mot Skåne 1523?' (*HT*, 1933); and R. Bergström, 'Stilleståndsavtalet mellan Berend von Mehlen och det skånska ridderskapet våren 1523' (*HT*, 1942).

IV. GUSTAV VASA

The principal source for the reign is the magnificent series *Konung Gustaf den Förstes Registratur*, I–XXIX (1861–1916), an almost inexhaustible mine of information on every aspect of policy and society, as well as a vivid reflexion of the king's personality: a collection of the better-known letters has been edited by Nils Edén, as *Brev av Gustav Vasa. Ett urval* (1917). Equally representative of the king, though in a different way, is Peder Swart, *Konung Gustaf I:s krönika*, ed. Nils Edén (1912), for this is an official history—the reign as Gustav Vasa wished it to be seen. It ends, however, at 1534: for a critical study, see Karl-Erik Wikholm, *Källkritiska studier till Gustav Vasatidens historia* (Uppsala, 1942). Its continuation, by Per Brahe (who was the king's nephew), is published as *Per Brahe den äldres fortsättning af Peder Swarts krönika* (Lund, 1897): though written by an admirer, it is much less tendentious and more personal, and is a valuable eyewitness account by a sympathetic observer: Rasmus Ludvigsson's Chronicle, printed in *HH* 20: 1, (1904) is pale and annalistic by comparison. The same vol. of *HH* has anonymous narratives of the king's last illness and death. An important source, which sheds much light upon the working of the finances in the latter part of the reign, is *Kammarrådet Nils Pedersson Bielkes konceptböcker 1546–1550*, ed. Lars Sjödin, which is printed in *HH* 33: 2 (1951); while *HH* 11: 1 (1880) gives itemized lists of revenues in 1530–3. In *Handlingar rörande Skandinaviens historia*, I (1816) is Olaus Magnus's account of his mission to the Netherlands; in *ibid*, IV (1817) some letters to the king from Luther and Melanchthon. *HH* 26: 3 (1924) prints the narrative of the Lübeck envoys on their fruitless visit to Sweden in 1541. Of cardinal importance for the history of the Reformation is *Olaus Petris Samlade Skrifter*, I–IV (1917); and a useful collection of materials on the history of the church is contained in P. Thyselius, *Handlingar rörande Sveriges inre förhållanden under konung Gustaf I. Reformations- och kyrkowäsende*, I–II (1841–44). Documents concerning 'the Vadstena *fracas*', which did so much to alienate the king from Prince Erik at the close of the reign, are printed in Carl Adlersparre, *Historiska Samlingar*, III (1797).

The best guide to Gustav Vasa's personality is his letters; but there is an excellent modern biography by Ivan Svalenius, *Gustav Vasa* (1950), and an agreeable popular alternative in Sven Wikberg, *Gustav Vasa*, I–II (1944–5). For an attempt to relate the king's public image to art-history, see Sven Alfons, *Gustav Vasa och Virginius* (1962).

In regard to the Reformation, the best general account is Holmquist's volume in *Svenska kyrkans historia* (see above). For the Swedish church on the eve of the Reformation, see the preceding volume in the same series, Yngve Brilioth's *Medeltidens kyrka 1274–1522* (1941); G. Kellerman, *Jakob Ulvsson och den svenska kyrkan*, I (1935); and Gunnar Olsson, *Stat och kyrka i Sverige vid medeltidens slut* (1947). The onset of the Reformation is discussed in detail in two important studies: Knut B. Westman, *Reformationens genombrott i Sverige* (Uppsala, 1912), and in the final section of Herman Schück, *Ecclesia Lincopensis. Studier om Linköpingskyrkan under Medeltiden och Gustav Vasa* (1959). See also the essays in Sixten Belfrage, *Studier i svensk reformationslitteratur*, I–V (Lund, 1931–2). The crucial meeting at Västerås is still a controversial topic. Among recent studies of it are Lars Sjödin, 'Västerås möte 1527. Ett fyrahundraårsminne' (*HT*, 1927–8); Lauritz Weibull, 'Västerås riksdag 1527' (*Scandia*, 1937); Hugo Yrwing, *Gustav Vasa, kröningsfrågan och Västerås riksdag 1527* (Lund, 1956); Sven Kjöllerström, 'Västerås Ordinantia' (*Scandia*, 1960): an older essay, now outmoded, is Harald Hjärne, 'Reformationsriksdagen i Västerås', printed in his *Ur det förgångna* (1912). The progress of the Reformation in Stockholm can be followed in Robert Murray, *Stockholms kyrkostyrelse intill 1630-talets mitt* (Lund, 1949); and see also Herman Lundström, 'Om det s.k. vederdöpareofoget i Stockholm under Gustaf I:s regering', in *Skisser och kritiker* (1903), and Knut B. Westman, 'Kultreformproblemet i den svenska reformationen' (*HT*, 1917). Sven Kjöllerström, *Missa Lincopensis. En liturgisk-historisk studie* (1941) describes an interesting attempt in the diocese of Linköping after 1536 to provide a Latin Mass which should make sufficient (but no more than sufficient) concessions to the new spirit. There are two good books on Olaus Petri: Robert Murray, *Olavus Petri* (1952), and Knut B. Westman, *Reformation och Revolution: en Olavus-Petristudie* (Uppsala, 1941). Sven Ingebrand, *Olavus Petris reformatoriska åskådning* (Lund, 1964), is designed for theologians only. Of other studies around Olaus Petri mention may be made of the following: Henrik Sandblad, 'Gustav Vasa, Ahitofel och Sankt Påvel' (*Lychnos*, 1960–1); Jan Eric Almquist, 'Dödsdömen över Olavus Petri den 2 januari 1540', in *Festskrift tillägnade Nils Stjernberg* (1940); Nils Ahnlund, 'Olavus Petri och Stockholm', in his *Tradition och historia* (1956); Lars Sjödin, 'Tillkomsten av Olaus Petris krönika' (*HT*, 1921); Gottfrid Carlsson, 'En historisk uppsats av Olavus Petri från 1530-talets början' (*HT*, 1925); Herman Lundström, 'Handlingar från rättegången med Olaus Petri och Laurentius Andreae i Örebro, 1539–40' (*Kyrkohistorisk Årsskrift*, 1909). The religious history of the period after 1540 has attracted, understandably, less attention than that which preceded it. The best guide is Ivan Svalenius, *Georg Norman. En biografisk studie* (Lund, 1937): see also Ingvar Andersson, 'Georg Norman, Laurentius Raimundus och *Visitatio Gustaviana*', in his *Svenskt och europeiskt femtonhundratal. Fynd, forskningar och essäer* (Lund, 1943). For the coming of Calvinism at the end of the reign, see Herman Lundström, 'Om Kalvins förhållande till Gustaf I', in his *Skisser och kritiker*: the same volume also contains a terse article disposing of the question of the Apostolic Succession. There is also a study of Gustav Vasa and the Reformation, from a Roman Catholic point of view: Jules Martin, *Gustave Vasa et la Réforme en Suède. Essai historique* (Paris, 1906). For the Reformation in Denmark, there is available in English E. H. Dunkley, *The Reformation in Denmark* (London, 1948). The critical period 1533–6 is dealt with in Hjalmar Heden, *Studier till Danmarks Reformationshistoria från Fredrik I:s död till slutet af Grefvefejden* (Göteborg, 1903).

The internal political repercussions of the Reformation, and other popular revolts, have been the subject of a number of studies. The career of Sten Sture's chancellor, and his final fall, are dealt with in R. Stensson's biography, *Peder Jakobsson Sunnanväder och maktkampen i Sverige 1504–1527* (Uppsala, 1947), and in the shorter study of Gottfrid Carlsson, *Peder Jakobsson Sunnanväder* (Lund, 1949). Folke Lindberg's 'Daljunkern', in *Studier tillägnade Sven Tunberg* (1942) argues that the evidence against the Daljunker's being Nils Sture is less decisive than has been thought: but see also Sixten Samuelsson, 'Till diskussionen om Daljunkern' (*HT*, 1948). Conflicting interpretations of the Västergötland rising are offered in Lars-Arne Norborg, 'Västgötaherrarnes uppror' (*Scandia*, 1961), and Sven Kjöllerström, 'Västgötaherrarnas uppror' (*ibid.* 1963), of which the latter, reaffirming the traditional view, seems the more persuasive: see also Jan Liedgren, 'Västgötaherrarnes uppror och den evangeliska läran' (*Kyrkohistorisk Årsskrift*, 1959). The 'church-bell rebellion' is the subject of Karl Hildeman's useful 'Klockupproret' (*HT*, 1946). The best estimate of the still somewhat obscure conspiracy in Stockholm in 1536 is Nils Ahnlund, 'Sammansvärjningen i Stockholm år 1536' (*S:t Eriks årsbok*, 1951): Kjell Boström discusses the painter of the picture of the *parhelion* which hangs in the Great Church, in *Jacob Matham och vädersolarna över Stockholm* (1958). The most modern and convenient book on the Dacke rebellion is Alf Åberg, *Nils Dacke och Landsfadern* (1960): related studies are Folke Lindberg, 'Upprorsledaren Jon Anderssons öde efter Dackefejden' (*HT*, 1934), and Gottfrid Carlsson, 'Nils Dackes första framträdande som upprorsman', in his *Från Erik Segersäll till Gustav Vasa* (1961). Dacke's connexions with the Habsburgs and other foreign powers are examined in Idem, 'Nils Dacke och Europa', in his *Engelbrekt, Sturarne, Gustav Vasa* (Lund, 1962). It was Gottfrid Carlsson also who first furnished a critical and balanced account of the career of the unfortunate Wulf Gyler, in his two long and fascinating articles 'Wulf Gyler i svensk tjänst' (*HT*, 1922, 1924); to which he later added a study of Gyler's propaganda-campaign against Gustav Vasa, 'Wulf Gylers polemiska författarskap', in his *Från Erik Segersäll till Gustav Vasa*. The intrigues of the other exiles are surveyed in another article by the same author, 'Flyktingars öden och "praktiker"', in *ibid.* His conclusions about Gyler were reinforced by Rudolf Bergström, 'Wulf Gylers framtidsplaner efter flykten från Sverige. Ett bidrag till frågan om hans "förräderi"' (*HT*, 1945).

At this point domestic disturbances shade into foreign policy. Sweden's relations with Lübeck during the whole of the sixteenth century are conveniently surveyed in Johannes Paul, *Lübeck und die Wasa im 16. Jahrhundert* (Lübeck, 1920). A more detailed examination, beginning in the fifteenth century and extending to the 1560s, is Kjell Kumlien's indispensable *Sverige och Hanseaterna. Studier i svensk politik och utrikeshandel* (1953). An older work which treats foreign policy in relation to foreign trade is Albert Falk, *Gustaf Vasas utrikespolitik med afseende på handeln* (1907); but this is now mostly supplanted by Sven Lundkvist's masterly dissertation *Gustav Vasa och Europa: svensk handels- och utrikespolitik 1537–1557* (Uppsala, 1960), which is essential reading. Two important articles are Sven Lundkvist's 'Sverige och Nederländerna, 1524–1534' (*Scandia*, 1961), and Hugo Yrwing, 'Lybeck och den nordiska förbundstanken efter unionsupplösningen', in *Gottfrid Carlsson 18.xii.1952* (Lund, 1952). Gottfrid Carlsson's 'Johannes Magnus och Gustav Vasas polska frieri' (*Kyrkohistorisk Årsskrift*, 1922), discusses relations with Poland, Gustav Vasa's overture for a Polish marriage, and the circumstances of Johannes Magnus's final withdrawal from Sweden. The same author's 'Gustav Vasa och den evangeliska Tyskland', in his *Engelbrekt, Sturarna, Gustav Vasa*, examines Sweden's relations with the German Protestant princes; and his 'En påstått kungsmord under Grevefejden', in *Från Erik Segersäll till Gustav Vasa*, explains the diplomatic consequences of rumours of Gustav Vasa's death. For the 1540s and 1550s there are two major works: Georg Landberg, *De nordiska rikena under Brömsebroförbundet* (Uppsala, 1925), and Poul Colding, *Studier i Danmarks politiske Historie i Slutningen af Christian III:s og Begyndelsen af Fredrik II:s Tid* (Copenhagen, 1939), to which may be added Paul-Erik Hansen, *Kejsar Karl V og det skandinaviske Norden 1523–1544* (Copenhagen, 1943). See also Ingvar Andersson, 'Tyska anfallsplaner mot Sverige 1555–7', in his *Svenskt och europeiskt femtonhundratal. Fynd, forskningar och essäer* (Lund, 1943). The only biography of Christina of Lorraine is Julia Cartwright's rather trivial *Christina of Denmark* (London, 1918). The origins and progress of Gustav Vasa's Russian war are all-too-exhaustively dealt with in Arvo Viljanti, *Gustav Vasas ryska krig, 1554–1557*, I–II (1957).

As to the economic and administrative history of the reign, one famous book which deals with both aspects—Hans Forssell's *Sveriges inre historia från Gustaf den förste med särskilt afseende på förvaltning och ekonomi*, I–II (1869, 1875)—is really no more than an heroic torso, for the author was compelled to leave his original scheme unrealized. It has chapters devoted to the royal administration and *förläningar*; to the aristocracy; and to the state's gains from the Reformation: they are followed by massive, pioneering statistics, especially of Sweden's foreign trade, which were to have been the basis for later chapters; and finally by notes on currency, weights and measures, and on commodity prices. The completed chapters can still be read with great profit; and the statistics remained unrivalled until the collective enterprise sponsored by Eli Heckscher. Of more modern studies two may be particularly recommended: Ingvar Peterzén, *Studier rörande Stockholms historia under Gustav Vasa* (1945); and Ingrid Hammarström, *Finansförvaltning och varuhandel 1504–1540* (Uppsala, 1956), which has altered our views of this period in many important respects. Shorter studies worth attention are Erik Lönnroth, 'Gustav Vasas finanspolitik 1538–1542', in his *Från svensk medeltid* (1959); Ingvar Andersson, 'Gustav Vasa och den ekonomiska politiken. En biografisk studie', in his *Svenskt och europeiskt femtonhundratal* (Lund, 1953); Alf Johansson, 'Penningeväsendet under Gustav Vasas regering' (*HT*, 1926); Per Nyström, 'Avelgårdsprojektet. Några anteckningar' (*Scandia*, 1936); Ingvar Peterzén, 'Gustav Vasas äldsta tulljournal' (*HT*, 1933). On the constitutional side, Gottfrid Carlsson discusses Gustav Vasa's coronation oath in 'Gustav Vasas kröningsed' (*HT*, 1946); possible models for the *arvförening* are examined in Ingvar Andersson, 'Förebilder för Gustav Vasas arvförening' (*Scandia*, 1931), and in Karl-Gustaf Hildebrand, 'Gustav Vasas arvförening. Dess medeltida bakgrund och förutsättningar' (*HT*, 1934); and the background to the king's Testament is discussed in Birgitta Odén, 'Gustav Vasa och testamentets tillkomst' (*Scandia*, 1963). Some footnotes to the administrative history of the reign are offered in Gottfrid Carlsson, 'Doktor Johan Rheyneck, Gustav Vasas första tyska kansler'; in 'Gustav Vasas kanslivanor' (both printed in his *Från Erik Segersäll till Gustav Vasa*, 1961); and in his 'Konrad von Pyhys föregåenden' (*Personhistorisk tidskrift*, 1961). Finally, the standard of civility attained at Gustav Vasa's court may be collected from a good short study by Gustaf Upmark, *Om Gustaf Vasas hof* (1912).

V. ERIK XIV

Though there is henceforward nothing to compare with Gustav Vasa's *Register*, a good deal of primary material bearing on the reign is in print. Sweden's relations with England, Poland and Lorraine provide the material for 'Handlingar rörande Sveriges utrikespolitik 1561–1566', ed. Ingvar Andersson and Sture Arnell, in *HH* 33: 1 (1946). In *De la Gardieska Archivet*, ed. P. Wieselgren, I (1831) is a collection of letters and instructions from the king, mainly on foreign policy (pp. 129–83), and on the war (pp. 183–207);

and there is another, mainly on military matters, in Carl Adlersparre, *Historiska samlingar*, II (1795). Anders Fryxell prints documents concerning Erik's search for a wife in his *Handlingar rörande Sveriges historia ur utrikes arkiver samlade och utgifvna*, II (1836), and in *ibid.* III (1839) documents concerning Johan's Polish marriage and the resulting quarrel with Erik: there is another collection on the same topic in *Handlingar rörande Skandinaviens historia*, III (1817). In the same volume is a collection of letters of Jöran Persson. 'Anteckningar från åren 1560–81 ur Hogenskild Bjelkes samlingar och med egenhändiga rättelser af hans hand', in *HH* 20: 1 (1914), is valuable for details of naval actions, and for the events at Uppsala in 1567. Sven Elofsson's 'Paralipomena', in *Handlingar rörande Skandinaviens historia*, XII (1825), which begins in 1556 and continues to 1579, is a valuable memoir by a man who stood at the centre of affairs: he was unfortunately a prisoner in Poland from 1563 to 1567, but he has much of interest on the last year of the reign. The internal crisis is illuminated by the collection of documents bearing on the murder of the Stures, printed in *Handlingar rörande Skandinaviens historia*, IV (1817), and also incidentally by 'Kongl. Kansliets Diarium öfver ingångna skrifvelser 1566' (*HH*, 8: 2 (1879)). 'Konung Erik XIV:s nämnds dombok' (*HH*, 13: 1 (1884)) prints the judgments of his High Court.

The first life of Erik XIV was written as long ago as 1774, by Olof Celsius, and still retains some interest; but the acknowledged authority for all aspects of the reign is now Ingvar Andersson, whose *Erik XIV* (new edn., 1948) is one of the classics of Swedish historical biography: see also, for Erik's personality, two studies by the same author, 'Erik XIV och astrologien' (*Lychnos*, 1936), and 'Erik XIV och Machiavelli' (*Scandia*, 1931). A penetrating examination of the bearing of Erik's ideas upon his political behaviour, which challenges Andersson's conclusions on some points (e.g. on Erik and Machiavelli), is Gunnar Annell, *Erik XIV:s etiska föreställningar och deras inflytande på hans politik* (Uppsala, 1945). Viktor Wigert, *Erik XIV. Historisk-psykologisk studie* (1920), is the work of a professional psychologist, whose views as to the nature of Erik's illness must be accepted, though historians have reservations about some of his other conclusions. Wigert's opinion that there was hereditary insanity in the Vasa line is corroborated by Hans Gillingstam's 'Nils Grip. Till belysning av Vasa-ättens sinnessjukdom' (*Personhistorisk tidskrift*, 1961). Information about another eccentric member of the family is collected in F. Ödberg, *Om prinsessan Cecilia Vasa* (1896); while Sture Arnell provides a solid but agreeable biography of Erik's queen in *Karin Månsdotter. Tolv kapitel om en drottning och hennes tid* (1951).

The opening of the Baltic question, with Erik's intervention in Reval, has been the subject of a historical debate which still continues. The economic explanation of Swedish policy was first put forward by Ingvar Andersson in *Erik XIV:s engelska underhandlingar* (Lund, 1935), which was reinforced by Artur Attman's celebrated book *Den ryska marknaden i 1500-talets baltiska politik, 1558–1595* (Lund, 1944), and by Sven Svensson's *Den merkantila bakgrunden till Rysslands anfall på den livländska ordensstaten 1558* (Lund, 1951): see also Artur Attman, 'Till det svenska östersjöväldets problematik', in

Studier tillägnade Curt Weibull (Göteborg, 1946). Reservations about the economic interpretation have been expressed in Kjell Kumlien, *Sverige och Hanseaterna* (1953), and in Gunnar Annell's book, mentioned above: they seem to me to have weight. The course of events in Estonia and Livonia is narrated in Claes Annerstedt, *Grundläggningen af svenska väldet i Livland* (Uppsala, 1868); in Sture Arnell, *Die Auflösung des livländischen Ordensstaates* (Lund, 1937), which however extends only as far as Johan's marriage in 1562; and in Walther Kirchner, *The Rise of the Baltic Question* (Newark, N.J., 1954), a valuable synthesis hampered by the repetitiveness and confusion which arise from the plan upon which it is constructed. General surveys of the Baltic question, with a strong Polish emphasis, are Adam Szelągowski, *Der Kampf um die Ostsee* (Munich, 1916), and Wacław Sobieski, *Der Kampf um die Ostsee von den ältesten Zeiten bis zur Gegenwart* (Leipzig, 1933). Władysław Konopczyński, *Dzieje polski nowożytnej*, I (Warsaw, 1936), is a standard history, useful for the period 1560–1611. See also G. Jenš, 'Rivalry between Riga and Tartu for the trade with Pskov in the XVI and XVII centuries' (*Baltic and Scandinavian Countries*, 1938). Other aspects of Erik's foreign policy are discussed in three studies by Ingvar Andersson: 'Erik XIV och Europa'; 'Erik XIV:s weimarska praktiker'; and 'Erik XIV och Island', all from his *Svenskt och europeiskt femtonhundratal* (Lund, 1943); and in his 'Erik XIV och Lothringen' (*Scandia*, 1933). F. Ödberg, 'Om den engelske köpmannen Johan Dymoch och hans förhållande till det svenska konungahuset (1560–1593)', in his *Tidsbilder ur 1500-talets svenska häfder* (1896), begins the exploration of a fascinating subject. Harald Hjärne, *Svensk-ryska förhandlingar 1564–1572. Erik XIV:s ryska förbundsplaner* (1897), deals with relations with Ivan IV. For relations with Denmark before the war, see Poul Colding's book, listed above, p. 481; for Danish diplomacy in Germany during the war, see August Fröbe, *Kurfürst August von Sachsen und sein Verhältnis zu Dänemark bis zum Frieden von Stettin 1570* (Leipzig, 1912).

For the Seven Years War of the North there is a valuable discussion of the sources (which also extends to other topics than the war) in Hasse Petrini, *Källstudier till Erik XIV:s och nordiska sjuårskrigets historia* (Lund, 1942). For Swedish strategy and tactics see respectively Artur Stille, *De ledande ideerna i krigföringen i norden 1563–1570* (Lund, 1918) and Generalstabens krigshistoriska avdelning, *Axtorna. En studie i organisation och taktik* (1926).

For the church under Erik XIV the best book is Sven Kjöllerström's *Striden kring kalvinismen i Sverige under Erik XIV* (Lund, 1935). For the constitution and methods of Erik's High Court, Jerker Rosén, *Studier kring Erik XIV:s höga nämnd* (Lund, 1955), is indispensable: see also, in this connexion, H. Munktell, 'Tortyren i svensk rättshistoria. Ett bidrag till straffprocessrättens historia' (*Lychnos*, 1939, 1940). Sture Bolin's article, 'Erik XIV och "säterifrihets uppkomst"', in *Studier tillägnade Curt Weibull* (Göteborg, 1946) deals with an important issue; but see also Sven A. Nilsson, *Kampen om de adliga privilegierna* (Lund, 1952). The constitutional position and special privileges of the counts and barons, from Erik's reign onwards, are set out in Robert Swedlund, *Grev- och friherreskapen i Sverige och Finland. Donationerna och reduktionerna före 1680* (Uppsala, 1936).

The motives behind the murder of the Stures inevitably engage the attention of all Erik's biographers, and for this reference should be made to the works of Andersson, Gunnar Annell, and Wigert, listed above; but in addition there are several special studies by Rudolf Elander, who gave much attention to the problem. They are: 'Jöran Persson och Genewitz-brevet' (*HT*, 1926); *Sturemordens gåta* (1928); 'Sturemorden. Ett försök till gåtans lösning' (*HT*, 1933); 'Myten om den ljushårige mannen i Erik XIV:s historia' (*Scandia*, 1938), and 'Nils Sture och Erik XIV:s astrologi' (*HT*, 1939). For the rising which deposed Erik, see Thure Annerstedt, *Resningen 1568* (Göteborg, 1880); A. Wattrang, 'Striden vid Hölö den 29 augusti 1568' (*HT*, 1926); Birgitta Lager, 'Johan III övertar makten i Stockholm', in *Historiska studier tillägnade Folke Lindberg* (1963), and the lengthy account, in barbarous verse, in *Konung Carl den IX:des Rim-Chrönika*, ed. B. Bergius (1759), the beginning of an extended piece of unconscious self-revelation by the future Karl IX which was to continue until 1592. For Erik's captivity and death, see A. G. Ahlqvist, *Konung Erik XIV:s sista lefnadsår* (1878); the account in Ingvar Andersson's biography; and R. Caspersson [etc.], *Erik XIV. Gravöppningen 1958 i Västerås domkyrka* (1962), a lavish and minutely-detailed account of the exhumation in all its aspects, which makes it virtually certain that he died of arsenical poisoning.

VI. JOHAN III

Printed sources for the reign, in addition to those listed under sections II and V, above, include a further instalment of the calendars of *råd*-decisions edited by E. W. Bergman: 'Register öfver rådslag i konung Johan III:s tid' (*Meddelanden från Riksarkivet*, 1881); Erik Sparre's highly important formulation of the political theory of the aristocracy, *Pro Lege, Rege, et Grege*, in *HH* 27: 1 (1924); 'Handlingar angående mötet i Reval 1589', ed. Helge Almquist, in *HH* 23: 1 (1910), with which may be linked 'Kurbrandenburgske gesandten Georg Eckhardts skrifvelse till kanslären Kristian Distelmeyer . . . angående konungamötet i Reval', *HH*, 20 (1905); 'Correspondance de Charles Dantzai, Ministre de France à la Cour de Dannemark 1575, 1580–86', in *Handlingar rörande Skandinaviens historia*, VII (1819). In the same series, vol. XV (1830) are documents concerning Horn's surrender of Ivangorod in 1590; and in *ibid.*, XXXVIII (1857), papers concerning the Russian war. Harald Hjärne printed the letters exchanged between Johan III and Ivan IV from 1568 to 1573 in *Historiskt bibliotek*, VII (1880). The Finnish historian Henri Biaudet gathered together a large collection of materials bearing on relations with Rome, of which he published summaries under the title *Le Saint-Siège et la Suède durant la seconde moitié du XVIe siècle. Notes et Documents* (Paris/Helsingfors, 1906). This was intended to be the first volume in a series designed to extend up to the outbreak of the Thirty Years War; but though one further volume appeared in 1912, the project never got past 1577. There is a small collection of letters of Pontus de la Gardie in *De la Gardieska Archivet*, IV (1833). There is a good deal of correspondence of members and former members of the *råd* concerning their relations with the king at the time of their disgrace and afterwards, in *Handlingar rörande Skandinaviens historia*, VII (1819), and in *ibid.* VIII (1820). *Carl IX:des Rim-Chrönika* continues to afford insight into the state of its author's mind: bound up with it in the same volume are 'Project till Regemente för Riksens höga Ämbeten och Hof-Staten, 1571'; Karl's characteristic letter of refusal of Johan's invitation to his second marriage; Johan's 'Hard Patent' against the clergy of the duchy, 1588; and a collection of letters from Erik Sparre to J. de Mornay.

For domestic politics we have in the first place Hans Forssell, *Sverige 1571. Försök till en administrativ-statistisk beskrifning* (1872), which is a species of statistical survey of the state of the country in that year: a reservoir of information, rather than a book. The significance of such statistics is revealed, and the state of the royal finances clearly displayed, in Birgitta Odén's *Rikets uppbörd och utgift* (Lund, 1955), which is essential reading. A companion-study by the same author, *Kronohandel och finanspolitik 1560–1595* (Lund, 1966), unfortunately appeared just too late for the writing of this book. Two other studies by Birgitta Odén are likewise of importance: *Kopparhandeln och statsmonopol* (1960), and 'Studier om myntregalet under Vasasönerna' (*HT*, 1964). Both these, and the latter particularly, shed light on the political struggles of the reign, as well as upon economic policy. The plots against Johan's rule are examined in F. Ödberg, *Om stämplingarna mot Johan III åren 1572–1575* (1897): some of the defects of Ödberg's methods are revealed, and one critical incident fully examined, in an exemplary study by James Dow, *Ruthven's army in Sweden and Estonia* ([Stockholm] 1964). See also Rudolf Elander, 'Upprorsförsök mot Johan III och prästens i Böne anklagelser mot honom 1576' (*HT*, 1958). Johan's relations with his brother Karl are examined in two studies by Olof Söderqvist, *Johan III och Hertig Karl, 1568–1575* (Uppsala, 1898), and its continuation 'Studier rörande förhållandet mellan Johan III och Hertig Karl' (*HT*, 1903–4). The interplay of ducal pretensions, constitutional theories, and religious antagonisms, is well brought out in a masterly dissertation of Kerstin Strömberg-Back, *Lagen, rätten, läran: politisk och kyrklig idédebatt i Sverige under Johan III:s tid* (Lund, 1963), which makes a significant contribution to the debate on the nature and provenance of Erik Sparre's political theories (for which see also the works of Nordlund, Lagerroth and Erland Hjärne, above, p. 473). A short study of the constitutional position of the royal duchies is K. G. Lundqvist, *Om hertigdömenas statsrättsliga ställning till kronan i Sverige 1556–1622* (1895). A modern examination of Karl's government of his duchy is much wanted: K. G. Lundqvist, *Hertig Karl of Södermanland* (Nörrköping, 1898) is not much more than an outline sketch. The relations of the aristocracy to the crown are dealt with in the still-useful book of A. G. Ahlqvist, *Om aristokratiens förhållande till konungamakten under Johan III:s regering*, I–II (Uppsala, 1864, 1866), though a more modern study is desirable. For the crisis at the close of the reign, two complementary articles by Emil Hildebrand still keep their place: 'Om Kalmarestadga eller det "latinska brevet" 1587', in *Festskrift tillägnade Carl Gustaf Malmström* (1897), and 'Böneskriften i Reval och rikets stängande för konung Johan' (*HT*, 1897). The persecution of the disgraced members of the *råd* is described (in connexion with the punitive measures against Karl Henriksson Horn), in a more concise and less discursive style than is usual with this author, in F. Ödberg, 'Om Konung Johan III:s förföljelse mot ståthållaren Karl Henriksson Horn och hans bröder 1590–1592' (*Västergötlands fornminnesföreningens tidskrift*, 1904). In 'Det svenska statsrådets ansvarighet i rättshistorisk belysning' (*Scandia*, 1939), Fredrik Lagerroth discusses the emergence, from the crises of 1590 and 1600, of the idea of ministerial responsibility; and in 'En pamflett av år 1592 mot Vasahuset' (*HT*, 1930), Lars Sjödin comments on a pamphlet (probably written by Axel Leijonhufvud) attacking the conduct of the royal brothers, and especially of Karl. The emergence of the office of *landshövding* is illustrated in Folke Lindberg, 'Till landshövdingeämbetets äldsta historia' (*HT*, 1939), which deals mainly with the period 1570–1611.

Turning now to the history of ecclesiastical policy, the text of the Church Ordinance of 1571 is printed in *Kyrkoordningar och förslag dertill före 1686*, I (1872). Some of its antecedents, in the form of partial statutes and diocesan regulations, are examined in Sven Kjöllerström, *Svenska förarbeten till kyrkoordningen av år 1571* (1940). The circumstances in which the Ordinance was accepted by the church are set out in an important article by A. Thomson, 'Johan III och stadfästelsen av 1571 års kyrkoordning' (*Scandia*, 1965), which corrects some prevailing misconceptions. The great question of the *missio suetica* is treated in two works, one old and one new: Andreas Brandrud, *Klosterlasse. Et bidrag till den jesuitiske propagandans historie i norden* (Kristiania, 1895) is a biography, while Oskar Garstein's *The Counter-Reformation in Scandinavia*, I (Oxford, 1965) is a general survey of the whole enterprise, based on a very wide-ranging collection of sources: it seems to me to be weakened by a disinclination to admit the independence (and tenacity) of Johan's religious convictions, and by a misreading of his personality: I do not find myself convinced by the suggestion that he was really a Roman Catholic who was deterred from declaring himself by fear of the consequences. A more balanced account is that of Karl Hildebrand, in his *Johan III och Europas katolska makter* (Uppsala, 1895), though much of the book is concerned with foreign policy, and though Garstein's all-embracing researches have enabled him to modify Hildebrand's account in matters of detail. Of Sven Kjöllerström's important *Kyrkolagsproblemet i Sverige 1571–1682* (Lund, 1944), only the first two chapters deal with the period down to 1626. The liturgical struggle of the 1580s is dealt with in J. A. Hammargren, *Den liturgiska striden under konung Johan III* (Uppsala, 1896); in the earlier chapters of Ragnar Ohlsson's exhaustive biography, *Abraham Angermannus. En biografisk studie* (Lund, 1946); in Karl Henning, *Strengnäs stift under den liturgiska striden* (Strengnäs, 1893); and in Olof Jägerskiöld, 'Johan III:s aktion mot prästerskapet i hertig Karls furstendöme 1588', in *Historisk studier tillägnade Nils Ahnlund* (1949): in this connexion Karin Strömberg-Back's *Lagen, rätten, läran* (Lund, 1963) is also of importance. Two developments which began in this reign, and were to have a long history, are treated in Sven Göransson, *De svenska studieresorna och den religiösa kontrollen från reformationstiden till frihetstiden* (Uppsala, 1951), and Hjalmar Holmquist, *De svenska domkapitelns förvandling till lärarekapitel, 1571–1687* (Uppsala, 1908). Johan's restoration-work at Vadstena is described in Andreas Lindblom, *Johan III och Vadstena nunnekloster* (1961), and his patronage of the arts in general in August Hahr, *Drottning Katarina Jagellonica och Vasarenässansen* (Uppsala, 1940).

The foreign policy of the reign has most recently been surveyed in Wilhelm Tham's volume of *Svenska utrikespolitikens historia* (above, p. 472). This may be supplemented by a number of special studies. Relations with Denmark are the subject of a solid article by F. Westling, 'Sveriges förhållande till Danmark från freden i Stettin till Fredrik II:s död' (*HT*, 1919); but this has been complemented for the later part of the reign by the massive (but stimulating) dissertation of Sven Ulric Palme, *Sverige och Danmark 1596–1611* (Uppsala, 1942), which deals with this period in its early chapters. So too does Birger Steckzén, *Birkarlar och Lappar* (1964), which supplants J. Nordlander, 'Om birkarlar' (*HT*, 1906, 1907), and which, though its etymology is attacked by the experts, certainly breaks important new ground with its account of the fur-trade and fur-revenues. On the Danish attitude to the White Sea traffic, see A. G. Hassø, 'Den danske Regering og Kofferdifarten Nord om Norge i det 16. Aarhundrede' ([Danish] *Historisk Tidsskrift*, 1932–4), and Walther Kirchner, 'England and Denmark, 1558–1588' (*Journal of Modern History*, 1945). One crisis in Swedish–Danish relations is illuminated by Ingvar Andersson's 'Anfallsplaner mot Danmark 1576–77', in his *Svenskt och europeiskt femtonhundratal* (Lund, 1943). For relations with Poland and the Habsburgs the standard work is Karl Hildebrand, *Johan III och Europas katolska makter* (Uppsala, 1898): it may be supplemented by Hildebrand's article 'Antonio Possevinos fredsmedling mellan Polen och Ryssland', in *Festskrift tillägnade Carl Gustaf Malmström* (1897); by Helge Almquist's substantial study, 'Johan III och Stefan Batori år 1582' (*HT*, 1909); by Johannes Paul's article, 'Die nordische Politik der Habsburger vor dem dreissigjährigen Kriege' (*HZ*, 1925–6); and by yet another of F. Ödberg's haphazard accumulations of useful information, this time centring round Sweden's diplomatic representative in Warsaw, *Om Anders Lorichs* (Skara, 1893). The nature of the Union with Poland, and the circumstances in which it came about, are discussed in Helge Almquist, *Den politiska krisen och konungavalet i Polen år 1587* (Göteborg, 1914), and more recently in a paper by Karl Lepszy, 'The Union of the crowns between Poland and Sweden in 1587', in *Poland at the XIth International Congress of Historical Sciences in Stockholm* (Warsaw, 1960), which is worth reading despite some very odd statements about Swedish internal politics: the relevant chapters in *The Cambridge History of Poland*, I (Cambridge, 1950) are also useful. And see *Etienne Batory, Roi de Pologne, prince de Transylvanie* (Kraków, 1935)—a joint publication of the Académie polonaise des Sciences et des Lettres, and the Académie des Sciences Hongroise. Relations with Poland and Russia, and a narrative of the fighting in Livonia, take up most of the space in Aegidius Girs, *Konung Johan III: des krönika* (1745), an account composed in the next generation which usually does not rise much above mere annals. Hedwig Fleischhacker, *Die Staats- und völkerrechtlichen Grundlagen der moskauischen Aussenpolitik* (Würzburg, 1959), brings out, as no other book does, the importance of Johan III's successful defiance of Ivan IV's ceremonial pretensions: see also Helge Almquist, 'En förolyckad moskovitisk besckickning. Ett bidrag till Östeuropas och Sveriges historia år 1575' (*HT*, 1938). Walther Kirchner, 'Die Bedeutung Narwas im 16. Jahrhundert' (*HZ*, 1951), provides a clear and compact exposition of a crucial topic. The beginnings of the Swedish empire in Estonia are described in B. Federley, *Konung, ståthållare och korporationer. Studier i Livlands förvaltning 1581–1600* (Helsinki, 1962).

There appears to be no biography of Johan III. It is a surprising *lacuna*, and one can only hope that it will soon be filled. In the meantime, Johan's own view of himself as king has been analysed by Sverker Arnoldsson, 'Johan III:s litterära självporträtt', in *Studier tillägnade Curt Weibull* (Göteborg, 1946).

VII. THE REVOLUTION

The triangular struggle between Sigismund, Karl and the *råd* is very fully documented in *Svenska riksdagsakter* (see above, p. 471); but a number of other printed collections are useful. E. W. Bergman, 'Register öfver rådslag i Konung Sigismunds tid' (*Meddelanden från Riksarkivet*, 1882), continues this valuable series. 'Handlingar rörande söndringen mellan Hertig Carl och rådsherrarne 1594–1600', ed. E. W. Bergman (*Historiskt Bibliotek*, II (1876)) prints correspondence between Karl and the *råd*: most of it later appeared in *Svenska riksdagsakter*. 'Acta ecclesiastica apud Svecos anno 1594', in *Handlingar rörande Skandinaviens historia*, I (1816), illuminates the crisis preceding the coronation. In *HH* 23: 1–2 (1910) are materials relating to Sigismund's first visit to Sweden in 1593–4, his second visit in 1598, and the Polish embassy of 1599; and *ibid.* 20 (1905) prints the narratives of Göran Silfverpatron and Karin Finke, as well as the memoirs of Karl's illegitimate son, Carl Carlsson Gyllenhielm, though the greater part of them deals with the period after 1600. If Gyllenhielm is naturally prejudiced in favour of his father, 'Knut Perssons krönika, angående Hertig Carls regering', in *Handlingar rörande Skandinaviens historia*, X (1822) is the witness of an adversary. *De la Gardieska Archivet*, IV (1833) includes documents from Jönköping *riksdag*, 1599. *Abraham Brahes tidebok* (1920) contains some vivid glimpses within the small space devoted to this period. The editor of *Konung Carl den IX:des Rim-Krönika* (1759) has annexed to Karl's verses a number of documents of interest bearing on the revolution: Karl's letter to Sigismund notifying him of Johan III's death; the Clergy's reply to Karl's inquiry concerning the danger from Roman Catholicism, 13 March 1600; and above all Anna Baner's justly famous account of the fate of the captive *råd*, and especially of her father Gustav Baner, from the time of their handing-over after the battle of Stångebro to their execution at Linköping: a most moving document.

The minutes of the High Court of Justice at Linköping in 1600 are printed *in extenso* in *Handlingar rörande Skandinaviens historia*, XIX: they should be read in conjunction with Sven Ulric Palme's article 'Rättegångsprotokollet från Linköpingsräfsten år 1600' (*HT*, 1938), and Idem, 'Två berattande källor om Linköpings riksdag 1600' (*HT*, 1936).

The 1590s are among the most intensively worked periods of Swedish history. On the Uppsala Assembly of 1593 there are two modern books: one, Hans Cnattingius' *Uppsala möte* (1943) sticks close to traditional interpretations; the other, Harry Hermerén's *Uppsala möte* (1944), sees in the summoning of the Assembly a political manœuvre by Karl: as will have appeared from the text, I do not find this view convincing. See also Herman Lundström's essay in his *Skisser och kritiker* (1903).

The general attitude of the aristocracy during the reign is analysed in S. J. Boëthius's *Om den svenska högadeln under Konung Sigismunds regering* (1877); and an extreme example of aristocratic-constitutionalism—a draft constitution probably drawn up soon after Johan's death by the erratic Axel Leijonhufvud —is discussed in Birger Lövgren's article 'Ett författningsprojekt från 1500-talet', (*HT*, 1913). Sigismund's first visit to Sweden is dealt with in J. A. Pärnänen, *Le premier séjour de Sigismond Vasa en Suède 1593–4* (Helsinki, 1933), which draws extensively on Italian archives, and replaces Harald Hjärne, *Sigismunds svenska resor* (1884): see also R. Lönnqvist, 'Nuntien Germanico Malaspina och planerna på Sveriges rekatolisering' (*HT*, 1937). The crucial problem of the significance of the resolution of the Söderköping *riksdag* in 1595 has recently been attacked afresh in Sven Ulric Palme's *Söderköping riksdag 1595* (Uppsala, 1952), and his arguments seem to me convincing: they are more or less corroborated by the account of the archbishop's policy given in Ragnar Ohlsson, *Abraham Angermannus* (Lund, 1946), though see Palme's review of Ohlsson in *HT* 1947. The project for marrying Princess Anna to a Hohenzollern, which did much to stiffen Karl's attitude, is the subject of a good article by Sven Ulric Palme, 'En polsk giftermålshandel' (*Personhistorisk tidskrift*, 1938). The period from 1597 has been covered, inch by inch, in a succession of detailed studies, beginning with Sven Tunberg, *Sigismund och Sverige 1597–8*, I–II (Uppsala, 1917), or the less recommendable Axel Jonsson, *Hertig Karl och Sigismund 1597–98* (Göteborg, 1906), and continuing with Helge Almquist, *Striden mellan Konung Sigismund och Hertig Karl, 1598–99* (Göteborg, 1914), and Daniel Toijer, *Sverige och Sigismund, 1598–1600* (1930), to which may be added Nils Ahnlund, 'Konung Sigismunds instruktion 1596 för sina svenska sändebud' (*HT*, 1957); Sven Ulric Palme, 'Samuel Laski om Sveriges tillstånd vintern 1597–98' (*HT*, 1944); L. Bachmann, 'Ett aktstycke från riksdagen i Uppsala 1598' (*HT*, 1939); Lars Sjödin, 'Om stadskrivaren i Stockholm Hans Bilefeldt' (*HT*, 1937); Sven Ulric Palme, 'Konung Sigismunds flotta i Östersjön 1599' (*Skrifter utg. av Sjöhistoriska Samfundet*, 1933); and Hugo Sommarström, 'Till slutakten av 1590-talets kris' (*HT*, 1933). Events in Finland are chronicled with almost equal minuteness in Pentti Renvall, *Klaus Fleming und der finnische Adel in der Anfangsphasen der Krise der neunziger Jahre des 16. Jahrhunderts* (Turku, 1939); Hugo Sommarström, *Finland under striderna mellan Sigismund och Hertig Karl* (1935); and Eric Anthoni, *Till avvecklingen av konflikten mellan Hertig Karl och Finland*, I: *Konfliktens uppkomst och hertigens seger* (Helsingfors, 1935). See also Nils Ahnlund, 'Före Klubbekriget', in his *Från Medeltid och Vasatid* (1933); and Arnold Soom's review of Pentti Renvall, *Kuninkaanmiehiä ja kapinoitsijoita Vaasa-kauden Suomessa*, in *HT*, 1951. The course of the revolution in

Estonia can be followed in B. Federley, *Kunglig Majestät, svenska kronan, och furstendömet Estland 1592–1600* (Helsingfors, 1946). Sigismund's relations with the Habsburgs are examined in Harald Hjärne, 'Bidrag till historien om Sigismunds förhållande till det Habsburgska huset, 1589–1604' (*HT*, 1883). The only separate history of the Linköping *riksdag* appears to be August Hallenberg, *Riksdagen i Linköping år 1600* (Uppsala, 1908).

VIII. KARL IX

Printed sources for the reign, in addition to those listed already, are not very extensive. The series of summaries of *råd*-resolutions is continued in E. W. Bergman, *Register öfver rådslag i konung Karl IX:s tid* (1883). Karl's draft of a recodification of the law, together with the so-called 'Rosengren draft', are printed as *Lagförslag i Karl den niondes tid*, ed. J. J. Nordström, in *Handlingar rörande Sveriges historia*, II Series, I (1864). The great collection of *Axel Oxenstiernas skrifter och brefvexling*, I Series, I (1888) now begins: this volume contains matter bearing on Oxenstierna's diplomatic activity, and also a valuable memoir on the internal situation and the affair of Hogenskild Bielke. In this connexion, also, Bengt Bergius appends to his *Konung Carl den IX:des Rim-Chrönika* (1759), the narrative of Olaus Martini and Petrus Kenicius, reporting Hogenskild's last confession; and *Handlingar rörande Skandinaviens historia*, XXVI (1843) includes papers concerning Karl's threat to abdicate, at the *riksdag* of 1606. Herman Lundström prints documents about Karl IX's action against the Uppsala professors for their former compliant attitude to Sigismund, in *Kyrkohistorisk Årsskrift* (1909). The most venomous of all the attacks by the exiles against the king, Jöran Knutsson Posse's *Hertigh Carls Slaktarebenck*, is available in a new edition (which clears up the question of authorship) by Tor Berg (1915). The rather highly-coloured reports of one of Sigismund's adherents upon conditions in Sweden are printed and discussed in Lars Sjödin, 'Hans Bilefeldts rapporter till Knut Persson åren 1602 och 1605' (*HT*, 1939). A large collection of documents bearing on the Lappmark controversy, from 1563 to 1610, but mainly falling in this reign, is printed in *Handlingar rörande Skandinaviens historia* (1858); and Harald Hjärne published a collection of excerpts from Russian chronicles in Swedish translation, mainly dealing with the campaigns of Jakob de la Gardie, in *Historiskt bibliotek*, VI–VII (1879, 1880). The earlier campaigns in Livonia are described in 'Egenhändiga anteckningar af Carl Carlsson Gyllenhielm' (*HH*, 20 (1904)), and in 'Grefve Johan af Nassaus relation om kriget i Livland åren 1601–1602' (*ibid.*). Karl's own deplorable account of why he lost the battle of Kirkholm is to be found in *De la Gardieska Archivet*, IX (1837). Two of his more notorious letters (to Klas Bielke in 1606; to Olaus Martini in 1604) are respectively in *ibid.* IV (1833), and in *Handlingar rörande Skandinaviens historia*, VIII (1820).

No king of Sweden is more in need of a modern biography than Karl IX, and the absence of any full study of him is among the most striking gaps in Swedish historiography, especially since the traditional estimate of him as the saviour of his country can scarcely any longer be defended. Sven Ulric

Palme's 'Karl IX—bondekonung?' (*Svensk tidskrift*, 1943) demolished the old view of him as the peasant's friend, and suggested the lines upon which a historical revision may probably proceed; but the same author's 'Till kännedomen om Karl IX:s muntliga framställningssätt. Några lybska bidrag' (*HT*, 1938), only reinforces impressions from other sources. Sam Clason, 'Historiska betraktelser af Karl IX' (*HT*, 1906) gives useful insight into his cast of mind by printing his comments on Swedish history. His religious opinions have been analysed in two studies, H. Block, *Karl IX som teolog och religiös personlighet* (Lund, 1918), and Otto S. Holmdahl, 'Karl IX:s förmenta kalvinism' (*Kyrkohistorisk Årsskrift*, 1919): as might be expected, they do not agree, in particular upon the question of how far he was really an adherent to Calvinist doctrines: see also Nils Ahnlund, 'Hertig Karls andra äktenskapshandel', in his *Storhetstidens gryning* (1918). In this connexion Claes Annerstedt, *Olaus Martini* (1902), is a helpful guide to the religious controversies of the reign; and the first volume of Herman Lundström's biography *Laurentius Paulinus Gothus*, I (Uppsala, 1893) is also useful. The problems raised by Karl's projected translation of the Bible are illustrated in Johan Lindblom and Hilding Pleijel, *Observationes Strengnenses* (1943). The concluding chapters of Ragnar Ohlsson's *Abraham Angermannus* give an account of Karl's harrying of the Uppsala professors. The most vivid picture of conditions at Uppsala, apart from Annerstedt's great history of the university (see above, p. 476) is afforded by Henrik Schück's admirable biography *Messenius. Några blad ur Vasatidens kulturhistoria* (1920). The same book has also information about the exiles, and about Messenius' work as Karl's pamphleteer. In this last respect a companion-piece to Schück is provided by Sven Ljung's dissertation on Messenius's enemy, and Karl's unscrupulous agent, *Erik Göransson Tegel* (Lund, 1939). The personnel of the *émigrés* is examined in Józef Trypucko, 'Svenskarna i Polen under Sigismund III:s tid' (*Svio-Polonica*, 1942). The early career of Axel Oxenstierna is treated in ample detail in Wilhelm Tham, *Axel Oxenstierna. Hans ungdom och verksamhet intill år 1612* (1935). It is especially valuable on the years 1609 to 1611, and it retains its importance despite the publication of Nils Ahnlund's masterpiece, *Axel Oxenstierna intill Gustav Adolfs död* (1940). Folke Wernstedt's *Ståthållaren Christoffer Wernstedt 1542–1627* (1929) has much interesting light on the duties of a *ståthållare* of Uppsala castle.

Two important books which appeared almost simultaneously have re-opened the whole question of Karl IX's attitude to the constitution: they are Nils Runeby, *Monarchia mixta. Maktfördelningsdebatt i Sverige under den tidigare stormaktstiden* (Uppsala, 1962), and Åke Hermansson, *Karl IX och ständerna. Tronfrågan och författningsutvecklingen i Sverige 1598–1611* (Uppsala, 1962). Both suggest that there was a less clear-cut division between Karl's views and those of his aristocratic opponents than has been thought to be the case in the past; but it seems to me that some of Hermansson's conclusions, though formulated with laudable moderation and caution, should be regarded with some reserve. On Karl's relations with the nobility, an old but still usable study is Severin Bergh, *Karl IX och den svenska adeln, 1607–1609* (Uppsala, 1882); and see also Carl Öhlander, *Bidrag till de adliga privilegiernas historia 1611–1626* (Uppsala, 1903). But the most weighty contribution to this subject is perhaps the chapter in Sven A. Nilsson, *På väg mot reduktionen. Studier i svenskt 1600-tal* (1964), which in this respect forms an epilogue to Nilsson's earlier studies (see above, p. 475), and should be read in conjunction with the same author's 'Reaktionen mot systemskiftet 1611. En linje i Gustav II Adolfs politik' (*Scandia*, 1950). Karl's relations with Duke Johan are dealt with in Folke Lindberg's article, 'Hertig Johan av Östergötland och hans furstendöme' (*HT*, 1941). For the background in popular superstition to the unrest at the end of the reign, see Nils Ahnlund, 'Helge broder Staffan', in his *Oljoberget och Ladugårdsgärde* (1924). A fresh look at the reasons for Karl's delay in accepting the crown (challenging Hermansson's conclusions on this point) is taken in Sven Lundkvist, 'Hertig Karl och kungakronan, 1598–1604' (*HT*, 1965). There are two studies of separate meetings of the *riksdag*, which, though old-fashioned, are still worth reading, even after the publication of Nils Ahnlund's *Ståndsriksdagens utdaning* (1933): they are G. O. Berg, *Riksdagen i Stockholm 1602* (1883), and N. F. Lilliestråle, *Riksdagarna 1609 och 1610* (Nyköping, 1888). Three articles discuss Karl's plans for law-reform and their consequences: Göran Setterkrans, 'Konungabalken i Karl IX:s lagförslag' (*HT*, 1964); Henrik Munktell, 'Mose lag och svensk rättsutveckling' (*Lychnos*, 1936); J. E. Almquist, 'Karl IX och den mosaiska rätten' (*Lychnos*, 1942). Göran Setterkrans, 'Karl IX:s högsta domstol' (*Scandia*, 1962), makes clear the king's attempt to use the *råd* as a permanent supreme court. S. Hedar, 'Karl IX:s förmogenhetsbeskattningar' (*HT*, 1937), deals with his imposition of a kind of income-tax. The special administrative machinery devised to manage the confiscated estates of the exiles is described in Tor Berg, *De särskilda fögderierna för förbrutna gods under Karl IX:s och Gustav Adolfs regeringar* (1927). Conditions in Finland are dealt with in Eric Anthoni, *Konflikten mellan hertig Karl och Finland. Avvecklingen och försoningen* (Helsingfors, 1927), which rounds off the story begun in his previous volume (above, p. 490).

In regard to foreign affairs, relations with Denmark (and much else besides) are best set out in Sven Ulric Palme's *Sverige och Danmark* (see above, p. 488): this now supplants K. Pira, *Svensk-danska förhandlingar 1593–1600* (1895). N. Enewald, *Sverige och Finmarken. Svensk Finnmarks-politiken under äldre tid och den svensk-norska gränsläggningen 1751* (Lund, 1920) still has its uses, however, and so also, for the Norwegian view of the question, and the substantial appendix of original documents, has O. A. Johnsen, *Finmarkens politiske historie, aktmaessig fremstillet* (Kristiania, 1923). A sidelight is afforded by Nils Ahnlund's short study 'Daniel Hjort', in his *Svensk sägen och hävd* (1928). But the only real modification of Palme's exposition is in Birger Steckzén, *Birkarlar och Lappar* (1964), which sheds new and even more unfavourable light on Karl's proceedings in the Arctic. Swedish relations with the rest of Protestant Europe are to some extent covered in Palme's book; they are shortly summarized in the opening chapter of Bertil Thyresson's *Sverige och det protestantiska Europa från Knäredfreden till Rigas erövring* (Uppsala, 1928). Tor Berg, *Johan Skytte, hans ungdom och verksamhet under Karl IX:s regering* (1920) is an important biography which touches many aspects of the history of the reign, and among them Karl's attempt to secure the alliance of England and the Dutch. As to Russia, a famous near-contemporary chronicle of the Time of Troubles is I. Massa, *Histoire des guerres de la Muscovie, 1601–1610*, I–II, trans. and ed. M. Obolensky and A. van der Linde (Brussels, 1866). There is a full-length treatment in V. O. Kluchevsky, *A History of Russia*, III, trans. C. J. Hogarth (London, 1913); but the best book on the subject from the Swedish point of view is still Helge Almquist, *Sverge och Ryssland 1595–1611* (Uppsala, 1907), and the most stimulating general account is Hedwig Fleischhacker, *Russland zwischen zwei Dynastien, 1598–1611* (Vienna, 1933). The course of the campaigns, and all other military matters, are expertly and exhaustively dealt with in Generalstaben, *Sveriges krig 1611–1632*, I, *Danska och ryska krigen* (1936), and *ibid.* II, *Polska kriget* (1936). Erik Grill, *Jakob de la Gardie, affärsmannen och politikern 1608–1636* (Göteborg, 1949), has little to say on this period. A sidelight is provided by E. Granstedt, 'Carl Carlsson Gyllenhielms fångenskap i Polen 1601–1613' (*Svio-Polonica, 1944–5*). French attempts at mediation are discussed in Helge Almquist, 'Henrik IV i sitt förhållande till Polen och Sverige' (*HT*, 1911).

Index

Index

Index